1/10/04

TERRY,

THANK YOU VERY MUCH FOR INVITING ME TO EXHIBIT MY GLOBAL POVERTY PHOTOGRAPHS AT THE FESTIVAL OF FAITHS. I REALLY ENJOYED SPENDING TIME WITH YOU IN LOUISVILLE.

PEACE and ALL GOOD,

Gerry Straub

The Sun & Moon Over Assisi

Paolo Grimaldi
MIA BELLA ASSISI
1998
Oil, tempera and gold leaf on panel

The Sun & Moon Over Assisi

a personal
encounter

with

FRANCIS
& CLARE

GERARD THOMAS STRAUB

ST. ANTHONY MESSENGER PRESS
Cincinnati, Ohio

The acknowledgments to copyright holders
of published texts are on the last pages of this volume.

Jacket design by Mary Alfieri
Book design by Sandy L. Digman and Mary Alfieri
Electronic pagination and format design by Sandy L. Digman
Map art and technical assistance by Constance Wolfer

Art, jacket front, p. ii: *Mia Bella Assisi,* painted by Paolo Grimaldi,
    1998, oil, tempera and gold leaf on panel, cm. 50 x 70 and
    p. 438: *Cielo d'Oro su Assisi,* painted by Paolo Grimaldi, 1997,
    oil, tempera and gold leaf on panel, cm. 30 x 40. Used with
    permission of the artist.

Art reproductions on pp. viii and 414 used with permission of
    Alinari/Art Resource, NY. Art reproductions on pp. 54, 342 and
    596 used with permission of Scala/Art Resource, NY.

ISBN 0-86716-393-3
Copyright ©2000, Gerard Thomas Straub
All rights reserved.
Published by St. Anthony Messenger Press
www.AmericanCatholic.org
Printed in the U.S.A.

☀ *With deep gratitude this book is dedicated to:*

Reginald A. Redlon, O.F.M.
and Liam McCarthy, O.F.M.

☽ *With special thanks to:*

Don Aldo Brunacci
André R. Cirino, O.F.M.
Hugh McKenna, O.F.M.
John J. Navone, S.J.
Briege O'Hare, O.S.C.
Ulic Troy, O.F.M.
Robert A. White, S.J.
Joseph Wood, O.F.M. Conv.
 and
All the friars at
Collegio Sant' Isidoro in Rome,
who warmly welcomed me
with space and solitude
(and lots of pasta)
and the use of their rich library
during the most critical phase
of the writing of this book
 and
All the fine people at
St. Anthony Messenger Press,
especially
Lisa Biedenbach and April Bolton,
 and
Kathleen Marie Straub,
my wife,
whose boundless love
and tireless support
gave me the freedom
to pursue my dream.

*Our real journey in life is interior; it is a matter
of growth, deepening, and an ever greater
surrender to the creative action of love and grace
in our hearts.*

—THOMAS MERTON

*Whatever I want to express in its truest meaning
must emerge from within me and pass through
an inner form. It cannot come from outside to
the inside but must emerge from within.*

—MEISTER ECKHART

*It is a good belief that our life is a pilgrim's
progress—that we are strangers on the earth...
our life is a long walk or journey from earth to
heaven.*

—VINCENT VAN GOGH

*Francis wished that everything should sing
pilgrimage and exile.*

—THOMAS OF CELANO

A Note on Attributions

In citations throughout this book, *Early Documents*
refers to Volume I of *Francis of Assisi: Early
Documents*, edited by Regis J. Armstrong, O.F.M.
Cap., J. A. Wayne Hellmann, O.F.M. Conv., and
William J. Short, O.F.M., and published by New
City Press in 1999. *Omnibus* refers to *St. Francis of
Assisi: Writings and Early Biographies: English
Omnibus of the Sources for the Life of St. Francis*,
edited by Marion A. Habig and published by
Franciscan Herald Press in 1973. Excerpts from
Thomas of Celano's *Lives* of Saint Francis are taken
from the *Omnibus*, unless otherwise noted. All
excerpts from the Liturgy of the Hours, Volumes III
and IV, are taken from the compilation, copyright
©1974, by the hierarchies of Australia, England and
Wales, Ireland, unless otherwise indicated. Excerpts
from Saint Bonaventure's *The Life of St. Francis* are
taken from Ewert Cousins's translation, published
by Paulist Press in 1978, unless otherwise noted.
Excerpts from the Acts of the Process of
Canonization and the Bull of Canonization are
taken from *Clare of Assisi: Early Documents*, edited
and translated by Regis J. Armstrong, O.F.M. Cap.,
and published by Paulist Press in 1988.

Contents

Giotto di Bondone
ST. FRANCIS GIVES HIS CLOAK TO A POOR KNIGHT
Late 13th century
Fresco, Basilica di San Francesco, Assisi

Part One

THE ATHEIST AND THE SAINT

The Journey Begins

THE ATHEIST

There are in the teaching of Christ as handed down in the gospels certain hard sayings: "take no thought for the morrow...go and sell all that thou hast, and give to the poor...turn the other cheek also...he who would save his life must lose it"—words that are often taken as said in particular contexts with particular and limited applications, but which can still perturb the individual conscience. It is because, in the records of history, few men have experimented more honestly in the literal practice of these sayings than Francesco Bernardone of Assisi, that his life-story has had such an arresting quality for men of very varied periods and temperaments. He had not only fearless sincerity, but also a persuasive personality, a poetry of action that attracted all who met him; and though his charm could not be defined, and no two friends could quite agree wherein it lay, yet it lives after him and continues its spell.

—T.S.R. BOASE, *ST. FRANCIS OF ASSISI*

I came under the influence of that spell in 1991. Since then, Saint Francis of Assisi has become my friend. But the seeds of the friendship had been planted long ago. As a child, I admired the gentle saint from Assisi and was captivated by the stories of his preaching to the birds and taming wild wolves. He seemed to embody the essence of Christianity. Francis not only believed the teachings of Christ, but also followed them—literally, completely and whole-heartedly.

For me, the advent of adulthood saw the decline of Christianity in my life. Francis, too, receded to the sidelines of my mind, where he stood as a symbolic relic from a pious fairy tale. Still, my heart retained a nostalgic soft spot for him, perhaps because my newly acquired secular and rational approach to life frequently left me feeling cold and isolated, and longing for those innocent, halcyon days of my childhood when my faith provided comfort and succor.

For most of my professional life I have been a television producer working in either Hollywood or New York, two places that are about as far from thirteenth-century Assisi as you can get. Several years ago, I made the transition to writing and was fortunate enough to have had two books published. The first, *Salvation for Sale*, takes a non-fictional look at the world of televangelism, as well as my own flirtation with fundamentalist Christianity; the second, *Dear Kate,* is a dark and brooding novel whose main character, pushed to the brink of suicide by his failure to find any meaning in life, probes his own life and faith in a series of letters to his daughter.

It was in the calm between the storms of the writing and publication of *Dear Kate* that Saint Francis trotted off the sidelines and back onto the playing field of my mind. I had been thinking about my next writing project. I had an idea for a novel in which a struggling writer who is battling a severe case of depression comes across a book of letters Vincent van Gogh had written to his brother, Theo. The letters speak so clearly to the writer's heart they sound as if they were written directly to him. Feeling the artist had become his personal friend, the writer begins to pen his reactions in a series of letters to Vincent. The writer eventually travels to France on a journey of self-discovery. The novel, as I envisioned it, would deal with the struggles the writer had with creativity and spirituality.

After a flurry of activity, and pages of notes, the idea stalled. One day, while looking for something in my basement, I came across a box of books I hadn't opened in years. I opened the box and the first book I pulled out was a short, poetic look at the life of Saint Francis entitled *Francis: The Journey and the Dream* by Murray Bodo, a Franciscan priest. Standing in my cold, damp basement, I thumbed through the book. The nostalgic feeling I always had for Francis was instantly rejuvenated. Still, within a few minutes, I put the book back in the box and sealed it up...which wasn't surprising, because at the time I was an atheist.

A few days later, while looking at one of van Gogh's self-portraits, one in which he made himself look rather monk-like, a mysterious flash of insight crossed my mind: I saw a connection between the saint from Assisi and the painter from Holland. It happened so fast I wasn't even sure exactly what I had seen or even what it meant...all I knew was Francis and Vincent instantly became brothers in my mind.

I hurried down to the basement and retrieved Father Bodo's book. While I was reading it, Saint Francis still seemed admirable, but, as an atheist, I felt he was someone with whom I couldn't relate because he was too far removed from my life and experience; nonetheless, I felt compelled to read more about him. I began rummaging through used-book stores and gradually accumulated at least three dozen books about Saint Francis, to go along with my bulging collection of books about van Gogh. For many months I did nothing but read and think about Francis and Vincent. Slowly an idea for a novel emerged. I felt a rush of excitement when a title popped into my mind: *The Canvas of the Soul*.

I'm not sure exactly when the title came to me, but it was sometime in early 1992. For the next four years, I relentlessly devoted all my time and energy to the book. At first the idea was vague; all I knew was an unpublished writer would travel to Assisi and Arles on a journey of transformation. In truth, I didn't even know what the transformation would be. I do know I was clearly more fond of Vincent than Francis; or perhaps it would be more accurate to say I was more interested in Vincent than Francis.

As the book began to take shape, I wrote a short summation of the novel, for use in my initial contact with potential publishers. Here is that summation:

> *The Canvas of the Soul* is a novel primarily set in two ancient towns, one in the Umbria region of Italy and the other in the South of France. It is the story of a modern writer's obsession with understanding the true nature of creativity and spirituality, and his desperate search to discover his own voice.
>
> A struggling writer named James Francis Howard travels to Assisi and then to Arles, as he explores the lives of the only two people he believes are capable of sparking his imagination:

Saint Francis and Vincent van Gogh...two artists who worked on *The Canvas of the Soul*. Traveling with Jim Howard is his 20-year-old niece, Bernie, a bright but discontented young woman who has yet to discover what she wants to do with her life.

As are many in this "post-modern" era, James Francis Howard is lost. The cultural myths and symbols of previous ages which provided fixed points of reference by which people could readily locate themselves in time and space have lost their power, energy and effectiveness, and so James Francis Howard has no reliable compass to help him find his way in these confusing times. The old reliable points of reference for those traveling down the path of life—God, church, society—have all but disappeared. *The Canvas of the Soul* follows James Francis Howard's search for some answers to the dilemmas of postmodern life.

By early 1995, progress on the novel had evolved to the point where I knew I had to actually travel to Assisi and Arles in order to complete it. In truth, I was desperate. I felt that I had perhaps wasted more than three years on an idea that didn't seem workable. The story had become bogged down. I was broke and exhausted...and had a meager 150 pages to show for all my work. Somehow, deep inside, I knew I had to make the trip before throwing in the towel; I knew I had to breathe in the air Francis and Vincent breathed, and had to walk the streets they walked.

On March 15, 1995, I boarded a plane at Los Angeles International Airport. I was alone and headed for Rome. I was exhausted and disillusioned...and ready to shred the manuscript, give up writing and try to get a job in television, where I had worked for nearly twenty years before I decided to quit in 1982 in order to pick up a pen and go in search of God and myself. If there was any hope I could finish the novel, it could only be found in traveling from Rome to Amsterdam via train, because that was the journey my main character, an unemployed and unpublished writer, was taking.

As soon as the plane reached cruising altitude, I pulled the white binder containing my novel out of my black canvas bag. I opened the binder and, glancing lovingly at the title, began reading the short synopsis of the novel and my brief bio which fit nicely together on one page, a page I prepared especially to introduce myself and my work to potential editors or publishers whom I hoped one day would be reading the manuscript. I've already shared with you the synopsis; here is the bio:

Gerard Thomas Straub is the author of *Dear Kate*, a novel published in the fall of 1992 by Prometheus Books. *Booklist* said
Dear Kate had "many philosophical pearls of wisdom throughout." *The Jerusalem Post* said *Dear Kate* "contained many brilliant sections." Mr. Straub's first book, *Salvation for Sale*, a nonfiction look at the world of televangelism, was published in
1986 by Prometheus Books, and an expanded, paperback edition was published in 1988. *The New York Review of Books* called
Salvation for Sale an "eye-opening book." The *Philadelphia
Inquirer* said it was "precise, well-researched, and frightening."
And *Booklist* said, "The sincerity and intensity of Straub's message are thought-provoking."

Gerard Thomas Straub is a former network television producer whose credits include a trio of popular soap operas:
General Hospital (ABC), *Capitol* (CBS) and *The Doctors* (NBC).

I suppose I should have felt proud after reading that page. After all,
I had written two books, and both had been published. No small
feat. And I once was a TV producer. I worked on some very popular
shows. During my TV career, I worked with a number of big stars—
Milton Berle, Elizabeth Taylor, Alec Baldwin, Demi Moore and many
more. Still, as I sat on the plane, I felt as if I were heading nowhere,
quickly. I didn't feel "brilliant"; I felt lost.

Before I tell you what happened in Rome, I had better fill you in
on some back story. Because the bulk of my writing during the past
dozen years was concerned with exploring the decline and death of
my Christian faith, which I chronicled in my two books, I will not
rehash my own spiritual odyssey prior to that trip in these pages,
except briefly to condense the experience in order to draw attention
to the extraordinary events that helped me make the journey from
not believing in God to writing a book about two saints who loved
God beyond measure.

I was raised in a Catholic home. Very Catholic. My parents loved
the Church and fully participated in its sacramental life. Daily Mass
and the rosary were part of the fabric of our lives. I had an aunt and
a cousin who were nuns; another cousin was a missionary priest. I
went to Catholic grammar school and high school. The saints were
my heroes. Catholicism not only was in my blood but also was an
intricate part of the architecture of my mind.

As a teenager, I entered a Vincentian minor seminary in hopes
of becoming a missionary priest. I dreamed of going to China and
spreading the Good News of the gospel. The dream died. Quickly.

The cause of death: a severe case of doubt. I left the seminary after six months and entered a Catholic high school run by the Vincentian Fathers.

The Needlepoint of My Life

The doubt I encountered as a teenager, which resurfaced with renewed intensity in my mid-thirties, became the central theme of both my novels, Dear Kate *and* The Canvas of the Soul. *Here is a short excerpt from the latter work that hints at my early doubts.*

A neighborhood poet once told me the real reason for writing a poem was rarely clear to him until long after the poem was written. His insight into the creative process suggests my real motive for telling my story is hidden in uncharted regions of my soul, and I may not discover it until the tale is fully told. So, rather than try to invent some clever reason why I'm going to pen my own story, I'll just call it fate.

Fate...the word no sooner tumbles out of my mouth and it's pummeled by conflicting interpretations. Is our fate something we create or our predetermined destiny?

A great poet once wrote, "Fate loves to invent patterns and designs. Its difficulty lies in complexity. But life itself is difficult because of its simplicity. It has only a few things of grandeur not fit for us. The saint, rejecting fate, chooses these, face to face with God." The poet was Rainer Maria Rilke; he penned those words in a fictional memoir which had strong autobiographical underpinnings. To be honest, I don't really understand the last sentence of that quote, perhaps because I don't understand God...or saints. But I'm intrigued by the idea of fate inventing patterns and designs. However, my hunch is the exact opposite is closer to the truth, that is, patterns and designs create fate.

For the past six years, I've been looking at the pattern and design of my existence, trying desperately to make sense of my life, and, even harder, make some sense of life in general.

My grandmother was a major part of the pattern of my life. She didn't seem to be bothered by life's countless mysteries. Her understanding of life, which was colored by her profound faith in God, was too simple to be subjected to the torments of probing the mysteries with endless questioning and thinking. Her faith yielded a bountiful harvest of calmness and equanimity. Neither troubled by the past nor worried about the future, she took life as it came...one day at a time. Everything she saw in life taught her about life...even needlepoint. Grams loved doing needlepoint. And she also loved doling out homespun wisdom. When I was a teenager, I was troubled by the puzzle of life; nothing I saw made any sense, none of the pieces fit together. One day, while sitting in her rocker doing a needlepoint, my grandmother held up the back of the cloth and said, "Jim, life is like this needlepoint. When you look at the back, you see a tangle of different colored threads. It looks like a meaningless mess. You have no idea what it is. This is how we view our lives. But, turn the cloth over and suddenly the tangle is an orderly design, a thing of beauty...this is how God sees our lives."

Just as no poem is self-evident, neither is any life.

My life seems to be a tangle of unconnected threads. I miss my grandmother. I miss her calmness, the way she used to gently soothe life's aches and pains for me. I wish I could turn over the needlepoint of my life and see something that makes sense. But I can't, so I'm stuck in the tangle of questions about the meaning of life.

Mercifully, this book helped me turn over the needlepoint of my life. For sure, many of the questions are still there, unanswered. But I'm no longer stuck in their tangle...they have been quieted by faith.

THE WORLD OF MAKE-BELIEVE

After high school, I landed a summer job at CBS-TV in New York City. I planned to start college in the fall. Those plans died quickly...because I was bitten by the show biz bug. I loved the excitement of the television industry: the lights, the cameras, the entire magical world of make-believe. I rose through the ranks fairly quickly, becoming an executive by my twenty-first birthday. As I immersed myself in the world of television, I gradually lost all interest in my Catholic faith. The saints were no longer my heroes. I worshiped at the altar of entertainment.

During my twenties, I never stepped inside a church, except for family funerals or baptisms. In my early thirties, during a crisis in my life, a family member took me to a charismatic prayer meeting held in the basement of a Catholic church. Despite my initial discomfort with their exuberant form of prayer, I found myself being attracted by the genuine sense of love and devotion I found within the group. During a dark and troubled period in my life, I suddenly found warmth and succor within the arms of the Church. Once again, daily Mass was a vital part of my life. I even entered a program to prepare for ordination as a permanent deacon. But once again, my plans were derailed...this time by the most unlikely of events.

THE BACKWATERS OF RELIGIOUS TELEVISION

One day during the summer of 1978, I was sitting in my office at CBS in New York. The TV was on, tuned to a local station. I was paying no attention to it until a program featuring a televangelist began to air. I can't recall what it was, but something caught my ear. And I listened. And as I did, I brushed aside whatever judgmental feelings I had about televangelists. I found myself nodding in approval of the things he was saying. A gentle, unexpected thought crossed my mind: This guy is at least trying to do something...call him. Within a few days, I wrote a simple letter outlining my professional experience and my recent renewal of faith and offered my services. I was invited to fly to Virginia Beach to meet the evangelist and his top lieutenants. I was impressed by him and his operation. He was impressed by my experience with CBS. They offered me a big job and I accepted it. I thought it was a way to fulfill my childhood dream of bringing the gospel to foreign shores. By means of satellite communications, then in its infancy, the evangelist's programs were broadcast around the world. I quit my job, sold my home and moved to Virginia. On my first day of work, I attended the mandatory daily noon prayer meeting, during which I felt as if I had died and gone to heaven: I was being paid to pray!

But I was not in heaven. Far from it. Trouble loomed on the horizon.

In quick order, I went from assistant director of network operations to the assistant director of network programming, a move which was prompted by their discovery that I was technically inept, so they moved me to the creative side of the operation, where I was given the mandate to create family programming. I created a soap opera entitled *Another Life*, which aired in syndication around the world for nearly five years. From a job point of view, everything was wonderful. I had the kind of creative freedom I had never enjoyed at the network. Besides the drama, I was also working on a news program. I produced and wrote a musical special that was filmed on location in Colorado, and a children's show that was filmed on location in Texas. I directed a live broadcast from Jerusalem. And, eventually, I became the producer of the evangelist's talk show, which aired live for ninety minutes, five days a week. The work was exhilarating and challenging.

But from a spiritual point of view, the picture was far from rosy. The faith experience I encountered in many of the other employees, as well as the evangelist himself, was dark and brooding. It was a faith that had all the answers while not allowing any questions. They saw sin and evil everywhere. Their unbending rigidity and intolerance made them unable to live harmoniously within a pluralistic society. The evil enemy was anyone who disagreed with their prophetic vision and understanding of God. Dissenters were devils who needed to be exorcised from their closed society. I was stunned to hear the evangelist defend the use of genocide as an acceptable tool for eliminating evil. There was no room in the evangelist's mind for any social perspective or political system that differed from his inspired views, which he learned directly from the mouth of God. Staff members routinely confused their own personal thoughts, desires, fears and emotions with the inspiration of the Holy Spirit. Of course, among them there were many good, decent people who truly wanted to follow Christ, but the overall atmosphere was not beneficial to me in my spiritual quest.

HOLLYWOOD

We stumble and fall constantly even when we are most enlightened. But when we are in true spiritual darkness, we do not even know that we have fallen.

—THOMAS MERTON, IN CLAUDIA SETZER,
THE SOUL: AN ARCHEOLOGY

After two and a half years of working with the televangelist, we parted company and I returned to the world of network television. Rather than return to New York, I elected to go to Hollywood and seek a fresh start in life. Shortly after my arrival, I landed a big job on the hottest soap opera on television, ABC's *General Hospital*. What a wild transition, going from faith healing to "Luke and

Laura" on the run. The high-pressure job of producing a number-one soap opera consumed all my time and energy. I was in the studio twelve hours a day, and on the weekends we often worked on location, filming in places like downtown Los Angeles and Catalina Island. Besides dealing with all the production details, such as set and costume design, I devoted much of my time to massaging the incredible egos of the stars and fielding their insane demands. About eighteen months into the job, I collapsed in my office and was taken to the hospital in an ambulance. This wasn't some fictional drama, this was real life and it was very scary. I was diagnosed as having a transient ischemic attack (TIA), which has all the outward appearances of a stroke, but is far less serious. Blood flow to my brain was temporarily blocked, causing me to lose feeling in one arm and rendering me unable to speak for a few seconds. I spent four days in the hospital, undergoing a barrage of tests.

While recovering, I was able to step back from the frantic pace of my life long enough to realize just how popular the show was. Men and young people were watching, expanding our audience beyond the traditional female market. Professional athletes confessed to being hooked on the show. Major stars—Elizabeth Taylor, Milton Berle—appeared in guest-starring roles. While I was in the hospital, I was treated as a celebrity, because I knew what was going to happen to "Luke and Laura." Female patients gave me the flowers their husbands had given them. They walked past my room in hopes of catching a glimpse of an actor visiting me. For some odd reason, the crazy idea of writing a book about the show and its phenomenal success crossed my mind. Discounting the reality that I was not a writer, I set pen to paper and began. I returned to work, but the notion of writing a book on soap operas so consumed me that I resigned one of the best jobs in television in order to sit alone in my dining room and write a book. I did not even own a typewriter. Heck, I wasn't even sure how to use verbs.

BACK TO THE BIG APPLE

Within three months the book was finished. I then realized I had absolutely no idea how to find a publisher. Within short order, I discovered that publishers had little interest in a book on soap operas, because they felt the people who watched soap operas were not smart enough to buy a book. They also felt that tabloid magazines devoted to soap operas contained all the info a fan would want, making a book superfluous. Then, out of the blue, I received a phone call from NBC, offering me the job of executive producer of *The Doctors*, which was taped in Rockefeller Center in New York City. I jumped at the chance. An executive at NBC introduced me to a literary agent (who had discovered John Grisham), who salivated at the chance of peddling a book on *General Hospital*. Within weeks, he had a deal lined up with Little, Brown and Company, publishers. There was one catch. They wanted me to cut one of the chapters. I refused. They withdrew the offer. It was a stupid thing for me to do. One day during lunch with the agent at a fancy Manhattan restaurant, the subject of my past association with the televangelist came up. The agent, as a member by birth of more than one group the evangelist had condemned, detested the evangelist. He all but begged me to write a book about the person and his ministry. The idea intrigued me, but I wasn't sure it was something I wanted to do. The idea just simmered on the back burner for a few months. When the news came that NBC was cancelling *The Doctors*, despite its steady improvement in the ratings under my leadership, I was confronted with a major decision which would alter the course of my life. Pleased with the work I did on the show, NBC offered me a position on another soap opera, one taped in Burbank, California. It was a tempting offer. But I rejected it and chose instead to go into exile.

MAKING SAUSAGE WITH MONKS

I packed up everything and headed for upstate New York, and the tiny hamlet of Cambridge, nestled on the border of Vermont, and began my search for God, a search that would take more than ten years. But back at the beginning of the journey, I had no idea I was embarking on a search for God. My goal was far more modest. I would write a book about my experience with the televangelist. And I had no idea the book I would write would cause me to embrace atheism and thrust me into the middle of a presidential campaign.

I had a one-room apartment over an antique store. The store was next to one of the oldest hotels in upstate New York and it boasted of being the home of pie à la mode. It tickled my fancy to be living next door to a place where the first person in recorded history had the amazing idea of putting a scoop of ice cream on top of a hot piece of pie. I forget the year, but it must have been in the mid-

1800's. It was one small scoop for man, but a huge step toward a more tasty life for mankind. But more important than living next door to a place of such historic importance to dessert lovers, I was living in a town that was home to a group of men who were lovers of God. Cambridge was located at the base of a small mountain. On the summit of the mountain was an Orthodox Christian monastery, and the monks became my friends. The monks called me Brother Hollywood, although one monk, my favorite, called me "the jerk."

It was the dead of winter. The bone-chilling temperature rarely got above freezing. I spent all of my time in my humble apartment or up in the monastery, helping the monks make sausage, which they sold out of their gift shop and also distributed to area supermarkets. I shared many meals with the monks. The writing went painfully slowly, primarily because I really did not have a clear idea of how to approach the book. In truth, I wasn't sure what I wanted to say. The literary agent wanted me to write a scathing exposé, revealing all the televangelist's dirty laundry, and there was plenty of dirty laundry to put on public display. But doing so did not appeal to me. I had no interest in writing a mean-spirited or vindictive book attacking someone else's beliefs, no matter how dangerous they may have been. Once I found myself alone in this frozen outpost, I burned with a desire to figure out how I got there, how I went from studying to be a deacon, to producing an evangelical Protestant television show, to producing hot and steamy soap operas in Hollywood and New York, to living in exile making sausages with monks. Within five tumultuous years, I went from being a devout Catholic who spent his spare time working in a shelter for runaway teenage hookers in Times Square, to being a thoroughly confused man who did not have a clue what to believe. What happened?

I read everything I could on theology, Church history and biblical studies. I consumed books. I even had a part-time job in a bookstore in Cambridge and I took my pay in religious books. I engaged the monks in debates about everything from the virginity of Mary to the divinity of Jesus. I questioned, I probed, I read, I pondered. I made a serious and sustained effort to really look at the Catholic faith, as well as the evangelical expression of Christianity. I began exploring Eastern religions. I found Zen Buddhism to be attractive. The deeper I went into my examination of religion, the more confused I became. The only ray of hope I saw was the faith of the monks. They lived what they believed. They lived in simplicity, tranquillity and brotherhood, welcoming anyone who knocked on their door. I was immensely drawn to their way of life. I even considered joining them. But that seemed crazy considering I had so many doubts about the Christian faith. The abbott said my spirit could not be contained on the mountaintop. I think he was telling me I had to roam around the desert a bit longer. Years later, I realized that a seed was planted in my soul during my time with the monks, a seed which eventually would bear fruit in an empty church in Rome. But, I am getting ahead of myself. Back to the book.

Slowly, a concept for the book began to emerge. What I found most reprehensible about the faith of the televangelist was its narrow-mindedness. It was his way or no way. He knew the truth and all others were doomed to hell, even other Christians, especially those who did not speak in tongues. His understanding of the gospel made prosperity a measure of faith; his God rewarded him with a wonderful array of material gifts, such as fine cars, a big home and a stable full of horses. In alternating chapters, the book would examine life inside the video "Vatican" of evangelical television through a series of short vignettes that together would present a real portrait of a very unreal world. The chapters between would look at my life and spiritual odyssey. While I was rather tough on the televangelist, I was even tougher on myself, revealing hidden secrets and sins. The book was an honest, sincere examination of my confused religious experience. In the process, I took a few cheap shots at the Catholic Church and Pope John Paul II.

Because the book's focus was split between exposing the televangelist and scrutinizing my spiritual journey and doubts, it was not an easy manuscript to sell. But it was eventually picked up by the premier publisher of secular humanist and atheist books, who was delighted to have a book that took a few jabs at the televangelist. The book was published in hardcover in 1986, and received a smattering of good reviews, including one that appeared in the *New York Review of Books*. The publisher seemed happy with the sales. Two years later, the televangelist ran for the presidency of the United States and actually did rather well in some early primaries. The publisher asked me to write a more hard-edged extra chapter dealing with some of the evangelist's extreme political ideas. I eagerly complied and an expanded paperback edition of the book was published in 1988. I did over twenty local television interviews, and I was featured in three different network news stories on the evangelist, including a long segment airing on the *NBC Nightly News* with Tom Brokaw. Moreover, I did over three hundred radio interviews. The televangelist began vilifying me on TV and radio, and I received death threats from some of his more fanatical followers. It was a wild and crazy experience. I was asked to speak at secular humanist and atheist conventions, occasionally as the keynote speaker. I was even featured on the cover of the nation's leading humanist magazine. My disdain for the televangelist and his radically dangerous political views, which threatened many of our freedoms, eventually turned into a disdain for all organized religions. Slowly my agnosticism was hardening into atheism. God was forced off the playing field of my life. In a cultural climate in which the human capacity to know the truth of anything is doubted and moral judgments are assumed to be mere statements of personal preference, my life was being eaten away by anguish, riddled with insipid problems and unanswerable questions. I swallowed a double dose of poison: materialism and skepticism. Following the mood of the time, I was hell-bent on suc-cumbing to the lure of instant gratification. I wanted riches and leisure, and I wanted them now. I felt I was losing myself in frantic and frenetic activity...while doing nothing that seemed to matter. Life was empty and meaningless.

Frustrated by the restraints of nonfiction writing, I began work on a novel about an unpublished writer who had lost the will to live. Listless, depressed and suicidal over his inability to discover any meaning to life, the writer retreats to his study and begins to write a series of long letters to his ten-year-old daughter, Kate, who lives in another state with his ex-wife. The letters attempt to explain what he is about to do: kill himself. His plan is to entrust the letters to a friend, who will ensure Kate gets them after she turns twenty-one. I described the book as fictional memoir in the form of an epistolary novel. In the book, I blamed the author's malaise on his strict Catholic upbringing and the guilt and fear instilled in him by the Church. The publisher claimed the book threw a "cold light on the oppressive religious, social, and cultural forces in contemporary life that undermine personal self-worth and identity." The novel, *Dear Kate*, was published in 1992...and I don't recommend you read it. For all practical purposes, it was the unhappy, unpublished writer from that novel—*me*—who a few years later would walk into a Franciscan friary in Rome...and walk out ten days later a new man. But I am getting ahead of the story.

Salvation for Sale

Writing Salvation for Sale *was a transforming experience. It forced me to look long and hard at all aspects of my life, especially what I believed. Once the book was published, I suddenly became a public figure and had to discuss very personal issues on radio and television shows. And the publication thrust me into the arena of atheism. I met some truly wonderful, moral, noble and honorable men and women who lived their lives without the need of any belief in a higher power. Suddenly, most of my friends were people who placed a very high value on rationalism, and were intensely distrustful of anything that smacked of the transcendental. I began reading more and more rationalist and humanist material, and in doing so I became more and more skeptical of even the most modest claims of religions. Faith in God was for losers.*

While I considered myself to be an atheist, I still harbored a faint hope for God. I was still drawn to the idea that God might exist, but that all religions somehow managed to deform or distort God's existence into an excuse for irrational behavior. Events like the Inquisition truly troubled me. I was an atheist who was attracted to the mystical. The epilogue of the book displayed that side of me. Here are a few brief excerpts:

> There is more faith in honest doubt and sincere searching than in half the rules and tenets of any religion....
>
> We dislike and frequently fear what we do not understand. When the subject is as complex as the deeply rooted views of humanity, then a true understanding might be impossible. Ultimately we may never understand, but we must persist in our efforts to try....
>
> Our future survival rests on our ability to listen to and to love one another, to know and respect one another. Dialogue and understanding must become part of our existence.

About a year ago, I thumbed through the book, mostly out of curiosity. It had been at least a half dozen years since I had opened it. I was quite surprised to find this paragraph in the epilogue:

> Perhaps our common prayer should be inspired by that gentle flower from Assisi, St. Francis—easily a saint for all faiths whose unselfishness, openness, defenselessness, and love for all creation make him a model for dialogue—who asked God to help him understand rather then be understood. He must have realized that there are no shortcuts to understanding and that he

would need plenty of help. And so do we. Francis traveled the road from sinner to sainthood by not giving up. And so must we, because there are no shortcuts to sainthood or salvation.

Today, I find it very interesting, that back in my darkest days of doubt and unbelief, Saint Francis still managed to tug at my heart and offer me a ray of hope. Years later, one of his followers would lead me back to God. The hardcover edition of the book ended with this paragraph:

> I respect the tenets of all faiths without fully accepting the dogmas of any religion. The abbot of an Orthodox Christian monastery in Cambridge, New York, once told me that "Christianity is not a religion, it is a way of living." If the truth of that sentiment were a reality in the lives of Christians, then those who offer salvation for sale on television would be out of business faster than a flick of the dial on a television set. Until that time, I will continue to seek, to doubt, to wonder, to ponder, and to question. I support secular humanism and consider it to be a breath of fresh air battling the pollution-filled smog that religion pumps into the atmosphere. The Christian zealots who dominate television are living examples of Winston Churchill's definition of a fanatic: "A fanatic is a person who can't change his mind and won't change the subject."
>
> My spiritual odyssey and the writing of this book have taught me that truth and serenity lie sleeping in silence and solitude.

Wow...that last line was prophetic. God does work in mysterious ways.

A CHANCE MEETING

In the fall of 1988, I was invited to be a guest on a local television show taped in Secaucus, New Jersey, and broadcast throughout the metropolitan New York City area. The host was the acerbic comedian, Jackie Mason. The topic of the show was the dangerous rise of fundamentalist expressions in all religions. The format pitted the host against an array of guests representing liberal and conservative branches of Christianity, Judaism, Hinduism and Islam. I was invited to attack the beliefs of fundamentalist Christians. The show had absolutely no interest in airing a free and informative exchange of ideas in order to facilitate understanding. Its goal was pure and simple, or rather impure and simple: stir up confrontation and conflicts in order to boost the ratings. Rather than a cordial discourse between opposing factions, the producers wanted a mud fight. And they got it. As the sole atheist on the panel, I was given preferential treatment by the host. I was tossed softball questions and allowed to speak without being rudely cut off.

I can't recall too much about my appearance on the show, but I will never forget what happened prior to the show. I was mingling in the green room with the other guests, waiting for the taping to begin. Suddenly I noticed two priests enter the room. I instantly recognized one of them, a Franciscan friar named Reginald A. Redlon. Before I moved to Virginia and went to work for the televangelist, Father Redlon was my pastor. At the time I was living in Little Falls, New Jersey, and attending the Franciscan parish of Our Lady of the Angels. I was very fond of Father Redlon. During my training for the diaconate, he allowed me occasionally to deliver a Sunday homily. I had not seen him in ten years. We had lost track of each other. He had no idea I had left my job with the televangelist and had moved to Hollywood and then back to New York. But as soon as we both caught sight of each other, our affection for each other swept across our faces. With a broad smile, the normally reserved friar moved toward me, exclaiming in a buoyant voice, "Gerry...what are you doing here?"

"I'm a guest," I responded, as we gave each other a warm embrace. I asked him if he was also a guest on the show. He said he wasn't, explaining he was just accompanying a friend who was a guest. He said, "I figured I should come with him for moral support. I'm sure this will be a circus atmosphere. By the way, who are you representing?"

"Atheists."

My answer stunned him. A look of disbelief crossed his face.

"I don't understand. How can that be?"

I then gave him a very brief account of what had happened, and told him about the book. We agreed to meet after the show.

We exchanged phone numbers and promised to stay in touch. I also promised to send him a copy of my book. Over the next few years, we had lunch in a Jewish delicatessen once or twice a year. I was living in Philadelphia at the time, and Father Reginald was assigned to a parish in Fairlawn, New Jersey, and then to a parish on the upper east side of Manhattan. Only the distance between our homes curtailed us from visiting more often. But every time we did get together, it was magical for me. Father Reginald respected my unbelief, while talking freely about his belief. I had great respect for him and welcomed our discussions of theology and philosophy. We had many wonderful chats about *Dear Kate* and the new novel I was writing, *The Canvas of the Soul*. He was intrigued by my pairing of Vincent van Gogh and Francis of Assisi. He was the only person to whom I showed copies of the earliest drafts of the book. He always encouraged me. He never pressured me into accepting Christianity. He said that I was a deeply spiritual person, and while I may profess to be an atheist, I thought about God every day. He knew I was on a search, and he supported that effort without trying to steer me in any direction. He had faith in me...and in God, and he was willing to allow us to work it out. He simply held out his hand in friendship.

In early 1995, shortly after moving back to Los Angeles, I knew I had to go to Assisi and to Arles in the south of France in order to complete *The Canvas of the Soul*. In truth, the trip was a crazy idea. After four years of working on the book, I was dead broke and the book was in bad shape. But I just knew I had to go. I called Father Reginald to tell him, and also to ask if he thought I might be able to stay in a friary in Assisi. He said he would check and call me back. Within an hour, the call came. He said that staying in a friary would be impossible, for a number of reasons, one of which was my inability to speak Italian. However, he gave me the phone number of a guest house in Assisi operated by American Franciscan sisters. I thanked him, and just as the conversation was about to end, I casually mentioned that I would be spending about ten days in Rome before going to Assisi. Asked where I intended to stay, I told him I had no real plans, and that I was just going to try to find a cheap hotel when I arrived. He warned against that, saying the only cheap hotels are in dangerous areas, and even they are not that cheap. He told me that he might be able to help me find a place, and that he needed to make a phone call and he would call me back. Within twenty minutes the phone rang and he greeted me with the news he had made arrangements for me to stay in a friary in Rome. A year or so earlier, Father Redlon had attended a six-week course on Franciscan spirituality given at the friary, and during his stay he had become friends with the guardian of the friary, Father Liam McCarthy, O.F.M. Father Reginald told Father Liam about me, and asked him if I could stay there. Father Liam said yes, even though such a request was unusual and rarely honored. And that "yes" changed my life.

AN EMPTY CHURCH IN ROME

It only takes a moment for God to enrich you.
—THOMAS KEATING, *OPEN MIND, OPEN HEART*

Rome is the city of Michelangelo, the city of Raphael. Rome is a city whose splendor and grandeur are, well, eternal. Rome is a city almost beyond description. You could easily run out of superlative adjectives long before you ran out of superlative sights to describe. Rome is a city so richly endowed with exquisite treasures that it is almost impossible to taste them all in full. Most tourists can only breeze past a fraction of the timeless delights the city has to offer, barely nibbling at the bountiful banquet of antiquity spread before them: the Pantheon, the Colosseum, the Catacombs, the Roman Forum, the Temple of Venus and Roma, the Vatican, and churches dating back to the earliest days of Christianity, such as San Giovanni in Laterano and Santa Maria Maggiore.

Rome is a city of sights, a feast for the eyes. Rome is a city of basilicas, churches and museums, a city of palaces, plazas and villas, a city of statues, fountains and gardens, a city of magnificent arches, ancient bridges and ornate stone gates. Rome is all those things to me. But it is much, much more than history, art and beauty. Rome is where I found what I had lost...God. For me, the most beautiful and most holy place in all of Rome is a simple seventeenth-century church hidden behind the walls of a Franciscan friary.

I landed at Leonardo da Vinci Airport just a few minutes behind schedule. Flying from John F. Kennedy Airport to Leonardo da Vinci Airport symbolically conveys the sense of history which was about to wash over me. The celebrated painter, sculptor, architect and engineer died in 1519, 398 years before the thirty-fifth president of the United States was born. Time in Rome is marked by centuries, whereas in America we speak of decades.

I retrieved my bags and passed through Customs without any problem. And with relative ease, I found my way to the commuter train for Rome. Gradually the green rolling hills near the airport gave way to city blocks crowded with old, dreary apartment houses from which most of the windows had laundry hanging and whose rooftops sprouted a jungle of antennas. It is not an inspiring approach to Rome. The forty-five-minute train ride offered no rising sense of excitement or heart-lifting views; it just unceremoniously dumps you in the massive Stazione Termini, Rome's main train station that connects with inter-city buses and the metro subway system.

As soon as I stepped outside the station, I noticed the 2300-year-old Servian Wall that abuts the massive train station, creating an interesting juxtaposition of slick modernism and crumbling antiquity. Tired and anxious to get to my destination, I elected to avoid dealing with the subway and jumped into a cab for the short ride to Collegio Sant' Isidoro.

Because the narrow street that fronted the friary was blocked by double-parked cars, the driver let me off about a half block from the entrance. Unfortunately, the short walk was uphill, and it was made tougher by having to lug the bags. Inside, a female secretary told me that the guardian was out and would not be returning until later in the afternoon, but that he welcomed me to join him for dinner. I was led to my room on the second floor. After unpacking and freshening up a bit, I decided to explore the friary grounds. After strolling through the gardens and the cloister, I entered the church, which was empty.

I sat down.

On the seat next to me was a prayer book, a condensed version of the Divine Office that included only the morning and evening prayers. I picked it up and randomly opened it to page twenty. My eyes were drawn to a psalm which began about halfway down the page. It was Psalm 63, and in bold print the text summarized the thrust of the psalm: "A Soul Thirsting for God."

I read those few words and something happened, something mysterious and unexplainable: I began to cry, uncontrollably. I sat there and sobbed for at least five minutes. I was washed in the feeling that the entire trip was really a ruse to help me quench my soul's thirst for God. I read the psalm:

O God, you are my God, for you I long;
for you my soul is thirsting.
My body pines for you
like a dry, weary land without water.
So I gaze on you in the sanctuary
to see your strength and your glory.

For your love is better than life,
my lips will speak your praise.
So I will bless you all my life,

in your name I will lift up my hands.
My soul shall be filled as with a banquet,
my mouth shall praise you with joy.

On my bed I remember you.
On you I muse through the night
for you have been my help;
in the shadow of your wings I rejoice.
My soul clings to you;
your right hand holds me fast. (1-8)

There is something you need to understand. I have never enjoyed reading the psalms, or for that matter, any of the Old Testament. To my mind, the psalms were antiquated expressions of an alien piety with which I could not connect. Yet, as I read the above passage, my soul seemed enthusiastically to sing the words with great feeling and emotion, and without any concern for the fact that I didn't believe God existed.

I closed the book. I looked at the tabernacle and prayed. The prayer was at once a plea for help from God and at the same time a litany of complaints against the Church. A day or two later, I jotted down the essence of the prayer in my journal:

Dear God, help me. You know how I have struggled with the issue of faith. You know I want to believe in You, but I can't. My brain is all thumbs when it comes to figuring out all the big questions of life which plague me. I'm so easily confused. The Bible is filled with so many contradictions and absurdities that I can't possibly believe it is your Word, or even the one and only word You have ever spoken. Every religion has its allegedly inspired scriptures. I'm baffled by it all. And the issue of Jesus being God and Man is hard to comprehend or accept. And I find it barbaric that he had to die on the cross to make you happy. The resurrection is another thorny issue. All the Church teachings about Mary and her virgin birth and bodily assumption into heaven sound preposterous. Then I get crazy when I read about all the bad popes down through the ages, power-hungry, pleasure-seeking men who had mistresses and fathered illegitimate children. And I hate the Church's disdain for women. As far as I am concerned, all religions pump out symbolic narratives that make unverifiable claims to ultimate truth. The New Testament makes you sound like an egomaniac who cares more about whom we worship than how we treat each other. Yet, God, here I am crying, thirsting for you. Please help me understand all this stuff. Help me believe in you, help me know you.

After finishing the prayer, I was overtaken by a sense of peace, a peace which sprang from the sudden realization that God does exist, and, moreover, does love me. I felt as if I were floating in a sea of love. I closed my eyes and sat in tranquil silence for a few minutes. This was the moment of grace which changed my life.

I did not understand what was happening. Where did this sudden knowledge or sensation that God exists come from? It made no sense; there was no rational explanation for the deep conviction that gripped me. I felt as if a giant light bulb had been illuminated inside of me, chasing the darkness of unbelief away, making everything clear. But almost as quickly, shadows of doubt began dimming the light. I recall thinking, "This has got to be some kind of an odd manifestation of jet lag."

I got up and started walking toward the door, which was to the right of the main altar. As I walked, I felt the urge to genuflect before the tabernacle. I felt myself smile as an image from my childhood skipped across my mind. Sister St. Dorothy was chastising me for "sloppy" genuflecting. "Remember, Gerard, you are making a gesture of respect before the King of the Universe, not picking up a marble off the floor and running home with it." Rather than genuflect, I simply paused and bowed in front of the tabernacle. It was a deep bow. As I bowed, a sincere sense of reverence washed over me. The very act of bowing seemed like the most natural thing in the world to do at that moment.

I returned to my room and washed my face. Looking at myself in the mirror, I thought I looked the same. Yet, I felt very different. Lighter. Calmer. But I was also confused by what had happened. I thought perhaps the incident was nothing more than an emotional reaction to the loss of the innocence of my childhood faith.

I took a leisurely stroll around Rome, not venturing too far from the friary. I visited the Trevi Fountain, the Piazza di Spagna, and the Pantheon. Dinner at the friary was very pleasant. Father Liam welcomed me with great warmth and cordiality. I never mentioned what had happened in the church. Instead, I entertained the friars with stories from my days as a TV producer in Hollywood.

After dinner, I returned to my room and closed the door behind me. I took off my jacket and tossed it onto the bed. I felt confined in the sparsely furnished, small chamber. I briefly longed for the space and warmth of my home. I took a deep breath. Whatever anxiety I felt I chalked up to a normal reaction to the drastic change in setting and the uncertainty of what lay ahead. I sat at the desk and opened my journal and began writing:

> Long day. I'm beat but still somewhat energized. This place isn't bad. The atmosphere seems very relaxed and informal. No austere Trappists in sight. In fact, the seminarians are down in the courtyard, playing their acoustical guitars and singing old Simon and Garfunkel songs. The familiar tunes are comforting.
>
> I wish I knew what happened in the church this morning. In a flash, the reality of God became more real than the reality of time and space. I suppose it may have been some kind of transcendental experience, but I'm a bit leery of quickly attaching metaphysical or mystical significance to things that could just as easily have more natural causes...like indigestion. Still, I felt this wave of tranquillity wash over me. It was followed by a radically different feeling within me. I felt myself lost in...how shall I say it?...lost in the embrace of an Absolute hug, a hug so tight that my "self," the me I know, became lost in a...no-self. Ugh. I hate this futility of words. I simply cannot express the change that took place within me as I read that psalm.
>
> I can't find the words to describe what happened. Every metaphysical expression that comes to mind doesn't adequately convey the experience; worse, they mislead or give birth to irreconcilable contradictions once they are exposed to the light of critical thought.
>
> Yet, something did happen. For a fleeting moment, perhaps longer, for time seemed suspended, I felt the presence of...God. Not a person or theological formula. I felt at One with something bigger and beyond my imagination. I know how to put it: I felt at home...and that feeling had nothing to do with the actual church.
>
> I had this thought during dinner that perhaps I should talk with Father Liam about what had happened. But if I can't explain it in the privacy of this journal, home to all my thoughts, no matter how trivial or unorthodox, how am I going to explain it to a virtual stranger?
>
> I'm going to bed.

I awoke early, slightly before 5:30 a.m.; still, I felt rested. As I lay in bed, I realized how quiet it was. I hadn't heard a sound all night. The thick walls of the old building insulated the inhabitants from the clamor of the traffic and commerce beyond the gates, creating a pocket of silence and stillness here in the heart of noisy and pulsating Rome. I felt a similar calmness within me. This is a safe place. I remembered Father Liam telling me that the community gathers for morning prayer at six in the choir loft. I had not planned to attend. But, *when in Rome, do as the Romans do*. Seeing as these Romans pray at the ungodly hour of six in the morning, I jumped up and joined them, even though I did not believe in the efficacy of prayer.

As I entered the choir loft, I was greeted by silent smiles and nods of good morning. One of the students gave me the Office of the Hours. At precisely six o'clock, Father Liam stood and on his cue so did the rest of the community. "In the name of the Father, and of the Son, and of the Holy Spirit," he said, before offering a short prayer. When he finished everyone sat down. One of the friars then sang the opening line of a psalm. On the second line, all the friars on the left side of the choir joined in singing the entire stanza. The second stanza was sung by those on the right side, where I was seated. I did not sing. I listened.

The singing wasn't that good, but it had a hypnotic and graceful quality to it. They sang from conviction, and it was convincing. As they chanted a second psalm, I felt as if I wanted to join in, and did so very tentatively, my voice barely rising above a whisper. I can't sing, not even in the shower. But this was praying. At that time, I didn't pray either—not even in a church. I wondered what I was doing, what was going on. I felt pulled in two directions... toward their faith and away from their beliefs. I managed to turn my mind off and just enjoy the harmony of the moment, the men joined together in one voice humbly offering their day and lives to something bigger and better than they are. As they chanted the uncompromising verses of the psalms, they were calling out to God, acknowledging their broken lives...something I could not do or even understand.

Later in the day, I sat alone in the choir loft and penned these thoughts in my journal:

> After living so many years in a world where God did not exist, I find myself exhausted to the point of despair from my secular search for meaning. Ironically, I had swallowed Sartre's tempting notion that a godless world would foster a radical human freedom which would enable us to continually create our own

existence based purely on our experience and understanding. It seems as if his existentialist view instead unleashed a cyclone of confusion which has left us in a state of perpetual disorientation. Life has no center. We are buried under tons of disjoined and unconnected pieces of information, a virtual blizzard of ideas and images hurled at us from all directions. Life today is fragmented, fast-paced and alienating. But not in this choir loft. Are these men, who gather in this place three or four times a day to pray, being deceived, living in an illusion? Or have I been tricked into believing in nothing?

At the conclusion of the morning prayer, which lasted about twenty minutes, the friars silently rose and walked downstairs to the church for the celebration of the Eucharist. I hadn't anticipated this and wasn't sure what to do. I hadn't been to Mass in at least a dozen years. I really didn't want to stay for Mass. Yet, I really didn't want to leave either. I stayed. I was surprised I hadn't forgotten any of the ritual; the words all sounded as fresh as if I had heard them yesterday. Even the rubrics, when to stand, to sit or to kneel, were instantly familiar. The Introit, the Kyrie, the Gloria, the Offertory, the Canon and the Consecration...the entire liturgy was, in fact, part of the fabric of my being, and standing among a small group of men praying as intently and sincerely as those followers of Saint Francis filled me with awe. Especially moving was the Consecration, the high point of the liturgy when the celebrant intones the most sacred words of the ancient ritual: *This is My body....* As the celebrant elevated the host high into the air, I pressed my hands together in prayer, an outward sign of my appreciation of the mystical moment. As the consecrated host was placed back down on the altar, the priests and seminarians, standing in a semicircle around the altar, all bowed in unison. I bowed my head slightly, ignoring the fact that I no longer could believe the bread was now the Body of Christ.

When it was time to distribute Communion, one of the friars took a bowl of consecrated hosts from the celebrant and placed one in each of the cupped hands. When he came to me, I did not extend my hands. I wanted to, but I knew I couldn't, for I was not in a state of grace, having not been to confession in years. The priest seemed surprised, but he gracefully covered himself and walked past me. I felt left out.

When Mass was over, I remained in the church, and sat in silence, alone, trying to figure out why the simple ritual of morning prayer and the Mass so deeply moved me. I couldn't make any sense of it.

After breakfast, Father Liam gave me a map of the city and pointed out a few important sights to see. During the day, I explored a number of magnificent churches, and during each visit, I felt myself being pulled farther into the mystery of God. In each church, I lit candles and prayed for an understanding of what I was feeling within myself. During dinner that night, I spoke with Father Liam about my novel and tried to explain the connection I perceived between Vincent van Gogh and Saint Francis of Assisi. He seemed intrigued by the idea and we had a truly stimulating conversation.

I set my alarm to ensure I got up in time to attend morning prayer. The early morning light gently washed over the choir loft. I noticed the antiquity of the carved wooden stalls in which we sat. I wondered how many men had sat in these very seats over the past three centuries, praying these same prayers. The wooden kneelers were actually slightly bowed in the middle from countless knees pressing upon them. The organ looked very old also. The walls hadn't been painted in many years, and had a few cracks in them. It seemed as if a cherished tradition was dying. Only a dozen men, a few of them very old, were carrying on the tradition. Yet when they opened their mouths in song, chanting the ancient psalms, the dusky, old choir loft was transformed into a thing of beauty. I sang a little louder that second day, and wanted to believe the prayers being prayed were being heard by someone outside the choir loft. I once again attended Mass. And even more than the first day, I wanted to receive Communion, but I did not.

The rest of the second day and the third day passed in a similar fashion. Between joining the friars for prayers and meals, I toured the city. The beauty of the churches astounded me. I had with me a literary guide to Rome, containing the impressions of writers upon visiting the city. One church, the Patriarchal Basilica of Santa Maria Maggiore, had captured the imagination of a number of writers. Stendhal called it "magnificent." Hawthorne was impressed by its "noble simplicity." George Eliot thought it "exquisitely beautiful." According to the legend, back in the year 352, the Virgin Mary appeared simultaneously to a wealthy Christian and to Pope Liberius. The Virgin told them that she wanted a church built in her honor on a hill known as Esquiline. The question of exactly where to build the church was resolved the next day when a summer snowfall not only fell on the spot where the Virgin wished the church to be built, but also neatly outlined the exact shape of the church.

More than any other church in Rome, the interior of Santa Maria Maggiore has maintained its medieval appearance. Its elegant nave is almost unchanged since the fifth century. Over the years, popes have added enormous side chapels and the building has grown, as efforts to enhance the church's beauty continued into the nineteenth century. Gold brought by Columbus from the New World glitters on the ceiling. So astonishing is the visual feast spread out before you, your eyes don't know where to focus. I was drawn to the beautifully sober harmony and coloring of the splendid classical columns lining the nave, and to the intricate gildings and moldings of the coffered Renaissance ceiling. But more amazing than the columns and the ceiling, and the most enchanting feature of the church, is the elegant grandeur of the nave. In *Italian Hours* (1809), Henry James marveled at "its perfect shapeliness and rich simplicity."

But the thing that made the deepest impression on me during my visit to the church had nothing to do with the building's miraculous history or its legendary beauty. I was standing outside the church taking a close look at the Baroque facade, constructed in the middle of the eighteenth century, when a sad, solitary figure suddenly distracted my attention from the brilliance of the facade and the steady flow of tourists entering the church. An old woman, darkly dressed in worn clothing, sat on the top step, her hunched back leaning against a column, her veiled head bowed and a hand outstretched in hopes of receiving a few coins. I inched a little closer to get a better look. Her hands, worn by age and weather, were leathery and gnarled. Her face was deeply wrinkled, clearly showing signs of a hard life. She said nothing. She never even raised her head to look at those passing by. She was virtually ignored by all. Two old women gave her some spare change.

During the evening of my fourth day at Collegio Sant' Isidoro, my life changed. It was unexpected and wonderful. After dinner I was walking in the Wadding Cloister when I ran into Father Liam. We no sooner exchanged pleasantries, than he said, "Gerry, would you like to talk?"

I said, "Yes, I really would."

He said, "Come on. Let's go somewhere private."

We walked to a little sitting room near the front office. It was about 8:30 p.m. Without realizing it, I was about to go to confession.

Our conversation lasted for nearly three hours. I told him everything I could about my life and how I wound up in Rome, alone and lost. Father Liam was wonderful, kind and gentle. He listened intently, occasionally offering tidbits of insight. But mostly he listened. I felt totally at ease baring my soul before him. Sometime after eleven o'clock, he said, "Do you want to pray?"

"Yes."

He said the most beautiful prayer I've ever heard, asking God's blessing on my life. Afterward, I asked him to hear my confession formally, even though I had pretty much told him everything that needed confessing already. I got more specific in recalling my sins. After he offered me absolution, he said, "Let's go into the church."

We got up, and walked to the church, which was just across the enclosed Spanish Cloister. Upon entering the darkened church, Father Liam switched on a single light over the main altar. We knelt in the shadows and prayed together. We read the night prayer from the Divine Office. Afterward, we stood up and hugged each other. As we separated, Father Liam said, "I'll see you at Mass in the morning." I said, "You can count on it." I then floated off to bed, completely renewed, a new man.

The next morning, a Sunday, I woke up with this thought on my mind: I'm going to receive the Eucharist today. I was very much looking forward to it, happily anticipating the thought of fully sharing in the liturgy. Fittingly, Father Liam was the principal celebrant. Shortly after the consecration of the bread and wine, I stood before him as he held up the host before me and said, slowly and deliberately, "This is the Body of Christ."

I said, with deep conviction, "Amen," as I devoutly held out my cupped hands. With a gentle and loving smile on his face, Father Liam placed the host into my hands. I paused briefly to look at the thin wafer, took a deep breath, and consumed it.

I returned to my seat and sat in silence, bathed in a feeling of warmth and peace. All my theological doubts were quieted. I felt myself breathing in and out. Each breath I inhaled carried the silent name of Jesus, and with every exhale, I softly said with words unspoken, "Have mercy on me." Inhale, Jesus. Exhale, have mercy on me. Over and over. With each breath, gradually I grew in calmness and serenity. Everything seemed new and aglow. I wanted to hug everyone present.

That was March of 1995. Since then, for the most part, I have been attending daily Mass and receiving the Eucharist. The Liturgy of the Hours became the foundation of my prayer life. Over the next three years, I stayed at Sant' Isidoro four times, for a total of more than six months' accumulated time. In the fall of 1998, I asked Father Liam if I could stay there again the following year when I returned to teach, and he said, "Gerry, you never have to ask if you can come home."

I am eternally grateful to Father Liam and to all the friars of Sant' Isidoro for allowing me to feel so at home in their home. And for bringing me home to God.

Later that day, I returned to Santa Maria Maggiore. The old woman was still on the steps, still being ignored. I sat in a quiet corner of the church and said a rosary. As a child, I had been drawn to the image of the Blessed Virgin Mary. As an adult, I was often torn over the issue of whether or not the virgin birth was fact or fiction. But as I sat in the church on that Sunday afternoon, that issue was far from my mind. Instead, I was graced with the ability to enter into the symbolism of the virgin birth. The symbol itself awakened in me a new awareness of the inner meaning of life. Mary is what I wanted to be. I hungered to surround, hold, embrace and possess, as a mother does her child in the womb, God.

The pilgrimage began.

WE HAVE A TABLE FOR FOUR READY

My ten days at Sant' Isidoro changed my life, but I had no idea what impact that "inner" change would have on my personal and professional life. One change was almost immediate, and made a trip to Rome an annual event for me. While I was at Sant' Isidoro, I was introduced to a Jesuit priest who was the director of the Interdisciplinary Centre on Social Communication at the Pontifical Gregorian University. Students at the center, mostly priests and nuns, learn how to better communicate the gospel through mass communications, such as film and television. Their studies of communication are combined with studies in the fields of theology, philosophy and social sciences. During my stay in Rome, I was invited to give a lecture one evening at the Gregorian. Actually, it wasn't really a lecture. I would simply give a few opening comments about being a television producer from Hollywood and then open the floor up for questions from the students. It was an exhilarating evening. Afterward, the director, Robert White, S.J., and I had dinner together, and during the course of the meal, he asked if I would return to the university in the fall and give a two-week seminar on television writing and directing to a select group of students. The course would run five hours a day, five days a week.

After those amazing days in Rome, I headed for Assisi and the rest of my planned trip, still convinced I was writing a novel about Vincent van Gogh and Saint Francis. After Assisi, I traveled to Arles, in the south of France, then to Paris and Auvers-sur-Oise, and on to Amsterdam. It was an exciting trip. Through arrangements I made beforehand with the Van Gogh Foundation, I was permitted to spend fifteen minutes alone in the room in Auvers where Vincent died.

After the trip, I returned home and continued working on the novel. In the fall of 1995, I returned to Rome to teach the course. I had thirteen students from eleven nations. They taught me more than I taught them. Plus I had the chance to spend more time in Assisi. More and more, Francis was sinking into my consciousness. During this trip I met Father John Navone, S.J., who, after reading a rough draft of the novel, suggested I write a book on Saint Francis. I spent the entire year of 1996 working on the book.

Near the end of 1996, I was introduced to a friar who started a soup kitchen in the slums of Philadelphia. I was struggling to understand Francis' ideal of poverty, and so I spent some time at the soup kitchen. Eventually, the idea to do a film on the soup kitchen was born. I lived with the friars for about three weeks while making the film. I learned about poverty. One night, I found myself in a courtyard outside the soup kitchen door. It was dark and very cold. About three hundred people were lined up, waiting for the meal to begin. The St. Francis Inn, located in the heart of what many consider to be the worst slum in America, was a very unusual soup kitchen. Their guests were invited to sit at a table, where they would be served a hot meal by volunteers who waited on them as if they were in a restaurant. This afforded the guests a degree of dignity. Because of the limited space at the Inn, they have room for only ten tables, which means about fifty people can be served at a time. The line waiting for a table sometimes stretches around the block. As I stood among the poor, my mind was flooded with doubts about making the film. How could I capture the spirit of what was happening here? Would it be too depressing? Who would watch it? How could we make a film on such a paltry budget, which was less than a normal production would spend on lunch?

Suddenly, the side door opened and a diminutive, gray-haired

Franciscan sister, dressed in jeans and a sweatshirt, said, in an almost angelic voice, "We have a table for four ready." The contrast between that stark, cold reality of the plight of the hungry and this sweet voice sounding as if she were the hostess at a fine restaurant struck a chord deep inside me. The words rang in my head. Instantly, I knew I could make the film, and those words would be the film's title.

The film aired on about fifty PBS stations around the country, which triggered donations to the St. Francis Inn from people of all faiths, as well as from some atheists. With those donations, the friars were able to expand the kitchen in order to better serve the poor.

The next fall, I showed the film to my students at the Gregorian. The students from Africa had no idea there was such devastating poverty in the United States. The film was also shown at an international conference of Franciscan priests and sisters. Somehow, thanks to that moment of grace in the empty church in Rome, my life was slowly being transformed. I went from being an atheist novelist to a Christian writing a book on Saint Francis, making a film on Franciscans feeding the poor and teaching a course every fall at a major Catholic university in Rome, which then afforded me the opportunity to go on a pilgrimage, spending more than three months in Italy. That experience became the heart and soul of this book.

Amazing Grace

A chance meeting in a TV studio with my former pastor, a man I greatly respected; it was just a moment in time, but that moment changed everything. I was lost, searching for meaning. But grace broke through my doubt and confusion. It would take time for it to flower. A half dozen years later, another brief moment in time...a phone call to the former pastor who had become my friend, and then another moment in time, when in the stillness of an empty church in a foreign land God broke through the silence. Days later, in the same church, another moment, on my knees, starting over.

Father Reginald, my former pastor, and Father Liam, who held my hand and led me home, are my heroes.

WRITING ABOUT FRANCIS

More biographies have been written on the life of Saint Francis than any other saint, a fact that clearly supports the oft-repeated claim that he is "everybody's favorite saint." Entire libraries are dedicated just to him. A collection of the numerous accounts of his life written within a hundred years of his death fills up more than two thousand printed pages. The smallest details of his life have been carefully examined and hotly debated by scholars. Year after year, still more books appear, each author presenting another dimension of the charismatic saint. Francis of Assisi has the longest single bibliography of any person in history. Even Marvel Comics has published a best-selling version of his life, entitled *Francis, Brother of the Universe*. Moreover, within a century of his death, Francis was the subject of thousands of works of art; in Italy alone, more than 150 paintings of the saint survive from the thirteenth and early fourteenth centuries. Today, people from a wide variety of religious backgrounds, who are concerned with such issues as ecumenism, interfaith relations, the sanctity of creation and animal rights, all point to Francis as an example and spiritual focus. Eight centuries after his death, Francis still has the power to inspire people.

Paul Sabatier, in his introduction to his *Life of St. Francis of Assisi*, writes: "One must not ask too much of history. The more beautiful a sunrise is, the more difficult it is to describe it." Sabatier's book was published in 1892 and was the first modern biography of the saint. Paul Sabatier, a learned and skeptical man, claimed he had a hard time preserving a comprehensive viewpoint regarding Francis' life; for instance, he came to accept the authenticity of the saint's stigmata, while rejecting many of the miracles attributed to Francis. Sabatier accentuated Francis' charm and downplayed the supernatural elements found in the early Franciscan sources. The complexity of Saint Francis' life opens it to all kinds of speculation and interpretations. And distortions. His story, crammed with drama and pathos, has the inevitability of myth; separating fact from legend alone would require the patience of a saint. During the past 750 years, much of Saint Francis' life has been embellished to such a degree that the real Francis is almost totally obscured, making it all the more difficult to distinguish between the mass of truth and apocrypha about the saint.

While historical accuracy was an utmost concern of mine, the story I'm about to tell is hardly a complete history of the two beloved saints. *The Sun and Moon Over Assisi* is simply a bouquet to a friend...and his best friend. In essence, I'll share what I found fascinating about Francis and Clare and try to tell their story in a fresh way. My words will form a patchwork quilt consisting of bits and pieces of their lives, along with some of their ideas about spirituality, a sampling of things they wrote, occasional personal reflections on the lives of the two saints, a few brief excerpts from some of the many books written about them, and a look at the art that graces the walls of the churches of Assisi, along with a guided tour of those magnificent churches.

One final observation about this book, or, more specifically, about the personal reflections that are sprinkled throughout the text. The reflections are easy to spot and each reflection is titled, such as "Finding Joy in Sadness" and "The Crib and the Cross." My intention is to offer reflections that help make various incidents from Francis' and Clare's lives more relevant to the modern person. In truth, I hoped to make their lives more meaningful to me. For instance, after reading the story of how Francis embraced the leper, I attempted to discover a lesson from that story which could be applied to my life, and my effort yielded a reflection entitled "I'm Hungry." Likewise, my attempt to more fully understand Saint Francis' love of poverty resulted in a reflection entitled "We Have No Potatoes."

On Pilgrimage

In the spring of 1997, as I was nearing the completion of this book, I was handed a once-in-a-lifetime opportunity: to participate in a month-long study pilgrimage to Assisi with a group of Franciscan friars and sisters. The pilgrimage was to be a time of spiritual renewal as modern-day followers of Saint Francis from six nations traveled to the origins of the Franciscan way of life. They would reconnect themselves to their Franciscan heritage and deepen their journey with Christ as they walked, slowly and prayerfully, through all the places that played a key role in the lives of Francis and Clare.

Before the trip, I intuitively knew that the pilgrimage would dramatically alter the tone and character of this book. As I walked in the footsteps of Saint Francis, I often paused to jot down my reactions to the places and events that I had come to love so much. Those reflections are all titled "Pilgrimage Diary," and each entry is numbered, from "Pilgrimage Diary 1" through "Pilgrimage Diary

118"...and they, along with the personal reflections, are the heart of the book.

The writing of this book has been a pilgrimage back to God...and my true self. In the introduction to his book *Through the Year With Francis of Assisi*, Murray Bodo, O.F.M., succinctly expresses the pilgrimage experience:

> The way of the pilgrimage is the way of death leading to life. You leave behind loved ones and home, entrusting their safety and care to God, who is drawing you away from them. It is God who leads the pilgrim as he leads the dying person, and you follow shyly, awkwardly, fearfully, at first; then letting go somewhere along the way, you surrender what you've left behind into the very hand that is clasping yours on the journey.
>
> It is not so much where you are going as the going away, the leaving itself, that matters. It is consigning to God what you thought was so dependent upon your presence: your loved ones, your affairs. You leave, not knowing for certain that you will return. You embark upon a journey of faith, from faith to faith.
>
> It is not that one place is more in God's hearing than another, so that he hears me better "there" than "here." But it is what happens to my own hearing in the traveling "there" to listen, when the things and people "here" begin to speak too loudly for me to hear my own inner voices and the voice of the Spirit. (pages 7-8)

The French painter and sculptor Jean Dubuffet (1901-1985) offered this startling observation: "Unless one says good-bye to what one loves, and unless one travels to completely new territories, one can expect merely a long wearing away of oneself and eventual extinction."

A pilgrimage is a quest for grace. The word "pilgrimage" comes from the Latin word *peregrinum* which means one who comes from a foreign land...a stranger. A pilgrim is a displaced person whose normal routines and relationships have been suspended. To be a pilgrim is to be marginalized, stripped of the familiar, forced to listen to the call of the Divine. To be a pilgrim is to be freed from the prosaic details of everyday preoccupations and responsibilities, free to contemplate and respond to God. A pilgrimage is not about tourism or postcards; it is about change.

Pilgrims are on a journey to the unknown. They pass through

unfamiliar territories in search of wholeness and completeness, in search of a meeting place of the human and divine. No matter what direction they travel, the destination of every pilgrimage is home. Pilgrims travel to the core of their being, to the Center of reality.

In recent years, pilgrims from all walks of life have been visiting pilgrimage sites around the world in record numbers. The October 12, 1993, edition of *The New York Times* contained this headline: "Pilgrims Crowding Europe's Catholic Shrines." In 1993 an estimated twenty thousand people a day visited Lourdes; and seventy thousand "pilgrimage certificates," indicating that a person had walked at least a hundred kilometers along the medieval pilgrim path, were issued at Santiago de Compostela in Spain—up from only two thousand issued in 1983. Pilgrimages fill a need.

In an essay entitled "Pilgrimage: An Enduring Ritual of Humanity," Virgilio Elizondo says, "In the midst of growing secularism and modernity...people are seeking the stable and unchanging rootedness of sacred truth. It seems that pilgrimage sites are responding to this deep anthropological need of the human soul to be connected to mother earth."

Following the pilgrimage, I was graced with the opportunity to spend a month in solitude and reflection at a Franciscan friary in Rome. On the morning of July 26, 1997, during the communal recital of morning prayers from the Liturgy of the Hours, we read five verses from Ezekiel. I understood the middle three verses in a way I never had before. The words resounded for me:

> I will sprinkle clean water upon you,
> and you shall be clean from all your uncleannesses
> and from all your idols I will cleanse you.
>
> A new heart I will give you,
> and a new spirit I will put in you;
> and I will take out of your flesh the heart of stone
> and give you a heart of flesh.
>
> And I will put my spirit within you,
> and cause you to walk in my statutes
> and be careful to observe my ordinances. (36:25-27)

The pilgrimage helped me to see more clearly the abundance of God's goodness, and in the light of that awareness I could better see my own shortcomings and insignificance. This book was not written by someone whose life is being lived in harmony with the ideals of

Saint Francis...no, it was written by a sinner seeking to better understand Francis' message. I'll let Murray Bodo explain. He wrote:

> There is always in the pilgrim's way the way of the penitent. For as we embark upon a journey to God, we are immediately aware of how far we really are from him for whom we long, toward whom we are journeying. That is the main reason why the words of Saint Francis sound at times rather negative, rather deprecatory of what is earthly, even what is human. He is not saying that the body, the world, the human person are evil. He is only saying that apart from God, without God, in comparison to God, we and everything else that exists are really nothing. Of ourselves we are worthless and vile. Of *ourselves*, on our own, as it were. (*Through the Year With Francis of Assisi*, page 9)

I am still a sinner who stumbles all too frequently. I am not "clean of all my uncleanness." I still harbor a few false idols. My heart of flesh is still all too easily hardened into stone. But my life is no longer about falling...it is about getting up, about accepting God's love and grace. Despite its weaknesses, my heart has been changed, and is growing stronger.

During the pilgrimage, I came to see that conversion is a continuing process rather than a single moment or event in my life. Francis' life was filled with conversion moments. And the process of conversion includes a constant need for repentance and renewal. Conversion, at its root, is a change of heart; it turns us away from the notion that we are the center of the universe. Conversion often means listening to the events in our lives that change our perspective. The fruit of conversion is a release from the burden of self-groundedness so we can enter into the freedom of being grounded in God, which will create a complete recentering of our passion and a complete realignment of our affections. But it takes time and effort. Each day, I need to be cleansed, to be given a new heart and a new spirit. On the morning of July 26th, I felt, ever so briefly, that cleansing, that new heart, that new spirit. Incarnation is a daily event.

Francis and Clare were saints of incarnation. There was a visible manifestation of the conversion process going on inside of them. They preached by the witness of their lives. Their lives were their sermons. And those sermons still have something to say to us today.

DEATH IN ASSISI

On September 3, 1997, I spent nearly three hours in the Basilica of St. Francis. I was carefully studying the frescoes and thinking about the gospel message the art so vividly illustrated. The bulk of that time was spent admiring the frescoes on the walls of the upper church which comprise Giotto's "life cycle" of Saint Francis. I imagined how I would film those magnificent frescoes and use them as a basis for a film documentary on the life of Saint Francis. The profusion of creative genius on display in the upper basilica is unsurpassed in the history of Italian art. Theology and art had merged to tell the moving story of a saint who lived poverty with joy. The pictorial text that covers the walls has spoken loudly and clearly to everyone who has entered the basilica during the past seven centuries. My dream was to bring the same degree of innovation and artistry to our most popular modern story-telling form: film.

My visit ended near the main altar of the upper church, where I offered a silent prayer that the film that had been playing in my head for many months would somehow be produced and be seen by a world in need of hearing afresh the message of the poor man of Assisi. After completing my prayer, I looked up, as if pleading to heaven, and my attention was arrested by the four majestic, triangular-shaped frescoes that adorn the cross-vaults directly over the main altar. I could never have imagined that twenty-three days later part of the ceiling would collapse killing four people, including a friar and a young postulant.

In the early morning hours of Friday, September 26, at 2:33 a.m., an earthquake measuring 5.5 on the Richter scale rocked Assisi, causing minor damage to some of the frescoes which grace the walls of the upper church. The Sacro Convento attached to the basilica sustained severe damage, especially in the refectory, and had to be evacuated. The basilica remained closed on Friday in order for the friars to inspect the damage and conduct a complete safety check. Shortly before noon, at 11:42 a.m., a second stronger earthquake measuring 5.7 struck the area. Inside the basilica, about twenty people were assessing the damage from the first quake when the vault over the altar gave way and a huge section of the ceiling plummeted to the floor. Seconds later, another section of the ceiling from the cross-vault at the rear of the church crashed down, crushing to death two friars and two government surveyors from the Cultural Ministry.

They were buried under nearly ten feet of rubble.

Sixty miles away in Rome, I was in a classroom on the third floor of the Pontifical Gregorian University. The class on television writing and directing that I was teaching was coming to an end when the massive building began to sway. For about ten seconds, the students and I were paralyzed by panic. An hour later, I learned of the disaster in Assisi. It was the 96th day of my pilgrimage, a pilgrimage that had been joyful, peaceful and inspirational. Suddenly, I found myself crying, not only for the loss of four lives, but also for the loss of the priceless art which so inspired me. For the rest of the pilgrimage, I carried within me the pain and sadness that would normally accompany the death of a family member.

In a Pilgrimage Diary at the end of the book, I've written an account of that dreadful day, and document the damage caused by the earthquakes and the hundreds of aftershocks that rattled Assisi.

One year later, on October 13, 1998, I returned to Assisi and was given the rare privilege of entering the still-closed upper church in order to write more accurately about the damage and the recovery process. The book ends with that dramatic visit.

THE SAINT

In the galaxy of Christian saints, the star of Saint Francis burns brightest, a saint whose appeal is universal and timeless, a saint who is cherished by people of all faiths and is even admired by people who live without the aid of any faith in a Supreme Being. In the fall of 1926, *The New York Times* published an account of preparations in Assisi for the commemoration of the 700th anniversary of the death of Saint Francis. The headline read: "Simple Homage Paid to Saint Francis." The story claimed: "No saint in the roster of Rome has as many admirers outside the circles of orthodoxy as the saint who went his way singing not in the official language of the Church but in the language of the plain people. By writers of every nation, representing every shade of religious belief, the husband of Lady Poverty has been proclaimed as an apostle of humanity, and one of the possessions common to all mankind."

Imagine, *The New York Times* suggesting Saint Francis belongs to all of humanity. Seventy years after the paper carried that story, Saint Francis' popularity continues to increase. He seems to be a saint not only for all people, but for all seasons as well. Yet Francis is truly a product of his time and place. He lived eight centuries ago in a small city that sits on the side of a mountain overlooking a lush valley located in the heart of Italy. However, this man, who chose poverty for his bride, managed to transcend the thirteenth century and his small city and is still able to attract followers and admirers from all around the world.

In the fall of 1992, a special edition of *Time* magazine dedicated to a look at the coming new millennium selected Saint Francis of Assisi as one of the top ten major figures of this fading millennium. The list included Galileo, Michelangelo, Gutenberg, Shakespeare, Jefferson, Mozart and Einstein. For a man who didn't discover any galaxies or continents, who didn't create any great works of art or write any literary masterpieces or compose any enduring music, who didn't invent anything or solve any of the mysteries of the universe, and who instead chose a life of prayer and poverty, Francis ranked in some pretty impressive company.

Still, it's far easier to admire Francis than to understand him. He can charm us with his gentleness or chill us with his unfathomable asceticism and long fasts; he can be seen as a nature lover, a social worker, a humanist, a lyric poet, a rebel, a radical, a dropout and an extremist. Especially an extremist. He was, in fact, the saint of excesses: excess in sacrifice, excess in love. And then there is the perplexing matter of the stigmata. Francis can be many different things to many different people. The Francis I want to present will not be a plastic, pious saint, a simple man who tamed wolves and preached to birds and loved nature, but a complex man who was demanding and uncompromising, yet who above all else loved God with his entire being. Francis is a human saint, a saint who could laugh and make mistakes, including misunderstanding what God was telling him.

Francis is an unlikely hero of the Church. He wasn't a bishop or an abbot or a theologian...*he wasn't even a priest!* Francis had no theological training, and he remained a deacon, either out of humility or because he simply did not find himself so moved by the Spirit to pursue priestly ordination. After his conversion, Francis never set out to be a religious. He never intended to form or head a new religious order, and he never imagined writing a rule of life for others to follow; all these things were done only when Francis was asked to do them by the pope in order to provide structure and direction for the thousands who chose to follow his radical, full-gospel way of life. Moreover, Francis wasn't well-versed in the Bible or the lives of the saints, and he had no interest in scholarly pursuits.

Francis wasn't at home in high, ornate pulpits; he preferred to speak directly to the peasants he encountered along the road. But when he did stand behind a pulpit, he didn't preach, he conversed. He didn't concern himself with complicated reasoning or developing a theme; he merely said, simply and directly, what came into his mind. He lacked any real oratorical style, and his sermons were devoid of dogmatism, theological quotations or pompous phrases. Francis' words came freely from the inspiration of the moment. Having lived, loved and suffered, Francis knew about life and had not forgotten its trials and sorrows...or its joys. He spoke and acted from the heart, and above all else he was profoundly human, and a man who gloried in his own commonness.

Francis' life took on heroic proportions because he became the *Poverello*—God's poor little one.

Saint Francis, the one true follower of the naked, crucified Christ, was devoted to poverty and embraced it as if it were his bride. He believed what Jesus said was true: "Blessed are the poor in spirit, for theirs is the kingdom of heaven." Because he loved God, Francis became detached, both in mind and heart, from all worldly possessions. During his life he grew systematically poorer, while finding true joy in penance and self-deprivation. He wanted none of the excesses of wealth. He didn't merely reject the excess of wealth but, more importantly, he rejected its sufficiency. Francis believed voluntary poverty was quintessential to a holy life; for him, God alone was sufficient. The saint took Christ's words literally, and Christ said it would be as difficult for the rich to enter heaven as it would be for a camel to squeeze through the eye of a needle.

In his early twenties, Francis began to experience two sensations which have caused countless mystics to take the first step along the road to illumination: self-hatred and a dissatisfaction with life. During the torturous agony mystics call the "dark night of the soul," a psychic transformation occurred and Francis, following the gospel admonition, turned his back on life, left his family, even stripped himself of the clothes his father had given him, and went off to lead the demanding life of a hermit and beggar. At first, he was ridiculed by the people of Assisi; even his friends called him mad. To the worldly, the saint always appears mad; and to the spiritual, worldly values seem insane.

Near the end of the twelfth century, just a half dozen years after Francis was born, the citizens of a small town in Belgium asked the king for permission to set up a clock in a public square and strike the hours in order to regulate business hours. Before then, knowing the correct time was not important. Besides, church bells already divided the day into three periods of prayer (morning, afternoon and evening) and that was sufficient. But now people felt a need to divide the day into shorter intervals, which created more deadlines. "Beat the clock" was the new game in town. In the beginning of the fourteenth century, the world's first public mechanical clock was installed in Milan, not all that far from Assisi. The clock marked the beginning of a new age: "Modern Times."

Francis saw it coming and rejected modern times and its unquenchable thirst for progress which eventually led to atom bombs and computers and our own explosive times that are measured by milliseconds. Francis wanted no part of modernity; he wanted people to look back and refocus on the life of Christ and follow him, because Francis believed Christ was the true way to progress. And Francis, an idealist who put his ideals into practice, followed Christ the way Scripture suggests: in complete poverty, giving up all and trusting fully in the Lord. He didn't want to own anything, except the bare essential minimum of clothing, which amounted to a hooded robe fastened about the waist with a rope. Francis had no books; in fact, he was skeptical of the printed word, except for the Word of God. He did not wish to feed his spirit on anything apart from God. He would have ignored "Must See TV" on NBC.

Francis had only one desire: the reconciliation of humanity with God, itself and nature. Of all those who have responded to Christ's plea to sell all they own and give the proceeds to the poor, Francis was the most literal, the most ardent and the most successful. Francis wanted to own absolutely nothing but the rags he wore. Mystics have always seen poverty as a key to spiritual wealth, because without resources one must rely totally upon God. Francis was so aware of this principle that he once threw away his belt buckle, considering it too grand a thing to own, and used instead a piece of rope. (I still rely on the lord of cash...and if that is lacking, I put my trust in my Visa card.)

Machiavelli said, "Christianity was dying; St. Francis resurrected it." Without Francis, Christianity may very well have vanished. Francis, in a sense, rediscovered Christianity, which had lost its luster and was seen as merely a lifeless formula. Yet, in that dead formula, Francis saw life itself. Staring at the face of a painted Christ on a cross, he experienced the revelation of the Passion, a revelation that gave birth to completely new forms of sensibility. For Francis, an ounce of transcendence was worth more than a ton of reasoning. (In contrast, for most of my adult life "reason" was my God, and the transcendental was a temptation to be assiduously avoided.)

Francis was the first saint to smile, at least in the Christian communion of saints. He enjoyed life. As a young man, Francis was full of vitality and enthusiasm; he loved clothes, splendid feasts and music...he was, in short, a playboy. Even after his conversion and new path of asceticism, he truly delighted in life and began singing the praises of God and nature. But in his day, religion was serious, God was a stern judge and life was violent, and so when people encountered anyone as happy as Francis, they assumed that the person must be sinning. But Francis was filled with a holy joy, a joy that infected all who came in contact with him.

Saint Francis' spirit renewed everything around him; as Dante wrote in Paradiso (Canto XI), "Like the sun that rises behind the mountain of Assisi," Francis made Italian art, poetry and even drama flourish. His mission was simple, yet profound: to humanize the Divine. For the people of Assisi, God was in heaven and had nothing to do with their miserable lives. Francis boldly preached a joyful God willing to be born into a messy world. This idea slowly infiltrated religious art, which began to reflect the radiant aspects of Christianity: goodness, gentleness and love. The effulgence of Christ could be seen on the faces of the saints portrayed on the walls of the churches. Art and literature before Francis had become stiff and formal; forms of convention stifled inspiration. But that changed with Francis. Poor Francis was a rich source of inspiration for artists such as Cimabue, Giotto and Dante. The glorious, unfettered spirit of the Renaissance can be traced back to the soaring spirit of a humble saint clothed in rags.

Charity and love, the essence of Christianity and the secret of the Gospels, were never better expressed—either before or after—than they were during the thirteenth century. Biblical scenes were suddenly populated by knights and common folks doing ordinary things...and God was in the picture! Francis and his followers began singing the praises of God and his saints—the "lauds"—in the vernacular. Little by little, Italian was substituted for Latin in the chanting and hymns. The mobile new friars, wandering from town to town preaching in Italian, managed to reach more people than the great monastic orders, secluded and stationary, could ever hope to.

It is interesting to note that within two hundred years, by the fifteenth century, art presented primarily images of suffering and death. The naked, suffering Messiah, crowned with thorns, offering his wounds and blood was the lesson artists taught. Christianity was no longer a religion of love, but a religion of suffering. The serene art that was born of the Franciscan spirit had given way to the somber art of the fifteenth century. The Triumphant Christ of the High Middle Ages became the Suffering Christ of the Late Middle Ages. The printing press made the transition possible.

Before the printing press, faith was spread and nourished by the spoken word, and preachers preferred to talk about Christ's birth and resurrection rather than his passion and death. For instance, Saint Anselm did not weep over Christ's passion, because through the passion, he had been saved. Even artists avoided the details of Christ's death. But books began to present meditations on the death of Christ, meditations often inspired by visions experienced by the mystics, such as Saint Brigitta of Sweden, a member of the Third Order Secular of Saint Francis whose fervent book *Revelations* described how Jesus' jaws were swollen, his tongue bloodied and his stomach so sunken that it touched his backbone. The Virgin Mary "told" Saint Brigitta just how badly her son suffered, how his eyes and ears and beard streamed with blood...and Saint Brigitta told the faithful in gory detail.

Francis was no stranger to the suffering Messiah, but for him the wounds of Christ became portals to the unfathomable love of God. Francis' love of God embodied the principle of unity which embraces the multiplicity of creation. Love of the Creator made Francis love all creation and creatures. Francis had a purity of heart which allowed him to embrace chastely the entire universe. In contrast, the impure (of whom I count myself) embrace things lustfully.

Purity of heart, for Francis, had nothing to do with sex; it was simply a manifestation of an uncluttered heart. Jesus alone was enough for Francis, and this reality in his life freed him from all the complications which entangle most humans, and the fruit of this freedom was true simplicity. Everything that Francis did flowed from the purity of his heart which strove only to give glory to and be in union with Jesus.

His concept of the spiritual life is as simple as it is energetic, and it rests on three points, which were nicely summarized by Martial Lekeux, O.F.M.:

First, plow the road to love by renunciation, that is, by complete deprivation: one that is primarily interior but which will be exterior as possible. In doing this, we must follow directives given in the gospel and make the imitation of Christ our rule of life.

Having in this way purified, simplified, and refreshed our life and heart, the next step is to arouse affective love in our souls by the assiduous contemplation of Christ, especially of his passion, and the continual raising of our souls to God, whom we have sought and recognized in all things.

Finally, this love must be put to work by conforming ourselves to Christ, our love, and by the perfect practice of every virtue, our one and only concern being to please him. (*Short Cut to Divine Love*)

Francis' awareness of God came from his deep awareness of himself, where he discovered God was the very ground of his being. This awareness of his true self fostered a greater awareness of God within others, including nature, which filled him with a profound sense of reverence for all he saw. The essence of Francis' spiritual outlook can be found in the words of Saint Amadeus of Lausanne, who died just about a quarter of a century before Francis was born: "He who does not know himself does not penetrate to the deep things of God."

Francis personalized and sanctified all of creation, including inanimate creation, and so he could no longer treat things as things. The sun, the moon, the stars, the trees, the birds all became his brothers and sisters, members of his family, and as such he was able to speak to them lovingly. From a rationalist point of view, this was very foolish. From a spiritual or mystical point of view, it was profoundly wise.

Assisi

It wouldn't be wise to try to tell Francis' story without first saying a few words about Assisi, because no other city or town is so closely identified with a saint. Assisi molded Francis, and Francis illuminated Assisi. Ironically, Assisi, a straggling medieval town, walled, gated and turreted, and forever tied to the memory of a man known as "an instrument of peace," has a blood-soaked, war-torn past. First the Romans conquered the Umbrian-Etruscans, and they in turn were conquered by the Goths, who eventually succumbed to the Lombards. Later transitions from an independent commune to a royal fiefdom to a papal state were marked by ferocious battles.

Francis was born in the imperial period, when Assisi was often threatened by the neighboring towns of Perugia, Urbino and Milano. The large fortress which overlooks the city was built by German feudal rulers; it was later enlarged by the popes, and was once the home of Emperor Frederick II. When Francis was a young man, the fortress was the site of some fierce battles between the aristocrats and the common people. Francis even fought in some of the battles. In Assisi, violence, brutality and war had become a way of life. Battles fought with stones and blunt instruments left combatants maimed for life. Bloody skirmishes with the neighboring comune of Perugia were waged with fierce intensity, and captured prisoners were subjected to unspeakably cruel torture. Assisi was truly a place in need of an "instrument of peace," and Francis would slowly transform himself into one.

Geography played a vital role in Assisi's history, because the city is situated high on the slope of a mountain, and therefore it held a great strategic importance in the Middle Ages for the control of the roads that led from Foligno to Perugia.

Assisi was a small crowded town in Francis' day. Few people living there could read and even fewer could deal with abstract concepts; the people of Assisi were walled off from the world of ideas. They had full confidence in the Church's answers to the few questions they asked. They believed in supernatural powers and the power of prayer. Angels and saints protected them; evil and natural disasters were the handiwork of the devil. The clergy were the elite members of society as well as the most educated; the Church was corrupt and riddled with simony and debauchery.

The physical reality of life in the Middle Ages is an important part of Francis' story. Johan Huizinga in *The Waning of the Middle Ages* notes that everything in those days was marked by stark contrasts, the likes of which the modern mind can hardly imagine. He writes, "The contrast between silence and sound, darkness and light, like that between summer and winter, was more strongly marked than it is in our lives. The modern town hardly knows silence or darkness in their purity, nor the effect of a solitary light or a single distant cry" (page 2).

In Francis' time, when it was night, it was night, pitch black; and when it was silent, it was so silent that even a distant cry in the night was startling. The differences between suffering and joy, between illness and health, between misfortune and happiness, between town and country, were also more sharp and striking. Back then, the cold and darkness of winter were so severe they were experienced as real evils. Huizinga writes, "We at the present day, can hardly understand the keenness with which a fur coat, a good fire on the hearth, a soft bed, a glass of wine, were formerly enjoyed" (page 1). Nature was a cruel tyrant whose whim could make every aspect of life utterly miserable. (Nature, as the people of Assisi learned in the fall of 1997, can still be cruel and make life miserable.)

Life was shrouded in mysteries, and many daily events, everything from marriages to funerals to common tasks to journeys, were performed under the rubrics of countless civil and religious formalities and ceremonies. Huizinga writes, "All things presenting themselves to the mind in violent contrasts and impressive forms, lent a tone of excitement and a passion to everyday life and tended to produce that perpetual oscillation between despair and distracted joy, between cruelty and pious tenderness which characterize life in the Middle Ages" (page 2).

And then there was the unspeakable physical misery and suffering. William R. Cook writes, "We can only speculate how many people were missing limbs and teeth, how many were deformed and disfigured from birth, diet, disease, war or accident. Many injuries and diseases that today are minor inconveniences left permanent marks on people in the Middle Ages. Most horrible of all were the lepers. Their grotesqueness and smell brought disgust to many who saw them..." (*Francis of Assisi*, page 20).

In short, life was hard...more brutal, more exciting, more dangerous, more mysterious, more glorious, more ritualistic than anything we can imagine. Each day presented new battles requiring fresh heroism. I would have lasted about a week.

Today, Assisi, with its ancient gateways, narrow medieval streets and stone houses with shuttered windows, is an endearing and charming little town, rising in a series of shelves or terraces on the mountainside. Paul M. Allen and Joan deRis Allen write:

> As one approaches Assisi, crossing the Umbrian plain from the west, particularly at the hour of sunset, the town appears as a dreamlike mirage, resting on a spur of the western slopes of Mount Subasio. An almost magical grouping of houses, towers, churches, spires, walls, gateways—all of them made from a local stone of a rosy-pink hue, and roofed with terra-cotta tiles in the local tradition—appear together in a harmonious oneness in the light of the setting sun. (*Francis of Assisi's Canticle*

of the Creatures, page 13)

It is fitting to apply the words "dreamlike" and "magical" to any description of Assisi.

Rome is known as the Eternal City, but Assisi feels like an Eternal Shrine, honoring not only Francis and Clare, but also the mirror of their love, Christ. Christ, through Francis and Clare, hovers over this enchanted, saintly city. Its twisting, climbing streets seem to lead straight to heaven. Grace and hope are in the air. Assisi soothes the soul and stirs the spirit. God's smile can be seen even on a cloudy day.

Assisi lies roughly halfway between Florence and Rome, in the center of Umbria, the only Italian province that lacks either a coast-line or a border with a foreign nation. The dark, wooded Mount Subasio looms behind Assisi like a massive hump, 4,900 feet high; the vast Valley of Spoleto lies below Assisi, a lush, green carpet thir-ty miles long and five miles wide, covered with meadows, vineyards, fields of wheat and maize, groves of olive trees and stands of cypress and oak trees. This gentle valley, with its peaceful rhythm of life, greeted Saint Francis each morning, easily enticing the sensitive young man to fall in love with nature and instilling in him a joy of life that eclipsed the fear of death in his religious outlook. Saint Francis sang the praises of the lush valley and smiling hills of Assisi all his life. He said, "I've seen nothing lovelier than my Valley of Spoleto." For Francis, the beauty of the valley and hills and sky—indeed, the wonders of all of nature—made a fitting altar for the worship of the Infinite.

Both the valley and the mountain are bathed in the brilliance of the golden Umbrian sunlight, creating a halo above the entire scene. The stone walls of the ancient churches and homes glimmer in the sunlit air that vibrates with freshness and purity; in the glow of sun-set, the soft light dances gently on the dark forms of cypresses stand-ing erect on the hillside, like knights protecting the holy shrines. During the day, the landscape below the calm azure sky speaks as loudly as the church sanctuaries and the frescoes. It is easy to see how Francis saw God's life-giving radiance and flame of divine love in the face of Brother Sun as it rose over Assisi.

The entire landscape—the humped mountain, the walled city, the wooded hillside, and the fertile plain—seems to shout a joyful hymn of praise to the Creator. It is a sight that stirs the unfath-omable yet radiant majesty of God and leaves one speechless...and calm. Harmony and communion abound in Assisi; they can be seen in nature and art, towers and churches, trees and shrubs, hills and fields. Peace is in the air, a peace you can almost touch, a peace that trancends the intellect. In Assisi, the Franciscan motto—*Pace e Bene* (Peace and Blessing)—fits like a glove. Francis is so real here, you expect him to pass under some archway or poke his head out of some alley.

In her charming book of poetry and pen-and-ink sketches, *Footsteps in Assisi*, Sara Lee Jobe suggests:

> Assisi has become a bridge
>   that spans the chasm created by time,
>   that separates the places called "past" and "present."
>
> The element of time has little significance
>   when one climbs the streets
>   where Francis joyfully greeted his neighbors,
>   or spends time in a chapel
>   he lovingly repaired,
>   or walks quietly in the garden
>   where Clare so often prayed.
>
> Awe and wonder
>   move with their own accord, unbidden,
>   pulling the seeker into the presence of the saints.
>   (page 23)

Life in Assisi is still measured by the sounds of church bells, some ringing mightily, others brightly. Added to the peace and charm which grace the town is something easy to overlook: the flowers. Flowers enliven the town on every side. They bloom in window boxes and in pots, they cascade from balconies and are hung in festoons from ancient walls and archways, giving an air of festivity to Assisi. The olive trees which cover the slopes of the hills below Assisi are considered to be the oldest in Italy; for centuries upon centuries their silvery leaves have shimmered under the bright sun. Fields of giant, bright yellow sunflowers dot the valley below; they all seem to be smiling at the city kissed by God.

In Assisi, there is a synthesis between poetry and prayer, between sanctity and song, between asceticism and aestheticism. Assisi taught me that simplicity, serenity, sincerity, silence and song are the heart of the Franciscan spirit. Assisi is an eternal shrine, in which Francis' candle still burns brightly.

To help the reader form an accurate picture of Francis in his or her mind, here is a brief physical description of the saint, excerpted from *Richest of the Poor*, a 1948 biography written by Theodore Maynard:

> It is also clear from what Celano says [Brother Thomas Celano was born in 1185 and wrote the first biography of Francis, whom he knew], listing details with the bluntness of a catalogue, that Francis was not very handsome: slight, rather undersized, round of head, with a long straight nose that was a trifle too prominent, a low forehead, eyes dark and bright, ears standing out somewhat but fortunately small, thin lips, and a swarthy complexion. The picture is far from prepossessing. Not only did he lack good looks, he struck one at first glance as insignificant.
>
> That this was so, however, makes it all the clearer that his charm must have been immense. Those dark eyes of his were bright with candor and affection and a good will that was boundless and simple. Except for such times as he had an air of melancholy (and that, too, was attractive), he was radiant in his joy.... [T]here was nothing about him that was not delicate or refined; this shone in his face and was materialized in his thin fingers and his small feet. Though he might appear undistinguished, everybody became conscious almost immediately that this utterly unself-conscious man was the most remarkable personality they had ever encountered. (page 25)

I'll conclude this section with a few words about a writer who came to Assisi a little over a hundred years ago, and how the magical little city turned his life upside down when he "encountered" the "remarkable personality" of the "utterly unself-conscious" saint whose spirit still mystically hovers over the city. The writer's name was Johannes Jörgensen. Jörgensen was at the core of his being a searcher—a searcher for truth. Writing, for him, I imagine, was a tool to reach a greater understanding of what he really thought. Born in Denmark, Jörgensen was raised in the Methodist Church, against which he rebelled, turning instead to theosophy, which gave way to agnosticism, which eventually evolved into atheism (a perfectly logical and reasonable progression), even though he never stopped desperately wrestling with a God he didn't believe existed.

Jörgensen was a gifted but tormented poet. He read all the decadent French writers that were in vogue in his day (late 1800's). He traveled to Italy in order to write about the Church. His friends expected a book that was brilliant, skeptical and witty...and filled with caustic comments about the superstitious Church in the south. But something happened in Assisi, and Jörgensen instead produced a book which glorified faith...and Francis.

As Jörgensen was making his way to Rome, he met a painter who invited him to spend a few days in Assisi. A chance encounter? Or fate? The simple invitation from the painter, who had recently converted to Catholicism and who eventually became a Benedictine monk, would lead to a complete transformation of Jörgensen's life. One moment on a road changed the direction of his life. When Jörgensen arrived in Assisi in July of 1894, he was a miserable, penniless writer overflowing with a deep hatred of bourgeois society. Worse, he loathed himself. But Assisi made him look at everything in a different light. Initially, he stayed in Assisi for three months. He was especially drawn to the Church of Santa Maria degli Angeli (St. Mary of the Angels). During those three months, Francis invaded Jörgensen's heart and soul, and changed his life. Suddenly, poetry embraced prayer and song sang of sanctity. Eighteen months later he converted to Catholicism. After several visits and writing his book, Jörgensen settled in Assisi in 1915, where he lived for most of the rest of his life. After years of spiritual conflict, the peace and joy of Assisi eventually soothed his soul. Until his death in 1956 (at age 89), Jörgensen was devoted to writing about Saint Francis. Today, the street which passes in front of the house where Jörgensen lived in Assisi is named after the Danish author.

Jörgensen's beautifully written and highly praised biography of Saint Francis was published in 1912 and is still considered to be the most notable contribution to Franciscan literature in modern times. The book is still in print, having been translated into countless languages.

I find Jörgensen's arrival in Assisi as an unbeliever and his subsequent dramatic transformation to be extremely interesting. Imagine, nearly seven hundred years after his death, Saint Francis still had the power to turn a modern, skeptical, talented writer's life upside down, and completely change the way he viewed the world.

To come to Assisi and to walk in the footsteps of Francis is, ultimately, to walk in the footsteps of Christ. During my first visit to Assisi, I found myself being drawn to Francis' radical interpretation of the message of Christ, and how that message transformed Assisi and the legends of Francis' followers down through the centuries. In his own time and for all time, Saint Francis is the tireless messenger of Love, continuously singing Incarnation's song. Saint Francis is a towering figure because of his simplicity, which reduced the entire Christian faith to one word: Love. As he neared the end of his earthly pilgrimage, Saint Francis of Assisi did not judge, reject, hate or condemn anyone or anything...he merely loved...all, equally, passionately.

"Merely"...as if it were that simple.

Saint Francis was a spiritual artist—in the sense that great artists are really...simplifiers. Vincent van Gogh thought Christ was the greatest artist of all time. Francis, I believe, finished a close second. He did not paint or sculpt; Francis was an artist whose medium was life itself. His story is a human drama with universal appeal, a story of an ordinary man who accomplished extraordinary things while transcending his time and place on his way to becoming the brightest burning star in the galaxy of Christian saints.

Simone Martini
St. Francis
c.1317
Fresco, Basilica di San Francesco, Assisi

Part Two

SAINT FRANCIS OF ASSISI

A Joyful Light

TROUBLED TIMES

*I*t is never possible to gauge in any just manner the life and
work of any really great man, unless we realise, as fully as
may be, the circumstances of his time.

—W. J. KNOX LITTLE, *ST. FRANCIS OF ASSISI*

Francis was born in 1182, smack in the middle of an era of heated
hostility and confrontation. The second half of the twelfth century
was a turbulent and tense period for Europe and the Western
Church. A great schism had rocked the Church. Heresies sprouted
and spread like weeds. Monasticism was on the decline. Critics of
the rich and powerful clergy expressed open hostility toward the
Church hierarchy. The laity were demanding a more active role in
the Church. Meanwhile, the Church set out to conquer and convert
the pagans of the Moslem east. It was the era of the crusades, when
violence was employed by the Church as an instrument of the
Kingdom of God. The Inquisition was soon to bring terror to the
homes of many in Christendom.

Here is Carlo Carretto writing as Saint Francis:

> Religion in my day was badly lived. Parishes were only half
> alive, and were for the most part cults rather than life. Priests in
> their sermons sought to terrify people with the usual discourses
> on eternal punishment, while the Gospel was buried in a heavy
> and inexorably clerical tradition. There was no room for the
> laity, married people, country folk. Only the religious counted.
> Above all, joy was missing. To be a Christian meant to be sad—
> especially for women, who stifled their femininity in a thou-
> sand fears. (*I, Francis*, page 26)

After centuries of governing every aspect of social life, the land-
rooted feudal system, solidly structured from top to bottom and
ruled by a small number of powerful lords, was on the verge of collapse and a new, more mobile society of merchants and craftsmen
was slowly emerging. And the emerging market system gave rise to
an unprecedented desire for wealth, goods and power. Additionally,
there was a dramatic population explosion which created a doubling
of the population between the years 1000 and 1200, giving birth to
a powerful trend toward urbanization. It was a time of profound
social upheaval and transformation. People and ideas were on the
move, and new cities were being formed.

But change did not come easily. By the thirteenth century, grue-
some urban riots were sweeping across Europe. Economic conflict
erupted in the towns, pitting apprentice against master. Peasant violence spread like wildfire in the countryside. Barter slowly disappeared as the crusades sparked an unprecedented increase in commercial trade in the West. Money became a part of everyday life, as
banks set up exchange branches in all the major cities throughout
Europe. Merchants, bankers and shipbuilders accumulated enough
money, prestige and power to rival aristocratic nobles, and a new
class of "haves" emerged. The entire social order was being over-
turned. In his book on Saint Lutgarde of Aywieres, *What Are These
Wounds?*, a Cistercian nun and mystic born in the same year as Saint
Francis, Thomas Merton writes:

> [The thirteenth century] saw the climax of many centuries of
> Christian culture and it witnessed a turning point in the social
> and religious history of the western world. Feudalism was com-
> ing to an end, a powerful commercial class was beginning to
> play a dominant part in civil life, especially in the great cities of
> western Europe. A gradual but fundamental economic revolu-

tion was taking place, with profound effects on the whole structure of society, and the spiritual life of the Catholic Church was
bound to be affected by it.

The thirteenth century was an age of conflict and contradiction. It was a century of great saints and great sinners, great
greed and great charity, great mercy and great cruelty. The
schoolmen were contemplating the deepest truths of theology
and philosophy with a limpid serenity of vision that has never
been equaled; but already, around them, less capable and less
spiritual minds were preparing the decline of Christian thought
by a sterile intellectualism without spirit and without insight.
There were already powerful heresies abroad, heresies which
affected thousands with unrest. (pages 1-2)

At the close of the twelfth century, Assisi had its own specific troubles: it was caught in the vise of an intense international power
struggle for control of the entire Italian peninsula. Vying with each
other for the Spoleto Valley were the Normans, struggling to hold on
to the southern Sicilian states; the German forces of the north, with
their eyes on the Holy Roman Empire; and the papacy.

Besides these external political pressures, Assisi itself was a community awash in conflicts between the newly-rich merchants, which
included Francis' family, and the old aristocracy, which included the
family of Saint Clare, and between the rich and the poor. It was a
city where the extremes of greed and misery lived side by side. Regis
Armstrong, O.F.M. Cap., writes: "The ancient Umbrian city was
internally torn by a struggle based on a social inequality that
widened the gap between the social classes and solidified sharp
social barriers." He adds:

> Assisi was at the crossroads. The economic structures that for so
> long governed its way of life were crumbling and with them the
> political machinery that had vacillated between one power and
> another was exerting itself in a revolutionary way. Citizens were
> now expressing themselves in new ways: destroying the city's
> fortress, once a symbol of domination by foreigners, proclaim-
> ing themselves a "Commune," and breaking new gates into the
> old city walls that new trade routes might be encouraged. Popes
> as well as emperors were keeping careful watch on the so-called
> "Commune of Assisi" and were attempting to keep it within
> their own power and control. (*Clare of Assisi*, pages 9-10)

Somehow, in this extremely volatile religious and political environment Francis grew into an apostle of peace and justice, preaching reconciliation and restitution, and the joy of holy poverty. In an essay entitled "This Dark Mystery: The Franciscan Vocation of Saint Clare of Assisi," appearing in the October 1993 issue of *The Cord*, Dr. William C. Zehringer writes:

> One of the most remarkable insights of the saint was his ability to judge, correctly, that a band of begging friars, praising God and ministering to the stricken poor in the lost corners of the world, could show his society the way out of the pride, selfishness and despair that were tearing at its very foundations.
>
> Indeed it was so. For it was in those very Italian cities that have been made immortal by Francis' sojourns in and around them, that there first began to emerge, in his century, "the capitalist rational economy" that Octavio Paz so brilliantly dissected [in *Conjunctions and Disjunctions*]: "At the same time that gold disappears from the dress of men and women and from altars and palaces, it becomes the invisible blood of mercantile society and circulates, odorless and colorless, in every country."
>
> And so, the divine calling to which Saint Francis directed not only Clare but also his first companions, had everything to do with opposing the headlong foolishness and largesse of all Lovers of the Living God to the spirit of calculation and profit that was to so seam the face of the modern world. And so they did, with singular panache and inspired song, down the roads of Europe and far beyond them.

IN THE BEGINNING

The more we indulge in soft living and pampered bodies, more rebellious they will become against the spirit.

—SAINT RITA OF CASCIA

Francis was born into a relatively wealthy family. His father, Pietro Bernardone, was a hard-working cloth merchant and shrewd businessman who had reached the highest level of the city's mercantile class. His shop in Assisi sold precious fabrics, which Bernardone acquired during his many trips to France. Francis' father owned a number of homes in Assisi, and even to this day, it cannot be determined with absolute certainty exactly which one was the actual house in which the saint was born. Down through the centuries no less than six or seven places in the town have claimed this honor. Today, it is possible to visit three houses where the saint allegedly was born. I visited each of the birthplaces and was happy to celebrate the saint's birth in each of them.

Very little is known about Francis' mother, whose name was Pica—although there is even some doubt about that. It seems probable that she was born in France, perhaps in Provence, where Pietro often traveled in search of fine cloth. Francis' early biographers bathed her in the gentlest of lights, illuminating a devout, quiet woman who worried about her son's future and frail health.

Pietro was in France on business when his son was born. Actually, "in France on business" sounds too modern, too soft. A grueling expedition comes closer to reality. Pietro was traveling with a long train of heavily baled pack horses and mules to a distant fair. Trips to France might have lasted for a couple of months. While he was away, Pica named the child John, in honor of John the Baptist. Upon his return to Assisi, Pietro promptly changed his son's name to Francis—or Francesco—perhaps to celebrate his good fortune on the expedition to France or simply to honor his wife's native land. Whatever the reason for the name change, the nickname stuck, even though, as the saint's first biographer points out, the name was rare—"singular and unusual"—at the time. The young Francis would grow to become singular and unusual in his own time.

There is precious little recorded information about Francis' early childhood or cultural formation. Most of the biographical sketches show Francis as a lively child, prone to playing pranks on neighbors and friends. Everyone seemed to like the affable young boy. By all accounts, he had a sweet temperament and was well-mannered. He was likeable and gregarious. Saint Bonaventure, who was just a young boy when Francis died and who eventually became the minister general of the Order, writes in his *Major Life*: "His gentleness, his refined manners, his patience, his superhuman affability, his generosity beyond his means, marked him as a young man of flourishing natural disposition" (*Bonaventure*, page 186).

His education was modest at best, but more than adequate to the needs of a future cloth merchant. He attended school at the Church of San Giorgio, where he learned to read and write. Decades later, Francis was provisionally buried in the very same church. Today, the Chapel of the Blessed Sacrament in the Basilica di Santa Chiara is located on the very spot where Francis learned to read the psalms in Latin and began his religious education.

Francis' knowledge of the Bible appears to have been gleaned from his active participation in the liturgical life of the Church rather than any systematic biblical study. Despite his regular church attendance, Francis was not considered especially pious. As a teenager, he enjoyed drinking and singing with his friends. In fact, Thomas of Celano, in his *First Life* of the saint, written shortly after his death, says that the young Francis lived "in sin with the zeal of youthful passion and was driven by the feverish impulse of his age to satisfy all his youthful desires as he pleased, since he did not know moderation he was easily driven to evil..." (1 Cel. 2).

Thanks to his parents' social status, Francis was free from every care, and tested all the pleasures that money could buy. Burning with cupidity, the teenage Francis lived closer to the state of indigence than to the state of grace. Hans Urs von Balthasar, S.J., wrote, "It is difficult to make young people understand the real mystery of Christ, because the mystery of weakness runs counter to the impulses of youth" (*The Last Grain of Wheat*, page 57). Perhaps this was true for Francis.

In place of solid facts about Francis' early years, we are left to fill in the gaps with our imaginations, as we try to place the future saint in the ancient streets of medieval Assisi. Chiara Frugoni paints a reasonable portrait of young Francis in the old city:

> Francis will have played on the narrow pavement in front of the church [San Giorgio]. At that time children and adults in fact lived much of their lives in the street, since the houses were small, squeezed within the surrounding walls which made space both precious and rare.
>
> It must have been good to go out into the open air like this and to enjoy the panorama around Assisi even without being aware of it. In the summer the green fields, the woods and the olive trees were mixed with areas of ripe corn, and coloured patches of flowers. The powerful sound of bells, marking the times of prayer and work, filled the air and drowned human voices and shouts. The town criers would pass through from time to time, to announce to their trumpets the decisions of the authorities. Sometimes acrobats and jugglers gave a show, to the sound of fifes, viols and tambourines. These were not the only noises of the city; the grinding of the cartwheels, the rapid and rhythmic clip-clop of horses' hooves striking the pavements, were mixed with the cries of a host of animals: geese, chickens, sheep, goats, pigs and cows. In the eyes of a child, horses are

gigantic animals, which is why it is so good to be able to master them. Francis watched them pass, ridden by noblemen dressed in precious and colorful clothes, and his imagination transformed them into heroes and paladins. He, too, will have galloped on a broomstick, using it as a hobby-horse. Perhaps he even had a horse on wheels, to play at jousting; and when he said his prayers in the evening perhaps he asked God not to make him a better person but to give him a magnificent horse, a real one. (*Francis of Assisi*, page 4)

As a young man, the spirited and jovial Francis loved the songs of the troubadours. He wore expensive clothing and used his parents' hard-earned money to fund lavish feasts and drinking bouts. He dreamed of romance and becoming a soldier. And like his mother, Francis also loved poetry.

The Face of God

The youthful Francis loved life and lived it to the fullest. He loved to party, to have a good time in everything he did. His being pulsated with life, eagerly greeting each new day with overflowing exuberance. And while those early years gave no hint of his saintly future, no hint of his looming total dedication to God, there was something different about him, something that clearly separated him from his fellow revelers. In his youthful coarseness, there was a hidden gift...the capacity to see beauty in all its purity. He was a wordless poet, easily intoxicated by a sunflower, ready to fly to the moon on the wings of a dove. He heard birds speak and saw stars sparkle. For Francis, beauty led to contemplation. In time his love for the beauty of nature was transformed into a love of the beauty of God. God was Beauty and made everything beautiful. Francis began to see beauty even in ugliness. And Francis' response to Beauty was wonder and worship, and the growing knowledge that the earth was sanctified by the very fact of its creation.

Creation became the revelation and manifestation of God.
The sun became the face of God.
The poet became the saint.

I have always loved the beauty of nature. Watching the sunset over the Pacific Ocean from the beach in Carmel-by-the-Sea never failed to fill me with wonder and awe. And peace. But beauty speaks to me in a whisper compared to the way it spoke to Francis. Perhaps I am too busy to hear it speak any louder than a whisper.

Ever since that day in Rome when for a fleeting fraction of a second I caught a veiled glimpse of the reality of God, the natural world has been more beautiful than ever. Still, I am more often than not overwhelmed by the ugliness of life. Ours is a coarse age. I need to cultivate the poet within me, to enlarge the sphere and capacities of my heart, so I, too, can see the face of God in the ugly ghetto of my daily life and experiences.

IN HIS FATHER'S FOOTSTEPS

In the middle of the journey of our life
I came to my senses in the dark forest
for I had lost the straight path.
        —DANTE ALIGHIERI, THE INFERNO

When Francis was five years old, Jerusalem fell to Islamic forces under the leadership of Saladin, setting off the crusades, an enormous enterprise which would directly influence Francis' life. When he was sixteen, a civil war erupted in Assisi, a conflict that could be boiled down to "old money" vs. "new money."

At fourteen years of age, Francis followed in his father's footsteps and became a member of the merchants' guild, which marked his formal entrance into the civic life of Assisi. Within two years, he was deeply involved in the revolt of the bourgeoisie of the city against the established nobility. The conflict turned violent and culminated in 1198 with the destruction of the Rocca Maggiore fortress which overlooked the city. In 1202, when Francis was twenty, Assisi went to war with its archenemy, the city of Perugia, its neighbor across the valley. The violent brutality of the battle was vividly described by a Perugian poet who wrote:

> Fallen are the lords of Assisi, and their limbs are all mangled,
> Torn apart and defaced, so their own cannot know them;
> There is no head where the foot is, their entrails are scattered.
> The eye no longer looks from the socket, its one-time window.
> (quoted in Elizabeth Goudge, *My God and My All*, pages 23-24)

Francis participated in the opening battle at Ponte San Giovanni (St. John's Bridge) between the two cities, where he endured the humiliation of being taken prisoner. Assisi was conquered.

Life in prison was hard. During his yearlong imprisonment in Perugia, Francis suffered a series of illnesses, and he grew weaker and weaker. While the harsh, filthy conditions in the cold, gloomy underground dungeon took their toll on his body, Francis' indomitable spirit remained strong. He took it upon himself to keep morale high among his fellow prisoners. He laughed at his chains and rejoiced in the Lord. But eventually, his delicate health crumbled under the privations of prison, and he became very ill with either malaria or paludal fever. Suddenly the frail youth was in a battle for his very life. Fortunately, his father came to his rescue. Pietro Bernardone paid the ransom required to release seriously ill prisoners, and liberated his son, who was still in the grip of a high fever. Francis returned home to Assisi, a sick and defeated young man. And the effects of his illness plagued him until his death.

Prison and illness brought Francis face-to-face with his own personal limits, and forced him to take a deeper look at himself and the meaning of life. During this time, Saint Bonaventure says, "The hand of God weighed heavily on him." Back in Assisi, while convalescing, Francis felt deep sadness for the first time in his life; not even the sight of the broad, shimmering valley and vineyards, and the poppies in the wheat fields below the city could lift his heavyheartedness. Pierre Brunette, O.F.M., writes that "his captivity, his sickness, his liberation, and his convalescence have their effect on him; a definite disenchantment with worldly affairs." A worldly withdrawal was noted by Thomas of Celano:

> Francis gradually perceived his inner world being transformed. Then his health returned. Using a cane, he was able to walk around in his home.... One day he went out thrilled at the prospect of seeing the surrounding countryside. But everything which was pleasant to see—the beauty of the fields, the loveliness of the vineyards and the woods—had lost its charm. He was stupefied by the changes which so suddenly had taken place in himself and he labeled as supreme folly any attachment to any of these things. (1 Cel. 3, in Brunette, *Francis of Assisi and His Conversions*)

Francis was beginning the long, hard process of transformation. The poet in him seemed to be dying; the saint was not yet ready to be born. Francis was depressed, uneasy and anxious. He even became irritated at a beggar asking alms in the name of Christ, and turned him away. It was an empty time of transition for Francis, a time of increased isolation. As Paul Sabatier eloquently noted: "The miserable emptiness of his life suddenly appeared before him; he was terrified at his solitude, the solitude of a great soul in which there is no altar" (*Life of St. Francis of Assisi*, page 16). For the first time in his life, Francis now knew failure and suffering, and as a result, he began to see things differently.

Grace was at work in Francis' life, but he would run from it and chase after his dream of knightly glory.

The Grinding Process

A pilgrimage is a fitting simile for the spiritual life. Spirituality is essentially a journey in which we move from what we are to what we will be. Francis was just beginning to learn that life is a journey to weakness. We truly learn to live when we begin to explore our weaknesses. Every experience of weakness is an opportunity of growth and renewed life. Weaknesses transformed by the reality of Christ become life-giving virtues.

The emptiness we feel stems from not realizing we are made for communion with God. If we are not growing towards unity with God, then we are growing apart from God. Francis would learn that he had to be still in order to move into a greater union with Christ. In stillness he could enter into a dialogue with the Savior. We need to bring to Christ what we are so that in time we become what he is. Francis would learn this lesson. But not quickly. There would be years of growth, years filled to overflowing with pain and struggle. Christianity leads to the cross, and it doesn't offer an easy way around it.

The grinding process had begun. Francis eventually would be ground into God.

DREAMS OF KNIGHTLY GLORY

To become a true disciple of Jesus means accepting a spirituality of the cross and renouncing a spirituality of glory.
—RUTH BURROWS, TO BELIEVE IN JESUS

By 1204, Francis was fully recovered, and he set out for the south of Italy on another military expedition. This was no petty, intercity skirmish, but a big-time battle in which Francis could at last achieve knightly glory. The forces of Emperor Frederick II and of Pope Innocent III were at war over the mastery of Sicily. A local count was raising a force to serve under the pope's general; the count was so impressed by Francis' fiery spirit that he ignored his less-than-robust frame and accepted Francis as a squire with the promise of knighthood, should Francis prove worthy on the battlefield. Francis saw the expedition as a heaven-sent chance for glory. He wanted big things for himself, a slice of fame and renown. He bought the brightest and best armor his father's money could buy and headed south. But Francis didn't get far, only to Spoleto, just down the valley, where he had a dream which dramatically altered his personal dream of knightly glory.

On the road to Spoleto, Francis encountered a brave but very poor knight who was dressed in shabby clothes and wearing dented armor. Francis was ashamed that a seasoned warrior should have such poor accoutrement while he, a frail, untested combatant, should be outfitted in the best that money could buy. Francis gave the knight not only his armor, but also his horse, in exchange for the knight's horse and armor. When word of this absurd incident reached Francis' father, it must have truly irritated him. But this was just the beginning....

The next night, Francis had the first of two dreams that would change the course of his life. In the dream, Francis saw himself in his father's warehouse, but instead of bales and bolts of cloth, the warehouse was filled with military equipment, saddles, swords, lances and shields emblazoned with crosses. Gradually the warehouse faded away and was replaced by a large, magnificent castle. Inside the castle was a beautiful bride. A voice told Francis the castle and the bride were his, and the munitions of war he had just seen were also his to furnish the knights under his command. Francis awoke, convinced the expedition to Apulia near the heel of the Italian boot was going to bring him more glory than he ever imagined. Saint Bonaventure writes: "...he judged the strange vision to be an indication that he would have great prosperity; for he had no experience in interpreting divine mysteries nor did he know how to pass through visible images to grasp the invisible truth beyond" (*Bonaventure*, pages 187-188).

When the expedition reached Spoleto, Francis had a second dream. Actually, it wasn't really a dream. In the shadowy state of half-sleep between dream and waking, Francis heard a voice ask, "Do you wish to go to war in Apulia?" Francis responded by saying that was his whole purpose.

Again the voice spoke, this time asking, "Is it better to serve the lord or the servant?"

Francis responded, "The lord, of course."

The voice replied, "Then why do you serve the servant?"

Francis suddenly awoke and cried out, "Lord, what would you have me do?" The voice told him to return to Assisi and then he would be told what to do. At dawn, though dazed and perhaps disappointed, Francis nonetheless got up and joyfully returned to Assisi, even though that very act would make him look like a coward.

In answering that question, Francis, the carefree, self-indulgent son of a wealthy businessman, began to search for a radically different way to fulfill his dreams of knightly glory.

The Pilgrimage Road

Francis...changes his carnal weapons into spiritual ones and in place of military glory he receives the knighthood of God.

—*THOMAS OF CELANO,* SECOND LIFE

Francis is now on the pilgrimage road. As he walks, his pride, arrogance and independence will begin to fall by the wayside, along with his illusions of worldly ambition and glory. As he moves from disillusionment to transformation, the road will be rocky and difficult. Tested, his faith will be strengthened as the Vinegrower prunes the old, carnal ways in order for the fruit of illumination to blossom.

As he travels, Francis will have periods of weakness, times when his vision becomes clouded, and days of discouragement and despair, but he always remains confident in the constant faithfulness of God.

God, grant me the grace to remain strong as I journey on my earthly pilgrimage.

PILGRIMAGE DIARY 1

Lady Limo

The geographical pilgrimage is the symbolic acting out of an interior journey.

—THOMAS MERTON, MYSTICS AND ZEN MASTERS

I *too, am joyfully returning to Assisi. And I'm going in style...unfortunately, it is not the simple style recommended by Saint Francis, who advised the friars to take nothing for their journey. I'm taking two large suitcases filled with far more stuff than I'll need.*

Wanting to minimize the stress and anxiety I might encounter just getting to the Los Angeles airport, my wife graciously treated me to a limo ride to the airport. She arranged for a chauffeur-driven Town Car to pick me up. Because there were no Town Cars available on the day of my departure, the company sent a stretch limo. While I was authentically embarrassed by the sight of the long, black car as it pulled up to my home, I also felt a twinge of gladness at the thought of riding to the airport in such grand style.

The car was equipped with a stereo system, CD player, TV, phone, sunroof, tinted windows and a well-stocked bar, including elegant, long-stemmed wineglasses. The car was so long, it seemed as if the driver was in another city. As the limo raced along the freeway, I smiled at the irony of beginning a pilgrimage to the land of a saint who took poverty as his bride by traveling in such high style. The limo had more space than Francis had in his cave at the top of Mount Subasio.

As the limo made its way to the airport, I thought about how joyfully Francis embraced poverty, delighting in her presence. Thomas of Celano, speaking of Francis' love of poverty, writes:

> The holy father, placed in the valley of tears, scorned the common riches of the sons of men as so much destitution; and ambitious of more exalted heights, he longed after poverty with all his heart; considering that she was the familiar friend of the Son of God, he strove in everlasting charity to espouse her, now that she was cast off by all the world. (2 Cel. 55)

Am I ambitious of more exalted heights than a stretch limo? I think
so, yet the lure of the limo and the riches it symbolizes are still a
powerful tug.

Thomas of Celano says, "No one was so greedy of gold as he
[Francis] of poverty." Poverty gave Francis a clearer understanding of
both human and divine life.

Gazing out the tinted windows of the limo, I fear I must be
content to gather only a few crumbs from Francis' bountiful table,
especially in regard to the more intimate mysteries and joys of the
spirit which he found in poverty.

TIME ALONE

*It is in solitude that the soul makes great progress and penetrates
the secrets of the Scriptures. In solitude the soul finds a fountain
of tears which purifies itself. And the more it withdraws from
creatures, the more it approaches familiarity to God.*

—THOMAS À KEMPIS, *THE IMITATION OF CHRIST*

Back in Assisi, Francis spent a great deal of time alone, seeking refuge
in solitary places in order to understand and nourish his spiritual
conversion. He gradually withdrew from his circle of fun-loving
friends. He was seeking a spiritual perfection which he assumed
required the abnegation of most of his former life. His friends feared
he had gone mad, a fear which was confirmed when Francis told
them that he no longer wanted to be "The Master of the Revels" (or
"Lord of the Feasts") during their nightlong parties known as *sere-
natas*, which were wild affairs, filled with loud singing and jubilant
dancing. In June of 1205, Francis attended his last *serenata*. He wanted his heart to be filled only with the sweetness of the Lord.

Francis was experiencing the truth which Saint Augustine had
grasped: "God must be loved first and loved to the extent that we
reach the point where, insofar as possible, we forget ourselves."
Francis was moving to that point.

PILGRIMAGE DIARY 2

A Needle in a Haystack

In silence we touch our emptiness, our loneliness, our longing.
—*BASIL PENNINGTON, O.S.B.*

I'm staying at a Franciscan friary in Rome for a few days before joining the pilgrimage. My room in Collegio Sant' Isidoro is small and simple: A bed, a chair, a desk, an armoire...just the bare basics. The second-floor window looks out to the cloister, which is graced with fruit trees and a fountain. The walls of the room are painted white, adorned only with a simple crucifix. The tile floor is partially covered by a faded throw rug. There is no TV, no radio. No noise. I'm struck by the silence.

We live in a whirlwind of noise. Our homes and cars have elaborate entertainment centers. Cell phones allow us to talk while driving or walking in the woods. Cable and satellite TV serve up news, sports and movies twenty-four hours a day. Computers link us to the Internet and chat rooms...and Web sites featuring triple-X porn stars. And, of course, crass commercialism is always screaming something at us. Finding silence is harder than finding a needle in a haystack. Our culture is so riddled with turmoil and confusion it is easy to seek refuge in the noise of idle entertainment, channel surfing through endless hours of tedious programs.

I want to be alone with God, but the barren silence of my room scares me. I miss the security blanket of noise.

So much of life distracts us from Life.

Francis knew he needed time alone in order to be present to God. He needed a desert experience.

In the barrenness of the desert we can experience the fullness of life. The desert is a place of silence where we can find the quiet to hear.

Wearing a Hole in My Pants...and My Sins

Not long ago a very learned man told me that souls who do not practice prayer are like people with paralysed or crippled bodies; even though they have hands and feet they cannot give orders to those hands and feet.

—*SAINT TERESA OF AVILA*, THE INTERIOR CASTLE

This morning I noticed a hole in my jeans in an odd place—just below the waist near the front left pocket. Then I remembered that about a year ago I developed a habit of tucking one of the keys on my key ring between my belt and the pants whenever I got out of the car. It seemed like a better idea than having the bulky key ring take up space in my pocket. Over the course of a year, the friction of the key rubbing against the jeans eventually caused a small tear in the pants. I noticed this as I was entering church for daily Mass.

In another habit I developed about a year ago, I began to say two prayers each day during Mass. The first prayer is known as the Prayer Before the Crucifix, which I say before the Mass. The prayer begins with this plea: "Behold, O kind and gentle Jesus, I kneel before you and pray that you would impress upon my heart the virtues of faith, hope and charity, with true repentance for my sins and a firm purpose of amendment." The second prayer is called Anima Christi, which I say just before receiving Communion: "Soul of Christ, sanctify me; Body of Christ, save me; Blood of Christ, inebriate me; Water from the side of Christ, wash me; Passion of Christ, strengthen me; O good Jesus, hear me; Within your wounds hide me; Separated from you, let me never be; From the Evil One protect me; At the hour of my death, call me; And close to you bid me; That with your saints, I may be, praising you forever and ever. Amen."

After saying the first prayer today, as I sat silently waiting for the Mass to begin, I thought about the tiny tear in my pants. I realized that I never thought about the effect the key rubbing up against the same spot in the pants day in and day out would have, and now suddenly I have a hole in my pants. The key just quietly went about wearing a hole in the pants without my noticing. My mind then drifted to something that happened yesterday. Actually, to something that didn't happen yesterday. For a very long time, I've had a proclivity towards a certain sin. I never seem to be able to resist it. And I have tried. But yesterday, I did avoid it. In fact, during the past month I've often been able to avoid it. Then I realized that for the past few weeks, it has become increasingly easier for me to resist the temptation. Suddenly, the image of the key wearing a hole in my pants dashed across my mind...and I saw a connection between the pants and my sins. Slowly and quietly over the course of the past year without my noticing, those two little prayers had begun to wear a hole in my sins, just as the key had worn a hole in my pants.

We want action. We want "quick fixes"—instant redemption and salvation. It doesn't work that way. Change is evolutionary, often so utterly slow you hardly notice the process. The daily repetition of those two prayers slowly increased, by God's grace, not only my awareness of a sin that had become habitual, but also my ability to resist it. Slowly, I began to catch a distant glimpse of the fact that the essence of sin was saying no to God's perpetual invitation for us to partake fully in the reality of his love and to reach our full potential as human beings. When I sin, I settle for mediocrity, denying myself the chance to reach my full potential, which can only be realized by living in unity with God. Gradually the dichotomy between my prayer and my life began to narrow. I still have a way to go. A long way to go. But every little bit of growth increases my capacity to respond to God's call to go further.

For Francis, the way to go was by way of poverty and humility. He emptied himself in order to encounter a liberating God who freed him from his slavery to himself. Over time the two prayers I prayed each day helped me see the wisdom of Saint John of the Cross, who wrote in his book Ascent of Mount Carmel: "The soul must empty itself of all that is not God in order to go to God."

Saint Francis said, "Poverty is the root of all sanctity." Father Ignacio Larranaga, O.F. Cap., explains why in Sensing Your Hidden Presence: "When our interior is liberated from interests, ownership, and desires, God can become present there without trouble. On the other hand, as long as our interior is occupied by selfishness and egotism, then there is no place for God. It is occupied territory" (page 208). All God wants is a surrendered heart.

Temptations show us what we, in our weakness, are capable of becoming. They are invitations to virtue. Specific sins invite us to develop specific virtues to overcome the sinful inclinations. Temptations give us a chance to turn to God.

I'm going to stop tucking my key between my belt and my pants, but I'm not going to stop saying those two prayers each day. O good Jesus, hear me, within your wounds hide me, separated from you never let me be, help me to keep wearing a hole in my sins, so my heart may be filled with your sweetness.

PILGRIM'S PROGRESS

Poor human reason when it trusts in itself substitutes the strangest absurdities for the highest divine concepts.
—SAINT JOHN CHRYSOSTOM

In the spring of 1206, Francis traveled to Rome as a pilgrim. This is where the apostle Peter preached and was martyred. The tomb of Saint Peter was a magnet that drew pilgrims from all over the world. Francis went straight to St. Peter's Basilica and knelt before Peter's tomb. In prayer, he asked Saint Peter to help him discover the treasure of gospel poverty. Afterward, he noticed other pilgrims making small donations of a few coins, which disappointed him, and, in one generous gesture, he threw all the money he had into the donation box. He left the church and was confronted with the sight of beggars clutching the clothing of those entering and leaving the church, begging for a few coins out of love for God. Arnaldo Fortini dramatically sets the scene:

> As he went out of the atrium he was struck by the turmoil of the bustling crowd—a spectacle, an unsavory and unexpected mixture: penitents who because of their great sins could not enter the church asking prayers of the pious faithful, pilgrims hurrying to the fountain to wash their hands according to the rite of purification, the poor lounging about the columns and along the stairs.
>
> There were an incredible number of poor; in accordance with an ancient custom, all the beggars of Rome gathered in the atrium. They pleaded, lamented, muttered prayers, stretched out their hands. Some of them suffered from the most repugnant infirmities—monstrous sores, maimed and crippled bodies, blindness, paralysis. (*Francis of Assisi*, page 204)

Francis found their poverty to be loathsome and wondered if he could ever stand to be so poor. In a dramatic decision, he exchanged his tailored clothes for the rags of a beggar and panhandled for alms in front of St. Peter's. "In his way," writes Saint Bonaventure, "he would learn to make light of what the world esteems and arrive gradually at the perfect observance of the Gospel." Francis had known the poverty of riches, and he was about to learn the riches of poverty.

PILGRIMAGE DIARY 3

A Tiny Spark

The real voyage of discovery consists not in seeking new lands,
but in seeing with new eyes.

—*MARCEL PROUST*

*F*rancis went to Rome on a pilgrimage. The first step any pilgrim
takes is a step in faith, a moving from the known to the
unknown, from the security and comfort of his or her home to the
unfamiliar terrain and language of a foreign land. The pilgrim strips
himself or herself of everything familiar in hopes of experiencing
something new, something deeper. Pilgrims go knocking on God's
door. The pilgrim seeks new ways of seeing and understanding; ever
restless, one combs the unknown land for new information and
insights. Questioning is at the heart of spiritual pilgrimages.
Removing themselves from their own personal duties and dramas,
pilgrims go on a search for answers to the questions that burn within
them. The pilgrim is not someone who is running away from
something...he or she is running to something. The pilgrim is an
explorer, an adventurer, a dreamer.

The Christian pilgrim hopes to meet Jesus on the road to
Emmaus.

Francis, whose entire life sang pilgrimage, first journeyed to
Rome in response to the new desires in his heart. He desired to root
himself within the tradition of the Church. Kneeling in front of the
tomb of Saint Peter, he desired to follow in the path of Saint Peter, a
path which led to martyrdom. Francis was on fire with desire to
proclaim the "Good News," and he went to Rome seeking direction
from the Lord—through the inspiration of Saint Peter—on how best
to do so. During his life, Francis occasionally returned to Rome to
renew his faith and to seek the wisdom of the gospel.

I came to Rome looking to ignite my tiny spark of faith into a
flame. It's been just a little over two years since that spark—that gift
of faith—was rekindled in my heart. But it has remained only a
spark, often in danger of being blown out by...me, my doubt, my sin,
my weakness, my selfishness, my ego. I still live for the most part not
by faith in God but by faith in myself, a prisoner of my own
impoverished inner life. My heart still beats with lust, a desire to

*possess and dominate; it forgets that love, real love, serves, that God
manifests himself in the form of a servant.*

I came to Rome looking for what Francis found, looking for a
way to tame the wolf that prowls the darkened forest of my soul,
ever ready to devour my timid faith in the most high, all-powerful,
all-good Lord whose praise Francis sang until his final breath. My
pilgrimage is about an interior movement toward a deeper self. The
exterior, geographical journey, as Thomas Merton suggested, is
symbolic of an inner journey. A pilgrimage is a time of transition.

While I stood humbled in the massive Basilica of St. Peter's and
was overwhelmed by its size and spectacular array of statues and art,
it was too noisy, too busy for me to feel anything other than chaos.
Until I saw a simple act of faith. I was walking down the right side of
the church, past all the side altars, including one housing the
magnificent Pieta by Michelangelo. About halfway to the main altar,
there is a small chapel reserved for quiet prayer and meditation.
Inside the chapel, the Blessed Sacrament was exposed. I went in and
sat down for a few minutes, but my mind was too jittery to enter into
any kind of contemplation or worship.

As I left the chapel and became engulfed in the sea of people
working their way either up or down the crowded aisle, some with
video cameras pointing to the elaborately decorated ceiling, I spotted
a nun dressed in a full, traditional habit, including the headdress. She
looked peaceful, calm, unhurried. As she walked past the chapel
where the Blessed Sacrament was exposed, she paused, turned
toward the chapel, knelt down and prostrated herself so her veiled
head almost touched the marble floor. She remained in that position
for several seconds. She then stood up, turned toward the front of the
church and continued walking. Her silent, devout act of reverence at
merely passing the chapel caused me to cry. I returned to the chapel,
knelt down and prayed. It was a time of sweet communion.

Later in the day, I saw the same sister in the piazza in front of the
basilica. I went up to her and told her of the impact she had on me.
She said, "With any experience of tears, God is trying to get in touch
with us."

We hugged. And after she urged me to pray the rosary each day,
we parted—her memory firmly emblazoned on my mind.

Jesus was present in the little chapel, and alive in the humble
nun.

My soul glorifies the Lord,
and my spirit rejoices in God my Savior.... (Luke 1:46-47)

A KISS OF A LEPER

To beggars he wished to give not only his possessions but his very self.

—SAINT BONAVENTURE

Upon his return to Assisi, Francis still was a pilgrim without a goal. He did not have a clear idea of what he would do with his life or how his inner sense of conversion would be materially manifested; all he knew at this point was that his life would be dedicated to serving God through religion. Solitude grew deeper and deeper.

One thing that did change in Francis' life shortly after his return from Rome was an unaccountable interest in lepers. This is significant because prior to this Francis had such a disdain for lepers that he was physically repulsed by the very sight of them. In those times, lepers represented the height of hopelessness. There were about nineteen thousand leper hospitals in Europe, doing their best to look after these unfortunate souls, who were actually regarded as legally dead. Even the Church contributed to their misery by citing lepers as an image of sin. In 1179, the Third Lateran Council issued a decree which demanded that lepers be forced to live outside the city walls. Their exclusion from the rest of society bordered on being absolute. Those lepers permitted to come near a village were required to wear distinctive clothing and to beat a clapper to warn people of their approach.

Francis was fastidious in his avoidance of any contact with this deadly and most loathsome of diseases. He would go as far as two miles out of his way to avoid contact with a leper, and even at that distance he held his nose to avoid even a hint of their stench, even though the faint and disagreeable smell emitted by lepers does not in fact carry very far. In short, Francis was horrified by lepers...but he would soon conquer this horror, set himself free from his past and be totally open to a new future.

In his commentary on the Gospel of John, Saint Cyril of Alexandria, a bishop and Doctor of the Church who died in 444, wrote: "It can easily be shown from examples both in the Old Testament and the New that the Spirit changes those in whom he comes to dwell; he so transforms them that they begin to live a completely new kind of life." Francis, led by the Spirit, was about to embark on a radically new kind of life.

One day, Francis was praying for guidance in the small church of St. Mary of the Angels, a decaying shrine hidden in the woods. Francis was very fond of this chapel, built in 352 by pilgrims returning from the Holy Land. After an hour of prayer, Francis heard a voice, not audibly as in Spoleto, but in his heart. The words he "heard" were these: "Francis, all those things that you have loved after the flesh, and desired to have, you must now despise and hate, if you would do My will. Then the things that before seemed sweet and delightful shall become unbearable to you and bitter, and from those that you once loathed you shall drink sweetness and delight without measure."

Francis left the church, got on his horse and headed back to Assisi. As he came out of the Portiuncula woods, the countryside became completely open, not even a hedge or boulder or a bush on either side of the dusty road...nothing in sight except a leper, dragging himself along, coming slowly toward Francis. Immediately, out of sheer habit, horror and disgust began to mount inside of Francis. He lifted his arm toward his nose to block out the stench that he would soon encounter. Then this thought ran across his mind: "You are not a knight of Christ if you are unable to conquer yourself."

This was a great moment, the crisis of a battle...and Francis did not back down, but bravely faced it.

He nudged the horse into a full gallop, rushing toward the leper. He heard the clapper and watched the leper draw to the side of the road to give him room to pass without contamination. Disgust surely must have seized him, as the putrefying stench filled the air. Francis dismounted and walked toward the leper. The leper's face was half eaten away and swollen. In an impulsive and courageous act, Francis embraced the astonished leper. Then he kissed the leper's hands, which had only stumps of fingers, before putting money into them. Finally, in a supremely bold gesture, Francis kissed the leper on the mouth.

This was a moment of true grace for Francis...and the leper.

Imagine what must have gone through the leper's mind when Francis embraced him. Moments before, the leper must have felt nothing but contempt and hatred for Francis, because the cloth merchant's son represented all the pampered, middle-class people who had resoundingly rejected him and forced him to live in lonely exile...until that moment, until that embrace in which both men felt the love of God.

It was a transcendent moment, a true turning point in Francis' life. There was no turning back now...he was on the road to glory, a glory beyond his wildest imagination.

In unpolished, spare and concise prose, Francis recalled this moment of conversion in his *Testament.* He wrote:

> This is how God inspired me to embark upon a life of penance. When I was in sin, the sight of lepers nauseated me beyond measure, but then God himself led me into their company, and I had pity on them. When I had once become acquainted with them, that which previously was bitter to me became a source of spiritual and physical sweetness for me. After that I did not wait long before leaving the world. (*Omnibus*, page 67)

Francis summarized his life before his dramatic encounter with the leper in four words: "I was in sin." And with a kiss of a leper he embarked upon a "life of penance."

A Life of Penance

We don't like the word "penance." For us, it's an ugly word, bearing connotations of guilt and shame. Yet, the foundation of Francis' spiritual life is built on penance. Harsh penance. Francis' sense of penance bordered on the extreme edges of asceticism. The people of Assisi were dumbfounded by the near-inhuman aspects of the austerity of his life. Saint Bonaventure tells us that the saint "curbed the stimulus of the senses with a discipline so rigorous that at great pains did he accept what was necessary for his sustenance."

Lent was not merely a season for Francis, but a way of life.

If conversion and faith require this kind of change—the "metanoia" of the New Testament—then we are not interested in it. But for Francis, his understanding of penance, manifested in the extravagances of austerity, was not tied to punishment. For him, penitential mortification was a means for growth, creating a "new man." Francis wanted to put his abounding passions to death so that their creative power could be put to the service of a higher goal, namely holiness. Francis wanted only to serve God in a full and radical way, and personal privations and penance made up the path he chose to follow.

In time, as Francis began to attract followers, he did not demand that his brothers emulate his relentless drive to subjugate his own earthly passions. On the contrary, Saint Bonaventure notes, "he rejected [for others] excessive severity [in penance] that was not, at the heart, clothed in mercy, nor sprinkled with the salt of discretion." Francis was only hard on himself, which made it easy for him to be soft with everyone else...especially with the poor and the poorest of the poor, the lepers.

For Francis, profound penances were the gateway to his profound humanity. His gentleness was derived from the strength and discipline he acquired while silencing everything within him that was not in harmony with the love of God.

I need to learn to be able to say no to the things in my life that are blocking me from a fuller relationship with God. The spirit behind Francis' desire for a life of penance tells me that small acts of mortification in my personal life can be effective teachers.

PILGRIMAGE DIARY 4

The Streets of Rome

*W*alking the streets of Rome, I see an abundance of wealth. Amid the affluence and fashion, the poor are clearly visible, too. In the shadows of ancient architecture, I've seen some of the poorest, filthiest and most desperate-looking people I've ever encountered. I can't imagine embracing them, kissing them.

I think of Francis as I walk, and I can't help but wonder...who are the lepers in my life?

Intersecting Lifelines

The encounter with the leper was the most critical moment of Francis' life. His attitude and expectations were turned upside down the moment he accepted God's role in the event. Before, he was unable to include the leper, a lowly, ugly outcast, in his understanding of the cosmic love of God. It was Francis who did the excluding. God, he would learn, excludes no one. With the kiss of the leper, Francis began to learn he and the leper were one and the same, and there was no difference between them. And he lived the truth of that realization.

Francis would claim everybody is worthy of the love of God. I don't always agree with that idea...I would have no trouble making a list of people I would consider unworthy of God's love. Sadly, I do a lot of excluding. The leper story tells me of the importance of searching for the infinite in the finite. By embracing the flawed and the finite, Francis discovered perfection and the infinite. He met the Lord, and that changed his life. He discovered true freedom. The story also shows the role of ongoing conversion in Francis' life. Growth came through pain, conflict and confrontation...and chance meetings?

What I find most intriguing about the story is that this most critical event in the saint's life appears at first to be the product of chance. Was the meeting between Francis and the leper a coincidence? Or is there a reason for everything? The questions make me look at my own life, and force me to look carefully at the endless parade of "coincidences" that lead me to crossing paths with Francis in the ancient city of Assisi, half a world away from my home in California. A few years ago, I would have answered the first question with an unqualified and resounding "yes"— for I fully believed all of life was ruled by nothing more than a random mass of chaos, and there was absolutely no reason for anything...it was all chance.

The story caused me to spend a little time reflecting on my own life, and the twisting road that I followed to Assisi. Reflection allows time for perspective to emerge, and gives us a chance to see things in a different light. It is so easy for me to forget about how my life has intersected with so many other lives, each encounter playing a role leading me out of the desert of unbelief into the garden of faith. Reflection gives me the chance to stop, pause, and see the interconnectedness of everything. God leads us to people we never expected to meet and to places we never expected to go. Without the leper, Assisi would not have become known as the home of a great saint, but would be just another charming Umbrian town sitting handsomely on a hill.

Who are the lepers in your life? Who is giving you a chance to encounter the infinite in the finite?

There is no such thing as coincidence...every encounter is charged with meaning and possibility...and grace.

Francis responded to grace the moment he got off the horse.

He got back on the horse a new man...for he had embraced God.

PILGRIMAGE DIARY 5

A Gateway for Growth

When your ship, long moored in harbour, gives you the illusion
of being a house...put out to sea! Save your boat's journeying
soul, and your own pilgrim soul, cost what it may.
—*ARCHBISHOP HELDER CAMARA, IN GREGG LEVOY, CALLINGS*

*Just as the leper was isolated from society, I am fragmented in my
relationship with myself, with other people, with the world and
with God. The isolation and dividedness are ugly and painful. For so
very long, I was torn apart by my inner conflicts and contradictions.
They hurt me and they caused me to hurt others. The leper reminds
me of my brokenness and my divided self. I've begun to mend the
wounds, but the past is still very much present. I am still in need of
healing, still looking for wholeness. Wholeness isn't easy; it doesn't
come in a flash. The cross offered no shortcuts to Christ. There are
no simple answers, no perfect healing. To think there are is an
illusion. We carry our wounds and anguishes with us. We must learn
to live with the pain and use it as a gateway for growth.*

*Francis was on the verge of learning that Christ accepts us as we
are, with all our weaknesses and confusions. The healing begins
when we look at ourselves honestly and open ourselves up to the
transforming love of God. It is the love of God that makes all things
possible and allows us to move toward a healing.*

This pilgrimage is a journey toward wholeness.

I'm Hungry

There is no need to search for a remedy for all the evils of the
time. The remedy already exists—it is the gift of one's self to
those who have fallen so low that even hope fails them. Open
wide your heart.
—*RENE BAZIN, REDEMPTION*

*The story of Francis and the leper is not an easy story to hear...or under-
stand. Trying to understand embracing and kissing a leper, my mind
drifts back a few years to a story from my own life, one which I had near-*

ly forgotten. At the time, I was living in Philadelphia. It was the dead of winter. For nearly two weeks the temperature never rose above freezing. One of the few benefits of being a writer is the fact that you don't have to venture out of the house when the weather is so nasty. When the cold spell finally broke, I was eager to get out of the house, and a Sunday stroll around historic downtown was the perfect antidote for my cabin fever. I planned on browsing in a used-book store and stopping for a cup of cappuccino—simple pleasures. What I hadn't planned on was an encounter with a homeless woman, whose body was sprawled on the ground at the corner of Walnut and 19th Streets, just a few blocks from the Liberty Bell and Independence Hall.

The homeless can trigger such diverse emotions. One can't help but notice their growing numbers. At the time of this story one could hardly traverse a block in downtown Philly without confronting a "street person" extending a paper cup toward you and imploring, "Can you spare some change?" For many, such requests are easy to ignore. Tough times make us callous. Even though as a writer my paydays are infrequent and insignificant, I usually toss a few coins into at least one cup. The problem is the number of cups. Worse, the homeless to whom I have to say, "I'm sorry, I can't," frequently respond with, "God bless you. Have a nice day."

What an annoying, sarcastic response. Don't they realize there are just too many outstretched cups to respond to each and every one?

No...they don't.

Still, hearing them say "God bless you" really irritates me. Then I get annoyed at myself for getting annoyed at them. I can't imagine what it would be like to live on the streets, not to have a home, a warm bed, food to eat, and people who care about me. How did they survive the weeks of sub-freezing weather? I couldn't have. Do they ever feel any joy, any relief from their misery, or even the simple comfort of a hug? What do they think when they see people going into Barnes & Noble Books or Victoria's Secret, people with enough extra money for books and sexy lingerie?

I guess I would be sarcastic, too. And bitter, also.

Back to the body I saw sprawled on the ground, hugging a manhole cover in order to stay warm from the steam flowing through its holes. As I approached the body, I expected to see a man, probably old, perhaps black. As I looked down, my expectations were confounded. It was a woman. A young woman. A young, white woman.

I took two or three steps past her. What I had seen took a few seconds to fully register. I stopped, turned and looked back. I'm not sure why, but I felt drawn to her. I was curious. I wondered how old she was and how she wound up in such a sad state. Then I noticed how no one else seemed to notice her. I moved toward a building, where I could inconspicuously stand in the shadows and observe this American tragedy. For twenty minutes, I stood silently watching. Her clothes were tattered and soiled. She wasn't wearing socks and her sneakers had holes and no laces. The section of her long, brown hair which wasn't covered by her frayed woolen cap was snarled and grimy. Every once in a while she would twist her body around in an effort to get comfortable. She would roll from her left side to her right side and then back again. Occasionally, a hacking cough sent shudders down through her nearly-frozen body.

But no one noticed her.

Scores of people walked past her, few even bothering to glance at her. There were couples who strolled by, hand in hand. There were families who strolled by, some pushing baby carriages. There were people walking alone, accompanied only by their thoughts. But no one noticed her. One walker was a talker, having an animated conversation on his portable telephone as he walked past the woman, practically stepping over her. Some people had shopping bags from the Banana Republic, others from Ann Taylor. But no one noticed her. Some had just come from the historic Episcopal Church of the Holy Trinity, all decked out in their Sunday best. And they all just walked by—lovers, families, talkers, shoppers, worshipers—they all just walked by.

But no one noticed her.

I watched in silence and wondered if the recession the country was in at the time had caused a fatigue of compassion. I wondered also if we had become so jaded by the onslaught of tragic headlines from around the globe telling us about the unfathomable suffering in such places as Somalia, Rwanda, Haiti, India, northern Iraq and Bosnia that we no longer can see the suffering in our own backyard. The new world order (whatever that is) has done little to ease the agony that plagues so much of the world, a world that seems to be "out of order." Suddenly a series of coughs forced the woman to sit up. It was time to stop wondering. It was time to act.

I walked over to her, bent down and asked, "Is there anything wrong?"

As the words tumbled out of my mouth, my brain thought, "What a stupid question! No, there is nothing wrong, she just likes sleeping on the cold sidewalk!" She looked right into my eyes. Her soft, blue eyes reflected the pain that gripped her life. I could see she was slightly retarded. Her teeth were crooked and yellow. Her face was smudged with dirt from the street. She said, "I'm hungry."

I handed her a five-dollar bill, and said, "I'm sure you can get something to eat with this." She took the money and said, "Thank you." She immediately stood up and started walking toward Chestnut Street, a main street where food could be found.

I'm not sure why, but I followed her. I was surprised when she walked past a convenience store. She walked for another block and then she entered an unpretentious, brick-faced diner with the upscale name of St. George IV Restaurant. I looked in the window. She was seated at the counter. She ordered something. The waitress headed for the kitchen and quickly returned with a brown paper bag. The woman took the bag and handed the waitress the five dollars. The waitress gave her some change. She got up, and walked out of the restaurant. I turned my back; she didn't see me. She started walking back toward Walnut Street, and the corner where I found her. She stopped at a traffic light. I approached her. She saw me and smiled. I said, "Here's five more bucks so you can get some more to eat tonight." She looked right into my eyes and said, gently and directly, "Thank you."

She shoved the money in her pocket. The light changed green and she crossed the street. I watched for a few seconds and then headed for my car. Who was she? Why was she alone and homeless? Does anyone miss her? A few minutes later, I drove past the spot where I first saw her sleeping on the ground. She was sitting on the same manhole cover, eating her food.

No one noticed her.

I'm glad I did. I fed Jesus...in his "distressing disguise."

When Francis embraced the leper, he was embracing God. As Francis grew in faith, he saw God in every living creature and in all of creation, which made it impossible for the saint to ignore any suffering he encountered. I could not embrace the guileless, young homeless woman...I could only hand her a few bucks and quickly forget her. I'm not a saint.

Down through the centuries, countless people, including numerous saints, believed that we can't find God alone, that we need each other to find our way. It seems to me that the lives of many modern people are marked by isolation. Many people don't even know their next-door neighbors. We tend to deny our interdependence. At the beginning of D. H. Lawrence's essay "We Need One Another" is this powerful observation: "We lack peace because we are not whole. And we are not whole because *we have known only a tithe of the vital relationships we might have had. We live in an age which believes in stripping away relationships."*

Saint Paul said, "We are all members one of another." Awareness of our interdependence is the true basis of compassion. As our isolation deepens, our compassion weakens...and the homeless become faceless. The homeless, along with those afflicted with AIDS, are today's lepers.

Listen again to D. H. Lawrence:

> Everything, even individuality itself, depends on relationship....
> The light shines only when the circuit is completed.
>
>   My individualism is really an illusion. I am part of the great
> whole, and I can never escape. ("We Need One Another")

Jesus said, "I was hungry and you fed me." Since that wintry day, the meaning of Jesus' words has slowly begun to dawn on me. The young woman, in some mysterious way, was Jesus. When we touch a person in need, we are touching Jesus. The mercy we share with broken people is the mercy Jesus returns to us. The next time you see a homeless person, filthy, covered with sores, begging for food, stop and listen, and you may hear these haunting words: "This is my body."

ACTS OF CHARITY

He is truly great who is great in charity.
—THOMAS À KEMPIS, *THE IMITATION OF CHRIST*

After the incident with the leper, Francis made daily visits to a nearby leper colony, bringing them alms...and love. He wiped their sores, washed them and bandaged them as best he could, even though the lepers railed obscenities that cursed heaven for damning them to such an unbearable hell. Francis' compassionate heart and poet's imagination understood their anger and ingratitude.

For Francis, Christ the crucified became Christ the leper.

Francis was now beginning to have some sense of the presence of God in all his creatures. He was beginning to feel a kind of brotherhood with all created things, including lepers and lambs and flowers. More and more, he saw the image of Christ in the poor and the afflicted. It was as though in looking at a leper he saw the broken and bleeding body of Christ his brother. And Francis would never again be able to treat another human being, no matter how lowly or disfigured, with indifference or contempt.

> The consequences of Francis' gesture [embracing the leper] are as important as the gesture itself. He attains greater harmony between his heart, his prayer, and his behavior. The lepers lead him both to an inner unity within himself and an outward unity with others. The drama which occurs brings him to a deep inner conviction of the need to go beyond himself in serving others. As he associates with the lepers, the others, he discovers himself to be other than what he thought. And now these others, repugnant as they may be, become like brothers to him. What is more, they initiate him into a life of penance. His spiritual quest now takes shape and becomes a way of life. It is no longer a momentary act of generosity, but on the contrary, becomes a necessity which will animate every one of his relationships. (Brunette, *Francis of Assisi and His Conversions*, page 42)

The face of the impoverished leper became the face of the humiliated Christ. Pierre Brunette goes on to say, "Every leper incarnated the Christ who is near and disfigured. He is a brother who requires special attention. The leper by the wayside is a brother on the same level as the Friar Minor, a privileged reflection of the Creator and a living portrait of Christ."

Saint Francis set a very high standard.

Becoming Marginalized

As Francis and his brothers toiled among the lepers on the outskirts of the city, one thing soon became clear: Work with the marginalized and you will become marginalized. The brothers felt this, and, quite frankly, some did not like it, and they told Francis so. Francis' response to their concerns was simple and direct: this is where Christ is...we are living in Christ's world.

The friars did not choose to be poor. They merely followed Christ and became poor as a result. Francis had no choice but to leave the city of Assisi, because all facets of the society within the walls were striving for something he was no longer interested in. He left and found himself among the poor, the lepers.

I have not followed Jesus to the margins of society, opting to live and work in the slums, feeding the homeless. Nonetheless, by following Jesus I feel myself slowly becoming marginalized in a different way. The things

I used to do and enjoy, such as watching TV and going to the movies, no longer interest me. Conversation with friends about everything from sports to politics no longer holds my interest. I'm no longer interested in merely making money. More and more, I am finding myself, at least emotionally, on the outskirts of society. And it is uncomfortable. Perhaps that is the point.

Blessed Are the Merciful

No man who ignores the rights and needs of others can hope to walk in the light of contemplation, because his way has turned aside from truth, from compassion, and therefore from God.
—*THOMAS MERTON*, NEW SEEDS OF CONTEMPLATION

Eileen M. Egan is a writer who traveled extensively with Mother Teresa. In an article in the September 20, 1997, edition of America *magazine, she described a 1955 visit to Calcutta, during which Mother Teresa gave her a tour of her Home for the Dying.*

I wondered how they could do this day after day. "Our work," Mother Teresa explained, "calls us to see Jesus in everyone. Jesus told us that he is the hungry one, the naked one, the thirsty one. He is the one without a home. He is the one who is suffering."

She looked around at the rows of pallets in the caravanserai [a kind of hostel or inn once used to house poor traveling pilgrims]. "They are Jesus. Each one is Jesus in a distressing disguise." She said it with a sort of luminous conviction. As I came to know more of her work and saw it grow in India and the world, I realized that this conviction was its bedrock. Each person was to be treated as a repository of the divine. If disfigured by the filth of the street, by leprosy, by anything that diminished his or her dignity, the person had to be envisioned in the light of the divinity behind the disguise. The infinite inviolable dignity was always the same.

How often do I see "a repository of the divine" in people I meet? My honest answer would have to be: rarely.

Hiding in the Shadows

Francis found God not in pomp and glory, but in infirmity and foolishness. He found God in what we throw away. Francis found the God of endless light hiding in the shadows, on the margins of society.

I think I was looking in all the wrong places.

PILGRIMAGE DIARY 6

The Way of Poverty

Fix your hope in heaven, and be certain help will ever be yours. Love God above all things, and believe that poverty is the sinew and bone of our religion.

—*BLESSED AGNES OF PRAGUE*

*D*uring a free afternoon in Assisi, as I was wandering down a narrow street just off the Piazza del Comune, I spotted an English-speaking pilgrim center operated by The Little Portion Franciscan Sisters. I went in, and much to my delight I found a collection of books about Saint Francis. They weren't for sale. Pilgrims were encouraged to sit, relax and read for as long as they wished. I was familiar with most of the books, but of the few I had never seen, one caught my attention. It was written by Leonardo Boff, a former friar from Brazil. His name had been mentioned during the morning lecture, so I sat down and took a look at his book, opening it at random to a section where Boff was addressing the issue of poverty. I read only that one page, which gave me much to think about. Here it is:

> The poetic structure of the Franciscan soul and of Christian faith are indispensable ways of understanding his [Francis'] way of being; the key, however is not found there, but rather in a new praxis of Saint Francis. At a definite moment in his youth he is converted. As in every authentic conversion, a *conversio morum* takes place, a change in the way of behaving and relating. A break occurs. One world dies and another is born. Francis began to identify himself with the poor and to do difficult penances. A painful process of interior purification was begun. He retired to the caves; long vigils; fasts and penances so rigor-

ous that he had to be merciful to his own body, which he tenderly called Brother Ass. The core of this effort at interiorization centered around the theme of poverty. Poverty, fundamentally, does not only consist in not having things, because individuals always have things: their body, their intelligence, their clothes, their being-in-the-world. Poverty is a way of being by which the individual lets things be what they are; one refuses to dominate them, subjugate them, and make them the objects of the will to power. One refuses to be over them in order to be with them. This demands an immense asceticism of the renunciation of the instinct to power, to the dominion over things, and to the satisfaction of human desires. Poverty is the essential path of Saint Francis, realized in the physical place of the poor. The poorer he was, the freer and more fraternal he felt. Possession is what engenders the obstacles to communication between human beings themselves and between persons and things. The more radical the poverty, the closer the individual comes to reality, and the easier it is to commune with all things, respecting and reverencing their differences and distinctions. Universal fraternity is the result of the way-of-being-poor of Saint Francis. He truly felt a brother because he could gather all things devoid of the interest in possessions, riches, efficiency. Poverty is thus a synonym for humility; this is not another virtue, but an attitude by which the individual is on the ground, in the earth, at the side of all things. Converting oneself to this way of being, and in the measure of its realization, one is rewarded with the transparency of all things to the divine and transcendent reality. In this way, universal reconciliation and a cosmic democracy is achieved. (*St. Francis, A Model for Human Liberation*, page 39)

That one paragraph was enough to bring me to the realization that I see things, not through things.

Francis was able lovingly to accept people as they were. Francis would tell us to listen, truly listen, to the people in our lives without trying to judge or change them. His approach could be reduced to a simple maxim: Don't try to convert each other...instead, be Good News to each other.

A Mouse Losing Weight

Almost every effort of the human mind is directed, not toward lightening the work of the laborer, but toward making more pleasant the idleness of the leisured.

—*LEO TOLSTOY*, A CALENDAR OF WISDOM

Recently, with great fanfare, the media in America heralded a possible treatment for obesity that has helped mice lose weight. For much of the world's population, famine is a reality, but for us a mouse losing weight is big news.

I need to go on a diet. I need to shed all that is unnecessary and superfluous from my life. We live in a world dominated by appearances, acquisitions and achievement, all of which hinder our ability to enter into true interior simplicity.

Rather than seeking the latest diet craze, I struggle to follow the advice of Saint Bernard of Clairvaux: "Seek God in the simplicity of your heart."

TAKE UP YOUR CROSS

The consciousness of each of us is evolution looking at itself and reflecting.

—*PIERRE TEILHARD DE CHARDIN, S.J.*, THE PHENOMENON OF MAN

These were trying and confusing times for Francis. Julian of Speyer, in his *Life of St. Francis*, which he began to write six years after the saint's death, tells us: "In his soul there was an alternation of joy for the spiritual sweetness he tasted, and a burning desire to realize his plan." Francis spent a great deal of time in fervent prayer, and eventually God graced him with another moment of illumination.

> One day while [Francis] was praying in such a secluded spot and became totally absorbed in God through his extreme fervor, Jesus Christ appeared to him fastened to the cross. Francis' soul melted at the sight, and the memory of Christ's passion was so impressed on the innermost recesses of his heart that from that hour, whenever Christ's crucifixion came to his mind, he could scarcely contain his tears and sighs, as he later revealed to his companions when he was approaching the end of his life.

Through this the man of God understood as addressed to himself the Gospel text: "If you wish to come after me, deny yourself and take up your cross and follow me." (*Bonaventure*, page 189)

At that moment, Christ stepped out of the pages of history and the Bible and became vividly real to Francis. He saw, felt and knew God's love and it was in the form of Jesus hanging on a cross. In that moment, Francis bore the stigmata on his soul...long before those wounds would appear on his body. Saint Bonaventure goes on to say that the experience gave birth to "an attitude of profound compassion."

Francis was changed, emotionally and psychologically.

He was a new man...in Christ.

Still, Francis did not yet have a clear idea of what God wanted him to do. His life was divided between serving lepers and praying in abandoned churches. But he wouldn't have to wait long before once again a voice heard in an empty church would show him the way.

A Divided Heart

Within his heart, Francis could feel the beating of contradictory impulses. He felt a call to prayer and a call to service.

Contradiction is a part of life. I am often pulled in two (or more) directions at the same time. It causes me to feel fragmented and disoriented. When the psalmist speaks of a divided heart, I know what he is talking about. When what I feel and what I do are in conflict, it leaves me paralyzed. Francis felt contrary forces tugging at him, causing him to endure periods of confusion and unrest. Some days I want to chuck everything and go serve the poor full-time at a soup kitchen. Some days I want to become a hermit, devoting myself completely to prayer. Then there is the urge to write. And the crazy urge to make films that will inspire people. I need to find equilibrium, a sense of unity within myself. Eventually Francis found a way to have the contradictory forces battling within him to join together, enabling the tensions to become life-giving.

Like Francis, I need to find balance in my life. I need to find time to work and time to pray. I need time alone and time with loved ones and friends. I have yet to discover the true rhythm of my life, a life nurtured by the natural contradiction of growth and decline, of light and dark, of

dying and rebirth. I need to find myself in those contradictions, for they
are me, and they are able to reveal my hidden wholeness.

The Divine Office

The early Franciscans had their Divine Office, and found in it
the hidden manna for mental prayer.

—*FATHER JAMES, O.S.F.C.,* THE FRANCISCANS

*N*o, it's not where God works. It's a book, a prayer book
consisting of four large volumes which correspond to the
seasons of the liturgical year. Priests, monks and nuns recite the
prayers and readings from the books every day, either in private or in
a communal setting, where parts of the office, especially the psalms,
are often chanted or sung. The Divine Office marks the hours of the
day, spiraling the soul in and out of psalmody, uplifting, descending,
flying to God, returning to earth. The Divine Office divides the day
into six periods of prayer; lauds and vespers (morning and evening
prayer) are the two primary periods.

To chant the Divine Office is to enter again and again into the
ageless mystery of Christ. Season by season, liturgical texts teach the
heart, and renew the spirit. The Divine Office has been a vital part of
the Church since the early days and is an attempt to fulfill the Lord's
command to pray without ceasing. Down through the centuries, the
Divine Office has been the heart and soul of monastic life, and a joy
and comfort for countless Christians. Hour by hour, it can prompt the
conversion of our hearts and cement our union with God.

The psalms are the heart and soul of the Divine Office. They are
also the oldest prayers in the Judeo-Christian tradition. The psalms
are a lexicon of the human condition, assuring us that our hopes and
fears and desires are just like the rest of humanity's, and that God is
with us always.

In short, the psalms, which Thomas Merton called "one of the
most valid forms of prayer for men of all time," are the most
significant and influential collection of religious poems ever written,
summing up the theology of the Old Testament and serving as daily
nourishment for the devout. Over time, the words of the psalms

slowly enter the heart and become a real presence, transcending the ideas and images they contain. Throughout history, the psalms have been the mainstay of monastic prayer. My own personal appreciation of the psalms as a gateway to contemplation was greatly enhanced by reading Merton's excellent book on the psalms, Bread in the Wilderness.

Following the study pilgrimage, I lived at the Collegio Sant' Isidoro in Rome for three months. Founded in 1625 to train seminarians from Ireland, today Sant' Isidoro is a friary under the jurisdiction of the Province of Ireland and is home to friars from around the world who are studying, working or simply visiting Rome. I spent the better part of most of my days at Sant' Isidoro in their main library, which contains a large collection of books about Saint Francis and Franciscan life and spirituality. I'm sitting in the library as I write this, and just a few minutes ago I was holding in my hands a copy of the Divine Office printed in Rome in 1744...a magnificent piece of craftsmanship.

Each day I also joined the friars in their communal prayers, which consisted of reciting together the Divine Office in the morning, at midday and in the evening. Day in and day out, we read aloud portions of sacred Scripture, some of which I was hearing for the first time. Some days, the readings opened my eyes to new ways of seeing and opened my heart to new ways of feeling.

In the third chapter of the Rule of 1223, *Francis urged the brothers to say the Divine Office. Francis based his life on Scripture, which guided and comforted him. And so, I thought it would be fitting to occasionally interrupt the text of this book in order to share some of the Scripture readings that touched me. I'll identify these asides as "The Liturgy of the Hours," which is another name for the Divine Office.*

Here is the first one.

The Liturgy of the Hours

If you trust in the Lord and do good,
then you will live in the land and be
   secure.
If you find your delight in the Lord,
he will grant you your heart's desire.

Commit your life to the Lord,
trust in him and he will act,
so that your justice breaks forth like
   the light,
your cause like the noonday sun.

Be still before the Lord and wait in
   patience;
do not fret at those who prosper;
those who make evil plots
to bring down the needy and the poor.

Calm your anger and forget your rage;
do not fret, it only leads to evil.
For those who do evil shall perish;
the patient shall inherit the land.

A little longer—and the wicked shall
   have gone.
Look at their homes, they are not
   there.
But the humble shall own the land
and enjoy the fullness of peace.
(Psalm 36 [37]:3-11)

THE LITTLE FIELD CHAPEL

*Through the fountain-fullness of the Word came the embrace of
God's love, which nourishes us into life, is our help in perils,
and—as a most profound and gentle love—opens us up for repentance.*

—HILDEGARD OF BINGEN

There was another small church that Francis loved to visit. The
church was named for Saint Damian, a saint revered by both Eastern
and Western churches for his charity. The church was not as old as
St. Mary of the Angels, but it, too, was owned by the Camaldolese
Benedictines of Mount Subasio. Both churches were perfect for
Francis' solitary prayer; both were simple and poor.

San Damiano is located just a mile downhill from the walled city
of Assisi, an easy walk for Francis. The little field chapel, half in ruins
following years of neglect, was empty. Francis, who was now in his
mid-twenties, longed to know God's will for his life. Kneeling in
front of a large, painted Byzantine cross above the main altar,
Francis prayed for guidance. Thomas of Celano tells us that Francis
was "devout and humble" in his supplication before the Lord.

Light was flooding in through the collapsed roof, creating pools
of light and shadows which surrounded Francis as he knelt in prayer.
We don't know how long he knelt before the crucifix, but I imagine
it could have been for hours. Perhaps he grew weary or melancholic,
wondering if God would answer his plea. Finally, in the calm stillness of the abandoned church something happened:

> [T]he painted image of Christ crucified moved its lips and spoke.
> Calling him by name it said, "Francis, go, repair my house
> which, as you see, is falling completely to ruin." (2 Cel. 10)

Francis took the words he heard as a direct order to restore it, and
set about the task of rebuilding the church, brick by brick.

Upon leaving the church, Francis spotted an elderly priest sitting in the sun. He approached the priest and gave him money,
instructing the priest to use the money to buy oil for the lamp before
the crucifix, so that it would be constantly burning, adding that
when the oil ran out he would furnish additional money to replen-
ish the oil.

Editing

The account I just presented of perhaps the most significant event in Francis' life is strikingly different from the one I had originally written. Time for a confession: I had based my original version on an amalgamation of accounts of the incident at San Damiano as they had been described in a number of biographies which I had read. Reluctantly, I must admit that in this instance, I failed to consult the actual sources myself. (By sources, I'm referring to the original accounts of Francis' life, written soon after his death by, for the most part, friars who knew him or his original companions.)

The impression I had from all that I had read was that Francis heard a voice, basically saying, "Rebuild my church." A book published in recent years by two friars poetically described the scene this way: "Yet just as self-pitying defeat seemed imminent, a whisper of sound broke through the gloom...Francis heard the grand symphony of silence."

Beautifully written. But no moving lips.

I didn't mention them either. I didn't know about them.

I had written: "In the quiet of his heart, Francis heard a voice tell him, 'Restore my church.' [Note the theological difference between "restore" and "rebuild."] Francis looked around and saw no one. [I made that up.] He was convinced God had spoken the words to him."

That's a very different telling of the story than the one told by Thomas of Celano.

Nobody knows exactly what happened, exactly what Francis saw or heard. I decided to cut my original version and give it to you straight, including the moving lips on the painted crucifix, which sounds awfully hokey. "In the quiet of his heart" Francis heard "a grand symphony of silence" sounds much more palatable to our modern ear.

But even the sources raise difficult questions. For instance, Thomas of Celano never mentions (in either of his lives of the saint) the powerful story which Saint Bonaventure told, the one where Christ had earlier spoken from the cross to Francis in a vision; and so Thomas of Celano says it was from this event in San Damiano that "the memory of the Lord's passion was deeply impressed on his heart."

I read one account where the author quoted those words from Thomas of Celano's Second Life and added, "so that, in the words of St. Bonaventure, 'he could hardly keep from weeping and sighing whenever the crucified Christ came into his mind.'" The author combined two dif-

ferent events into one narrative, which is fine if you're writing for television and you include a disclaimer in the credits advising the viewer that
some events have been altered or combined for dramatic purposes or in
consideration of time constraints.

After reading the early documents on the life of Saint Francis, I have
a new respect for historians and their tireless quest for accuracy.

PILGRIMAGE DIARY 8

The Cross of San Damiano

The noblest prayer is when he who prays is inwardly transformed into what he kneels before.

—ANGELUS SILESIUS

*T*he cross is crucial in Francis' conversion and spirituality. When
Francis knelt at the foot of the large cross which hung in the
small chapel of San Damiano, his life was transformed. Francis was
educated by what he saw: creation, beggars, lepers, his followers.
And he looked hard and long at the cross of San Damiano. And the
cross told a story, a visual story with a profound theological message
which acted as a portal through which Francis could enter into the
mystery of God. To the untrained Western eye, icons appear at first
glance to be rather odd and strange; the figures and their expressions
seem exaggerated and out of proportion. The first few times I looked
at the cross of San Damiano, I saw little more than the figure of
Christ on a cross. I was totally unaware of the symbols employed by
the iconographer, a twelfth-century monk, and did not know how to
"read" the picture he had painted. For instance, the tiny shells that
form the border around the entire cross symbolize eternity, beauty
and endurance. The cross itself was a mystery to me; but two books
helped me learn how to read and understand the icon—The Icon of
the Christ of San Damiano *by Marc Picard, O.F.M. Cap., and*
Franciscans: Conventual Friars of the Community *by Robert Melnick,
O.F.M. Conv., and Joseph Wood, O.F.M. Conv.*

The icon is a visual text which artfully retells the story of Christ's
passion as it is presented in the Gospel written by John. The story the
cross tells highlights humanity's continual struggle between good and
evil, and the Gospel message that death no longer has a power over

us thanks to the Resurrection of Jesus. At the very base of the cross, below the feet of Christ, there is a rock, carrying two messages. The first suggests the Church was founded on the rock of Peter, and the rock represents the authority of the pope. A second interpretation of the meaning of the rock has more personal implications. Jesus said that anyone who listens to his words and acts upon them is like a person who builds his or her house on a strong foundation of rock. Surrounding the crucified Christ are a host of figures, including Mary, his mother, John, the beloved disciple, Mary Magdalen, the centurion and a number of angels. The resurrected Christ on the cross is wearing a crown of glory instead of the crown of thorns. His body, though still bearing the wounds of his death, is luminous. At the top of the cross, above the head of Christ, there is a smaller figure of Christ ascending into heaven from inside a circle representing perfection. Melnick and Wood write: "But Christ is breaking out of that circle, going beyond perfection into the unimaginable abundance of God. Christ now carries the cross as a scepter. He has transformed the instrument of torture into a sign of hope, the royal crest of the Kingdom of God" (page 7). Above the ascending Christ, there is a hand gesturing a blessing. It is the hand of God the Father.

If you go to Assisi, prior to kneeling before the crucifix of San Damiano, read about the painted cross in these two excellent books, and it will greatly enhance your visit. Among other things, it will help you understand why the artist used the colors he did, why the eyes of Christ are so large (and why they gaze at a spot between heaven and earth), and why the neck of Christ is so thick. This icon is virtually a picture book, and knowing the visual language employed by the artist magnifies its power and beauty.

The San Damiano incident, which occurred midway through the year 1206, demonstrated Francis' humanity, showing that he was a saint who made mistakes. Francis misunderstood the message he heard. He took the words literally and began to repair the church. Eventually, he came to understand God had much more in mind than the restoration of that one church.

The followers of Saint Francis believe that the "church" God was talking about was not a building but the institution, and that God wanted Francis to restore the Church universal, which was on the verge of collapse. Even the papacy had been corrupted. I once heard a Zen Buddhist who had a great love for Francis say he thought the *"church" God had in mind was neither a building nor an institution, but Francis himself. Interesting. Here's a thought: perhaps God gave Francis a series of progressively more difficult tasks which allowed the saint to build up his spiritual strength by first restoring a building, then an institution, and finally the job requiring the most strength, restoring himself.*

Restoration

The opposition of the "dark tyrant" within us [to divine union] is so powerful that this self must slowly be broken up to the last grain, like a rock under continual attack of the waves. It must crumble away, rot, burn up, until it is finally open.
—HANS URS VON BALTHASAR, THE LAST GRAIN OF WHEAT

"When I was in sin...." That's the way Saint Francis described himself before his conversion, before he "put on the mind of Christ" and began to live his life through Christ in the spirit and slowly started to die to his self. We don't much like the word "sin." I don't, even though I am acutely aware that I am a sinner. Despite my progress in wearing a hole in my sins, I still sin a lot. Sin, the way I understand it, is a failure to love. I fail often. I fail when I put myself first.

Conversion involves a "metanoia," a turning away from sin and becoming a "new creation." In that sense, Francis did not restore himself because restoration implies a return to an original condition. According to Christian theology, we were born in sin. In other words, thanks to original sin, sin has always been a part of our nature. In that light, Francis was not engaged in a process of restoration but one of elimination.

Eliminating sin in my life is proving to be a difficult chore. I can't seem to get out of my own way, and my own way always reverts to a self-seeking persona that is not in harmony with the life of Christ. Francis let go of his own way, let go of everything he knew and loved, and, leaving all behind, jumped into the unknown abyss of God, where he became so united with God that he became a new person, a new creation. The old man had died; Adam no longer lived within him. Adam is still alive and kicking within me. I still listen to him, along with a dense cacophony of other voices, rather than to God, and so true union with God is not possible. Sin keeps me alienated from the fullness of God. Recently, my frus-

*tration with my inability to significantly reduce sin in my life has dimin-
ished because I've started to look at the process from a new perspective,
one I gleaned from reading the writings of Thomas Merton.*

*Merton saw sin as a symbol of our state of alienation from God...and
our true selves. Nowhere is Merton's understanding better articulated
than in James Finley's book,* Merton's Palace of Nowhere: A Search for
God Through Awareness of the True Self. *A former monk at the Abbey
of Gethsemani, where Merton was his novice master, Dr. Finley writes:*

> ...Merton's whole spirituality, in one way or the other, pivots on
> the question of ultimate human identity. Merton's message is
> that we are one with God. What Merton repeatedly draws us to
> is the realization that our own deepest self is not so much our
> own self as it is the self one with the "Risen and Deathless
> Christ in Whom all are fulfilled in One" [from *Mystics and Zen
> Masters*].
>
> Merton leads us along the journey to God in which the self
> that begins the journey is not the self that arrives. The self that
> begins is the self we thought ourselves to be. It is this self that
> dies along the way until in the end "no one" is left. This "no
> one" is our true self. It is the self that stands prior to all that is
> this or that. It is the self in God, the self bigger than death yet
> born of death. It is the self the Father loves forever. (page 17)

*The "self that dies along the way" is our false self, the descendant of
Adam's disobedience, an egocentric act which caused our spiritual death
by destroying our relationship with God. The resurrected Jesus restores
that relationship and allows us a way to once again become grounded in
God, to become who we were meant to be. James Finley writes:*

> Christian life is clearly presented in the New Testament to be
> primarily a participation in the life of Christ. We are called "to
> die with him" by "dying to sin" so that we might "rise with
> him." Life in Christ does not begin at biological death, but
> rather begins now in a death to self, in a conversion, a
> metanoia, in which we "put on the mind of Christ" and live a
> life through Christ in the Spirit. (page 24)

*Living a "life in Christ" is something that does not just happen; it's not
like putting on a new coat. It is a process, a long arduous struggle. Why?
Because we stand in our own way...our false self resists and rebels every
step of the way, fighting for its own way, the way of sin, the way of self-
seeking pleasures. To live a life in Christ means we must die to this false*

self. For Christ to flourish, our false self must vanish. Finley writes, "To sink into the unknown depths of God's call to union with himself is to lose all that the false self knows and cherishes."

But the false self still wants to listen to the serpent's song of lies and illusions instead of God's song of true harmony. Dr. Finley writes:

> There is something in me that loves darkness rather than light, that rejects God and thereby rejects my own deepest reality as a human person made in the image and likeness of God.
>
> Sin is the word we most often use to refer to this latter aspect of human experience in which we find ourselves negating our own intrinsic relationship to God. Sin taken in this sense does not...refer simply to the isolated actions we call sinful. Rather, such actions are seen as symptoms or manifestations of sin taken as the state or condition of alienation in which we find ourselves. As Paul expresses in Romans, "...I am weak flesh sold unto the slavery of sin. I cannot understand my own actions. I do not do what I want to do but what I hate.... What happens is that I do, not the good I will to do, but the evil I do not intend. But if I do what is against my will, it is not I who do it, but sin which dwells in me" (Rom 7:14-20).
>
> Of sin considered this way, Merton writes [in *New Seeds of Contemplation*]:

> > To say I was born is to say I came into the world with a false self. I was born in a mask. I came into existence under a sign of contradiction, being someone that I was never intended to be and therefore a denial of what I am supposed to be. And thus I came into existence and nonexistence at the same time because from the very start I was something I was not.

> Here Merton equates sin with the identity-giving structure of the false self. This in itself is significant. The focus of sin is shifted from the realm of morality to that of ontology. For Merton, the matter of *who* we are always precedes what we do. Thus, sin is not essentially an action but rather an identity. Sin is a fundamental stance of wanting to be what we are not. Sin is thus an orientation to falsity, a basic lie concerning our own deepest reality. Likewise, inversely, to turn away from sin is, above all, to turn away from a tragic sense of mistaken identity concerning our own selves.

This then is the false self, in that it ends up with less than nothing in trying to gain more than everything which God freely bestows upon his children. The false self is a whole syndrome of lies and illusions that spring from a radical rejection of God in whom alone we find our own truth and ultimate identity. (pages 27-28)

The first time I read about the concept of a false self and a true self, my intellect understood the theological principles underpinning it, but the idea didn't resonate in my heart. Gradually I began to see the inner struggle that was going on inside of me really was a matter of my old self, my false self, resisting my efforts to live a life in Christ. Prayer was not easy. Often it was dry, arid. It was difficult to see God in the daily, mundane events of my life; God still seemed distant, beyond my reach. Years of unbelief and skepticism caused me often to question the merit of trying to live a more God-centered life, trying to live a life in Christ.

Sometimes during Mass, my mind will wander and entertain the thought that my attendance is a waste of time, that the Mass is nothing more than an antiquated, lifeless ritual or that the concept of transubstantiation was nothing more than theological mumbo jumbo and that the consecrated host is merely a symbol and not the Body of Christ, so there is really no need to eat a symbol. The false self has a very active mind, continually questioning, doubting and constantly trying to restore itself to the throne of my life, trying to force God to abdicate. I'm also troubled by my frequent inability to resist the temptation to sin, which in some cases had become rather habitual. Yes, I had professed Christ with my lips and in my heart, yet my false self shouted back, "No...you alone are all you need. Jesus is a fairy-tale messiah and God does not care. Wake up. Live for yourself. You are your own ultimate fulfillment."

In the two years since my rebirth in Christ, I have slipped and betrayed him often. But grace and mercy help me to get back up and try again to live a life in Christ. Day by day, little by little, the false self dies. I have no idea how long it will take for the rebellious Adam who lives within me to vanish. James Finley notes:

Adam is not seen as some historical figure who committed a particular act that brought about a kind of ontological birth defect that is handed down from child to child. Rather, Adam is now. Adam is ourselves in disobedience to God. The garden of Eden prior to the fall is just as much in the future as it is in the past. Both heaven and hell live not only beyond us but also within us, and it is through the door of ourselves that we enter both. (page 30)

The false self makes life hell. I know, I've been there. Dr. Finley correctly points out:

> ...the serpent's lie is a dark and twisted echo of God's creative act in which he made us sharers of his own divine life. Indeed, for us to want to be like God is simply for us to want to be who God created us to be in his own image and likeness....
>
> The spiritual life for Merton is a journey in which we discover ourselves in discovering God, and discover God in discovering our true self hidden in God. (pages 30, 31)

Saint Francis made that journey. It was a long, hard trip, and he suffered greatly along the way. He discovered what Thomas Merton expressed centuries later: "The secret of my identity is hidden in the love and mercy of God." Merton went on to say:

> [T]here is only one problem on which all my existence, my peace and my happiness depend: to discover myself in discovering God. If I find Him I will find myself and if I find my true self I will find Him.

Saint Francis, the helper and the hermit, discovered his true self and God through his selfless service to others and in the inner desert of prayer and contemplation. In the process, he removed the shackles of sin and the mask of illusion and was able to have a face-to-face relationship with God.

Again I recall Francis' description of himself before his encounter with the leper: "I was in sin." Thomas Merton identifies sin with the illusions of the false self which hinder us from recognizing Christ. He writes:

> Every one of us is shadowed by an illusory person: a false self.
>
> This is the man I want myself to be but who cannot exist, because God does not know anything about him. And to be unknown of God is altogether too much privacy.
>
> My false self and private self is the one who wants to exist outside the reach of God's will and God's love—outside of reality and outside of life. And such a self cannot help but be an illusion.
>
> We are not very good at recognizing illusions, least of all the ones we cherish about ourselves—the ones we are born with and which feed the roots of sin. For most people in the world,

there is no greater subjective reality than this false self of theirs, which cannot exist. A life devoted to the cult of this shadow is what is called a life of sin. (*New Seeds of Contemplation*, page 34)

Saint Francis, help me to walk out of the shadow of sin and into the glorious sunshine of God's presence. Help me liberate myself from anxiety and fear and inordinate desire. Help me undo Adam's destructive journey. Help me keep the flame that was rekindled two years ago burning and don't let the winds of doubt and skepticism blow it out. And finally, dear Francis, help me sincerely pray the prayer written by Saint Ignatius Loyola:

> Lord Jesus Christ...all that I have and cherish you have given me. I surrender it all to be guided by your will. Your grace and your love are enough for me. Give me these, Lord Jesus, and I ask for nothing more. Amen.

In his book, The Heart of the World, *Thomas Keating, a Cistercian priest, monk and abbot, writes: "When we work to surrender our own desires, world view, self-image, and all that goes to make up the false self, we are truly participating in Christ's emptying of himself."*

I was frustrated by my failure to fully live a life in Christ. I've come to see that the transition from the false self and a life of sin to the true self living in oneness with God is a very slow and long process. That doesn't mean I'm satisfied with the pace of my progress; it only means I won't become depressed or distressed by my inability to instantly and completely make my false self vanish. He's been around for a long time, and he's a stubborn cuss.

The spiritual life is a journey...a journey of elimination and restoration.

The Liturgy of the Hours

A portion of a reading from the homilies of Saint John Chrysostom:

Here then are the five high-roads to repentance: first,

acknowledge one's sins, second forgiving the sins of others, third prayer, fourth almsgiving, fifth humility. Do not be idle then, but day by day set out along these roads.

SUMMONS AND RESPONSE

Interior experience is geared to action. It is designed to soften up our self-centered dispositions, to deliver us from what is compulsive in our motivation, and to open us up completely to God and to genuine service of others.

—THOMAS KEATING, *THE HEART OF THE WORLD*

God had broken through the silence at San Damiano and Francis would respond with every fiber of his being. His own private, self-made world came to an end and a new world appeared within him and around him...a world where the impossible became an everyday experience.

Francis responded immediately to Christ's request that he rebuild the church. There was no debate, no planning; there was only action, instantaneous and spontaneous. William R. Cook writes:

> It would have been easy and rational to take some time to think about precisely what Christ's words meant. It was not every day that Christ spoke to him, and in a previous vision [the vision of a palace filled with weapons], his first interpretation of what Christ had said proved to be quite wrongheaded. Yet Francis responded as best he could in obedience to the words of Christ as he understood them at the moment. Francis never lost his instinct of beginning with what the words clearly meant in a literal sense and allowing deeper meanings to emerge as he lived out their most obvious meaning. This is an important kind of faith—God tells us enough to get us started and he will aid us as we move in deeper ways to His call. It is also an expression of humility—I will respond in obedience, which [St.] Benedict called the first step of humility. It is a matter of trusting God's words more than one's own intellect or will. (*Francis of Assisi*, page 37)

Today, some Franciscans joke that they act first, think later.

The Liturgy of the Hours

The Lord is compassion and love,
slow to anger and rich in mercy.
His wrath will come to an end;
he will not be angry for ever.
He does not treat us according
    to our sins
nor repay us according to our
    faults.
(Psalm 102 [103]:8-10)

Stone by Stone

It is as if a single holy desire impelled him [Francis] at length:
to cast more and more of what is earthly into the flame Christ
had kindled, so that the flame in turn might light up the world
so much the more.

—*REINHOLD SCHNEIDER,* THE HOUR OF ST. FRANCIS OF ASSISI

*First, the leper, then the vision of Christ hanging on the cross, and final-
ly the crucifix of San Damiano—three critical events in the life of Francis.
God was knocking on the door of his soul, and as he knelt in front of the
crucifix he was at last willing to throw the door fully open. And the hand
of God, says Celano, came upon him and changed him. Before the vision
and that divinely-charged moment before the crucifix, Francis had been
troubled and confused by what was happening inside himself. He was
tormented by conflicting thoughts. Peace was nowhere to be found, nor
could he find delight in the things which once pleased him, especially*

nature. *Emptiness was part of the process of change, and Francis was still trying to flee the hand of God. God gently extended a hand to Francis. But Francis could not give what he didn't have. Despite his own weakness, he began to rebuild himself. Stone by stone, his own inner fortress was pulled down and rebuilt in the image of Christ. A heart hardened by vanity and a lust for money, fame and glory was slowly being transformed. As he wandered about Assisi, dazed and distracted, it was clear to all that he was no longer the jubilant troubadour. In the midst of his weakness, at low tide emotionally and spiritually, he is graced with a vision, and shortly afterward, comes to San Damiano, and kneels down before the poor, naked, crucified Christ. In the rubble of the church, Francis doesn't have one stone fixed upon another in his own life. Yet, the more he surrenders to God, the more God visits him with consolations. God gives him a mission, a plan for his life.*

Touched by God, filled by God, Francis now burned with a desire to help others believe in their own goodness. He invites us to rebuild our lives in the image of God, whispering in our ears, ever so gently, "God is simply waiting for your response."

Francis' mission was clear: help people find reconciliation with themselves, others and God...stone by stone, rebuilding individual lives, communities and the world.

PILGRIMAGE DIARY 9

Thoughts Scribbled While Walking

Settle yourself in solitude, and you will come upon Him in yourself.

—*SAINT TERESA OF AVILA*

During the course of this pilgrimage, I managed to take at least one solitary walk each day. On a good day, the walk might last up to an hour. I always carried a small reporter's notebook with me, in order to jot down random thoughts. The practice of carrying a little notebook to record my thoughts began about a year ago, and has proven to be a handy tool that helps me recall and give permanence to passing moments of insight, such as these:

Contemplation requires tranquillity and patience.

*The art of contemplating divine truths grows out of the art of
remaining still.*

To be a contemplative is to be receptive to the divine Word.

*It is possible to find solitude while standing in line at a supermarket
or bank.*

Kindness is essential for reconstructing our Garden of Eden interiorly.

*Within each of us, without exception, there is a longing to pass
beyond finite things.*

Without prayer, God dies in our hearts.

Each day needs to be a pilgrimage into my own heart.

I need to stand before God in a stance of constant conversion.

Humility is the heart of Christianity, and the gateway to prayer.

NAKED IN THE SQUARE

*All this strengthened Francis in alacrity to carry through his res-
olution, and he patiently endured the blows and hard words.*
—FROM *THE LEGEND OF THE THREE COMPANIONS*

The experience of San Damiano eventually led Francis to a painful
break with his family and the world of business. He realized the
restoration of the church would require a lot of money. While his
father was away on business, Francis took (or as G. K. Chesterton
puts it with brutal frankness: "He stole...") cloth from his store and
traveled via horse to Spoleto. He sold the cloth—and the horse,
too—to raise money to restore the tiny church. He returned to the
church with the money, and tried to give it to the old priest. But the
priest would not accept it. He suggested that Francis spend some
time in prayer and offered to let Francis stay with him, either in his
house or in a cave near the church. Francis left the money in the
church and retreated to the cave, where he embarked on a period of
prayer and fasting. Meanwhile, Francis' father returned and was out-
raged when he discovered that Francis had taken the horse and the
cloth. He immediately began looking for his son, determined to drag
his son home and knock some sense into him.

Pietro Bernardone's search eventually led him to the church.
Francis, learning of his father's anger and imminent arrival, fled in
fear. The old priest returned the money Francis had left behind.
Once he recovered the money, Pietro gave up his search for his son

and returned home. Francis, now in hiding, continued his fasting and prayer for nearly a month. During this time, Christ was no longer in the throne of his heart...fear was. Francis agonized over his father's recrimination, the scorn of his neighbors, and the mocking disdain of his friends. He must have been in the grip of fear and must have wondered if he was making a huge mistake. Thomas of Celano says, "He prayed always with a torrent of tears that the Lord would deliver him from the hands of those who were persecuting his soul, and that he would fulfill his pious wishes in loving kindness; in fasting and in weeping he begged for the clemency of the Savior, and, distrusting his own efforts, he cast his whole care upon the Lord" (1 Cel. 11).

This was a time of real anguish, and Francis clung to the hope God would hear his prayer and help him cast off his fears. In this "darkness," Thomas of Celano tells us that one day (perhaps in April of 1207) "a certain exquisite joy," beyond anything Francis had ever experienced before, penetrated the void, and the "fire" from this joy prompted Francis to abandon his hiding place and return to Assisi, knowing full well that he was about to "expose himself openly to the curses of his persecutors."

When Pietro spotted Francis walking down the street, he was horrified by his son's appearance. His emaciated body was covered with dirt. His eyes had dark rings under them and his hair was disheveled. Children were tormenting Francis as they followed him down the street, calling him names, shouting insults, and throwing stones and garbage at him. "You're mad; you're demented," they shouted. Saint Bonaventure notes: "But the Lord's servant passed through it as if he were deaf to it all, unbroken and unchanged by any of these insults." Hearing the commotion, Francis' father ran to the street to see what was happening. Pietro Bernardone, filled with sorrow, shame and anger, became so enraged at the sight that he seized his son "with many blows and dragged him home" (*The Legend of the Three Companions*, 16) and locked him in the store's dark basement.

Francis remained a prisoner in his father's basement for weeks. His father only provided Francis with bread and water, in hopes of somehow breaking his son's spirit and curing him of his crazy ideas. According to *The Legend of the Three Companions*, Pietro "used threats and blows to bend his son's will, to drag him back from the path he had chosen." While Pietro's treatment of his son was harsh and cruel, it reflected the fact that he desperately wanted the "old"

Francis back, wanted his son to be "normal," to enjoy life and follow in his footsteps and help him run the business. Francis stood firm. The situation filled Pica with anguish. She could see that her son's mind "was irrevocably made up and that nothing would move him from his good resolution" (*The Legend of the Three Companions*, 18). Eventually, when Pietro was away, Pica, "filled with tender pity," released her imprisoned son. Upon his return, Pietro was so angry he denounced his son as a thief and set legal proceedings in motion to disinherit him.

Francis repudiated his father in a public square in front of the bishop's residence, giving back to him all he owned, including the clothing he was wearing. Standing naked in the square, Francis declared he would call no one "Father" except God. Francis was now free...free to follow the Lord. Some saw it as a bold act of faith; for some, it was a foolish act. Either way, Francis was from that day on going to follow the gospel...he had forsaken everything, picked up his cross, and walked in the footsteps of Jesus. And the earth must have thrilled beneath his footsteps. And as it was for Jesus, Francis' ascent along the road that lay ahead of him ended with the cross.

Don't Ask

> Prayer can be dangerous; when it is real, prayer pits against me all the world that rejects Jesus.
>
> —*ROBERT FARICY, S.J.*, PRAYING

A number of people from Assisi, including Bishop Guido, who covered the naked Francis with his cloak, surrounded Francis in the square as he made his bold and daring break with his father...and his past. It is hard for me to imagine anyone publicly performing such a radical act.

I know I couldn't.

But what if I thought—fully believed—God was asking me to do something equally as radical.

Could I do it?

Would I do it?

Please God...don't ask.

It's hard enough for me just to do the right thing...even when no one is looking, so I can't imagine doing something so bold when all the eyes around me were looking at me as if I were mad, the way the crowd must have looked at Francis that fateful day in the square.

Murray Bodo, O.F.M., in his delightful and inspirational book Tales of St. Francis, *offers this prayer:*

> Cover me with your cloak, O Lord, for I am afraid of the naked-ness I sometimes feel in trying to love you. I am so exposed out here where you've led me. I need to know that your arms sur-round me. Come, Lord Jesus, and be my tent, my coverlet, shielding me from the eyes of those whose gaze seems at times to penetrate my thin, vulnerable skin. (page 36)

To which I can only add, "Amen."

Additional thought: being more interested in pleasing other people than God, I couldn't do anything as foolish as Francis did. Francis, on the other hand, was unconcerned about what his friends and family thought; his only concern was pleasing God and doing the will of God.

I doubt I will ever become a man of prayer, if I continue to seek to be held in esteem by humans. The grace of prayer is given to the pure of heart, those who seek only the Lord with all their heart and soul.

PILGRIMAGE DIARY 10

Interruptions

I hate interruptions. The phone ringing while I'm working or reading makes me nuts. The dog whining to go out when I am in the middle of writing a sentence annoys me. Much of family life is about interruptions. "Oh, Dad, can you help me with my homework?" "Oh, dear, can you put out the garbage?" Most people do not like being interrupted; family life teaches us how to handle interruptions gracefully. God knows I interrupt the lives of everyone who lives with me.

Just off the main piazza in Assisi is the church known as Chiesa Nuova, the new church. At least it was new in 1619, when Philip III of Spain had it built on what was presumed to be the site of Pietro and Pica Bernardone's home and shop. In the small piazza in front of the church there is a statue of Francis' father and mother. Inside the front door of the church, on the left side, is an opening leading, according to tradition, to the dark cell where Francis was locked up by his father. Another tradition claims the main altar was constructed on the very spot which once was Francis' actual room. Historians cast some doubts about whether or not the church marks the spot where Francis grew up. The historical accuracy of the tale that the church occupies the place where Francis spent his childhood is not very important to me. I am more interested in the symbolic value of the church, which forces one to think about family.

Francis' family was part of the merchant class, whose values and ideas were planted in his impressionable young mind. For instance, merchants gave money to the poor because they felt it would induce God to favor them in return. The Church held a dim view of the merchant class because the merchants, with their increasing wealth and independence, threatened the feudal system which supported the Church. Francis eventually reached a point where he had to break with the values of his family, his class and his Church, and in doing so, he interrupted everyone.

Pietro wanted Francis to follow him in the family fabric business, and when Francis rejected his father's plan, the father became irate. Some would say Francis was the child of an abuser. Francis interrupted his father's vision of family life. The bishop embraced the merchant's son because he detected a flicker of divine inspiration within the young man's rebellion.

The essence of being a child involves interrupting your parents, for everything from changing diapers to transport to Little League games. If Francis had not interrupted his family's life, I would not be writing this book. If Francis had not interrupted the life of his Church, he would have been a Benedictine. The dream to write a book about Saint Francis interrupted my life.

Chiesa Nuova invites us to ponder the interruptions in our lives. I am grateful that Francis of Assisi interrupted my life, and I am learning to be more tolerant when members of my family, including the dog, interrupt my life.

Interruptions are opportunities for grace, both to be received and to be given.

As I sat alone in Chiesa Nuova this question tiptoed into my mind: Has Christ interrupted your life?

The question took my breath away, because I feared the answer was...not really. Or not enough to dramatically change my life, or the lives around me. Christ interrupted Francis, and Francis interrupted history.

Stripped of Everything

Only through poverty of spirit do we draw close to God; only through it does God draw near to us. Poverty of spirit is the meeting place of heaven and earth, the mysterious place where God and we encounter each other, the point where infinite mystery meets concrete existence.

—JOHANNES METZ, POVERTY OF SPIRIT

Today, we place a great emphasis on clothing. We make fashion state-ments, and all too readily judge others solely on the basis of what they are wearing. And nudity is common in movies and television. Magazines and the Internet use nudity to attract subscribers. For Francis, clothing and nakedness were very symbolic, and a means of expression. He dressed as a troubadour, in the finest of silk, in his party days. He dressed as a knight to enter battle. He wore a beggar's rags in the early days of his search for God. Eventually, he created and wore a habit which perfectly reflected his devotion to poverty and simplicity.

Francis truly wanted to imitate Christ. And Christ died naked on the cross, even though we don't show the slain Lamb of God naked on the cross, because we simply couldn't take such a graphic image. We need to cover Christ up; and we need to cover ourselves up, and not just with clothing. By removing his clothes in public, Francis stripped himself of his fear and pretense. He stripped himself of his parents and their influ-ence, prestige and security. He stripped himself of his friends and neigh-bors. He stripped himself of his past and his future family wealth. Naked, only the thin wall of flesh stood between him and God. Naked, he had nothing and had nothing to lose. Naked, he had no plans, no prospects for the future. Naked, both literally and symbolically, Francis was the freest man in the world. Naked, Francis had to rely on God for everything. Naked, his faith was lived on a minute-to-minute basis. Naked, Francis only wanted to be clothed in the glory of God.

The symbolism of his spectacular gesture prompts me to ask myself a very tough question: what in my life needs to be stripped away? Am I willing to stand naked in front of God, stripped of everything that stands between myself and the Divine?

A STATE OF PENANCE

Voluntarily disengaged from all worldly connections, and enjoying the true liberty of the children of God, Francis retired now for a while into solitude, to listen more attentively to the sweet whispers of divine Grace.
　—EMILIUS CHAVIN DE MALAN, *THE LIFE OF ST. FRANCIS OF ASSISIUM*

For nearly two years Francis lived as a hermit, calling himself a penitent and living according to the gospel as he understood it. It was a time of prayer and fasting, and living in a "state of penance." For Francis, penance was the most effective way of entering into the unceasing renewal required to achieve the gospel imperative of *metanoia*, a complete change of mind and heart through renouncing all self-love, all self-will and all self-seeking. Francis practiced acts of vigorous mortification as a means of breaking down any resistance within himself toward fully living the life of Christ in his own life.

It was also a time of restoring small, dilapidated chapels in the countryside near Assisi. Without any money and possessing nothing but the warmth of his personality and the fire of his faith, Francis went from town to town begging, often asking only for stones to use in rebuilding the Church of San Damiano. He carried the stones on his own shoulders. He quickly learned the skills of a stonemason. He also cared for lepers, going door-to-door with a bowl begging for food for them to eat. He even briefly worked as a servant in a Benedictine Abbey near Gubbio. In short, Francis was a beggar and a homeless, itinerant worker. Worse, he was cursed by his father when they crossed paths.

The gospel life certainly wasn't an easy life. God, it seems, asks hard things of those who love him. Yet all the accounts of this time of Francis' life indicate he endured all these hardships with great joy in his heart, and often a song on his lips.

Out of the darkness of detachment and utter deprivation, Francis slowly emerged to sparkle with sunshine and mercy.

Finding Joy in Sadness

My faith in God is so easily shaken that it is hard for me to understand how Francis overcame the loneliness of his new life and the numerous set-

backs he encountered along the gospel road. He was just one man. And a frail man at that. Yet, he undertook the Herculean task of fighting the physical decay of crumbling churches and suffering lepers. He didn't weigh the hugeness of his task, a task far beyond the reach of one frail man. He didn't see the obstacles. He only listened to his heart. Stone by stone, he restored the churches. Bowl by bowl, he fed the lepers. He did what he could, and left the rest to God.

I couldn't. I would have caved in under the enormity of the problem. The decaying churches would have filled me with sadness...and doubt. Was the truth of the faith upon which these temples were built not true? I would have looked into the tormented face of a leper and wondered why a good and merciful God would have permitted such agonizing suffering. Yet Saint Francis faced the hardships and heartbreaks with hope and joy.

In contrast, the joys I've experienced in life have all been lined with sadness. For me, joy has been fleeting; sadness, enduring. And I know I'm not alone in that regard. All around me, I see people fighting to suppress the sadness by searching for joy in a wide array of ways: sex, power, fame, fortune, drugs. We crowd into gigantic malls and gobble up all the goodies on display. We consume more than we need because we think we need more than we have. Credit cards in hand, we chase after the hottest fashions, the fastest cars, the quickest computers, the latest electronic gadgets in order to find happiness and dull the sadness. But the sadness remains.

Saint Francis...show me how you were able to find joy in the midst of so much sadness.

THE TABLE OF THE LORD

Love softens all things and makes every bitter thing sweet.
—THOMAS OF CELANO, *SECOND LIFE*

Life during these first solitary years wasn't easy for Francis. Change is always hard, and Francis was remaking himself, and the process of making the gradual transition from a life of easy prodigal self-indulgence to one of heroic self-abnegation in imitation of Christ was painful. In essence, Francis was conquering himself, so God could rule.

Early one evening, Francis went up to Assisi to beg for oil which he needed for the lamp he always kept burning before the crucifix at San Damiano. When he saw a house with lamps burning, he walked up to it, but before he could knock on the door, he noticed through the window a gathering of his old friends inside the house. They were having a party. Francis must have recalled the days when he was the life of such parties. Suddenly, he was too ashamed to knock on the door. Not wanting to cause embarrassment for either them or himself, he turned and walked away from the house. Within a few steps, Francis knew that his own weakness was causing him to be a coward. He returned to the house. His old friends let him in. They must have been stunned by his appearance. His worn, patched clothing must have looked strikingly out of place. As they looked on in astonished silence, Francis proclaimed he was a coward too ashamed to enter the house. His confession must have baffled them. He then asked them for some of their oil for the love of God. In moments like this, Francis found opportunities for self-conquest.

Sometimes, victory was hard. For instance, the old priest at San Damiano, who came to love Francis, grew increasingly distressed over how exhausted Francis was at the end of a long day's work restoring the little church. The priest was so worried about Francis' frail health, he began preparing hearty meals for him. But Francis saw this kind gesture as a temptation that could easily divert him from his commitment to true poverty. Francis realized that even a simple meal in the humble surroundings of the poor priest's home could be as addictive and comforting as all the luxuries he had once enjoyed in his father's house, and so he refused the food and opted instead to beg for his meals.

This last story can be found in Thomas of Celano's *Second Life* (Chapter IX, 14) and in *The Legend of the Three Companions* (Chapter VII, 22). According to the latter source, Francis, thinking about how his being pampered by the priest might eventually cause him to forsake his profession of poverty, began the following reflection:

> Wherever you may happen to go, do you suppose you will find another such priest who will treat you so kindly? This is not the life of the poor such as you wished to choose: rather you should go, bowl in hand, from door to door, and driven by hunger, collect the various morsels you may be given. It is only thus that you can live voluntarily for love of Him who was born poor, lived poor in this world, and remained naked and poor on the cross.

Elizabeth Goudge, in her life of Francis, *My God and My All*, picks up the story:

> And so he took a bowl and went up to Assisi and begged for his food from door to door, for the love of God. The astonished housewives gave him such scraps as they had and when he had enough to make a meal he went away to a quiet place and sat down and looked at the nauseating fragments in his bowl. Fastidious as he was his gorge rose [that is, his stomach turned to the point he felt ill and nauseous at the sight of the food]. How could he possibly swallow this disgusting mess? But this was the sort of food that poverty had to eat, and he was vowed to poverty, and he must eat it. So summoning all his courage, shuddering with revulsion at every mouthful, he set to work.
>
> As he ate a strange thing happened to him, for the feeling of nausea passed and he began to eat with appetite, and not only that but to feel a glow of happiness all through him. For with the self-conquest there had come to him one of those moments of light that came so often when he prayed, and the light illuminated many things. He realized that this poor meal was a sacrament of the providence of God. God spreads a table for His little ones, for the birds and beasts and for the poor who put their trust in Him, and is Himself their servant, as Christ was the servant of His disciples when he knelt before them to wash their feet and gave them His body and blood to be their food. He saw also that the providence of God is a circle of loving and giving, God serving His poor through the bounty of His rich, and His poor offering up their thanks to Him. And he saw more deeply into the meaning of the Trinity, the love that gives and the love that accepts, returning love again, and the love that is gift between them, Father, Son and Holy Spirit. And entering a little more deeply into the meaning of poverty he saw that it can be more blessed to receive than to give. Until now he had only given, he had poured himself out in love and service, and perhaps his giving had not always been quite free from the taint of pride; for the power to help others, even though it may seem wholly good, is still a power; but he had not set himself humbly to receive the service of God and man. With this humble receiving, he understood now, true humility must begin, and without it there is no true poverty. To Peter's cry of, "Thou shalt never wash my feet!" Christ had answered, "If I wash thee not thou hast no part in me," and unless he can learn to say with Peter, "Lord, not my feet only, but also my hands and my head," he

would have no part in the poverty of Christ. From that day onwards he had a great reverence for beggars because they were to him the symbol of this humble acceptance, and he called the eating of this food that had been begged for the love of God eating at the table of the Lord.

Day by day now he ate nothing except these scraps of food that he begged in the streets. It was not the bread of idleness, for idleness in any sort or form was always abhorrent to him, it was the bounty of God that gave his body strength for the rebuilding of God's church and the nursing of His sick. (pages 55-57)

Attitude Adjustment

Francis' imprisonment and subsequent illness eventually brought him face-to-face with the realization that worldly possessions and fame were worthless trophies that did not have the power to fill the void within him. Money and possessions no longer were the focus of his attention. While he personally shunned them, Francis did not condemn money and wealth, nor did he criticize those who devoted themselves to storing up earthly riches. Francis simply saw money and possessions as roadblocks to true joy. Rather than condemn them, he merely adjusted his attitude toward them.

When I see the extraordinary wealth of some people, I find myself getting angry at those who have so much money when so many have so little. Francis would rebuke my anger and gently tell me that money, big houses and fancy cars are not the problem...the problem is people's attitudes toward worldly treasures. Money is a tool, not a god. Francis continually forces me to reevaluate my relationship with money and material possessions. Do I own them or do they own me? Most lives are preoccupied with thoughts of money...how can I get more money, how can I save more money, do I spend too much money?

Money makes the world go 'round...or does God?

The Liturgy of the Hours

My heart is ready, O God;
I will sing, sing your praise.
Awake, my soul;
awake, lyre and harp.
I will awake the dawn.
(Psalm 107 [108]:1-2)

Incessant Wanderings

Francis' willingness to follow God anywhere is what made him so simple, pliant and totally responsive to even the slightest prompting of the Spirit. No wonder the worldly people of Assisi could not tolerate his incessant wanderings. They could only sneer at the future saint, because they acted out of their own self-interest, and any other kind of behavior was incomprehensible.

Could I have understood Francis' behavior had I been living in Assisi in his time? I doubt it, because it is hard for me today to understand not acting out of my own self-interest...although, Francis is certainly making me aware of it.

OUR LADY OF THE ANGELS

After finishing the restoration of San Damiano, Francis began the work of restoring a small, abandoned chapel hidden in the woods in the valley below Assisi known as the Portiuncula, or little portion of earth. The church was named Santa Maria degli Angeli—"St. Mary of the Angels." In his *Major Life*, Saint Bonaventure tells us:

When he finally completed this church [San Damiano], he

came to a place called the Portiuncula where there was a church dedicated to the Blessed Virgin Mother of God, built in ancient times but now deserted and cared for by no one. When the man of God saw how it was abandoned, he began to live there in order to repair it, moved by the fervent devotion he had toward the Lady of the world. According to the name of the church, which since ancient times was called St. Mary of the Angels, he felt that angels often visited there. So he took up residence there out of reverence for the angels and his special love for the mother of Christ. The holy man loved this spot more than any other in the world. (Chapter II, 8)

The church and the land around it were owned by the Benedictine monks of Mount Subasio. When the restoration was completed, Francis continued to live in a camp near the church and on occasion a monk would come down to celebrate Mass in the rebuilt church. Francis had prepared a home for the Eucharist and the Word, and his reverence for churches where the Word could be proclaimed and the Eucharist celebrated gave birth in his heart to a prayer he would teach his followers, a prayer still said by the friars today:

We adore you, most holy Lord Jesus Christ,
here and in all your churches throughout the world;
And we bless you because by your most
holy cross you have redeemed the world.

Planted on the Periphery

The roots of sanctity are planted in the depths of human frailty.
—LEONARDO BOFF

According to the Legend of Perugia *the Portiuncula was "the poorest of churches of the whole region around Assisi." One cannot overlook the symbolism at work here. The institutionalized Church at the time was rich and powerful. The Church was a dominating, secularized feudal power which owned half the land in Europe. Even monks were rich in land and material goods. Rather than enter into the "system," Francis moved to the periphery, where he found the environment ripe for creatively responding to the call of conversion. On the margins of society, far from the center of power, Francis chose the path of foolishness, following the Crucified Christ in absolute poverty and simplicity.*

Prophets are always planted on the periphery. Even the Son of God was born on the periphery of Jewish society.

The Liturgy of the Hours

A reading from the catechetical instructions of Saint John Mary Vianney:

> Prayer is nothing else than union with God. When the heart is pure and united with God it is consoled and filled with sweetness; it is dazzled by a marvelous light. In this intimate union God and the soul are like two pieces of wax moulded into one; they cannot any more be separated. It is a very wonderful thing, this union of God with his insignificant creature, a happiness surpassing all understanding.

PILGRIMAGE DIARY 11

Dazzled by a Marvelous Light

Silence is a gift of God, to let us speak more intently with God.
—*SAINT VINCENT PALLOTTI*

Francis was "dazzled by a marvelous light," of this I have no doubt. Oh, how I long for the sweetness of a pure heart that is united with God. Yet I ignore the very means of obtaining it: prayer. Francis committed himself to prayer. He didn't just squeeze prayer into his schedule; for at least half his life, prayer was the only thing on his schedule. Saint John Vianney wrote:

> [There are those who] immerse themselves as deeply in prayer as fish in water, because they give themselves totally to God. There is no division in their hearts. O, how I love these noble souls!

Saint Francis of Assisi...used to see our Lord and talk to him just as we talk to one another. (The Liturgy of the Hours, Vol. IV)

When I pray, I pray as if I've got a plane to catch. Lord, help me slow down and spend more time with you in prayer. And help me plunge into the deep water of real prayer, into the Ocean of the Love of God.

Mary's Example

Jesus sleeps in peace under the folds of your veil.
—*SAINT THÉRÈSE OF LISIEUX*

Purity of heart does not imply an absence of sin. Nor is it simply a matter of chastity. Purity of heart reflects the faithful heart of Mary. A pure heart holds nothing back, constantly giving God everything. Mary's most pure heart desired only that God's will be done. With purity of heart, we are called to follow Mary's example, and bring Jesus spiritually into today's modern, confused world, a world in need of a mother's unselfish love.

A NEW MISSION

During these years Francis had not preached to anybody; the idea of preaching, still less of founding an Order, had never entered his head. He had simply followed a clue which led him by painful happenings and along a dark path into a close union with God.
—H.F.B. MACKAY, *THE MESSAGE OF FRANCIS OF ASSISI*

It was in the restored church of Our Lady of the Angels that Francis made the transition from hermit and restorer of churches to apostle and evangelist. The change happened during a Mass being celebrated in honor of the feast of Saint Matthew the Apostle. As Francis listened to the priest reading from the Gospel of Matthew, he believed God was talking directly to him, and so the words of the Gospel became marching orders for Francis:

Jesus sent out these [disciples] after instructing them thus.... As you go, make this proclamation: 'The kingdom of heaven is at hand.' Cure the sick, raise the dead, cleanse lepers, drive out demons. Without cost you have received; without cost you are to give. Do not take gold or silver or copper for your belts; no sack for the journey, or a second tunic, or sandals, or walking stick. The laborer deserves his keep. (Matthew 10:5-10)

Those powerful, challenging words spoken by Christ reverberated through Francis' mind and heart. This is what he had longed for with all his heart. His pulse must have been racing.

Still, Francis humbly exercised caution and prudence...at least until he heard the priest say, "*Ite missa est*," and the Mass was over. Every word of the Gospel reading made a profound impact on his mind...it can be seen in his Rule, his Testament, and in all his writings. Christ had given Francis the formula of unreserved abnegation...he heard it with his own ears and his soul danced in delight: *This is it!*

Damien Vorreaux, O.F.M., in his book *First Encounter with Francis of Assisi*, describes Francis' reaction to the words of the Gospel:

> Here were honest, everyday words, perfectly familiar, neutral, inert—pure clichés. Ages ago they had been tamed, stripped of beak and claw, taught to roll over and play dead: real word-mummies. But this morning they seemed strangely new and pure, compact, stocky, literally unforgettable. This morning the words *made sense*. This sleeping gospel suddenly awoke. Francis wanted to seize its uncluttered heart. (pages 25-26)

But Francis needed to be sure he had correctly understood the words of the Gospel, and after Mass had ended he rushed up to the priest and breathlessly asked the priest the meaning of the text. I can almost hear Francis pleading: "How can we deny those words? Are they not a command from God?"

What a solemn moment! Francis' whole future hung on an impromptu consultation with a humble priest in a shabby little country chapel. But the meaning of the text was clear, even though no one, not even the priests, seemed to adhere to it, and so its true meaning could not be explained away.

Damien Vorreaux continues: "The old priest went over the text with him point by point, and Francis, ecstatic with joy, drunk with the Holy Spirit, said, 'This is what I want, this is what I've been looking for!'"

From then on, Francis was certain of his calling and mission, and he set out to preach the gospel around the world and to every creature. According to Thomas of Celano, Francis said, "This is what I long to do with all my heart."

The Liturgy of the Hours

A reading from the treatise of Saint Robert Bellarmine,
The Ascent of the Mind to God.

> O Lord, good and forgiving and
> abounding in steadfast love, who
> would not serve you with all his heart,
> when he has begun at least to taste the
> sweetness of your fatherly rule.

Simple Words

When Francis began his preaching mission to the people of Italy, it was a rather bold move, because at the time it was the custom for only bishops to preach. Sadly, many bishops were more interested in amassing money than in tending to their flock. The common people had little instruction in spiritual matters, and as a consequence sank deeper into an abyss of spiritual ignorance and superstition. Sin was more prevalent than prayer. These were truly dark days for the Church, until Francis appeared as a joyful light. He came as a poor man to serve the poor, carrying with him a message of peace and love. With outstretched arms he welcomed everyone. He spoke from the depths of his heart, and his simple words penetrated the souls of his listeners. This seemingly illiterate man, the very antithesis of the pedantic clergy, had the power to hold and sway an audience...and he gave all the credit to God.

Thoughts Scribbled While Walking

*T*he acknowledgment of our own weakness is the first step
toward an acknowledgment of Christ's strength.
*In condemning others, I am avoiding the more difficult task of
knowing myself.*
Only the pure of heart see God in everything.
Cling to yourself and you will lose yourself.
Communion with God is life; separation from God is death.
*Praying creates an awareness of God; and that awareness elicits
a response.*
*When it comes to following Christ without reservation, I know
what to do. What I lack is the courage to do it.*
Walk humbly behind Christ.
Love and trust are the heart and soul of simplicity.
By recognizing my weakness I become strong.
God is humble. God lives in our poverty and weakness.
To run from the experience of poverty is to run from God.

AN OUTER HABIT

*The poor man who is naked will be clothed and the soul that is
naked will be clothed by God with his purity, satisfaction, and
will.*

—SAINT JOHN OF THE CROSS

Francis knew what he had to do; now he had to do it. He had to act
on the words...he had to go out into the world, proclaiming the
kingdom of heaven was near. Selecting the coarsest material he
could find, he made himself a habit shaped in the form of a cross.
He fastened the simple habit about his waist with a rope, and off he
went. Dressed like a peasant, he walked barefoot through the countryside and towns, bringing the peace of Christ to all who wished to
receive it. He preached the word of God in public squares, always
beginning his sermon by offering a blessing to those assembled:
"The Lord give you peace." Filled with conviction, he spoke with
great passion. His enthusiasm and assurance electrified his simple,

plain words, giving them power to move his listeners.

All He Needed

The Gospel said to take nothing for the journey, not even a pair of san-dals. And so Francis took nothing, trusting God for all he needed. Unlike Francis, we wouldn't literally follow such harsh—and even foolish and senseless—directives. We know better. We would take ample supplies and have contingency plans drawn up. Still, this Gospel does challenge us to travel lightly...after all, Jesus always stressed that our identity and secu-rity are not to be found in material possessions or clever strategies, but in God alone.

Francis took nothing for his journey, and still he had all he needed.

God alone...is not yet enough for me. I still need more than that. Still want more than that. And so I never seem to have enough.

PILGRIMAGE DIARY 13

Crazy or Inspired

*F*rom the time Francis heard Matthew's Gospel he was certain of his calling. Certainty...I wish I could feel it regarding my "calling." To be frank, I'm not sure I know what my calling is...and I've already passed my fiftieth birthday. At times, I think writing this book—and consequently coming on this study pilgrimage—is exactly what I should be doing. At other times, I think this is the craziest thing I've ever done (and I've done a lot of crazy things!).

Was Francis' impulsive and literal reaction to the Gospel story he heard mumbled in Latin crazy or inspired? Thinking about the priest whom Francis asked to explain and interpret the Gospel text, and wondering what answer Francis would receive today, Adolf Holl, in The Last Christian, *writes:*

> One can easily imagine what a modern theologian—of whatev-er denomination—would have said to Francis. The theologian would have conceded that Jesus' instructions to his disciples were historically credible, that they derived from a very old tra-dition. But he would have pointed out that a literal adherence to them after so long a time and under such altered cultural

conditions would be an anachronism, an exaggeration. He would have added that they were only practicable in a country like Palestine, with its warm climate: Jesus had only formulated them for his preaching among Palestinian Jews, as was evident from the text itself. He would never have intended to fashion a rule that was valid for all times and places. Francis might observe in this regard what Jesus had said on another occasion (cf. Luke 22:35-36), namely at the Last Supper, just before his death. He asked the Apostles, "When I sent you out with no purse or bag or sandals, did you lack anything?" The Apostles had answered, "Nothing." To which Jesus replied, "But now, let him who has a purse take it, and likewise a bag. And let him who has no sword sell his mantle and buy one."

Of course, this was a dubious passage, which may have only gotten into the Gospel after Jesus' death. But one could infer from it that even the very first Christians in Palestine had realized that people couldn't always go about anywhere in the world as carefree and unprotected as in Francis' text from Matthew. So clearly Francis was on the wrong track if he meant to guide his life by a single passage from the Gospel. Such one-sidedness was too sectarian; one must keep the totality of the Christian message in mind.

We also know how Francis would have reacted to the theologian's remarks—with greatest deference. "We ought to honor and revere all theologians...as those who minister to us spirit and life." Thus he wrote in his Testament, obviously without any reservations. At the same time Francis would never have dreamed of attaching any importance whatsoever to the theological lesson.

He would have listened politely and then given the same reply he gave on a similar occasion to a respected theologian who had joined the Friars Minor and asked Francis whether the clerics in his fellowship were allowed to have books: "I say to you, brother, what is my original and final desire, my first and last word. No friar shall have anything except a tunic with a cord, and a pair of drawers."

I like to imagine Francis in heaven chatting with all the Christian theologians, with Augustine and Karl Barth, Aquinas and Rudolf Bultmann. Francis asks them what they would be without their books. They can't find a good answer. He tells them, "Without your books, perhaps you might have become Christians."

I'll leave it to others to judge whether Mr. Holl's judgment of theologians is too harsh. Francis urged his followers to criticize only themselves and not others.

The point I'm making in all this is simple: knowing how to interpret the gospel is a very difficult task for most people today.

Should it be?

What would Francis of Assisi say to us?

Would his response have any relevance in our time and culture?

How we answer those questions determines how we interpret the gospel...and also, how God speaks to us.

Francis said, "I have done what was mine to do; may Christ teach you what you are to do."

Francis doesn't want us to do what he did; he isn't interested in people becoming copies of him. Francis knew each person is an individual, a unique creation loved by God as an individual. Francis would have agreed with the Japanese poet Matsuo Basho (1644-1694) when he wrote (in The Narrow Road to the Deep North): "Do not seek to follow in the footsteps of the men of old; seek what they sought." Francis would tell us to listen, listen intently with a pure and humble heart, and we will know what we are to do.

I am doing what is mine to do.

And the doubts I feel at times come from some dark corner within me where my false self is clinging to the hope it can still get its own way, that it can knock God off the throne of my life.

But I know that nothing finite can ever satisfy the infinite longings of my heart. Julian of Norwich said it best: "In the Only I have all."

Listen. Listen.

Buying Bewilderment

The painter Paul Gauguin claimed he shut his eyes in order to see. The Sufi mystic Rumi advised selling your cleverness and buying bewilderment. What they are saying is that the heart sees what the eyes can't. Francis learned that lesson very well, and was willing to let God flip his world upside down. Conversion is listening to the events of your life that change your perspective. Francis understood he had a need for an ongoing change of heart, an ongoing change of perspective that allowed him to see the way God saw. It was his willingness to be "grasped" by God that made him unique. He approached each day with a simple, very childlike attitude: God, what do you have in store for me today? This outlook released him from the burden of self-groundedness and into the freedom of being grounded in God, thus allowing himself to experience a realignment of his passion, and a complete re-centering of his affections.

For Francis, conversion was a liberating experience, freeing him from the prison of self-rule.

THE MADNESS OF THE GOSPEL

In *I, Francis*, Carlo Carretto, who lived a life of intensive silence and prayer as a hermit at Spello near Assisi, put these words in Francis' mouth:

> The social struggle in my day was very lively and intense, almost, I should say, as much so as in your own times. Everywhere there arose groups of men and women professing poverty and preaching poverty in the Church and the renewal of society. But nothing changed, since there was no change of heart.
>
> When the poor agitate, and their agitating succeeds and they become rich, they grow arrogant like the rest of the rich, and forget their old companions in misery.
>
> This is what happened then, and this is what is happening to you.
>
> Revolutionaries, who battle for the freedom of the working classes for instance...but having themselves become the State and achieved power and wealth, they then suppress those members of the working class who think differently from themselves and who naturally feel cheated....
>
> No, brothers and sisters, it is not enough to change laws. You have to change hearts. Otherwise, when you have completed the journey of your social labours you find yourselves back at the beginning—only this time you are the ones who are the tyrants, the rich, the exploiters of the poor....
>
> This is why I took the Gospel path. For me poverty was the sign of liberation, yes, but of true liberation, the liberation of hearts. This was the thrust that shot me out of the middle-class mentality, which is present to every age, and is known as selfishness, arrogance, pride, sensuality, idolatry, slavery.

I knew something about all that.

I knew what it meant to be rich, I knew the danger flowing from a life of easy pleasure, and when I heard the text in Luke, "alas for you, who are rich," my flesh crept. I understood. I had run a mortal risk by according value to idols that filled my home and would have fettered me, had I not escaped....

You can reproach me, go ahead. But I saw, in the Gospel, a road beyond, a path that transcended all cultures, all human constructs, all conventions.

I felt the Gospel to be eternal; I felt politics and culture, including Christian culture, to be within time.

I was made to go beyond time.

In the quest for justice and human equality, the Old Testament would have been enough. It would have sufficed to read Deuteronomy, the Book of Kings, Leviticus.

There, one is taught to build the State along the lines of good sense, and the old theocratic mentality.

There one learns perhaps to make war, take captive, divide booty, kill, torture perhaps in the name of God, just as was sometime done in my day, and is sometime done in yours.

But the Gospel was another matter.

The Gospel is the madness of a God who is always losing, who gets Himself crucified to save humanity.

The Gospel is the madness of a people, who, in the midst of tears, need and persecution, still cry out that they are blessed.

I had grasped all this, and I understood why the wise and well-balanced would have destroyed me. So I called on the madness to save me. And I was happy to have found the true madness, the saving madness of the Gospel. (pages 20-22)

Francis heard the Word in the silence of his heart, where it was welcomed and given space to grow and creatively animate his life.

No Fatted Calf for the Good

Near the end of Part One, I mentioned that on my first visit to Assisi I began to be drawn to Francis' radical interpretation of the gospel. Since that trip, I've come to better appreciate just how radical the gospel itself is. The truly radical nature of the gospel is clearly evident in the parable of the Prodigal Son. In this story, Christ says, in essence, that the just person who has never sinned will be less well received in heaven than the person who has sinned and has repented. So it seems straying from the straight and narrow path has its rewards, as long as you return to the path. There was no fatted calf or feast for the son who did not kill or steal or commit adultery, and who instead obeyed all the Commandments. This is hard for us to understand, because it goes against our nature. We want to reward the good and punish the bad. The prodigal son's brother was enraged and filled with bitter indignation at his father's joyful reaction to the return of the brother who had brought shame to the family. The father's response: Your brother who was dead is now alive, he who was lost is now found. That response recurs again and again in the gospel, like a leitmotif with endless variations: for the one who exalts himself shall be abased; and the one who humbles himself shall be exalted; and the first shall be last, and the last, first.

Jesus didn't spend all of his time with the good and the just. He consorted with outcasts, with publicans and sinners. He ate with prostitutes and with vagabonds he found along the highways and hedges. Why? Perhaps because they, like the prodigal son, were capable, in the extremity of their evil or pain, of a sudden awakening that enabled them to convert their utter deprivation into a new reality and true clarity. Moments of great suffering and failure often lead people to scale the heights of their souls...perhaps because they have nowhere else to go. Crying out for God in the darkness isn't something an honest person, who believes he or she stands well with himself or herself, society and God, is likely to do. The prodigal son risked all and lost all, and yet in the moment of loss, he came nearer to God than ever before.

It's not the way most of us would have organized things. But that's what makes the gospel message so radical. And truly hard to follow...at least for me.

PILGRIMAGE DIARY 14

Nada

I remembered some words of St. Francis de Sales to the effect that to get up after a fall, over and over again, was more pleasing to God than if we did not fall. I grasped this; that trust which would go on, in spite of continual failure, must please God.

—*RUTH BURROWS*, BEFORE THE LIVING GOD

*There is one area of my life where poverty is very real: My
prayer life is impoverished. If I had to choose one word to
describe my prayer life, it would be: empty. A big, fat nada. Perhaps
the reason my experience of prayer is empty is because Jesus is still
outside of me—not within me in a way which I can feel. And so, my
prayer seems "outward" and lacks the true intimacy of being
"inward," a sweet communion within me, as I imagine it was for
Francis and all the other saints.*

*I often experience prayer as a blank inertia. Once in a great
while, the blankness or void gives way—ever so fleetingly—to
something more substantive, as if God, though still hidden, is really
present. When I experience prayer as a void, I lack the trust in God
to continue anyway. I flee the darkness, the emptiness.*

*I've tried setting more time aside for quiet prayer—just sitting still
before the Lord—but the noise of my own thinking, my own
consciousness, makes it virtually impossible for me to sit still for
more than a few minutes.*

*Saint Teresa of Avila may have had an interior castle, but I have
an interior prison—blank, cold, barren.*

*Even though I love God and sincerely long for a deeper
relationship, I consider myself a spiritual failure because of my
inability to pray more effectively, to feel more connected to God on
a daily basis. Sin seems nearer than God does.*

Oh dear God, please give me the courage to trust fully in you
when my prayer leaves me feeling alone; give me, sweet Lord, the
grace of perseverence to sit still in my inner prison until you unlock
the door.

*Saint Augustine writes, "Go back inside yourself, for truth dwells
in the inner man."* Come, Lord Jesus, enter my heart with your
Presence and Fullness.

No Strings Attached

There is no wilderness so terrible, so beautiful, so arid and so
fruitful as the wilderness of compassion. It is the only desert
that shall truly flourish like the lily....

—*THOMAS MERTON,* THE SIGN OF JONAS

On my desk at home is a small picture card featuring a detailed look at the father and son from Rembrandt's famous painting The Return of the Prodigal Son. The back of the card features the prayer of serenity. The picture for me represents the ideal of the all-merciful, all-forgiving father from the Gospel story told by Jesus. The painting does not tell that a father in the patriarchal social context of the biblical story would never run to embrace a son who had dishonored him. That would have been an act far too undignified for the venerable head of a family to perform, especially since the son had not yet even sought forgiveness. Moreover, the son had thrown away any privileges he may have had; he lost all his money and was on the brink of total ruin. In those times, the son would have been considered a complete disgrace to all, and not worthy of the father's trust or affection. Yet, the father forgave the son without asking him for any reparation or proof of the sincerity of his repentance.

For those who heard Jesus tell this parable, it was truly an astounding story, because he was telling them that God's forgiveness was an easy thing to obtain. You simply have to walk into God's loving arms. God gives Love away. There are no strings attached, no conditions to be met. It is ours for the asking.

The father's embrace of the son healed the son of the disastrous effects of his wrongful behavior. When you experience that level of generosity, totally unmerited, you become more acutely aware of your failures, and you make a sincere effort not to repeat them. That is the transforming secret of confession.

The story of the Prodigal Son tells us that we do not have to feel guilty over the reality of our human frailty and weakness. God is not standing behind some bush waiting to jump out and sternly judge us. No...God, Jesus says, is running down the road toward us, eager to wrap his arms around us and kiss us better. The enormity of God's love, which is so vast it is beyond measure or comprehension, creates in me an awareness of the depth of my insufficiency. But that awareness does not trigger feelings of unworthiness or emptiness. Rather it creates a sense of poverty which allows me to trust fully in God, and abandon myself fully in God's bountiful love.

The painting and the parable also remind me of my need to forgive others, without hesitation and without question. And without question, that is hard to do, which only illustrates more clearly the radical nature of the parable and of God's love.

Jesus says, "Be merciful, just as your Father is merciful." (Luke 6:36)

A NEW FORM OF LIFE

*Soon the fragrant odour of his virtues attracted disciples to the
standard of Francis.*
   —EMILIUS CHAVIN DE MALAN, *THE LIFE OF ST. FRANCIS OF ASSISIUM*

By 1209, Francis' austere way of life began to attract others.
Impressed by Francis' kindness, sincerity and holy demeanor, men
from all walks of life asked to join him in his new way of life. The
first to follow him was Bernard of Quintavalle, a wealthy citizen of
Assisi and, according to Saint Bonaventure, "a venerable man"; he
was followed by Peter Catanii, a lawyer, and then came Giles, an
illiterate layman with a great gift of prayer who was known for his
heroic virtue. They set out on preaching tours—to the Marches of
Ancona, a hilly country northeast of their native Umbria; to the
Valley of Rieti, to the south; and to Florence in Tuscany, to the
north.

PILGRIMAGE DIARY 15

The Only Question

Humility is an attitude of honesty with God, oneself, and of all
reality. It enables us to be at peace in the presence of our powerlessness and to rest in the forgetfulness of self.
   —*THOMAS KEATING*, OPEN MIND, OPEN HEART

*T**he fuel that propels this pilgrimage for me is the desire to
better understand and enter into a more mystical expression of
my Christianity. The first step on the road to mysticism seems to be
an overwhelming consciousness of God. This consciousness for me
tends to dominate all my thoughts and eclipses all other interests;
God is always on my mind. One time when Saint Francis was
praying in the house of Bernard of Quintavalle, it was reported that
he repeatedly said, "My God, my God, what art thou? and what am
I?" Of course the question was also asked by Saint Augustine, but it
nonetheless represents Francis' frame of mind: This was the only
question he thought worth asking. And it is the question every mystic
asks as he or she begins a journey to God...and sometimes the*

answer is discovered by the end of the quest.

Francis protected and deepened his overpowering consciousness of God by constant prayer. The nineteenth-century Russian Orthodox bishop-turned-monk Theopane the Recluse advised, in addition to prayer, those graced with a hunger for God must add humility: "Guard this feeling, given to you by the mercy of God. How? First and foremost by humility, ascribing everything to grace and nothing to yourself. As soon as you trust to yourself, grace will diminish in you; and if you do not come to your senses, it will cease to work completely" (The Art of Prayer: An Orthodox Anthology, page 60).

Prayer and humility go hand in hand: Prayer deepens humility and humility deepens prayer. Theophane the Recluse observed: "Growth in prayer has no end. If this growth ceases, it means life ceases."

Go In, Go Out

I'm torn. Discordant currents within me pull me in many different directions. This hardly makes me unique. Humans are steeped in complexity, loaded with strengths and weaknesses, gifted with vast potential and cursed with severe limitations. Tension is a natural part of life. I want to write books, which is an internal, solitary act of contemplation, and I also want to make films, which is an external, communal form of action. Earlier in these pages I said I felt a desire to work in a soup kitchen, a desire which stands in opposition to another desire I have, to be a hermit devoted to prayer. When I'm reading a book on spirituality or theology, I feel as if I should be feeding the hungry. The other day I was running an errand for an elderly, feeble neighbor, and while doing so pages from unread books danced in my head. How do I find balance and harmony?

People are always talking about the importance of unity, either within families or communities or the workplace. Forget that stuff—how do I find unity within myself? God seems to be telling me that I need to be still. But I also feel God wants me to change, to move into a new reality of life. The call to conversion implies the continual need to grow, to change. More tension. Even a casual reading of the lives of the saints tells me I must face the darkness in order to experience the light. Christ, being fully human, also lived a life of tension and contradiction. While hanging and dying on the cross, Christ became the apex of contradiction:

promising the fullness of life in the barrenness of a cruel death.

Saint Francis saw God in the tensions and conflicting forces within himself. He accepted his own complexity, and created something new and fresh for himself. He responded to the Christ he saw in everyone by living a life of service to others. But he also paid attention to his need for solitude by finding a time and place for withdrawal so he could enter fully into contemplative prayer. He went in, and he went out...living a life of prayer and service. He was able to do this because he centered his life on Christ, listening to and experiencing both the suffering Messiah and the risen Lord in his daily life. Christ himself went into the marketplace, preaching and curing the sick, and he also went into the desert, praying and seeking the will of the Father. Francis found the unity for his life by imitating the life of Christ.

Is there another way? I don't think so...at least not for me. But I am not sure I have the courage and strength to imitate Christ. Am I able to be content with what I have? Can I rejoice in the way things are this very moment, whether good or bad? Am I capable of not acting in anger when I am wronged? Can I avoid nursing a grudge? Can I bear injuries patiently? Can I pray for my enemies? Am I willing to put the needs of the poor ahead of my own selfish desires? Can I treasure chastity and shun arrogance? Am I ready to bury jealousy and envy? Can I avoid grumbling or speaking ill of others? Can I stop engaging in foolish, idle chatter and immoderate behavior? Can I rid my heart of all deceit? Can I acknowledge my own sinfulness? Am I willing to devote myself to prayer? Can I place my hope in God alone?

Can I say yes to any of those questions?

No.

God give me strength to turn my "no" into "yes," to turn my old ways into your ways. Help me say yes to you, yes to Life.

PILGRIMAGE DIARY 16

Buon Giorno, Buona Gente

Anyone who has really understood that God became human can never speak and act in an inhuman way.

—KARL BARTH

The Valley of Rieti was practically a second home to Francis. Only his beloved Valley of Spoleto occupied a higher place in his heart. The Valley of Rieti, located northeast of Rome and far to the south of Assisi, was the site of Francis' first efforts at preaching, but in time it came to represent the contemplative dimension of the Franciscan charism. Francis loved the mountains that ring the valley. The valley floor, which once was a lake until it was drained by the Romans, is covered with wheat fields, olive trees, vineyards and flowers. The city of Rieti is an ancient city that sits on a low hill at the southern end of the valley; the city is still partially surrounded by medieval walls. Near the end of his life, Francis traveled to Reiti seeking a cure for his eye disease, and during his stay he was consoled during a night of prayer by the sweetness of heavenly flute music. Four important Franciscan sanctuaries are located in the valley: Greccio, Fonte Columbo, La Foresta and Poggio Bustone. The pilgrimage spent a week in the valley, exploring each of the four locations. The four sanctuaries resonate with the simplicity and humility of Francis' spirit. Nature and silence take precedence over art and architecture.

Poggio Bustone is located about sixteen kilometers from the city of Rieti, and is the northernmost Franciscan sanctuary in the valley; it sits in a high, rugged and remote area which provided Francis ample solitude. The Convento di San Giacomo is believed to have been founded by Saint Francis in 1217. Down a flight of stairs from the Convento is a small hermitage where Francis planted a cross to remind him of his redemption. There is a steep path leading from the Convento up to the crest of the hill. Along the path, there are six little chapels. At the end of the path there is a small hermitage cut out of the rock.

Francis first came to Poggio Bustone in 1209. As he entered the little village, he greeted the inhabitants with the cheerful words: "Buon giorno, buona gente"—"Good morning, good people." The greeting reflects the saint's ability to see good in everyone.

Poggio Bustone was a place of pardon for Francis. One day, Francis found a place for solitary prayer and stayed there for a long time. He was concerned about the future of his little band of friars, and was praying for some sense of direction. While praying, he became preoccupied with the sins of his past. He began to repeat over and over again the words, "O Lord, have mercy on me a sinner." Eventually the repetition of his plea gave way to a great joy. The depths of his heart were washed in a soothing sweetness. And then his spirit danced in the certainty that all his sins had been forgiven and his soul was filled with an abundance of fresh grace. God showed his humble servant that his little band of men would increase into a great magnitude who will announce the Good News of salvation to the world.

Francis' compunction over his sins was not a simple matter of feeling sorrow about wrong actions. It was a sincere attempt to separate himself from those things within him which were harmful to his relationship with God. He no longer wanted any behavior from his past to have any power over his present, which was consumed by a love of God and a desire to grow closer to God. God heard his cry and graced Francis with an unshakable peace and joy.

I climbed to the peak with two friars. As we made our way up the hillside, we spoke about how driven our society is by the need to be useful. One friar mentioned how he always feels this need to at least have the appearance he is working, even during his own personal free time. It is as if we fear what lies beyond our usefulness. The other friar spoke about how monks are viewed with suspicion in our society because our materialistic culture, which is at its heart irreligious, finds the idea of devoting your life to seeking God to be incomprehensible because it produces nothing. I joked that some monks produce wine and cheese, but the underlying sad truth we discussed was that society is focused on chasing the transient quest of business and pleasure.

Places like Poggio Bustone help us restore a sense of balance between our intimate relationship with God, which is nurtured in contemplation, and our communal relationships with our families or communities and our co-workers. But our drive for usefulness, for action, seems to far outweigh our desire to be still. One friar observed, "We want to just plunge immediately into deep contemplation, but it doesn't happen. It takes a lot of time to still the restless movement within us." We all understood his frustration. We are doers, performers who always have an itch to be acting. It is hard for us to simply sit before God and listen. How can we speak about God, or share God's love, when we haven't fully experienced it ourselves? Francis knew he had to spend time listening to God before he could speak to others about God.

When we reached the summit, we decided to split up and take about fifteen minutes by ourselves before heading back down. As I sat looking out over the beautiful Rieti Valley, the vastness of creation heightened my awareness of my need to spend more time contemplating God. I recalled something I heard earlier in the day during one of the lectures. Someone suggested, "You become what you gaze upon," and they asked us to reflect on how we spend our time, so we might become more aware of the focus of our attention. My attention is not always focused on God. During the week before this pilgrimage, I spent more time watching baseball on television than I did listening to God in prayer. I need to spend more time on the most important relationship in my life.

Glorifying Banality

Music's only purpose should be for the glory of God and the recreation of the human spirit.

—*JOHANN SEBASTIAN BACH*

The deeper I travel into the life of Saint Francis of Assisi, the more concerned I become about the state of what passes for popular entertainment these days, especially in film and television. As a culture, we are becoming obsessed with entertainment, and actors are becoming icons of all we hope for and admire. The following astute observation comes from The Lessons of St. Francis *by John Michael Talbot and Steve Rabey:*

One day Francis was staying in the town of Rieti. As was often the case, some of those around Francis at the time were musicians and artists. Suffering from a variety of physical ailments, the saint asked a brother who had worked as a musician before joining the Franciscan movement to play his zither to ease his pain. The saint also talked to the brother about an issue that was on his heart, saying, "Brother, the children of this world have no understanding of the things of God. Formerly, the saints used such musical instruments as the zither, psalteries, and others to praise God and console their souls: now these instruments promote vanity and sin, contrary to the will of the Lord."

We can see the truth of these words today. I'm continually amazed at how little true goodness there is in the music and entertainment of our modern world. Our stereos, radios, and televisions seem to play constantly. Mass-produced entertainment is everywhere: in our homes, our cars, our offices, and even in our public elevators and restrooms. But with so much mass-produced culture surrounding us, doesn't it seem strange that there is so little that offers anything of true and lasting beauty? We're engulfed by a nonstop barrage of technically proficient, well-produced and expertly marketed entertainment, but so little of it uplifts our soul. In fact, much of popular culture glorifies banality, ugliness, and violence. What a mess we've made of this beautiful gift of God, which was designed to heal and bless us.

When I began making my living producing soap operas, I had this lofty idea I was making art. In time, I came to see that the economic, commercial and editorial constraints of the soap opera genre stifled individual artistic expression and prevented serious exploration of the important issues of life. I wasn't producing art...I was manufacturing a vehicle that delivered commercials. It was all about ratings.

Today, I watch very little television. (Or, more truthfully, far less than I used to watch.) It is becoming increasingly difficult for me to stomach the nearly constant diet of banality and triteness which is served up by television. All too often, most characters are dysfunctional, sex is casual, gratuitous and self-serving, violence is excessive and comedy is mean-spirited. Finding an uplifting show is becoming harder and harder. Still, my nonviewing is not rooted in an elitist attitude that says all TV is garbage. My viewing is decreasing because I have come to realize the importance of silence in the spiritual life. Moreover, I no longer have the same need for escapism, which is what TV primarily peddles.

In a country in which the vast majority of people believe in God, it amazes me how we have been so seduced by the power of entertainment that we no longer have the will to simply turn it off.

Day in and day out we are drenched by a torrent of words. Words,

words, words...but little silence in which the Word may reside.

We must be still in order to move into a greater union with Christ. We must give Christ our time regularly, day in, day out, coming before him just as we are, wounded and weak.

Without silence there is a deep level of our being which is not contributing to our wholeness. We are incomplete without the fruit of silence and solitude.

But withdrawal from the endless possibilities for stimulation modern life offers is painful. It takes faith and hope to give God time.

PILGRIMAGE DIARY 17

Thoughts Scribbled While Walking

Simplicity safeguards the spirit from distractions and leads it to God.

Enjoy without owning.

God alone calms and satisfies all our desires.

You can't be converted without becoming naked and seeing clearly all your faults and weaknesses.

Do not judge others; instead, live with God.

Stop measuring your progress. In fact, let go of the idea of "progress."

Self-indulgence leads to spiritual dryness.

Desires give birth to desires.

Consume less.

Everything belongs to God. Nothing belongs to us.

The seduction of property blinds us to the needs of the poor.

We must become the poor Christ...offered up and given away.

SEEKING PAPAL APPROVAL

By the spring of 1209, their number grew to twelve, and Francis found it necessary to write a rule of life for himself and his followers. Using simple words, Francis based the Rule on the solid foundation of gospel principles, adding, according to Saint Bonaventure, "a few other things that seemed necessary for their way of life in common." After having written the Rule, Francis harbored a hope it would be endorsed by the pope, in part because some people thought Francis and his followers were heretics or just another radical fringe group. And so he and a few of his friars set out for Rome seeking approval for their form of life (*Forma Vitae*) from Pope Innocent III. But approval of his gospel way of life would not be easy to obtain. During that time, many different sects which the Church considered heretical were sprouting up under the leadership of laymen, some of whom even espoused the same kind of evangelical poverty as did Francis. Francis could easily have been viewed as the leader of yet another politically-tinted splinter group, such as the Albigenses or the Humiliati or the Waldensians or the Cathars.

It is almost impossible to imagine the initial meeting between the pope and the pauper, the former an icon of power and the latter, an icon of humility. Francis, dressed in rags and dirty from the ordeal of the long, grueling walk from Assisi, was a simple penitent whose coarse hands gave clear evidence that his primary "ministry" was little more than rebuilding crumbling churches. And this insignificant little man was about to stand before a towering figure, Pope Innocent III, whose papacy, which began in 1198, brought the Church's temporal power and influence to its zenith. Innocent was a famous and greatly learned man whose books on the Mass were among the best-sellers of medieval times. Moreover, he was a skilled statesman, a consummate politician and a fiery orator. He was thirty-six years old when he was elected pope, and went on to be one of the most powerful pontiffs in the history of the Church. Innocent loved order and beauty, and was the first pope to use the title *Vicar of Christ*. While he lived simply and chastised wealthy clergy for their excesses, his sponsorship of the crusades darkened his page in papal history. He is remembered more for his political ruthlessness than for his pastoral activities, which were considerable, including encouraging the Humiliati, a poverty-based reform movement, to return to the Church.

The following description of what happened when Francis arrived in Rome was added to Saint Bonaventure's *Major Life* by Jerome of Ascoli, minister general of the Order from 1274 to 1279, who later became Pope Nicholas IV. According to Professor Cousins, whose translation I will use, Jerome heard the story of how Francis and the pope met from Cardinal Riccardo degli Annibaldi, who was a relative of Pope Innocent III.

When he arrived in Rome, he was led into the presence of the

Supreme Pontiff. The Vicar of Christ was in the Lateran Palace, walking in a place called the Hall of Mirrors, occupied in deep meditation. Knowing nothing of Christ's servant, he sent him away indignantly. Francis left humbly, and the next night God showed the Supreme Pontiff the following vision. He saw a palm tree sprout between his feet and grow gradually until it became a beautiful tree. As he wondered what this vision might mean, the divine light impressed upon the mind of the Vicar of Christ that this palm tree symbolized the poor man whom he had sent away the previous day. The next morning he commanded his servants to search the city for the poor man. (*Bonaventure*, page 204)

They found Francis in a nearby hospice and immediately brought him to the pope. Francis humbly explained his gospel way of life and how he wanted his followers to live and act. Saint Bonaventure writes that the pope detected Francis' "remarkable purity and simplicity of heart," his "firmness of purpose" and his "fiery ardor of will," and he was inclined to approve the Rule. However, the pope hesitated because a number of cardinals who were present felt the radical way Francis wanted to live was too innovative and far too difficult to follow.

But Francis found a worthy advocate in John of St. Paul, a cardinal who was impressed by his unselfishness and love of the poor. Addressing the pope and his fellow cardinals, he said, "If we refuse the request of this poor man as novel or difficult, when all he asks is to be allowed to lead the Gospel life, we must be on our guard lest we commit an offense against Christ's Gospel. For if anyone says that there is something novel or irrational or impossible to observe in this man's desire to live according to the perfection of the Gospel, he is guilty of blasphemy against Christ, the author of the Gospel" (*Bonaventure*, page 205).

Struck by the force of the cardinal's reasoning, the pope asked Francis to seek God's will on the matter in prayer, and after doing so, if he were still certain of the path God was leading him down, then he should return to him and he would eagerly give Francis' new community his blessing.

HOLDING UP THE BASILICA

After a period of prayer, Francis returned to the Lateran filled with conviction. He boldly told the pope a parable based on the Scriptures, concluding that if Jesus had promised us eternal life, surely he would not deny us the things we need here on earth. After listening to Francis, the pope fully believed that Christ had spoken through the poor man from Assisi. The pope then recounted a vision that he had recently had in which an insignificant poor man was holding up the Lateran Basilica, which was on the verge of collapse. Francis, according to the pope, was the fulfillment of that prophetic vision. He said, "This is truly a pious and holy man by whom the Church of God shall be restored." The pope then gave Francis his verbal consent and ordered the Brothers to live strictly according to the gospel.

PILGRIMAGE DIARY 18

Basilica di San Giovanni in Laterano

*F*ew sights in Rome can match the Basilica of St. John Lateran
in significance to the Catholic faith. The basilica, which is the
cathedral of Rome, began life as a sign of Christianity's acceptance.
In 312, Constantine triumphantly entered Rome after defeating
Maxentius in battle. He immediately forbade the persecution of
Christians. To demonstrate his full embrace of Christianity,
Constantine chose the site of Maxentius's bodyguards' barracks to
construct a monument to Christ, the Holy Redeemer, and in doing so
he destroyed one of the signs of his enemy's greatness. The land was
originally owned by the Laterani family, and Constantine gave the
property to Pope Melchiades. Two years later, Pope Sylvester I took
up residence in the Lateran, a group of buildings comprising the
basilica, a palace and a baptistery. The palace became the pope's
official residence.

The basilica was badly damaged during the invasion of the
barbarians in the fifth century. Further damage was inflicted by an
earthquake in 896. And following its near destruction by fire in
1308, the building was rebuilt during the Baroque era. Until the late
nineteenth century, the basilica was almost constantly being rebuilt,

restored and embellished by a virtual who's who of Italian artists and architects.

During its long life, the Lateran was home to some of the most decisive councils in the history of the Church. One cannot overestimate the importance of the Lateran in the life of the Church. Crusades where launched from here; important doctrines of faith were defined here.

The Lateran captivates me for two reasons: its beauty and its significance in the life of Saint Francis, who came here seeking the pope's approval for his radical way of life.

As you approach the basilica, your attention is first caught by the gigantic statues along the balustrade (top) of the eighteenth-century facade. The central statue, and the highest, depicts Christ. He is flanked by John the Evangelist and John the Baptist. The remaining dozen statues, all seven meters tall, represent the Doctors of the Latin and Greek Churches.

The interior of the church is a visual feast. A pilgrim risks straining his or her neck looking up at the imposing ornamentation of the ceiling, with its lavish gilded finish. The central nave, with its Latin cross plan, measures a staggering 130 meters in length. Along the sides are twelve niches housing statues of saints. Each niche is bordered by columns of ancient green marble. Above each niche, in stuccoed high relief, are scenes from the Old and New Testaments. The transept is adorned with frescoes, marble and gilding. The apse contains the papal altar, and the chair of the bishop of Rome. The mosaic in the apse is dominated by the figure of Christ in the clouds, surrounded by angels. Below are the figures of the Blessed Mother, Saints Peter, Paul, John and Andrew. Two other figures stand among these pillars of the early church: Francis of Assisi and Anthony of Padua. The tomb of Pope Innocent III, who died in 1216, can be found in the right transept. Pilgrims can also visit the baptistery, which dates back to the fourth century, and the charming thirteenth-century cloister, decorated with fragments of antique marble.

A pilgrim following the trail of Francis is encouraged to begin at the Basilica of St. John Lateran because no other building in Rome is more closely connected with the life of Saint Francis. Francis walked these grounds. Francis' inner strength came to light in this spot and was recognized by the pope. The basilica is the baptistery of the Franciscan Order.

THE BREAD OF TEARS

He who is willingly poor is free, and without the cares of this world's goods.

—JOHN RUYSBROECK, *THE SEVEN STEPS*
IN THE ASCENT OF SPIRITUAL LOVE

Having secured the pope's blessing, which gave them juridical status, Francis and his followers returned to Assisi. Depending totally on God's providence for their food, the brothers vowed never to turn their back on holy poverty. Saint Bonaventure tells us, "They spent their time praying incessantly, devoting themselves to mental prayer rather than vocal prayer because they did not yet have liturgical books from which to chant the canonical hours" (*Bonaventure*, page 208). Francis often taught them lessons from the Scriptures. They set up camp at Rivotorto, located just a few miles from Our Lady of the Angels Church, where they lived in a large mud and stone hut for nearly two years. This wasn't some happy-go-lucky camp-out. Poverty for Francis and the friars was not merely a matter of living simply. No, poverty, for them, was true poverty...they were dirt-poor, living without sufficiency in a constant state of need. A story from Lawrence Cunningham's *Saint Francis of Assisi* illustrates Holy Poverty as practiced by Francis:

> An old and poor woman who had two sons as friars once came to Saint Mary of the Angels to beg alms from Saint Francis. The saint went immediately to Brother Peter of Catania (who was the minister general at the time) and asked if there was anything to give the woman, adding that a mother of one friar was a mother of all friars. Brother Peter answered, "The only thing in the house is a copy of the New Testament, which we use to read the lessons during the night office." Saint Francis said to him, "Give her the Bible; it will be more pleasing to God that she should have it than we should read from it." Thus, she got the first New Testament that the brotherhood owned. (page 70)

During those early days of the brotherhood, they worked hard and barely subsisted, "drawing nourishment," Saint Bonaventure writes, "more from the bread of tears than the delights of bodily food."

Francis' love of poverty flowed from his belief in God as the creator, and that all creatures belong to God and owe their existence to God's sovereignly free love. Eric Doyle, O.F.M., writes:

Francis could not call anything his own which belonged by love to Another, for this would have been to commit spiritual adultery. Poverty was a way of expressing his relationship as a creature with the Creator. He knew his being was the gift of generous love. When he stripped himself in front of the bishop his very nakedness proclaimed that one must renounce all ownership, even possession of self, and go to God with no barriers between his love and self, and stand naked before him, for whom the mountains skip and the rivers clap their hands, because he gave them life and beauty. Only when we go to God in this way is it revealed how much he loves his creatures. And nothing can teach the inherent value of creation more clearly than that.

Poverty, therefore, is not a rejection of the world but a renunciation of ownership and possessions. The grace of freely embraced poverty brought Francis into a new relationship with creation: a brother among many brethren. When he renounced his earthly inheritance in the square it will be recalled that he also addressed God at that moment in the words *our Father*. The brotherhood of creation takes its origin from the Fatherhood of God, just as the inner life of the Trinity begins in an eternal procession from the Father and returns to him in the love of the Holy Spirit. The foundation of the universal brotherhood is Christ, the First-born of creation and the brother of all.

In his poverty Francis had real self-knowledge. He knew that he was a creature, and therefore that his meaning was not to be found entirely in himself, but primarily in God's love by which all creatures come to be. He knew also that he was a brother of Jesus Christ and this gave him the key to everything. His self-knowledge led him into union with all creatures because he knew he was one of them. (*St. Francis and the Song of Brotherhood and Sisterhood*, pages 35-36)

Before my first trip to Italy in March of 1995, I thought the meaning of my life resided solely within me...and after years of searching I found none. I simply existed, trying to squeeze moments of sweetness out of the bitterness of life. But during that trip I discovered the meaning of my life could only be found in responding to God's love for me. Knowing and loving God has helped me know and love myself...and others, too.

A FISTFUL OF COINS

Another piece of advice for his friars was that they should put the same value on money as on dung.

—THOMAS OF CELANO, *SECOND LIFE*

Alexandre Masseron, in *Memorable Words of Saint Francis*, tells the following story in connection to the above quotation:

> This contempt for money was to attract to the Order one of its first members. Bernard of Quintavalle had just sold all his possessions and "with great joy," as we read in the *Fioretti*, distributed to the poor of Assisi the money he had received. A group of loiterers was gathered one morning in St. George's Square. They were naturally watching with interest everything going on in the market place, especially when it concerned Francis. Bernard was rich. Francis was with him and was taking good care of him. A priest who had sold stone to the youthful Francis Bernardone when he was repairing the church happened to pass. The stone had not been fully paid for. The priest thought this was a good opportunity to press his claim. Thomas of Celano describes him as "moved to ravenous avarice" (2 Cel. 109), but these words seem to us an exaggeration in the light of later events. However...Francis did not argue with the priest. He simply plunged his hand deep into Bernard's pocket, took out first one and then another fistful of coins and gave them to the priest. Francis, who was delighted at the unexpected opportunity to clear off his debt, said:
>
> "Now, sir, are you paid in full?"
>
> The priest, surprised to receive so much, went away happy. Later, however, his conscience troubled him when he thought of his own greediness compared with the detachment of the young man. Soon after, the priest, too, became a friar. He was called Brother Sylvester and he was the first ordained priest to join the Order.
>
> Contempt for money was becoming contagious. If heaven should send us another Francis of Assisi, endowed with the same holiness and the same genius, would it be the same today? Would the golden calf, before which men bow so low today, be treated in the same way?

Francis knew that money and possessions were not bad in and of themselves, but that they could easily become a hindrance to enriching one's spiritual life. In *The Essentials of Mysticism* Evelyn Underhill writes, "Mystics know that possessions dissipate the energy which they need for other and more real things; that they must give up ownership, the verb 'to have,' if they are to attain the freedom which they seek, and the fullness of the verb 'to be'" (page 167).

Francis believed in the liberty of poverty rather than in the power of money.

We Don't Have Any Potatoes

[W]e do not fully welcome Christ if we are not ready to welcome the poor person with whom He identified Himself.
—*RANIERO CANTALAMESSA, O.F.M. CAP.,* POVERTY

The cornerstone of Franciscan spirituality is poverty. Francis took Lady Poverty for his bride. Of course, for us moderns, poverty is a strange choice for a mate. The goal of our lives is to escape or avoid poverty. We chase after Sister Porsche or Brother BMW. When we look at the millions of indescribably poor people around the world, people living in unthinkable squalor in far-off places, such as India, or in the shadows of our own cities, such as in the Kensington section of Philadelphia, we cannot even remotely begin to picture poverty as an ideal.

For Francis, a life of poverty didn't just mean living a simple, uncluttered life. Francis knew poverty, at its core, was a condition of being perpetually deprived, of being in a state of constant need. The virtue of poverty is that it leads one to recognize that God alone can provide us with what we truly need. Francis believed that to travel down the road to God required him to rid himself of all possessions. Buddha understood the same thing. He was born a prince—Prince Gautama—and was raised in a luxurious palace. When he was around age thirty, he left his father, his wife, his son, the palace and his fortune and set out to solve the problem of human suffering. He knew that the road to enlightenment was paved with detachment, and that he had to break free from all desire and karma.

Down through the ages, mystics of all faiths have claimed that God speaks in the quiet of our hearts and we can hear the voice only when we silence the noise of our selfish desires. Francis turned his back on all the things of the world which might turn his heart away from God. With the help of Lady Poverty, Francis gladly gave up all his desires except one—to do the will of God. Joy, he discovered, was in giving, not in having.

I understand the spiritual concept of poverty, too. Or do I? Even though I'm drawn to Francis' ideal of poverty and have no consuming desire for riches, nonetheless the last thing I want to be is poor. I don't want to have to beg for food or not be able to buy a book I want to read. Yesterday, I had no trouble spending fifteen dollars for the latest recording of Gregorian chant by the Benedictine Monks of Santo Domingo de Silos. I can't help but think perhaps Francis took the idea too far and his impetuous literalness which demanded he own nothing but one ragged, old, brown robe was a mistake. Mahatma Gandhi didn't think it was a mistake. Gandhi said that Francis' renunciation of every conceivable human consolation was so complete and profound that he "made himself zero." In effect, Francis created a void in his life, a void which could only be filled by God. Francis' understanding of poverty didn't leave room for him or his followers even to live in the security of a sturdy building or to have the assurance of daily food. Francis wanted his friars to live from moment to moment, trusting completely in God, and giving "no thought for the morrow"—just as the Gospel said. He called money dung, and became angry when a friar even touched a coin. This is hard to understand or appreciate.

While writing this book, I had the opportunity to see Francis' concept of poverty in action. In the fall of 1996, I agreed to write and direct a documentary film on the work being done by a team of Franciscan friars, nuns and lay volunteers who minister to the poor and homeless in the Kensington section of Philadelphia. The area, known as "The Badlands," is one of the worst slums in America; the soup kitchen the Franciscans operate is called "St. Francis Inn." Besides the soup kitchen, which feeds 300 to 500 people a day, the team also runs a men's shelter that accommodates ten men a night, a women's center which offers counseling during the day to prostitutes and drug addicts, and a thrift-shop that provides clothing for the poor. In order to write the script, I made two trips to Philadelphia and lived at St. Francis Inn for a total of nine days. What I saw shocked me, saddened me and, eventually, inspired me as I slowly gained insight into the spiritual wisdom of poverty.

I went to Kensington expecting to find a soup kitchen. What I found was a community of remarkable yet very human people offering not just a hot meal to the poor and homeless, but also love to all those who were hungry and hurting. The staff gave their all to those who had nothing. As

I observed them, I saw people who saw Jesus in people most of us do not even see. They looked at the broken, dirty and disheveled people who live on the margins of society and saw a spark of divine beauty and goodness. The drug addicts, the prostitutes, the mentally ill, as well as the poverty-plagued elderly and families who live each day without hope or enough to eat, come to St. Francis Inn and are treated with dignity and respect.

One young Franciscan volunteer minister told me that when she goes home and hears people talking in a condescending manner about drug addicts and prostitutes, she gets angry because they are talking about "my friends." That was the amazing and unexpected part...the staff don't just feed the guests, they enter into a relationship with them. They listen to them. They laugh with them. They cry with them. They hug them. They encourage them. They pray for them. In short, they give them-selves—completely and without reservation—to the guests. And what is even more unexpected, the staff claim it is the guests who give to them, enriching their lives in innumerable little ways each day.

Before I spent time in Kensington, the plight of the homeless always troubled me, but the problem was beyond, not only my comprehension, but also my ability to do anything about it. It's hard to care about the homeless when you don't know anyone who is homeless. My time in Kensington helped me put a face on the homeless...the face of Sheila from Tent City, whom I came to care about very much. Tent City is not a campground. Located on an empty, corner lot, it consists of a collection of small, ramshackle dwellings made of cardboard, scraps of discarded wood and large pieces of plastic. A dirty mattress, standing on its side, formed a wall of one of the dwellings. Perhaps a dozen people live in the four or five huts. I tagged along with one of the friars, Father Francis Pompei, who was delivering some leftover food that had to be eaten before it spoiled.

It was a damp, cold night. As we loaded the van, the light drizzle began to intensify. I began to shiver as we drove, which made me wonder how the homeless endure the winter nights. I don't think I could. As we pulled up to the lot, we could see a group of people gathered around a fire. Some were standing, warming their hands over the bright flames; others, bundled under blankets wrapped around their heavy coats, were seated on the old junk furniture which encircled the large barrel in which scraps of wood were being burned. The friar introduced me to his friends, who were thrilled by the surprise late-night food delivery. "Hey, we got some good stuff here. It came from a gourmet Japanese restaurant. It was left over from their Sunday brunch. It won't last long. Gotta eat it quickly."

No need to worry...starving people do not need to be told to eat quickly. Sheila asked me to sit on the tattered couch with her. I did, though it felt awkward sitting on a couch which sat in the middle of a vacant lot. The friar sat down on a wooden crate. As they ate, we talked about all kinds of things. Perfectly normal conversation. I couldn't help but feel as if we were in their living room...except it was raining in this living room, and the occasional loud truck that passed made it difficult to hear each other. The main topic of discussion was the coming winter. The temperature at night will regularly get well below freezing. Some of the people were going to try to find an abandoned building in which to squat. They needed to get their hands on a kerosene heater, which would be instrumental in helping them survive the winter.

I don't know why, but I was attracted to Sheila. Perhaps it was her broad, infectious smile and hearty laugh. If this littered lot were my living room, could I manage to smile or laugh? But beyond her smile, Sheila's eyes told a different story. In them, I could see deep sadness. The sadness of someone who couldn't break the addiction to drugs. The sadness of a mother who had her daughter taken away by the state because she was not able to care for the child. The sadness of a woman who confronts relentless suffering and violence on a daily basis. The sadness of a woman whose home was a cardboard hut in a lot off a busy street. In the distance, through the drizzle and over the roofs of the boarded-up buildings, I could see the skyline of Philadelphia, the City of Brotherly Love. Sheila and her friends experience very little brotherly love. Rejection is their lot; hopelessness, their brother.

During my two visits to Kensington, I ran into Sheila a number of times. She often came to the Inn to eat. Whenever I drove past Tent City with one of the staff, I asked to stop for a few minutes to visit Sheila. I asked if I could photograph her. She let me. She was a large woman. Her face was round, and her smile made her cheeks look puffy. Her skin was weathered by constant exposure to the harsh winter. Her teeth were crooked. Her thrift-shop clothes fit her poorly. Yet, she was beautiful. Beautiful in her openness.

One morning, during my second visit, I saw her waiting by the side door of the Inn. The poor are always waiting; they are powerless to do anything else but wait. When I approached, I could see she had been crying. There were no smiles that morning. She was clearly troubled by something, so I asked her what the problem was. I wasn't ready for what

I heard. Sheila and a couple of other people from Tent City had moved into an empty building to escape the bitterly cold nights. It was a crack house. One of the women living there had a young baby, whom Sheila had grown very fond of. She missed her own daughter very much, and so Sheila showered her motherly affection on the infant. The baby's mother was a crack addict. Sheila made it her business to look after the child when the mother was stoned. Sheila heard the baby crying in the middle of the night, but she didn't get up to see what the problem was. She said, "I was cold and tired. I thought about getting up, but I couldn't. I fell asleep."

When Sheila came downstairs that morning, she made a horrific discovery. The mother and child had been sleeping on the couch. During the night, the mother had rolled over on top of the child. The child must have cried, but to no avail. Under the weight of her drugged mother, the child suffocated. Sheila and the mother screamed as they shook the baby. Someone ran to a pay phone a few blocks away and called for an ambulance. The paramedics said the infant had lapsed into a coma. They rushed the child to the hospital, where she was reported to be in critical condition. Sheila blamed herself for not responding to the cries in the dead of the night. I tried to comfort her. But there was little I could do. I expressed the hope that the hospital could help the baby and everything would end up OK. Sheila needed some change to take a train to a clinic, where she had an appointment. She had been troubled by pains in her stomach for over a month. I gave her the money. As she walked toward the train station, I thought about just how tough her life was. If living in a crack house in order to escape some of winter's bite wasn't tough enough, now she had the added burden of guilt over a child's tragic accident, not to mention her own chronic stomach pains.

Later that night, Sheila was in the courtyard of the Inn, waiting her turn to come in and get a hot meal. They were serving turkey soup. I noticed a woman come up to Sheila and say something to her. Sheila began crying. A couple of women surrounded her and tried to comfort her. I went over to see what the problem was. One of the women whispered in my ear, "The little baby from the crack house died." I backed off in order to give Sheila and her friends space. Besides, what could I say? After a few minutes, Sheila left the courtyard and began to walk alone under the Kensington Avenue elevated train. I ran after her. As I approached her, a train roared by overhead. I just looked at her. Her eyes were filled with tears. She said, "The baby died." I could hardly hear her. I said, "I know.

I'm sorry." The train passed. Stillness suddenly filled the dark night, as we stood alone looking at each other. I gave her a hug. And as I did, I said something that was so unplanned it caught me by surprise as the words punctuated the cold stillness of the night: "I love you." She hugged me even tighter and said, "I know. Thank you." There was a brief pause as we both looked at each other. "I'll be OK," she said. We parted. I stood watching her as she walked alone under the elevated tracks as another train loudly rumbled past. It was a moment I shall never forget. I felt a real, vital connection to a homeless, black woman who was a drug addict. Before spending time with the friars in Kensington, I would have considered such a person to have been repulsive, someone I could never embrace.

By embracing the lepers whom he found repulsive, Saint Francis of Assisi was able to discover their beauty. That same miracle of discovery happens every day in Kensington.

The staff at St. Francis Inn thought I was doing them a favor, offering my time and expertise to make a film about their ministry. No way. It was the community of St. Francis Inn who did me a favor, showing me the true meaning and beauty of Lady Poverty. By becoming poor themselves, the staff depends completely on God for everything. They are fed each day at the altar, where they receive the strength in turn to feed the poor. The spiritual poverty Francis espoused for himself and his followers recognized that there was nothing wrong with material things, but he did not want the friars to appropriate anything for themselves. Not owning anything meant they had nothing to defend. Francis did not want to even cling to his own ego...that was Adam and Eve's mistake. During a homily, Father Charles Finnegan, O.F.M., a former provincial of the Holy Name Province, quoted the martyred archbishop of San Salvador, Oscar Romero: "Without poverty of spirit there can be no abundance of God."

During my stay at St. Francis Inn, I learned that I needed to empty myself in order to be filled by God. Creating that void isn't going to be easy. I'm still clinging to my own understanding, my own ideas; I want to be in control of my life, which, I now see, means God can't be. The friars, nuns and lay members that form the community at St. Francis Inn showed me a better way, a much richer way, the way of Lady Poverty. While they were feeding the poor, they also were spiritually feeding me...and for that I'm very grateful. At the St. Francis Inn, I learned that charity is the antidote to the poison of self-absorption.

Saint Francis of Assisi would feel very much at home on this island of hope in the midst of a sea of despair. He would be glad to see his followers depending on God for everything and living simply so others might simply live. Saint Francis would have smiled had he been in the kitchen the day a volunteer asked Brother Xavier de la Huerta, O.F.M., "What are you making, Brother?"

"Potato soup," Brother Xavier answered without hesitation.

The volunteer looked around the kitchen for a few seconds and then asked, "Where are the potatoes?"

"We don't have any potatoes," responded Brother Xavier.

A perplexed look crossed the volunteer's face. "How can you make potato soup then?"

Brother Xavier's answer reflected his faith: "The Lord knows what we need, and he will provide."

And he did. Within twenty minutes there was a knock on the side door. The volunteer opened the door and standing before him was a man who said he had been to a farmer's market, adding, "When I saw the potatoes I had this sudden thought that I should pick up a couple of fifty-pound bags for the Inn. I hope you can use them."

Embracing Lady Poverty means learning to admit...we don't have any potatoes. It also means letting go of self and entrusting ourselves to God. The essence of Lady Poverty is fulfillment and inner freedom. Lady Poverty is not rich because she has given up much but because she has found much. God's love and grace are all the riches she needs.

The Liturgy of the Hours

Happy are those who consider the
poor and weak. (Psalm 40[41]:1)

What Is Poverty?

The detachment of poverty grew into a great liberation of love and the disinterested enjoyment of all things. The only one who can taste the world, without denaturalizing its reality, is the one who renounces the spirit of possessing it. Only then does it cease to be threatening and is introduced into the arena of human fraternity.

—*LEONARDO BOFF*, ST. FRANCIS: A MODEL FOR HUMAN LIBERATION

I will turn to a friend, Professor Lawrence S. Cunningham, Chair of the Department of Theology at the University of Notre Dame, for a definition.

Simplicity of life and poverty are not the same. There are many people who live in very simple lives, either by choice or circumstance, who are not poor. Poverty does not simply mean a lack of money or goods. In its essence poverty means radical insecurity about the basic means of life. Poverty is literally not knowing where the next meal is coming from, or the frantic fear of getting ill because there is no money for a doctor, or the gnawing despair when one recognizes the gap between the next possible time when money will come and the actual needs of the household. It is, in short, a knowledge that the world is not solid, secure, and benign. Poverty is not only want; it is the fear and dread that derives from want. (*St. Francis of Assisi*, page 58)

It is so easy to depict Saint Francis as some kind of care-free minstrel who loved simplicity, as if it were a poetic virtue to be cherished. Francis of Assisi didn't just have an inclination toward simplicity. The simplicity that underlines his life was simply a by-product of his love of poverty. Francis loved the radical insecurity of poverty because for him it was the ultimate act of faith in the providence of God. To imitate Christ, which was his sole goal in life, meant living a life of extreme self-denial. But self-denial as practiced by Francis never gave way to some twisted form of self-loathing. While denying himself everything, he fully loved everything, joyfully entering into a healthy relationship with all creation. Following the self-emptying example of Christ and trusting fully in the providence of God enabled Francis to see the entire world as a free gift of God and a manifestation of God's presence and love.

A HOTEL FOR DONKEYS

One goes more quickly to heaven from a hut than from a palace.
—SAINT FRANCIS OF ASSISI

Francis and his followers stayed at Rivotorto for nearly two years. Rivotorto takes its name from the winding, serpentine brook that crosses the plain, a brook in which Francis most surely washed his feet. It was at Rivotorto where Giles joined Francis. This humble settlement of humble men was the cradle of Franciscanism.

But Francis and his entourage didn't get a chance to plant their roots in Rivotorto because they were practically chased from the site by an ill-tempered peasant who insisted on boarding his donkey in the main hut. One evening, shortly after dusk, the man approached the hut, and, thinking it was vacant, decided he and his donkey would take shelter there for the night. When he entered the hut he was surprised and angered to find the friars silently praying. He caused a great deal of commotion, pushing the donkey into the hut, tripping over the friars and interrupting their prayer time.

Francis humorously claimed he wasn't running a hotel for donkeys; in response, the man began to shout, cursing the brothers. Even though Francis abhorred profanity, he remained calm, trying his best to see what God was trying to tell him through the foul mouth of the mule driver. Francis told his brothers that God was giving them the opportunity to liberate themselves from the temptation of claiming ownership of the hut, reminding them that where there is ownership, there is security, and where there is security there is no room for his beloved poverty. Rejoicing, Francis told his brothers they must vacate the hut immediately. Without another word, they abandoned their dwelling and headed for St. Mary of the Angels, where they set up camp not far from the Portiuncula.

Shortly afterwards, Francis went to the abbot of Mount Subasio and asked his permission to occupy the chapel and the surrounding "little portion of earth." The abbot, impressed by the holiness and growing numbers of men entering the new order, gave the little chapel, the poorest church his order owned, to Francis, without any restrictions or payment. Francis was delighted, especially because the church was so poor and had such a humble name— Portiuncula—yet he could not accept ownership of the church. Each year he insisted on sending a basket of small fish to the monks of

Mount Subasio as rent in return for the privilege of being allowed to stay in the church.

Anglican Bishop John Moorman, in his monumental book *A History of the Franciscan Order From Its Origins to the Year 1517*, writes:

> Once the brothers were settled at the Portiuncula, their number was more than doubled by the arrival of several new men. The first was probably the priest Sylvester, who, having repented of his avarice, now came to join the poor men. After him came Leo, Rufino, Masseo, Juniper, Illuminato, Augustine, Stephen, Leonard, James of Assisi, Theobold, Simon of Assisim, Simon Collazono, and John de Laudibus. (page 20)

The friars preached throughout the towns and villages of Umbria and Tuscany. They served lepers and ministered to the needs of the poor. And the Order continued to grow. Moorman writes:

> At Perugia Francis appears to have enrolled a man who spent many years as a hermit. At Cortona the saint and his companion were given hospitality by a rich young man called Guy who, touched by the words and example of Francis, gave all his goods to the poor and joined the fellowship. At Arezzo Francis converted a nobleman called Benedict Sinigardi who afterwards lived for many years as a mystic, telling strange stories of what had been revealed to him. At Florence a lawyer called John Parenti gave up his profession and, with his son, joined the Order of which, in time, he became Minister General. At Pisa two youths were accepted, Agnellus who lived to become custos of Paris and the leader of the first expedition of friars to England in 1224, and Albert, a future Minister General. (page 23)

These were the golden days for Francis.

But soon, not only would the number of his followers dramatically increase, but also the number of his problems. And many of the problems stemmed from the way some of his followers interpreted their vow of poverty.

Lady Poverty

The Lady Poverty was his own symbolism of a spiritual principle. The principle was liberty. Poverty freed him from things of earth, it liberated him from the cult of self; his spirit could then wing its flight to God.

—FATHER JAMES, O.S.F.C., THE FRANCISCANS

Poverty fueled all of Francis' thinking and teaching. He required, for himself at least, an exact and strict adherence to Christ's words, and, in what is known as the Apostolic command, Christ said, "Take nothing for the journey."

For Francis, that is the end of the story.

But is it?

Did Jesus hold such a rigorous view of poverty in his teachings or in the way he lived? He did not. In fact, in Mark's Gospel, Jesus tells the apostles to carry a purse with them when they travel to preach. A nun on the pilgrimage carried a Calvin Klein purse. Very stylish.

The real reason Francis loved poverty, I think, is that the Lord had made himself poor by entering into the world, and that Jesus, the Son of the all-powerful God, was not ashamed to be so poor as to be born in a stable. Moreover, Christ was poor, suffering, naked and hung on a cross. Jesus not only dedicated himself to a preference for the poor, but also shared their social condition. For Francis, Christ made poverty a royal virtue, and so he clung to it with an inviolable fidelity. Poverty was a means of liberation and freedom. The end and aim were love. Love was the unifying force of his life and personality. Poverty removed all obstacles blocking the full glow of love. Love of poverty was really love of Love.

A hundred years after Francis' death, the papacy, employing reasonable biblical exegesis, condemned the Franciscan doctrine of poverty. In the view of the papacy, Francis was holding poverty to a higher standard than Christ did.

The problem is simple: Francis isn't practical...and neither is the gospel. I believe I'm very sympathetic to the plight of the poor...but you won't catch me selling everything I own and giving the proceeds to the needy. I wish I could. Instead, I'll be content to try to be more generous in giving to the poor and try to develop a broader sense of spiritual poverty. These things may make me a better person...but they will not make me a saint. Saints go to the extremes; they give everything.

Sadly, the word "saint" has no real meaning to the modern world.

LADY CHIARA

For both of them [Saint Francis and Saint Clare], Jesus was their first and greatest love. They loved him in each other, just as he revealed his love separately in each of them.
    —AUSPICIUS VAN CORSTANJE, O.F.M., *FRANCIS: BIBLE OF THE POOR*

During the winter of 1212, Francis preached in the Cathedral of San Rufino in Assisi. A young noblewoman heard his words and was profoundly moved; her name was Lady Chiara...Clare, as she is known to us. She chose to follow the "life of the gospel" portrayed by Francis. Eloi Leclerc, O.F.M., in *The Wisdom of the Poor One of Assisi,* writes: "Better than anyone, Clare had perceived the hidden splendor of this way of life and she became so imbued with it that it radiated from her." On Palm Sunday, Clare left her family's house and went to the little church of St. Mary of the Angels in the fields below Assisi. Francis cut her hair, gave her a plain tunic, and the Poor Ladies (known today as Poor Clares) were born, though it would take forty years for Clare to receive papal approval of her rule for the sisters, which finally came in 1253, shortly before her death.

Without Clare's story, Francis' story would be incomplete. I'll tell her story in Part Three.

PILGRIMAGE DIARY 19

Thoughts Scribbled While Walking

*P*rayer is hanging on to God, stubbornly clinging to God.
    Beg for the grace of prayer.
The universal lack of an interior life is a key element behind the rash of violent political and religious conflicts that plague so many nations.
Humility is the first fruit of honesty with oneself. True humility plunges one into adoration of God.
Physical solitude is nothing without an inner solitude.
Seek God in the ordinary events of daily life.

The Cross is a sign of eternal charity.
Prayer is being present.
God never shouts to be heard over our noise. Only silence gives
  God a chance to speak.
God's ways are so profoundly different from ours that it is
  impossible to understand them.

Small Talk

When he [Francis] pronounced the word "Jesus" or heard someone say it, he was filled with joy and seemed to be completely
transformed, as if he had suddenly tasted something marvelous
or caught the strain of a beautiful harmony.

—*SAINT BONAVENTURE,* MAJOR LIFE

Thomas of Celano tells us:

The brothers who lived with Francis knew how his daily and
continuous talk was of Jesus and how sweet and tender his conversation was, how kind and filled with love his talk with them
was. His mouth spoke out of the abundance of his heart, and
the fountain of enlightened love that filled his whole being
bubbled forth outwardly. Indeed, he was always occupied with
Jesus; Jesus he bore in his heart, Jesus in his mouth, Jesus in his
ears, Jesus in his eyes, Jesus in his hands, Jesus in the rest of his
members. Oh how often, when he sat down to eat, hearing or
speaking or thinking of Jesus, he forgot bodily food....(1 Cel. 15)

Thoughts of Jesus never distracted me from eating. Even though the pic-
ture of Francis presented by the biographer in his first life of the saint was
intended to show Francis as a saint, I doubt Celano was exaggerating
very much when he says Francis' "daily" conversation was filled with
"continuous" talk of Jesus.
  What is our conversation filled with?
  Certainly not Jesus.
  If we mention Jesus in our conversation just once during the course
of the day that's a lot. We prefer small talk. It's easier, less troublesome.
  Some food for theological thought:

We talk too little about God in the Church or we talk about him
in a dry, pedantic fashion, without any real vitality. We have

learned too little of the incomprehensibly noble art of a true initiation into the mystery of experience of God and therefore also apply it far too little. That is why, in the face of world-wide atheism, we have a feeling of being merely on the defensive. This impression—which in the very last resort is false—arises of course also to a large extent because we interpret the *mysterious presence* of God and its history, neither of which we can obviously correspond to our expectations, as the absence of God or we dig up a "Death of God" theology, not knowing at all what the word "God" means. (Karl Rahner, S.J., *The Shape of the Church to Come*)

Francis knew what the word "God" meant. It was a reality that burned in his heart. Saint Bonaventure wrote: "Jesus Christ crucified reposed continually on the breast of Francis like a bouquet of myrrh, and the fire of love with which he burned made him desire to be entirely transformed in Jesus" (Omnibus, page 6).

The fire of love needs to be lit in our hearts.

Pilgrimage Diary 20

A Child Talking

There is but one road which reaches God; if anyone shows you another, you are being deceived.

—*SAINT THÉRÈSE OF LISIEUX*

*H*ow is it that I rarely forget to wear my Tau cross around my neck, but frequently forget that I carry within me the Holy of Holies, the living presence of God? If the indwelling presence of the Creator truly permeated and influenced my life, how utterly changed I would be.

Humans are very complex beings. I think we all too frequently bring that complexity into our relationship with God. Saint Francis came to understand that God, on the contrary, is the mirror of simplicity, and consequently the simpler we are, the closer we come to God. In Matthew's Gospel, Christ tells us "to be as simple as doves." Instead, I fritter away my time philosophizing about God instead of talking with God. Francis sought God in the simplicity of his heart. And he spoke to God in a simple, unaffected way, as a *child talking with his father. That, I'm beginning to see, however dimly, is the essence of true and real prayer.*

Scarcely a Single Hour

Endeavor to enter into your inner treasure house and you will see a heavenly treasure. The ladder leading into the kingdom of heaven is hidden within you, in your heart. And so purify yourself from sin and enter your heart; there you will find the rungs of the ladder by which you can climb to the heights.

—*SAINT ISAAC OF SYRIA*

If our daily conversation is hardly imbued with talk of God, perhaps it is because of the dryness of our daily prayer life. The Pilgrim Continues His Way, *the sequel to the spiritual classic* The Way of a Pilgrim, *contains a passage in which a priest helps the pilgrim prepare for confession. The essence of the text points to the fact that an honest examination of conscience would reveal that we love neither God nor our neighbor, that our religious convictions are shallow, and we are full of pride and sensual self-love. The following excerpt deals with the proof of our lack of love for God.*

"A Confession which Leads the Inward Man to Humility"

Turning my eyes carefully upon myself and watching the course of my inward state, I have verified by experience that I do not love God, that I have no love for my neighbors, that I have no religious belief, and that I am filled with pride and sensuality. All this I actually find in myself as a result of a detailed examination of my feelings and conduct, thus:

1. *I do not love God.* For if I loved God I should be continually thinking about Him with heartfelt joy. Every thought of God would give me gladness and delight. On the contrary, I much more often and much more eagerly think about earthly things, and thinking about God is labour and dryness. If I loved God, then talking with Him in prayer would be nourishment and delight and would draw me into unbroken communion with Him. But, on the contrary I not only find no delight in prayer, but even find it an effort. I struggle with reluctance, I am enfee-

bled by sloth, and am ready to occupy myself eagerly with any unimportant trifle, if only it shortens prayer and keeps me from it. [*That last sentence hits nightmarishly close to home, acknowledging a reality for me that I would never admit.*] My time slips away unnoticed in futile occupations, but when I am occupied with God, when I put myself into His presence every hour seems like a year. If one person loves another, he thinks of him throughout the day without ceasing, he pictures him to himself, he cares for him, and in all circumstances his beloved friend is never out of his thoughts. But I, throughout the day, scarcely set aside even a single hour in which to sink deep down into meditation upon God, to inflame my heart with love of Him, while eagerly giving up twenty-three hours as fervent offerings to the idols of my passions. [*For me, this is tough to read...because the truth hurts.*] I am forward in talk about frivolous matters and things which degrade the spirit; that gives me pleasure. But in consideration of God I am dry, bored and lazy. Even if I am unwillingly drawn by others into spiritual conversation, I try to shift the subject quickly to one which pleases my desires. I am tirelessly curious about novelties, about civic affairs and political events; I eagerly seek satisfaction of my love of knowledge in science and art, and in ways of getting things I want to possess. (pages 146-147)

I say I love God, yet I wonder if I could prove it in a court of law. Saint Francis de Sales reminds us: "The will loves only by willing to love." Which I take to mean that I must act "as if" I truly loved God, despite the compelling evidence to the contrary. Hypocrisy? No. Faith is more than mere feeling or human calculation. God doesn't measure the quality of our love. We can't, no matter how perfect and selfless our love might be, earn God's love. It is pure gift. Grace is everything. No matter how poorly I may love God, I am always guaranteed full access to God and assured of a divine embrace. My imperfect love can only be perfected by prayer.

Vatican II instructed us that "action is subordinated to contemplation." Moreover, the gospel tells us we should pray ceaselessly. But it doesn't tell us how we can possibly do such a thing. It sounds totally unreasonable. The Way of a Pilgrim and The Pilgrim Continues His Way not only help bring the soul of Eastern Christianity to light, but also go a long way in answering the question of how exactly we go about praying ceaselessly.

Francis knew the importance of prayer, and his life reflected the rich-

ness of his prayer. Here are two short passages that, for me, call Saint Francis to mind.

> He who has attained true prayer and love has no sense of the differences between things: he does not distinguish the righteous man from the sinner, but loves them all equally and judges no man, as God causes His sun to shine and His rain to fall on the just and the unjust. (*The Way of a Pilgrim*, page 97)

> The soul which is inwardly united to God becomes, in the greatness of its joy, like a good-natured simple-hearted child, and now condemns no one, Greek, heathen, Jew nor sinner, but looks at them all alike with sight that has been cleansed, finds joy in the whole world, and wants everybody...to praise God. (*The Pilgrim Continues His Way*, page 160)

I've got a long way to go. Francis, I'm sure, would advise us not to become overly troubled by the dryness of our prayer. Instead, he would gently suggest we await with patience the fruit of persevering in prayer, and encourage us to set up an altar to God in our hearts where we can pray wherever we are, no matter what we are doing. He would whisper to us: Fly to God on the wings of prayer. Pray always, no matter how poorly, and do not be disturbed by anything. Rest in God. Free yourself from the servitude of your passions; disengage yourself from those amusements of the mind and attachments of the heart which distract you from God, who is your only delight. In humility, make the effort to pray, for this much is within your power, and grace will surely purify your prayer. And remember the words of James: "pray for one another so that you may be healed" (5:16).

Pray for me.

THE SOURCES

> *Whether or not all the details of his [Francis'] life and miracles withstand our standards for biographical accuracy, the impact of Francis's [sic] unique personality on the thirteenth century and beyond is irrefutable. The legend of his life that we glean from the surviving records is the story of a man who found God's will for his life by first turning inward and then living his inner vision in the outer world.*
>
> —SUSAN W. McMICHAELS, *JOURNEY OUT OF THE GARDEN*

This brief history of the life of Saint Francis only takes us up to the actual formation of the Friars Minor, at which point his story really swings into high gear. Before proceeding with a streamlined summary of the major events and themes of the rest of Francis' life, I need to pause briefly to present a "truth in advertising" caveat.

At the risk of taking this book down a scholarly path, which I am ill-equipped by temperament and training to do, I'd like to offer a brief observation on the history of the history of Saint Francis. The earliest known writings about Francis are known as "the sources," and they consist of (besides everything Francis himself wrote, including prayers, admonitions, rules and letters) everything written about the saint during the first hundred years after his death. These early documents are the source of everything we know about the saint. Most of the writers were friars, including Thomas of Celano, Julian of Speyer, Bonaventure of Bagnoregio, Thomas of Eccleston and Jordon of Giano. These men wrote in a style very familiar to their times. The kind of writing employed by medieval writers writing about saints is called hagiography. I'll let a story define the word.

In the early days of the world-famous evangelist Billy Graham's ministry, he preached to small crowds in tents he pitched on the outskirts of towns and small cities. He was, practically speaking, invisible and unheard. One day, he took his fledgling crusade and its fiery message of salvation to the Big Top...New York City, where his words were bound to fall on deaf ears. Somehow, the young evangelist, with his wavy blonde hair and chiseled good looks, caught the attention of the newspaper baron William Randolph Hearst. Hearst sent a brief memo to the editors of all his papers; it said, essentially, "Puff Graham." In newspaper parlance, those two words meant the editors should only run stories that showed the Reverend Graham in the best of lights. Coming from Hearst, "Puff Graham" was not a suggestion, it was an order. Thanks to the friendly and flattering press coverage in important papers, Billy Graham's crusades drew larger crowds and his fame rapidly grew.

The early books which presented the life of Saint Francis were not written by investigative reporters or journalists; they were written by friars who wanted to spread the saint's fame, to increase devotion to him. In works of hagiography, the writers essentially put pen to paper in order to "puff" a saint, to carefully place a halo on his or her head. The writers were biased; they were devoted to the saint, and their writing is intended to boost devotion in the heart of the reader. The hagiographers of old are not simply biographers of saints, and their books should not be confused with the modern concept of a biography, which we expect to be objectively true and based on verifiable facts. The hagiographer was concerned with verifying holiness; he or she wanted to convince the reader that this holy person was, in fact, a saint. Facts could be hedged because the primary purpose of the writing was, according to William R. Hugo, O.F.M. Cap., "to edify the reader, to verify the subjects' sanctity, to increase the reader's devotion to the saint, and to move the reader to moral change." In his book *Studying the Life of Francis of Assisi*, Hugo writes:

> Exaggeration in hagiography is like salt in a stew; it spices things up and brings out the flavors that are already there. We, in our century, criticize exaggeration in historical writing, from our perspective, it distorts the truth. However, from the medieval hagiographer's perspective, exaggeration promoted the truth. It helped them illustrate the saint's holiness and moved readers to astonishment and the desire to change their lives. Medievals would think of exaggeration in hagiography more as embellishment than deception. (page 23)

Pious embellishments were liberally employed when it came to miracles. In the Middle Ages, one could never be considered a saint unless he or she performed miracles. Incredible signs and wonders were indispensible and tangible proof that God was working in and through the holy person. Do miracles happen? Hugo, a Franciscan friar, says in his book that he does not believe in miracles. What about me? I'm skeptical. Very skeptical. Many of the miracles performed by Saint Francis, especially those found in works written long after his death, can be shown to be additions to his story. However, despite my skepticism, I believe in the possibility of miracles. I think they do happen, but they are very rare events, rarely subject to scientific verification. The point that is important to remember when reading the sources is that not every word of every story is the gospel truth or even historically accurate.

[Note: Those interested in reading some of "the sources" are in luck, because New City Press published in 1999 the first volume of a three-volume series entitled *Francis of Assisi: Early Documents, Volume I: The Saint*. This long-awaited compilation of the writings of Saint Francis and the early Franciscan witnesses is an indispensable resource, essential for anyone interested in seriously studying the life of Saint Francis and is included in the bibliography at the end of this book.]

PREACHING TO THE BIRDS

The creator must be sought through the creatures.

—SAINT TERESA OF AVILA

Both Thomas of Celano's *First Life* and Saint Bonaventure's *Major Life* contain the charming story of Saint Francis preaching to the birds. It is one of the best-known stories from the saint's life. Here is Bonaventure's version of the story, as translated by Murray Bodo, O.F.M.:

> Once near Bevagna in the Spoleto valley St. Francis saw a large flock of birds of various kinds. There were doves and crows, and those popularly called daws. Now Francis was always fervent towards creatures and showed them great tenderness, so as soon as he saw these birds, he left his companions and ran eagerly to the birds. And when he got close to them, he greeted them in his usual way. They seemed to be waiting for him; they didn't fly away as he expected them to do. And so, filled with joy, he begged them to listen to the word of God. Among other things, he said this to the birds: "My Brother Birds, you should always praise your Creator and love him. He covered you with feathers and gave you wings to fly with and granted you a kingdom of pure air. He cares for you, too, without any worry on your part, though you neither sow or reap."
>
> At these words, as Francis and his companions later reported, the birds acknowledged his words in a wonderful fashion. They stretched out their necks and flapped their wings, and gazed at him with beaks open. And St. Francis walked among them in fervor of spirit, brushing their heads and bodies with his tunic, and not one of them moved until he made a sign of the cross over them and gave them permission to fly away. And Francis and his companions went on their way, as well, praising and thanking God whom all creatures venerate and humbly acknowledge. (*Through the Year With Francis of Assisi*, pages 173-174)

Thomas of Celano goes on to offer us a bit of commentary:

[Francis] was already simple by grace, not by nature. After the birds had listened so reverently to the word of God, he began to accuse himself of negligence because he had not preached to them before. From that day on, he carefully exhorted all birds, all animals, all reptiles, and also insensible creatures, to praise and love the Creator, because daily, *invoking the name* of the Savior, he observed their obedience in his own experience. (1 Cel. XXI, *Early Documents*)

As you leave the upper church of the Basilica of St. Francis in Assisi, your attention is drawn to a famous fresco that graces the rear wall to the right of the main door. The fresco beautifully depicts Francis preaching to the birds. Following closely the story from Celano and Bonaventure, the fresco contains birds of varying sizes and species. Birds of different species normally don't mingle. The story and the fresco are trying to tell us something.

First, we must understand that Francis was not merely a nature lover. That's too simple. Francis loved God...and because God created nature, Francis loved nature. The different kinds of birds symbolize people—people of all races, nationalities and personalities who together make up a single diverse flock of humanity. And Francis has gathered them all together so they can hear him proclaim the Good News of the gospel. Francis is telling us that we must not only take care of nature and each other, but we must also share the Good News with all creation.

I have no doubt that Francis preached to birds. Whether they listened doesn't matter—but I have a hunch some did.

A dodo bird named Gerry did.

PILGRIMAGE DIARY 21

Tall Testaments

The economics of affluence demands that things that were special for us last year must now be taken for granted....
—*DAVID STEINDL-RAST AND SHARON LEBELL*, MUSIC OF SILENCE

A s the bus traverses the rolling green hillsides and valleys of Umbria—what a delightful feast for the eyes! We've rolled past a bucolic collection of old stone farmhouses, remnants of medieval castles, winding dirt roads, sleeping dogs, grazing goats and lambs, *lush gardens, fields of sunflowers, bright and happy, and long lines of olive trees marching in line towards the horizon. Off in the distance, the ancient towns seem to grow out of the mountains without intruding on the holiness of the landscape, but rather as if they are essential to the mountains' existence.*

We've just passed Foligno. The hills are covered with stone buildings crowded together. The highest hill is crowned with a large church. Interestingly, churches dominate the landscape of all the medieval hill towns we've passed. Today, tall office buildings owned by banks dominate our cities. We accentuate what is most important to us; what interests us we embellish. Skyscrapers are our cathedrals, tall testaments to the religion of economics. The modern cityscape loudly proclaims money is more important to us than God. The landscape of Umbria quietly proclaims the opposite message.

I once bought into Nietzsche's notion that "God is dead." In time I learned that God's alleged death gave birth to absurdity, nausea, loneliness, nothingness, and that without God, earth became a desolate, cold and confused planet. Moreover, God's death robbed us of something irreplaceable: God alone was capable of helping humanity escape from its egocentric prison, thereby giving us the freedom to discover the joy of living. Dostoyevski said, "It is impossible to be human and not bow down; if God is rejected, before an idol we bow." And bow I did...to idols of all sizes, shapes and forms, idols which provoked and captivated my heart, while absorbing and enslaving my humanity. For most of us, money is the primary idol before which we bow and which becomes our absolute value. And the rest of our pantheon of popular idols includes power, sex, hedonism, permissiveness, and drugs; they are all gods of slavery, robbing us of joy, filling us with fear, and surrounding us with loneliness...and separating us from each other and God.

Francis discovered that God alone could liberate us from the idols that oppress and dehumanize us. God alone is willing to accompany us on our long pilgrimage through the desert, showing us the verdant path of surrender, forgiveness, grace and mercy.

A Little Bread

The gate of heaven is very low; only the humble can enter it.
—*SAINT ELIZABETH SETON*

The same Jesus Christ who humbled himself at the Incarnation, "when he came down from his heavenly throne," continues to do so every day, Francis emphasizes in his First Admonition, for he "comes to us and lets us see him in abjection, when he descends from the bosom of his Father into the hands of the priest at the altar." Francis saw in the Eucharist a continuation of the self-emptying of Christ, which took place not only at his birth but throughout his earthly life. In fact, Francis cannot contain his wonder when he contemplates Christ's continued presence among us in such humility...God in the form of bread! Francis beautifully expressed his love for the Eucharist in his Letter to the Entire Order *(which is also known as* A Letter to a General Chapter*):*

> Let everyone be struck with fear,
> let the whole world tremble,
> and let the heavens exult
> when Christ, the Son of the living God,
> is present on the altar in the hands of a priest!
> O wonderful loftiness and stupendous dignity!
> O sublime humility!
> O humble sublimity!
> The Lord of the universe,
> God and the Son of God,
> so humbles Himself
> that for our salvation
> He hides Himself
> under an ordinary piece of bread!
> (*Early Documents*, page 118)

In the mystery of humility, poverty and weakness—in the mystery of the cross—Francis discovered the fullness of love and the omnipotence of God, who lives with us in our condition.

Thoughts Scribbled While Walking

Desires rob us of freedom.
Dependence on reason is unreasonable.
Sanctify the present moment.
My poverty is a cry to God.
Humility is an expression of the reality of our littleness and powerlessness.
When I pray using my mind, I find I have nothing to say. Prayer is a gift of the Spirit.
The more I pray, the deeper I enter into the darkness of the absence of evidence.
No moment is insignificant. Incarnation may break through at any time.
Mary is a model for meekness. Meekness is truly a divine disposition.

Hail Mary, full of grace, help me to pray.
O most pure Theotokos, teach me childlike humility
of heart and purity of spirit.

A Living Tabernacle

Jesus is sacramentally present in the Eucharist; He is also present, in a different way, in the poor. Saint John Chrysostom saw the connection between the presence of Jesus in the Eucharist and his presence in the poor. In a homily on the Gospel of Matthew, the great saint of the Eastern Church wrote:

> Would you honor the body of Christ? Do not despise Him in His nakedness, that is, in the unclothed poor; do not honor Him here in church clothed in silk vestments, and then pass Him by unclothed and frozen outside.... What is the use of loading Christ's table with gold cups while He Himself is starving? Feed the hungry, and then if you have any money left over spend it on the altar table. Will you make a cup of gold and

withhold a cup of water? What use is it to adorn the altar with cloth of gold hangings and deny Christ a coat for His back?... Adorn your house if you will, but do not forget your brother in distress. He is a temple of infinitely greater value. (The Liturgy of the Hours, IV)

The once visible Christ who walked on earth, while now present in the Eucharist, has existentially passed to the poor and to all those whom Jesus referred to when he said, "You did it to me." Raniero Cantalamessa makes this clear when he writes:

The poor person is Jesus, still roaming the world unrecognized, rather like when he appeared in different guises after the resurrection, to Mary as a gardener, to the disciples on the road to Emmaus as a traveller, to the apostles on the lake as an expert fisherman standing on the shore—waiting for their eyes to be opened with a cry of recognition: "It is the Lord!" (Jn 21:7). If only that same cry of recognition—"It is the Lord!"—could issue from our lips even once, at the sight of a poor person." (Poverty, page 10)

Saint Francis, who strove to combine radical detachment with loving care of the downtrodden, learned to see the poor person as a living tabernacle of the poor and despised Christ. Oh dear Saint Francis, help me gain the sensitivity and courage to have that same vision.

FASTING AND MORTIFICATION

A conversion is a turning around, a change of heart; and mortification is the process of saying good-bye to what is not of God, to what is preventing us from experiencing true peace and joy.
—MURRAY BODO, *THE WAY OF ST. FRANCIS*

In his book, *The Sacred Exercises of the Love of Jesus*, published in 1623, a Franciscan friar named Severin Ruberic wrote: "Throughout the entire life of our Seraphic Father St. Francis we see, on the one hand, nothing but the bitterness of sacrifice and penance, and on the other, the sweetness of God's impulses. He began by ridding himself of his possessions and went on to the utter stripping of himself, seeking nothing but God."

The twin pillars of Francis' life were love and abnegation.

For Francis, the soul's love of God increased in direct proportion to its detachment from and renunciation of its own selfish interests. Love of God covered all his actions, including his extreme acts of abnegation, which he undertook to weed out the roots of self-love and all its carnal inclinations and all-consuming passions which prevent the soul from uniting itself with God.

But love came first. Francis knew that renunciation, either internal or external, had no meaning or merit apart from and without love. Love took possession of Francis, devouring his heart while burning away everything earthly within him. Francis became so riveted to Christ through holy compassion for all creation that he bore on his body the wounds of his crucified love.

Underlining Francis' fasting and acts of mortification was his belief that it was not possible for him to be interested in himself and interested in God at the same time. He knew God loved him more than he (Francis) loved himself. And so, he made a decision to no longer be concerned about himself or his needs, but instead he strove with every fiber of his being to enjoy only the delights of God and trust completely that God would take care of him. Francis totally disregarded his own misery and suffering, trusting God would either dispose of it or help him bear it. He gave his full attention to God's all-embracing goodness, finding in God's clasp true joy.

Francis no longer offered incense to vanity or his own satisfaction. His only aim was to please God alone. Fasting and mortification helped Francis die to himself so he could live fully for God.

Lord, root out of my heart all self-love and give me in its place a perfect love of you. Take away the heart of a slave and give me the heart of a son.

PILGRIMAGE DIARY 23

Following the Wrong Road

*P*rogress along the spiritual road seems painfully slow. As I listen to the stories of the friars and sisters with whom I'm traveling, I'm somewhat surprised by the common thread that runs through them: Why, after so many years of prayer and varying degrees of asceticism, years of trying to lead a more spiritual life, must we struggle with the same weaknesses, the same faults. I've already expressed in these pages my own frustration with the slowness in which I am able to eradicate sin from my life. Is this just the way it is, or are we missing something, doing something wrong...or worse, are we following the wrong road altogether? Why not ask Saint Francis?

As I looked more closely at the ascetical life of Francis, one thing became clear: the purity of his motivation. Often for us moderns, spirituality has become just another tool to help us become better people. That is to say, our spirituality is egocentric: What is it doing for me? Not so for Francis. Francis' goal was not self-perfection; his goal was God alone. Asceticism for Francis was inspired and animated by a simple principle, found in the sixth chapter of the book of Deuteronomy: "Thou shalt love the Lord thy God with thy whole heart, with thy whole soul, and with thy whole strength" (6:5). To deviate from this reality is to return to a self-centered perfection which misses the essence and profound purpose of Christianity.

Francis took seriously the words of Christ, and in John's Gospel, Jesus said, "Without me, you can do nothing." Taking those words to heart changed Francis' entire outlook: God alone must be the source and expression of all his actions. As we grow in awareness that of ourselves we can do nothing but that in Christ we can do all things, we will no longer be discouraged by our own faults, nor will we be proud of the virtuous acts we perform through the promptings of God's grace. Once Francis arrived at the realization that he was nothing and that God was all, his own weaknesses and failings were no longer obstacles, but instead were transformed into a means through which his faith was strengthened by the exercise of heroic acts of self-sacrifice, echoing the words of Paul in his Second Letter to the Corinthians: "Gladly will I glory in my infirmities that the power of God may dwell in me" (12:9).

I must learn to trust in God and mistrust my own strength. Only then will love motivate my actions and purify my intentions.

Blessed Are the Poor in Spirit

God desires to possess our heart completely; if we do not empty it of everything other than himself, he cannot act nor do there what he pleases.

—BROTHER LAWRENCE OF THE RESURRECTION, O.C.D.

Francis understood that it was impossible for a soul that still finds some satisfaction in other creatures or in any created thing to completely enjoy a truly deep level of divine intimacy without first emptying itself of everything other than the divine, pruning away every vestige of self-interest, and it was equally clear that the best way to accomplish this was through the mortification of the senses. To be with God meant to abandon everything else. He also knew that mortification of the senses was in and of itself useless, unless it stemmed from the purest of motivations...that is, unity with God, not self-improvement or to avoid the detrimental effects of sin. Listen to the words of Saint Francis:

> There are many who, while insisting on prayers and obligations, inflict many abstinences and punishments upon their bodies. But they are immediately offended and disturbed about a single word which seems harmful to their bodies or about something which might be taken away from them. These people are not poor in spirit, for someone who is truly poor in spirit hates himself and loves those who strike him on the cheek. (*Early Documents*, pages 133-134)

To be truly "poor in spirit" requires that we count absolutely nothing as our own, including our reputations, possessions and positions in life. Francis said in his early Rule, "We may know with certainty that nothing belongs to us except our vices and sins." Imagine being so poor in spirit that we claim ownership of only our sins. Francis believed we had to despise everything that caused us to be self-centered or selfish. Why? Because only that level of poverty of spirit will allow us to become so free in God that we will be immune from offenses or insults hurled our way, which will allow us to not merely turn the other cheek, but rather to respond in love. Francis knew that fasting and other acts of self-denial practiced only for the sake of avoiding sin was not enough if we are not willing to surrender everything in order to love God more fully.

To enter more fully into the presence of God, to experience the Divine from moment to moment in even the most mundane things of life, we need to let go of everything that is not of God. As the heart empties itself of everything but God, it inherits the riches promised by Christ to those who are "poor in spirit."

The consuming fire of divine Mercy which Francis fully experienced created within him a tremendous purity of life which allowed him to see the Creator in every creature.

PILGRIMAGE DIARY 24

No Television

Solitude is the furnace of transformation. Without solitude we remain victims of our society and continue to be entangled in the illusions of the false self.

—*HENRI J. M. NOUWEN*

I haven't watched television in forty-nine days. Today is August 10, a Sunday, and it's 7 p.m. If I were home, my wife and I would be sitting down in our living room for our Sunday night ritual: pizza and 60 Minutes. Every Sunday night my wife makes a pizza, and she plans it so it comes out of the oven just seconds before 60 Minutes goes on the air. As I thought about our pleasant little ritual, I suddenly realized how long it has been since I last watched any television. It seems almost unthinkable to have gone so long without seeing NYPD Blue, Homicide: Life on the Streets, ER or The CBS Evening News With Dan Rather. Forty-nine days without CNN or Baseball Tonight on ESPN. Unthinkable.

Yet—amazingly—I don't miss it.

I think again of the candid observations of the unknown man traveling across rural Russia in the 1850's found in The Way of a Pilgrim, and how he laments his sloth and is troubled by how eagerly he occupies most of his time with any unimportant trifle and does not spend the time alone with God.

I can't begin to imagine how many hours I have wasted in front of the television. Taoism suggests that when the mind is wild, the spirit is distracted. The onslaught of images and ideas from both the frivolous programs which pander to our basest instincts and from the commercials which often use sex and empty promises to stimulate sales, combine to create a wild mind...wild in the sense of being over-hyped or stimulated. For many people, if not most, television offers a distraction from the cares and pressures of the day. Even though we sit passively in front of the television, the effect it has on us is far from calming. As a Taoist would say, "When the spirit is distracted, it will attach itself to the ten thousand things."

The distracted mind is running wild with things of the world: fame, fortune, passion, possessive love, alcohol and drugs, sex, riches and out-of-control emotions. Out of this distraction, craving and desire emerge, and the mind is disturbed. The mind is attracted by what it sees, giving birth to cravings, and subsequently the desire to satisfy those cravings. Slowly, the forces of earth become stronger than the forces of Heaven. Yet, out of our worldly desire and craving, stress and anxiety emerge, and the peace of heaven is hidden. This may sound simplistic, yet out of this notion arises the understanding the saints had of the importance of detachment.

I'm slowly coming to see that detachment is forged in the furnace of solitude. And silence. Thomas Szasz writes, "Man cannot long survive without air, water, and sleep. Next in importance comes food. And close on its heels, solitude." You don't hear sentiments like that on television, which claims we need the latest fragrance of perfume or the fastest new car for survival. Detachment frees us from the control of others and introduces us to the indwelling presence of God. Saint Augustine exhorts us: "Enter into yourself; it is in the interior man where Truth is found."

Solitude, by enabling us to be genuinely alone, frees us from the panicked need for acquisitions, approval and acclaim. From his time alone, Saint Francis learned to be prompted not by the opinions of others but by the divine Center within him.

Walking hand in hand with solitude is simplicity, a virtue exemplified by Saint Francis. His simpler life-style freed him from the tyranny of striving to be affluent. His solitude fostered a simplicity of heart.

Søren Kierkegaard wrote, "Oh, blessed simplicity, that seizes swiftly what cleverness, tired out in the service of vanity, may grasp but slowly."

Perhaps prayer has been difficult for me because I enter into it in an agitated state, distracted by thoughts, desires, fears and anxieties. I find it hard to "let go" and be still, be silent. I am learning that it is in the silence of the heart that distractions are diffused and the artificiality of modern life crumbles. In order to grow spiritually, I need to feed on a steady diet of silence.

When I get home, I hope I have the courage to unplug my television.

STORMY SEAS

Once satisfied that the call of his brotherhood was not to contemplation but to preaching, it was impossible that St. Francis should be satisfied with missionary efforts in Italy alone.
—W. J. KNOX LITTLE, *ST. FRANCIS OF ASSISI*

In the summer of 1212, Francis felt the urge to be a missionary, and to expand his preaching beyond the limits of Italy and Christianity. He wanted to bring the Word of God to the Muslims living in Syria. Perhaps he wanted to convey a message of peace to counteract the violence of the latest crusade (known as the "Children's Crusade" because hordes of German and French youth marched into battle), launched to liberate the tomb of Christ from the hands of the "infidels." If he could convert the Muslims, countless lives could be spared. His faith, his piety and his heroic spirit filled him with the belief he should undertake such a risky venture. But being an obedient servant of the Church, Francis first traveled to Rome in order to seek permission from Pope Innocent III, despite the fact the pontiff believed that force alone could be effective against the "infidels."

As he journeyed to Rome, he stopped in marketplaces along the way and preached the gospel. While he was preaching in Todi, the cries of swallows swooping overhead caused such a disturbance the people could not hear Francis speaking. Francis told the birds to be quiet and listen to the Word of God. And they did. And they remained silent until Francis concluded his message. In Rome, Francis preached in the streets and alleys while waiting to see the pope. His preaching was so effective, a number of new men—and one woman—joined the brotherhood. It was at this time that Francis met Jacoba de Settisoli, a young woman married to a Roman nobleman. They became lifelong friends, and Francis always referred to her as "Brother Jacoba." After gaining permission from the pope, Francis returned to Assisi and appointed Peter Catanii to lead the friars during his absence. Francis and a companion left Assisi and headed for a port on the Adriatic, where he hoped to catch a merchant ship heading for the Middle East. It is not known how Francis paid for the voyage. Perhaps he begged for passage on the ship, or he might have performed some menial task on board in exchange for the fare. Somehow, he got on board, but the ship did not get far before it encountered a severe storm which threw it off course.

It was a terrifying and perilous trip, which mercifully ended when the ship managed to come ashore in Slavonia. It is not certain what Francis did in Slavonia, but eventually he was forced to return to Italy, because passage to Syria from that port was impossible for at least another year. (In Francis' day, travel via ship was a slow and dangerous enterprise. Ships were powered by oars and sails.) He learned of a ship sailing to Italy...now all he had to do was try to get on it.

With no money, the friars pleaded with the captain to allow them to board the ship out of a love for God. The plea was denied. A pious sailor aided Francis and his companion by helping them board the return ship as stowaways. Once they were hidden, another sailor provided Francis and the brother with food for the journey. This trip also encountered a storm which threatened its survival. Thanks to the foul weather, the ship veered way off course, thereby increasing the length of the journey so that the food ran out long before they reached Italy. The passengers and crew feared starvation. This was not the "Love Boat." Word of their plight reached Francis in the cargo hold. Realizing that the sailors were facing starvation, Francis came out of hiding to share his meager food with them. Legend has it that Francis blessed the food he and his companion had not eaten, and the provisions were miraculously multiplied as they distributed them to the hungry sailors. The sailors said the ship made it to Italy only because God answered Francis' prayers. After docking in Anconia, Francis returned to Assisi. His first missionary adventure may have been aborted, but he would try again.

Meanwhile, Francis continued going from city to city in Italy, preaching with great effectiveness.

SPAIN

Later the same year, or perhaps early in 1213, Francis attempted to go, via Spain, to Morocco, where the gospel was either unknown or hated. Perhaps his first experience at sea persuaded Francis to try a mostly land route, walking across Italy and southern France and into Spain, where he would catch a ship to Morocco. He had hopes of meeting and converting the famous Sultan Mohammed-ben-Naser, who had recently suffered a serious defeat at Las Navas de Tolosa and had been forced to flee Spain and take refuge in Africa. The defeat spelled the end of Muslim domination of the Iberian peninsula. Francis wanted to visit the sultan in exile and extend an olive branch of peace, presenting him with the gentleness of the gospel. And he was more than willing to suffer martyrdom if necessary. But once again, Francis never reached his destination.

Not much is known of this trip, which only Thomas of Celano mentions, and then only in his first life of the saint. There is some speculation that Francis visited the sanctuary of Santiago de Compostela, which was the most venerated shrine during the Middle Ages. All we know for sure is that Francis became seriously ill while in Spain and was forced to return to Italy. But he would not give up his dream of preaching to the Muslims, even if it meant losing his life.

Larger Than Life

As someone who earned his living producing television dramas, I cannot help but be struck by the sweeping, colossal drama of Saint Francis' life. For instance, just think about his two failed attempts at reaching the Holy Land. Those two trips pack enough dramatic potential to make a number of compelling films, yet they are not even mentioned, due to lack of space, in many of the biographies of the saint. Try to imagine the faith—and the foolishness—of attempting such daring missions. Try to imagine the stress and strain of the harrowing storms at sea, the strenuous walk across Europe, the illness, the heroism...it is difficult to conceive of his personal courage, strength and determination to overcome any obstacle. Those two stories are littered with numerous side-stories detailing humorous and sad and uplifting events along the way, each biographer picking one or two to tell. Even though I am not even attempting to write a biography, I could not fail to mention the story about his telling the swallows to shut up so the people could hear his sermon. It is no wonder that no one book, no one film could present a full and accurate portrait of a saint who truly was larger than life.

The Liturgy of the Hours

The angel of the Lord is encamped
around those who revere him, to
 rescue them.
Taste and see that the Lord is good.
He is happy who seeks refuge in
 him.
(Psalm 33[34]:8-9)

PILGRIMAGE DIARY 25

And an Angel of the Lord
Appeared in a Volkswagen

*H*alfway through the four-week pilgrimage, we were given a
free weekend to go anywhere and do anything we wanted.
*Forty-six people elected to travel together via bus to Florence for a
day of sightseeing, shopping and visiting the city's great art
museums. Two others chose to stay in the reflective silence of Assisi.
Two others ventured off on a side pilgrimage to Cortona.*

*I was one of the two who went to Cortona. The trip wasn't my
idea. In fact, I had never heard of Cortona. My traveling companion
for the day, an American friar who works in Mexico, didn't know
very much about the city, but he had a burning desire to go there
because it is the home of Saint Margaret of Cortona. I didn't know
anything about Saint Margaret of Cortona either. The friar's parish in
Juarez, Mexico, where he is pastor, is named in honor of Saint
Margaret of Cortona, and so he wanted to visit her shrine and collect
as many religious articles and information about the saint as he
could to bring home to his parishioners. After he told me about Saint*

Margaret's life, and I had read about the city and the saint's amazing
story, I decided to go to Cortona with the friar. I'm glad I did. It was,
perhaps, the best single day of the pilgrimage.

Saint Margaret of Cortona

*Saint Margaret of Cortona was born in 1247 in Tuscany, not far from
La Verna (the mountain where Francis received the stigmata), in the
little town of Laviano in the Diocese of Chiusi. She was a beautiful
young girl and an only child, whom her parents had no difficulty in
spoiling, even though her father was a poor farmer. As a teenager,
her beauty made it easy for her to win the attention and affection of
men, even those whose social status was much higher than the
working class of her parents. After her mother died, her father
remarried and life turned sour for young Margaret. Her father was
moody and violent, and the new stepmother found Margaret's
willfulness and independence to be unacceptable.*

*The home was rife with conflicts. And Margaret, unlike other
young females of that time, was not about to tolerate the situation at
home. She had a thirst for affection, and finding none at home, she
walked out of her family and followed her quest for love. She was
seventeen years old. With the help of her beauty and wit, she soon
became involved with a nobleman from Montepulciano and lived in
his castle as a servant. The relationship quickly progressed from lord
and servant to lord and mistress. After they had a child, the
nobleman promised to marry her someday. But someday never came.
The nobleman, his mistress and the child lived together for nine
years. Margaret lived a life of leisurely luxury. She was twenty-seven
years old when the noble left the castle on a long journey. A few
days later, his dog returned without its master. Margaret and the dog
set to out find him. She did. He had been robbed and killed in the
forest.*

*Margaret was forced to face not only the death of her lover, but
also the disgrace she encountered when she returned to Laviano as a
fallen woman with an illegitimate child. Her father, with prodding
from his wife, said Margaret had disgraced him and would not allow
her back into his home. She was homeless with a young child,
condemned and cast out by her own town. In her loneliness and
rejection, she turned to God. She knocked on the door of a*

Franciscan friary, and the friars greeted her with mercy and kindness. After experiencing the healing balm of confession, Margaret embarked on a life of penance and severe practices of mortification, which the friars advised her to moderate.

The Tuscan penitent followed closely the example of Saint Francis. She began to beg for her food, accepting only broken bread and scraps of leftovers. The people of Cortona refused to treat her like a common beggar and offered to give her whole loaves of bread and full portions of food. At first she refused to accept their generosity, insisting that she be treated no better than the poorest of the poor, because of Christ who had nowhere to lay his head. Eventually, she began to accept the whole loaves, and immediately gave them away to the poor. She reserved for herself only scraps of bread and other food, which she ate only after feeding everyone else who was hungry. And if there was nothing left over, she did not eat. When people gave her clothing, she exchanged it for the threadbare garments of the poor. She tended to the sick, nursing them as best she could. She became known as "the mother of the poor."

She began to work with the friars, helping them minister to the poor and the sick. She went from a life of self-seeking pleasures to a life of repentance and giving herself completely to those in need. Three years after joining the friars in their work with the poor, Margaret entered the Third Order of Saint Francis, and became a secular Franciscan. She soon became famous for her sanctity. She was a mystic who actively cared for the poor and sick, skillfully blending contemplation and action. She founded a community of women who cared for the sick; she also founded a hospital in Cortona. Soon, the people of Cortona were coming to her for spiritual advice. Word of her visions and healing powers spread all over Italy, and into France and Spain. Her son became a Franciscan friar. Margaret died in 1297 at the age of fifty. Seven centuries later, her incorrupt body lies in a glass coffin under the altar of a basilica which bears her name.

Cortona

In a word, Cortona is spectacular. The ancient city sits atop the southern spur of Monte San Egidio on the border of Tuscany and Umbria. The view of the valley below stretching to Lake Trasimeno is breathtaking. The slope of the mountain causes significant variations in height within the city; almost every street appears to be climbing up or going down. The winding, twisting, ascending and descending streets and narrow alleys form a labyrinth running through centuries-old buildings, palaces and churches. Unofficially, I counted seventeen churches, and may very well have missed some. The Church of San Francesco was built in 1245; the infamous Brother Elias is buried in the floor of the choir. The fifteenth-century Church of San Niccolo was founded by Saint Bernadine of Siena and contains a fine bust of Saint Francis in terra-cotta. The sixteenth-century convent and Church of Santa Chiara breathes an air of quiet contemplation. The magnificent Basilica of Santa Margherite, located on the highest part of Cortona, contains the mortal remains of the city's most famous resident, Saint Margaret of Cortona. The steep uphill path to the basilica is lined with the Stations of the Cross created by a Cortonese artist in 1947, in thanksgiving to Saint Margaret for protecting the city from bombing during World War II.

The art in all the churches contributes to Cortona's name as "city of art." The city also has two excellent museums. The Museo Diocesano contains a number of paintings by Fra Angelico, including one of his masterpieces, The Annunciation, which the Dominican artist painted in 1433. The piazzas are among the most charming in all of Italy. The city truly retains all its medieval flavor. Walking down Via del Gesu, bordered by twelfth- and thirteenth-century houses joined in a very irregular fashion, you can easily imagine you are in the Middle Ages. Via Dell'Orto Della Cera runs through one of the oldest sections of Cortona, and the restored homes retain the charm and patina of a distant past. Just beyond the ancient gate of Porta Montanina remnants of an Etruscan wall which once circled the city are clearly visible. Cortona is a city of history, art and spirituality.

The Day

I met Father Larry in front of Papa Casa Giovanni at eight o'clock in the morning. It was already hot. I was surprised to see him wearing his habit, thinking he would be uncomfortable traveling on trains and buses, and walking around an ancient city in this heat. But, before the day was over, I was glad he wore it. We took the bus down to the train station. The seventy-five-kilometer train trip was pleasant; I *never tire of looking at the Umbrian countryside. Shortly after the idyllic town of Passignano on the shores of Lake Trasimeno, the train headed north for the final leg of the journey. When we disembarked from the train we had to take a bus up the mountain to Cortona. The bus ride up the winding road continually afforded us extraordinary views of the valley.*

Within minutes of arriving, we knew we were in a very special place. The outdoor markets were buzzing with activity, offering for sale everything from fine leather goods to cheap T-shirts. It didn't take us long to figure out that our primary destination, the Basilica of St. Margaret, was at the opposite side of town from where the bus let us off, and more importantly, the entire walk to the basilica would be uphill. I felt like saying, "I bet you're sorry you wore that heavy habit." But I refrained. As we walked, we stopped at many of the city's churches for quick visits. We also breezed through the Museo Diocesano, pausing only long enough to admire the work of Beato Fra Angelico. As we walked through the maze of visually stimulating streets, I felt as if I could spend a week in Cortona in order to fully absorb all the city's charms. The medieval architecture was stunning. Within two hours, I was suffering from sensory overload.

Eventually, we made it to the far side of the city, and began the most arduous part of the climb, to the highest part of the city. The Basilica of St. Margaret is isolated from the rest of the city, sitting majestically atop the hill overlooking the busy city and lush valley below. I knew I was out of shape, because I could not keep up with Father Larry, who seemed to be almost jogging, despite being dressed in his hot habit. We made it to the entrance of the church just as it was about to close for three hours for the afternoon siesta. I knew I would never make the climb back up the hill. Father managed to use his limited ability at speaking Italian to convince one of the sisters who cares for the shrine to allow us in. I'm sure his habit helped. The kind sister gave us a private tour of the church. Unfortunately, the gift shop had already been locked, so Father Larry would have to return if he wanted to pick up some materials for his parish in Mexico. We thanked the sister, and headed back down the hill for lunch.

At lunch, Father Larry revealed a little secret he had hidden up his oversized sleeve. We were going to visit a friary called Le Celle, a hermitage founded by Saint Francis in 1211 during one of his early apostolic missions through Perugia, Cortona, Arezzo and Florence. The name predates Francis' arrival at the secluded mountainside location, and it refers to the small buildings that were part of an abandoned mill which once drew power from a forceful stream known as Vigone Torrent, now running through the heart of the hermitage. Once I heard that Saint Bonaventure and Saint Anthony of Padua had both lived in Le Celle, I was more than eager to visit the shrine maintained by the Capuchins since 1537. After a fine meal of pasta, we set out for the hermitage.

We left the city through the Porto Montanina with the understanding that the hermitage "wasn't that far up the road." After walking nearly an hour along the side of a narrow, twisting, gently climbing road, we were...nowhere. All we could see was forest, and not a hint of the hermitage. I was beginning to have my doubts about the directions and if we would ever find Le Celle. Further, I was worried we might not make it back to Cortona before dark. While I was ready to give up and turn back, Father Larry blithely kept walking, saying, "God will take care of us." I lacked his confidence. Suddenly, a little Volkswagen zoomed past us. Then I noticed his brake lights go on. The car stopped and began backing up. A young, handsome man leaned over, rolled down the passenger window and said, in English, "Where are you guys going?" Father Larry responded, "Le Celle." The young man said, "Get in, I'm going there, too." We drove for at least ten minutes, at a rather brisk pace, before arriving at the hermitage. During the drive we learned that the young man was to enter a Capuchin novitiate in the fall, and he had stopped because Father Larry was wearing his habit...thank God.

Le Celle

The highlight of our visit to the hermitage was spending time in a small cell once used by Saint Francis. The narrow quadrangular room was built using a natural recess in the rocky mountainside as one of the walls. Adding wooden walls to the natural niche created an ideal place for solitude. Hanging on one of the walls is an icon of the Madonna and Child in front of which Francis used to pray.

Over the years, many additional buildings were added, including a small chapel, a refectory and a dormitory. The chapel contains the altar at which Saint Anthony celebrated Mass.

Thomas of Celano writes, "He always sought a hidden place where he could adapt not only his soul but also his whole body to God. When he suddenly felt himself visited by the Lord in public, lest he be without his cell, he made a cell of his mantle. At times, when he did not have a mantle, he would cover his face with his sleeve so that he would not disclose the hidden manna" (2 Cel. 94). The Legend of Perugia *reports Francis as saying, "Wherever we are, wherever we go, we bring our cell with us. Our brother body is our cell and our soul is the hermit living in that cell in order to pray to God and meditate"* (Omnibus, section 80).

Le Celle reminds us to keep a hidden place for the Lord. Not only is it important for us to have a quiet place reserved for prayer, even if it is only the corner of a room, but we need also symbolically to take that cell with us as we move about the world. The idea of imagining my soul as a hermit living within the cell of my body is an effective way to help me maintain a more prayerful attitude no matter how busy I am. I can recall being told as a kid that my body was a temple or tabernacle of the Holy Spirit and, as such, we had to treat the body with respect and reverence. Imagining my soul as a hermit works better for me. My body must play the role of Martha, caring for the hermit who is busy being mindful of God.

Return

As Father Larry and I began our walk home, we could not help but be mindful of the quickly darkening skies. A rainstorm was on its way, and would more than likely hit while we were still a long way from Cortona. Again, while I was concerned about the coming rain, Father Larry was unfazed by the prospect of getting drenched. As we entered the parking lot on the lowest level of the hermitage grounds, we saw our angel and his Volkswagen. He said, "I figured you guys would need a ride back to Cortona, so I waited for you."

About halfway on our journey back to Cortona, the skies opened with a loud chorus of thunder and bolts of lightning. The young man drove us directly to the Basilica of St. Margaret of Cortona, where Father Larry was able to buy the things he needed for his parish in Mexico. We stayed in the church until the storm passed and then began our journey back to Assisi. It was a great day...thanks to our angel in the Volkswagen.

Later that night, as I reflected on the day, I was impressed by Father Larry's ability to accept whatever the day had to offer. The day had begun with his not being able to find his eyeglasses, which had fallen behind the bed. He had asked me to help search for them, and as we had done so, I had become increasingly annoyed at the prospect of our missing the only train to Cortona. Father Larry had showed no signs of tension or concern; in fact, he had been ready to scrap our plans and stay in Assisi...and pray. When we had found the glasses, we had made a mad dash to the train, arriving at the station with only minutes to spare.

Worry is not a part of Father Larry's life; he has replaced it with surrender. I don't think it would have made much difference to him had the angel not appeared. Whatever God wills, Father Larry accepts. Still, next time I hope he is more careful with his glasses.

FOURTH LATERAN COUNCIL

Francis' fame and popularity were reaching epic proportions. Talk of his performing miracles was everywhere. In his first life of the saint, Thomas of Celano reports, "When he entered any city, the clergy rejoiced, the bells were rung, the men were filled with happiness, the women rejoiced together, the children clapped their hands; and often, taking branches from the trees, they went to meet him singing" (1 Cel. 62). Even accounting for some exaggeration in the level of exuberance which greeted Francis as he traveled about, there is little doubt he was having a positive impact on the spiritual lives of the people he encountered.

However, while Francis was effectively enflaming the faith of the people, it was still a dark time for the Church in general. The Fourth Lateran Council, convened by Pope Innocent III in 1215, addressed many of the problems confronting the spiritual decline within the Church. Documents from the council condemned the licentious and avaricious behavior of some of the clergy, such as priests living luxuriously, being drunk in public, engaging the services of prostitutes and neglecting to perform religious rites. Many priests spoke more about commercial affairs than spiritual matters. Churches were falling into disrepair. Masses were being shortened, and the words of the liturgy were being carelessly spoken. Clerical posts were being sold. Bribes had become commonplace. Unqualified priests were being promoted. Church funds were being lavished on personal comforts and pleasures, such as fine clothing and palaces. Relics, and even the sacraments, were being sold. Priests were fathering children. In his opening address, the pope deplored the scandals that were bringing great dishonor to the Church. It is no stretch of the imagination to think the Church was on the verge of collapse. While Francis was earnestly attempting to rekindle the flame of faith, the Church seemed to be doing its best to blow it out by creating a climate for skepticism and distrust to flourish because of the deplorable behavior of some of the clergy. Innocent III, though scheming and ambitious, was a man of lofty character, and so the decline of the Church must have caused him great anguish. He felt the only remedy would come through the might of papal force. Little did he know that a gentle breeze stirred by the poor man from Assisi would be a far more powerful agent of change.

As the head of a religious order, Francis, in all likelihood, attended the Fourth Lateran Council, where it is believed he met Saint Dominic for the first time. More than four hundred bishops, along with eight hundred abbots and priors, crowded into the Basilica of St. John Lateran for the opening session on November 11th. Among other things, the Council authorized mounting a fifth crusade to reclaim the Holy Land. The Council also dealt with some serious theological matters. The doctrine of transubstantiation was proclaimed. Also, the Council began to formulate the doctrine of the Holy Trinity, which eventually would lead to a split between the Eastern and Western Churches. At the Council, some speculate that Francis began to see more clearly his role in helping to reform the Church. Francis confronted the deep troubles of the Church with even deeper faith.

PILGRIMAGE DIARY 26

Insignificant

*P*ope John Paul II is in France where he is attending a world youth festival in Paris. A poll taken by a French Catholic newspaper, La Croix, and French television, and released on the day the pope arrived (August 21st), found that religion played no significant role in the lives of sixty-three percent of French people between the ages of eighteen and thirty.

UNLETTERED AND POOR MEN

He was like the morning spread upon the darkness. At his rising
the whole face of the countryside changed and put on a smile.
—THOMAS OF CELANO, *FIRST LIFE*

There is plenty of evidence of the extraordinary power exercised by
Francis over all classes and kinds of people. One unsolicited testi-
monial came in the form of a letter from a priest who became a
respected historian. A portion of the letter was included in an essay
written by A. G. Little and published in a collection called *Franciscan
Essays II*:

> ...the small band of brothers had grown into a multitude, and
> had been joined also by a band of sisters. It is interesting to see
> how they struck a contemporary who did not belong to the fra-
> ternity. Jacques de Vitry, bishop-elect of Acre in Palestine, later
> famous as the historian of the crusades, arrived at Perugia on
> the day of the death of Innocent III, 16 July, 1216, and soon
> afterwards wrote a letter to his friends in France describing his
> journey and experience: "One comfort I found in those parts:
> many of both sexes, rich and poor, clergy and laity, having left
> all things for Christ were fleeing from the world: they were
> called Friars Minor. They are held in great reverence by the Pope
> and Cardinals. They are in no way occupied with temporal
> things, but with fervent love and eager zeal labour every day to
> save perishing souls from the vanities of the world.... And
> already by God's grace they have reaped a great harvest and
> gained many.... They themselves live according to the form of
> the primitive church, of whom it is written: the multitude of
> them that believed were of one heart and one soul. By day they
> come into the cities and towns that they may win souls, living
> the life of action; at night they go back to a hermitage or soli-
> tary places devoting themselves to contemplation. The women
> live together in diverse lodgings near cities; they accept nothing
> but live by the work of their hands. But they are often much
> distressed because they are honored by clergy and laity more
> than they would wish. The men of the Order assemble with
> manifold advantage once a year at an appointed place, that
> they together may rejoice in the Lord, and feast; and they then,
> with the advice of good men, make their holy regulations
> which are confirmed by the pope. After this they are dispersed

through the whole of the rest of the year throughout Lombardy and Tuscany and Apulia and Sicily.... I believe that to the shame of the bishops, who are like dumb dogs unable to bark, the Lord by these unlettered and poor men wills to save many souls before the end of the world."

A SOARING EAGLE

Love is the abridgement of all theology.

—SAINT FRANCIS DE SALES

Francis' spiritual wisdom even impressed theologians. In his book, *The Mysticism of St. Francis of Assisi*, D.H.S. Nicholson tells a story whose origins can be traced to Thomas of Celano's *Second Life* and Saint Bonaventure's *Major Life*:

> One time when he was at Siena a member of the Order of Preachers visited him and talked for some time of the life of the spirit. The visitor was a doctor of divinity, and when he asked St. Francis his opinion on a text from Ezekiel which he could not understand, St. Francis naturally demurred to instructing a man who was evidently more learned than himself. But the other insisted, and put his question again. What, he asked, was St. Francis' understanding of the saying, "If thou proclaim not to the wicked man his wickedness, I will require his soul at thy hand," because he himself knew many people who were in mortal sin whom he had not denounced. The answer which St. Francis gave shows the naturalness with which he applied the saying in a way which made it referable to all the details of life. If the passage were to be taken as a general application, he said, he took it to mean that what was demanded was that a man should live in such a way as to reprove the wicked, as it were, automatically, by the example of his life and the purity of his conversation. Avoiding the obvious interpretation that it was incumbent on every man to go about proclaiming the wicked-ness of his neighbors, he turned the tables on those who might be inclined to do so, and insisted that what was fundamentally necessary was a shining example in their own lives. The answer is said to have given immense edification to the visitor, and caused him to remark as he went away that "this man's theology, based on purity and contemplation, is a soaring eagle, while

our learning crawls with its belly on the ground."

The comparison is not justified; the higher faculty which, awakened by long periods of contemplation, enters into a region where the intellect cannot come, gains a source of comprehension from which the logical faculty is debarred by its very nature. St. Francis' theology was not an intellectual acquisition, but was of the nature of his inner intuitive sight which knows instead of propounding theories: it pierces through the external into the very core of the mystery. As Celano put it, "the lover's affection entered within, whereas the knowledge of masters remains without."

PILGRIMAGE DIARY 27

Hold My Hand

G od, help me let go of my own thoughts and theories. My best thinking has gotten me nowhere. I desire to live only for you. Help me to let go of my own ideas and imagination. Help me even let go of my own daydreams. I desire to think only of you, not myself. But this is so difficult. It seems almost impossible not to put myself first. You are not always the center of my universe, the crazy, confused world within me. I want to love what you love. I want to let go of all that is not of you, all that keeps me from becoming closer to you. When I spend time alone with you, my mind too easily drifts, is too easily distracted. Hold my hand in prayer, give me strength.

Help me feed on you alone. Help me labor for you alone. Pour streams of living water into my heart, washing away all traces of its meanness and self-centeredness.

Today, Lord, show me how to share your love with those I encounter.

PREACHING TO THE POPE

By 1217, the brotherhood had increased to such a size, many friars were now sent to foreign lands to preach. They went to France, Germany, Spain, Portugal, Hungry, Greece, Tunis and elsewhere, and their efforts were met with mixed success. The friars encountered strong resistance in Germany, where many were tortured and martyred. Following the death of Innocent III in July of 1216, Cencio Savelli was elected pope, choosing the name Honorius III. The new pope was old and pious, and lacked a thirst for power. Francis' friend and confidant Cardinal Ugolino wanted him to meet the new pope. While Honorius III was a decent man, who had given much of his personal fortune to the poor, he was surrounded by prelates and clergy who were still very much absorbed in temporal affairs. Ugolino, fearing that Francis, in his simple purity, would not make a great impression on the pope and his calculating curia (many of whom had no sympathy with his doctrine of poverty and viewed him as a simpleton), suggested that he prepare his remarks to the pontiff beforehand, committing them to memory. Francis wasn't very good at delivering prepared sermons. He always preferred to speak extemporaneously, and if he had nothing to say to a crowd he would simply bless them and dismiss them. Nonetheless, Francis followed the cardinal's advice and prepared his remarks, perhaps with Ugolino's help, before meeting the pope.

When Francis appeared before the pope in 1218, the speech that had been carefully crafted, composed in immaculate Latin and committed to memory flew out of his mind and he could not recall a word of it. He humbly knelt before the pope and asked for his blessing. Then he stood up and, burning with a love of God, delivered a passionate and eloquent sermon in the Tuscan language to the pope and the cardinals in attendance. He became so ecstatic as he spoke, he literally began joyfully dancing before his audience. One of Giotto's frescoes in the upper basilica depicts Francis preaching before Pope Honorius III. The pope and the cardinals, rather than being put off by his exuberant speech, were deeply impressed by his sincerity and holiness. Francis asked the pope to appoint Cardinal Ugolino as a special protector of his Order because he was becoming increasingly distressed and troubled by the onerous prospects of governing his rapidly expanding fraternity. The request was honored. The following year, the pope issued the bull *Cum dilecti*, in which he assured the bishops of the world that there was no doubt about the "catholicity" and religious zeal of the Friars Minor and instructed the bishops to fully embrace, without a hint of reservation, the wandering friars.

Become Like Children

A great man is one who has not lost the child's heart.
—*MENCIUS (372-289 B.C.)*

*A*t Mass a few days ago, the Gospel reading came from
Matthew's Gospel. It told the story of the disciple who asked
Jesus a question: "Who is of greatest importance in the Kingdom of
God?" A very human question. Instead of answering immediately,
Jesus asked a child in the crowd to come stand next to him. With the
child at his side, Jesus told the disciple that in order to get to heaven
he would have to become like a child, adding, "Whoever makes
himself lowly, becoming like this child, is of the greatest importance
in heaven."

I thought of Francis, who became lowly and childlike. Today, I
spotted a book on a shelf of books which had not yet been
catalogued. I could see only the spine of the dust jacket:
Navone...Personal Witness. Could it be? Yes...it was! The author was
John J. Navone, S.J., a professor at the Pontifical Gregorian
University. I had met Father Navone in the fall of 1995, when I
taught a two-week course on television writing and directing at the
Gregorian. He had agreed to read an early draft of The Canvas of the
Soul. After reading it, he had written me saying, essentially, that the
novel did not work, and had suggested I write a book on Saint
Francis. I had thought the idea was ludicrous. (In fact, it was...and if I
had known just how ludicrous it was, I would never have undertaken
the writing of this book.) I had dismissed the idea and had continued
working on my novel.

A few months later, however, his suggestion had popped back
into my mind. I was sitting at my kitchen table; it was late at night,
and I was editing that day's work, a few new pages of the novel,
pages that went into the Assisi section of the book. Suddenly, I
thought, "Why not?" And so it began. I had put the novel on a shelf,
where it still sits, and had begun work on a book about Saint
Francis...this book.

In the Collegio Sant' Isidoro library, I opened Father Navone's
book and looked at the inside flap of the dust jacket. And there
staring back at me was a very young-looking Father Navone. He was

thirty-seven years old when Sheed & Ward published the book in 1967. The bio blurb said he had recently received his doctorate in theology from the Gregorian. Today, he is a highly respected and much-loved professor there, where his courses are among the most popular offered, and he has authored numerous books.

I randomly opened the book to page 161. Amazingly, Father Navone was discussing there the very same story from Matthew's Gospel. He wrote:

> Jesus describes the process of conversion as becoming like a child (Mt 18:3): "Unless you are converted and become like children, you will never enter the kingdom of heaven." Conversion is not here understood as something completed; it clearly involves a process of change and development in which one progressively humbles himself before God as a child (18:4). Becoming like a child suggests the development of an attitude of complete dependence and reliance upon God, which would be opposed to one of self-reliance. It suggests a parallel in the final attitude of the prodigal son, who returns to his father, helpless and humbled after the folly of a disastrous self-assertion. Conversion involves the constant recognition that everything a man is and possesses is a gift of God.

Including friendship.

Francis' life is fueled by the conviction that the central mystery of Christianity is our transformation from world-wise, self-sufficient "adults" into abiding children of the Father of Jesus by means of the grace of the Spirit.

The Liturgy of the Hours

A portion from a reading from the letter of Saint Francis of Assisi to all the faithful:

> We should not be wise and prudent according to worldly standards, but rather we should be simple, humble and pure. We should never desire to be above others, but rather we

should be servants, and subject for the Lord's sake to every kind of authority. Upon all who do these things and endure to the end will rest the Spirit of the Lord; he will make his dwelling place and home in them and they will be children of their heavenly Father, whose works they do; they are the spouses and brothers of our Lord Jesus Christ.

THE WOLF OF GUBBIO

If your heart is upright, every living creature will be a mirror and a book of holy devotion.

—THOMAS À KEMPIS, *THE IMITATION OF CHRIST*

The most famous story about Saint Francis is the one in which he tames the fierce wolf that was threatening the people of Gubbio. And that story can be found in the most famous book on Saint Francis, *The Little Flowers of St. Francis.* Written by an Italian Franciscan, who lived about a hundred years after Francis, to capture the spirit of the Franciscan way of life, the book has been the most widely read book on the saint during the last hundred years. The book ignited controversy and debate, and its history is in itself a fascinating story.

The Little Flowers grew out of the debate over how to live the dream of Saint Francis. The uniqueness of Francis' way of life was part of the problem with trying to follow it. Francis combined an active ministry of going among the people and sharing the good news of salvation with a deeply contemplative life of isolated prayer in caves far from the public square. If I were a friar back in those early days of the Order, I would have been attracted to the contemplative streak within the saint. The chasm between the active and contemplative sides of the Franciscan charism nearly killed the founder's dream. Francis' ideal was so towering, and the growth of the Order was so staggering that after Francis' death the meaning and reality of living his dream had still to be figured out.

And figuring it out was the problem, because three distinctly different approaches to following the dream had evolved. One group of friars felt that a certain amount of modification to the saint's vision was needed in order to serve the needs of the Church, which was asking them to work in parishes, universities and in the foreign missions; subscribers to this position were known as moderates. Another group was more radical in its departure from the ideals of Saint Francis, especially those concerning ownership of property, and for them the ascetical practices of Franciscan poverty and contemplation became more symbolic than practiced. And the third group, known as the *zelanti* or spirituals, considered the Rule of St. Francis to be almost equal in merit to the Gospels and felt that it should be strictly followed without a trace of compromise, no matter how impractical it might be. The century after the death of Francis was marked by a bitter conflict among the three groups. One saint, three ways to follow him. The dream was splitting apart, thanks in part to the human weakness of those trying to live it.

A moderate friar, who was sympathetic to some of the ascetical ideals of the spirituals, became frustrated by the fact that many of the wonderful stories about Francis and his first companions and the early days of the Order told by second-generation friars were missing from the authorized life of the saint, written by Saint Bonaventure. Fortunately for us, the friar, Ugolino di Monte Santa Maria, was a talented writer who felt it was important to preserve these vivid stories because they offered a more complete portrait of the saint. Sometime around 1325, he began compiling the stories and weaving them into a compelling narrative that has enchanted readers for centuries. His masterpiece was titled *Actus Beati Francisci et Sociorum Ejus*, or, in English, *The Deeds of St. Francis and His Companions*.

The book was later condensed and published in Italian in 1476 as *I Fioretti di San Francesco—The Little Flowers of St. Francis*, and it became an instant classic and was translated into numerous languages. In Italy, the book was so popular it was known as "the breviary of the Italian people." While the book occasionally lapses into excessiveness when portraying some of the miraculous legends surrounding the life of Francis, it has remained a favorite of people around the world because of its simplicity, charm and eloquence in communicating the spirit of Saint Francis.

I have only presented you with the lightest sketch of the important story behind the writing of *The Little Flowers*. Readers interested in learning the full story should read the introduction to Raphael Brown's translation of the book, published by Image Books.

The power of the *Fioretti* lies in the art of story-telling and its ability to connect us to our common humanity. Stories touch the heart, which is why Christ told stories as a way of conveying his message. The story the *Fioretti* tell is really the story of faith. Through the magic of story, the faith of Francis and his friends is linked to our faith, enhancing and enriching it. *The Little Flowers* is a book of faith to be read in faith.

Here are three of the stories, beginning with the story of the wolf of Gubbio.

The Wolf of Gubbio

Gubbio is a charming city located about twenty-five miles north of Assisi. The city, 2500 years old, quietly sits in a gorge between steep cliffs high atop a green mountainside. The city flourished in Roman times, and one of the first things a visitor spots is a large, well-preserved first-century Roman amphitheater. The windy slopes of the Apennine hills of Gubbio are lined with straight rows of rugged gray stone houses, many of which date back to the thirteenth century. The historic core of the city is composed of five main streets, each on a different level, linked by sloping alleys. The tower of the Palace of Consuls, built in the fourteenth century, looms over the delightful Piazza della Signoria, which easily transports you back to the Middle Ages when Francis walked these streets.

One day Francis visited the city and learned about a very fierce and ferocious wolf who was attacking animals and people. The entire city was so terrified of the wolf that no one dared go beyond the city gate. Francis decided he would go and find the wolf and tell him to stop terrorizing the people. The people warned Francis not to undertake such a foolish mission, because the wolf had already devoured a number of people and surely would kill him. Francis ignored their warnings. He blessed himself and placed his hope and safety in the hands of God. People lined the city walls to witness the encounter between the saint and the wolf.

Not far from the city gate, the wolf came charging toward Francis. The wolf's mouth was open and his sharp teeth were set to rip into Francis' flesh. Francis made the sign of the cross toward the wolf. The wolf slowed down and stopped. He closed his mouth. Francis called to the wolf and told him to come closer. When the wolf got to Francis, he ordered the wolf not to attack or hurt anyone again. The wolf lowered his head and lay down at Francis' feet.

Francis then preached to the wolf, reminding him how terrible it was to harm God's creatures. Francis told the wolf he deserved to be put to death for devouring humans who were created in the image of God. However, Francis said he wanted to show the wolf mercy, and as long as the wolf promised never to harm anyone again, he could go free. The wolf shook his head, indicating he understood and accepted Francis' offer of mercy and peace. Francis then told the wolf he would ask the people of Gubbio to give him food every day, so that the wolf would not suffer from hunger. The wolf put his paw in Francis' hand to seal the deal. The wolf then gently walked next to Francis as he entered the city.

A huge crowd surrounded Francis and the wolf in the main square, and Francis delivered a stirring sermon, imploring the people to give up their sinful ways. The people were so astounded by what they had witnessed and heard they gave praise to God. And from that day on, the people of Gubbio and the wolf lived in harmony. The wolf went door to door each day and was fed by the people. So wondrous was the miracle, that dogs did not even bark at the wolf as he strolled through the city. The wolf grew old and died two years later, causing the city great sadness.

The wolf is immortalized in a bas-relief over the door of a little church on Via Mastro Giorgio. A few years ago, workers renovating another church unearthed the skeleton of a giant wolf buried beneath a slab.

The Turtledoves of Siena

One day, a boy from Siena captured a number of turtledoves in his snare. He placed them in a cage, and was on his way to the market to sell them when he ran into Saint Francis. The sight of the caged birds filled Francis with pity. Francis had great compassion toward gentle animals, and he knew these defenseless birds would be sold and killed. Francis asked the boy to give him the birds, because the Scriptures said doves are symbols of purity and humility, and therefore they should be treated with kindness.

The boy gave Francis the doves. Francis held them to his breast and spoke kind words to them. The wild birds instantly became tamed. Francis then took the birds to a place where the brothers were living and made nests for each of them. The doves became a part of the brotherhood, becoming very friendly with the friars.

Before taking the doves, Francis prayed with the young boy. He then told the youth he would one day become a friar and serve Christ with distinction. When the boy grew up, he joined the Friars Minor and lived an exemplary life.

From Murderers to Friars

One day, Saint Francis was walking near Borgo San Sepolcro when he was approached by a wealthy young nobleman. The young man told Francis that he wished to become a friar. Francis said that perhaps his wealth might make it difficult for him to live a life of poverty and hardships. The young man said that with the grace of Jesus, he would be able to endure anything. Francis blessed him and immediately accepted him into the brotherhood, giving him the name Angelo. Not long afterward, Francis appointed Angelo as the guardian of the Hermitage of Monte Casale.

Around that time, three notorious robbers who were murderers approached the hermitage and asked Brother Angelo if he would give them some food. Angelo refused their request, saying they were unworthy to share the food that had been given to sustain the servants of God. The three men left in anger. No sooner had they departed than Francis arrived, carrying a sack of bread and a jug of wine he had begged. Angelo told Francis about the men and his refusal to feed them. Francis sternly rebuked the guardian, telling him that sinners are more easily returned to God by acts of kindness than by cruel reproofs. He reminded Angelo that Christ came to heal sinners and that he often ate with them.

Francis gave Angelo the bread and wine he was carrying, and ordered Angelo to find the robbers and give it to them. Furthermore, Francis said, after you give them all the bread and wine, get down on your knees and confess your sins of cruelty. When Angelo left in search of the robbers, Francis prayed that the robbers would repent of their misdeeds and return to the Lord. The robbers were so moved my Angelo's gift of food and wine, and the humility of his confession, that they returned with him to the hermitage, and, after assuring them of the mercy of God, Francis accepted them into the brotherhood.

The Fullness of Joy

What is grace but the beginning of joy, and what is perfection
of joy but grace complete?

—*RICHARD ROLLE*

*During evening prayer at Sant' Isidoro, we frequently chanted the won-
derful hymn to Mary, The Magnificat, taken from Luke's Gospel:*

My soul glorifies the Lord,
my spirit rejoices in God, my Savior.
He looks on his servant in her lowliness;
henceforth all ages will call me blessed.

The Almighty works marvels for me.
Holy his name!
His mercy is from age to age,
on those who fear him.

He puts forth his arm in strength
and scatters the proud-hearted.
He casts the mighty from their thrones
and raises the lowly.

He fills the starving with good things,
sends the rich away empty.

He protects Israel, his servant,
remembering his mercy,
the mercy promised to our fathers,
to Abraham and his sons for ever. (1:46-55)

*I can see more clearly now that before my conversion in 1995, I was
indeed starving. Yet I didn't know how to satisfy the hunger that gnawed
away at me. Of course the hunger was for God, who has truly filled me
with good things. But God doesn't force-feed us...we must open wide and
accept his nourishment. Among the good things the Lord does give us is
joy. Before my conversion, I easily became depressed. Joy was unknown. I
know that during the past three years, my tendency toward depression
has almost completely disappeared. Still, the joy I now know is rather
fragile because I have failed to enter fully into the mystery of the cross the
way Francis did, and therefore draw nearer to God. I still have a lot of
self-interest which must be nailed to the cross before I can hope to experience the perfect joy which Francis knew. The crucifixion of self is essen-*

tial to full knowledge and service of God. I want the fullness of joy with-out walking up the hill of Calvary. But I must. Grace is calling me. God must become everything to me, and myself, nothing, before I exclaim, with Blaise Pascal, the great scholar and tormented soul who suddenly experienced the presence of God, "Joy! Joy! Tears of Joy!"

A FARMER NAMED JOHN

The following story doesn't come from *The Little Flowers*. I found it in a pictorial biography of the saint by the noted Swiss photograph-er Leonard von Matt. The book's narrative was written by the Reverend Walter Hauser, a parish priest from Switzerland. Father Hauser called the story, simply, "Farmer John Joins St. Francis":

> A great characteristic of St. Francis was his simplicity, and he loved to see true simplicity in his brethren.
>
> As he went about preaching, he was often pained to notice how dusty and dirty some churches were. He would then approach the priest in charge of them, and ask him quite humbly to keep the church cleaner out of reverence for God. Often he would set to work with a broom himself.
>
> Once he entered a chapel which was sadly neglected and he immediately began to sweep it. A farmer named John, who at the time was ploughing in a field nearby, hastened to the chapel and asked Francis if he might be allowed to help him. So they worked together, and when they had cleaned the whole chapel, John turned to St. Francis. "Brother," he said, "for a long time I have wanted to come and serve God together with you and the brethren, but I didn't know how to get in touch with you. Now God has arranged it, and I am ready to do what-ever you tell me."
>
> Francis was delighted and explained to him that if he want-ed to join them, he must sell his property and give the proceeds to the poor, as it says in the Gospel: "If thou wilt be perfect, go, sell what thou hast, and give to the poor."
>
> John thereupon went back to his oxen in the field, unyoked the animals, and brought one of them to Francis, saying: "Brother Francis, my inheritance is small enough, because I have always worked in my own family; but I am claiming this ox as my share, and I am giving it to the poor." But when his parents heard what he was going to do, they came along with

his younger brothers and made a great fuss. They seemed to be more distressed about the loss of the animal than about the young man's departure. Francis, however, gave them a meal and consoled them, saying: "I can't give you back your brother, because he belongs to God; but since you are poor, I am ordering him to give up the ox and give it back to you." The young man did so, and was then clothed in the habit of penance.

Brother John was so simple that he thought he should imitate whatever he saw Francis doing. When Francis was praying, John imitated every movement: When Francis knelt down, he knelt down; when Francis raised his hands, he raised his hands, and so forth. He even imitated his way of sighing or coughing. When Francis eventually noticed this, he scolded John but in a very kindly way, because he was amused by his simplicity. John lived only a short time, but even in that short time he acquired a reputation for sanctity.

Later on, Francis often used to tell the story of John, though he did not speak of him as "Brother John," but always as "the holy John." (pages 41-42)

A Clean Sweep

In that last story, I love the part where Francis "would set to work with a broom himself." We all love doing the big, important jobs. I know I do. But we would rather not tackle the humble tasks. I'd prefer to preach to a full church than to take a broom to an empty church. Not so Francis. He did either with equal love.

Back in the brotherhood's infancy, when Francis and his brothers were living in the Portiuncula, they often visited nearby villages, proclaiming a message of penance and conversion. And Francis always took his broom, in case he needed to clean a church. After he had preached to the people, he would speak privately with the priests, imploring them to keep the churches clean for the celebration of the Eucharist.

The story clearly shows Francis' humility and his love for and devotion to the Eucharist. For Francis, a church was God's home...in fact, not theory. He fully believed that God was truly present during the sacrifice of the Mass. And the depth of his belief compelled him to treat both the church and the celebration of the Eucharist with great respect. His quietly sweeping an empty church is the best sermon he could preach on the subject.

My Emotions

For most of my life, I have been ruled by my emotions. They are used to running wild, free to pull me in any and all directions. Did I say "my emotions?" Hardly, for they in fact owned me; I was their slave. Christ was fully aware of the importance of emotions in human life. Many of his miracles were in response to emotional needs, such as pleas from grief-stricken parents. When I began to focus my attention on God, it set off a chain reaction of events which eventually led to my gaining a degree of mastery over my unruly emotions.

In order to love God, I had to learn how to love my neighbor. But before I could even begin to love my neighbor, I had to learn to love myself. Before I could love myself, I had to get to know myself. Acquiring self-knowledge means learning about your emotional needs. I craved affirmation from others, and would do anything to elicit it. A disapproving word would send me into a tailspin. I feared not being held in high regard by others. Without some kind of outside approval, even if it was artificially induced, I was confronted with my own emptiness. I feared my own poverty. Now I am free to enter into my own intrinsic littleness, because I am confident of God's love for me, a love which I did not have to earn nor could I ever merit, no matter how hard I tried. As I grew in awareness of God's love for me, it was easier for me to unearth my own inner weakness.

What freedom! I no longer have to chase after the security that I found only in affirmations from others, because I know the loving hug of God's compassion and mercy. Now I take responsibility for my emotions, which no longer are obstacles to my experiencing the fullness of God.

A FISH STORY

Here is a story from Father Hauser's book. It captures the essence of many of the stories that dot the landscape of Saint Francis' life.

A certain fisherman once caught a large fish in the lake of Piediluco, and presented it to Francis. Francis accepted it politely, but then began to talk to the fish and to address it as a brother. He then carefully put it back into the water and began to pray aloud. As long as the prayer continued, the fish would not leave the side of the boat in which the saint was sitting. But when the prayer was ended, and Francis gave the fish leave, it swam gaily away. (page 45)

Without prayer, I'm a fish out of water.

SHEEP, LAMBS AND RAMS

If your heart is straight with God, then every creature will appear to you as a mirror of life and a sacred scripture. No creature is so small and insignificant as not to express and demonstrate the goodness of God.

—THOMAS À KEMPIS

The fish story can be traced back to Saint Bonaventure's *Major Life*. Chapter Eight of the biography is filled with delightful animal stories, stories featuring lambs, rabbits, birds, crickets, pheasants and wolves; the chapter has an unwieldy title...

ON
HIS AFFECTIONATE PIETY
AND
HOW IRRATIONAL CREATURES
WERE AFFECTIONATE TOWARD HIM.

Here are two of those stories, both from the translation by Professor Cousins:

When Francis was traveling near the city of Siena, he came upon a large flock of sheep in a pasture. When he greeted them kindly, as he was accustomed to do, they all stopped grazing and ran to him, lifting their heads and fixing their eyes on him. They gave him such a welcome that the shepherds and the friars were amazed to see lambs and even rams frisking about him in such an extraordinary way.

Another time at St. Mary of the Portiuncula the man of God was offered a sheep, which he gratefully accepted in his love of that innocence and simplicity which the sheep by its nature reflects. The pious man admonished the sheep to praise God attentively and to avoid giving any offense to the friars. The sheep carefully observed his instructions, as if it recognized the piety of the man of God. For when it heard the friars chanting in the choir, it would enter the church, genuflect without instructions from anyone, and bleat before the altar of the Virgin, the mother of the Lamb, as if it wished to greet her. Besides, when the most sacred body of Christ was elevated at mass, it would bow down on bended knees as if this reverent animal were reproaching those who were not devout and inviting the devout to reverence the sacrament. (page 256)

What should a modern person who is aware of the importance of critical thinking think of that last story, a story featuring a lamb that not only genuflects, but also can identify a statue of Mary and understands the sacredness of the transubstantiation? Of course we can simply dismiss it as a pious fairy tale, but does the story have anything to tell us? I happen to like the story. At the risk of sounding naïve or jejune, I'll even admit that I harbor a secret wish that the story was factually true. But then again, I liked the movie *Babe*.

The Soul of a Poet

Do not have Jesus Christ on your lips and the world in your hearts.

—*SAINT IGNATIUS OF ANTIOCH*

With the soul of a poet, Francis placed a greater emphasis on value than on utility, and he dreamed rather than planned. He stripped away all his illusions, masks and pretensions, leaving himself (and his followers) exposed and vulnerable. His heightened sensitivity deepened his suffering. He faced the unpredictability of life with true innocence. These qualities made people feel uncomfortable around him, because he brought them face-to-face with the stagnation in their own life and faith. I confess that at times I find the saint annoying, wishing he would lighten up and let the rest of us live with our comforting illusions.

But he never lightens up.

Francis keeps telling us we must keep looking at Jesus and base our lives on the values of Jesus. His message is simple and consistent: transcend yourself through a denial of your self-sufficiency. He is always telling me: free yourself from the tyranny of your ego, the slavery of your notion of self-importance. He whispers, "Forget yourself and serve others. Take a broom to the church...and your life."

I pretend I don't hear him. But I do. And it makes me feel uncomfortable. Which makes him smile.

THE SONG OF THE BIRDS

In the pious simplicity of his pure and holy soul, St. Francis made the smallest insect in creation instrumental to excite him to divine praise—even the worm crawling on the earth was to him a striking memento of the great Creator.
—EMILIUS CHAVIN DE MALAN, *THE LIFE OF ST. FRANCIS OF ASSISIUM*

The importance of all the animal stories from the life of Saint Francis is that they tell us something about the saint. In *Francis: Bible of the Poor*, Auspicius van Corstanje, O.F.M., writes:

> The animal stories in the life of St. Francis bear witness not to a man who at certain times felt a need to seek refuge in a world of fantasy but to a mystic who experienced the real world in a way that we can hardly imagine. When we hear the birds chirruping and singing, we hear only sounds. Francis heard words. He experienced in their song the sweetness of God's presence.... (page 69)

The intimacy Saint Francis felt between God and creation made his spirit dance to the song of the birds.

I cherish my own romantic notion of Saint Francis as a man who expressed extraordinary kindness to all animals. His best friends seemed to be birds. I like that Saint Francis very much. Yet Saint Francis' love of nature was only part of who he was. The most essential aspect of his life was his total devotion to God. His love of nature flowed from his far greater love of God.

PILGRIMAGE DIARY 29

Two Loaves of Bread

*H*alfway through our pilgrimage, we needed a break, some space and time for quiet and reflection. Whenever Francis wanted to be alone with God, he always sought out some mountaintop cave which would become his hermitage, but there was one notable exception. In the year 1211 (or possibly 1213), Francis spent Lent on an island. Isola Maggiore is one of three small islands located in Lago Trasimeno (Lake Trasimene), the largest lake in the Italian peninsula. Lent, of course, is a time of fasting and penance,

which were both important elements in Francis' spirituality. Penance,
for Francis, was an open channel to complete absorption in God.
Fasting helped him curb his appetite for anything not of God, so God
alone could fill his heart and his entire being.

Prior to Lent that year, Francis had been preaching in the hilltop
city of Cortona, which is not far from the shores of Lake Trasimene.
The Fioretti *tell us that Francis was staying in the home of a devoted
friend when, during the night, he was inspired to spend Lent on an
island in the lake. Before dawn on Ash Wednesday, his friend ferried
Francis to the island in his small boat. Francis instructed the man not
to reveal his whereabouts in order to secure his privacy. He also
asked the man to return for him on Holy Thursday so he could spend
Easter Sunday with the friars living at Le Celle. According to the
boatmen, Francis took with him to the island two small loaves of
bread.

Each pilgrim traveled to the island carrying two small loaves of
bread. And that is the end of the similarities between our one-day
visit to the island and Francis' extended stay. We journeyed to the
shoreside town of Passignano on a huge chartered bus. We then
boarded a ferry for a delightful, sun-drenched, twenty-minute cruise
to the island. The great stretch of water flashing in the rays of the sun
was encircled by undulating hills covered with olive trees and
vineyards. The tranquil panorama was a welcome antidote to two
weeks of lectures held in stuffy classrooms and visits to crowded
shrines.

According to a legend still told by the people living on the island
(but which can't be found in the Franciscan sources), there was a
storm on the day that Francis crossed the lake in his friend's boat, yet
he managed to keep a candle alight for the whole trip. Likewise, on
the return trip there was another storm, this one of far greater
intensity and, according to the legend, Francis calmed the fury of the
lake by merely holding up his hand.

The important part of the story has nothing to do with keeping a
candle lit in the wind or calming a storm. The heart and soul of the
story is the forty days Francis spent in rigorous fasting. Raphael
Brown's translation of The Little Flowers *has it that Francis, after
being dropped off by his friend, "went into a very dense thicket in
which thorn bushes and small trees had made a sort of little cabin or
hut. And he began to pray and contemplate heavenly things in that

place. And he stayed there all through Lent without eating and without drinking, except for half of one of those little loaves of bread. His devoted friend came for him on Holy Thursday, as they had agreed. And of the two loaves, he found one whole and half of the other. It is believed that St. Francis ate the other half out of reverence for the fast of the Blessed Christ, who fasted forty days and forty nights without taking any material food. And so with that half loaf he drove from himself the poison of pride, while according to Christ's example he fasted for forty days and forty nights" (pages 57-58).

I fasted about forty minutes before eating one of my two loaves of bread. About two hours later, I ate the other loaf, along with an apple I purchased at a local market. Just before we boarded the ferry for the return trip, I had a cappuccino and a small pastry...cream-filled, no less. Quick fast.

What drew Francis and his brothers to fasting and penance? Murray Bodo in The Journey and the Dream suggests a reason: It was a way for them to "be united with God on a new level of conscious-ness and understanding." Father Bodo goes on to say, "So the pain of detachment was only a means of union. It was a stilling, of quieting everything that would prevent them from hearing that hushed knock of God within. That is why Francis left his father. Pietro's world, his values and what he lived for, clamored so loud in Francis' ears, he could not hear the Voices in the heart of his real self. That is why he was willing and able to bear the insults and hooting of the citizens of Assisi; he heard a voice within him that was even louder and more real than all the citizenry of the world. That is why he mortified his body when it clamored so loudly for attention that it threatened to drown out the peace of the 'Voice' inside. Everything then that he and the brothers had done and suffered was for union with God, who dwelt inside them. They had sacrificed everything that their love might be consummated..." (page 104).

Upon arriving on Isola Maggiore, we walked together in silence along the western shore. One main road encircles the island. The section of road along the western shore, where the island's inhabitants live and work, is paved with vertically laid bricks and bordered on both sides by fully restored buildings, some built in the thirteenth century. We walked past the tiny church of Buon Gesu (or Holy Jesus), and the restored church of San Salvatore, which was built in 1155. Outside the little town the road gently winds around and we found ourselves walking past luxuriant hills covered with olive trees, cypresses, pine trees and poplars on the right, and to our left was the rocky shoreline and the vast expanse of Lago Trasimeno.

Halfway down the eastern shore was a statue of Saint Francis which commemorated his landing at that point on the island. After a short prayer service, each of the pilgrims headed out one-by-one for a day of silent reflection. Some, including me, climbed to the top of the hill which dominates the island. Along the way, we visited a tiny chapel containing the flat rock that served as Francis' bed during his forty days on the island. Talk about a firm bed! Farther up the hill is the charming Church of St. Michael the Archangel, a thirteenth-century structure recently restored and containing a number of fine frescoes, one of which is a copy of Cimabue's depiction of the Assumption of the Virgin gracing the apse of the upper church of Saint Francis in Assisi. Over the altar is a large Byzantine crucifix featuring Francis and Mary Magdalen kneeling just below the pierced feet of Christ. The summit offers a sweeping panoramic view of the lake and the mountains, hills and lakeside villages on the distant horizon.

After visiting the churches, I found a quiet spot on a large rock on the shore below the remains of a former Franciscan friary. After gazing at the lake and thinking about all I had seen during the first two weeks of the pilgrimage, I decided to read Saint Bonaventure's The Soul's Journey Into God. Just as I reached Chapter Two—"On Contemplating God in His Vestiges in the Sense World"—a couple walked down the path leading to the shore. They spread out a blanket on a small patch of sand located about twenty yards from where I was sitting. After arranging the blanket, they walked up the shoreline a short distance and disappeared into a thicket of bushes and shrubs. I returned to my reading. A few minutes later, heralded by giggles, they emerged from the bushes and strolled back to the blanket. The woman was topless; the man was wearing the smallest, tightest bathing suit I had ever seen worn by a man. The woman was wearing an even skimpier string bikini bottom which left virtually nothing to the imagination.

I tried to ignore them. I looked back down at my book, and read: "For through sight enter the sublime and luminous heavenly bodies and other colored objects...." I chuckled to myself, closed the book, got up and walked completely around the island, rejoicing in the island's beauty.

One Reality

Holiness is the infinite capacity to love. Only God is truly holy, because only God is infinite. But I am called to grow in holiness, to grow in capacity to love others and to receive their love.

—*ROBERT FARICY, S.J.*

Francis loved his little brothers and everyone he met just as they were, and not as he hoped they would be. He loved them for what they were, unique individuals, and he never tried to manipulate them into being what he thought they should be. He knew every person is ultimately a mystery created in the image and likeness of God. And if God is unknowable and inexhaustible, so, too, are his creations. We are all different, and Francis' respect for this reality underlined his ability to live with others and to give himself so fully to everyone. His understanding that everyone was sacred and had the right to develop to his or her full potential created in him a sense of reverence that made him handle all creation with care. Francis knew every person is of great worth to God, and he only wished to give them space to grow. As Francis entered more deeply into the mystery of the Gospels, he saw things with more clarity. It was all rather simple and boiled down to one reality: Love is the key to growth.

Without love there is no growth.

PILGRIMAGE DIARY 30

Being One

God does not create poverty, we do, because we do not share.

—*MOTHER TERESA*

One day at lunch at Sant' Isidoro, we were joined by an elderly friar who had just spent some time in Colombia, South America. He said he had visited a region that was "beyond the limits of poverty." His description of the impoverishment tested the limits of lunchtime conversation.

We can pretend it doesn't exist (and we're great at doing so), but there is a widening gap between rich and poor, overabundance on the one hand and desperate need on the other, and this deep division is leading to injustices on worldwide levels. Leonardo Boff writes: "The meaning of human life is found not in creating riches but fraternity; it is supported not by having but by being one with and compassionate with all creatures" (St. Francis: A Model for Human Liberation, *page 1*).

The Liturgy of the Hours

Lord, make haste and answer;
for my spirit fails within me.
Do not hide your face
lest I become like those in the grave.

In the morning let me know your love
for I put my trust in you.
Make me know the way I should walk;
to you I lift up my soul.
(Psalm 142 [143]:7-8)

STRIPPED OF EVERYTHING

Love lives without desire, knowledge without intellect; the will chooses to do the will of God. I live and yet not I; my being is not my being; so great is this paradox that I can't define it. Poverty is to have nothing and not to wish to have anything and yet to possess everything in the spirit of liberty.

—JACOPONE DA TODI, *LAUDA LX*

According to Saint Bonaventure, Francis "used to say that poverty was the foundation of the Order, on which the entire structure of their religious life so basically depended that it would stand firm if poverty were firm and collapse completely if poverty were undermined" (*The Life of St. Francis*, page 84). Francis never tired of extolling the virtues of poverty, as the following story bears witness.

> One day as the friars gathered around him [Francis] they asked which virtue pleased Christ most. He replied:
>
> "You must know, my brothers, that poverty is the most excellent way of salvation, for it is the root of perfection, and it nourishes humility. Its fruits are many but they are not recognized. It is, in effect, the treasure hidden in a field of which the Gospel speaks (Mt. 13-44), the treasure that can be bought only by selling all that one has. The purchase price in no way compares with the value of what one has to sell. Those who wish to attain this peak of perfection must renounce not only worldly prudence, but even learning. They must do this in order to contemplate in its nakedness the power of the Lord and to be able to offer themselves stripped of everything to the Crucified One. For the man who within himself clings to his own way of thinking has not completely renounced the world." (Masseron, *Memorable Words of Saint Francis*)

Poverty and its interpretation were a perennial problem for the followers of Saint Francis, a problem of such immensity that it eventually led to friars being "burned alive by their brother friars for no worse fault than obstinate devotion to the strict Rule of St. Francis." (See *From Francis to Dante* by G. G. Coultan; this book traces the life of the Franciscan Salimbene [1221-1288], a friar who chronicled the early years of the Order.)

Over one hundred friars who were members of a branch of the Order known as Spirituals were burned at the stake as heretics; many others were imprisoned and exiled because of their involvement with Joachimist teachings, which claimed, based on an interpretation of the Book of Revelation (14:6) by Joachim of Fiore, a Cistercian abbot, that a new age ruled by the Holy Spirit was about to dawn on humanity. The Spirituals believed Francis had been chosen by God to usher in this new age.

Imagine—if you can—friars burning friars over the issue of poverty and how to interpret it. The complexity of gospel poverty not only eludes a simple definition, but also renders a univocal understanding impossible.

The Importance of Detachment

Detachment liberates the wings of our heart so that we can rise to the grateful enjoyment of life in all its fullness. We must open our hand and let loose what we hold before we can receive the new gifts that every moment offers us.

—*DAVID STEINDL-RAST*, A LISTENING HEART

Obviously, my favorite saint is Francis of Assisi. And my favorite "spiritual" writer is Thomas Merton. And I guess it should come as no surprise that things I am trying to understand about Francis are often made clearer by Merton. For instance, as I tried to understand the importance of detachment in the spiritual life, it was Thomas Merton's writings which helped me understand detachment is a means for arriving at a mindset which does not strive to possess or control people or things, but rather sees the inner mystery of life, allowing everyone and everything to be itself. God owns everything, and merely loans us what we need. We don't own, we borrow. In The Silent Life, *Merton writes:*

As soon as we take them to ourselves,
appropriate them,
hug them to our hearts,
we have stolen them from God,
they are no longer His, but our own. (pages 25-26)

Life is becoming more and more complex and divisive. Detachment helps us rid ourselves of what is unnecessary. As we trim the excess from our lives (which is no easy task), we are better able to enter the interior simplicity that is the hallmark of genuine prayer. Prayer is hard because our inner and outer worlds are so fragmented. The turbulence of being pulled in so many different directions leaves me feeling disordered, confused and overwhelmed. Detachment helps me focus on one thing: God. As God slowly becomes the center from which all things flow, the fragmentation gives way to unity, to wholeness. I think there is a hunger for unity in the world today.

Accumulating possessions was for Francis a sin against poverty. He had to uproot ownership from his life because it blocked him from a deeper experience of God. I cannot emulate him on this score, and actually divest myself of everything but the bare minimum of clothing. But what I can do—and must do—is adopt a spirit of poverty, which will allow me to be content with sufficiency rather than striving for superfluity.

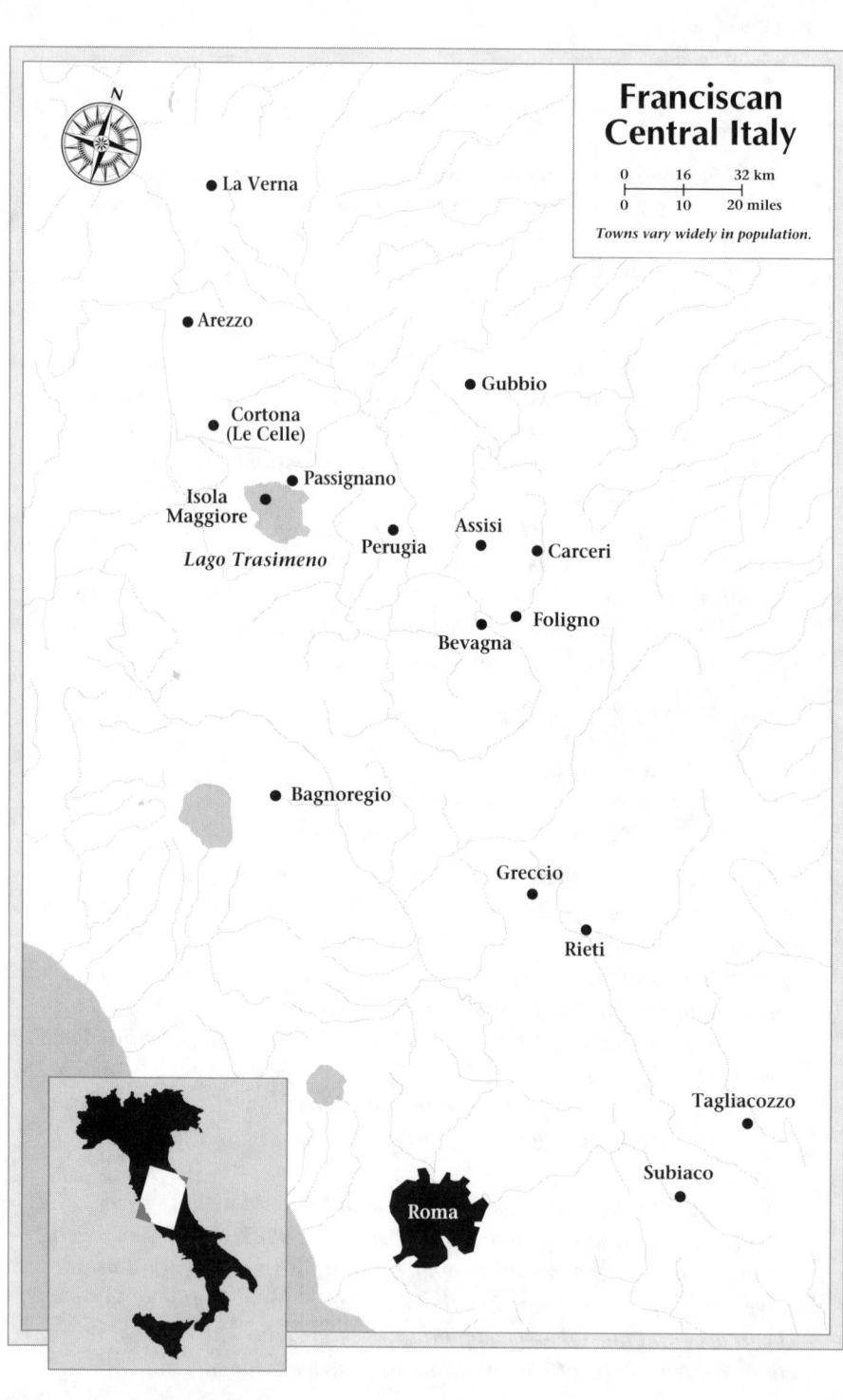

Franciscan
Central Italy

0   16   32 km
0   10   20 miles

Towns vary widely in population.

● La Verna

● Arezzo

● Gubbio

● Cortona
(Le Celle)

● Passignano

Isola
Maggiore

Lago Trasimeno

● Perugia

Assisi
●

● Carceri

● Foligno

Bevagna

● Bagnoregio

Greccio
●

Rieti

Tagliacozzo
●

Subiaco
●

Roma

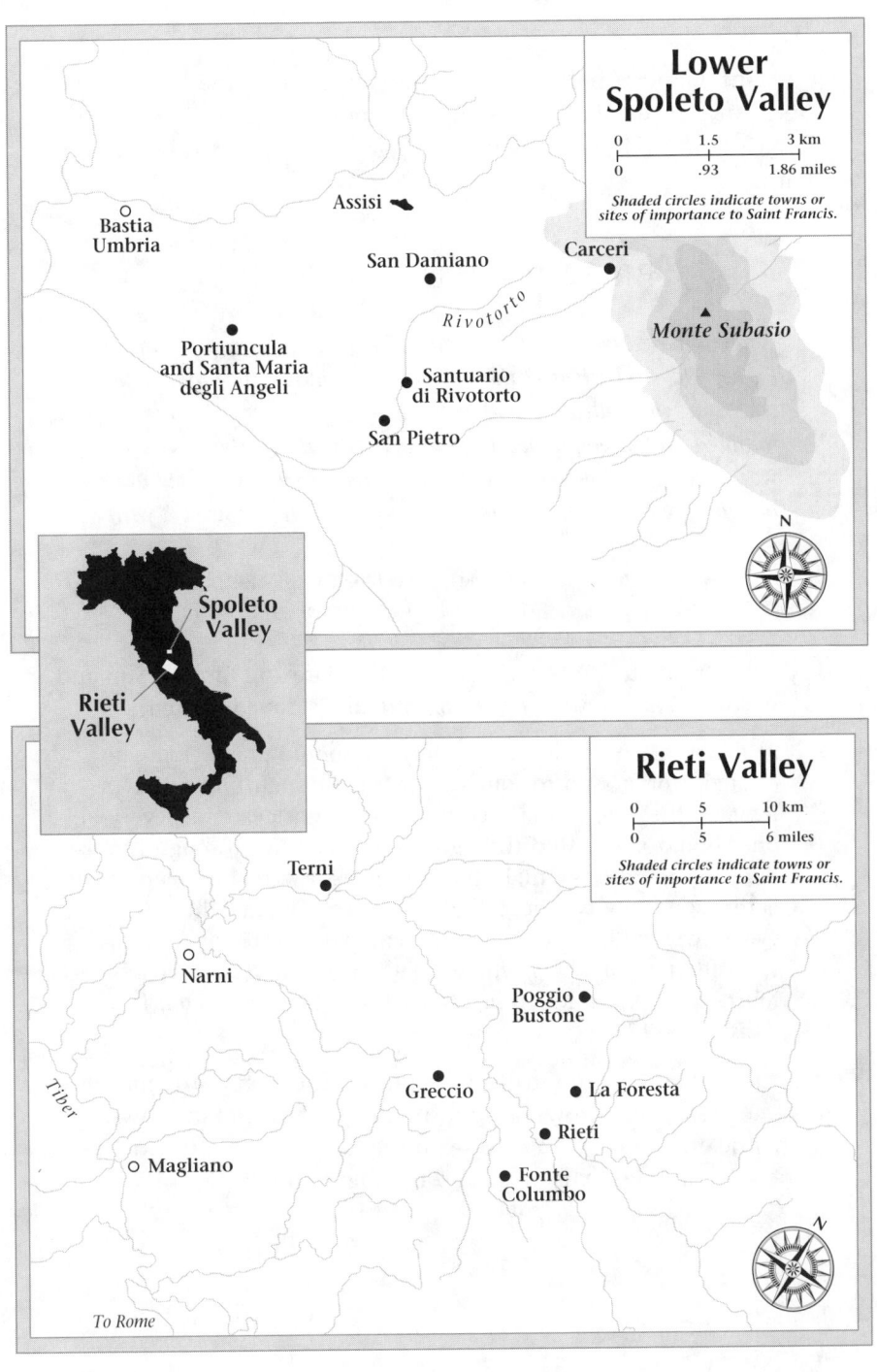

Lower Spoleto Valley

| 0 | 1.5 | 3 km |
| 0 | .93 | 1.86 miles |

Shaded circles indicate towns or sites of importance to Saint Francis.

Bastia
Umbria

Assisi

San Damiano

Carceri

Rivotorto

Monte Subasio

Portiuncula
and Santa Maria
degli Angeli

Santuario
di Rivotorto

San Pietro

N

Spoleto
Valley

Rieti
Valley

Rieti Valley

| 0 | 5 | 10 km |
| 0 | 5 | 6 miles |

Shaded circles indicate towns or sites of importance to Saint Francis.

Terni

Narni

Poggio
Bustone

Tiber

Greccio

La Foresta

Rieti

Magliano

Fonte
Columbo

N

To Rome

Saint Francis, help me to better distinguish the people and things in my life that are helpful in my quest for a deeper unity with God, from those people and things that will only distract from that goal.

BROTHERS SUN AND FIRE

God composed the world from all its elements for the glory of his name. He strengthened the earth with winds, illuminated her with stars and filled her with creatures of every kind. He thus surrounded and strengthened human beings with all there is in the world, giving them great power. All of creation was destined to be a helpmate for them, for humans can neither live or survive without the elements.

—HILDEGARD OF BINGEN, IN RENATE CRAINE,
HILDEGARD, PROPHET OF THE COSMIC CHRIST

Let's turn from burning brothers to Brother Fire and Brother Sun and a story from *The Mirror of Perfection* of Francis' love for them:

At dawn, when the sun rises, everyone should praise God who created Brother Sun for our service, for through him our eyes light up the day; in the evening, when night descends, everyone should praise God through Brother Fire, for through him our eyes light up the night. We are all, as it were, blind, and it is through these two brothers that the Lord gives lights to our eyes. We should praise the Lord, then, in a special way for creatures and for the others, who serve us day by day. (Translated by Murray Bodo, O.F.M., from *Through the Year With Francis of Assisi*, page 172)

The closer Francis came to God in prayer, the deeper his humility became. Humility grows as our proximity to God narrows. An authentic encounter with God—coming face-to-face with God, as it were—can only leave us meek and humble of heart.

A LITTLE DOG

Love is swift, sincere, pious, pleasant, generous, strong, patient, faithful, prudent, long-suffering, manly, and never seeking her own; for wheresoever a man seeketh his own, there he falleth from love.

—THOMAS À KEMPIS, *THE IMITATION OF CHRIST*

The following comes from *The Mirror of Perfection* and illustrates the depths of Francis' humility, which was so profound he even gave up the privilege of choosing his own companion to travel with him.

> On another occasion he gave up all his companions to his Vicar, saying, "I do not wish to appear alone in the privilege of having an especial companion of my own. Let the friars accompany me from place to place as the Lord shall move them." And he added, "Recently I saw a blind man who had only a little dog to guide him on his way, and I do not want to seem better than he."
>
> For it was always his glory to renounce every trace of privilege and ostentation so that the virtue of Christ might dwell in him. (*Omnibus*, page 1166)

SISTER LARK

Be moderate in all things except the love of God.

—SAINT FRANCIS DE SALES

Here is one more story from *The Mirror of Perfection*, which reflects the natural wonder and childlike charm which exuded from Francis and his early companions:

> Sister Lark has a hood like a religious and is a humble bird who gladly goes in search of any little grain, and even if she finds something in the garbage, she picks it out and eats it. In flight she sweetly praises God like good religious who, detached from worldly things, turn ever toward heaven and who long only to praise God. The lark's garb, her plumage, is the color of earth. Thus she offers religious an example of how not to wear elegant, flashy clothes, but moderately priced things, of the color of earth, the humblest of elements. (Translated by Murray Bodo, O.F.M., from *Through the Year With Francis of Assisi*, page 174)

A Wild Flower

Each moment of our lives is like a grain of sand lying just alongside the ocean of mystery.

> —*KARL RAHNER,* LITURGY OF THE WORLD

*The way Saint Francis was able to view the ordinary things in life in an
extraordinary way reminds me of William Blake's poetic insight:*

> To see a world in a grain of sand
> And a heaven in a wild flower,
> Hold infinity in the palm of your hand
> And eternity in an hour. ("Auguries of Innocence")

*There was a holy fire that burned within Francis that transformed every
encounter he had into a living experience of spirit and life. Francis so
cleansed the window of his own perception that everything he saw
appeared as it truly is—the gift of the infinite God. He saw things in their
native purity. The windows of our perceptions are dirtied by self-interest.
I'm guilty of not seeing things as they are, but how they affect me.
Mystics like Francis, schooled in self-simplification, humility, contemplation and detachment, are able to brush aside all obstacles blocking
their ability to see the hidden Reality of the Invisible in all things visible.
For them, there is no separation betweeen heaven and earth, between the
sacred and the profane, and the whole of creation is holy and open to
God.*

PILGRIMAGE DIARY 31

Thoughts Scribbled While Walking

*eek, knock, ask, plead.
   In solitude, seek God, not consolation or ecstasy.
   I was becoming smug about my spiritual progress when I was
      knocked off my high horse by this thought: I still harbor
      aspirations beyond Christ.
   Prayer is about loving and being loved.
   The sacred dwells in the secular.
   Simplicity is in harmony with contemplation.*

*Spiritual life involves struggle and effort. Anyone who wants to
love distrusts whatever is easy.*
Adoration is not optional.
Prayer deepens with purification of faults.
You grow into what you dwell on.
*Test your love for God; love wants more than anything else to be
in the presence of the beloved.*

Lovers of the Cross

*There seem to be two sides to Francis: the light side and the dark side.
The light side preaches to birds; the dark side engages in unthinkable acts
of penance and mortification. We like the "light" Francis, the poet who
sings praises to God. Elizabeth Goudge in* My God and My All *suggests
we need to look carefully at the dark side, too.*

Pope Pius XI wrote of Francis, "The herald of the Great King did
not come to make men doting lovers of flowers, birds, lambs,
fishes or hares; he came to fashion them after the Gospel pattern, and to make them lovers of the cross." This is a warning
most of us need, so prone are we to think of Francis only as the
happy troubadour singing God's praises over the hills and
through the valleys, as the storyteller who could keep crowds
rocking with laughter at his jokes and as a man who so loved
animals, birds and flowers, that he would preach to them and
talk to them as though they were his human friends. We dwell
on this sunny side because it seems to us easy and happy and
turn aside from the other because it is grim and difficult. We
would rather not think of the penitent who scourged himself
until blood ran down, of the man who was not ashamed to go
weeping through the world for the passion of Christ, of the fasting and the night-long vigils in darkness and cold. We would
like to think of poverty in terms of spiritual freedom and sunny
days in the woods, not in terms of hunger, lice-infested rags,
pouring rain, lepers, disease and death. The dark side of the picture presents a challenge it is not easy to meet and we are not
altogether sure that we wish to be made into lovers of the cross.

*To follow Francis, we need to be lovers of the cross. The way of the cross
is the way Francis traveled. For him, there was no other way.*

PILGRIMAGE DIARY 32

Barring the Crucifix

Followers of Jesus are called to believe that nonviolence, poverty, openness and forgiveness are the surest way for them and
their communities to receive life from God and to give life,
peace and unity to the world. It is on our weakness that the
power of God is manifested through the Paraclete, the Holy
Spirit.

—*JEAN VANIER*, COMMUNITY AND GROWTH

A *below-the-fold headline on page one of the August 19, 1997,
edition of the* International Herald Tribune *read: "Crusade
Against the Crucifix: Does Bavaria Have a Prayer in Court?" Last year
when an electrician in the tidy Bavarian town of Bruckmuehl, a
serene pastoral community twenty-five miles southeast of Munich,
took his six-year-old daughter to school on her first day of class at a
local public school, he had no idea his life was about to be turned
into a nightmare. His troubles began when he told school officials he
did not want his child to study in the shadow of the crucifix and
asked to have it removed from the wall of her classroom.*

*German law gave him the right to ask. Two years ago, Germany's
Supreme Court struck down a Bavarian law requiring the display of
crucifixes in classrooms because it violated a constitutional
requirement of "religious neutrality" in public institutions. That ruling
was the result of a ten-year crusade by a Bavarian artist who did not
want to send his three children to schools in which they would be
horrified by what he called the "image of a bleeding, half-naked
male corpse" that depicted Jesus Christ dying on the cross.*

*But the people of Bavaria protested and ignored the ruling. The
crucifixes remained on the walls. The Bavarian government, which
represents Germany's second most populous state, crafted new laws
to circumvent the court's ruling. It amended the law to allow the
removal of a crucifix from a classroom or public building if
somebody who objects gives sufficiently valid reasons for taking it
down.*

*Enter the electrician who said that a religious symbol has no
place in a classroom, "especially if it represents a church that is anti-
democratic in nature and practices sex discrimination by refusing*

*equal rights to women, such as the chance to become priests." He
also noted what he believed to be the Catholic hierarchy's opposition
to science. His appeal was rejected by the school on the grounds it
was "too polemic and not sufficiently personal." The electrician
responded by saying, "How can any school or court decide that
reasons must be personal and not political? It's like saying it is only
acceptable to object to Hitler because of his ugly mustache and not
because he persecuted Jews and other minorities." He decided to
fight back by challenging the ruling in court.*

And how did the good people of Bruckmuehl respond?

*With hatred and vindictiveness and trying to turn the electrician's
life into a living hell. There was a stream of anonymous death
threats, and phone calls warning that his daughter would be
kidnapped. Motorists cruising down his street tossed burning
packages onto his lawn. And a neighbor planted a ten-foot-tall
crucifix in front of his house—and then obtained a court order
prohibiting the electrician from attempting to force him to remove it.*

*The paper reported that more than seven million foreigners now
live in Germany. They include Turkish and Iranian Muslims, Russian
Jews and Asian Buddhists. In addition, many secular Germans are
questioning why organized religion should play so central a role in
their political culture.*

*I wasn't sure how to respond to the article. As a former atheist, I
understand the electrician's concern. As the author of a book that
took a critical look at an evangelical Christian TV ministry, I know
firsthand about receiving threats from people who took exception to
what I had to say. I also strongly decry the hostile way in which the
Catholic citizenry attacked the electrician for exercising his
constitutional right to object to religious imagery.*

*Last night I was walking along the Via del Corso. The wide
street, lined with stores peddling everything from videos and perfume
to jewelry and clothing, was crowded with shoppers. I entered the
Church of San Giacomo. A priest was saying Mass for a few
worshipers. A side chapel contained a large crucifix. I knelt down in
front of the bleeding, half-naked Jesus...and prayed. I'm not sure how
long I knelt there, but my silent meditation moved me to tears.*

*Twelve hours later, I'm reading this article and find myself siding
with the electrician.*

Perhaps if the cross were more than a symbol, but also a lived reality in the lives of Christians, then people like the electrician wouldn't object to the image that inspires noble behavior.

Francis of Assisi was an evangelist. He burned with the desire to spread the gospel, to save souls. That same desire doesn't consume me, perhaps because I'm sensitive to the delicate balance of life in a multicultural society. We need to respect the beliefs of others. Yet, how do we do that while trying to convert them to our beliefs?

Francis and his brothers used to enter a village and knock on doors to announce the Good News of salvation. Nothing gets me angrier than when Jehovah's Witnesses knock on my door trying to sell me their truth...I find it presumptuous and obnoxious.

I really have no answer to offer.

Francis wisely said, in effect, that our lives are our best sermons. Making death threats is a lousy sermon.

God grant the electrician peace.

The Liturgy of the Hours

My song is of mercy and justice;
I sing to you, O Lord.
I will walk in the way of perfec-
tion.
O when, Lord, will you come?

I will walk with blameless heart
within my house;
I will not set before my eyes
whatever is base.
(Psalm 100 [101]:1-3a)

HOLY WATER

The following story comes from a sermon preached by Saint Bonaventure in Paris on October 4, 1262.

> I want to tell you something that happened in the Province of Reiti.... There was a fatal epidemic which attacked the animals of the region so that they could not take food. Suddenly, all the animals were dying and the people did not know what to do to save them. One of the local people went to see a devout man and told him how the animals were dying and asked his advice. The devout man advised him to get some water in which St. Francis had washed his hands and feet, sprinkle it all over the animals and they would be cured. He did this and the animals came running for their food. I was told this by someone who saw it happen. (From *The Disciple and the Master*)

PREACHING TO THE SULTAN IN EGYPT

The ardent desire of laying down his life for Christ, continually urged Francis to the commencement of his Eastern mission, there to scatter unsparingly the seed of his eternal truth, and irrigate with his blood, if necessary, that once fertile soil of Christianity.
—EMILIUS CHAVIN DE MALAN, *THE LIFE OF ST. FRANCIS OF ASSISIUM*

In the year 1217, Francis, despite his own personal failures at missionary work, devised a plan to send the friars out on various missionary enterprises. He dispatched friars in pairs to foreign lands, instructing them to walk humbly and prayerfully. To show that he was willing to share in the hard work and endure the shame and hunger that came with preaching abroad, Francis elected to go to France. However, Cardinal Ugolino convinced Francis to stay in Italy. The friars who traveled to France and Spain encountered no unusual difficulties, because they were led by men familiar with the customs and language of those lands. The friars who were sent to Germany and Hungary encountered unbearable difficulties. They were beaten and endured the harshest of humiliations; disheartened, the friars eventually returned to Italy.

By 1219, during the fifth crusade, Francis was determined to set out on a mission. This time, the cardinal did not try to stop him. The

Franciscan attempt at confronting Islam had met with great resistance. Friars in Tunis and Morocco were beheaded, some after having first been rolled in broken glass. (Down through the centuries, religious persecution, no matter what flavor, always produced the ugliest atrocities of which humanity has been capable.) When Francis left for Egypt, it seems plausible to think that he himself fully expected his journey to end in martyrdom. Perhaps he even hoped for such an ending to his life. In an article entitled "St. Francis and Islam," published in 1981 in *Concilium* magazine (number 149), Francis de Beer writes: "Francis' only reason for setting foot on the soil of Islam was his desire to offer his life as a holocaust for his Moslem brothers." Before leaving, he appointed two vicars to govern the order in his absence.

In *Exile and Tenderness*, Eloi LeClerc, O.F.M., puts these words into Francis' mouth:

> "Beloved brothers, before I go overseas to the Saracens in compliance with God's inspiration, I wish to ask once more, and for the last time, what the Lord expects from us above all, so that no question may ever be raised among you concerning the path you are to follow. O my brothers and my sons forever blessed, listen to me, listen to your father's voice. When at the beginning the Lord gave me brothers, nobody showed me what I should do. I consulted the Gospel with Brother Bernard. And the Lord himself revealed to me that we should live according to the norm of the holy Gospel. That is why I, Brother Francis, your worthless little poor man, wished and still wish to follow the example of the most high Son of God by serving the Lord in humility and poverty. You likewise, my sons, who have received the name of Friars Minor, walk and abide in that way. We are small and poor, with no goods, no power, nothing assured in this world, but we are heirs to the Kingdom of Heaven.
>
> "As the Lord sent his apostles through the world, so do I likewise send you today, and I give the same instructions: Do not provide gold or silver. You have received without payment, give without payment. And for the journey, take neither wallet, nor staff, nor shoes, nor any kind of provisions, for the laborer has a right to his maintenance. And to whatever house you enter, say as you cross the threshold, 'Peace be to this house.'
>
> "Listen with attention, brothers! The Lord's first requirement is that his messengers be poor men and men of peace." (pages 40-42)

When Francis announced his plans to go to Egypt, so many friars volunteered to go with him that they all could not fit on the ship. Francis had to select which friars would be permitted to accompany him. Not wanting to show favoritism or to disappoint those not chosen, Francis said he would leave the selection in the hands of God. How would God choose? In a method that was very typical of Francis. Francis called on a small boy to pick eleven friars out of all those assembled at the port. Randomly, the little boy touched one friar after another, saying, "This one." And so in June of 1219, the twelve men set sail from Ancona.

It was a long and grueling trip. After a brief stop at Cyprus, the ship reached the seaport city of Damietta in the Nile delta of northern Egypt near the end of July. Damietta, a city of eighty thousand, was well fortified, defended by a triple ring of walls with many high towers. The city was under siege by the crusaders, who only a few days earlier had won an important victory. But the last day of July, the attack on Damietta was beaten back, and in the process the Christian army suffered considerable losses.

Horrified by the scandalous and excessively cruel behavior of the crusaders that he had witnessed—a virtual orgy of slaughter and debauchery—Francis was filled with a deep sorrow and became depressed. From a distance, Francis the idealist believed the crusades were a sacred venture; up close, Francis the humanist viewed the crusades as a sacrilegious act.

Perhaps Francis saw how the crusades violated the ideals of the gospel. Those ideals had been honored by the early Church, which instructed the people not to return evil for evil; instead, the Church promoted a spirit of reconciliation. God's people, according to the early Church, had to be a people of forgiveness. Violence was never advocated. By the thirteenth century war and violence had become a way of life. Crusaders ruthlessly slaughtered Moslems, Jews, pagans and even Christians whom the pope declared to be enemies of the faith. The crusades were considered to be a holy war and killing Saracens was thought to be a religious act. Worse, the mass slaughter was blessed by the Church as fulfilling God's purposes on earth...*Deus vult* (God wills it) was the battle cry of the crusaders. Killing was justified and sanctioned, and the victims were looked at as less than human. Saint Bernard wrote, "To kill a Muslim is not homicide." The popes called for the crusades to eliminate rather than to convert the Saracens. Moreover, the crusades exploited the penitential system to raise funds to exterminate unbelievers.

Christianity had taken on a warlike spirit, and it used an iron sword instead of the sword of the spirit.

Domine Deus, miserere nobis...Lord our God, have mercy on us.

In his biography of the saint, Morris Bishop writes:

> Francis' ideal was fundamentally at odds with that of the crusaders. They wanted to cleanse the land of its pollution by eliminating the polluters [i.e., Arab Muslims]; the less idealistic simply coveted land, money, promotion, jobs. Francis' ideal was to purify the world by correcting its errors, by the aid of God's grace, which would manifest itself in support of His agent's design. It was all so obvious! God was simply waiting for Francis to act. (page 121)

The crusaders planned on storming the city again in late August. Francis believed God was telling him the forces of the cross would suffer a great defeat. Risking ridicule, Francis warned the crusaders, even taking his plea directly to the Christian commander, Cardinal Pelagius, but his warning fell on deaf ears. On August 29 the crusaders launched an offensive that was handily turned back. Six thousand crusaders were killed or captured.

It was time for Francis to act, to do what he came to do: preach to the Sultan Malek el Kamil. It was a foolhardy mission, especially in light of the fact that the Sultan had offered a gold ducat for every Christian head presented to him. Accompanied only by Brother Illuminato, Francis fearlessly marched toward the enemy line, where he was immediately seized by soldiers armed with curved swords known as scimitars. Francis repeatedly shouted the sultan's name. The soldiers believed he must have been an emissary sent to seek a peace treaty and therefore elected not to lop the saint's head off right there on the spot and instead beat and bound Francis before escorting him to the sultan's palace.

Exactly what transpired during the meeting is not clear. Hard facts are clearly outnumbered by tall tales. We do know that the sultan, who was a nephew of Saladin, was a cultured and courteous man with a skeptical mind who was not averse to debating the merits of the gospel and the Koran as an intellectual exercise. Perhaps the sultan consented to see Francis merely to amuse himself. The sultan asked Francis for a letter of accreditation, assuming his visit was connected with the crusades and was sponsored by some diplomatic authority. Francis said he was sent by God, not man, to announce the Good News and that his visit had nothing to do with the crusades. Francis then told the sultan about Christ the savior and the Trinity, and his fervor and boldness impressed the sultan. It seems safe to conclude he was charmed and intrigued by Francis, for Francis did leave the palace with his head still attached.

An Authentic Revolutionary

Self-imposed poverty, Francis would discover, prevents violence. It allowed him to work freely in the middle of danger because he had nothing to defend. My hunch is that the sultan saw Francis as a self-emptied man who claimed nothing, not even his very life, as his possession. Francis was an authentic revolutionary because his total detachment permitted him the freedom not to compromise his beliefs in order to protect himself or his property.

TRIAL BY FIRE

One story which seems to have garnered historical acceptance claims that the sultan tried to trick Francis by spreading before him a carpet with crisscrosses woven into the design. The sultan said if Francis walked on the crosses he would accuse the Christian of insulting his own God; and if Francis refused to walk on the carpet he would accuse Francis of insulting him. Francis' response to the challenge displayed the same degree of ingenuity as the challenge itself. Francis said the crosses on which he walked belonged to the thieves between whom Christ had been crucified and so he was not ashamed to tread on them.

Giotto (the artist whose life and work will be explored in Part Four) depicts in the upper Basilica in Assisi a scene whose historicity has never been fully proven. The scene shows Francis and the priests of the sultan standing beside a fire. Francis, in an effort to prove the superiority of his faith, proposed a trial by fire in which he offered to throw himself into flames on condition that a Muhammedan priest do so also. Francis told the sultan that he should believe in the faith of whomever emerges from the fire unharmed. The sultan, being a wise man and noticing that his priests did not like Francis' proposal, declined the offer. Francis then said he would still throw himself into the fire, if the sultan would only pledge to accept Christ if he was not consumed by the flames. The sultan was touched that a man who did not even know him would be willing to throw himself into a fire for the sake of the sultan's own soul and salvation. He offered Francis gifts of gold and silver. Of course, Francis, concerned only with souls, refused. The sultan was even further impressed with the saint and marveled at his contempt for worldly goods.

The sultan asked the religious leaders of the palace what he should do with Francis. Behead him, was their response, because he had preached against the law of Muhammed. The sultan told Francis that he would not behead him because he couldn't put to death someone who was willing to give his life for another's salvation. The sultan ordered that Francis be set free and further decreed that he and his companion be permitted to travel without restriction through the Holy Land.

In *God's Fool*, Julien Green offers the following observation: "There seems to be no doubt that Malik al-Kamil was unforgettably impressed by Francis, and that Francis himself discovered a new humanity in the person of his host. The notion that he had of Islam had to be modified: The essence of faith—belief in God—could be found outside of Christianity, and that belief deserved respect. This broad view of the problem of religion had enormous, almost revolutionary, force. The only way to win over souls is by gentleness and honest example" (page 205).

It should be noted that Saint Bonaventure in his *Major Life* of Francis does not even mention the "trial by fire" episode. However, a horn given to Francis by the sultan, which the saint eventually accepted at the sultan's insistence, is kept on display in the Sacro Convento di San Francesco in Assisi. According to a passage in *The Little Flowers*, the sultan secretly converted to Christianity, a claim which has no historic foundation, but is simply a legendary embellishment that has been believed by some people for centuries.

I believe that Francis as a little brother desired first to befriend (not convert) the sultan, and that is the real reason why the saint left the palace with his head still attached.

Francis, the Inventor

A few years after meeting the sultan, when Francis was writing a new Rule, he included a chapter aimed at those friars who would be going among the Saracens and other nonbelievers. He told the brothers to live among the people and to submit to them, respecting their beliefs, religion and culture, and only preaching when circumstances permitted. In other words, Francis did not want the brothers to live as strangers among the people, holed up in their own little world. He instructed them to be prudent and as simple as doves, and not put on an air of superiority, and warned them not to become engaged in arguments or disputes, but instead be peacemakers.

Francis wanted his brothers to simply live spiritually among the people, bringing peace to everyone they met. It was fine to preach the gospel, but it was wrong to attack the belief and faith of those who follow Muhammed. Calling the prophet a traitor and liar was not an effective way to approach Muslims. Francis had developed a sensitivity for the good that God worked in the people of other faiths, and sought to open up a dialogue with them. Francis wanted to establish equality and peace among people of differing faiths. This was a far cry from the goals of the crusades, which wanted only to root out the infidels, crushing them into submission. Francis' approach to dealing with Muslims was radically new, and clearly demonstrates that he was a liberating visionary.

Christians in the early thirteenth century viewed the prophet Muhammed as a devil, and those who followed him as heretics living outside God's order of salvation. Francis saw them far differently. For him, Muslims were people of faith among whom God was present through grace. He was impressed by their prayerfulness, answering to the call of the muezzin five times a day. His approach to Muslims was simple: Accept the "other" as brother. (Actually, that approach was not so simple when you consider that Christians of that time hated Muslims.) Francis proposed that his friars be nothing more than a simple, peaceful presence among the Muslims, a gentle witness to the depth of the Christian life, and not to engage them in useless polemics or try to refute their religious convictions. He told the friars to preach only "when they see that it pleases the Lord"; but to do so in a manner that allowed reverence and respect for the Saracens to vibrate through their words. This truly was a revolutionary approach. Many in the Church went among the "infidels" with power and a sword. Francis went among the people in humility and with a spirit of nonviolence and peace. Many in the Church sought destruction; Francis sought fellowship.

Francis has much to say today to those who are interested in interreligious dialogue...after all, he invented it.

The Crib and the Cross

Francis failed in his attempts to get the crusaders to scale the heights of the true Christian ideal; he wasn't even able to lift them out of their debauchery. He also failed in his preaching of the gospel of Christ to the sultan. Surely these setbacks must have saddened the saint.

The sultan allowed him to travel to the Holy Land. There is no record of what happened there, but we can only imagine what it was like for Francis to visit the sacred sites of the life of Christ. Oh, how it must have nourished his soul! Father Augustine, O.F.M. Cap., writes, "With what adoring reverence must he have knelt upon the hill of Calvary, and stood upon the ground where the shepherds had listened to the angels sing" (Some Lives of the Seraphic Saint, *page 57).*

I bet Francis heard angels sing, also. Their song never reaches my secularized ears. I can only imagine the sweetness of the sound.

Imagine Francis entering the Church of the Nativity and kneeling where his savior was born. Francis' vivid imagination must have transported him back twelve hundred years to the very spot where "the Word was made flesh." Meditating on the mystery of the Infant God must have enraptured his soul, must have magnified his understanding of the depths of the Gospel according to Saint John, which exquisitely proclaims: "God so loved the world that he gave his only Son."

Francis loved Christmas. "He called it," says Thomas of Celano, "the Feast of Feasts, because on that day the Most High Son of God became a poor little child." Traveling to the land of the crib and the cross must have wiped Francis' sadness away and filled him with holy joy.

Often in my life, I have known the pain of sadness and failure. Not knowing what to do with the pain, I simply carried it with me for far longer than I needed. When life knocked Francis down, when he failed to accomplish what he thought God wanted him to do, he knew how to reach out to God for a helping hand, a hand which never failed to lift him back up.

Francis knew how to look to the crib and the cross for all that he needed, and he experienced both mysteries every day at the altar.

A TRUE BROTHERHOOD

Years ago, long after I had lost my faith, I read about the crusades in detail for the first time. I was horrified by the brutality employed by the Church and sickened by the political corruption that had infected the Church. My reading helped reinforce my belief that God did not exist. Now, rather than focus on the abuses of the past, I prefer to follow Vatican II's wise counsel which is found in "Declaration on the Relation of the Church to Non-Christian Religions":

> The Church has also a high regard for the Muslims.... Over the centuries many quarrels and dissensions have arisen between Christians and Muslims. The sacred Council now pleads with all to forget the past, and urges that a sincere effort be made to achieve mutual understanding.... (*Vatican Council II: The Conciliar and Post Conciliar Documents*, pages 739, 740)

It should be noted that Saint Francis' spirituality grew out of the tumultuous times in which he lived; it was an age of tremendous social change and horrific violence. In his thought-provoking book, *Francis of Assisi: Return to the Gospel*, Eloi Leclerc, O.F.M., writes:

> We need to outgrow the over-simplified idea that Francis found his vocation through a simple reading of the Gospel, independently of the current circumstances. He read it as a man who felt within himself the seething passions of his epoch, and who was carried along by the tidal wave of a human movement welling up from the depths of society. Francis read the Gospel with new eyes, in the light of the major aspirations of his time. In return, this reading of the Gospel made it possible for him to liberate those aspirations from their limitations, and to make them blossom forth into a more complete vision of man and his destiny.
>
> What gives to the Franciscan Gospel experience its true dimension and its seductive power is precisely this combination of the Gospel with the deepest aspirations of man, and the encounter between the message preached by Jesus and the creative forces of history. Not that Francis ever sought, in the least, to adapt the Gospel to his times. The fact is at once simpler and far deeper. The Gospel became life and light in this man because in him it came into contact with all the vital forces he bore within himself, and which were those of his times. It was in Francis's very heart and in a living manner that this mar-

velous encounter took place.

Paul Sabatier was right when he wrote: "By an ineffable mystery, he (Francis) felt himself to be the man of his century, the man in whose bosom were pent up the efforts, the desires, and the longings of peoples; with him, in him, humanity yearned to renew itself and, to speak as the Gospel speaks, to be born again.... Yes, Saint Francis was aware of the incessant labor of transformation taking place in the depths of humanity, struggling toward its divine destiny" (*Life of St. Francis of Assisi*, page 379).

Because he himself assumed his full share in this labor of transformation, along with the humblest and poorest of his fellow men, Francis discovered an aspect of God very different from that current among the adherents of ecclesiastical principalities and holy wars. For him, God ceased to be the external, dominating, and Transcendent One, the Lord in a more-or-less feudal dress. To him, God appeared as mysteriously present in our history, bereft of all trappings of power, bound instead to what was weakest and most despised in man's world. Francis rediscovered God's humbleness, God's humanity. Not merely as an object of devotion, but as a new principle on which to reconstruct society. He understood that if one acknowledges the God of the Gospel, then one can no longer be satisfied with just any form of social organization. This acknowledgment is bound to bring about a transformation in human relationships; it involves seeking and bringing into being true brotherhood, a brotherhood that excludes nobody. The God of the Gospel lets himself be seen through other men, where there are no more lords and no more subjects, where no one is kept out. The dawn of true brotherhood is the light in which God is truly found. (pages viii-ix)

The ideal of a true community of all people, excluding no one, is still, eight centuries later, a long, long way from being realized. The blueprint which Francis discovered in his time in the gospel is there for us to discover.

PILGRIMAGE DIARY 33

This Old Man

*B*efore the pope's most recent visit to Paris, the French seemed bored by the prospects of the visit. Even Church officials in Paris feared the turnout for the pope would be small, perhaps even smaller than the huge crowds who were drawn to a gay pride parade in early summer. The most optimistic expectation was that three hundred thousand young people would sacrifice their vacations and endure being scorched by the August heat.

To everyone's surprise a half million young people showed up for the first major event of the pope's four-day visit when he spoke in the vast park at the base of the Eiffel Tower. Saturday night there was a vigil service held on a racetrack on the outskirts of Paris and 750,000 young people from 160 nations attended. During the service, the weak and frail-looking pope baptized several young people. Sunday Mass was celebrated under a blazing sun and drew over a million people—the largest crowd ever assembled in Paris.

The public's boredom quickly turned to curiosity. People wondered why the youth were flocking to hear a pope whose views on moral questions were seen as outdated at best. Everyone was talking about it. Young people were interviewed by the media. Many of them said they were skeptical about the pope's hard-line stance on birth control, abortion, women's ordination and a litany of other issues. Yet they came because they wanted to see and hear the pope.

They came because they saw the pope as a man of principle, a man of integrity and courage, a man of transparent faith and conviction. A newspaper columnist wrote, "Thus they are drawn to this old man who really does believe in God, divine revelation, sacrifice of self, and an objective morality."

They did not come out of faith; they came in search of faith.

They came to see this old man, this old man of faith. And he gave them new insights into an ancient truth.

A young person at the closing liturgy held up a sign for the pope to read. It read: "You are our youth."

THIS UNTUTORED MAN

Humble self-knowledge is a surer way to God than searching the depths of learning.

—THOMAS À KEMPIS

A few years before his death, Francis was preaching in Bologna, and among the crowd gathered to hear him was a man named Thomas, an archdeacon from Spoleto. Later, Thomas recorded his impression of Francis and his sermon.

> In that year (1222), I was residing in the Stadium of Bologna; on the feast of the Assumption, I saw Francis preach in the public square in front of the public palace. Almost the entire city had assembled there. The theme of the sermon was: "Angels, men, and demons." He spoke so well and with such sterling clarity on these three classes of spiritual and rational beings that the way in which this untutored man developed his subject aroused even among the scholars in the audience an admiration that knew no bounds. Yet, his discourses did not belong to the great genre of sacred eloquence: rather they were harangues. In reality, throughout his discourse he spoke of the duty of putting an end to hatred and arranging a new treaty of peace.
>
> He was wearing a ragged habit; his whole person seemed insignificant; he did not have an attractive face. But God conferred so much power on his words that they brought back peace in many a Seignorial family torn apart until then by old, cruel, and furious hatreds even to the point of assassinations. The people showed so much respect as they did devotion; men and women flocked to him; it was a question of who would at least touch the fringe of his clothing or who would tear off a piece of his poor habit. (*Omnibus*, pages 1601-1602)

There is a lot of information packed into those two paragraphs. I was struck by the physical description of Francis. He looked insignificant. His face was far from attractive. He wore a ragged habit. Slight, ugly, poorly dressed...sounds as if poor Francis didn't have much going for him. Yet he drew a large crowd and many, including the educated, were moved by his words...in fact, they were so moved, they were compelled to change their behavior. Why? It wasn't his eloquence. In fact, his address was peppered with caustic comments that scorned the failures of the academic community to right soci-

ety's wrongs. Yet, his words were warmly received even by the educated.

When Francis spoke, people listened, because he spoke from
experience and he spoke straight from the heart. Contemplation
increased the intensity and simplicity of Francis' love for God and
all humanity and creation, and this intensity and simplicity infused
his preaching. Francis did not present theological formulas. He presented himself, a life changed by a deeply personal encounter with
the living God.

The people listening to Francis in the public square in Bologna
that day in 1222 heard someone real, someone fully alive.

PILGRIMAGE DIARY 34

Thoughts Scribbled While Walking

*O*nly God understands God.

It is easier to be self-centered than to be patient and loving.

*Holiness seems beyond our grasp, so we settle for
mediocrity.*

*I must empty my heart of all selfishness, before God can fill
it with love.*

*Prayer stimulates a mindfulness of God, which in turn
stimulates acts of love and mercy.*

*Love is service. It is the emptying of self. It is losing in
order to find.*

*Acknowledging my own weakness increases my ability to
be more merciful to others.*

*The Christian life can be reduced to this: Live the
beatitudes.*

*Every moment is a moment of grace—if my eyes and heart
are open.*

*Handle all life, and every moment of your life, with care,
respect and love.*

*In the state of emptiness, you are better able to encounter the
fullness of God.*

THE SECOND RULE OF SAINT FRANCIS

The imitation of Christ in accordance with the Gospel in poverty and humility is the ideal proposed by St. Francis in the Rule, an ideal which every brother attempts to practice in the spirit of fraternity and humility toward his brothers in vocation and towards all men; what is more, he tries to live in brotherhood with the whole of creation, since God is father of all.

—LAZARO IRIARTE, O.F.M., *FRANCISCAN HISTORY*

Francis spent a great deal of time and anguish on the writing and ratification of a new Rule for the Order. Every serious biography of the saint devotes a significant number of pages to the painful evolution of the new Rule. Volumes upon volumes have been written in which the differences between the Rule Francis wrote in 1220 to 1221 and the one that was eventually approved in 1223 are examined and debated. Moreover, as Cajetan Esser, O.F.M., points out, during the course of the Order's history, "radically divergent views have been advanced and vigorously debated regarding the original form of life of the Order and the original ideals of St. Francis." I was tempted to skip this part of Francis' story because the process of evolution from the early form of life to the final Rule was riddled with politics (often dirty politics) and smacked too much of "inside the [Franciscan] beltway" to be of any great interest to the vast heartland of lovers of Saint Francis. But, because of the Rule's overall importance, I've resisted the temptation and will present the story of the Rule in the broadest of strokes, touching lightly on the key twists in the story's plot.

All religious orders have rules which govern them, and they generally reflect the charism of their founder. In the beginning, the only rule the followers of Francis had—or needed—was the actual life of Francis. But as more and more men joined the little brothers, a need for a more definitive rule increased also. The first Rule, orally sanctioned by Pope Innocent III, consisted of little more than quotations from Scripture and a few basic regulations deemed necessary for living a holy life. The Rule did not survive in its primitive form, but it is clear that it was written in few words and in a simple manner. In his will (or Testament) written near the end of his life, Francis said the Lord revealed to him the way he and his followers should live and "I had it written in a few words and simply; and the Lord Pope confirmed it for me."

Over the course of the next dozen years, additions to the original Rule were made in response to the needs of the rapidly growing
Order. For instance, the establishment of fixed residences, the institution of chapter meetings, the formation of provinces and the
appointment of provincial ministers, and regulations governing the
reading of the Divine Office, the reception of the sacraments and
fasting were all codified. These and other changes eventually crys-
tallized by 1221 into a Rule that abounded in scriptural citations and
long pious admonitions. In a chapter meeting in 1220, Francis
announced his intentions of writing a new rule, and he held con-
ferences in which the ministers were given a chance to voice their
opinions. For instance, Francis wanted the new rule to say that the
Holy Spirit was the minister general of the Order, but the motion did
not pass. (This reminds me of a funny story. While I was at St.
Francis Inn working on my documentary, I heard that a police officer came to the Inn in response to a report that a guest was carrying
a concealed weapon. The officer knocked on the side door and was
greeted by Brother Xavier. The cop said, "Who is in charge here?"
Brother Xavier answered, "The Lord." The policeman, frustrated,
said, "If you don't mind, I'd like to speak to someone more earth-
bound.") The chapter agreed on the essential points of the new Rule
but left the form and the details to be worked out by Francis at his
leisure. The ministers of the Order, along with officials at the Papal
Curia, wanted a Rule that would present a clear pattern of thought
and contain very definite statutes and regulations.

The Rule of 1221 contained twenty-four chapters, many of
which consisted of a series of sweet yet urgent exhortations, such as
a call to love all and to have hatred only for their own vices and failings. The Rule lacked the precise articles of a code of law. In the Rule,
which was more pastoral than legislative, Francis sounds like a
father urging his children to live a life in perfect conformity with the
crucified life of Christ. Chapter 23 amounts to a long prayer of praise
and thanksgiving. The prayer mirrors Francis' enthusiasm and fervor
for the glory of God and Christ. The Rule reveals Francis' belief that
disciplinary rules are not needed if a friar has given his heart to God.
And Francis can't imagine a friar not doing so, and therefore he was
quite incapable of incorporating a rigorous code that accounted for
the faults and perversity of human weakness. Francis did not want a
detailed code aimed at enforcing his ideal on weaker people, for that
ideal is without meaning unless it is openly embraced with love and

enthusiasm. The Rule did not meet with universal acceptance. It had too many loopholes and it lacked precision; moreover, its organizational provisions were primitive.

The rift between the ministers and brothers who wanted a softening of the primitive rigor of the Rule and the partisans of Francis grew deeper. In his book, *The Franciscans*, Alexandre Masseron writes:

> The cleavage between the partisans of Francis and those of the Ministers cut deeper and deeper into the fraternity. Bitterness, anxiety, doubt, discouragement, even anger, replaced the ineffable joy of the pristine years in the soul of the Saint. Jeers, insults, hunger, cold, physical suffering—all these he had borne joyfully. But now his sons were in revolt against Heaven and against himself. The Order threatened to be unfaithful to its vocation.
>
> Words of indignation, cries of anguish, rose to his lips. "I love the brethren with all my heart," he cried out, "but if they followed my footsteps I should love them even more, I should not become a stranger in their midst. For there are Superiors who lead them into other ways, setting old examples before them and paying little heed to my counsels. In the end we shall see what they are doing." And again: "Who, then, are these men who have wrested out of my hands my Order, the Order of brothers?"
>
> Francis feeling himself a stranger in the midst of his own followers—what cry of distress could be more poignant? The heart from which this despairing appeal burst forth had never known or promulgated any laws but those of love. But this cry sums up the whole history of the struggle of Francis against the Ministers.

As the need for a clear, definitive rule, officially sanctioned by the Church, intensified, Francis began to work on a new rule, one which would take into consideration an Order consisting of men who had strong and frequently differing ideas on how they should live. Francis knew that not all the brothers had the same tender attachment to absolute poverty that he clung to so tightly. Seeking solitude, Francis went to the hermitage at Fonte Columbo with Brother Leo and Brother Bonizio, where after a period of fasting and prayer he wrote the new Rule, which was shorter and better organized than his Rule of 1221.

Francis returned to the Portiuncula and submitted his modified rule to Brother Elias, the new minister general. Elias, who had his own plans for the Order, was not pleased with the paucity of concessions Francis had incorporated into his new Rule and so he promptly "lost" the manuscript. Without uttering a word of reproach upon hearing that Elias had lost the Rule through carelessness, Francis, exercising great patience, returned to the serenity of Fonte Columbo and dictated the Rule to Brother Leo for a second time.

The new Rule was presented at the next chapter meeting, where anguished discussions between Francis and the assembled ministers resulted in a number of modifications. The Rule was endorsed by Pope Honorius III in a bull dated November 29, 1223. The Rule of 1223 (also known as *Regula Bullata*) has remained in effect ever since.

There is a considerable difference between the unapproved Rule of 1221 and the approved Rule of 1223. *The Marrow of the Gospel*, translated by Ignatius Brady, O.F.M., contains this observation regarding the style of the later Rule:

> The style of this Rule reveals that someone other than Francis had a hand in its composition. In place of the simple and sometimes awkward and even repetitious style of the saint, as we know from his writings, we meet throughout an unusual smoothness and even elegance of style.

Whose hand?

In *The Franciscan Adventure: A Study of the First Hundred Years of the Order of St. Francis of Assisi*, Vida Dutton Scudder writes that in the latter Rule...

> ...the hand of Cardinal Ugolino, Protector of the Order, and the hand of Brother Elias, can clearly be traced. Very astutely are the changes inserted. Even as it finally stood, the Rule retained enough of Francis' spirit and standards to prove a great embarrassment in later times. The ideal of Poverty is still implicit in it. It is a noble Rule, and has been to this day the guide of a noble Order. In it the genius of a great ecclesiastical organizer softens and modifies, but does not destroy, the genius of an uncompromising and intuitive saint. But that it expresses Francis' full mind few would dare to claim.
>
> The most careless reader perceives that between the two Rules much water has run under the bridge. Principles are hard-

ening into laws...authority and organization are tightening. Gone are the great quotations from Scriptures, which had been Francis's marching orders; gone was the command to take nothing on the way, replaced by the vague admonition to live as strangers and pilgrims—and one must respect the honesty of the candid implication that the plain commands of Christ are for no mortal to obey. The injunction to work is softened into a phrase which might mean something or nothing, and the significant allusion to menial service has been dropped. The paragraph now reads: "Let those brothers to whom the Lord has given the grace of working, labour faithfully and devoutly, so that in banishing idleness, the enemy of the soul, they do not extinguish the spirit of holy prayer and devotion, to which all temporal things must be subservient. They may, however, receive as the reward of their labour things needful for the body, for themselves or their brothers, with the exception of coins or money."...Again, the statement is omitted or twisted, through Ugolino's clever persuasions, in which the Rule of 1221 said clearly that obedience to the ministers is not obligatory should their injunctions contradict the rule of poverty, to which the first allegiance of the brothers is due. Ugolino received the saint's permission to reword his statement, and replaced it by an ambiguous injunction to the ministers to be charitable to rebels, whereby, as Jörgensen dryly says, those who, to the thought of Francis, had been approved warriors of the good cause, were changed into sinners under discipline, or patients needing treatment!

Francis could only acquiesce in these alterations, some of them necessarily, and all cleverly, planned in conformity with commonsense. To his "irreducible minimum" he clung firmly; the last Rule like the first prohibited ownership of houses or land or any traffic with money. A person true to it would have been a close friend of Madonna Poverta.

The Marrow of the Gospel offers this assessment of the differences in the content between the two Rules.

Considered in terms of content, the final Rule appears to be a brief extract of the Rule of 1221. Certain precepts are, of course, entirely new; but as a whole, the text is a repetition in very short form. For example, in the Rule of 1221, Francis laid great stress on the complete dedication of heart and mind needed for the observance of the Rule, and in consequence was often profuse in his warnings, exhortations and counsels. There is little of this left in the final Rule. When he does admonish and exhort, his words are much briefer and concise, almost as though he feared to repeat anything a second time. This may be the reason too why the text of Holy Scripture is so seldom quoted.

After the approval of the Rule of 1223 in Rome, Francis headed for Greccio. Abbe Leon le Monnier, in his *History of St. Francis of Assisi*, writes: "He liked the monastery [correct term: friary] in the town because he believed it richer in poverty than many others."

It was time for Francis to celebrate Christmas.

CHRISTMAS AT GRECCIO

God is born in the empty soul by discovering himself to her in a new guise without guise, without light in divine light.
—MEISTER ECKHART, "SERMONS AND COLLATIONS"

During the Christmas season in 1223, Francis journeyed to the little village of Greccio, where he spent time alone in a hermit's cave high on a mountain owned by a noble and pious friend. Below the cave was a level space. Francis asked his friend if he could use the space for a Midnight Mass, adding that the Mass would be preceded by a pageant he hoped would evoke a vivid memory of the child born in Bethlehem. With his friend's help, Francis mobilized the whole village and they set to work, clearing the site, cutting torches, making candles and building a manger scene. Reflecting on the fact that a manger is an animal feed-box, someone suggested that the birth of Jesus must have been witnessed by the oxen, horses and mules housed in the stable. Mention of animals caused Francis to recall a verse from the prophet Isaiah: "The ox knows its owner, and the donkey knows the manger of its master." And so, he procured an ox and an ass to be part of the scene. Because Matthew's Gospel mentions soothsayers were in attendance, and Luke's Gospel proclaims the presence of shepherds, Francis enlisted the help of some of the townfolk to represent them.

On Christmas Eve, great crowds of people came and the forest echoed with their voices raised in song. The night was lighted by hundreds of torches. Saint Francis standing before the crib, his heart overflowing with love and compassion, preached to the people about the birth of the poor King, whom he called the Babe of Bethlehem. Thomas of Celano, in his *First Life* of Saint Francis, said that Francis was "filled with a wonderful happiness." He also writes that the priest celebrating the Mass was filled with "such consolation as he had never before known." Thomas of Celano goes on to report:

> The saint of God was clothed with the vestments of the deacon...and he sang the holy Gospel in a sonorous voice. And his voice was a strong voice, a sweet voice, a clear voice....Then he preached to the people standing about, and he spoke charming words concerning the nativity of the poor king and the little town of Bethlehem....His mouth was filled more with sweet affection than sweet words....At length the solemn night celebration was brought to a close, and each one returned to his home with holy joy. (1 Cel. 86)

The moving ceremony, designed to rouse the hearts of those weak in faith, clearly demonstrated Francis' creative imagination, and helped to popularize the use of a crèche, or Christmas crib, in the Christian world. But of greater importance, Greccio tells us something about the depth and resiliency of Francis' faith. He came to Greccio in defeat. In an article published in 1981 in an issue of *Concilium* magazine that was devoted to Saint Francis (number 149), Bertrand Duclos, O.F.M., writes:

> The Rule he had composed, steeped in the gospel, had been "lost," to be replaced by a canonically "arranged" Rule. He understood that the game was humanly lost, just as the death of Christ seemed to corroborate the judgment of the law-makers. He knew that the road of the Incarnation is a road of contradictions, but that it was the only road. Hence the extraordinary episode at Greccio. He wanted "to represent to himself the sufferings and discomforts that Jesus endured from childhood to save us." All the Rules in the world with all their canonical astuteness can do nothing against the fact that God came, poor among the poor. That fact cannot be erased.

And Francis had no intention of erasing it; he desired only to magnify it.

Downwardly Mobile

The Gospels gave us the narrative, each adding different details of that night of nights. But it was Francis' devout spirit that gave birth to the picturesque iconography that has come to symbolize the birth of Christ. But over the centuries, the humble Franciscan crib has been supplanted by a comforting, greeting-card sweetness that conceals the true and revolutionary message of the Gospels.

On that first Christmas night, in silence and simplicity, God became downwardly mobile, embracing humanity and entering into its suffering with boundless love. The very substance of humanity was placed in an animal feed-box at birth. A king who would never claim any worldly authority was presented to the outcasts of society. Greeting cards erroneously depict the shepherds as gentle, pastoral men. But, in truth, shepherds were ostracized in that time and place because they were considered to be common thieves who stole animals and illegally allowed their flocks to graze on land they did not own. Shepherds were despised in Jewish circles yet they responded to the birth of Jesus with piety and adoration. The message was clear: God incarnate came to embrace, forgive and save all people.

From the very beginning, Jesus identified himself with the poor and the rejected, showing us that divine truth and power lie waiting where the world never thinks to look. Seeking the compassionate response of God is the only path to peace.

PILGRIMAGE DIARY 35

Christmas in July

*A*fter our visit to Greccio, as the large tour bus transported us back to the friary where we were staying, someone started singing Christmas carols. Within minutes, everyone on the bus had joined in the celebration of Christmas in July. It was so silly, yet so refreshingly honest to be singing hymns to the Christ child on a bus in the middle of the summer, because our hearts had been touched in Greccio, thanks to Francis' vivid, childlike imagination.

For Francis, every day was Christmas—and Good Friday and Easter, too. Most days, I forget those three important days in the life of Christ.

The Liturgy of the Hours

A reading from the Sermons of Saint Bernard *on the* Song of Songs.

Love is self-sufficient; it is pleasing to itself and on its own account. Love is its own payment, its own reward. Love needs no extrinsic cause or result. Love is the result of love, it is intrinsically valuable. I love because I love; I love in order to love. Love is a valuable thing only if it returns to its beginnings, consults its origin and flows back to its source. It must always draw from that endless stream. Love is the only one of the soul's motions, senses and affections by which the creature in his inadequate fashion may respond to his Creator and pay him back in kind. When God loves, he wishes only to be loved in return; assuredly he loves for no other purpose than to be loved. He knows that those who love him are happy in their love.

My Stuff

Saint Francis compels me to look at my relationship to all the material things in my life. I moved not too long ago, and as I packed I was dumbfounded by just how many possessions I had. And I enjoy most of the stuff I own. Some things, such as my books, may actually own me, because I can't imagine living without them. Francis makes me take a second look at the very concept of "ownership," suggesting that in truth everything belongs to God, who in his infinite love allows me to use them. Adopting that attitude prevents me from guarding what is "mine," and, instead, fills me with a sense of gratitude for the generosity of God who has loaned to me all the things I need. That shift in consciousness lifts a tremendous burden from my heart. Rather than clutching what I own, I enjoy what has been temporarily loaned to me. The books that surround me are God's, not mine. I'm free to enjoy them, and, more important, I'm free to give them away.

Everything is gift. Everything is God's. Francis has taught me that I am merely a humble steward gently holding things in trust, enjoying God's bounty without becoming attached to anything.

But it is not always an easy lesson to put into practice. I still do clutch some things, tightly, especially my numerous van Gogh prints. A priest friend in Albany, New York, Father Peter Young, is seventy years old and still works tirelessly, up to sixteen hours a day, serving convicts and drug addicts. I was in his home one day, and I mentioned to him how much I loved a beautifully framed icon of the Blessed Mother hanging on his wall. He took it off the wall, handed it to me, saying, "Take it." I hung it back on his wall, but I took with me a valuable lesson in love and freedom.

A mutual friend told me of a similar story. One day, Father Young was driving a drug addict to a counseling session, and the young man complimented him on his hat. The guy was just making conversation. Still, Father Young took the hat off and gave it to him. "Gerry," my friend said, "don't ever tell Father Young you like anything of his, unless you want it. I've seen him give away coats and gloves he had been wearing. One night, he met a man who was unable to find a job because he had no shoes and was too embarrassed to go for an interview. Father Young took his shoes off and gave them to the guy, and then walked to his car in his stocking feet...and it was snowing at the time, the temperature hovering around zero. Another ex-convict had no car to get to work in, and Father Young gave him his car, and then spent the next month driving an old school bus around town until he got another car."

Father Young is the freest man I know. He knows everything is a gift, freely given and freely given away. I can only dream of such a spirit of detachment.

FREEDOM FROM ATTACHMENTS

Simplicity is no more and no less than being ourselves, knowing that we are loved.

—JEAN VANIER, *COMMUNITY AND GROWTH*

In Francis' life, poverty and freedom joined together, inseparable and equal. As one author succinctly put it:

> Only the free are really poor. A beggar that yearns for posses-
> sions is no freer than a wealthy person that is dominated by his
> possessions. Francis was so free that he tolerated no ill-will
> toward people richly-appareled. At Montefeltro castle he calm-
> ly surveyed those knights and ladies in their festive regalia,
> remarking: "God is their Lord, too, and any time he pleases he
> can call them and make just and holy people of them."
>
> The mystery of the individual soul and its course demanded
> respect anywhere. Love for souls and the realm to which they
> belonged allowed of no barriers, no prejudice against them.
> Francis found entry among nobility, as a witness to the truth
> who resolved "to live not for himself alone but for everybody,
> moved therefore by the example of Him deigned to be the one
> to die for all." Young count Roland dei Cattani accosted Francis:
> "Father, I should like to talk with you about the welfare of my
> soul." But Francis directed him back to the festive gathering,
> saying, "First of all go and enjoy dinner with your friends...
> Then we can talk it over with all quiet and composure." That is
> how he attracted souls, with the serene, equable force radiating
> from a life devoted to the truth, from his freedom of attach-
> ment to the goods and possessions, the aims and prejudices of
> mortal men." (Reinhold Schneider, *The Hour of St. Francis of
> Assisi*, page 46)

From the simplicity of disentangled living Francis learned how to
enter the fullness of integrated life. He possessed nothing while
enjoying everything.

Holy Simplicity

I recommend to you holy simplicity.
—*SAINT FRANCIS DE SALES*

*These are complex times. And we lead complex lives. We live in a hectic,
fast-paced society that is filled with moral dilemmas, financial worries,
ecological disasters, criminal violence, racial bigotry, corporate greed,
decaying inner cities, global political unrest and economic instability,
and deadly wars fueled by religious differences which pit neighbor against
neighbor. We are stressed and anxious, as we breathlessly chase after*

more and more possessions. Our passion to possess blinds us to the reality that much of the world is enduring poverty and starvation on a scale unmatched in human history. About eight hundred million people do not have access to adequate food and nutrition. I read somewhere that four hundred people a day die of starvation. Every minute of every day twenty children die of hunger, or diseases related to hunger. It seems unthinkable. But the sad truth is that countless millions of malnourished and aimless people are living on the edge of extinction.

What can I do? I think Saint Francis would recommend that I take a close look at the virtue of simplicity. By way of simplicity, Francis was able to enter into the deep silence of his heart.

Simplicity is hard. Attaining it will not eliminate the complexity of modern life and all its intricate personal and global problems. I think simplicity allowed Francis to live in harmony with the ordered complexity of his day. As his heart grew in simplicity, he was better able to understand the Lord and the world around him.

Francois Fenelon, in his book, Christian Perfection, *wrote: "It is a wise self-love, which wants to get out of the intoxication of outside things" (page 196). Before I can free myself from the lure of material things I have to become more sensitive to the things of the spirit, which will diminish my chances of being dazzled by the superficial, such as the latest sports car from BMW. More important will be the latest revelation from God on how I can love my neighbor while at the same time deflecting my own self-centered greed. Through simplicity we learn that self-denial paradoxically leads to true self-fulfillment. Simplicity allows us to hold the interests of others above our self-interest. Real simplicity is true freedom. The constant drumbeat of materialism is no longer deafening. We desire less, and are happy with less.*

Simplicity is the best method of stripping away excess baggage that weighs us down and all nonessential adornments that surround us. As these distractions disappear, the reality of God becomes clearer. Simplicity is a much more profound concept than voluntary poverty, which is much smaller in scope, because simplicity not only reduces material possessions it also diminishes desire for them. Simplicity immunizes from the plague of consumerism.

Alexander Solzhenitsyn said, "On our crowded planet there are no longer any internal affairs." Our future depends on more and more people learning to live more simply. It has been said that the world has enough resources to meet everyone's need, but not enough to match every-

one's greed. Americans make up six percent of the world's population, yet we gobble up more than thirty percent of the globe's resources. If the rest of the planet follows our greedy example it will spell disaster for humanity. Large segments of the world's population are already living without hope, tottering on the brink of cruel death by starvation. Simplicity is not an option, it is a vital necessity. Reckless, out-of-control consumption must be curtailed before it destroys us. Unlimited growth, which fosters a throw-away culture, is a dangerous illusion. Voluntary denial is liberating. As Christians we must become advocates of the poor and the forgotten. We must become poor ourselves, living simply so others can simply live.

I'll let Saint Augustine have the last word: "All plenty which is not my God is poverty to me." Amen.

Pilgrimage Diary 36

Il Beato Tommaso da Celano

*T*he interesting thing about a pilgrimage is that it connects you physically to places that are spiritually uplifting. Something happens when that connection is made. The spiritual dimension is given shape and form, is made tangible. The abstract becomes concrete. The starting point of the lectures during the pilgrimage was an examination of the life of Thomas of Celano, because he laid the foundation for all the information we have about Francis. The lectures taught me much about Thomas, and about the kind of writing, hagiography, in which he excelled. But facts in and of themselves are lifeless. Thomas, for me, was a faceless character adrift in a sea of information, far beyond my sensory perception. But not for long.

One day, we took a trip to Tagliacozzo, where Thomas of Celano is buried. The trip made the lifeless story of the biographer spring to life. The antiquated town is a little more than an hour's drive east of Rome, and it lies in a charming valley that is encircled by the rugged mountains of the Abruzzi region. The faded stone buildings, with their arched doorways, shuttered windows and balconies laden with flowers, along with the narrow streets and wide plazas of the town make it easy to transport yourself back in time to an era when Thomas of Celano walked these very streets. Today, I walked along Via Beato Tommaso da Celano—"the street of Blessed Thomas of Celano."

Thomas was born and raised in the town of Celano, which is about sixteen miles from Tagliacozzo. Near the end of his life, Thomas came to Tagliacozzo in search of a quieter life as a chaplain to the Poor Clares, who occupied a monastery in the town. Shortly after the death of Saint Clare, Pope Alexander IV asked Thomas to write a life of Clare. Thomas completed the book in 1256. It was his last major literary work. He died in 1260 and was buried on the monastery grounds. The Poor Clares abandoned the monastery in 1476, at which point the property was taken over by the Conventual Friars. Thomas's body was placed inside the Church of St. Francis.

Along the left wall of the church, there sits a small coffin. One side of the coffin is made of glass, allowing a view of the remains of the first biographer of Saint Francis. Normally, such morbid displays would repulse me. Yet, as I sat in silence in front of the writer's decayed body, I felt engulfed in a sea of tranquillity. Thomas, clothed in his habit, his hood covering his head, was resting on a red mattress. His hands were folded over his breast. It was the hands that touched me. I imagined him holding a pen, writing about Francis. I felt an electric connection to this man who not only knew Francis, but also devoted his life to writing about him. I said a prayer, asking Thomas of Celano to help me also to write about Francis of Assisi.

I think he heard the prayer.

I purchased a postcard featuring a portrait of Thomas with a quill pen in his hand standing before a table covered with books. I framed the card (the frame cost about twenty times the price of the postcard), and it hangs on the wall near my computer. During my brief visit to Tagliacozzo, Thomas of Celano stepped out of the pages of history and became very real to me.

LA VERNA

Mystics are explorers and all that now happened beyond the bridge happened in a far country.
—ELIZABETH GOUDGE, *MY GOD AND MY ALL*

In May of 1213, Francis and Brother Leo were preaching in the Marches when they came across a small village that was busy prepar- ing a banquet celebration to honor a count who had been made a knight. Francis and Leo entered the courtyard of the castle of Montefeltro and climbed on a low wall and began to preach. Slowly, Francis' eloquence began to draw a crowd who listened and were spellbound by his words. One of the guests at the castle was a rich count who was deeply moved by the impromptu sermon. He asked to speak privately with Francis, and following their conversation, the count told Francis he owned a mountain called La Verna which was located just over the Tuscan border and that it was a perfect spot for a hermitage, and so he wanted to give Francis the mountain.

Today, La Verna stands next only to Assisi as a Franciscan shrine. Even to the skeptical, its history seems directed by destiny. It is an Apennine summit, a heap of tumbled rock standing 4,160 feet above the Casentino Valley. It has been called an altar raised in the very heart of central Italy. Saint Teresa of Avila called it a great castle of the soul.

It was at La Verna, on September 14, 1224, the feast day of the Exaltation of the Cross, that Francis lay in one of the rocky interstices of the mountain caves and received the stigmata.

Francis had great devotion for Mary Queen of Heaven and for the archangel Michael. In his day, many people observed a special fast in honor of Mary and Michael. The fast, known as Angel's Lent, lasted from the feast of the Assumption on August 15th until the feast of Saint Michael on September 29th. As the fall of 1224 approached, Francis wanted to spend Angel's Lent on the mountain at La Verna, also known as Monte Alvernia. Seven of his closest companions—Leo, Angelo, Masseo, Rufino, Silvestro, Illuminato and Bonizio—accompanied the saint to the holy mountain. (Some historians question the presence of the last three brothers.)

Leaving Assisi, the brothers set out for the long journey across Umbria and into Tuscany. They walked north through valleys bursting with grapes that would soon be harvested. They walked through villages and forests. They walked over hills and along the banks of the Tiber River. They traveled in their usual manner, keeping silence and stopping only to say the Divine Office at the prescribed hours. At day's end, hungry and thirsty, they would beg for scraps of bread while seeking the lodging the Lord had prepared for them, sometimes sleeping in abandoned churches. It was a lengthy and grueling trip, covering more than seventy-five miles, and by the time they reached the foot of the mountain, Francis was far too weak for the steep climb to the summit, where the count had built a little chapel named after the Portiuncula, Santa Maria degli Angeli, as well as huts made of clay and interwoven branches. The hermitage was on a plateau at the edge of a cliff, and offered a spectacular view of the valley below.

Seeing how exhausted Francis was, the brothers borrowed a donkey from a peasant farmer. When they told the farmer they needed the donkey to carry Francis up the mountain, the farmer was anxious to meet Francis because he had heard so much about him. After being introduced to Francis, the farmer warned Francis that he should take care to be as good in reality as he is in the stories people tell of him, because so many have put their trust in his preaching. It was a bold, almost insulting admonishment for a farmer to address to a man renowned for his holiness. And Francis loved it. Being told by a peasant to be what people think he is moved the saint to get down on his knees and kiss the poor farmer's feet. Francis humbly thanked the man for reminding him of his responsibility to live as he preached.

Francis mounted the donkey, and the brothers began their trek up the mountain. The farmer said he would walk with them, but he soon grew weary because of the stifling heat. He told Francis he was dying of thirst. Francis got off the donkey, knelt down and prayed. As he prayed, the brothers saw a spring of water bubbling up near a rock. After refreshing themselves, they continued their torturous ascent. After climbing through the woods of the lower slopes, they stopped by some large rocks to sit and rest. Francis sat under a tree and marveled at the great view stretched out before him. All the charms of Tuscany and Romagna were on display for as far as the eye could see, all the way to the horizon. Little villages dotted the landscape below. The foothills were covered with vineyards and olive trees. The Arno River crossed the valley, past proud castles and modest homes, twinkling in the sunlight. In the distance, shimmering in the heat, another mountain touched the puffy white clouds. Francis was at home. He loved the valleys and ravines his tired eyes soaked in, and perhaps he became lost in the memories of all the paths he walked during his life, preaching and healing as the Lord had prompted.

Then, according to *The Little Flowers*, a large flock of birds shattered the profound silence of the mountain. The birds were exuberantly singing and fluttering their wings. They surrounded the resting saint, some even landing on his shoulders. Some of the birds walked on Francis' feet. The brothers were enchanted by the sight. The joyfulness of the birds filled Francis' heart with wonder. He told the brothers that Jesus was so pleased that they were going to be praying on this solitary mountain that he sent the birds to welcome them with sweet songs and open wings. But what lay ahead for Francis was far from sweet. Farther up the mountain, the most mysterious moment in his life was waiting for him in the silence.

As the brothers continued their climb, news of their arrival on the mountain reached Count Orlando. He was so delighted Francis had returned to the hermitage that he and his servants set out for the mountain, carrying with them a supply of food for the brothers to eat during their stay. When they arrived at the hermitage, the brothers were praying. Francis and the brothers greeted the count with love and joy. They sat down and spoke. The count told Francis and the brothers that he did not want them to be uncomfortable or endure any unnecessary hardships while they were on the mountain, and so he instructed them to send word to his castle if there was anything they needed, adding he would be angry if they did not ask for what they desired. Francis thanked the count for his generosity and kind offer of assistance.

After the count departed, Francis told the brothers that he was distressed because he feared that being pampered by the count threatened their loyalty to Lady Poverty. He told them they must cherish in their hearts the love of poverty, instructing them not to heed the count's offer. Francis then told the brothers that he believed his death was approaching and that he wished to be alone with God so he could lament his sins. He said Brother Leo could bring him a little bread and water, when he felt prompted to do so, but other than that he wished not to be disturbed, either by the other brothers or anyone who came to the hermitage looking for him. He blessed them and retreated to his hut, apart from the others' hut, under a beech tree.

According to tradition (or more accurately, according to local folklore), the deep, dramatic rifts and chasms in the mountain at La Verna are the result of an earthquake that took place at the death of Jesus. At the place formed (even if only poetically or piously) by Calvary, Francis was going to endure the sufferings of Calvary.

As Francis entered deeply into the solitude of the mountain, he was troubled about the future of the Order, which was headed in a direction he felt to be wrong. As he prayed in a rocky crevice under a great overhanging stone, he committed his fraternity into the hands of God, in essence, giving back to God what God had given to him. Afterward, when Brother Leo visited his hut to give him some bread and water, Francis asked his friend to randomly open the "book of the Gospels" in three different places (in honor of the Holy Trinity) and read to him whatever passages his eyes fell upon. All three times, Leo opened to accounts of Christ's passion on the cross. Francis took this as an indication his remaining days on earth would be filled with suffering, and he resigned himself to fully accepting God's will.

That night Francis was unable to sleep. As he lay on his hard bed, an angel appeared to him in a vision, saying he would soothe Francis' restless spirit by playing the violin the way it is played before the throne of God in heaven. The angel gently moved the bow across the strings just once, but that was enough to fill Francis with unimaginable joy and sweetness. Francis was approaching a kind of all-transforming union with God that only a few mystics have experienced. He was being submerged in a fathomless fountain of happiness. The next morning, while recounting the vision, he told the brothers that had the angel drawn the bow across the strings a second time, his soul would have left his body from uncontrollable happiness.

The Abbot le Monnier picks up the story:

> They celebrated the Feast of the Assumption of Our Lady with the brethren at the convent, and then Francis began his usual fast in honor of the Holy Angels, and retired into solitude. He spent the first days in almost continual prayer. In this long period of contemplation his mind became absorbed in God, and his whole soul was filled with unutterable sweetness and grace. Never before had he been in such close intimacy with God, and he profited by these favours from the Almighty to endeavor to penetrate more closely into the mysteries of his Divine Friend. "Not," says S. Bonaventura, "as a gazer on the ineffable Majesty who would deserve to be overwhelmed with its glory, but as a faithful and prudent servant, seeking to know the will of God to which he ardently desired to conform himself entirely." He entreated God to show him the way in which He desired him to walk for the remainder of his life. The answer was less prompt and less explicit than he might have expected. All that he understood was that great sufferings were in store for him. He declared himself entirely submissive and ready to endure any anguish of mind or any bodily torture; one thing only he asked, that the Divine Will might be manifested to him. (*History of St. Francis of Assisi*)

Francis' days of solitude following the Feast of the Assumption were spent in a secluded spot on the far side of a deep ravine, where he surrendered himself to pray. In order to gain access to it, he had to cross over the ravine by crawling across the large trunk of a fallen tree, a natural bridge for the saint. A fierce-looking falcon built a nest near Francis' hut. The falcon lost all his predatory instinct and would gently wake the sleeping saint with a beating of his wings so Francis could get up in time for matins. Francis told Leo to visit him only twice a day, once to bring scraps of bread and a little water, and again at night to call him for matins. They set up a secret code for the night prayer. Leo was to stand on his side of the ravine and shout out the first line of the prayer: "O Lord, open my lips." And if Francis from the other side of the ravine responded, "And my mouth shall declare your praise," then Leo should cross the tree and say matins with Francis. But, should Francis not respond, then Leo should return to his hut, knowing that Francis was in such a state of rapture that he was unable to pray with his friend.

One night, Leo stood by the side of the ravine and shouted out the verse from the psalm. And when he did not hear any response, he elected to crawl across the tree trunk anyway. Francis was not in his hut. Leo heard sounds which he thought might have been Francis praying, and so he went to investigate. When he got near the saint, he stood quietly in the shadows and listened as Francis prayed aloud. Over and over again, Francis announced to God that he was a worthless, useless little worm of a servant. Leo accidentally made a noise, which arrested Francis' attention. As Francis approached Leo, the brother feared Francis would be angry at him for disobeying his orders. But his love for Francis was so great, he had to cross the ravine to see if Francis was all right. Francis, while not happy with the intrusion, seemed to understand Leo's dilemma. Leo asked Francis why he was praying in such a manner, calling himself a worm. Francis said that during his contemplation he was graced to see God in the depth of his infiniteness and also see himself in all his lowliness. The gulf between humanity and Divinity was greater than Francis ever imagined. After blessing Leo, Francis asked Leo not to spy on him again, and told him to return to his hut.

The days and nights of deep solitude rolled by, until the feast of the Exaltation of the Holy Cross, celebrated on September 14th, arrived. Since the days in San Damiano, Francis always had a deep reverence for the cross of Christ. Before dawn on the day of the feast, Francis lifted his hands into the fading darkness of night, and pleaded with God to allow him to experience in his soul and body as much as he possibly could the suffering of the crucified Christ.

And the prayer was answered.

A seraph with six radiant wings descended from heaven and approached Francis. Francis was both frightened and delighted. The saint was infused with the knowledge that he was about to undergo a great suffering, but not the suffering of a martyr. An inner flame would transform him into the likeness of the crucified Christ, whose very wounds would be manifested on Francis' frail body. The marks of the nails that pierced the flesh of Christ began to appear on Francis. Blood flowed out of a fresh wound in his side.

Out of humility, Francis tried to hide the wounds from the brothers. But it was not possible. Blood had soaked through his habit. His wounded feet made it impossible for him to walk. Francis was in great pain. The brothers took turns nursing him and washing his clothes. But only Brother Leo was permitted to see and swathe the saint's wounds. The brothers knew something wonderful yet mysterious had happened. Even the falcon let Francis sleep longer in the morning. The stigmatization caused great joy to spread across the hermitage. On the feast of Saint Michael the Archangel, Francis asked Leo to bring him some parchment and a pen. Francis then wrote a litany of praise to God. When Francis handed the parchment back to Leo, the brother feared that Francis loved God so much now that he could no longer love him. Francis sensed what Leo was feeling, and so he took the parchment back, turned it over and wrote a blessing for Leo: "The Lord bless you and keep you. The Lord show His face to you and have mercy on you. May the Lord turn His countenance to you and give you peace."

On September 30th, Francis rode a donkey down Mount La Verna for the last time. He slowly made his way back to Assisi. Along the way, as he passed through towns like Borgo San Sepolcro, Monte Casalle and Citta di Castello, crowds rushed to greet him, hoping to kiss his hand, chanting *"Ecco il Santo"*—"Here comes the saint." But Francis was oblivious to their veneration. As they traveled they encountered early snows, and even the bitter cold that penetrated his threadbare habits did not seem to disturb the saint, whose heart and soul were still transfixed by the beauty and pain he experienced on Mount La Verna. And amazingly, after a short rest in the town of his birth, the merchant's son set out on yet another missionary trip to the surrounding towns. Throughout the rest of his life, Francis remained silent on the subject of the stigmata, and so we have no idea of what he thought about it.

For obvious reasons, people speak of Mount La Verna as the Calvary in Saint Francis' life. But Saint Bonaventure suggests that La Verna is really symbolically closer to the biblical Mount Tabor, because on this holy mountain Francis was transformed into the image of the Savior.

Taking Us Further Than We Want to Go

It is hard for a former atheist with a strong skeptical streak, even one who has returned to Christianity, to accept the validity of the events alleged to have happened on Mount La Verna. It would be easy to poke holes in all the stories that form the narrative of Francis' last visit to the mountain, which Dante described as a harsh crag between the Tiber and the Arno rivers. In the Chapel of the Stigmata, I got down on my knees, bent over and touched my head to the spot that has been venerated for centuries as the place where Francis received the stigmata. As I rose, I believed the events happened. That is all I can say. There is no use trying to intellectualize or explain my belief.

And that is not to say I am comfortable with the belief that Francis truly did bear the marks of the cross of Christ on his body. I would be too embarrassed to tell some of my atheist friends about my belief, because I know they view Francis as an emaciated ascetic saddled with cultural and mystical symbols of his time who is a victim of an illusion induced by weeks of isolation on a mountain. But the story fits; it seems eminently plausible and credible. The story was not born in the fertile imaginations behind Fioretti. *Thomas of Celano, who was well educated and intelligent, included the event in his life of the saint. Francis was the first person in history to experience the phenomenon of the stigmata. I cannot bring myself to believe the story was a hoax. Besides, should we not all desire to share in the suffering of Christ, even if we are too frightened of the pain to ask for the wounds to be visited upon us the way Francis did? I must confess that before my first visit to La Verna, I certainly entertained doubts about the stigmata. Up until then, I put the matter aside, figuring it was not essential to understanding and appreciating the life and message of Saint Francis of Assisi. It still is not; I just happen to believe it, and my subsequent visits to the holy mountain only deepened my belief.*

Entering into the experience of the stigmata forces me to look more closely at the passion and death of Christ. In doing so, I better understand the depth of Christ's love...and the shallowness of mine.

Francis always takes us further than we want to go. Further in poverty, further in love. And with the stigmata, he takes us further into the mystery of salvation. Don't try to understand the stigmata of Saint Francis; simply enter into it and allow it to deepen your faith.

A Human Possibility?

One who does not seek the Cross of Jesus is not seeking the glory of Jesus.

—*SAINT JOHN OF THE CROSS*

The stigmata of Saint Francis force us to look at the unity between the sensory world of creation and the unseen world of the spirit. The stigmata were an external, physical manifestation of Francis' interior spiritual harmony with Christ. Francis' inner identification with Christ was made visible through the stigmata, and his body itself became a prophetic statement that humans can truly become like Christ through total immersion into his suffering. Francis so completely entered into the humanity of Christ, that the wounds of Christ became the best and most natural way for God to sanction his experience.

In his first life of the saint, Thomas of Celano suggests we, too, can have this same experience, a revolutionary suggestion that was purged from his second life of the saint because the Church wanted to underline the doctrine that God could only be accessed through the sacraments. Celano's first interpretation said, in effect, that the incarnation was open to everyone who entered fully into the suffering of Christ. God will come down from heaven and enter into the humble abode of our frail bodies. That interpretation was far too radical for the Church. Celano later explained the stigmata as an extraordinary event reserved only for a saint as special as Francis, and it was far beyond the reach of the rest of us mere mortals. The stigmata became a unique symbol of God's favor on Francis, rather than something that was possible for anyone who imitated Christ as closely as Francis did.

There is a world of difference between the portrait of Francis as a profoundly holy person from the moment of his birth, which we find in

Celano's second life of the saint, and the portrait of Francis in his first life, which shows him to be as imperfect as everyone else, but slowly evolving into someone who became like Christ in everything, including the reception of the wounds of the cross.

Francis experienced the immanence of God in his flesh. The lesson of the stigmata is that the Incarnation is not only a divine event that broke through history but also a human possibility that can break through our lives.

Embraced by the Cross

Dante explained the significance of the stigmata:

> Then he received from Christ, upon the bare
> Ridge between Tiber and Arno, that last seal
> Which two years long his body lived to wear.
> (*Paradiso*, Canto XI)

Medieval Florentine artisans used seals to identify their wares. Dante's "last seal" would refer to the third brand that members of the Wool Guild used as a guarantee of authenticity and excellent quality. Readers have interpreted Dante to mean that Francis wears the seal of the stigmata as assurance that in him is a true and authentic image of Christ.

For Francis, the road to Christ began with a crucifix speaking to him and it ended with his being embraced by the cross.

PILGRIMAGE DIARY 37

The Shrine of La Verna

*T*he mountaintop Shrine of La Verna is a sprawling complex, consisting of numerous chapels and churches. The shrine, rich in history and abounding in sanctity and mysticism, cultivates an attitude of prayer and meditation within anyone who visits it.

The Chapel of Santa Maria degli Angeli was built between 1216 and 1218. More commonly known as the "Chiesina," or the little church, the chapel was dedicated to Our Lady of the Angels because Mary appeared to Francis and told him where to build the first little church of La Verna. The church is divided into two parts; the first consisting of the original structure, and the second an addition built

sometime after 1250 to accommodate the growing number of
worshipers. The two sections are divided by a wrought-iron screen.
The chapel was solemnly consecrated in August of 1260 under the
watchful eye of Saint Bonaventure, who was the minister general at
the time. The concrete walls of the humble chapel are bare. Wooden
choir stalls line the side walls of the original church. The stalls pull
your attention to the church's most notable feature, a stunning
representation of the Assumption of Mary located on the wall behind
the altar and made from brightly painted terra-cotta.

The fifteen enameled terra-cotta reliefs which grace many of the
churches at La Verna were created by a family of Florentine sculptors
known for their high technical and aesthetic standards during the
fifteenth and sixteenth centuries. The family name—Della Robbia—
became synonymous with the enameled terra-cotta art form. The
glazing process by which stannic enamel is applied to terra-cotta was
perfected by Luca Della Robbia (c. 1400-1482), who adapted the
process to monumental sculpture. Luca passed on his secrets to his
nephew Andrea (1435-1528), who created most of the enameled
terra-cottas at La Verna. Luca and Andrea, along with five of Andrea's
seven sons, formed the Della Robbia School. Andrea Della Robbia's
other two sons joined the Dominican Order. The two dominant
colors of the reliefs are blue and white. All the figures in the terra-
cotta reliefs are painted a very bright white, and they are placed in
front of a deep blue background. Other colors are minimally
employed on other objects in the scene, such as trees or flowers. All
the figures are exquisitely sculptured. In the "Annunciation," which
is located in the basilica, the sweet humility of Mary is delicately
rendered.

Andrea Della Robbia's Assumption in the Chiesina features Saint
Francis and Saint Bonaventure kneeling in adoration. The newer
section of the chapel features two terra-cottas created by Giovanni
Della Robbia, Andrea's son. Count Orlando, who gave the mountain
to Francis, is buried under the floor of the chapel.

Next to the Chiesina is the basilica. Construction on this larger
church began in 1348. It houses a number of Della Robbia terra-
cottas and the Chapel of Relics. The most prized relic is a piece of
cloth stained with the blood of Saint Francis. Among the artifacts
preserved is a bowl used by Francis when he dined at Count
Orlando's home.

Outside the basilica, to the right as you leave, is the tiny Chapel of the Pieta. An archway on the left side of the chapel leads to the Corridor of the Stigmata. This 250-foot-long corridor was built in 1578 to allow the friars to process to the Chapel of the Stigmata. The left side of the corridor is lined with windows offering a delightful view of the wooded terrain. The upper half of the right side of the corridor is covered with frescoes illustrating episodes from the life of Saint Francis.

About halfway down the corridor, a small door on the right leads to a cave in the rocks which houses Saint Francis' bed. The bed, under a huge overhanging rock, is rather hard...because it is made of stone. It was on this large flat stone that Francis slept whenever he wasn't praying. The cave gives you a sense of the way Francis lived while at La Verna. I could feel the cold and dampness, and the severity of his devotional life. When Francis occupied this cave, it must have been very dismal and desolate. Yet in this darkened hollow of cold, hard rock, Francis prepared his soul for the most important and mysterious event of his life. The Seraph's swift flight was quickly approaching the saint.

At the end of the corridor, on the right side, is the entrance to the Loddi Chapel. Loddo Loddi was a nobleman from the area who built the chapel in 1581 on the site of an early community cemetery. From the chapel a short flight of dimly lit steps leads to a slightly larger Chapel of the Cross. This chapel is located on the spot of Francis' second cell, a crude shelter in which the saint endured the agony which preceded the reception of the stigmata. This chapel features a dramatic terra-cotta statue of Saint Francis, bearing the marks of the stigmata, sitting on a rock next to an open book of Scriptures, with his friend, the falcon, sitting on a branch next to him. At the far end of the Chapel of the Cross is the entrance to the Chapel of the Stigmata.

Construction on the Chapel of the Stigmata began in August of 1263. The wall behind the altar is covered with a depiction of the crucifixion created by Andrea Della Robbia. Christ dying on the cross is flanked by four pairs of angels. At the foot of the cross, Saint Francis receives the stigmata in the presence of the Blessed Mother, Saint John the Evangelist and Saint Jerome. The side walls of the simple chapel are lined with wooden choir stalls. In the middle of the marble floor, directly in front of the altar, the spot where Francis received the stigmata is covered by glass.

As you turn and head back out of the chapel, stairs on the right side lead you to a narrow corridor to the Oratory of Saint Bonaventure. The seventh successor to Francis, who was made a cardinal shortly before his death, used this tiny stone room to pray and contemplate. Perhaps he conceived his monumental book, Itinerarium Mentis in Deum ("The Soul's Journey Into God") in this very room. I sat for ten minutes in this room, and was deeply moved by the experience.

Down a short flight of steps from the Chapel of the Stigmata is the Oratory of Saint Anthony of Padua. Saint Anthony lived in this small stone room for several months before his death in 1231.

The shrine has other interesting sites, including the Precipice, a fantastic rock formation that offers a spectacular view of the valley below, Brother Leo's cell, the first cell of Francis, the Chapel of Blessed John, the massive projecting rock under which Francis often came to meditate and, one of my favorites, the Chapel of the Birds, which is downhill from the main portion of the shrine. The tiny Chapel of the Birds commemorates the place where the birds welcomed Francis with a symphony of joyful chirping.

The day we spent at La Verna made a deep impression on me. I had been fully aware that some friars think the wounds that manifested themselves on Francis' body might have been the result of his contracting leprosy. As a skeptic, I was more comfortable with that sort of rational explanation. But as I knelt in the Chapel of the Stigmata, words from Saint Bonaventure's The Soul's Journey Into God, which he began writing at La Verna, resonated with my spirit: "There is no other path but through the burning love of the crucified."

I don't know about the Seraph, with his many wings, but I believe that the burning love of Christ penetrated the flesh of the saint. Believing it, however, does not imply that I understand it. It simply means that I accept that the course of Francis' life, with his ever deepening love for God, might naturally wend its way to such an unprecedented, supernatural encounter with God, who granted Francis the desire of his heart. For Francis, the stigmata seemed inevitable, even if it had never happened before during the history of Christianity. Francis had the simplicity and originality to want what no one ever dreamed of...to experience the pain and suffering of

Christ in order better to feel the depths of the Savior's love.

At La Verna, Francis was crucified and transformed. It was his destiny.

Mount La Verna is holy ground.

THIS DARK MYSTERY

As the soul becomes more pure and bare, and possesses less of created things, and is emptied of all things that are not God, it receives God more purely, and is more completely in Him; and it truly becomes one with God, and it looks into God and God into it, face to face as it were; two images transformed into one.

—MEISTER ECKHART

The Franciscan mystic and poet, Jacopone da Todi, offered this word meditation on the stigmata in *The Lauds*:

I have no words for this dark mystery;
How can I understand or explain
the superabundance of riches,
the disproportionate love of a heart on fire. (*Laud* 61)

The stigmata lift Francis out of the birdbath by shattering our romantic notions about his being a gentle, warm friend of the birds. Of course this animal-loving image of Francis is the one we hold dearest, because that Francis helps us think we can be happy without giving of ourselves, that love demands no sacrifice. The image of Francis bleeding from the wounds imprinted in his flesh tells us a different story, the story of salvation won through the agony of the cross. Francis did not spend his time avoiding suffering; rather, he embraced it fully, because by the suffering and death of Jesus, we have won the promise of the Resurrection.

Talking to birds is easy; dying to self is hard.

Francis did both.

PILGRIMAGE DIARY 38

Thoughts Scribbled While Walking

My awareness of God's mysterious presence within me helps me become more aware of the same presence within others.

To love others as Jesus loves them is difficult, if not impossible, yet it must be our primary goal as Christians.

Compassion is far removed from pity and sympathy. Compassion grows out of an awareness of our common humanity.

The key to attaining happiness is to give it away. But we love hanging on to what we've got.

Divine love is not fickle. It has only one desire: total self-giving.

I live in an overcrowded house of false values.

Poverty helps me see beauty in an earthenware pot.

A homeless, naked, dying man on the cross asks: Are you reasonably comfortable?

Mary gave God a human heart. She gives me Christ's heart.

Stop brooding over the incomprehensible.

Recapture your childhood faculty for make-believe. Let go of your sophisticated ways.

Stand before God in a stance of conversion.

The Bread of Life

Communion is the nature of ultimate reality.

—*CATHERINE MOWRY LACUGNA,* GOD FOR US

The focal point of the faith and holiness of Saint Francis was his love and imitation of Christ. His spirituality grew out of his unconditional love of Christ. Eric Doyle, O.F.M., and Damian McElrath write:

He dedicated himself to Christ absolutely, loved as really and truly present in creation, in the Scriptures, in the Eucharist and in the church. The presence of Christ was all but visible and tangible to him. So deep was his faith in Christ and so ardent his love of him, that Francis longed to do what he had done, to say what he had said, to suffer what he had suffered, above all in his passion and death. In a word, he wanted nothing else save to walk in the very footsteps of Christ. At Greccio on Christmas night 1223 he reproduced the circumstances of Christ's birth in Bethlehem. In memory of the Lord's forty days' fast Francis went out to fast on an island in Lake Trasimene. On at least three occasions, according to Bartholomew of Pisa, he reenacted the account of the Last Supper. Two years before he died he received the marks of the stigmata on his hands and feet and side. By this time his desire to follow Christ down to the last detail of his life was by God's grace for him fulfilled.

Francis' faith was nurtured, fed, sustained and deepened by the Word of God and the Eucharist. Doyle and McElrath write: "Francis was profoundly aware of Christ's true presence in the sacrament of the Eucharist and in the Word of God, the holy Scriptures. These for him are intimately connected because it is through the power of Christ's words that the Eucharist is consecrated."

Francis burned with love for the Eucharist. Again, Doyle and McElrath:

> He revered the Eucharist because it continues the revelation of God made in the Incarnation. It is Christ really present among us.
>
> There is only a difference of modality between this presence and his days on earth in Palestine, when he was truly and historically present. Francis makes this comparison most lucidly in the *First Admonition*:
>
> > He shows himself to us in this sacred bread just as he once appeared to his apostles in real flesh. With their own eyes they saw only his flesh, but they believed that he was God, because they contemplated him in the eyes of the spirit. We, too, with our own eyes, see only bread and wine, but we must see further and firmly believe that this is his most holy Body and Blood, living and true.

Just as God was present there when Jesus was asleep in the boat as a storm raged on the Sea of Galilee, so is he present now on the altar motionless and hidden, amidst the activities and hurly-burly of life. Francis had a profound love of the Eucharist. Celano tells us that he:

> burned with a love that came from his whole being

for the sacrament of the Lord's body and he was carried away with wonder at the loving condescension and the most condescending love shown there.

Through the Eucharist we are more intimately united to Christ, more closely to one another and more deeply with the whole world and the entire cosmos. The sacrament, constituted of a tiny piece of bread and a little wine in a cup, together with the transforming word, unites God and man, eternity and time, heaven and earth, church and world. (essay in *Franciscan Christology*)

Saint Francis of Assisi experienced the Eucharist as a Sacrament of Love in which God became his spiritual food. He needed the refreshment of Love's presence the way his lungs needed air. Nourished by Love, Francis was able to love in turn all of creation. As Christ's Body and Blood became one with Francis' body and blood, Francis was able to become Christ to everyone he met.

PILGRIMAGE DIARY 39

The Imitation of Christ

Those who have God are short of nothing; God alone is enough.

—*SAINT TERESA OF AVILA*

*T*he last Reflection began with my rumination about Francis' love and imitation of Christ. Imitating Christ should, I would imagine, be the goal of all Christians. For me the problem is how to begin imitating Christ. At first blush it seems like a task doomed to failure. For a start, the fickleness of my own heart can easily divert my attention. I seem to be ruled by my emotions, what I feel at any given time. There are days when I just do not feel like even following Christ, let alone imitating him.

I wonder about Francis, how he did it, how he managed to persist in striving at all times to become like his Savior in every way possible. Did he struggle with his emotions and feelings? He had to; he was human. (In fact, in The Legend of the Three Companions we read, "He [Francis] suffered great perplexity of spirit, and he did not rest until he had achieved the dreamed-of ideal; he was racked by diverse thoughts that harshly disturbed him.") So how did he remain focused for the long haul, undaunted by his doubts or weaknesses? I think the answer, in part, lies in his single-mindedness, which he put to the service of his understanding that a mystical union with God was best achieved through the evangelical counsels of poverty, chastity and obedience. Those virtues helped Francis strip everything from his life except what he desired most: union with God, through an imitation of Christ.

Recently, I have been drawn to reading the spiritual classic by Thomas à Kempis, The Imitation of Christ. Here there is a clear insight into the detrimental effects of the fickleness of my heart, with its ever-changing moods and desires.

When I read the words of Thomas à Kempis, "...for men pay ready attention to any pleasant thing that comes their way..." (Book Three, Chapter 33), I instantly recognize myself. In an age when we are bombarded with so many alluring and stimulating images and ideas from every form of media, and are constantly enticed by provocative advertising designed to create needs we don't really have, it is very easy to be distracted from keeping our eye on God. The modern person takes in such an overwhelming amount of information every day, that distraction and confusion are inevitable.

So, how do I conquer the fickleness of my own heart and acquire the purity and singleness of intention that is required for a genuine imitation of Christ? Perhaps Saint John of the Cross offered the clearest way to begin: "Do not feed your spirit on anything apart from God."

The Fruit of Asceticism

It is a wise self-love, which wants to get out of the intoxication of outside things.

—FRANÇOIS FENELON, CHRISTIAN PERFECTION

The aim of asceticism is the attainment of poverty of spirit. Poverty of spirit is the manger of gentle receptivity which allows the Divine to be born within us. To be wholly present to God, with all of our heart, mind and soul, we must be poor in spirit. This is the entire message of Saint Francis.

Poverty of spirit, as the saint clearly understood, is far more than material poverty. While material poverty may help to facilitate poverty of spirit, it is nonetheless important to realize that a person without possessions can still be possessed by a craving for things. It is the craving that makes us restless, distracting our hearts and minds from being present to God alone. Poverty of spirit frees us from being divided by false idols and uncurbed passions.

PILGRIMAGE DIARY 40

News From Around the World

Everything that is in the heavens, on earth, and under the earth is penetrated with connectedness, penetrated with relatedness.
—*HILDEGARD OF BINGEN*

*D*uring the past few weeks in Rome, I've been reading the International Herald Tribune *every day. Here are some actual headlines from the paper during that period. They reflect a world in chaos.*

Suicide Bomb Rocks Jerusalem Market: 15 Dead and
170 Wounded
Algerian Night of Slaughter Reported to Leave 300 Dead;
Many Decapitated
Kenya Death Toll Rises: Two Policemen Found Slain
Bloody Battle for Power in Mexican Drug Cartel
Crime Sweeps Brazil as Police Strike
U. S. Checking on Police Beating of Immigrant in New York
Over 400 Arrested in Germany as Neo-Nazis Mark Hess Death
Asia Chokes on Growing Pollution
Victims of Violence in U.S.: 1.3 Million a Year and Soaring
China Leads in Executions: 4,367 Executed in 1996

Every day, we are assailed by information and news, normally bad...often unbearably bad news. Previous generations, born before the advent of television, global communications and the information superhighway, didn't have to bear the troubles of the whole world every day in their minds and hearts, as radio, television, newspapers and the Internet invite us to do. Every age has had its share of wars, plagues, famines, bloody revolutions and natural disasters, but only recently have they all—from all around the world—come into our homes on a daily basis, bringing their heavy burden of distress, and in the process leaving so many people feeling overwhelmed and insignificant. What can we do about it?

In a previous reflection entitled "I'm Hungry" (page 81) I wondered if we had become "so jaded by the onslaught of tragic headlines from around the globe" that this had contributed to our succumbing to "a fatigue of compassion." The question still lingers as the headlines continue to give witness to the unfathomable suffering endured by so many.

Is wondering what we can do the only thing we can do?

If so, then we shall remain powerless to do anything, thereby increasing the hopelessness that can be felt between the lines of all the stories associated with these tragic headlines. Francis would beseech us to do something, to do what we can.

Saint Thérèse of Lisieux, who spoke more directly to the needs of our generation, not only demonstrated how to cope with the despair and angst that often accompany modern life, but she also showed how it is possible to make a profound difference from within the limited scope of the daily routine of our own lives.

Casting aside her dreams of being a warrior or martyr, Thérèse slowly realized that even in her littleness, she could make a difference, a life-giving difference, to others.

In the limited space of her convent, her carmel, she made a difference to the whole world, by doing everything, however small, out of love. In the limited space of our own homes and our own lives, we can do the same. Every act of kindness, performed in love, changes the whole world.

THE POETIC SUMMATION

From the day that the Saint had been wounded on La Verna his strength continually languished. His life from this time was to be far more an interior than exterior life.
—ABBÉ LEON LE MONNIER, *HISTORY OF ST. FRANCIS OF ASSISI*

It was the spring of 1225 and Francis was in the midst of the most painful period of his life. He had been very sick for months, forced to live in a hut hastily constructed in the garden at San Damiano, where Clare and her sisters cared for him. He was back where it all began, just a few feet from where he first heard Christ invite him to restore the church that was in ruin. Now, it was poor Francis lying in ruin. He was completely blind and his body was so racked with pain that he had hardly slept for nearly two months. The wounds from the stigmata bled constantly.

Almost twenty years after his conversion, Francis was in the eventide of his life; exhausted by fasting and illness, he was in the twilight of his final agony. His suffering must have pushed him to the limits of his endurance. Worse than his physical suffering must have been the suffering of his soul.

Rather than curse the darkness that enveloped him, Francis cried out to God, pleading for mercy. He cried out, "Lord, help me in my infirmities, so that I may have the strength to bear them patiently." In his poverty and pain, Francis heard good news, a voice proclaiming that he should be glad because his sufferings could not compare to the immeasurable treasure awaiting him in heaven.

Francis was instantly filled with joy, as if a brilliantly bright sun had risen in the darkness of his soul. Being a poet and a lover of song, Francis responded to the vision trumpeted by the voice with a poem that was meant to be sung. He knew his time and mission on earth were nearing an end and now he was reassured that his life-long dream of seeing his Creator in paradise was going to be fulfilled, that his way of suffering with Christ on earth was truly a way to the resurrected and risen Christ in heaven, and he wanted to sing for joy a poem of gladness for all the world to hear. Here is that poem, an inspired prayer of thanksgiving from the tender heart that continually thanked God for all living things.

The Canticle of Brother Sun

Most high, all-powerful, all good, Lord!
All praise is yours, all glory, all honor
And all blessing

To you alone, Most High, do they belong.
No mortal lips are worthy
To pronounce your name.

All praise be yours, my Lord, through all that you have made,
And first my lord Brother Sun,

Who brings the day; and light you give to us through him.
How beautiful is he, how radiant in all his splendor!
Of you, Most High, he bears the likeness.

All praise be yours, my Lord, through Sister Moon and Stars;
In the heavens you have made them, bright
and precious and fair.

All praise be yours, my Lord, through Brothers Wind and Air,
And fair and stormy, all the weather's moods,
By which you cherish all that you have made.

All praise be yours, my Lord, through Sister Water,
So useful, lowly, precious and pure.

All praise be yours, my Lord, through Brother Fire,
Through whom you brighten up the night.
How beautiful is he, how gay! Full of power and strength.

All praise be yours, my Lord, through Sister Earth, our mother,
Who feeds us in her sovereignty and produces
Various fruits with coloured flowers and herbs.

All praise be yours, my Lord, through those who grant pardon
For love of you; through those who endure
Sickness and trial.

Happy those who endure in peace,
By you, Most High, they will be crowned.

All praise be yours, my Lord, through Sister Death,
From whose embrace no mortal can escape.
Woe to those who die in mortal sin!
Happy those She finds doing your will!
The second death can do no harm to them.
Praise and bless my Lord, and give him thanks,
And serve him with great humility. (*Omnibus*, pages 130-131)

Francis composed the portion of the *Canticle* up to the verses about
pardon and peace in the garden of the Poor Clares' convent at San
Damiano. Though his spirit was housed in a broken, dying body, it
was able to sing a hymn of thanksgiving for all of creation. He wrote
a portion of the *Canticle* stressing forgiveness, suffering and
endurance after learning about the bitter feud between the bishop
and mayor of Assisi. He then had two friars sing the longer version
of the *Canticle* at a meeting he arranged between the bishop and the

mayor. During the meeting the two men set aside their grievances and peace was restored.

In his beautifully illustrated book, *St. Francis of Assisi*, Bernardino Farnetani, O.F.M. Conv., writes, "The single notes of love, which had grown in his heart during his entire life, have come together here in a great symphony of praise. It has been said this is the most beautiful poetry since the Gospel, and it could only be the work of one who had grasped the purest and most vital ideals of the Gospel." Adding:

> The world seen by Francis is the inner echo of his purity, in which he sees, as though in a mirror, the "goodness" of God reflected in all things.
>
> Today we are beginning to notice how right Francis was in his dream of love for creation. We are beginning to wonder anxiously what the future of our world will be like, if man continues in his violent ravaging of nature. The air and the water are becoming more and more polluted; many species of animals and plants are threatened by extinction; the balance of cosmic energy has been destroyed, and nature itself has become an object of conquest for man in his continual struggle for power.
>
> Saint Francis' love for nature was not mere sentimentalism. He recognized man's use and dependence on it and he made this "service" to man another reason for praising the Lord. Like poets, and more so, saints can discover God's presence permeating the world, the presence that preserves the world. And therefore Francis wants man to feel this divinity and respect it, overcoming his selfishness and his violence, in order to be able to read in it the "signification" of the "most high, almighty, good Lord." It was the song of his life, set to the rhythm of his love for God, who reflects His beauty in creation and His love in those men who know how to love. (page 100)

Murray Bodo, O.F.M., writes of the *Canticle*:

> *The Canticle of Brother Sun* is a sublime articulation of the secret of Francis' life: you integrate the depths of the self by leaving self and entering into what you can see and hear and touch and feel and smell. God dwells "deep down things" [Gerard Manley Hopkins], and you find Him when He finds you loving the world He has created and redeemed. (*The Way of St. Francis*, page 145)

In *The Canticle of the Creatures*, Francis is telling us that all of creation is united with God, the creator of all, and the essence of that union is best expressed and fully realized in a spirit of fraternity in which all of creation forms an unseen oneness.

The Canticle of Brother Sun, which has come to be called *The Canticle of the Creatures*, originally ended with the verse praising the Lord through Sister Earth. The sections which address those who grant pardon, endure in peace, and encounter death were added later...and later, I'll discuss those additions. But now I'll focus on Francis' skill as a poet, by sharing the following passage:

> Like a skilled and gifted painter, he [Francis] uses the light, life and color of language to move men's hearts and minds. The ultimate expression of his creative love of poetry reached its climax in the lines of *The Canticle of the Creatures*, written in the dialect of the Umbrian people. This work is generally considered to be the earliest example of lyric poetry in Italian—and is said to be the true historical source of Western nature poetry.
>
> This achievement alone would have been sufficient to ensure Francis of Assisi a lasting place in the history of Italian literature. Nevertheless, of far greater importance is the fact that, in addition to its qualities as an outstanding creative work of poetry, *The Canticle of the Creatures* is clearly the genuine outpouring of a heart immersed in deepest prayer and contemplation. The joy expressed in it is all the more extraordinary if one realizes that it was composed during his last illness when his body was racked with intense suffering. Yet the canticle itself expresses no hint of anything except deepest gratitude, reverent joy, and limitless love. It is a true hymn of thanksgiving!
>
> In the text of the Italian original, the word "per" (through) is repeated frequently, but is often overlooked by translators of the canticle into the English language, when in a number of instances the "for" is used instead of "through." This, however, alters a most fundamental point which Francis wished to express in the canticle—namely, that all creation is the means through which God himself is "praised and glorified"—not that God is to be praised and thanked "for" all things created by him. Therefore not only the sun, moon, stars, and the four elements, but even forgiveness, suffering, and death are shown to be the means by which the creator is "honored and blessed."(Allen, *Francis of Assisi's Canticle of the Creatures*, pages 100, 101)

The French-Jewish intellectual Simone Weil, who, besides being attracted to both Buddhism and mystical Christianity, spoke out against injustice and sided with the oppressed prior to her death at 34 in 1943, was drawn to admire the sheer beauty of Saint Francis' canticle because it so eloquently expressed his attitude of grateful dependency on all things as gifts of God. Weil writes:

> The example of St. Francis shows how great a place the beauty of the world can have in Christian thought. Not only is his actual poem perfect poetry, but his life was perfect poetry in action. His very choice of places for solitary retreats or for the foundations of his convents was in itself the most beautiful poetry in action. Vagabondage and poverty were poetry for him; he stripped himself naked in order to have immediate contact with the beauty of the world. (*Waiting for God*, page 160)

Father Michael L. Gaudoin-Parker offers the following observation on Simone Weil's thoughts on Saint Francis:

> Such a phrase as "immediate contact with the beauty of the world," that Weil exalts, catches the sublime symbolism of Francis' own imagery of a bride or spouse to express the Christian value he discovered in poverty. Only by experiencing and acknowledging his nakedness before God—in every sense of "being naked"—did this man know himself: not only as vulnerable, defenseless, and ridiculous in his pride, but as great too. For in his nakedness, and in no other condition, did he see that every human being is great because he is sought by God—as is brought out again and again in the Scriptures. (*A Window on the Mystery of Faith*, pages 41-42)

Francis' poetry, as well as his life, grew out of his love of poverty, which helped him penetrate the mystery of God-incarnate.

Even though Francis could no longer see or enjoy the beauty of creation, could no longer see other creatures, even though his eyes were so diseased that they couldn't even be exposed to the light of a fire let alone the glorious light of the sun, he was still able to express his innermost joy through material things, through the sun, the moon and the stars, through the wind and air, the water and fire, through the flowers and herbs and all of earth, and he could do so only because all of nature was being illuminated from within.

Father Eloi Leclerc, O.F.M., has this to say:

> There can be no doubt that Francis experienced the sacred in

the cosmos and entered into communion with God through the medium of created things and indeed in the very depths of created things. It is this aspect of his religious experience that *The Canticle of Brother Sun* expresses.

Real though it is, however, this aspect of his experience cannot be separated from another: his union with God along the lowly ways established by the incarnation of the Most High Son of God. In fact, all that is original in Francis' religious experience derives from the synthesis he effected between an interior and very personal evangelical mysticism and an ardent cosmic mysticism.

Francis unites, in a wonderful way, a life of union with the person of Christ and the profound religious feeling which pantheistic religions entertain toward the cosmos. He unites the Sun and the Cross. Max Scheler, the German philosopher, speaks as follows in his book on the nature and forms of sympathy:

> It was left to one of the greatest artificers of the spirit in European history to make the memorable attempt uniting and harnessing this [a non-cosmic personal love-mysticism of universal compassion], within a single life-stream, to the animistic sense of union with the being and life of Nature. This was the very remarkable achievement of the saint of Assisi.

The synthesis resulted in one of the most profound and fascinating spiritual experiences any human being has ever had.

The Canticle of Brother Sun is both praise of the cosmos and a hymn to the inner depths. (*The Canticle of the Creatures*, page xii)

Paul's epistle to the Ephesians states: "God has given us the wisdom to understand fully the mystery." The key to that wisdom has eluded me. Perhaps Francis, with his ability to embrace all of creation as the glory of God combined with his ability to let go of everything within himself which allowed him to simultaneously discover his true self and to experience the presence of God, found the key to that wisdom.

I hunger for that kind of wisdom.

PILGRIMAGE DIARY 41

Distant and Hidden

*B*eing back in Sant' Isidoro brings back lots of memories. I think about how empty my life was before my first visit here. Today, I fully understand that my life would be empty without God. For the first year or so after rededicating my life to Christ, I was filled with an inner peace and joy. I seemed intoxicated with God. God was always on my mind and in my heart. My time of prayer had a sweetness to it. But lately, the glow seems to have worn off. God seems distant and hidden, far beyond my humble reach. I find no consolation in prayer. Nor do I find consolation in anything else. Even a Yankees victory doesn't mean all that much anymore. Where did the joy go? I want to become closer to God, yet God seems further away. What is this emptiness? Is this a purging, a pruning? Can I outlast the darkness? The pilgrimage road is getting steeper. Even though I don't feel like it at times, I must stay faithful to the climb. I'm struggling to put my faith in God, and not in my feelings.

I suppose loving God is no different from any other kind of love. The excitement of the first encounter is magical, sparks flying, bells ringing. But the honeymoon eventually ends. The glow fades. Love has its dark spots, its troubling moments. The joy is always surrounded by the mundane realities of daily life. There is always laundry to do. And garbage to be taken out.

No matter how strong the love is, it always feels incomplete. There are valleys, and that is where authentic growth begins. The real test of love is its ability to continue to love through the dull times and even through the times of complete darkness. I need unquestioning trust in God's love for me. I need to remain faithful in prayer, confident that in God's perfect timing the sweetness will return...sweeter than ever.

Lord God, I abandon my life to you. Heal my sinfulness, my loneliness. I surrender everything to you and your transforming love.

Brother Sun and the Death Train

The story you are about to read is disturbing. It contains frank descriptions of extreme cruelty. Sadly, it is true. The story takes place on a Nazi death train. Why would I include a story of Nazi brutality in a book about a peace-loving saint? Because the story dramatically illustrates the power and purpose of The Canticle.

Standing on top of one of the towers of the fortress Rocca Maggiore, looking down on the city of Assisi and the valley of Spoleto, it is easy to imagine hearing The Canticle of Brother Sun *being sung. But to imagine the same beautiful canticle being sung on a Nazi death train crammed with poor souls headed for a concentration camp is impossible to imagine. But it was. Franciscan priest Eloi Leclerc was on the train when it happened. In* The Canticle of Creatures, *which, I am sorry to say, is no longer in print, Leclerc included an epilogue entitled: "The Language of the Soul's Night." The story, in the form of a journal, tells of his dreadful experience on that train. He sets the stage for the story, taken from pages 227 through 236 of his book, this way:*

> April, 1945: The Allied armies are penetrating deep into the heart of Germany. A lengthy freight train is moving slowly along the line from Passau to Munich, with thousands of exiles packed into its cars. They have been shut up there for twenty-one days now. Hundreds have already died; hundreds more are at death's door, delirious from hunger. The train started from Buchenwald and has made a long detour through Czecho-slovakia and the mountains of Bohemia; now it is heading for Dachau near Munich. Suddenly, incredibly, singing can be heard from one of the cars; it is Francis of Assisi's Canticle of Brother Sun! "All praise be yours, my Lord, through all that you have made, and first my lord Brother Sun...All praise be yours, my Lord, through Sister Earth, our mother."
>
> What can such a song mean in circumstances like these? The men who sang were hardly more than ghosts themselves, surrounded by the dead! What was going on in this railroad car?

Leclerc claimed, "Francis of Assisi's Canticle of Brother Sun *is not simply an expression of esthetic, or esthetico-religious, emotion at the spectacle of nature, but the expression of an experience that takes place in the night of the soul."*

It is not nature that inspired Saint Francis, but what the saint had seen inside of himself that allowed him to look at nature in a totally new way, a way that caused him to write The Canticle of Brother Sun *while in the shadow of death.*

Father Leclerc's story in diary form, "The Language of the Soul's

Night," describes his journey on the death train. The first entry is dated April 7, 1945.

He vividly paints the horror. Here are just a few mild examples:

Rocked by the swaying of the train, we sink into a boundless sadness.

We were forbidden to stand up, even to restore circulation to our legs. We were forced to remain crouching, day after day. For food, a few potatoes and a bit of bread; nothing hot, of course. Meanwhile a very cold fog descends....

We knock each other over trying to get a morsel of bread....

Here the suffering is limitless and everyone shares it. All differences fade away in the face of the common destiny. Lost in the mass of men, there are five of us who are sons of St. Francis.

For five long days, from April 11th to the 16th, the train sat at a small station. The prisoners were not permitted to get off.

The train stands still all day in this little station. In the evening, the dead are removed; nothing else happens all day. The same thing the next day; we spend all day without food, and in the evening they remove the dead. Life is tragically simplified for us now. We have only one occupation to fill our time: watching others die, while we ourselves wait for death. On the average, two men died each day in each car; that means a hundred deaths a day for the whole train.

These days spent motionless seem endless to us. But the nights bring a further torment. Alongside the dying, who are at their last gasp, some of the living fight for a bit of space in which to sleep; others go mad and pound their heads against the sides of the car in order to finish their nightmare. Over us, an SS man rains down blows with a club in order to restore quiet. But even all this is not the worst. The terrible, awful thing is to find oneself watching for a neighbor to die and telling oneself that tomorrow there will be more room to stretch out in.

The train finally moved. Through the slots of the freight car walls, the prisoners could see the wide-open beauty of the mountains of Bohemia, making their imprisonment even more torturous. The diary continues to describe the horror.

We are paralyzed by the cold. There is nothing hot for us to eat. Some of us, coming back from removing the dead, have managed to pick up some pieces of wood and a few bricks along the track. On the bricks we light a fire in the car. It's really more of a ghost of a fire. We crowd around it to get dry and warm, but the flame is too weak. Besides, skeletons can't get warm....

The dead! There are more and more of them. Many of our comrades die of dysentery; many of exhaustion. Others have contracted erysipelas and are the most horrible spectacle of all. Within a night or a day, these men become unrecognizable; their swollen fiery faces are completely distorted. Delirious with fever, these unfortunates fill the night with their yelling; they scream for water, but in vain.

And here is the final excerpt, which contains the point of the story:

These extremities of suffering plunge us into acute anxiety. It is no longer simply the anxiety that grips any living thing as death approaches. Amid our terrible distress there arises in us a strange feeling that eats away at those inmost certainties which till now sustained us. We have a growing impression that we have been handed over to some blind, savage power. There we are, thousands of men abandoned to hunger, cold, vermin, and death. The human being is completely crushed. Man, whom we had till now believed was made in God's image, now seems laughable: worthless, helpless, hopeless; a being caught up in a whirlwind of forces that play with him, or rather, pay absolutely no attention to him. Among the corpses that lie in the water of the car, eyes turned back, is a companion or friend. Everything we can see, every experience we must undergo, tells us we are in the grip of iron law, handed over to the play of blind forces—and that this, and this alone is reality.

Reality where the Father has no place! Experience that once in your life, and you will never again speak lightly of the "death of God." It is an atrocious experience. When the Father is absent, the Son is in agony. The Son's agony is always due to the Father's silence, the Father's absence. And where can the least sign of the father be found in this hell? Now we understand the words, "My soul is sorrowful enough to die."

Black night fills our souls. And yet, on the morning of April 26 when one of us is in his last moments and the light has almost left his eyes, what rises from our hearts to our lips is not a cry of despair or rebellion, but a song, a song of praise: Francis of Assisi's *Canticle of Brother Sun!* Nor do we have to force ourselves to sing it. It rises spontaneously out of the darkness and nakedness, as though it were the only language fit for such a moment.

What brings us in such circumstances to praise God for and through the great cosmic brotherhood? Theories have no place in our utter confusion of spirit; they offer no shelter against the storm. The only thing that remains and is priceless in our eyes is the patience and friendship this or that comrade shows you. Such an act by someone who, like yourself, is immersed in suffering and anxiety, is a ray of light that falls miraculously into the wretched darkness that envelops us. It recreates you, makes you a human being once again. Suddenly we learn all over again that we are men. And when such an act of friendly help has been done to you, you in turn are able to do it for another and thus respond to the reign of brute force with a freedom and love that bear witness to another kind of reality....

At such a moment, astounding though it seems, we experience wonder before the world; we experience the sacred in the world. Such an experience is possible only in extreme deprivation of soul and body. Only in utter distress and need can we fully appreciate a mouthful of bread, a sip of water, a ray of sunlight, and now and then, like a visitor from another world, the warm greeting of a passerby. The tiny drops of rain that tremble on the telephone wires in the evening light after a storm are filled, to the selfless eye, with boundless innocence. And the broad rain-washed heaven shows us—how luminous, how pure it is! All these lowly things that we can contemplate from the floor of our car are not the result of passing chance. They speak sweetly to the soul.

Where do they come from, this purity and innocence that suddenly lay hold of us through these humble realities? Whence the limpid radiance that bathes the world but is perceptible only amid extreme poverty? How innocent things are. Do you smile? Yet this experience can be matched by no other. Nietzche said: "One must...have chaos in oneself to give birth to a dancing star." We certainly have not been spared chaos. Devastation is everywhere, around us and within us. History has swept like a cyclone across our lives. And yet, over this heap of ruins, there now shines "the great evening star of poverty."

Surely, through this changeless transparency of things, it is the most primitive level of being that communicates with us; it is that indomitable, eternal reality that remains unchanged through the course of history. The man with the rifle can spread death and keep thousands of men in the thrall of fear; he can destroy a great deal. But he is powerless against this hidden spring of purity and innocence. Man's arm cannot reach to these depths.

The purity and innocence do not originate in us. They do, however, well up within us, at the deepest level of the soul, and when they do, they restore childhood there. It is not our gaze that brings them into being; on the contrary, it is they that enable us to see things once again as children do. But this purified vision is attained only through a kind of agony, when we have become poor enough to welcome such purity and innocence. What chaos we must have within us if we are able to see the world born once again into the light! It is always in the shadow of the crucified Christ that the Christian, at the end of his journey, recovers the vision of a child. His selfless gaze is then no longer fixed on some paradise. Rather, even at the heart of devastation and death, it expresses an immense will to peace and mercy. And, despite the seeming power of evil, it is such a man who is stronger. He is capable of defeating the most monstrous onslaughts of barbarism. Amid the furor of history, his eyes speak to the end. They do more than that: they sing of it.

Because this vision was given to us, we were able, on an April morning in Germany, to gather round our dying brother and sing of the sun and the stars, the wind and the water, the fire and the earth, and also of "those who grant pardon for love of you." "When he died, so light as to be nameless," there was no flight of larks overhead, but a supernatural peace had filled our hearts. That evening we carried his body away, accompanied by blows from the SS who felt we were not moving quickly enough. His was the last death in our car.

I once spoke lightly of "the death of God" because I had taken a close look at the world and saw nothing but random chaos, unfathomable suffering, blind hatred, and a wide assortment of unspeakable evils. And I never came close to riding in a boxcar of a death train. I was looking outside of myself for signs of a loving God. And I saw none. Things changed only when I began to look within.

Wandering Minstrels

Even after I read Father Leclerc's powerful story a number of times, it is still very difficult for me to imagine singing The Canticle of the Creatures *on a Nazi death train. Francis would have understood.*

I'll end this section on the Canticle *with the following passage:*

Francis composed a melody to go with the words of his poem, and sent some of the brothers to various places in order that in singing it they would convey its profound truth to their listeners. He instructed them in how to do this: like traveling medieval minstrels who sang of brave knights and their true loves, they were to form a circle in marketplaces and town squares, wherever people gathered. One of their number was to preach a sermon, and immediately afterward all of them were to sing Francis' *Canticle of Brother Sun*. The one who had preached was then to turn to the people and say, "We are the wandering minstrels of God and the only reward we ask is that you lead a life of true penitence."

In response to the brothers' surprise at thus being called "itinerant minstrels," Francis asked: "Who indeed are God's servants, if not minstrels who seek to move men's hearts in order to lead them into the joys of the spirit?" From this time onward, despite his steadily increasing weakness and suffering, for Francis it was sufficient to hear his Brothers sing his "canticle of joy," in order that he himself could find the courage and strength to bear every burden laid upon him. (Paul M. Allen and Joan deRis Allen, *Francis of Assisi's Canticle of the Creatures*, page 82)

But the struggle wouldn't go on much longer.

The Liturgy of the Hours

A pure heart create for me, O God,
put a steadfast spirit within me.
Do not cast me away from your presence,
nor deprive me of your holy spirit.
(Psalm 50 [51]:12-13)

PILGRIMAGE DIARY 42

The Light of the Soul

I *love looking at the really old books in the library at the Collegio Sant' Isidoro. If you're interested in reading the works of the great Franciscan theologian John Duns Scotus, the champion of the Immaculate Conception who died in 1308, the library has a number of editions of his works published in the 1580's. Want to see how the sacramental rites have evolved over the centuries? Just a few minutes ago, I was thumbing through a small book published in 1589, and it contained, in Latin, the complete Rite of Baptism, including three pieces of music. Another book, published in 1658, was four hundred fifty pages in length, but printed on pages no bigger than an index card, and it contained the rubrics and prayers of all the rites of the Roman Church. A third book, published in Dublin in 1820, contained the official prayers and rituals used in the administration of the sacraments; the prayers used during Extreme Unction and the blessing of the ill were beautiful.*

The cover page of an old book on Saint Francis read:

WORKS
OF
THE SERAPHIC FATHER

ST. FRANCIS OF ASSISI

TRANSLATED BY
A RELIGIOUS OF THE ORDER

R. WASHBOURNE
18 PATERNOSTER ROW, LONDON
1882

Part IV of this book contained short sayings of Francis. Each of the "sayings" was contained in brief stories, each with its own italicized title. Here is one I found interesting:

The Light of the Soul is to be Preferred to that of the Body

The doctor tried to persuade the holy Father to restrain his tears, if he wished to preserve his bodily sight. To which he replied: "Brother Doctor, it is not right to lose even the least spiritual light, for the sake of that light which we have in common with the flies; for the soul does not receive light for the sake of the body, but the body for the sake of the soul."

Francis wasn't a good patient.

THE LAST DAYS

Loving Christ, I wish to climb naked on the cross, and I wish to die, Lord, embraced by you; it would be a joy to me to experience death in your embrace.

—JACOPONE DA TODI, *LAUDA XLII*

In the summer of 1225, Pope Honorius III was living in Rieti, having been forced to flee Rome due to political unrest and riots. At that time, Francis was suffering because of his eyes, and the brothers wanted him to travel to the papal court so they could make arrangements for him to receive proper medical attention. Francis resisted, fearing an operation, which he knew would be nothing short of torture. The minister general, Brother Elias, convinced Cardinal Ugolino to write a letter ordering Francis to come to Reiti so he could be treated by the pope's physician. Francis traveled on foot from Assisi to Reiti, wearing special shoes the nuns at San Damiano made for him so he could walk more comfortably on his stigmatized feet.

Before arriving in Reiti, Francis stopped at the home of a poor priest near Poggio Bustone. News of his presence at the priest's home caused a crowd of people to surround the priest's humble residence. In the field next to the church was a small vineyard which was the tiny parish's main source of income. The crush of people trying to catch a glimpse of Francis trampled on the grapes, destroying most of them. And the grapes they didn't destroy, they ate. Francis knew the priest was upset because the vineyards' normal yield of thirteen barrels of wine was lost. Francis told the priest to allow the people to eat the grapes out of the love of God, and that God would reward him with a harvest greater than normal. The priest put his trust in Francis' promise of divine help, and allowed the people to remain in the vineyard and eat the grapes. When it was time to harvest the grapes, they produced twenty barrels of wine.

By the time Francis reached Reiti, his eyes had deteriorated to the point were he could hardly distinguish light from dark. The physicians decided his condition was so bad that they had to resort to a very drastic method of treatment. At the time, it was believed that applying red-hot irons to the temples surrounding the eyes could relieve such problems as ophthalmia, a condition causing a severe inflammation of the eyeball. The procedure was performed, without an anesthetic, at the hermitage of Fontecolombo, not far from Rieti. The doctors placed the cautery into a fire until it glowed. This must have been a moment of sheer terror. As the incandescent iron was about to be placed over the his eyebrows, Francis said, "Brother Fire, God has given you a splendor that has made you the envy of all creation. You are the most noble and useful of all creatures. Be kind and courteous to me, and temper your heat so that I am able to endure your burning caress." With that prayer, the terror Francis had felt riddling his body melted away into a sea of calmness. The brothers gathered in the room could not endure the awful sound of the hiss of his flesh as it was touched by the burning irons. They fled the room. Francis did not even flinch. When the physicians completed the treatment, Francis told them they could do it again—"cook it more"—if they needed to, because he had not felt a thing. The treatment no doubt increased the faith of the doctor, but it had no effect on Francis' eyesight.

From then on, Francis' life was a painful, downhill road to death. He spent the following winter in a hermitage north of Siena, where the milder weather and companionship made his pain more bearable. In the spring of 1226, following a night when he hemorrhaged badly, Francis was transported to the hermitage of Le Celle outside of Cortona. The brothers took two habits and two cloaks for the dying saint, which they continually changed and cleaned to conceal the flow of blood from the stigmata, which Francis wanted hidden from the world. His condition was deteriorating rapidly. His legs and feet were now swelling, and he was unable to retain food. He endured pains in his spleen and liver. His stomach was swollen. He vomited blood. Francis was wasting away from tuberculosis. The end was near, and Francis had only one wish: to see Assisi before he died. Before leaving, he told the friars to always love Lady Poverty.

Being a Pilgrim

I *miss my home, my family, my safe and comfortable routine. A pilgrim is a stranger, always on the move, never feeling at home. I miss making my own coffee first thing in the morning. I miss my CD collection, and the classical music that soothes me. Yesterday, I bought some fruit at an outdoor market. I could not help but think of the merchant at a fruit-and-juice bar near my home in Los Angeles. Two or three times a week I enter his tiny store. He smiles at me, and without a word he begins to prepare a fruit salad for me, knowing exactly how I like it. No need to tell him to add just a touch of honey, a little yogurt and extra bananas. He knows me. And I like that. No one knows me here in Italy. Unknown, I exist on the margins of their society, without any power or the security of family and friends. I'm cut off by language, isolated by unknown customs and traditions. Even making a phone call is a challenge. I need a map to go anywhere, and a calculator to figure how much 32,800 lire is in American money.*

While I have money in my pocket and the companionship of my fellow pilgrims, I nonetheless feel a sense of poverty and powerlessness. I feel naked, abandoned and solitary. I guess that is a normal state of mind for a pilgrim. I'm trusting it is a state of mind that ultimately will be helpful in my search. But right now, it is painful. I'm tired and lonely.

I'd love to hug my wife. I'd even love to take my dog for a walk...and clean up after him.

SISTER DEATH

The malady of Francis grew hourly more incurable and afflicting. He was frequently attacked at night by vomiting of blood, which, on many occasions, reduced him almost to the last extremity. His disconsolate flock shed a flood of tears; and encircling his dying couch, gave vent to their sorrow in loud and heart-rending sobs.
—EMILIUS CHAVIN DE MALAN, *THE LIFE OF ST. FRANCIS OF ASSISIUM*

Because of the increasing esteem for Francis' holiness, the friars transporting him back to Assisi feared that the people of Perugia might try to seize the dying saint (who was a living relic), in order to lay claim to his bodily remains after his death, and so they took a rather circuitous route. Somewhere near Gubbio and Nocera, the traveling brothers were met by a body of armed men dispatched from Assisi to safeguard the saint's return. As they made their way to Assisi, they walked beneath a scorching summer sun. For Francis, the road became his *via dolorosa*. He was in unbearable pain. Sister Death was waiting to embrace him.

Fearing the Portiuncula was too unprotected, they elected to bring Francis to the residence of the bishop, who was away on a pilgrimage at the time. As they approached the city walls, news of the dying saint's return spread through Assisi like a wildfire. As evening approached, they processed slowly into the city. People lined the streets to see Francis. But Francis' eyes were so bad he was practically blind, barely able to distinguish shadows. One can only wonder what he heard or how he felt. Once inside the bishop's palace, Francis was surrounded by the brothers and some doctors. One doctor told Francis his disease was incurable and that he would not live longer than another month. Francis stretched out his arms and said he welcomed Sister Death.

He asked the brothers to sing *The Canticle of the Sun*, which of course they were happy to do. But they were unable to control their tears and emotions. While sobbing, they made beautiful music for Francis. And Francis added the last verse to the poem:

> Praised be thou, O Lord, for our Sister Bodily Death,
> from whom no living man can escape.
> Woe to those who die in mortal sin.
> Blessed those who have discovered thy most holy will,
> for to them the second death can do no harm. (Translated by Johannes Jörgensen)

Francis did not want to die in a palace, and so asked to be taken to the Portiuncula, a place he loved dearly. Accompanied by a great throng of people, the brothers carried Francis down the hill to the valley below. At a leper hospital halfway between Assisi and the Portiuncula, Francis asked the brothers to stop and turn him around so he could face his beloved city one more time and bless it. Through his blind eyes, Francis looked long and hard at the city, whose image must have been emblazoned on his mind. It was a moment of profound silence. Francis slowly raised his hands, and, while making a sign of the cross over the city, said, "Blessed be you, holy city, for the Lord has chosen you to be a home and abode for all those who in truth will give glory to Him and give honor to His name. And through you, holy city, many souls will be saved, and in you many servants of God will dwell."

While lying prostrate on a cot, close to death, Francis had a very unusual thought: He wanted a sweet cake made by his Brother Jacoba, the noblewoman from Rome who loved Francis and the brothers dearly. Francis knew she would be saddened if he died before she had a chance to say good-bye. And so he dictated a letter to be delivered to her. At the same time, Lady Jacoba had a premonition about his impending death, and so she set out for Assisi, bringing with her Francis' favorite sweet dessert, an almond cake known as *mostacciuolo*. When she arrived at his side, she offered him a piece of the cake. Francis seemed delighted and tried to nibble on it, but he was too weak. Despite the tears from Brother Jacoba and the brothers, Francis seemed at peace. He would live only a few more days. One by one, brothers came to say farewell to Francis. He dictated a letter to Sister Clare, consoling her with a blessing and absolution for any possible failures she may have committed against her vows. Francis gave the brothers one last sermon, admonishing them to be faithful to poverty.

As the moment of death approached, Francis asked to be stripped naked and placed on the bare ground. His wish was granted. Lying naked on the ground, Francis was still preaching, showing the brothers his fragility and his closeness to Mother Earth. He was without any defenses, without any pretenses. He was an artist of his own life and his last dramatic gesture was a symbol of his life, a life of vulnerability and humility, waiting for the final encounter with God. He told the brothers, "My work is done. May Christ teach you what is yours to do." Francis began softly to recite Psalm 141, his weakened voice barely audible. "With a loud voice I cry out to the Lord; with a loud voice I beseech the Lord" (Vulgate Bible). As the brothers chanted a psalm, Francis quietly died...naked on the ground, faithful to Lady Poverty until his final breath, which came late Saturday night on October 3, 1226. The larks flying over the Portiuncula sang their final farewell to their friend as his spirit ascended to heaven. Right up until his final breath, the chant of the Resurrection, the chant that expresses the fullness of life, of peace and of love, never ceased to be on Francis' lips.

The brothers dressed him in a new tunic, and on Sunday morning, they carried Francis' body on a stretcher for one last trip to Assisi. They were followed by a procession of people and clergy carrying olive branches and lighted candles and singing hymns. They stopped at San Damiano so the Poor Clares could say farewell. Clare watched in silence.

In a letter announcing the death of Francis, Brother Elias, the minister general, wrote:

> The thing I feared has come to pass, for me and for you. Far from us has gone the consoler, and he who carried us like lambs in his arms has set forth a pilgrim into a far country.... The beloved of God and man has entered the mansions of exceeding light.

PILGRIMAGE DIARY 44

No Greater Love

This is my commandment, that you love one another as I have loved you. No one has greater love than this, to lay down one's life for one's friends.

—*JOHN 15:12-13*, NEW REVISED STANDARD VERSION OF THE BIBLE

Fifty-six years ago today, on August 14, 1941, Father Maximilian Mary Kolbe, O.F.M. Conv., laid down his life for a fellow prisoner. Today he is known as Saint Maximilian because on that fateful day Father Maximilian lived this Gospel message to the fullest by giving up his life in exchange for a young married man with a family who was condemned to death by the Nazis. The following account of Maximilian's life was based primarily on Desmond Forristal's book, Maximilian of Auschwitz.

Maximilian Kolbe was born on January 7, 1894, in the small village of Zdunska-Wola in Poland. His parents, Julius and Marianna, were textile workers; they worked at home, a home crowded with looms. The village was very poor, and most of its inhabitants spent long hours on looms in their homes, selling the cloth once a week to merchants in the nearby city of Lodz. His mother was a pious woman who as a child dreamed of becoming a nun; but as she lived in a section of Poland that was under Russian control and the authorities had suppressed convents, it was virtually impossible for young Marianna to enter religious life. Instead, she frequently prayed for a devout husband. Julius was a secular Franciscan who diligently attended Mass and received Communion. They married on October 5, 1891. Maximilian, who was christened Raymond, was the second of five boys, of whom only the first three survived infancy. By the age of ten, young Raymond's life was already deeply rooted in prayer. Besides being an altar boy, he had a small altar hidden where he often went to pray without letting anyone notice. He had great devotion to Saint Francis of Assisi.

Despite his prayerfulness, young Raymond had a mischievous streak which occasionally got him in trouble. On one occasion, his mother scolded him saying, "What is to become of you, Raymond?" The boy was troubled by the question, and went to his little altar to pray and seek an answer from the Blessed Mother. Later, he confided to his mother that Our Lady had appeared to him, offering him two crowns, one white, symbolizing purity, and the other red, signifying martyrdom. "Which do you choose," asked Mary in the apparition. "Both," answered the young boy. The mystical experience ignited a lifelong devotion to Mary within his heart.

When young Raymond was thirteen years old, he attended a retreat, along with his parents and brothers, conducted by a Conventual Franciscan priest. It was the turning point of his life. Soon afterward, the two oldest boys entered a Conventual minor seminary. As they approached graduation, the boys had to decide whether or not to enter the Franciscan novitiate. Raymond was on the verge of deciding against continuing his Franciscan studies and instead becoming a soldier in the Polish army. Before he could formally announce his decision, his parents paid him a visit and delivered the news that their youngest son had decided to join his brothers as a Franciscan. Moreover, Julius and Marianna also decided to more fully dedicate their lives to God by becoming vowed religious themselves. Julius was entering a Franciscan monastery in Cracow, and Marianna was entering a Benedictine convent in Lwow. Marianna's childhood dream was not only going to be fulfilled, but she also was able to offer God the lives of her husband and three sons.

On September 4, 1910, the two oldest boys entered the novitiate. Raymond became Brother Maximilian. He made his simple profession the following year, and shortly thereafter, because of his great academic abilities, he was sent to the Pontifical Gregorian University in Rome to complete his studies. (Since its founding in 1551, the University has seen twenty of its graduates become saints, and over the centuries, sixteen popes have studied there.) He earned two doctoral degrees, one in philosophy, the other in theology. He was ordained a priest on April 28, 1918, in Rome. He returned to Poland after his ordination, where he worked until 1930, when he set sail for Japan, where he labored as a missionary for six years. In 1936, he left Japan to return to Cracow in order to attend a provincial chapter meeting, during which he was reassigned as superior of a friary in Niepokalanow, Poland. During these years Father Kolbe grew into an exceptional Marian theologian, seeing as deeply into the role of Mary in the work of the Trinity as fellow Franciscan John Duns Scotus had six centuries earlier. Kolbe formed the Knights of the Immaculate, a movement dedicated to spreading the message of Christ through love and devotion to Mary, whom he felt was the one fully human being who never strayed from total surrender of her will to God.

In September of 1936, after the German army crossed into Poland, the Polish authorities in the district where Father Maximilian was stationed told the brothers and seminarians to return to their hometowns and serve in the Red Cross. Father Kolbe elected to stay behind with one priest and thirty-six brothers to care for the wounded and maintain a presence in the friary.

On September 19, 1939, the Nazis took control of the monastery and Maximilian and the others were forced to board a train bound for the internment camp at Amtitz. Father Maximilian, with his great love for the Virgin Mary and rigorous devotion to the Immaculate Conception, immediately turned the prison camp into the City of the Immaculate. His tent became his monastery; caring for the other prisoners became his apostolate. For Father Kolbe, Mary truly was an "icon of the Holy Spirit." Looking at her, he could see the beauty of our humanity and the power of God's grace...even in a concentration camp.

A few weeks later, they were transferred to another camp and on December 8th—the feast of the Immaculate Conception—they were released after eighty-one days of imprisonment.

Father Kolbe returned to the friary at Niepokalanow and began work on a book about the Immaculate Conception. Two years later, for reasons which are not clear, Father Maximilian was arrested on February 17, 1941. He was taken to a prison in Warsaw. Soon after his arrival at the prison, Maximilian, wearing his habit, was confronted by a soldier who taunted him about his rosary, which hung from the cord he wore around his waist. The soldier reached for the crucifix, pulled it roughly from the rosary beads and asked, "Do you believe in this?" Father Kolbe said, "Yes, I believe." The soldier became enraged and punched the priest in the face. And then he asked the same question again. Again, Father Kolbe said he believed. Again his answer drew a blow to his face from the fist of the soldier. Looking directly at Father Kolbe's bloodied face, the soldier asked the same question for a third time, and for the third time he heard the same defiant response from Father Kolbe. Another powerful blow to the face. The beating resulted in Maximilian's being sent to the prison hospital. A few days later, he was assigned light work in the prison library.

On May 28th, a consignment of 305 prisoners was shipped from the prison to Auschwitz...among them was Father Maximilian Kolbe. In the darkness of the truck ride to the train station, Maximilian led the prisoners in song.

The train arrived in Auschwitz that evening.

The number 16670 was tattooed on Father Kolbe's arm. He ministered tirelessly to the needs of his fellow prisoners. There are numerous reports from survivors of the horror of Auschwitz telling how Father Maximilian not only helped others but also endured being mistreated and beaten with great patience and dignity. He prayed constantly and risked being punished by making the sign of the cross over the food before eating. On two occasions he secured scraps of bread and managed to say Mass and give Holy Communion to some of the prisoners. He lived in extreme self-denial and gave whatever was given to him—his meager rations, a pair of shoes— away to others. The frail priest, who had lost one lung to tuberculosis, often gave his food away, and he did so in a discreet manner that would not embarrass the recipients of his generosity—he gently placed scraps of bread into their pockets without drawing any attention to the exchange. He blessed food for people, bringing a ray of light into their ever-expanding darkness. Witnesses from the camp were unanimous is asserting Father Kolbe's modesty, meekness and humility, saying he never spoke of himself or his sufferings and *always placed himself last.*

Father Kolbe, weak from not eating and giving so much of himself, became sick with a high fever and pneumonia. Unable to walk, he was taken to the infirmary. The pneumonia passed but his temperature remained high and so he remained in the hospital. But he would not rest. Instead, he ministered to the suffering and sick and dying, doing what he could to lessen their pain. He told stories, heard confessions and recited prayer in common with them. He raised spirits. Day or night, he never refused to listen to someone who needed a consoling word. Witnesses say his words were simple and profound.

Near the end of July, he recovered sufficiently to be transferred to Cell Block 14. The following week, a prisoner managed to escape. To discourage future attempts at escape, the SS exacted a brutal retaliation: ten prisoners were sentenced to death by starvation in the cellar of Block 11, known as Death Block. Moreover, all future escapes would result in the same ratio of death sentences for other prisoners.

One of the ten prisoners chosen was Francis Gajowniczek, a forty-year-old sergeant who had served in the Polish army. The prospect of the horrible death he was about to endure filled him with terror. He began to cry because he knew he would never see his wife and children again. Suddenly, Maximilian Kolbe boldly stepped forward and said, "I want to die in place of this prisoner," pointing to Gajowniczek. Everyone was stunned, including the Nazi guards. Life for the prisoners was a constant battle for survival, and this act of complete self-abnegation defied their comprehension. How could this priest, who had been methodically and brutally stripped of his dignity and humanity, muster the will and love to sacrifice himself for another? Perhaps fearing the guards might not accept his offer, Kolbe played to the twisted Nazi philosophy of eliminating the weak and offered it as explanation for his proposal: "I have no wife or children, and I am old and not good for anything." Kolbe was in fact only seven years older than Gajowniczek. Kolbe went on to say that the stronger soldier would be more useful to the guards.

The swap was made. Gajowniczek was spared.

Maximilian and nine other men were led away. They were herded, naked, into the cell. They had entered hell. They were denied food, water and clothing. The cell was dark, with hardly *enough air to breathe. They endured severe hunger pains. When they begged the guards for a mouthful of water or scrap of bread, they were mercilessly clubbed and kicked. They became so desperately thirsty that some of the men drank urine from the slop bucket. They laid on the cold floor in fetal positions knowing there was no escape from a cruel death by starvation. Some went mad, attacking the others like feral dogs.*

In this chamber of unspeakable mental horror and physical torture, there was one calming force—Father Maximilian. He led the men in prayer and song. When the guards entered, they always found Kolbe standing or kneeling in prayer, usually saying the rosary. His eyes burned with such prayerful intensity the guards ordered him to look at the floor. Kolbe's calmness and serenity in the face of total deprivation and certain death haunted the guards, some of whom became traumatized by his unexplainable courage.

One by one, the men succumbed to excruciatingly painful deaths. After two full weeks, only five were still alive. Maximilian was one of them, and only he was still fully conscious. On August 14th, the authorities could wait no longer. They needed the cell for other prisoners. The head of the infirmary was summoned to the cell and ordered to inject the surviving prisoners with carbolic acid. According to a Polish interpreter who survived the camp, when the executioner entered the cell, Kolbe was sitting by the far wall, awake and alert. After administering the lethal injection into the veins of the others, the doctor approached the priest.

With a prayer on his lips, Father Maximilian Mary Kolbe, O.F.M. Conv., offered his executioner his arm. The needle broke through his skin and entered his vein. The acid quickly traveled to Father Kolbe's immense heart and snuffed it out.

A witness who entered the cell after the doctor had left reported that, except for Kolbe's remains, all the naked corpses where lying on the floor. They were filthy, and their contorted faces dramatically revealed their suffering. Father Kolbe's body, however, was leaning against the wall, still sitting upright. Unlike the others, his body looked clean and bright. His eyes were open; they were serene and pure. His face was beautifully radiant. Those who saw his corpse knew he was a saint. His body was taken to the crematorium, and the next day, on the Feast of the Assumption of the Blessed Virgin Mary, it was consumed by the flames.

Francis Gajowniczek survived the camp and lived for fifty-four more years, dying at the age of ninety-four.

I can image Saint Francis of Assisi, at the gates of heaven, greeting the future Saint Maximilian with wide-open arms, perhaps saying, "Well done, my son."

On the afternoon of August 14, 1997, I walked to the little church of San Andre delle Frate, located just a few blocks from Sant' Isidoro. In that church, at a side altar dedicated to Our Lady, a young Father Kolbe celebrated his first Mass on April 29, 1918.

The interior of the church is covered with frescoes and the main altar is adorned with two magnificent sculptures of angels created by Bernini for the Ponte Sant' Angelo (a bridge over the Tiber) but they were so beautiful they were put inside this church instead. As I knelt in silence, I realized the real beauty was inside Maximilian...and inside each of us.

Saint Maximilian and Saint Francis, help us see that beauty.

The Liturgy of the Hours

Bless your servant and I shall live
and obey your word.
Open my eyes that I may see
the wonders of your law.
I am a pilgrim on the earth;
show me your commands.
My soul is ever consumed
as I long for your decrees.
(Psalm 118 [119]:17-20)

PIGRIMAGE DIARY 45

Empty Hands

In order to become an instrument in God's hands, we must be of no account in our own eyes.

—*SAINT ANGELA MERICI*

I go to God with my hands full...and ask for more. Francis was willing to go to God with empty hands. For him, the only thing that really mattered was utter trust in God, and his adult life was a continual witness to the realization that total trust cannot exist until we have lost all self-trust and are rooted in poverty.

The deepest levels of self-denial which Francis reached present us with a huge gap in comparison to our feeble efforts at approaching perfect trust in God. What is it that keeps me from total surrender into the loving embrace of God? I know what God seeks, yet I hesitate. I know God loves me, and this love, I realize, does not spring from a reluctant heart; God stands always willing and waiting to love us even more deeply...yet we hesitate in accepting his love out of fear of losing ourselves and being buried in God. Rather than following the self-emptying example of Francis and the saints, I try the latest spiritual shortcuts to God. And I buy books. All I do is go around in circles, getting nowhere, slowly.

Francis said the road to God is straight and narrow: The road is poverty.

I'm still looking for an easier road, one that gently winds its way up the mountain to the summit where God dwells.

THE GENTLE EXTREMIST

The word which most quickly springs to mind when thinking about Saint Francis is *gentle.* Yet that mild-mannered word is ill-suited to describe a saint who was above all else a hard-nosed extremist. Every major event in Francis' life reveals an extreme interpretation of either the gospel or what he believed was God's will for his life. The middle ground was unknown territory for Francis; for him, it was all or nothing when it came to God. No middle-of-the-road "golden-mean" Aristotle for Francis. This posture is hard for us, for we strive for moderation, for the middle of the road, and look at the extremists on the far right and far left as crackpots. How was Francis able to be an extremist and still appear reasonable? And gentle, too. This is one of the many riddles of his life.

Saint Francis' life was riddled with startling paradoxes, some of which were nicely summarized by Marie Dennis and others in their thoughtful book, *St. Francis and the Foolishness of God*: "An enormously free and spontaneous person, he nevertheless adhered faithfully to the institutional Church; a fully alive human being, he embraced suffering; a true lover, he chose celibacy; born into relative affluence, he practiced a literal poverty" (page 8). Francis, I would add, was passionate, impulsive, extroverted, fun-loving and poetic; yet, he was also moody, mystical, demanding, introspective and, at times, even fearsome. Yet, we think of him as gentle.

When it came to applying the lessons he learned from his literal interpretation of the gospel to his own life, Francis did so with scrupulous exactitude. Consider Jesus' instruction from the Sermon on the Mount that we should "take no care for the morrow." Knowing the importance of planning ahead, a reasonable person wishing to follow Christ would look for the underlying principle in Christ's advice and perhaps come to the conclusion that Christ felt it was important to live in the present moment, that "now" was more important than "tomorrow." Different people, different cultures even, could interpret "take no care for the morrow" in different ways, reflecting the richness of the Gospel. But no one would come to the conclusion that Christ really meant "take no thought for the morrow" and make a concerted effort not to take any thought for the morrow.

No one but Francis, that is. For him, Christ's advice to take no thought for the morrow, literally meant just that: Take no thought for the morrow...period. With Christ's instruction in mind, Francis told Brother Cook never to put the next day's vegetables or beans or dried peas in water to soak overnight as was the custom, because that simple and practical action was in effect thinking about the morrow.

Is soaking beans for the next day's meal giving too much thought for the morrow? Was Francis just trying, through exaggeration, to make a point? Can anyone today match Francis' unswerving passion for the ideal as expressed in the Gospels, or is he just an example for us to try to emulate as best we can? What would happen if the entire world, for just one day, took no thought for the morrow? Francis is not the patron saint of calendar manufacturers.

Francis was a man of immense courage and profound determination. And it took all the courage and determination he could muster to follow the extremely difficult path he had chosen for himself, and he was very harsh with anyone who tried to persuade him to take an easier way. He wasn't content to just follow Christ; he wanted to be, as Celano observed, "conformed in every act with that of the Blessed Lord." It certainly was not easy to accept every recorded word of Christ at face value and scrupulously follow every command, completely disregarding the cost to himself...I know I have neither the courage nor the determination to so literally and completely follow Christ. Just stop for a second and think about the kind of courage and determination it would take to "set out upon the way of total perfection." That was Francis' goal...and nothing short of it would do. Personally, I am more impressed by the saint's courage and determination than by any of his other traits.

PILGRIMAGE DIARY 46

Drawn to Knowledge

*H*umans are drawn to knowledge. We thirst for it. While knowledge is important, understanding is vital. Knowing ourselves is the first step toward knowing the truth. True self-knowledge is the father of humility, which is the foundation of all virtues.

Sadly, we hate humility.

AN IGNORANT MAN

There is a contrarious stream that ripples through Francis' life. He vigorously protested against the evils of the institutional Church and, at the same time, he faithfully served the very same institution. In an age when priests were being disparaged for their decadence, Francis had an unwavering reverence for priests. In an age of beastly violence, Francis preached a love for peace.

Francis' love of animals—of all living creatures—is, of course, legendary. However, there was one minor exception which echoes his interpretation of the above Gospel story and his edict to the cook. Francis wasn't fond of ants. He commended their industry, but they weren't Franciscan enough to please him, because they stored up grain so providentially. Yet, he did, nonetheless, believe they were just doing the will of their Creator. It is interesting to note that Francis acted as special providence to a hive of bees when their honey ran short by giving them sugar and honey to keep them alive during a hard winter. Even though many of his ideas might have sounded very impractical, Francis still was a practical man.

Yet a practical man would certainly see the value of books and education. Not Francis. Francis was grieved when he saw learning pursued while virtue was neglected. He said, "My brothers who are led by curious craving for knowledge, will find their hands empty on the day of retribution. I would rather have them growing strong in virtue, that when the periods of tribulation come they could have the Lord with them in their distress. For tribulation is coming, such that, useless for people, their books will be flung out of windows and into cubby holes."

Eloi Leclerc, O.F.M., puts these words into the mouth of Saint Francis during a conversation with one of his followers:

> But all the books of the world, you see, are incapable of giving wisdom. You must not confuse science with wisdom. At the hour of trial, in temptation or distress, it is not books that will help us but simply the Passion of Our Lord, Jesus Christ. (*The Wisdom of the Poor One of Assisi*, pages 26, 27)

Once when he returned from a lengthy missionary trip, Francis discovered his friars had opened a house of studies in Bologna. Francis immediately ordered the house closed.

During his life Francis often referred to himself as an ignorant man. It's not that he was against education or the pursuit of knowledge and wisdom, but he thought all studying should be aimed at serving the proclamation of the gospel, and for that only a few books were required. Francis believed that his followers' actions would be their most effective form of preaching. He warned the brothers against "seeking the wisdom of the world," adding, "As for myself, I know Jesus Christ and him crucified, that is enough for me."

Why was Francis so strident about not seeking an education? Mario von Galli, S.J., gives one possible explanation:

> Francis possessed a knowledge about God that was based on his

own living experience. So strong and radiant were the sparks it gave off that book knowledge seemed pale by comparison; book knowledge could not enrich him. So we are confronted with a paradox: Francis chooses to be poor in scholarly knowledge so that he will not lose his own rich treasury of knowledge. Francis experienced God in everything, above all in prayer. (*Living Our Future*, page 98)

Guido Ferrando suggests that Francis did not scorn education, but rather "he merely felt that it was impossible for one to be devoted both to the pursuit of learning and to the cultivation of the mystical side of one's nature." (Christopher Isherwood, *Vedanta for the Western World*, in Gasnick, *The Francis Book*, pages 253-259)

Johannes Jörgensen offers another explanation:

What most displeased Francis was, perhaps in his inner-most heart, the pride of intelligence, egoism, the perversion of wisdom to a means of flattering the vanity of the ego. He did not desire that man should adorn himself with wisdom so as to be looked at and esteemed of men. It was much better, he felt, to fall on the knees and pray to God for your fellow men, alone and unknown in a grotto or a hermitage high up among the mountains, than in a cathedral with a soul full of vanity over what a fine fellow one is. (pages 232-233)

For Saint Francis, the crucified Christ was all he needed. The rest, including books, was dross.

But Francis' intolerance of education was aimed only at himself and his followers. He never forced his ideas outside of the Franciscan family, or claimed his ideas were the best and only path for people to travel. Francis was friends with Saint Dominic, whose own religious order stressed the value of education. Francis greatly admired Saint Anthony of Padua, who was a scholarly Augustinian monk before joining Francis, even after Anthony became a professor at the University of Bologna. Francis freely admitted there were other ways besides his own. But his way stressed the experience of God over the study of God. I think Francis would have readily agreed with something Henri Nouwen wrote: "It is sad that most ministers have more hours of training in how to talk and be with people than how to talk and be with God."

Francis' shunning of education was not the result of an anti-intellectual bias, but rather reflects the theological truth that God cannot be comprehended by thought. Listen to the words of the unknown fourteenth-century English mystic and author of *The Cloud of Unknowing*, a classic book which perfectly mirrors Francis' philosophy: "And so, I prefer to abandon all I can know, choosing rather to love him whom I cannot know. Though we cannot know him, we can love him. By love he may be touched and embraced, never by thought."

PILGRIMAGE DIARY 47

Brother Irony

*H*ow delicious is the irony! Francis preferred meditating on the image of the cross to reading books; yet, his life has given birth to countless books. Alexandre Masseron, in The Franciscans, nicely captures the irony:

> Men have erected to the glory of Saint Francis of Assisi innumerable monuments of all kinds. The most curious, and perhaps the most imposing, is that of erudition. Learned men have exalted the Poverello, that love of simplicity and somewhat intransigent adversary of bookish knowledge, upon a pedestal of books—a pedestal to which they add new material every day and which will probably never finish.

The seventh centenary of the death of Francis, celebrated in 1926, triggered a wave of Franciscan studies. Between 1920 and 1926, 254 books and essays on the life of Francis were published in Europe and the United States.

Out of curiosity, I tried counting the books in the Franciscana section of the major library at the Collegio Sant' Isidoro. I tired after reaching one thousand books, and I was only about halfway through the stacks. And for the most part, the library only features books in English and Italian. The library also has a section reserved for periodicals and scholarly journals devoted exclusively to Franciscan studies. Masseron was right—there seems to be no end to the material.

Purity of Intention

Francis knew that God seeks purity of intention, which dictates that people surrender their whole selves, so they may exist only by the grace of God. Guidance from God replaced books, ideas and self-assurance for Francis. God was his sole teacher and solitude his classroom. Theology for Francis began and ended on his knees. He put himself in God's hands, to be used as God pleased. In his pure and simple commitment to the will of God, each moment carried Mary's response to the angel: "Be it done unto me according to your word." That was it—a constant yes to God, even if it meant no to himself. In each moment, Francis only longed to see and rejoice in God; everything else was abandoned and forgotten.

I say yes to myself more than I do to God.

A GOOD PREACHER

Francis said, "There are so many eager for the climb to knowledge that the man is blessed who keeps himself barren of it for the love of God." And, "A man has only as much knowledge as he puts into action, and a religious is only as good a preacher as he puts into action. For the tree is known by its fruits."

And Francis was a good preacher; he put the directives of his heart into action.

Be Not Afraid to Be Alone

In Thomas of Celano's First Life, he tells us Francis "frequently chose solitary places so that he could direct his mind completely to God...." Solitude and focus were important elements of Francis' prayer life. They have no part in my prayer life, which may account for the impoverished nature of my prayer. Thomas of Celano says prayer was Francis' "safest haven," and that his prayer was of "long duration, full of devotion, severe in humility," noting that "if he began late, he would scarcely finish before morning." I can't remember the last time I spent a full thirty minutes in prayer. And it takes me just about that long to quiet my mind and push aside the events of the day.

PERFECT IMMOLATION

Too often you set your prayer and life against each other, service of God and service of your brothers, contemplation and action. The day when you know the depths of the mystery of Christ, there will be no more opposition.

—JEAN LAFRANCE, *PRAY TO YOUR FATHER IN SECRET*

In *I Know Christ*, Gratien de Paris, O.F.M. Cap., offers the following insightful observation:

Francis could not stop and compile a book of sublime thoughts, nor could he smugly delight in their beauty. His was that exalted wisdom which did not perfect the intellect alone by stopping at a theoretical knowledge, but one that enjoyed what it knew. It was a wisdom which knew because it loved and wanted to love better, whose knowledge was greater and deeper the more virtuously it acted. Knowledge is real and valuable only to the extent that it is a light and an incentive to action. "Man," he said, "knows only what he experiences, he really knows only what he puts into practice." Here we have one of the truest and most profound aphorisms of this simple man. His faithful disciple, Brother Giles, liked to say, "Our actions never measure up to our belief." Now Francis was obsessed with the need of acting proportionately to his faith. To preach the truth which one did not apply to one's self was in his eyes a sign of dishonesty and insincerity. The preacher would thus make his life a continual contradiction.

Observation had taught him how slow we are to put our resolutions into practice. We wear ourselves out talking and we believe that we have done all we should once we have voiced admirable thoughts, or told of the heroic actions of others. It alarmed him to see that *the exercise of the spoken word* so easily exhausted all vitality and energy of certain men that they hardly had any strength left for *the exercise of virtue*. He reacted against this common fault with all his strength.

For Francis, integrity demanded more than harmony between thought and action, between theory and practice. It further demanded an *eagerness* that would make its response prompt and generous. It brooked no delay in fulfilling its promise nor tardiness in executing the counsels of the Lord, who spoke to him either from the height of the cross or in the sublimity of the Gospels. Such was his temperament that he could not remain inactive. In fact, he suffered as long as he had not put into practice what he had conceived in his heart. Here is proof that this idealist and mystic was also a man of great action. He was not satisfied with desires, idle wishes, promises, nor even a generous impulse. What is more, he was never satisfied with the results obtained. With breathless haste, he always aspired to greater progress, for an even more perfect immolation of himself.

THE SUMMIT OF PERFECTION

[Francis] was not ashamed
to ask advice in small matters
from those under him,
true Friar Minor that he was,
though he had learned great things
from the supreme Teacher.
He was accustomed
to search out with special eagerness
how and in what way
he could serve God more perfectly
according to God's good pleasure.
As long as he lived
this was his supreme philosophy,
this his supreme desire,
to inquire from the wise and the simple,
the perfect and the imperfect,
the young and the old,
how he could more effectively reach
the summit of perfection.
(*Bonaventure*, pages 293-294)

Saint Francis of Brooklyn?

In my novel The Canvas of the Soul, *the main character, a writer named James Francis Howard, occasionally records his thoughts in a journal as he and his niece Bernadette travel across Europe. What follows is one of his journal entries, which he had written aboard a train going from Rome to Assisi.*

Perhaps there are two ways of seeing. The normal, everyday way, that is with our physical eyes. And the more rare way, with spiritual eyes. Our physical eyes see things the way they appear, flat, static, and looked at within the natural dimensions of time and space. Our spiritual eyes do not look at things, but through things, and so their vision is charged with different reality. Francis saw everything through spiritual eyes, which allowed him to see the innocence woven through all people and things, as though a shaft of sunlight danced over the most common of people and things, and made them look radiant.

I imagine it was easier for Francis to take a bold leap of faith than it is for post-modern humankind. The cultural myths and symbols of previous ages which provided fixed points of reference by which people could readily locate themselves in time and space have lost their power, energy and effectiveness, and so many of us today have no reliable compass to help us find our way in these confusing times. All the old reliable points of reference for those traveling down the path of life—God, church, society, a sense of self—have all but disappeared. Maybe that is what this trip (and this story) is really all about, a search for some answers to the dilemmas of post-modern life.

Throughout history, most people used a combination of religious faith and their knowledge of sacred histories and mythologies to help them make sense of the physical world in which they lived. Rightly or wrongly, they had an understanding of how the world worked and their part in it, and this understanding gave them a degree of comfort, along with a sense of belonging and security.

We, despite the help of technology that can explore the outer reaches of our galaxy and the availability of a mountain of information at our fingertips, have no such understanding. We live isolated, disjointed, incoherent and impoverished lives in a superficial, fast-paced, fragmented world where confusion, anguish, anxiety, banality, pessimism and a sense of lack of order prevail.

The collected wisdom of humanity has been shattered into a million little pieces, all being trampled underfoot by people powerless to put them back together again. Not only can we not find the truth, we've come to believe there is no absolute truth to be found. Everything is as true (or false) as everything else. In our eclectic society, values have become relative and reason has reached its limits. Life in the post-modern world has become meaningless.

During this century, rationalism has decidedly won its battle with religion, skepticism has triumphed over mysticism. For a long time, I thought this was a good thing. Religion had wielded its bloody sword for far too long, dividing people and stirring up centuries worth of hatred as countless people were ready to kill over inconsequential religious differences. But has rationalism, in all its triumphal glory, done anything to reduce the level of human misery, or has it simply just shifted the misery around?

Had Francis been born in Brooklyn, New York, in 1950, could he have scaled the heights of faith which he did? Or would it have been impossible for him to let go of that rational, critical, analytical side of the modern "self" and simply live as spontaneously and unreflectively as he did in thirteenth-century Assisi? Could he have taken the words he read in the Bible to be the literal truth? Would Francis of Brooklyn have possessed a sadly too-sophisticated realization of the mythical metaphor as a metaphor, making full participation in the metaphor virtually impossible? I think each of those questions would have to be answered in the negative...and that, I think, is a tragedy, the stillborn child of rationalism.

For many years, rationalism was my God. But I've come to realize humans are not rational beings. We merely have the capacity for reason; however, we also have the ability to recognize when reason is not sufficient. Mahatma Gandhi expressed this well: "There are subjects where reason cannot take us far and we have to accept things on faith. Faith then does not contradict reason but transcends it. Faith is a kind of sixth sense which works in cases which are beyond the purview of reason."

PILGRIMAGE DIARY 48

'Poor, Simple Francis'

I've settled into a gentle yet productive rhythm of life at Collegio Sant' Isidoro. I rise at 6:45 a.m., throw on some old clothes and head down the hill to a coffee bar for a cup of cappuccino and a pastry. Then I walk to the newstand and pick up The International Herald Tribune. *The 2,800-lire cost of the paper (just under two bucks) seems a bit steep to find out how the Yankees are doing, but I*

*pay it every day anyway. Besides finding out if Tino Martinez has
added to his league-leading home run total and if the Yankees are
gaining ground on the first-place Baltimore Orioles, I also learn
about all that has gone wrong in Europe and around the world
during the past twenty-four hours. Riots in Kenya, terrorists' bombs
exploding in Jerusalem, a priest in Ireland sent to jail for molesting
children, parents in France allowing their children to be featured in
pornographic movies, a passenger jet crashing in Guam because of a
software error in a computer. I seem far removed from the events that
move the world. I then head back to my room, huffing and puffing
my way up the long flight of steps that connect Piazza Barberini to
Via degli Artisti and Sant' Isidoro. (By the way, Via degli Artisti gets
its name from the time when German artists occupied Collegio Sant'
Isidoro when the friars were temporarily expelled during the
Napoleonic Wars.) Back in my room, I read the paper, shower and
dress for the day. All that takes about an hour and fifteen minutes,
and so by 8 a.m. I'm seated at my desk in my room. This is my quiet
time. For thirty minutes, I try to be still...to just be. I pray. And chase
away thoughts of writing postcards or doing something "useful." At
8:30, I bring the paper into the sitting room adjacent to the refectory,
and add it to the Italian papers and* The Times *of London which the
friars get every day.*

*I then walk around the cloister for about ten minutes, breathing
in the beauty and tranquillity. And history. The cloister has an aura of
immense antiquity and holiness. For centuries, men have prayerfully
walked the cloister. Each day I seem to notice a different fresco.
Yesterday, for instance, I looked closely at the one of Saint Margaret
of Cortona. I smiled, recalling the day I spent in the church and city
that honors her name. By 8:45, I wander into the church. Mass
begins (on the summer schedule) at 9 a.m. I sit in stillness before the
Blessed Sacrament for a few minutes, and then I read the office of
readings for the day. Morning prayer is combined with the
celebration of the Eucharist. By 9:30, I leave the church and climb
the three flights leading to the major library. I work until 12:55 p.m.
Then it's off to midday prayer with the friars, followed by lunch. By
2 p.m., I'm back in the library, where I work for two or three hours
more before heading out for a walk around Rome. Evening prayer is
at 7:45 p.m., followed by dinner. After dinner, I walk around the
moonlit cloister for a few minutes or take a short walk to the Spanish*

*Steps or the Trevi Fountain, sometimes stopping for a gelato.
Afterward, I read for a short time, and by 11 p.m., I go to bed.*

*Today is Sunday...which means there isn't a paper to read,
because the* Herald Tribune *only publishes Monday through
Saturday. So this morning I found myself looking for something to
read. My desk had a stack of books on Francis and Clare, books I
either purchased or borrowed from the library. But it's Sunday—no
work, no reading anything Franciscan. Besides, after yesterday, I
need a break.*

*Up until yesterday, my time in the library had been very pleasant
and fruitful. In fact, a few days ago, I was so immersed in the books I
had plucked from the shelf that I had lost all consciousness of time.
And dinner! I looked at my watch and it was 10:15 at night...I had
gone eight hours without ever noticing the time. But yesterday was
different.*

*Yesterday, my reading shifted from Francis' life to the aftermath
of his life. From the time he handed over the leadership of the Order
to Peter Catanii, there has been a great debate over the direction and
charism of the Order. And the debate was not always courteous or
even orderly. In fact, it rarely was. There was shouting and name-
calling, deep rifts and division. After Francis' death the Order
splintered into various factions. The divisions still exist. The First
Order of Friars Minor consists of three separate groups: The Friars
Minor (O.F.M.), the Conventuals (O.F.M. Conv.) and the Capuchins
(O.F.M. Cap.).*

*Yesterday, I got caught up in all the debate. The history of the
Order is as messy as all histories of human endeavor are wont to be.
As I read about the debates over the Rule, the role of poverty and the
Order's mission, I began to lose sight of Francis.*

*He was simple—or rather, his way of following the Christ was
simple: do what the gospel says. And he did. Literally, exuberantly
and totally.*

*I woke up this morning still feeling somewhat weighed down by
my time in the library the previous day. I was feeling confused and a
bit overwhelmed by all the arguments on how to follow Francis, how
best to live a Franciscan life. Is poverty poverty or a metaphor?
Should friars teach or preach? Serve or study? How do you blend
contemplation and action? So this morning, I didn't want to read
about Francis or Franciscans. And without a paper to read, I turned*

to the five books I brought with me:

A Confession—And Other Religious Writings, by Leo Tolstoy
The Cloud of Unknowing, edited by William Johnson
Mystics and Zen Masters, by Thomas Merton
The Evolving Self, by Mihaly Csikszentmihalyi, and
Prayer, by Hans Urs von Balthasar

I picked Merton, my favorite writer. I randomly opened the book to page 269, about fifteen pages into a chapter titled: "The Other Side of Despair: Notes on Christian Existentialism." I read the first paragraph on the page:

In religious existentialism the blank, godless, nothingness of freedom and of the person, Sartre's *neant*, becomes the luminous abyss of divine gift. The self is "void" indeed, but void in the sense of apophatic mystics like St. John of the Cross, in whom *nada*, or nothingness of the self that is entirely empty of fictitious images, projects, and desires, becomes the *todo*, the All, in which freedom of personal love discovers itself in its transcendent ground and source which we are accustomed to call the Love of God and which no human name can ever account for or explain.

I closed the book. Too heavy for a Sunday morning. Or any morning. Merton is best read at night.

While showering, I thought about my struggles with faith, the battles between belief and unbelief that have raged within me for so many years. Religion was riddled with absurdities. Atheism was laced with desperation. I found no answer to the problem of evil and suffering in the world. I alternated between belief that the world was created by God and the belief that the world was nothing more than a chemical accident. At times, the model of self offered by Christ, namely self-abnegation, charity before anger, passivity before action and not caring about tomorrow, seemed desirable, but impossible to follow. At other times, the way of Christ, the way of the cross, seemed like a disgusting ritual of self-punishing sacrifice demanded by a masochistic God. Yet, without the support of some kind of metaphysical hydraulics, life seemed hopeless.

Today, I know peace. As I walked to Mass I thanked God for that gift.

During Mass, I thought about the library here at Sant' Isidoro. So many books. Then I thought of poor Francis. Poor, simple Francis. Somehow he knew—and feared—that study, education and the pursuit of knowledge, if pursued to a greater degree than prayer and piety, would eventually lead to nothing but confusion and doubt.

Francis—poor, simple Francis—understood: the cross was all the education he needed.

After Mass, I went to the library. I felt much better. History is messy, even the history of those who follow saints. It's messy because it is human. We have a way of getting in our own way. We give in to pride, avarice, lust, anger and envy all too easily.

Francis—poor, simple Francis—told us how to get out of our own way: "Do not look to life outside, for that of the spirit is better."

Francis listened to the Word of God, and the light of grace penetrated to the incandescent center of his being, and his spirit responded to the Word's freedom by a corresponding readiness not only to continue to listen but also to accept and follow.

As for me and my interest in books, education and the pursuit of knowledge—I love books, and reading will always be a part of my life; nor will I stop my continuing education and determined search for knowledge. However, I acknowledge that these things have their limits and I can't allow them to have a priority in my life. The pilgrimage has taught me to put prayer first...Francis and Clare did.

When we try to make our own special order out of the disorder that is the absence of God, we are doomed to failure. My experience has taught me a valuable lesson: when the Divine flame is blown out humans are left in the dark without hope. I've been there. It's not pretty.

I looked for God in books, and found him not. I found God in a simple, pure moment of surrender and openness. I shouldn't forget that...I need to spend more time in prayer.

A Richer Way

Saint Francis believed in the absolute reality of God. Moreover, he believed that while God transcended the material world in which we live, God manifests Divine Presence in this world and in doing so has sanctified the world and made it real because it has been charged with the reality of God. Modern people, even those who claim to believe in God, are *far too "nonreligious" (or secularized) to believe the way Francis did. We either deny or find it hard to accept transcendence. Like many people, for most of my life, I harbored strong doubts that human existence had any meaning whatsoever. I saw none. I saw nothing but random chaos. I regarded anything sacred as a threat to freedom and an insult to the intellect. I couldn't see God in the resplendent beauty of nature. I equated transcendence with magic, something only the gullible could fall for. Saint Francis was far beyond my understanding. I thought his was an ancient and medieval faith that had all but disappeared. But, by the grace of God, Poverty's little Brother showed me a richer way.*

The Liturgy of the Hours

A reading from the Confessions of Saint Augustine:

Late have I loved you, O beauty so ancient and so new; late have I loved you! For behold you were within me, and I was outside; and I sought you outside and in my ugliness fell upon those lovely things that you have made. You were with me and I was not with you. I was kept from you by those things, yet had they not been in you, they would not have been at all. You called and cried to me and broke open my deafness: and you sent forth your beams and shone upon me and chased away my blindness: you breathed fragrance upon me, and I drew in my breath and do now pant for you: I tasted you, and now hunger and thirst for you: you touched me, and I have burned for peace.

PILGRIMAGE DIARY 49

'Late Have I Loved You!'

*R*arely—extremely rarely, actually—do I read something either ancient or new which captures the essence of what I am feeling. Yet, the excerpt I just quoted from Saint Augustine sums up perfectly the core of my experience during the past three years. I'm certainly not familiar with Augustine's writings or theology, or even his personal history beyond the basic broad strokes; nor do I dare to compare myself, with all my faults and deficiencies, both intellectually and spiritually, to this great Doctor of the Church. However, we did share in common the existential awareness of living without God and then suddenly living with God...our deafness being shattered, our blindness being lifted. We both feasted long and hard on earthly banquets, but having tasted the Lord, we hungered only for the Divine.

The experience—and subsequent change in me—makes absolutely no sense to my friends. They are puzzled, some even perplexed. And I understand. Had I read that passage from Augustine's Confessions before my first trip to Rome in 1995, I would have appreciated the eloquence with which he expressed his inner feelings, but I would have dismissed those feelings as a spiritual fantasy.

And then the "fantasy" happened to me. What was real became unreal; and what was unreal became real. And I am humbled by it and could never boast of it. The word "grace" has taken on new meaning.

Spiritual truth cannot be taught...it must be experienced. And once it has been experienced, one instantly realizes how much there is to learn. If you want a deeper experience of God, pray for it, search for it. For every sincere step we take toward God, God takes ten toward us.

PILGRIMAGE DIARY 50

Civita de Bagnoregio

*Y*esterday, Father Liam drove me to Bagnoregio, to visit the birthplace of Saint Bonaventure. It was as if we had traveled back in time. Earthquakes in 1297, 1349, 1695 and 1794 have left the oldest part of the medieval town isolated from the main part of the modern city...if an already centuries-old city can be called "modern." Remnants of the old town cling to the summit of a hill the centuries have kept carving away. At the outskirts of the city, there is a pedestrian bridge connecting the new and old cities.

The old city sits precariously atop a plateau that was formed by volcanic eruptions long before the birth of Christ. Near the top of the plateau, the trees and vegetation end, giving way to steep stone cliffs. Imagine a tightly compacted medieval city, with all the buildings snuggled close together, but instead of an ancient wall surrounding it, there is simply a ledge overlooking a cliff. Over the past two centuries, buildings on the outer perimeter of the city have slipped over the side as the plateau slowly erodes. From a distance, you can see the tower of a church rising from a cluster of buildings. The terrain surrounding the base of the hill is very rugged.

August is not the ideal time to cross the steep footbridge to the medieval Bagnoregio. The primitive beauty ahead and below us was only a mild distraction from the strain of the climb. At the far end of the bridge you enter the city through a gate that was added in the eleventh century to an existing structure that dated back to the Etruscan-Roman period. The old city is quiet and nearly empty. Seventy-five years ago, some six hundred fifty people lived here; today, about twenty-five people call this haven of silence home, and they are far outnumbered by cats and flowers. There are no cars, no hints of anything modern or new. A scholar could observe the buildings and easily trace periods of the city's history: Etruscan, Roman, medieval and into the Renaissance, where time stopped. You can walk up and down all the streets in under ten minutes. At the center of the tiny maze of buildings is a large square. Overlooking the square is the church. I could find no information on its history, except that the tower was built in the eleventh century.

Off the southeast corner of the square is a small street leading to where Saint Bonaventure's house used to be. The earthquake in 1695 destroyed the small Church of St. Peter's, once on the block where Bonaventure spent his youth. Only fragments of the foundation of the saint's house remain. Father Liam and I sat on what was the front step to Bonaventure's childhood home and read a few pages from The Soul's Journey Into God. Afterward, we said a brief prayer and headed back across the bridge.

In De Scientia Christi, Saint Bonaventure writes, "The soul is not satisfied with any good it grasps and comprehends, since no such good is the highest. It is satisfied only by a good of such a sort that the soul is taken captive by its greatness and super-excellence." As we made our way across the bridge, under the scorching heat of the sun, I understood the truth of that statement.

On our way back to Rome, we took a slight detour in order to go to the small town of Narni and visit the Hermitage of St. Urban. In 1213, Francis came to this remote mountain location in search of solitude among the rocks and woods of the region. The hermitage still contains a few buildings in which the saint stayed. The little Chapel of St. Sylvester was once a hut where Francis slept. It was in this place that an angel appeared to Francis during a serious illness and consoled the saint with music from a viola.

During that same illness, Francis was very weak and he asked for a sip of wine. But there was none, and so the brothers brought him some water instead. Francis blessed the water, and when it was poured it had been miraculously changed into the finest of wine. After tasting the wine poverty had denied him but holiness had given to him, Francis made a quick recovery. The story of the wine can be found in The Treatise of Miracles, written by Thomas of Celano between 1250 and 1253 at the request of Brother John of Parma, the minister general, and a shorter version can be found in Celano's First Life, at the very end of Chapter 21 of Book One. The well from which the brother drew the water is still visible behind the chapel; the actual bucket is a medieval warrior's helmet.

After spending a few minutes in the cave Francis used to enter to pray, we began our drive back to Rome. It was a wonderful day.

THE SAINT OF ECOLOGY

A merciful heart is a heart burning for all creation, for men, for birds, for animals and even demons.

—SAINT ISAAC OF NINEVEH

Those who passionately love Mother Earth and who are concerned about ecology and who work to curtail pollution have unoffically adopted Saint Francis as their patron saint. In an essay entitled "Celebrating the Death of St. Francis," Daniel P. Sulmasy, O.F.M., sheds some light on the Franciscan spirit of ecology:

> Bonaventure says that Francis was a man who had reached such a state of purity "that his body was in remarkable harmony with his spirit, and his spirit with God." It is in this ecology of *spirit* that the Franciscan spirit of ecology truly begins. Francis was a genuinely hylomorphic man—body and mind, deed and word. The rest of us, enlightened as we might think ourselves, often tinker with our own dualism, bracketing off the world from faith, people from our worship, action from our contemplation. That is why we are content to pollute our world. But Francis understood himself to be a creature. He understood his link to all other creatures. He knew himself as a creature of the love of God: the wild, exuberant, free love of God. It is because he understood this so well that he could call the sun his brother, and the moon his sister. He knew keenly that bodies, all bodies, are called into being only because of the love of God. He knew the power by which human bodies can participate in the love of God. It is that power that enabled him to kiss lepers and to preach peace to sultans.
>
> But he also knew the limits of bodies, the horizon of the material. This is the knowledge of Franciscan humility. He bore none of the contemporary delusions about being self-made, and so he called the earth his mother. He bore no delusions about being all powerful, and so he called Poverty his Lady. He bore no delusions about being immortal, and so he called death his sister. He truly lived in remarkable harmony: with himself, God, other people, and all creation. This is the harmony that supported the melody of his joyous song. Francis, the minstrel of God, directed the chorus of creation in a cosmic symphony of praise. His death marked only the beginning of the second movement. (*The Cord*, October, 1993)

VOICES

We should always be hearing, as with bodily ears, the gurgling wellspring of our origin in God.

—HANS URS VON BALTHASAR, S.J.

The tough thing about Francis' story for modern people to accept is the fact that he "heard" voices. We put people who hear voices in institutions. I think we have become hung up on the word "voices" or that Francis "heard" something. I believe the voice was inaudible, and was more like a flash of insight, a sense of knowing. The "voice" was so clear, so real, so authentic, so truthful, that Francis had no trouble following it because the "voice" was devoid of conflict, chaos, emotion or judgment...it was a pure thought, which he followed as he let the insight guide him.

In her book on Hildegard of Bingen, Renate Craine writes:

Listen, the Rule of St. Benedict advises, listen with the "ears of your heart." Listening with the ears of the heart refers to a type of contemplative listening, an experiential awareness of the Divine Mystery in circumstances of life. This kind of consciousness, of tasted intimacy with God, which like prayer arises from the depth of one's being, is beyond explanation. It can only be described by analogy to physical sense experience. Tradition, since Origen in the third century, has referred to this contemplative consciousness as the "spiritual senses." Just as we have five physical senses, so we have five spiritual senses, some of which can be awakened at a certain stage of the spiritual journey. Expressions like "hearing God," "seeing God," being "embraced by God," and even "tasting God" are poetic renderings that point to the perception of these senses. When the Rule of St. Benedict advises a listening with "ears of the heart," it refers to the consciousness spoken of as a spiritual sense. This kind of savoring of the love of God was taught in Hildegard's monastic formation. It is, however, the birthright of all God's children, a potential that needs focus and practice. We are all capable of "opening our eyes to the light that comes from God" as the prologue of the Rule advises:

"It is high time for us to arise from sleep" (Rom. 13:11). Let us open our eyes to the light that comes from God, and our ears to the voice from heaven that every day calls out this charge: "If you hear God's voice today, do not harden your hearts" (Ps. 94 [95]:8). And again: "You that have ears to hear, listen to what the Spirit says to the churches" (Rev. 2:7). And what does the Spirit say? "Come and listen to me and I will teach you fear of the Lord" (Ps. 33 [34]:12). "Run while you have the light of life, that the darkness of death may not overtake you" (John 12:35). (*Hildegard, Prophet of the Cosmic Christ*, pages 43-44)

The great Jewish scholar Rabbi Abraham Joshua Heschel offers lucid insight into how prophets "hear" voices:

The leading exponents of Jewish thought exhort us not to imagine that God speaks, or that a sound is produced by Him through organs of speech.... In being "told that God addressed the prophets and spoke to them," our minds are merely to receive a notion that there is a divine knowledge to which the prophets attain.... We must not suppose that in speaking God employed voice or sound. (*The Wisdom of Heschel*, page 347)

What Francis heard at the foot of the cross of San Damiano arose from the depth of his being and flowed out of his "tasted intimacy with God." It cannot be explained; it can only be experienced. And it can only be experienced if you take the time to listen.

Carlo Carretto puts these words into Francis' mouth: "One day as I gazed at the crucifix I had a clear impression that the lips were moving. [*Ah...you remember the moving lips, right?*] At the same moment I heard a voice saying to me: 'Francis, repair my house! You can see, it is all in ruins'" (*I, Francis*, page 14). The author felt the reader would need an explanation about "hearing a voice" and so, in a footnote, he has Francis explain what happened:

Oh, I do hope you don't get hung up about the lips I saw moving and the voice my ears heard. Now that I understand such matters a little better I can tell you about them, and it will help you not become falsely mystical or superstitious but to accept everything in a spirit of faith.

In reality, the lips of a wooden crucifix do not move. If, for instance, my father, Peter of Bernardone, had been standing next to me at that moment, being so rich and having such good sense, he would not have seen a thing: and especially, he would not have heard a thing.

It was I who did the seeing and the hearing, for I saw and heard in faith. No one has ever been able to explain how this phenomenon, on the borderline between human and divine, actually occurs. What is known is that it takes place entirely in the realm of faith, hope, and love, and that it is utterly personal.

God clothes our faith with vision, with light, with voice, in order to come to the aid of our poverty and to give clarity to our relationship with him. But the relationship itself has its validity in faith.

It was in faith that Abraham saw the angel, that Jacob saw the ladder that reached to heaven. It was in hope that Moses saw the burning bush, and in love that Joseph interpreted the dream that he should take Mary as his spouse.

But as far as we are concerned, nothing visible happens.

When Bernadette saw the Blessed Virgin in the grotto at Lourdes, there were thousands of people around her who did not see anything at all.

What counts—what gives value to our relationship with the divine—is the instrument by which God speaks to a human being: faith. (page 14)

And so, there you have it: It is faith that does the seeing and the hearing, not the eyes and ears. Francis saw everything through the eyes of faith.

Lord, increase my faith, and help me to see and hear more clearly.

Franciscan Spirituality

There are no Franciscans in heaven; just those who, while on earth, followed Jesus in the way of Saint Francis of Assisi.

—*ZACHARY GRANT, O.F.M. CAP.*

Within the Catholic Church there are six major spiritual traditions which have grown out of the uniqueness of their founders; they are the Augustinians (founded by Saint Augustine), the Benedictines (founded by Saint Benedict), the Dominicans (founded by Saint Dominic), the Jesuits (founded by Saint Ignatius of Loyola), the Carmelites (reformed and renewed by Saint Teresa of Avila) and, of course, the Franciscans. Each "order" has a distinct character, charism and spirituality. And what is the essential trait of those who follow Jesus in the footsteps of Saint Francis? The Capuchin friar Zachary Grant offers a succinct answer in his book, Paths to Renewal:

Franciscan spirituality directs us to the amazing truth that the

Son of God was born among us from the womb of a Virgin-Mother in order *to share our human condition*, to live simply and humbly among the poor, and then, taking on our sins, to suffer the injustice of a cruel death. *By imitating His style of life* and His servant-role as revealed in the Gospel, we respond to each other's needs *as brothers and sisters of Jesus* in joyful *praise* of God's goodness. We are called to remind the Church that she must always image the *poor and humble Son of God*. (page 134)

Another impression of Franciscan spirituality and its Christocentric nature is offered by the Conventual Friar J. A. Wayne Hellman, in an essay entitled "The Spirituality of the Franciscans":

Franciscan spirituality focuses on the passion of Christ and touches the heart of human, cosmic, and divine reality. Franciscan spirituality is not simply gazing upon the cross but entering into the experience of the poverty of the cross to know the compassionate wisdom of God from within God. Franciscan wisdom is to know God in the poverty of the cross of Jesus, in his identification with the suffering and rejected.... It is this wisdom which Bonaventure, in his second sermon on the nativity of the Lord, described as a union in which "immensity is tempered with smallness; strength by weakness; clarity by obscurity; immortality by mortality; divinity by humanity; and riches by poverty." Smallness, humanity, and poverty are the rich legacy of Francis of Assisi. His spirituality proclaims a radical denial of power in a power-hungry world. Franciscan love for Christ crucified bequeaths a compassionate tenderness toward all and a witness to what is possible in a world torn by war and tribulations. (*Christian Spirituality: High Middle Ages and Reformation*, pages 48-49)

The triptych of Franciscan spirituality is sharing, service and praise; and this is best expressed by a life of poverty and humility.

PILGRIMAGE DIARY 51

Thoughts Scribbled While Walking

*M*orning prayer is the most important prayer of the day...it sets the tone for all that will follow.
Our hearts are as great as our love.

We can only love truly when our hearts are free of the self-
centered desires of pride, ambition and lust.
When Christ reveals his heart to us, he also reveals our
sinfulness.
A true act of love is one that expects nothing in return.
The more aware we become of the Divine Presence within us,
the more we shall forget ourselves and become more serene
and pure of heart.
Transformation is a daily event.
Pray always.
Cling to Jesus.

A TEACHER AND A GUIDE

By slowly converting our loneliness into deep solitude, we create
that precious space where we can discover the voice telling us
about our inner necessity—that is, our vocation.

—HENRI J. M. NOUWEN, *REACHING OUT*

For a world that is currently searching for a spirituality that is not encased in rigid or lifeless religions, Francis serves as a model of someone who went beyond religious dogma and into the realm of pure spirituality, without condemning his Church, but instead renewing it.

Francis was a man of contemplation and action...a rare combination. He greatly loved and he suffered greatly. Pope Pius XI wrote, "In no man, we think, was the likeness of Christ our Lord or the Gospel's ideal more perfectly reproduced than in St. Francis."

To understand Saint Francis and fully to appreciate him, you must penetrate the mystery of his deep devotion to the humanity of Jesus, a devotion not born of a learned tradition, but which sprang directly from his heart and his personal experience of God's love. His devotion is appealing because it was not satisfied with merely imitating or following Christ, but it transformed Jesus into a friend whom Francis could embrace and be comforted by within the brotherhood of his own heart.

Saint Francis took the enshrined Jesus out of the cathedrals and monasteries, and let him walk among the people, touching them with his mercy, kindness and compassion.

Dante, in the poetic tribute to Francis he puts in the mouth of Saint Thomas Aquinas in Canto XI of the *Paradiso*, praises the saint's capacity for wonder, love, joy and the appreciation of beauty, and exalts Francis over all the learned Doctors of the Church and holy founders of monastic orders as the most perfect imitator of Christ. Saint Francis was a simple man who was enthralled by the mysterious beauty of creation. He delighted in everything he saw, for he saw the resplendent love of God in everything, and so he praised God for all of creation. Francis did not shun the world or try to escape it; he embraced it, fully and without reservation.

So many people today feel they must be able to express their religious beliefs in Hegelian or Heideggerian terms. They miss the point. In contrast, Saint Francis' life illustrates the power of total self-surrender to the Kingdom of God, giving up everything for the fullness of life in communion with the Creator, Sustainer and Fulfillment of all things. What do we not enjoy who enjoy God who enjoys all things? What do we not have who have communion and friendship with God who is Lord of all things?

Francis is the higher wisdom of those who know how to hold on to all things with open hands. All our great scientific and technological advances have somehow stripped us of our innocence and simplicity, leaving us feeling alone and disquieted. Saint Francis can help us recapture the pure simplicity and gentle innocence that are the cornerstones of human happiness.

Saint Francis can still be a teacher and a guide for the modern follower of Christ. In an article entitled "Poor Man of God," published in the October-November 1975 issue of *The Catholic Worker*, Dan Mauk wrote:

> If we are to capture the essence of the man called Francis, the animating force behind him, it would be an injustice to focus in on merely one aspect of his life: his love of poverty, his simplicity and joy, his life of prayer, etc. To see the whole of Francis is to see a man of God—one who saw how well bound together are the body and the world, the soul and God. When Francis knelt before the cross in the Church of San Damiano and heard the words of the crucified Christ, "Go, Francis, and repair my house," there took place in his heart a complete change that left him ever after burning with love for the Crucified One. In the years that followed, his joy and light-heartedness were also accompanied by times of deep and dark suffering. He knew well the "dark night of the spirit," suffering many physical illnesses,

seeing his quickly expanding order of brothers often falling into mediocrity and corruption. He was a man who attained mystical heights, planted deeply in suffering. But so in love with God was Francis, so filled with the Spirit, that even in the midst of darkness he would compose his famous poem and prayer, "The Canticle of Brother Sun." Accordingly, he calls on all creatures, the sun, the moon, the stars, even suffering and death itself, to pour out their praise to God.

Today, while scientists guide and direct the great technology overcoming the earth, and politicians, governmental authorities, and wealthy corporations dangle the world over the delicate fringes of destruction, we are still able to look to Francis as a great witness, teacher, and guide. We can share in that greatness and power that made Francis exuberant with joy, true joy, if we are courageous enough to become little ones, and join him in his prayer—

May the power of your love, O Lord, fiery and sweet as honey, wean my heart from all that is under heaven, so that I may die for love of your love, you who were so good as to die for love of my love.

To which I can only add my humble, "Amen."

Pilgrimage Diary 52

Old Books

*T*oday a friar from India visited Sant' Isidoro. The guardian gave him a tour of the house, which included a visit to the major library, where I was working. Adjacent to the library there is a small room which contains some very precious books and manuscripts, plus documents that trace the history of the college. The door to the room is locked and very rarely opened. The guardian opened the door to the room and invited the friar from India and me in for a look at some of the books.

The first book he showed us was a magnificent Bible printed in 1476. Next, he showed us a book about Saint Francis that was hand-printed in 1250. As we admired the workmanship, we discussed the patience required for such a tedious task. Next, he showed us a hand-printed book from the early 900's. Holding a book over a thousand years old filled me with awe.

The guardian then showed us a letter written in Latin in 1646 by Father Luke Wadding, the founder of the college, to his nephew. The letter began with "My dear son." Wadding was a famous and respected Franciscan historian; there are many portraits of him hanging in Sant' Isidoro. In fact, his stern image is frescoed onto the wall of the Aula Maxima (a large lecture hall). It was good to see this personal side of the man, that of a tender uncle writing to his nephew.

We then looked at an official document prepared by the Nazis during World War II. It stated that Sant' Isidoro should not be harmed in any way because it belonged to the government of Ireland. The proclamation had an official Nazi seal stamped onto it, and it had been posted on the front door.

We spent some time in the small room...and breathed in the history of this wonderful place.

IN HIS OWN WORDS

Saint Francis didn't leave us with much writing. The sum total of all his writings would fill perhaps one hundred fifty pages of an average-sized modern book. He preferred deeds to words. Still, he did write a few things down; mostly admonitions and instructions directed toward his followers. Here are some things from the *Omnibus* Francis said with his pen.

> A man's knowledge can be judged only by his works and the sermons of a religious are only as effective as his actions.

> It is no use walking anywhere to preach unless our walking is our preaching.

> Wherever we are, wherever we go, we bring our cell with us. Our brother body is our cell and our soul is the hermit living in that cell in order to pray to God and meditate. If our soul does not live in peace and solitude within its cell, of what avail is it to live in a man-made cell?

> I caution the friars and beg them not to look down upon or pass judgment on those people whom they see wearing soft or colorful garments and enjoying the choicest food and drink. Instead, each must criticize and despise himself.

While you are proclaiming peace with your lips, be careful to have it even more fully in your heart. Nobody should be aroused to wrath or insult on your account. Everyone should rather be moved to peace, goodwill, and mercy as a result of your self-restraint.

Where there is inner peace and meditation, there is neither preoccupation nor dissipation.

Where there is poverty and joy, there is neither covetousness nor avarice.

Where there is patience and humility, there is neither anger nor worry.

Where there is love and wisdom, there is neither fear nor ignorance.

Where there is mercy and discernment, there is neither excess nor hardness of heart.

Hold back nothing of yourselves for yourselves.

Blessed is the servant who esteems himself no better when he is praised and exalted by people than when he is considered worthless, simple, and despicable, for what a man is before God, that he is and nothing more.

How much interior patience and humility a servant of God may have cannot be known so long as he is contented. But when the time comes that those who ought to please him go against him, as much patience and humility as he then shows, so much has he and no more.

Blessed is the friar who loves his brother as much when he is sick and can be of no use to him as when he is well and can be of use to him.

All creatures have the same source as we have. Like us, they derive the life of thought, love, and will from the Creator. Not to hurt our humble brethren is our first duty to them; but to stop there is a complete misapprehension of the intentions of Providence. We have a higher mission. God wishes that we should succor them whenever they require it.

When you see a poor person, you are looking at a mirror of the Lord and his poor mother. So, too, in the sick you are contemplating the kind of infirmities he took upon himself for us.

We should love our enemies because their injurious conduct gives us an occasion to gain eternal life by returning love for hatred.

I consider you more a servant and friend of God and I love you more, the more you are attacked by temptations. Truly I tell you that no one should consider himself a perfect friend of God until he has passed through many temptations and tribulations.

God is charity and what He seeks above all is our heart, that, having put away all impediments and cares, we should serve, love, adore, and honor Him with a clean heart and pure mind. We should make our hearts a mansion for Him who is the Lord God omnipotent, Father, Son, and Holy Spirit.

Sanctify yourself and you will sanctify society.

When the soul is tepid and little by little cools to grace, then flesh and blood may leap forward to impose their needs.

Temptation overcome is the ring by which the Lord espouses the soul of his servant to Himself.

For what else are the servants of God than his singers, whose duty is to lift up the hearts of men and move them to spiritual joy.

Nothing belongs to us except our vices and sins.

Let us acknowledge that all good things belong to God.

Nothing must displease the servant of God save sin alone.

Simplicity destroys all the wisdom of the world and the wisdom of the body.

Charity destroys every temptation of the devil and of the flesh and every carnal fear.

Near the end of his life, Francis was too ill to attend a chapter meeting. Instead, he sent a letter to the chapter general and all the friars in attendance. In it, he wrote:

Almighty, eternal, just, and merciful God, have us poor wretches for your sake do what we know you want, and have us always want whatever is pleasing to you; so that cleansed interiorly, and interiorly enlightened and aglow with the fire of the Holy Ghost, we may be able to follow the footsteps of your Son, our

Lord Jesus Christ. Aided by your soul-saving grace, may we be able to get to you, who in perfect Trinity and simple Unity live and reign and triumph as God almighty world without end. Amen.

Amen indeed. Those two sentences give us a glimpse of the ascetic theology that emerges from Francis' interior life.

Thaddee Matura, O.F.M., suggests that the best way to get to know Francis is to learn about him through his own writings. Father Matura prefers the lyrical and mystical qualities of Francis' own writings to the "turgid" style of the thirteenth-century biographies and the tendency of modern biographies to be "repetitive and overly dramatic." And his point is valid. For readers interested in exploring more deeply the actual writings of Francis, they would be well served to pick up Thaddee Matura's excellent book, *Francis of Assisi: The Message of His Writings.*

Without Anything of His Own

The line from Francis' writings that most haunted me was: "We may know with certainty that nothing belongs to us except our vices and sins." I heard the sentiment of those words expressed by a follower of Saint Francis long before I actually read them. When I was making the film on the St. Francis Inn, one of the friars, Brother Xavier, told me the only thing he owned was his failures and sins. The line stuck in my head, perhaps because of the genuineness in which Brother Xavier expressed it. I felt he believed what he was saying, and that is what impressed me so much. Here was this truly wonderful man, giving totally of himself, all day long, to everyone he encountered. People called him on the phone or knocked on his door at any hour, knowing full well that he would always respond in love and generosity. Yet this saintly man spoke only of his "sins."

Like Saint Francis, Brother Xavier knew on a profoundly deep level that everything good we enjoy springs from Divine Goodness, and that we have no right to claim anything as our own except for the reality of vice and sin in our lives. Francis said, "We have failed through our own fault." God gives us nothing but goodness. We have defiled and restrained that goodness by choosing sin. By perceiving the immensity of the goodness of God, Francis was able to see clearly how contrary to the ways of God our behavior is, and this realization enabled Francis to view humanity, including himself, as "miserable and wretched, rotten and foul-smelling, ungrateful and evil." Without seeing the true goodness of God, we have no way of seeing the true lack of goodness within ourselves.

Burdened by the weight of the contradictions in his own life, Francis broke the shackles of his senses and their untamed desires, and escaped into the true freedom of love and built within himself a fortress of simplicity and light.

For Francis, conversion was always on his mind, which forced him continually to let go of everything that was not of God. By owning nothing but his sins, Francis gave God the glory for everything.

Following the example of Saint Francis, Brother Xavier's embrace of poverty transcended material things and enabled him to stand before God without anything of his own. Poverty that deep exposes us to the things in our lives that rob us from knowing the profound goodness of God.

PILGRIMAGE DIARY 53

The Word of the Lord

Humanity does not live by bread alone, but by every word that comes from the mouth of God.

—MATTHEW 4:4

*D*uring the pilgrimage, we celebrated Eucharist almost every day. During those liturgies there were numerous times when a sentence from either the first reading or the Gospel proclamation hit me with new impact.

Francis lived on the Word of God. Scripture was a source of both inspiration and comfort. Here are a few sentences from the Word of God that fed me in a special way during the pilgrimage.

Come to me, all you that yearn for me, and be filled with my fruits; you will remember me as sweeter than honey, better to have than the honeycomb. (Sirach 24:19-20)

Jesus said, "Stop worrying, then, over questions like, 'What are we to eat, or what are we to drink, or what are we to wear?' The unbelievers are always running after these things. God knows all that you need. Seek first God's reign, and God's justice, and all these things will be given to you besides. Enough, then, of worrying about tomorrow." (Matthew 6:31-34a)

All that matters is that one is created anew. (Galatians 6:15)

For God's foolishness is wiser than human wisdom, and God's weakness is stronger than human strength. (1 Corinthians 1:25)

We do not fix our gaze upon what is seen but upon what is unseen. What is seen is transitory; what is unseen lasts forever. (2 Corinthians 4:18)

The harvest of justice is sown in peace for those who cultivate peace. (James 3:18)

We are afflicted in every way possible, but we are not crushed; full of doubts, we never despair. (2 Corinthians 4:8)

Out of the Birdbath

"Rembrandt painted him, Zeffirelli filmed him, Chesterton eulogized him, Lenin died with his name on his lips, Toynbee compared him to Jesus and Buddha, Kerouac picked him as the patron of the 'Beat' generation, Sir Kenneth Clark called him Europe's greatest religious genius."

I found those words, on the back cover of The Francis Book. *I was rummaging in a used-book store when I spotted the book of well over a hundred excerpts from other books, essays, articles, poems, songs and documentaries written about Saint Francis, published in 1980 in celebration of Francis' 800th birthday. Titles of some of the excerpts include:*

"Francis, the Whirling Dervish?"
"Saint Francis and Russian Monasticism"
"Saint Francis and Sri Ramakrishna"
"Muhammad and Saint Francis"
"Saint Francis, Buddha, and Confucius"

The blurb on the back cover goes on to say: "Here is the book that takes St. Francis of Assisi 'out of the birdbath' and places him where he really is: at the heart of human and divine experience for Christian and non-Christian people all over the world. Here are the thoughts and visions of some of the greatest writers and artists of the past eight centuries, as they confront the enduring mysteries of a wealthy small-town merchant's son who became a 'mirror of Christ.'"

I was intrigued by the list of divergent contributors to the book. The list included novelist Nikos Kazantzakis, pop songwriters Donovan and Arlo Guthrie, poets Henry Wadsworth Longfellow and Alfred, Lord Tennyson. The list included well-known historians, theologians, art critics and journalists. The list also included Thomas Merton, Oscar Wilde and Albert Camus.

Imagine, Merton and Wilde...and Camus too!

Could anyone other than Francis bring three such different men together?

Francis can touch all kinds of different people, people with an infinite variety of ways of looking at things, because all kinds of different people are attracted to the way Francis saw things. The essays written by this unusual triumvirate of literary luminaries show three different aspects of the saint's life that attracted each one of them. Thomas Merton wrote about Francis' appreciation for solitude. Albert Camus wrote about the deeper meaning of Francis' love of poverty. Oscar Wilde had this to say (in a section entitled "Francis and Christ" in De Profundis):

> There is something so unique about Christ. Of course just as there are false dawns before the dawn itself, and winter days so full of sudden sunlight that they will cheat the wise crocus into squandering its gold before its time, and make some foolish bird call to its mate to build on barren boughs, so there were Christians before Christ. For that we should be grateful. The unfortunate thing is there have been none since. I make one exception, Saint Francis of Assisi. But then God had given him at his birth the soul of a poet, and he himself when quite young had in mystical marriage taken Poverty as his bride; and with the soul of a poet and the body of a beggar he found the way to perfection not difficult. He understood Christ, and so he became like him. We do not require the *Liber Conformitatum* [Book of Conformities] to teach us that the life of Saint Francis was the true *Imitatio Christi* [*Imitation of Christ*], a poem compared to which the book of that name is merely prose.... Indeed, that is the charm about Christ, when all is said. He is just like a work of art himself. He does not really teach one anything, but by being brought into his presence one becomes something. And everybody is predestined to his presence. Once at least in his life each man walks with Christ to Emmaus.

Emmaus is a village outside of Jerusalem where, according to the Gospel of Luke, Jesus appeared to two disciples the evening of his Resurrection. For me, my road to Emmaus ran through the heart of Rome...and I'll *talk about that experience in Part Five. But for now, back to Oscar Wilde for a second. Speaking of Christ, Wilde said that by just being brought into his presence a person cannot help but become something. It has nothing to do with what Christ teaches or says...it is merely his being, a being fully charged with the reality of God, that compels us to change, to become something bigger and better than we are.*

If Francis is indeed a "mirror of Christ," then it stands to reason that he, too, really doesn't teach us by words or example, but rather by just being in his presence we are compelled to at least try to follow his example. Francis was so hungry for God and so full of God that he was no longer himself...he had changed into a mirror of Christ. And when you come close enough to Francis to be able to look into that mirror, you see a reflection of the presence of Christ, "and by being brought into his presence one becomes something."

The Example of Saint Francis

I was surprised to learn that the author of the immensely popular novel, Siddhartha, *which is infused with Eastern thought, began his writing career by writing about Saint Francis of Assisi in trying to describe a way out of artistic alienation. I found the following paragraph in Lawrence Cunningham's book,* St. Francis of Assisi, *which is sprinkled with wonderful photographs by Dennis Stock.*

> Hermann Hesse (winner of the Nobel Prize for Literature in 1946), under the influence of nineteenth-century romanticism, wrote a short monograph on Saint Francis of Assisi in 1904. In that same year he published his first novel, *Peter Camenzind*, which showed that his interest in Francis was not merely historical. The eponymous hero of the novel overcomes his disgust with the bohemian life of Zurich and Paris by a visit to Assisi, where he learns that the life of an artist can be enriched by the humanism he senses in the town and from the continuing influence of the saint. The example of Saint Francis serves as a paradigm who teaches the hero of the novel the value of suffering and love while encouraging him to cultivate a tender love for the world of nature around him. Finally, the self-centered life of the artist gives way to the caring service of others as he learns to nurture and befriend an ailing peasant named Boppi. (page 104)

I am amazed at the power Assisi and Francis have to change lives.

The Example of Christ

Over and over again in the life of Saint Francis, in book after book, we read of the saint's determination not only to follow but also to imitate the life of Christ. Especially in poverty. There is no doubt that Christ was poor. He worked for his daily bread as a carpenter in a small, impoverished village. Lacking money or possessions was not what made Christ poor. Besides, he was far from destitute. He was poor—absolutely and totally poor—because no thing possessed him. He belonged completely to God, and whatever things Christ had he used as a visible manifestation of God's love. Following the example of Christ, Francis was poor in order that his inner emptiness could become a womb containing the fullness of God.

PILGRIMAGE DIARY 54

Ponte Matteotti

Francis' ideal, overwhelmed in every encounter with practical circumstances during seven hundred years, can still prick the cheap vanities of a civilization deceived by material successes.

—*RAY C. PETRY,* FRANCIS OF ASSISI, APOSTLE OF POVERTY

We celebrated the Feast of the Assumption at Sant' Isidoro with a special four-course meal at lunchtime. The meal was accompanied by some very nice red wine from Assisi. After the meal, I returned to the library to work...so many books, so little time. The air in the library was hot and stagnant. About 5 p.m., I still felt stuffed from the bountiful meal and I was beginning to feel drowsy from the stuffiness of the library. I thought a walk would be the perfect remedy for both conditions.

I elected to walk along the Tiber River, hoping Sister Breeze might be playing along its banks. But, alas, it seemed as if Sister Breeze had left town on feria with the rest of the Romans. Still, it was a pleasant walk, my mind tossing little pebbles into the river. When I reached Ponte Matteotti, I crossed the bridge and walked back along the opposite bank.

After crossing the bridge, I turned left and after walking a few yards, I spotted a man leaning against the low concrete wall, staring out at the Tiber. He appeared to be homeless, and filthy beyond measure or description. His long, black hair was matted and gnarled. His face was blackened from soot and grime. His pants were torn along both the inner and outer seams of both legs, leaving much of his legs exposed. His lower legs and bare feet looked as if they were encased in a crust of thick, black sludge. On the ground near his feet, he was surrounded by a dozen small, plastic bags containing— in all likelihood—all he owned. As I passed by him, I caught a whiff of the most vile odor. I thought of Saint Francis and how he used to avert his nose from the stench of the lepers. I continued walking for a minute or so, and then stopped. I looked back at the sad, lonely figure, still standing motionless and staring at the river. I assumed a similar position. As I leaned against the wall, I pretended to be looking at the river, but every once in a while I'd steal a glance his way. On my fourth or fifth glance, he caught me looking at him. We looked at each other for a few seconds and then he turned his head back towards the water. It was then that I noticed something.

Under the bridge, on both banks, were large arches that formed framed tunnels running the width of the four-lane bridge. As I looked into the tunnel nearest me, I spotted something, but I couldn't be sure what it was, though I had my suspicions. I walked back toward the homeless man leaning against the wall. He noticed me coming about the same time I became aware of the horrific smell emanating from his body and clothes. I got within a couple of feet of him and I stopped. I could see more clearly into the tunnel, and my suspicions were confirmed: people were living in the tunnel. Both walls were lined with bags, boxes and blankets.

I motioned to the tunnel and asked, "Do you live there?"

He didn't answer. He just looked at me. Of course, he probably didn't speak English. I reached into my pocket and took out three thousand-lire bills, worth under two dollars. I stuck the money out towards him. He grumbled something and turned away, not taking the money. I put the bills on the wall, knowing Sister Breeze wasn't around to blow them away. But before I could leave, the man made an annoyed-like motion indicating he didn't want the money. I picked the bills up and walked away.

As I walked, my mind turned to Saint Francis, thinking: "If

Francis were in Rome tonight, he'd be sleeping in that tunnel, laying his head down with the poorest of the poor." He would have looked at the homeless man by the wall and would have seen past the filth and have seen Christ. Francis would have walked into that dark, dirty, crowded tunnel and thought, "This is holy ground; Jesus sleeps here."

To be honest, these thoughts were causing me great frustration. What am I to make of Francis' love of poverty? How should I respond to it? Could I follow Francis, if he were here, into the tunnel? What can I do about the people in the tunnel?

Mercifully, these thoughts and questions began to recede as I drew near the Spanish Steps and my attention was captured by the fountain and all the people enjoying life as they sat on the steps eating ice cream and talking on cellular phones. Minutes from these steps is the famed Via Veneto and la dolce vita...the sweet life...of expensive restaurants and elegant stores selling the latest in fine fashion. But you won't find Francis on the Via Veneto...he'd be back in the tunnel living on the fringe of society with the forgotten people, the people we don't want to see.

I thought about skipping dinner, but the loneliness of my room compelled me to seek out the fellowship of the dining room table, even though I wasn't hungry. Earlier in the day, I had given one of the friars an article I had written which had been recently published in The Cord, a little magazine that bills itself as a journal of Franciscan spirituality. The article was entitled "Lady Poverty." [An expanded version of the article is in this book, as a reflection entitled "We Have No Potatoes."] The first two sentences of the article are: "The cornerstone of Franciscan spirituality is poverty. Francis took Lady Poverty for his bride." Simple enough. And true, as far as I was concerned. But the fellowship of the table was about to present a counterview. The friar said, "Gerry, I read 'Lady Poverty.' Very well done. However, you say Francis took Lady Poverty for his bride...well that's not exactly true."

The friar went on to tell me about a friar in Ireland, a very well-loved and respected man, who had recently published an article in which he claimed that when Francis spoke of Lady Poverty he was using the courtly language of the troubadours. After explaining what that meant, he said the friar suggested that Francis was merely honoring Lady Poverty, because she was the bride of Christ. The truth, as the friar from Ireland saw it, was that Lady Poverty was Christ's bride and Christ's alone, and Francis never claimed to marry poverty. Then our conversation shifted gear a bit, as the friar went on to talk about the abuses of trying to live in radical poverty.

I listened...in stunned, shocked silence.

I returned to my room. I immediately began thumbing through the writings of Thomas of Celano and Saint Bonaventure, the primary sources of our knowledge of Francis.

Thomas of Celano: "...he longed after poverty with all his heart; considering that she was the familiar friend [note: not spouse] of the Son of God, he strove in everlasting charity to espouse her, now that she was cast off by the world. Therefore, having become a lover of her beauty, in order that he might cleave yet more closely to her as his spouse..." (2 Cel. XXV).

Saint Bonaventure: "The holy man saw that poverty was the close companion of the Son of God, and now that it was rejected by the whole world, he was eager to espouse her in everlasting love" (Bonaventure, page 239).

Sounds to me as if Francis took Lady Poverty for his bride.

The next day I read the quotes from Celano and Bonaventure to the friar. Then I said, "Francis was more faithful to poverty than most men are to their wives. He never betrayed her. Right up to the end of his life he fought to have her play an important role in the lives of his followers, resisting all attempts to soften her significance."

The friar seemed pleased by my impassioned response to the troubadourian language nonsense. He suggested I write an article rebutting the article of the friar in Ireland. I had no interest in doing that, but I did enjoy the discussion we then had on exactly how we—a friar in Rome and layperson in Los Angeles—could respond to Francis' ideal of poverty.

After a long talk, we realized...we didn't know how.

Perhaps, we are both too rich to know.

Wrestling With Poverty

Poverty is the door to freedom...because, finding nothing in ourselves that is a source of hope, we know there is nothing in ourselves worth defending. There is nothing special in ourselves to love. We go out of ourselves therefore to rest in Him in Whom alone is our hope.

—*THOMAS MERTON,* THOUGHTS IN SOLITUDE

After spending more than three years thinking and writing about Saint Francis of Assisi, I'm still puzzled by poverty. Francis considered poverty to be a basic component of the Christian life. He urged his early follow-ers to "empty" their hearts of all attachment to earthly goods. He saw poverty as a road a person must walk down if he or she is to become transparent to the Lord, to neighbor and to self. I've got to work out my own response to Francis' ideal of poverty, a vision which has been severe-ly narrowed over the centuries.

Francis was a man of passionate impulses, which was part of his charm. But his simple, unsophisticated approach to life and his literal interpretation of the gospel also caused him to make illogical conclusions which gave birth to questionable obsessions, such as the extremes of self-deprecation, bodily abuse and the strict observance of poverty. Francis' ideal of poverty did not last long within the Franciscan Order; the ideal was far too severe and impractical for anyone to follow in its fullness. Even though Francis implored his followers to avoid the temptations of laxity and to preserve the spirit and truth of complete and radical pover-ty, it wouldn't be fair to say the friars betrayed the ideal, because it was impossible for the fragile idealism of the saint to survive the harsh reali-ties of daily life. In the pristine and uncompromising absolutism of his ideal of poverty, the saint was able fully to strip himself of all proprietary ambitions. But, who else, in either his day or ours, could follow his example, fully and without reservation? Very, very few, if any. The stan-dard Francis set was inhuman, far surpassing the limits of sound sense; it even exceeded the poverty which Christ lived. And so, after Francis' death, modification of the ideal was a natural and inevitable conse-quence, even though some factions refused to compromise and insisted on strict observance of absolute poverty. Still, attempts to reconcile devia-tions from the ideal caused, and continue to cause, mental strife and dis-tress within the Order.

It distresses me. I wrestle with the implications of Francis' ideal of poverty almost every day. He doesn't leave room for easy answers.

During the past one hundred years, historians from Paul Sabatier to Johannes Jörgensen to Father Cuthbert to J.R.H. Moorman have analyzed Francis' life and his relationship to poverty from every possible angle and have presented conflicting views about the meaning and importance of poverty in the mind of Francis. I'm not sure Francis had a systematic approach to poverty. His ideal of poverty didn't spring to his mind fully developed. He grew into it, through real-life experiences. He did not attempt to articulate a highly developed theology of poverty. His mind did not work that way. His thinking was always spontaneous and immediate. He spoke in personal terms, one-on-one with his followers and to the people he met along the road. He did not deal in abstract ideas; his ideas and responses to problems were always very concrete, very real. He did, however, think in images, and it was easy for him to jump from one image to the next. He spoke about real things—lepers, run-down churches, money—and offered real responses. He often employed simple parables to express himself. Francis simply wanted his practice of poverty to be a literal representation of the poverty of the gospel. Francis wanted to live a way of life that was a reproduction of the way Christ lived. No detail of the gospel was too insignificant for Francis to imitate, even nakedness. He did not care if a literal following of the gospel caused him or his followers discomfort or even placed them in danger. For Francis, the observance of poverty was an essential part of apostolic life. He could not permit himself to be richer than his Beloved. Francis had nothing and loved nothing in this world, so his soul could be free to love Christ alone.

Needless to say, Francis' ideas about poverty were so extreme, so severe, that it comes as no surprise that they were confronted with great difficulties when he asked his followers to put them into practice, causing deep splits in the brotherhood. Disputes over the nature and degree of poverty raged for centuries, especially between the Spiritual and Conventual branches of the Order. In 1317, Pope John XXII entered the fray, issuing a series of bulls which essentially condemned the doctrine of absolute poverty. The practical needs of the friars' communal life were so overwhelming that the ideal of absolute poverty became more devotional than dogmatic. For those interested in a detailed account of the evolution of the ideal of poverty in the Order during its first two hundred years, I would recommend reading Franciscan Poverty by Malcolm D. Lambert.

Francis had one goal: a total and complete imitation of the life of

Christ, with special emphasis on Christ's poverty. Francis' desire to live a life of absolute poverty is too radical a path for any layperson to follow. However, it would be a grave error to discount his love of poverty as something only he could espouse. We may not be able to embrace Lady Poverty as fully as he did, but we must keep his ideal ever before us. The extremes to which Francis went should challenge us to go further down the path of poverty than we would like to travel. The example of Francis should challenge us, upset us, and force us to respond. I do not want to become poor. I want poverty to remain symbolic in nature, not a fact in reality. I'm happy to have Lady Poverty point out that I could live on less, that I should share more of what I have with those who have less. But Francis does not allow me to be happy with my limited love of Lady Poverty. He gently nudges me to go further, to become poorer...in spirit and in flesh.

I may not be able to wed Lady Poverty, but I am happy to have her be a close friend, a friend who cares enough to tell me the hard truth I may not want to hear. I'm waiting for her to tell me to stop eating rich foods.

A Fountain in a Piazza

People think pleasing God is all God cares about. But any fool in the world can see [God is] always trying to please us back...always making little surprises and springing them on us when us least expect them.

—ALICE WALKER, THE COLOR PURPLE

Francis always expected little surprises, little unexpected and pleasing gifts from God. He was always looking with open eyes. Francis had a profound reverence for the holiness of all created things. He looked at the visible things before him—a bright, yellow sunflower, a shimmering cypress tree, a lazy lizard on the path to the Carceri, a glistening fountain in a piazza—and was able to see the glory and perfection of his invisible God. Francis saw the essence of things, and how they mirrored the essence of God.

God was always within his sight. Everything the saint saw was a sacrament. The incarnation was a daily event for Francis, as God spoke through all the material things in the world he so lovingly created...for us. What joy! Francis praised and thanked God every day for the simple things that revealed the grandeur of God.

Teilhard de Chardin, deeply influenced by St. Francis of Assisi, writes in The Divine Milieu: *"God, in all that is most living and incarnate in Him, is not withdrawn from us beyond the tangible sphere; He is waiting for us at every moment in our action, in our work of the moment. He is in some sort at the tip of my pen, my spade, my brush, my needle—of my heart and of my thought."*

Francis kisses the earth because he is keenly aware of the wonder of creation and he is telling us we must respect all of creation. Francis praised Brother Sun and Sister Moon because they were created by God and are reflections of God's love and beauty. When Francis praises all of creation, he is not doing so as a high priest of ecology; rather, he is making a mystical statement that claims we can have an experience of God through creation, because God is present in all of created matter, energizing it.

Saint Francis, help me see what is right in front of me. I too often see past things to the next thing, not allowing time for my eyes to really see and my mind to be truly mindful. Help me, Saint Francis, see God in everything.

Looking for Jesus

If you are looking for Jesus, you'll find him in the midst of those who are being crucified, rejected, alienated and oppressed. He is in the dark corners of your neighborhood, waiting for you to help him. Unless we stand shoulder-to-shoulder with the poorest of the poor, we will not find the crucified Christ, nor experience the richness of his resurrection.

Francis chose poverty as his bride because he wanted to imitate Christ. And Christ himself not only embraced poverty by becoming human, being born in the poverty of a stable as the son of a poor woman, but Christ also embodied God the Father's love of the poor, a love which is reflected in countless Old Testament verses, and transformed poverty into a thing of splendor. Poverty taught Francis how to love more perfectly. Lady Poverty is a real flesh-and-blood person, living within the destitute and the rejected, bestowing royal dignity upon the poorest of the poor. Francis passionately embraced that which Christ embraced. In a stable at Bethlehem and on the cross at Calvary, Jesus freely embraced poverty, freely endured humiliation and suffering. Francis constantly reminded his brothers that Jesus gave up the riches of heaven and became poor for us, and out of love for Christ the friars have chosen the path of poverty.

BRIGHT AND PRECIOUS AND FAIR

I'd like to end Part Two by quoting a passage from Susan Saint Sing's inspirational book, *Saint Francis, Poet of Creation*. The passage serves both as a meditation on the suffering of Francis and an introduction to Part Three, which looks at the life of Saint Clare. The essay is entitled "The Lady Clare," which Susan Saint Sing begins by quoting a phrase from Francis' *Canticle of Brother Sun* in which he praises Sister Moon and the stars.

> In the heavens you have made them, bright
> and precious and fair.

In my own life, I often think of Francis as the saint, canonized, and in heaven. It is so easy to forget his suffering. In fact, his physical poverty sometimes seems a lightness, a nice carefree way to stroll the world. How often we would all like to walk away from our possessions and the responsibilities they demand.

It is absurd, of course, to think that Francis led a carefree life. He brought such joy out of poverty that we identify with the ideal and rarely with the reality: day-to-day discomfort, lack of proper food and shelter, not to mention the struggle with conscience. The struggle between his dream and his very human self. Was he right? Was it right for others? His followers were mounting. Did he have the right to lead them among lepers? Was his vision of God so clear that he should point the way for others? And what about Clare? Should she be asked to live in such hardship?

It seemed especially at night that these doubts came. There is a folk legend about Francis and Brother Leo traveling one moonlit evening from Siena. They hadn't been well received: Francis was quiet, thinking of his spiritual sons and daughters. Would they also one day be so rudely treated? Would their example of Christ's love shine forth to people, or in their austere poverty would they give up, lose faith, and sicken in body and spirit? Consumed especially by his concern for Clare, he dragged himself to a well and stared into its depths.

Suddenly he called to Brother Leo.

Little lamb, do you know what I have seen in the water?

Leo peered over the rim and replied, *The moon, Father Francis.*

No, Leo, not Sister Moon but Sister Clare, the true face of Clare and the purity and joy of her resolution to live in perfect poverty. My fears have vanished! For I know, even as we walk, our Sister receives great joy from her love of God and his gift of holy poverty.

"Bright and precious and fair." You can almost hear the original utterance, whispered in ecstasy. Francis capsulizing his love in the magic he drew from the deepest well and the darkest nights. (page 57)

Pietro Lorenzetti
ST. CLARE
c.1330
Fresco, Basilica di San Francesco, Assisi

Part Three

SAINT CLARE OF ASSISI

The Shining Light

A DIFFERENT LOVE STORY

C
lare, who shines through her radiant merits, is now shin-
ing in Heaven in the light of Glory, and on earth through
sublime miracles.

—POPE ALEXANDER IV, *THE BULL OF CANONIZATION*

Saint Bonaventure said Saint Clare "was the first flower in Francis' garden, and she shone like a radiant star, fragrant as a flower blossoming white and pure in springtime." No one captured the heart and spirit of Saint Francis' message more than Saint Clare, and no one ever came closer in following or reaching the Franciscan ideal than she. Echoing Saint Bonaventure, Johannes Jörgensen called her "the flower of the Franciscan Order." If you want to know about Francis, talk to Clare; she understood him better and loved him more than anyone else. She was, in short, his soulmate. And she died fighting to keep his dream alive. But that is only part of her story.

Francis and Clare...theirs is a love story, a love story of extraordinary—even divine—proportions.

At the risk of having my poetic license revoked, I'll introduce the story of their undying love by comparing their love, at least in its earliest stage, to one of the most famous romances of all times, that of Cyrano and Roxane. Cyrano de Bergerac was a seventeenth-century soldier and adventurer. Like the young Francis, Cyrano lived life to the fullest. He was fearless, exuberant and poetic. And secretly in love with the beautiful, young Roxane. But, believing he was too ugly because of his grotesquely huge nose to ever win her love, the eloquent Cyrano helps the object of Roxane's desire, a handsome, tongue-tied young soldier named Christian, win her affection through a series of poetic love letters Cyrano writes for him.

Close your eyes and imagine the scene from Edmond Rostand's dramatic play where Cyrano stands in the shadows beneath Roxane's balcony as he gently whispers words that Roxane thinks are coming from Christian. The power of Cyrano's words not only enters Roxane's ears but also penetrates her very soul. Your heart breaks as you see Roxane falling in love with Cyrano's soul yet ending up in Christian's arms. Circumstances contrive to prevent Roxane from ever consummating her love with either Christian, who dies in battle, or Cyrano, who dies seconds after Roxane. She has lived in a convent since Christian's death, finally realizing it was Cyrano she has loved through all the years since her soul was first stirred on the balcony by Cyrano's words.

Of course, Francis and Clare's story is far different from Cyrano and Roxane's; however, it bears a close resemblance in one sublime detail. Imagine the Cathedral of San Rufino in Assisi centuries earlier, in the year 1212. Sitting in a pew during a Lenten service is a beautiful young girl named Clare. Listen to how novelist Julien Green describes the scene in, *God's Fool*:

> When Francis was preaching in the cathedral of San Rufino, he had no idea that a young girl, seventeen years old, accompanied by her mother and sister, was listening with passionate attention to the great seducer of souls who spoke of God's love. Francis was not what is called handsome, and he was twelve years older than she. But that didn't matter because, as unsurpassingly beautiful as she was, she welcomed each of his words with an indescribable emotion. He wrenched her out of herself. Together with him she fell in love with Love—and how can you separate Love from Love's messenger? Had the two kinds of love interfused? We have only one heart to love God and his creatures. If Clare had been told that she was in love with Francis, she would have been horrified and would not have understood. But after she got home, his voice, at once gentle and vehement,

kept following her, preaching penance, scorn for riches, mortification of the flesh.

    She could no more resist the impulse to love than he could.
It was in their nature, his and hers, but this was the first time
she had heard him extolling Love, and he revealed to her that
their passion was the same: the infinite desire to be one with
God. (pages 143-144)

Like Roxane, the exquisitely beautiful Clare had been seduced by the
power and tone of an unsightly man's words. And Francis, dressed
in his torn and tattered habit, like Cyrano, used the power of his
own words, electrified by his deep understanding of Love, not to
draw love to himself, but to be put to the service of another, who in
Francis' case was his God.

    But the love Francis and Clare shared was nothing like the kind
of romantic love to which we are attracted. In *This Living Mirror*,
Sister Frances Teresa, O.S.C., explains their special kind of love:

> Deep in our hearts, we sense that Clare and Francis attained
> something for which we all long, though we do not always
> realise that the deep taproot of their love was their shared call
> from God. It was not a transcended romance, though we often
> see it as such. The romanticism, in fact, is ours and fairly inac-
> curate; the bond between them was not based on natural attrac-
> tion or affinity, but a shared commitment, a shared sharing in
> God, far more precious than natural affinity. In an essential
> and, almost, in an existential sense they had a shared life. They
> exemplified in their relationship what they most deeply
> believed in, namely the Incarnation of Christ, as if, singly and
> together, they each personified God's union with humanity.
> When we look at them now, we see them glowing with the fire
> of love, God's love for them, theirs for God and their love for
> each other, and it all seems to us one burning furnace in which
> they are as united as it is possible for two people to be. They are
> like the three young men, themselves tossed into a furnace,
> walking about in the heat of it, glowing red-hot and yet not
> destroyed, and the presence of God walking with them. It was
> not a godly substitute for marriage, but something altogether
> beyond marriage, something nearer to the union of Christ and
> humanity, of which marriage is an analogue. Surrendered to the
> Gospel, they lived and related in this life as we shall all do in
> the Kingdom which is to come. This was the real wonder of it.

    Permeating their love was their shared vocation which flourished once it was firmly planted in the soil of God. When Clare speaks of herself as a little plant of Francis she is not saying something which we might find rather twee but possibly justified by love; on the contrary, she is making a statement about the gestalt, the setting of their lives. They lived in God as plants in soil, drawing nourishment from humanity, the humus, of Christ, and giving back the service of their fruits. By claiming this title of little plant, Clare is saying that Francis had planted her in the best soil going, for God is our natural habitat, the finest soil for all our lives and loves. (pages 87-88)

Almost a century ago, Paul Sabatier captured the special nature of their love: "It is possible to meet souls...who are so pure, so little of this world that with one step they enter into the holy of holies, and once there, the thought of any other union would not be so much a fall as an impossibility. Such was the love of Francis and Clare."

By comparing Francis and Clare to Cyrano and Roxane, clearly I *should* have my poetic license revoked.

Sister Frances Teresa began her chapter on Clare and Francis with a fitting quote from Ezra Pound's *Canto LXXXI*:

What thou lovest well, remains,
the rest is dross.
What thou lov'st well shall not be reft from thee,
What thou lov'st well is thy true heritage....

NOBLE BY GRACE

When the human person responds to the offer of God's grace in an appropriate way, the basic effects of this response may be seen in a firm sense of fidelity to God, a strength of character in one-self, and an increasing generosity and love of one's fellow beings.
—ZACHARY HAYES, O.F.M., "BONAVENTURE," IN
THE HISTORY OF FRANCISCAN THEOLOGY

Thomas of Celano describes Clare as "of noble parentage, but she was more noble by grace; she was a virgin in body, most chaste in mind; a youth in age, but mature in spirit; steadfast in purpose and most ardent in her desire for divine love; endowed with wisdom and excelling in humility; Clare by name, brighter in life, and brightest in character" (1 Cel. 18).

Long before that day in the cathedral, Clare already had a reputation for holiness and piety. In fact, she lived a nun-like life, despite her family's wealth and social status. For example, Clare had a desire not to be seen by anyone, and avoided all the social gatherings young girls her age enjoyed. In public, she dressed elegantly, as was expected of members of her family, but beneath her fine outer garments, Clare wore a rough woolen shirt against her skin. She always set aside part of the lavish meals that were served at her parents' table, and gave the food to the poor. From the beginning, Clare's heart was attracted to religion. Thomas of Celano wrote: "With a docile heart she learned from her mother's lips the rudiments of faith and as the Spirit worked within and formed her into a most pure vessel, she became known to men as a vessel of grace."

Clare was known to spend hours in prayer. Thomas of Celano noted: "Holy prayer was her constant companion...." She was gifted in the things of the spirit from childhood; her sister Beatrice described her as "angelic" as a little girl. As she matured, she was drawn to a life of solitude. When she was a teenager, a suitor came to visit Clare and, much to the young man's frustration, she only wanted to talk about fasting and alms-giving. At seventeen years old, Clare made a decision to live in virginity and poverty, clearly indicating that a lay penitential spirituality, a long-standing movement in the Church but rarely associated with any member of the noble class, was fully flowered in her life. In short, Clare was destined for a life dedicated to God long before she joined Francis on the road to sainthood.

Ingrid J. Peterson, O.S.F., in her 1993 biography, writes:

> Although it is frequently said that Clare followed Francis, the story of Clare begins with a call from God and her response, which came from an inward gaze. The starting point of Clare's life was the God she found dwelling within her flesh, a God whose traces, later in time, she came to recognize in Francis. (*Clare of Assisi*, page 1)

Sister Ingrid goes on to say:

> Clare's sainthood is valid in her own right without Francis of Assisi. However, without the popularity of Saint Francis, who provided the masculine approval that seems essential to validate a woman's life, the story of Clare as a saint might have remained hidden. (page 2)

Francis had heard stories of Clare's holiness before he met her. The early sources also indicate that Clare wasn't the first woman to follow Francis. Reading between the lines of the sources, some scholars find it reasonable to imagine that Francis spotted a talent in Clare and went after her because he needed a recognizable figure to lead the women who had already answered the call to a more radical following of the gospel.

Francis and Clare's relationship was based solely on their mutual desire to imitate Christ, especially in poverty and humility. Theirs was, at heart, a spiritual friendship that served them both well. Margaret Carney, O.S.F., in *The First Franciscan Woman*, writes:

> The relationship of Francis and Clare should be characterized as a communion of mutual charism and mission. Clare, a woman touched by the Spirit and committed to the path of holiness, found in Francis the perfect guide for the aspirations that had earlier moved her towards a form of evangelical witness. Francis, for his part, found in Clare a leader who could give shape to the hopes of women who sought to share the call to penance and poverty that the friar's preaching announced. Much of the mutual influence that these two leaders and mystics exerted upon one another is found in the writings they have left us. (page 241)

A Good Catholic Girl

Clare was a good Catholic girl before she met Francis. She went to church, did good works and avoided evil. Yet, when she encountered Francis, she was introduced to something radically different from just being good. She suddenly realized that God wasn't interested in our "just being good." God desired far more than that...God wanted us to be so united with him that we become reflections of the divine.

Francis inspired Clare to dedicate herself to live in full accordance to the highest demands of the gospel. She put the whole gospel into her whole life. She lived for nothing but God. Her mind and heart were constantly centered in God. She entered fully into the most rigorous demands of poverty. She gave herself in charity to all. Prayer became her very breath. She lived love, and radiated with sanctity. Clare's undying fidelity to the Lord and her vocation inspired everyone who knew her. Pope Alexander IV called Clare a "lofty candlestick of holiness."

The light from that candlestick shimmers with one unequivocal message: God wants our all. God wants our trust, our humility, our openness, our hearts...God wants our entire beings, so his perfect love can be born again into the world.

How do I respond to that message?

I must begin by renewing my commitment to God every day. I must try every day to deepen my relationship with God.

Clare calls me to ascend the ladder of contemplation.

Bookends

The title of this book refers to Clare in terms of her relationship to Francis. In doing so I am guilty of a form of male chauvinism, though certainly none is intended. After immersing myself in the lives of Francis and Clare, I remember telling a friend that I thought I might have an even greater admiration for Clare than I do for Francis. One of the first people who read an early draft of this book was a friend, another television director who was only marginally familiar with the lives of Francis and Clare. His first comment to me after reading it was, "I really like Clare. She was something else."

In my heart, she is on equal footing with Francis, a saint in her own right. Still, in virtually all the books I have read, Clare is presented as only a part—albeit a very important part—of Francis' story. What I never stopped to consider was that all the books were written from a distinctly male point of view, a view which stressed the superiority of the male. Listen to these words from a biography of Saint Francis written by a Franciscan friar, Omer Englebert:

> A woman is usually worth what the ideas of the man she admires are worth, and her capacity for sacrifice allows her to attain the heights of heroism when the man shows her the way. Thus it was with Saint Clare, who, better than anyone else in the world, and nearly as well as the Poverello himself, realize his ideal. (page 160)

The book was first published in French in 1947. I almost gagged when I read those lines, because I certainly do not think any woman needs to measure her worth against a man she loves or admires. Still, as I told the story of Francis and Clare, I, too, told their story from the perspective that Clare came closest of anyone in history to following the ideals of Francis.

I certainly didn't mean to infer that Clare somehow was less than Francis, but I suppose I did.

Without realizing it, after reading book after book on Francis, all written from a distinctly male point of view, I subconsciously came to view Clare only in light of Francis, even though I had great admiration for her as an individual. My eyes were opened to the centuries-long chauvinistic approach to the lives of the two saints from Assisi by reading Sister Ingrid. She writes:

> The problem with some of our contemporary approaches to Clare of Assisi is related to patriarchy. In a patriarchal system, where the world centers around men and the events of their lives, the male becomes the norm and the female is measured in relation to that "ideal." None can dispute the church's patriarchal bias, which has permeated our culture since before the time of Francis and Clare, and which came to be gathered together in the teaching of Thomas Aquinas, who proclaimed as dogma that man is the perfect species and that woman is somewhat—or quite a bit—less than perfect. It has been a given for two thousand years of Western culture that women are inferior: physically, socially, intellectually, and morally. Moreover, woman is the cause of evil and sin, and she is a temptation to masculine virtue.
>
> No wonder then, in the eight hundred years since the time of Francis, that Clare is frequently assessed in relationship to Francis, measured, held up according to his standard, and even praised because she is "almost" as perfect as Francis. Recall familiar approaches: Clare was the first true follower of Francis, Clare lived Francis' ideals, Clare preserved Francis' way of life after his death, Clare imitated Francis, or Clare is Francis' little plant. Clare herself used the metaphor of the little plant; therefore, it is argued, the concept must have validity for today. Starting with a particular bias, the point worth knowing is always Francis: to know more about Francis. Look at Clare as a means of understanding the ideals of Francis.
>
> The translation of such a patriarchal bias: if we want to know more about how holy men live, look at Clare who—despite the fact that she was female—helps to show us Francis' way of perfection. Ignore that Clare is worth knowing for her merits as a religious person who happens to be a woman. Disregard that Clare was the first woman to write a rule for religious women. Presume that Clare "followed Francis," that a female could not

find the way to God unless directed by a male. (pages 5,6)

I think Sister Ingrid should be read by any woman interested in learning about Clare's life and spirituality. I recommend it even more highly to any man interested in the same subject. She does not write some feminist spin on the life of Clare. It is a thoughtful and informative study of Clare and the times in which she lived, and also of the lives of her female family members and friends who followed her way of life at San Damiano.

I think that Francis drew more strength from Clare than Clare drew from him. I think Clare was a source of true comfort and inspiration to Francis. To me they are truly equals, bookends of the Franciscan way of life, who together present the wholeness—the yin and yang—of a united male and female outlook.

By referring to Francis and Clare in my title as the sun and moon over Assisi, I do not mean to diminish Clare's own brightness; the title is merely a poetic expression, which should not be taken as a chauvinistic metaphor.

THE TREASURE

This witness also said she heard from Saint Clare's mother when she was carrying this child and was standing before the cross praying that the Lord would help her in the danger of childbirth, she heard a voice that told her she would give birth to a great light which would greatly illumine the world.

—THE ACTS OF THE PROCESS OF CANONIZATION

Clare was born in 1194, possibly on July 11th, into one of the richest and most powerful noble families in Assisi. Her ancestry can be traced back to Charlemagne. Her father was Count Favarone di Offreduccio. Her mother, Donna Ortolana, was from the noble Fiumi family. They, along with two younger sisters, Catherine and Beatrice, lived in a fortified palace, guarded by valiant knights, on the Piazza San Rufino, in Assisi's most fashionable quarter; the family also owned a country castle. According to people who knew her as a teenager, Clare was "of beautiful countenance." "Her face was oval, her forehead spacious, her color dazzling, and her eyebrows and hair very fair. A celestial smile played in her eyes and round her mouth, her nose was well fashioned and slightly aquiline...." (See

The Process of Canonization, witnesses 18 and 19.) With sparkling eyes and radiant color, Clare was tall and shapely, a beautiful young lady. Surrounded by her loving family, admiring friends and fawning suitors, with willing servants and the security of wealth in an unsteady, shifting age, Clare was no doubt the envy of the ordinary girls of Assisi. There are very few details about Clare's early life. But we do know that part of her early childhood was disrupted and spent in political exile.

> When Clare was a small child, the political situation in Assisi became so dangerous for women and the children of the noble class that they fled to nearby Perugia [which was under Papal control]. The merchant class was forcing its way into power, thus crippling the feudal system. New city-states began forming throughout Italy. During the first decade of the thirteenth century, the social order in Assisi stabilized enough for the young Clare to return to the city with her mother and two sisters. (Ingrid Peterson and Ramona Miller, *Praying With Clare of Assisi*, page 15)

Clare's father would most certainly have been deeply involved in the political struggles between the nobility and the citizens, and consequently not actively involved in Clare's daily life. Her mother was a pious woman who went on numerous pilgrimages, visiting shrines in Rome and the Holy Land. Clare's education prepared her for a future life as the wife of a nobleman, in which her duties would include running a large household. From all accounts Clare was an engaging young girl who treated the servants in a kindly manner; she was also sensitive to the hardships of the poor and generously shared her food with the less fortunate.

As a young teenager, Clare must have heard of Francis and perhaps even saw him, especially given the small size of Assisi. The bold, dramatic turn in Francis' life, as he went from a youthful, fun-loving, free spirit to a man dressed in rags, caring for lepers and restoring old churches, must have fired Clare's imagination. She must have watched as Francis and his group grew, both in numbers and in spiritual maturity; after all, two of Francis' early disciples were Clare's cousins, Rufino and the priest Silvester. The sensitive young girl undoubtedly recognized that Francis was doing far more than wearing a hair shirt under a silk blouse or giving away crumbs from a rich table; Clare had to see and understand that Francis was following Christ's command to forsake all and follow him.

Murray Bodo, in his meditative book *Clare: A Light in the Garden*, paints a beautiful portrait of the attraction between Francis and Clare:

> She followed him because she loved the treasure. She heard him speak of what he had found, and a passage in her heart had opened up. They had found the same treasure in different caves, and they would share it with whomever they met in that secret place below the surface of life. She was Clare and he was Francis, and together they would show the world its hidden heart. (page 5)

The determined, restless young woman had no choice but to follow Francis' example...it was really a matter of when. But, we must remember that young girls living in thirteenth-century Assisi did not have the right to determine their own future...Clare's future was not her own. During the Middle Ages, noblewomen were expected to marry well and increase the family wealth. By the time she reached eighteen, Clare was already well past the marriageable age, and her parents were lining up suitors for her, and firmly pressing her to accept one of the many advantageous offers of marriage available to her. Actually, her parents had wanted her to marry shortly after her twelfth birthday, but Clare had managed to get them to delay their plans. Clare had a much different marriage in mind—she wanted Francis to take her hand and give it to Christ. Her choice not to marry caused great turmoil and anguish in the household, and greatly disrupted the peace within the Offreduccio palazzo. It took great courage and determination for Clare to follow through on her dream to have no other spouse but Christ. First, she had to renounce her privileged position in the nobility, and, second, she had to refuse to follow the conventional monastic tradition (that was one of the few options open to women) because it, too, seemed to represent wealth and security.

During the Lenten season of 1212, Francis preached a series of sermons in San Giorgio and the Cathedral of San Rufino. Clare must have attended a number of these. Considering her love of beautiful sermons, Clare must have been captivated by the fiery improvisations of this preacher-poet who was once known as "the king of the youth" and who was now inebriated with God's love. She, too, felt she had to make a decision, a decision to follow Francis' example and walk in the footsteps of Christ.

But it is important to remember it wasn't Francis' words that motivated Clare; what moved Clare was what she heard in her heart. Listen once again to Ingrid J. Peterson:

> When Clare was influenced by Francis' preaching, it wasn't because his personal life was a model for her. It was not because she finally found her knight in shining armor, the man of her dreams; it was because Clare had a hunch that what Francis said about the Gospel and the poorness of Jesus is what she could put into action in her own soul. What Francis said touched Clare's heart. In the thirteenth century, for a woman of the aristocracy to choose to live without property as a means of support was a risk, even of life itself. (page 9)

As a young girl, Clare saw the deep divisions within the community of Assisi; she was troubled by the conflict between the merchants with newly acquired wealth and the old aristocracy, and by the ever widening chasm between the rich and the poor. Many members of the Church hierarchy, driven by a hunger for power and money, behaved so scandalously, they sparked the birth of numerous religious movements consisting of laypeople who wanted to live a more gospel-centered life, animated by penance and a radical following of Christ and the apostles. Clare's sensitive soul responded to the extremes of greed and misery she witnessed by dedicating herself completely to the service of Christ's poor. And so, the soil of Clare's soul had been well-tilled and was ready to receive the message sown by Francis. Clare had already made a private vow of virginity and service to the poor. She was living as a penitent and was planning to give away her inheritance to the poor. The words she heard in San Rufino issuing forth from the mouth of Francis just hastened her along on her spiritual journey.

PILGRIMAGE DIARY 55

Private Chaplain

*O*ne morning at Sant' Isidoro, Mass was celebrated for a congregation of one: me. The students were on holiday in Ireland, and all the friars except one, Father Hugh McKenna, O.F.M., were otherwise engaged. Father Hugh entered the sanctuary, bowed before the tabernacle at the rear of the apse, turned, kissed the altar and then, smiling, began the Mass saying, "It's just the two of us."

The first reading came from the third chapter of Paul's letter to the Colossians, which contains the admonition to "Clothe yourselves with compassion, kindness, humility, meekness, and patience. Bear with one another and, if anyone has a complaint against another, forgive each other; just as the Lord has forgiven you, so you also must forgive." (3:12-13, The New Revised Standard Version Bible)

Here is the Gospel reading (from the sixth chapter of Luke). Jesus speaks to his disciples:

"But I say to you that listen, Love your enemies, do good to those who hate you, bless those who curse you, pray for those who abuse you. If anyone strikes you on the cheek, offer the other also; and from anyone who takes away your coat do not withhold even your shirt. Give to everyone who begs from you; and if anyone takes away your goods, do not ask for them again. Do to others as you would have them do to you.

"If you love those who love you, what credit is that to you? For even sinners love those who love them. If you do good to those who do good to you, what credit is that to you? For even sinners do the same. If you lend to those from whom you hope to receive, what credit is that to you? Even sinners lend to sinners, to receive as much again. But love your enemies, do good and lend, expecting nothing in return. Your reward will be great, and you will be children of the Most High; for he is kind to the ungrateful and the wicked. Be merciful, just as your Father is merciful.

"Do not judge, and you will not be judged; do not condemn, and you will not be condemned. Forgive, and you will be forgiven; give, and it will be given to you. A good measure, pressed down, shaken together, running over, will be put into your lap; for the measure you give will be the measure you get back." (Luke 6:27-38, *The New Revised Standard Version Bible*)

After reading the Gospel, Father Hugh sat down. Believing this would be a time of silent reflection, I thought about the line from a Gospel rich in advice running counter to normal human behavior: the admonition that we should not judge. In my heart of hearts, I am quick to judge some people rather harshly—and often unfairly and incorrectly. But my fledgling thoughts were stifled by words of wisdom from Father Hugh.

He began by saying, "Paul tells us we should forgive each other as soon as a quarrel starts. That sounds good in theory but when you're in the heat of a quarrel with someone, the last thing that comes to mind is forgiveness." He then made the obvious connection to Luke's Gospel, pointing out the need to love our enemies because there is little credit in loving only those who love us...even sinners love those who love them. The ability to love our enemies is a trait only found in humans, albeit very few.

But then Father Hugh surprised me by skipping to what he thought was a very relevant precept from Jesus' discourse: Lend without expecting to be repaid. He turned that idea upside down by saying: "And why should we lend without hope of repayment? Well, just think about how generous God is in giving to us without any hope that we will give back to him."

My mind was instantly flooded with the remembrance of the countless gifts that life has showered on me. On this trip alone, so many people have been generous in their support of my work. One friar, whom I shall not embarrass by naming, paid my airfare. I've been loaned everything I need without any thought of repayment. And how much greater is God's love, how much more God wants to give us...with no strings attached. I've accepted all these generous gifts, and not only have I not responded in kind, giving back to the Lord, but I have instead often responded by thoughtlessly turning my back on God...and I do so whenever I fail to love, whenever I put myself first...and I do that more than I care to admit.

Today, the Lord loaned me a private chaplain...and I'm giving you, dear reader, the gift he gave me. Earlier in these pages, I said the gospel was difficult. It really isn't difficult...it is surprising, in that the behavior it requires is so unexpected. Our human nature, corrupted by our sinfulness, does not respond to events of life in a divine way. But when we throw off our old self, and put on our new self, clothed in the divinity of Christ, our responses to people and situations we encounter slowly begin to resemble the divine way God treats us. The difficulty comes in that our first reaction, conditioned by habit, to those who hate us, hurt us, cheat us, steal from us and quarrel with us, is often far more human than divine. Those habits—thoughtless, unloving, selfish acts—are broken only by prayer and a deepening awareness of the divinity within.

Paul said it best: "[Y]ou have stripped off the old self with its practices and have clothed yourselves with the new self, which is being renewed in knowledge according to the image of its creator."

(Colossians 3:9-10, New Revised Standard Version Bible)

Thanks to Father Hugh's generosity in sharing his insights with his congregation of one, I am going to make an effort to remember—and to be more aware of—how much God gives to me each day, and with that increased awareness, I am going to try to live more in the spirit of thanksgiving and generosity to those I meet, giving out of love. [That resolution, expressed honestly and sincerely, faded rather quickly...the gospel is difficult.]

After Mass, I said to Father Hugh, "I've never been to a Mass at which I was the only person attending." He said, "Well, today you had your own private chaplain."

THE DECISION

Clare was much struck by Francis' decision [to become a penitent]. *The dramatic thoroughness of the saint's conversion impressed her greatly and it always remained her model for her own choice of life.*

—MARCO BARTOLI, *CLARE OF ASSISI*

Filled with intense emotion, and with the help of her aunt, Clare arranged a secret meeting with Francis in which she planned to tell him of her desire to leave all for Christ. Clare was distressed by the prospect of marriage, something her parents had been pushing on her for years, and she wanted to open her chaste heart to the little brother who spoke so wonderfully about Christ and seek his wise advice. One cannot help but wonder what Francis' reaction was to the proposed meeting with the young noble Lady Clare. After his conversion, Francis, with a few exceptions (most notably Lady Jacoba, a lifelong friend) severed all contact with women; he even avoided looking at them. Moreover, he instructed his followers not to even speak to women, unless under certain cautious guidelines. To put it simply: Francis essentially removed women from his world.

Still, Francis agreed to the meeting; but not without first taking precautions to guard against the possibility of temptation or hint of impropriety. Clare had to be accompanied by a safe relative, Madonna Buona di Gualfuccio; and Francis was accompanied by Brother Philip the Tall.

We can only wonder at their reaction to each other. Julien Green, with the perhaps overblown flourish of a novelist, suggests a possible scenario:

> This was love, mystical love, two souls flying toward each other above and beyond the demands of the flesh. Here too they had to be careful. The terrain was dangerous. Can we imagine the ancient adversary, as Dante calls him, passing up such a rare opportunity? A man facing a woman, both of them saints, but neither of them disembodied spirits. Don't tempt the devil, the proverb says. Did they realize they were doing just that? Francis was in his thirtieth year; as he looked at that young girl in her exquisite beauty, how could he not fall in love with her? A fall would have been an incalculable disaster, because it would have hurt the millions of souls who were to find salvation under their guidance. But miraculously there wasn't even a shadow of fault. (*God's Fool*, page 145)

Green suggests that nothing improper happened between the future saints because grace was already visibly at work on Francis' humanity, and that Clare was far too in love with Christ.

Clare told Francis that she wanted to surrender her life to Christ. Francis told her to despise the ways of the world and its vanities and perishability, and not to follow the wishes of her family regarding a marriage, but to keep her body as a temple for God alone. Undaunted, and with the same calm courage and persistence that graced her entire life, Clare did exactly what Francis told her to do. As a result, Clare knew that living under the same roof with her parents was incompatible with following her desire to live only for Christ, and that she had to make a decision about leaving home.

Quickly, the day of decision drew near. Palm Sunday fell on March 18th. Clare went to Mass that morning with her family; she was fully aware of her dramatic plans for the evening. Omer Englebert, in his biography of Saint Francis, sets the scene:

> Clare, adorned like a bride, went with her family to [the Cathedral of] San Rufino; but when it was time for the distribution of the palms, her heart failed her. Here she was about to leave her mother and sisters forever, and this was the last time that she would pray with them in the church where she had been baptized. It almost seemed to Clare as though her secret would suffocate her. She could not stir from the pew and the bishop had to descend the sanctuary steps to place the blessed

palm in her hands. (*Saint Francis of Assisi, a Biography*, page 162)

THE RENDEZVOUS

Clare saw conversion as a break which signified the beginning of a completely different life.

—MARCO BARTOLI, *CLARE OF ASSISI*

Later that night, Clare made her break from her past. Here is the way Mark Hegener, O.F.M., describes Clare's secret plan in his small book, *The Poverello*, which takes an almost poetic look at Francis' life and mission:

> Deep in the night of Palm Sunday Clare unbarred a secret door of the family mansion, hitherto blocked with beams and heavy stones. Without farewell she stepped out in the world of spiritual adventure. In Assisi they point out Clare's house and show you the door from which she fled. In ancient Umbrian homes, special doors were made for the passage of the bodies of those who died within. Living persons never used those doors. Clare's using the so-called "Door of Death" to elope to the convent was a splendid piece of symbolism: dying to the world by leaving her father's house through the "Door of Death," seems like one of those dramatic actions characteristic of St. Francis himself. (pages 37-38)

Clare had an accomplice in her middle-of-the-night escape. Her cousin Pacifica di Guelfuccio was waiting on the other side of the *Porta di mortuccio*—or "door of death." Clare had to move in order to clear a passage, a task which required strength that should have been beyond her ability to reach, but reach it she did, thanks to her determination and strong will.

There is far more drama to the events of Palm Sunday than is evident on the surface of the story. The secret plan was well thought-out, but it involved more than enough people to have given it away on every hand. To begin with, when Clare approached Francis about her desire to live a life of perfection according to the gospel as proclaimed by him, it presented a real dilemma for Francis: how could a woman live in all respects as did the friars? Theodore Maynard, in his 1948 biography of Saint Francis, writes: "Francis and his disciples could adopt absolute poverty and living by doing odd jobs or by begging; but how was this going to be possible for a woman, especially one who was completely alone?" (*Richest of the Poor*, page 123).

Verifiable historical facts are sparse and so we can only offer conjecture as to how Clare broke with her family and followed Francis. It seems reasonable to assume Francis took the perplexing problem of Clare's desire to follow his way of life to Bishop Guido of Assisi and the two men most likely decided on a plan where Clare would live temporarily with the Benedictine nuns. When the bishop noticed Clare sitting in her seat during the distribution of the palms, he must have realized that she was overcome by emotion in the face of the giant step into the unknown that she was about to take. By descending from his throne in the sanctuary and placing a strand of palm in Clare's hand, the bishop was, in effect, offering Clare encouragement. The act seemed to signify heaven's favor for her purpose. Bishop Guido could just as easily, and with just cause, have tried to dissuade Clare from taking such a drastic step, perhaps suggesting that she merely become a Benedictine nun, which was something many women of her class did. But Clare was the only woman determined to follow Francis.

After Clare and her cousin made their way along the narrow, twisting streets of Assisi, they reached the wall that surrounded the city. As in any medieval Italian city, the city gates were closed at sunset, and the keys entrusted to the mayor. With hostile Perugia only fifteen miles away, the gates were surely locked when Clare reached them. How were the gates opened to the two women? No one knows for sure. Perhaps someone was bribed, but somehow they got out.

After making her way through the darkness, Clare arrived at the Portiuncula to find the brothers waiting for her with torches in their hands. It must have been an exhilarating moment as the ragged men led the elegant Clare into the dimly lit chapel, where she laid aside her rich dress and put on the rough Franciscan habit. After Francis sheared her long, golden hair, she made her vows to him. This, too, was extraordinary, and also uncanonical, because this function was normally designated to a bishop, and Francis wasn't even a priest! It is assumed that Guido had delegated to Francis the necessary authority, and he also had cleared the way for Clare to stay, at least temporarily, at the Benedictine convent of San Paolo in Bastia. After tonsuring her hair and accepting her into his way of life, Francis and Brother Philip accompanied Clare to San Paolo, which was about a two-mile walk, where she offered herself as a poor woman without any dowry to present to the convent. So the evening was fraught with danger...and crowned with heroism as the complex plan went off without a hitch and with perfect timing. But the future held still more problems to be overcome.

It is easy to view Clare's elopement to St. Mary of the Angels and her consecration to the Lord through rose-tinted glasses, as if it were merely a story from a romantic adventure. But Mother Mary Francis, P.C.C., asks:

> Can we likewise rouse ourselves to a vital concept of what courage a girl of eighteen, wealthy, lovely, cherished, and pursued, required to become the first daughter of the Poverello? Francis was an enigma to those to whom he was not an object of suspicion. His little ragged band of friars had no official status in the Church at the time. He had no security to offer the beautiful young Clare, not even to the extent of the next day's dinner (and one wonders where he contrived to get the shabby habit he threw over her satin gown!)—nothing, in effect, but a dream as mad as the Gospel and his personal guarantee, as his daughter, she would always be entitled to nothing at all. (*Spaces for Silence*)

Such a deal!

Clare had the courage to stake absolutely everything on a principle she knew to be sound and true. I know that I lack that same kind of courage.

THE REACTION

The next day, Clare's family awoke to find her missing. When they discovered where she had gone, they were bitter, very angry and determined to get her back. Led by Clare's Uncle Monaldo, a few of Favarone's men, who were armed, stormed off to retrieve Clare. They were ready to use force to reclaim her. The men caused quite a stir at San Paolo, but Clare stood firm, literally clinging to the altar, and refused to return home. The ninth section of the *Legend of St. Clare* tells the story:

> [A]fter the news reached her relatives, they condemned with a broken heart the deed and the proposal of the virgin and, banding together as one, they ran to the place, attempting to obtain what they could not. They employed violent force, poisonous advice, and flattering promises, trying to persuade her to give

up such a worthless deed that was unbecoming to her class and without precedent in her family. But taking hold of the altar cloths, she bared her tonsured head, maintaining that she would in no way be torn from the service of Christ. (*Clare of Assisi: Early Documents*, page 197)

Yielding to Clare's vehement objection to leaving the convent, the men decided against using force and returned to Assisi without her.

But the prioress of the convent was worried. She sent word to Francis that she was concerned that Clare's father would return and forcibly remove his daughter. The prioress felt Clare's presence was jeopardizing the monastery and the safety of the other nuns. Francis took Clare either to another Benedictine convent, St. Angelo in Panso, or (as recent scholarship suggests) to a settlement of Beguines, but it was clear to both Francis and Clare that they had to find a home where Clare would be free to follow the Franciscan path.

There was one more dramatic event in the early days of the Poor Ladies, as Francis called Clare and her Sisters. Johannes Jörgensen relates the incident this way:

Angry as Favarone had been, he now was more furious than ever, when his young daughter Agnes [Agnes was her religious name; her given name was Catherine], sixteen days after Clare's flight, also left her home and went to Sant' Angelo to be there received into the Sisters' life. Of her he had great hopes; she was engaged and the marriage already settled. And now she was taken also with the same madness! Wild with rage and indignation he asked his brother Monaldo to take twelve armed men and get Agnes back.

The nuns in the convent of Sant' Angelo drew back alarmed from the weapons that confronted them and deserted Agnes. The young girl, scarcely more than a child, made a vigorous resistance and the men had to adopt strenuous measures. Blows and kicks were hailed upon her, they pulled her by the hair, and thus drew her out of the convent. "Clare, Clare, come and help me!" the unhappy one cried in vain, as locks of her hair and bits of her clothes were left hanging on the bushes by the roadside.

Clare was in her cell and asked God to help her in this hour of need. And then it suddenly came to pass that twelve strong men were unable to bring Agnes's body one inch further. She became suddenly so heavy that she might have been of stone. The men pushed and pulled her, but in vain. "She has eaten lead all night," said one of them, grinning. "Yes, the nuns know what tastes good," answered another. But her uncle Monaldo became so furious over this unexpected obstacle, that he lifted his armored fist to crush with one blow the contumacious girl's head. But it came to pass that he too was petrified and stood powerless, with lifted but helpless arm. Meanwhile Clare came to the scene, and the half-dead Agnes was abandoned to her. The family made no further attempt to prevent the two girls from following their vocation; later the third sister Beatrice joined them, and after Favorino's death, Ortolana also. (pages 128-129)

It is of interest to note that the various biographies of Saint Francis treat this scene with varying degrees of piety, some stressing the miraculous events—Agnes becoming too heavy to move, Monaldo's arm freezing in place preventing him from hitting Agnes—while others downplay them somewhat. For instance, Julien Green states a miracle took place; however, he never mentions that Clare prayed, instead he suggests that Clare ran to Agnes's defense and "began to harangue the men so forcefully that they abandoned their prey and went back sheepishly to Assisi, while the two sisters returned to their cells" (page 149). Also, Agnes was a name given to Clare's sister by Francis symbolizing purity safe from the clutches of the world. *Agnes* is derived from the word *agnello*, meaning lamb, and Francis gave Catherine this name because she had sacrificed herself like a lamb to the divine Lamb.

PILGRIMAGE DIARY 56

Thoughts Scribbled While Walking

The loud drumbeat of fear and anxiety can be quieted by contemplation.

Jesus does not promise happiness. He proclaims the beatitudes.

Contentment is the daughter of simplification.

If Christ is the center of my life, then I am not. This is good.

Tell your ego to shut up.

Let yourself be loved; let yourself be acted upon by God.

Poverty is another term for "letting go."

Detachment makes one powerful.

To keep silence is to keep listening.

A HOME FOR THE POOR LADIES

She was the princess of the poor, the duchess of the humble, the mistress of the chaste, the abbess of the penitent...her very life was for others a school of instruction and doctrine.
—DOCUMENT OF CANONIZATION, IN MURRAY BODO, O.F.M.,
CLARE: A LIGHT IN THE GARDEN

Shortly after her sister joined Clare, Francis was given (either by the Caldomese monks of Mount Subasio or by Bishop Guido of Assisi) the little church of San Damiano as a home for the Poor Ladies. The generous gift caused Francis to weep tears of joy, perhaps because he was enough of a poet to realize that everything symbolic must begin with the literal. Francis had taken literally the voice he heard before the crucifix in San Damiano, "Francis, go and repair my church." In time, the church he had repaired was in the caring hands of his most extraordinary follower. Taking the Lord's words literally was perhaps not a mistake, for in his simplicity, Francis had prepared a fitting home for Christ's brides. Francis had restored the church and this church would help restore the Church universal. At San Damiano, the symbolic and the literal were joined as one.

In this little house of penance
the virgin Clare enclosed herself
for love of her heavenly spouse

Here
she imprisoned her body
for as long as it would live
hiding it from the turmoil of the world

In the hollow of this wall,
the silver-winged dove, building a nest
gave birth to a gathering of virgins of Christ,
founded a holy monastery,
and began the Order of the Poor Clares.

Here
on a path of penance
she trampled upon the earth of her members,
sowed seeds of perfect justice,
and showed her footprints to her followers
by her own manner of walking.

In this confident retreat
for forty-two years
she broke open the alabaster-jar of her body
by the scourgings of her discipline
so that the house of the Church
would be filled
with the fragrance of her ointments.

How gloriously she spent her life
in this place
will ultimately be told
after it is revealed
how many and how great
were the souls
[who] came to Christ
through her.

For within a short time
the reputation of the holiness of the virgin Clare
has spread through the neighboring areas
and from all sides
women ran after the odor of her ointments.

—FROM *THE LEGEND OF ST. CLARE*, IN *CLARE OF ASSISI:*
EARLY DOCUMENTS, PAGES 198-199

SHARING LIFE AND POVERTY

God wishes to dwell in us in poverty without any of the trappings
for which we win so much praise. All he wishes is to be the sole
object and only enchantment of the present moment.

—JEAN-PIERRE DE CAUSSADE,
THE SACRAMENT OF THE PRESENT MOMENT

In her book, *Clare: Her Light and Her Song*, Sister Mary Seraphim,
P.C.P.A., offers a fine miniature portrait of the early years at San
Damiano:

Night descends on the Spoleto valley gently as the twilight
fades. The gates of Assisi are securely locked and gradually the
city grows quiet. Even in the palazzos of the wealthy the inhabitants retire not long after the sun goes to rest. As a young

moon rises, the Umbrian countryside is drowsing peacefully.

On the hillside outside the walls of the city, the little monastery of San Damiano stands silent under the stars. Only the feeble glow of the sanctuary lamp relieves the velvety blackness enveloping the cloister. Nearly all the sisters are asleep after a strenuous day.

After praying Compline, the night prayer of the Church, together, most of the sisters had retired. Some linger awhile in the chapel, among them is Sister Clare. Thomas of Celano, drawing on the memories of these sisters writes: "For long periods after Compline, Clare would pray with the sisters...and after the others had gone to their hard couches to rest their tired limbs, she would remain watchful and unwearied in prayer, that while sleep lay hold of the others, she might 'by stealth' as it were 'catch a whisper of God.'"

In these dark hours, quietness seeps into Clare's spirit as she yields herself to the silent but irresistible call of her Lord. "She opens wide the depths of her soul to the streams of divine grace" and silently savors the gift of God. She endured the cares of the day just past and entrusts the unknown tomorrow into her Father's hands. As the night grows deeper, Clare abandons herself to the Lover who is seeking her.

Prayer in these early years may have often been just mute yearning, a wordless longing that torments rather than satisfies Clare. She experiences keenly her helplessness, her radical inability to bridge the great gulf that seems to separate her from the "most high Lord." Words are wholly inadequate. Tears spontaneously release her pent-up affection and are so sincere that "the others also are moved to weep."

In time all the other sisters leave, and Clare watches alone before the altar. Her aching desire causes her to fling herself on the floor where, face to the earth, she allows the very posture of her body to express the unspeakable longing of her spirit. "She bedews the ground with her tears and caresses it with her kisses, and thus seems to clasp her Jesus on whose feet these tears and these kisses are imprinted," records her biographer.

The intensity that is hers by nature, the wholeheartedness with which Clare gives herself to whatever she does, characterizes her prayer as fully as it does all other areas of her life. Her extremes in fasting and mortification are due in part to this same trait.

Although this almost ruthless drive to do nothing by halves forms the natural cornerstone on which Clare's future holiness will be built, at this early stage it is almost her undoing. Fortunately, Clare also possesses remarkable common sense and a delicate perception of the movements of grace which prevent her from becoming eccentric. The proof of this is her sunny and balanced disposition.

Not all saints in the making are a pleasure to live with, but, according to her sisters in religion, Clare was. Celano sums up their impressions: "Although severe bodily mortification usually begets affliction of spirit, quite the opposite was seen in Clare, for in all her mortification she preserved a joyful, cheerful countenance, so that she seemed either not to feel bodily austerities or to laugh at them. From this we gather that the holy joy which flooded her within overflowed without; for the love of the heart lightens the chastisement of the body."

The "love of the heart" is the deep and truest explanation of all that Clare does. She is discovering the Heart of Love in Jesus that Francis's fiery zeal is illuminating for all their contemporaries. From his conviction that "the love of him who loved us much is much to be loved" flows the prayer: "May the power of your love, O Lord, fiery and sweet as honey, wean my heart from all that is under heaven, so that I may die for love of your love, you who were so good as to die for love of my love."

Clare is learning that what attracts the divine Lover most powerfully is not eloquent prayer but tongue-tied helplessness, not elaborate rituals but mute poverty, not a wealth of words but silent emptiness. To her helplessness, her poverty, her emptiness, the great and good Lord will bow down. He himself will cross the abyss to reach her. She remembers with emotion that once he came "despised, needy and poor (himself) into this world, that men and women who were in dire poverty and want, and suffering absolute need of heavenly nourishment might become rich in him by possessing the kingdom of heaven."

Clare is so overwhelmed by this divine graciousness that she knows not whether to weep for wonder or to "rejoice and be glad. Be filled with a remarkable happiness and spiritual joy!" She does both.

The moon slowly rises as the stars wheel in their cosmic patterns. As the moonlight approaches, Clare rises from the floor. She lights a candle stub from the sanctuary lamp and shielding it carefully, picks her barefoot way up the steep, uneven steps to the dormitory, Her shadow wavers on the wall as she gazes tenderly over the sleeping sisters. It is the summer of 1214, only two years since she and Agnes were the sole occupants of this rough loft. But now, how many more sisters have come to share their "life and poverty."

Yakety-Yak

I talk too much. I delight in words. Silence is hard for me. I love using words, and without them I feel helpless. I can open a floodgate of words to assist me in getting others to see things my way. Frankly, words help me control and manipulate others. Words express my love, hate, joy, anger, pain, fear and a host of other emotions. With equal ease, I use them to heal some people and to condemn others.

Long ago, back in the seventh century, a Syrian monk named Isaac of Niniveh suggested that anyone who loves using words, even a person who says admirable things, is empty inside. That sounds rather harsh. Yet I think it might be true. The monastic traditions of both the Eastern Church and Western Church have always championed silence, claiming that if you love truth, you will be a lover of silence. Why?

I am not sure. What I have noticed from my awkward attempts at silence is that talking leaves me exhausted. I use words to defend myself and to express myself. And it takes effort. In silence, I confront myself. Silence is a schoolroom. It teaches me about longing and loneliness, about desire and emptiness. It teaches me to listen...to God, to myself, to others. Silence creates stillness within me, a stillness that refreshes and invigorates me.

Last night, as I reflected upon my day, I recalled a phone conversation I had with a friend. We spoke for nearly an hour, perhaps longer. We had an electric exchange of ideas, opinions and feelings. I recalled how after we hung up, I immediately took a deep breath in an effort to recover from the exhaustion (and exasperation) I felt. During the conversation, I thought I was listening to my friend. But, I wasn't. My mind wandered as he spoke. I thought about myself, things in my life. I thought about how to respond to him. I struggled to express with crafted exactitude how I felt about certain topics, one of which was prayer. As we spoke, it all seemed so important, so urgent. Yet later that night, I could barely recall anything significant from our chat. The effects of the hour on the phone stood in sharp contrast to the half hour I spent during the day in silent meditation, which left me feeling peaceful and centered.

Obviously, conversations with friends are a vital part of life. My friend has gifted me with many insights and has comforted me on many occasions. We are social animals. We need each other. Yet, our culture does not value silence, nor does it appreciate solitude. I'm struggling to learn how to balance my love of words and conversations with friends with my growing need for silence and solitude.

Silence is teaching me the value of simplicity. It is helping me see the power of renunciation to overcome my bondage to things that are not good for me. Silence is helping me to die to the opinion of others.

A few weeks ago, during a period of silent meditation, two phrases popped into my head: Be quiet, be compassionate.

Slowly, I am seeing that silence and compassion are sisters who support each other.

WITHIN THE WALLS

Blessed are the ears which hear God's whisper and listen not to the murmurs of the world.

—THOMAS À KEMPIS

Saint Clare spent the rest of her life within the walls of San Damiano, more than forty years. In 1215, Francis asked that Clare officially assume the administration there with the title of abbess. Prior to this, Clare had refused to assume any title or style of religious superior. In response to Francis' request, she begged, in sweet humility, that Francis give another sister the position of headship. Francis declined, and Clare had to accept out of obedience, and, feeling the responsibility of her charge, only one thing preoccupied her: namely, to be the first in every virtue and the last in every concession. During her entire life at San Damiano, Clare's unconquerable faith was seldom discouraged by adversity.

Maria Sticco, in her 1962 biography of Saint Francis, writes:

> She [Clare] slept on the bare ground or on twigs, she wore a hair shirt, and ate only what was necessary. Yet, to see her smiling, with that bearing of a duchess in her worn tunic, patched but

clean, none ever would have said that she was wracking her body in penance. When the sisters were still sleeping in their little cots at dawn she rose, went into the church, lit the lamp and then, not without a twitch of pain for having to break their youthful slumber, she would call the others with a bell which prolonged its peals through the little convent. But even more silvery than the bell was the voice of Clare which rose above the others in the choir singing praises to the Lord. Late at night, she walked through the poor dormitory, observing the sleeping sisters one by one, covering them with love, stopping at the bedside of the sick, while for the younger, the weaker, the more tempted ones, she always had a maternal caress.

She never gave an order that she herself had not first carried out; she preferred doing to commanding, serving to being served. She always chose the most uncomfortable place, the stalest bread, the most tattered tunic, and she nursed the most repulsive illnesses. For humility she washed the feet of the lay sisters who came in from the outside. She not only nursed them materially as the Rule provided, but she also educated them. She taught them how to pray and read, she directed their labors, those beautiful embroideries which are sent to the poor churches and which are still one of the glories of Assisi. She kept them happy. And when she divined remorse or temptation in the heart of a sister, she would call her aside, knowing so well how to talk understandingly, going so far as to kneel before her so that the sister might confess her torment to her, that she succeeded in comforting her. (*The Peace of Saint Francis*, pages 120-121)

From Father Cuthbert's biography of Saint Francis:

Francis gave Clare no Rule of life [recent scholarship refutes this claim; see note following quotation]: he merely set before her the inspiration of absolute poverty and of trust in the infinite solicitude of God. For the rest, Clare shaped her daily course by the example of the brethren so far as a woman might properly go with them. She gave herself to prayer and manual labor; was helpful to the sick who came to her for comfort, and welcomed the brethren whenever they visited the sisters to discourse about Jesus Christ and the spiritual life. Her daily bread was provided for partly by the produce of a small vegetable garden which she cultivated; partly by the alms which the brethren begged for her and her sisters, even as they begged for themselves. It was a simple homely life at San Damiano, filled however with keen spiritual interests and a vital delight in the vocation of holy poverty. That vocation meant to them a great deal of liberty of soul; and in whatever fashion the soul finds its liberty, it finds its paradise. The enclosure of San Damiano might be narrow measured by the yard-tape, but what did it matter to those who lived constantly on the wings of a joyous faith and whose spiritual horizon was limitless as the heavenly love which was in their hearts? (pages 167-168)

[Note: Current research claims that Francis gave Clare a "forma vita," a form of life which one scholar, Jean Francois Godet-Cologeras, equates with Clare's Rule when ultimately written.]

TALES FROM THE LEGEND

This woman, the cornerstone and the foundation of her Order, from the very beginning sought to place the building of all virtues on the foundation of holy humility.

—THE LEGEND OF SAINT CLARE

The Legend of Saint Clare was written shortly after her death. Although there is some doubt about who actually wrote this official biography of the saint, the general consensus among historians is that it was written by Thomas of Celano. *The Legend* is based on interviews with those who personally knew Clare, along with all the information gathered during the Church's official examination of her life, which was published in *The Acts of the Process of Canonization.*

The Legend of Saint Clare is included in *Clare of Assisi: Early Documents*, and is a fine introduction to the life of Clare, containing all of her writings, including the wonderful letters she wrote to Blessed Agnes of Prague, her Testament and the Rule. It also includes numerous contemporary letters written to Clare by popes and cardinals, and many stories such as the following:

The Miracle of the Multiplication of Bread

There was only one [loaf of] bread in the monastery when both hunger and the time of eating arrived. After calling the refectorian, the saint told her to divide the bread and to send part [of it] to the brothers, keeping the rest for the sisters. From this remaining part she told her to cut fifty [pieces] according to the number of ladies and to place them on the table of poverty. When the devoted daughter replied, "It would be necessary to have the ancient miracles of Christ occur to receive fifty pieces from such a small [piece of] bread," the mother responded by saying: "Confidently do whatever I say, [my] child." The daughter hurried to fulfill the command of her mother; the mother hurried to direct her pious aspirations for her sisters to her Christ. Through a divine gift, the little piece [of bread] increased in the hands of the one breaking it and a generous portion existed for each one in the convent. (page 206)

That Miracle of the Liberation of the City

Another time Vitalis d' Aversa, captain of an imperial army, a man craving for glory and bold in battle, directed the army against Assisi. He stripped bare the land of trees, devastated the entire countryside, and so settled down to besiege the city. He declared with threatening words that he would in no way withdraw until he had taken possession of that city. It already had come to the point where that danger to the city was feared imminent.

When Clare, the servant of Christ, heard this, she was profoundly grieved, called her sisters around her, and said, "Dearest children, every day we receive many good things from that city. It would be terrible if, at a proper time, we did not help it, as now we can." She commanded that some ashes be brought and that the sisters bare their heads. First she scattered a lot of ashes over her own head and then placed them on the heads of those sisters. "Go to our Lord," she said, "and with all your heart beg for the liberation of the city."

Why should I narrate the details?
Why describe again the tears of the virgins,
and their *impassioned* prayers?

On the following morning, the merciful God *brought about a happy ending to the trial* (I Cor 10:13) so that, after the entire army had been dispersed, the proud man departed, contrary to his vow, and never again disturbed the city. A little later the leader of war was cut down by the sword. (pages 212-213)

During the history of the fraternity of Saint Francis, the little hillside enclosure of San Damiano was a constant witness to the pure Franciscan spirit. In the early days, the followers of Saint Francis felt the warm embrace of early hope and unwavering faith, but as in all human relationships, faith eventually clashes with earthly experiences and reality, and during the troubled years that lay ahead for the followers of Saint Francis, San Damiano stood as a lighthouse flashing out its message of warning or comfort in a storm. Saint Clare's clear vision and indomitable loyalty to the dream of Saint Francis and his ideal of poverty were a saving influence.

Waiting for God

[W]e need to appreciate that the only way to know God is to proceed in humility, simplicity, and poverty, enter God's silence, and there in patient prayer wait until divinity reveals itself according to its own good timetable.

—WILKIE AU, S.J., BY WAY OF THE HEART

In The Canvas of the Soul, *James Francis Howard, besides writing in his journal, also wrote short essays, which he called "parasketches"...a word he invented to describe short bursts of writing that he thought of as the literary equivalent to the countless, quickly-produced sketches Vincent van Gogh made in the process of teaching himself how to paint. Here is one of those parasketches.*

We're too modern, too sophisticated, too secular, too educated, too rational to hear God's voice the way Francis did. "Rebuild my church," a voice told Francis. And he did. With stones and spirit. And his very life.

"Write a book." Was that God's voice...or my own? I don't even need to hear God's voice—I'd happily settle to hear God's throat clearing. But even that is too much to hope for.

By the busload people pour into Assisi every day. Six million people visit every year. For many the place is simply a museum, a well-preserved 13th-century town crammed with fresco-covered churches. But many others come in hopes of hearing God's voice. They come in search of what Francis and Clare found...the peace, the sweetness, the stimulation—of knowing God's voice. We dash from church to church. We descend to the Portiuncula enshrined within Santa Maria degli Angeli, or we ascend to the Carceri perched atop a ravine on Mount Subasio. We pray. We light a candle. We buy a statue or a Tau cross. And we move on. The bus is leaving. Can we make it down the hill to San Damiano and back in an hour? No. Got to go. We gave the place a day, maybe two or even three, but we had to get going, had to visit Venice or Siena or Florence—Tuesday, Giotto; Wednesday, Michelangelo—had to visit Rome and Raphael.

But God doesn't talk in soundbites or in sync with the train schedule. God isn't worried about catching the 10:11 train to Foligno, with connections to Rome and Venice. God speaks to the still, not the restless or the harried tourist. God doesn't use a cellular phone to catch us on the run.

Do you want to catch God? Stop everything you're doing...and wait.

We're too busy, too sophisticated, too secular, too educated, too rational to stop everything...and wait. But that, I think, is what God wants, even demands. He is a God who comes, but only to those who wait. Francis knew how to wait. We're too busy, too busy to wait for God.

The Psalmist was wise when composing the challenge: "Be still and know that I am God." Stillness, silence and waiting are the portals through which we must walk in order to discover the deeper reality of God. To "be still" means to become peaceful and concentrated. Stillness creates space for deep looking and deep listening that allow us to gain a glimpse of the reality of God, and lead us to greater understanding and compassion. Stillness allows us to become mindful of each moment, and to realize that every moment is pregnant with the possibility of giving birth to God's transforming spirit. To become truly still, you must penetrate your own silence and enter into the solitude of your heart. In that gentle stillness, the mystics tell us, the voice of God becomes audible.

Thoughts Scribbled While Walking

Encourage playfulness.
Humility does not mean self-deprecation or condemnation.
We experience God's love in proportion to our experience of our
 own weakness.
The more you pray, the more you will become poor, plain and
 empty. And ready for God.
Prayer consists of becoming aware.
Detachment reflects the realization that God alone matters.
Do not be seduced by perishable things.
Be like the blind beggar at Jericho seated at the side of the road
 and stretch out open hands to the silence of God.
Solitude allows the soul to look upon everything and see unity.

CLINGING TO LADY POVERTY

Poverty in all things was in harmony with poverty in spirit which
is true humility.

—THE LEGEND OF SAINT CLARE

Clare was a strong woman, strong enough to stand up to Francis, the friars, cardinals and even popes. Part of Clare's strength was her special ability to make herself loved, and she was so persuasive that Francis, the cardinals and the popes themselves always came to appreciate—and yield to—her way of thinking.

To illustrate this point, I'll once again turn to Maria Sticco's artful biography:

> But where St. Clare most showed the identification of her thought with that of St. Francis was in defense of his bride, Lady Poverty. The virgins of St. Damian lived under a brief Rule similar to that St. Francis had given his friars. Around 1216 Clare requested [Pope] Innocent III for the privilege of poverty for herself and her sisters. [Note: The "privilege of poverty" Clare was seeking was permission to take a pledge of absolute or utmost poverty as observed by St. Francis, in which a friar promised not to own anything; essentially, Clare sought the

privilege to have no privileges.] The Pope granted it [only to Clare], indeed, he wrote the first words of the brief with his own hand, observing with a smile that such a request had never before been presented at the court of Rome. In 1219, while Francis was in the Orient, Cardinal Ugolino, who protected the Poor Ladies in the name of the Holy See, approved the very strict Rule, which had been suggested to him by Clare. [Recent scholarship refutes this claim, suggesting that Ugolino gave Clare a set of constitutions (often called Ugolino's Rule) in 1219; but Clare did not suggest anything that Ugolino approved.] When, after the death of St. Francis, the same cardinal became Pope Gregory IX, he told her that such poverty and such fasts were excessive for young women. In the belief that her resistance derived from her respect of the vow, he said, "If it is because of the vow of poverty, we absolve you of it." Clare rose up as if the ideal of the departed teacher were burning in her warrior blood, "Holy Father, absolve me from my sins, but not the vow to follow our Lord." (pages 123, 124)

The pope backed down, but Clare and her sisters continued to live without formal approval of a Rule, and the ideal of absolute poverty continued to be questioned. Maria Sticco writes:

The more some followers of Francis attacked the dream of the founder, the more the abbess armed herself to defend it in her fortress, gathering around her the most faithful who considered St. Damian as their bulwark and St. Clare as the surviving spirit of the inimitable teacher. Other convents came into the Second Order asking and receiving permission to own land and houses. Over this, Clare suffered acutely. How could they call themselves "Poor Clares" when they despised the admonition that the teacher had written for her, for them? "I, humble Friar Francis, desire to follow the life and the poverty of our most high Lord Jesus Christ and of His most Blessed Mother and I counsel you to live always in that very holy life and poverty, and keep watch attentively so that, either by the teaching or counsel of someone, you do not ever stray from it as long as you live." (page 124)

Clare never strayed, and Francis' words were her dominating thought. She knew how to put off death itself until Pope Innocent IV approved the Rule, written by her and fully in conformity with the principle of absolute poverty. In everything that did not infringe upon the essential nature and character of the Franciscan life Clare gracefully submitted to the will of the pontiffs.

In *Enduring Grace*, which examines the lives of seven women mystics, including Clare of Assisi, Carol Lee Flinders, coauthor, incidentally, of the immensely popular cookbook *Laurel's Kitchen*, writes about Clare's understanding of "the mysterious wealth and power concealed" within the Franciscan understanding of poverty. She writes:

> We cannot "place" our minds, our souls, or our hearts anywhere if they are absorbed somewhere else. Out of Clare's passion for poverty there had arisen the perfect detachment that allowed her to direct her attention, her devotion, her love, at will, wherever she chose. Christian contemplatives have always taught that poverty "of the spirit" leads to unitive prayer, prayer so undistracted and so deep that all barriers between oneself and God vanish. By undertaking spiritual disciplines, you free yourself from all attachments and all preoccupations, creating a kind of inner vacuum that God cannot help but fill. The fourteenth-century Rhineland mystic John Tauler wrote, "When we thus clear the ground and make our soul ready, without doubt God must fill up the void." To Clare, though, holy poverty had to begin with actual physical poverty: having nothing—having no *things*. No room here for the rationalizing impulse that says, "What's a warm cloak or two so long as I have my mind fixed on God?" For her, holy poverty was an expression of her union with God, not just a means for reaching it. If your mind is truly fixed on God, she seems to be saying, you won't need a warm cloak, because God's love will surround and embrace you. Indeed, what impressed others was not so much the deprivation of her daily life, though they do mention it, but the joy. "She was never upset," said one sister. "Never disturbed," said another, "always rejoicing in the Lord" (*Clare of Assisi: Early Documents*, page 51).

Furthermore, Clare appears to have been able to absorb herself so deeply in prayer that she went beyond ordinary levels of consciousness. On Good Friday one year, she experienced something of what Francis had at La Verna. For nearly twenty-four hours she was insensate—lost in union with Christ crucified. Sister Filippa persuaded her to revive and eat only by reminding her that Francis had ordered her never to let a day pass without taking bread.

The deficit Clare carved out of her own creaturely needs did not work as an advantage only to her. It became an unfathomably vast fund out of which she could give: give food, for she is credited with more than one "feeding miracle"; give health, for she is said to have healed a remarkable variety of ailments of body, mind, and soul. Give safety and bestow peace, for she is believed to have protected her convent from invading mercenary troops on one occasion and Assisi itself from an attacking army on another. It was written of her, "This clear spring of the Spoleto Valley furnished a new fountain of living water."

Once Clare had glimpsed the mysterious wealth and power concealed in the practice of holy poverty, it became the central work of her life to see that the right to live "sine proprio," with nothing of one's own, would be assured to her Poor Sisters forever. Francis himself had of course been called "Il Poverello," "the little poor man," and one of his first acts as a spiritual teacher had been to tell erstwhile drinking companions that he had married a beautiful woman—one whose identity he revealed as "Lady Poverty" only after he had teased them into a frenzy of curiosity. All of his followers, in turn, embraced the ideal of poverty. But it was Clare who lived out that teaching radically and unequivocally in the face of powerful opposition from church authorities. In the deepest sense, the wealthy young girl really did become Francis's cherished "Lady Poverty." (pages 24-25)

Unlike Francis, and in spite of the austere life she led, Clare lived to an old age; she died in her sixtieth year, on August 11, 1253. The last two and a half decades of her life, after Francis had died, Clare was a victim of numerous sicknesses. In the fall of 1252, she knew her end was approaching, but she still had important work to do—she had to get her Rule approved.

It's the Economy, Stupid

Life in America at the end of the twentieth century was all about the economy. Life in Assisi in the beginning of the thirteenth century was all about the economy. Francis and Clare walked out on the guiding light of money, and it sent shock waves through their culture. Many others followed their lead and pulled out of the system, saying they didn't want anything to do with it.

What about me? How do I respond to society telling me that it is all about the economy, stupid?

THE RULE

The spouse of Christ who longs to become perfect must begin with her own self. She must put aside, forget everything else, and enter into the secrecy of her own heart.

—SAINT BONAVENTURE, *HOLINESS OF LIFE*

Let's return briefly to the year 1219. Cardinal Ugolino has tried to impose upon Clare and her sisters a Rule of his own composition, which tended to form the sisters into a new order distinct from the Franciscan fraternity. Father Cuthbert writes: "With a gentle reasonableness in which there was no rancour, yet with an inflexible determination, she [Clare] wooed the authorities to recognize her Franciscan vocation; and her persistency regained one position, then another" (page 172). Clare reluctantly agreed to a revised Rule, but from then on, her life was a long struggle to maintain her Franciscan prerogatives and her inclusion in the Franciscan family. Once Cardinal Ugolino, who actually admired Clare, appointed a Cistercian monk to be the spiritual director at San Damiano's. It didn't take Clare long to have the Cistercian replaced by a Franciscan friar, Philip the Long, one of Francis' first companions. But Francis did not claim any jurisdiction over the Poor Ladies, and so they remained subject to the Rule composed by Cardinal Ugolino, much to the grief of Saint Clare.

On one occasion, her obedience to Pope Gregory IX resulted in a miracle. Nesta de Robeck writes:

> During Gregory's visit of 1228 there occurred a famous miracle at San Damiano described by Celano and other legends. The Pope accompanied "by many cardinals" had gone to her convent to hear Clare speak of celestial and divine things, and while they discoursed on divine matters St. Clare caused the tables to be set with bread that the Holy Father might bless it. When their spiritual discourse was ended, St. Clare, kneeling before the Pope with great reverence, besought him to bless the bread set on the table. The Holy Father replied, "Clare, thou servant and friend of God, I wish thee to bless it with the sign of

the cross to which thou hast dedicated thyself." Then Clare answered: "Holy Father, absolve me from such an act, for surely I should be worthy of harsh correction were I, a most miserable little woman, to dare to give such a blessing in the presence of the Vicar of Christ." The Pope, however, continued, "To the end that this may be imputed to the virtue of obedience and not to presumption, I command thee by holy obedience to make the sign of the cross on this bread and to bless it in the name of God." Then St. Clare being a true daughter of obedience devoutly blessed the loaves with the sign of the most holy cross. O wonder! On each of the loaves there immediately appeared impressed the sign of the cross, most fair to see. Then some of the loaves were eaten, and some, for the sake of the miracle, were set aside. "And when the Holy Father saw the miracle, he partook of the bread and departed leaving Saint Clare his blessing."

It was probably during this visit that Clare begged Gregory to ratify the privilege of poverty accorded by Innocent twelve years before....

[I]n a letter to Clare dated September 17, 1228, the Pope made a step in the direction she wished.

> Gregory, Servant of the servants of God, to Clare our beloved daughter and to the other sisters of San Damiano in the diocese of Assisi, health and apostolic benediction.

It is clear that in absolutely renouncing all earthly property you have had no other motive than to serve God. And now that you have sold your goods and given the proceeds to the poor, you propose to persevere in this complete renunciation in order to follow the steps of Him, Who being the Way, the Truth, and the Life for us became poor. You are boldly walking in His steps, and allowing nothing to turn you aside not even the lack of what is necessary because with the help of grace and the ordering of charity you have subordinated the flesh to the law of the spirit.

On His side, He Who gives the birds their daily food, and clothes the lilies will be your eternal sustenance in the glory of the beatific vision. Therefore, since you have besought Us, by Apostolic favour, We confirm your resolution to live in utmost poverty, and by the authority of this present letter we confirm to the privilege that no one can coerce you to receive possessions.

Let no man dare to lacerate this page, or to contradict it.

Should anyone have the temerity to do so, let him be warned of the indignation of Almighty God, and of the Apostles Peter and Paul.

Given at Perugia in the second year of Our pontificate.

Clare's life as abbess is sprinkled with stories of how she stood up to cardinals and popes when she thought they were wrong. For instance, Pope Gregory IX (the former Cardinal Ugolino), issued a decree forbidding the sisters from receiving spiritual guidance from the friars. Clare then renounced the material help the sisters received from the friars, and told the pope, "If we have to do without spiritual bread, we can also go without bodily bread." Clare then promised to go on a hunger strike, and Pope Gregory yielded and rescinded his decree.

On September 8, 1252, Cardinal Rainaldo of Segni, who was the protector of the Order, came to visit Clare at San Damiano. Clare was very ill. She submitted her latest Rule to the cardinal and it clashed with a Rule which the current pope, Innocent IV, had written. Clare forcefully demanded that her sisters be permitted to vow to "take nothing as their own, whether it be a house, or a place, or anything at all. Instead they are to be as pilgrims and strangers in this world." Clare continued, though physically weakened and near death, to push for the virtue of absolute poverty, which the Church continued to think was too severe a vow for women to take. Clare won over Cardinal Rainaldo who promised her he would intercede on her behalf to the Holy Father.

Pope Innocent IV himself came to visit the sick abbess. He made no attempt to conceal his admiration for her, yet he was still not prepared to accept her Rule. Clare asked for the pope's blessing and for absolution for her sins. The pope said, "Would to God, my daughter, that I had as little need for God's forgiveness as you!"

A few weeks later, the pope paid Clare another visit. Clare had been unable to take any nourishment whatever for more than two weeks; still, her presence of mind and spiritual strength remained intact, and she was able to wage her final combat. With great ardor she implored Christ's Vicar to grant her and her daughters "the privilege of most high poverty." Innocent buckled and allowed himself to be persuaded, and on August 9, 1253, just a few days after his second visit, he signed at Perugia the Bull "Solet annuere" which approved the new Rule.

Her daughters,
who would very soon be left as orphans,
stood around the bed of the mother,
a sword of sorrow piercing their souls.

Sleep did not restrain them
and hunger did not tear them away,
but,
forgetting their beds and tables,
the only thing that pleased them,
night and day,
was crying.

Among them was Agnes [her sister], the devoted virgin, filled
with salty tears and begging her sister not to depart. Clare
replied: "It is pleasing to God that I depart. But stop crying, because you will come to the Lord a short time after me. And the
Lord will comfort you greatly after I have left you." (*The Legend
of St. Clare*, in *Clare of Assisi: Early Documents*, pages 228-229)

The next day a friar hurried from Perugia to San Damiano to bring
Clare her longed-for papal bull. This was Clare's last joy on earth, for
the next day she died, with her sister Agnes, who for thirty years had
been separated from Clare as abbess of a convent near Florence,
kneeling at her bedside.

Clare was faithful to Francis and his vision until her very last
breath. She fought tenaciously for the right of the sisters to be guided by the friars, and for the sisters to be considered as one religious
family with the men. And she left her beloved community of San
Damiano firmly and forever established in the pure observance of
Franciscan poverty and in the essential Franciscan life...even though
at that very moment the friars were arguing over the wisdom of the
Rule Saint Francis wrote.

In her book, *Strange Gods Before Me*, Mother Mary Francis, abbess
of a convent of Poor Clare nuns in New Mexico, offered the following insight into the lives of Francis and Clare:

Saints see into the depths of earthly existence, which is the
immediate reason why they are fitted to receive from God
insight into eternal life. Saints never spend their lives standing
on the shore of life. They "strike out into the depths and let
down their nets." And they always bring up a catch. Neither do
saints dwell on the edge of their souls. They cast themselves
into the depths and discover who they are, why they are living,

and what the whole business is about.

This is certainly patent in St. Francis and St. Clare of Assisi. They held the key to life's mysteries because they did not just see things or people. They saw *into* things and people. To Francis and Clare, creation was a vast symbol, and they spent their lives deepening and sharpening their power of interpreting it. Everything was fraught with mystery, touched with symbolism, tingling with wonder. (page 22)

I know in my own life, my vision of the world and myself (and others, too) rarely focused much beyond the surface of things. Francis and Clare have taught me to use my restored vision of faith to look more deeply at my life and all of creation.

One in Essence

[Saint Francis] saw this God whom he so cherished in everything that exists, and he wanted all creatures to love and serve him.

—*EUGENE MARTIN*, THE CATHOLICISM OF ST. FRANCIS

Francis and Clare were mystics. Mystics are mysteries to us. Yet it was their mysticism that let them see so deeply into everything, that let them see God in everyone. D.H.S. Nicholson offers a possible clue to how this happened:

For the mystic, and perhaps in particular to the Christian mystic, the knowledge of his own inherent divinity, the conviction that God dwells within him in the kingdom that is within, gives certainty that he is no less immanent in everyone who comes into the world, however much that Presence be obscured and overlaid. It is the invariable postulate despite all appearances to the contrary, and whatever the accretions of selfishness and materiality and degradation that hinder its manifestation. The Incarnation is for him a literal and continuing fact, not regulated to the mists of history, but ever present and over-poweringly real today and every day. It is, in fact, the one unfailing reality which is his continual inspiration and the foundation of all his hope—the earnest of the fuller realization that comes with the entry of That which is incarnate into the consciousness.

Any suggestion, therefore, of loving God apart from the man in whom He dwells is impracticable. The love of the one necessitates the love of the other, since they are bound together and are one in essence if not realization. To love God is to love Him in all His aspects. (*The Mysticism of St. Francis of Assisi*)

Which is not easy.

NOBLE LADIES

Remaining enclosed
Clare began to enlighten the whole world
and
her brilliance dazzled it
with the honors of her praises.
The fame of her virtues filled the chambers of noble ladies,
reached the palaces of the duchesses,
and even the mansions of queens.

—THE LEGEND OF SAINT CLARE

Saint Clare's way of life attracted women from all classes of society. Besides the rich and poor, Clare's holiness also attracted women of nobility. Before her death, three noble ladies followed in her footsteps. The first was Agnes of Prague, who was the daughter of King Ottokar I of Bohemia. Elizabeth of Hungary, the daughter of the King of Hungary, joined the Third Order after the death of her husband, and so completely dedicated herself to the care of the sick and poor she eventually was canonized a saint. Salome of Crakow entered the Poor Clares in 1245.

The Liturgy of the Hours

A reading from the letter of Saint Clare to Blessed Agnes of Prague.

Happy the soul to whom it is given to attain this with Christ, to cleave with all one's heart to him whose beauty all the heavenly hosts behold forever, whose love inflames our love, the contemplation of whom is our refreshment, whose graciousness is our delight, whose gentleness fills us to overflowing, whose remembrance makes us glow with happiness, whose fragrance revives the dead, the glorious vision of whom will be the happiness of all the citizens of the heavenly Jerusalem. For he is the brightness of the eternal glory, the splendour of eternal light, the mirror without spot.

Looking into that mirror daily, O queen and spouse of Jesus Christ, and ever study therein your countenance, that within and without you may adorn yourself with the flowers and garments that become the daughter and chaste spouse of the most high King. In that mirror are reflected poverty, holy humility and ineffable charity, as, with the grace of God, you may perceive.

Gaze first upon the poverty of Jesus, placed in a manger in swaddling clothes. What marvelous humility! What astounding poverty! The King of angels, Lord of heaven and earth, is laid in a manger. Consider next humility, the blessed poverty, the untold labours and burdens which he endured for the redemption of the human race. Then look upon the unutterable charity with which he willed to suffer on the tree of the cross and to die thereon the most shameful kind of death. This mirror, Christ himself, fixed upon the wood of the cross, bade the passers-by consider these things: "All you who pass this way look and see if there is any sorrow like my sorrow." With one voice and one mind let us answer him as he cries and laments, saying in his own words: "I will be mindful and remember and my soul shall languish within me." Thus, O queen of the heavenly King, may you ever burn more ardently with the fire of his love.

Contemplate further the indescribable joys, the wealth and unending honours of the King, and sighing after them with great longing, cry to him: "Draw me after you: we shall run to the fragrance of your perfumes, O heavenly bridegroom." I will run and faint not until you bring me into the wine cellar, until your left hand be under my head and your right hand happily embrace me and kiss me with the kiss of your mouth.

In such contemplation be mindful of your little mother and know that I have inscribed your happy memory on the tablets of my heart, holding you dearer than all others. (*Clare of Assisi: Early Documents*, page 201)

[Note: This reading was featured on August 11th, the feast day of Saint Clare of Assisi.]

SAINT AGNES OF PRAGUE

The excerpt from Clare's letter to Agnes of Prague comes from the fourth (and last) of the known letters she wrote to the former princess. The first of these letters was written in 1234 and the last in 1253. Here is a brief historical sketch of Agnes:

> Agnes of Prague, daughter of King Premsyl Ottokar I of Bohemia and his second wife Queen Constance of the Hungarian Arpad dynasty, was born in 1205. Agnes was engaged at an early age to a son of the duke of Silesia and was sent to that court to live. Her education was taken care of by Queen, later saint, Hedwig.
>
> When Agnes was only three years old, the young duke died and the princess returned to Prague where she was placed in a Premonstratensian monastery for her education. Shortly after she was engaged to the son of Emperor Frederick II, the future King Henry VII, who was in residence at the court of Duke Leopold of Austria. Agnes was then sent to Austria to live, but, after some time, Agnes was jilted by the young Henry who married the duke's daughter. Once again Agnes returned to Prague where her angry father was preparing to wage war against Leopold, but the princess persuaded her father not to avenge

her. She next received offers of marriage from the royal court of England, and then from Frederick II whose wife had died. Her father did not accept any of these offers, however, leaving Agnes free to remain in Prague, devoting herself to charitable works.

At this time she met the Friars Minor who had arrived in the city in 1225. No doubt these friars spoke to her of Clare, the life of the Poor Ladies of San Damiano, and the ideals of Franciscan life. Agnes then set out fulfilling her own plans. In 1232 she obtained property from her brother for the erection of a hospice, which she built and turned over to the administration of the Crosiers of the Red Star. She also obtained a convent to house the "Poor Ladies" and a residence to satisfy the needs of the Friar Minors who would act as chaplains. When the building was completed, Agnes wrote to Clare and the Holy See, asking permission to establish the Poor Ladies of San Damiano in Prague and requesting sisters from Italy for the purpose.

In the spring of 1234, during an immense public celebration, Agnes, with seven other young women of the wealthiest noble families of Bohemia and five of the Poor ladies of Italy entered the new monastery. (*Clare of Assisi: Early Documents*, page 33)

PILGRIMAGE DIARY 58

Thoughts Scribbled While Walking

*D*ryness in prayer forces me to identify with the abandoned Jesus.

Jesus said he was meek and humble of heart. What am I?

Spiritual reading gives me the chance to spend time with remarkable men and women who have looked long and lovingly at the Real.

Prayer is an act of humility, stemming from a mindfulness of our inadequacy.

Humility is a miracle.

"This day is yours, Lord," I say each day upon rising. Yet, before I even finish my first cup of coffee, the day has become mine.

God reveals my sinfulness to me, not to make me feel guilty but to offer me forgiveness and freedom from the

bondage of sin.
Redemption isn't a ticket to heaven...it simply means a
soul has been redeemed—set free—from self-interest.
The soul that waits on God, patiently and unhurriedly,
will eventually be filled with the realization he or she is
infinitely loved.
Don't try to possess the object of your delight...kiss the
joy as it flies.

THE MAKING OF A SAINT

The only tragedy is that we are not all saints.
—CHARLES PEGUY

Was Clare a saint? In order to officially declare that she was, the Church had to examine her life thoroughly. The results of the examination were published and submitted to the pope. The report, known as *The Acts of the Process of Canonization*, was published in 1253, and quickly disappeared from sight until 1920, when a friar discovered the report in the library of the late Monsieur de Landau in Florence. The text was published in *Archivum Franciscanum Historicum*, Vol. XIII, Quaracchi, 1920.

Regis J. Armstrong includes a translation of the text, which presents an indispensable source of our knowledge of the saint, in *Clare of Assisi: The Early Documents*. (Nesta de Robeck's biography of the saint also includes a translation of the report.) Here is Father Armstrong's introduction to his translation.

Within two months of the death of Saint Clare, Pope Innocent IV issued a papal bull, *Gloriosus Deus*, Ocotober 18, 1253, in which he entrusted Bishop Bartholomew of Spoleto with the responsibility of promoting the Cause of her canonization. The Bishop of Spoleto, who had previous experience in these matters, took as his associates the archdeacon, Leonardo of Spoleto, Jacobo, the archpriest of Trevi, Brothers Leo and Angelo of the Friars Minor who were close friends of Saint Francis, Brother Mark, chaplain of the monastery, and a notary. On November 24, 1253, they went to the Monastery of San Damiano in Assisi and officially interviewed under oath thirteen of the sisters who had lived with Saint Clare. Two other sisters, one of whom was in the infirmary, were questioned on November 28, 1253, and, on the same day, Sister Benedetta, the Abbess of San Damiano, spoke in the name of the entire community and declared the willingness of all the sisters to testify concerning the sanctity of Saint Clare.

The same day, November 28, 1253, the Bishop and his official party proceeded to the Monastery Church of San Paolo in the center of Assisi to officially interrogate those citizens of the city who had known the saint or experienced her intercession. Thus they examined an elderly knight, Ugolino di Pietro Giraldone, the lady Bona Guelfuccion, Ranieri di Bernardo, and Pietro di Damiano, all of whom were associated with the family of Saint Clare and had known her intimately as a child. On the following day, the officials interviewed Iovani di Ventura who testified to one of the miracles that occurred after Saint Clare's death.

The text of the *Acts of the Process of Canonization,* together with the papal bull, *Gloriosus Deus,* comes to us in an Umbrian Italian version of the fifteenth century. Nonetheless, a critical, internal study of the text, as well as a thorough examination of the parallels that exist between it and the later *Legend of Saint Clare,* leaves little doubt as to its authenticity. It was only in 1920 that Zefferino Lazzeri, O.F.M., discovered and published the *Acts.* (page 125)

What follows is a brief synopsis of the testimony of three of the witnesses.

Sister Pacifica, a nun at San Damiano, asserted that Clare often passed the entire night in prayer, and that her fasts were so rigorous that they made some of the sisters sad, adding that Clare never ate on Mondays, Wednesdays and Fridays. She also testified that once when five sisters were ill, Clare healed them all instantly by making a sign of the cross over them. She mentioned that Clare was deeply humble and she loved the poor very much.

Sister Benvenuta, another sister from San Damiano, discussing the saint's humility, said Clare always performed the lowest tasks in the house. She said Clare had only one habit, made of home-woven material, which was coarse and was the shabbiest one in the house. She said Clare often wore a shirt made of boar's hide under her tunic, with the bristles of the hide rubbing against her skin. Sister Benvenuta told of the time she had lost her voice and Clare healed her through the sign of the cross. She also told of several other sisters who were healed of several different diseases by Clare. She recounted the story of a little boy from Spoleto whose life was in danger after he had put a stone up his nose and no one could get it out. The boy's mother, in panic, brought him to Clare. Clare made the sign of the cross on the boy's nose and the stone fell out. Likewise, the saint also healed a friar of a mental illness after Francis sent him to Clare.

Sister Filippa spoke of Clare's great compassion for all the sisters and for the afflicted. Sister Amata spoke of her assiduousness in prayer and contemplation. Sister Cecilia spoke of how Clare treated the sisters with great meekness and kindness. And so it went, witness after witness, twenty in all, testifying under oath about the holiness of Clare. Most told of episodes they had witnessed over the years that illustrated Clare's deep prayer life and her ability to heal the sick.

On August 15, 1255, Clare was canonized a saint by Pope Alexander IV. In a report during the proceedings for her canonization, it was said of Clare that "she saw herself [in Francis] as though in a mirror," and as such the example of her life was no less effective than Francis' own. I don't know if film director Franco Zeffirelli had in mind the notion of a reflection which is implied in that statement when he gave his famous film on St. Francis the title *Brother Sun, Sister Moon*, but Clare's light is indeed a reflection of Francis', even though softer and gentler, just as the moon reflects the light of the sun.

FRANCIS AND CLARE

Poverty is the pearl of the Gospel.
—SAINT BONAVENTURE, *DEFENSE OF THE MENDICANTS*

If I had to pick just one word to describe the essence and foundation of both Francis' and Clare's lives, it would be: poverty. Francis believed the Church's languishing spirituality could be directly attributed to her vast wealth and rise to great political power, and that the Church needed to be reminded of—and strongly exhorted to follow—the example of absolute and voluntary poverty, along with the resulting detachment of worldliness, as exemplified by Christ and the apostles.

Many critical observers, including members of his own order, think Saint Francis had incorrectly interpreted the Gospels and reached a wrong conclusion regarding what Francis saw as Christ's uncompromising attitude toward poverty. Francis' ideal of poverty caused him a great deal of suffering near the end of his life, as he witnessed many of his own followers turning away from poverty. Francis continued to stress all the biblical arguments in favor of absolute poverty, but it must be pointed out that Christ did not lay down hard and fast rules when he sent out his disciples, but adapted himself to existing conditions and desired the apostles to do the same. Although on their first tentative mission to Palestine, Christ told the apostles to take nothing with them (Matthew 10:9-10), a passage that was decisive for Francis, the command appears slightly modified in Mark 6:8-9; and when Christ sent his followers out beyond the frontiers of Judea, he even commanded them to take a purse, a scrip and a sword (Luke 22:36). Christ paid taxes, and Judas, the treasurer, accepted presents of money for the others (Matthew 17:24-25; John 12:6). But it seems obvious that Francis overlooked these passages. Thus, his ideal was narrower and more ascetical than that of Christ.

The discrepancy between Francis' mystical ideal of poverty and the actual teaching of Christ inevitably led to a heated conflict with many of his own followers, a conflict which nearly destroyed the order. Only Saint Clare steadfastly held on to the ideal of poverty that Francis espoused. Clare never disappointed Francis, unlike his own brothers who frequently let him down. Regis J. Armstrong, O.F.M. Cap., expressed it very succinctly:

> As friars, the memory of Clare should disturb us. History reminds us that, while Clare was fighting to preserve the charism of poverty, we were accepting one dispensation after another in order to have possessions which would enable us to be more efficient ministers of the Word. While Clare's vision of a life *sine proprio* became clearer and more focused, we friars were becoming more involved in resolving canonical distinctions and ambiguities. (from "Starting Points: Images of Women in the Letters of Clare of Assisi to Agnes of Prague," in *Spirit and Life*)

In his 1976 biography, Anthony Mockler quotes a passage Saint Francis penned in his "Last Wishes":

The brothers must be very careful not to accept churches or poor dwellings for themselves, or anything else built for them, unless they are in harmony with the poverty which we have promised in the Rule; and they should occupy these places only as strangers and pilgrims. (*Francis of Assisi*, page 165)

In a footnote to that quotation, Mockler wrote:

It may seem that Francis' attitude to property was hypocritical. He could hardly claim to live "without property" when he not only accepted but asked for a church and land for huts. The distinction between outright ownership and usufruct was academic in practice. This is a question that has always baffled the Franciscan Order and kept it in a state of perpetual tension. Father von Essen's view is that by the force of circumstances, as numbers expanded a community of monastic-style life grew with (a) fixed dwellings (b) punitive powers (c) studies. Certainly, at the present day, there is no distinction at all, as regards the possession of communal property, between the Franciscans and the Benedictines. The Order has completely abandoned not only the objections to outright ownership but the rule-of-thumb that Francis evolved—small, not large, churches; minimal furniture; dwelling-places in wood and clay, not in brick or stone; no estates or properties or houses bringing in rent. There has been a surrender to materialism all along the line; and, most shockingly of all, present-day Franciscans with their worldly common sense seem to have not the slightest uneasiness of conscience. The commercialization of the Portiuncula is particularly repellent. (pages 176-177)

Undoubtedly, Saint Clare would agree with Mockler's observation.

Theology of Poverty

Soar with the wings of Charity,
For charity is life-giving;
The love of God and of neighbor
Will sweep you up to the highest
peak.

—*JACOPONE DE TODI*, LAUDA XXXI

Over and over again in this book, I've returned to the subject of poverty. It can't be avoided. I'm going to give the last word on the subject to John J. Navone, S.J., and the following excerpt comes from his book Personal Witness. *The chapter is entitled "The Parable of the Banquet," and it begins with this sentence: "It is not by accident that St. Luke should refer to the 'poor, the crippled, the blind and the lame' as those invited to the great banquet (14:21)." A few pages later, Father Navone explains the importance and meaning of being poor.*

In Luke's theology of poverty the Messiah is born, lives and dies poor. "...the Son of Man has nowhere to lay his head" (9:58). Jesus' association with the poor is, for Luke, a sign that He is the fulfillment of the messianic promise: "The spirit of the Lord...has sent me to announce good news to the poor" (Is 61:1). When the delegation from John the Baptist asks Jesus whether He is the Messiah, Jesus calls their attention to the messianic sign: "Go and tell John what you have seen and heard; how the *blind* recover their sight, the *lame* walk, the *deaf* hear, the *dead* are raised to life, the *poor* are hearing the Good News. And happy is the man who does not find me a stumbling block" (7:22-23). Jesus asserts that He is the Messiah when He says that He does all the prophets said the Messiah would do. This explains why Luke so frequently calls his readers' attention to Jesus' association with these people; it is a basis for their confession of faith in Jesus as the true Messiah.

Are the "poor" to whom Luke refers the economically poor? The general lines of Luke's doctrinal context indicate the answer. The poor are basically those who are perceptive, who open themselves to the divine charity. The tax-gatherers, the Gentiles and the sinners like Mary Magdalen, who could purchase a costly ointment for Jesus, were all not economically poor. And yet they were poor in the sense that they recognized their poverty before God; they were *receptive* of His Messiahship, of His salvation, of the forgiveness of their sins. And for all these divine benefits repayment was impossible.

In another respect, however, economic poverty was included in a special way. Divisions within Jewish society at the time of Jesus were based more on religious than economic grounds, more on knowledge and the exact observance of the Law and poverty. The Scribes and Pharisees were highly respected because they were literate. And the special privileges and particular marks of respect which they enjoyed they owed more to their religious instruction than their wealth. All this is true. It is likewise true that the economically poor were not despised because of their poverty. Yet it happened that, precisely because of their poverty, they lacked the instruction in the Law and that ability to observe it carefully that is necessary for being highly regarded. Long work-hours precluded exact observance as well as the time for theological speculation. So it happened that the poor, the economically destitute, were the despised ones, the "sinners...."

In conclusion, then, we can say that, in Luke's theology, the poor were all those whom the religious leaders of Israel excluded from the Kingdom of God. They were the marginal men living on the fringes of Jewish society precisely because they deviated from the religious ideals of the Pharisees. Luke shows that the social and economic poverty actually fostered the receptivity requisite for the acceptance of the Messiah. (pages 84-86)

PILGRIMAGE DIARY 59

Thoughts Scribbled While Walking

A pure heart is an undivided heart.
Prayer creates a listening heart.
God demands a lot of time. In prayer, quantity produces quality.
Imagine...you can hold in your very being the One who holds
    the whole universe. Amazing. True.
Sit with Jesus and allow his heart to speak to your heart.
True poverty is total trust in God.
God reveals himself in simplicity, in the simplicity of prayer and
    the simplicity of bread and wine.
The road to holiness is paved with authentic penance.
A humble prayer offered with trust and perseverance is always
    answered.
Humility is fundamental to holiness.
Stop trying to be relevant. It is a trap. Only God is relevant.

THE PATRON SAINT OF TELEVISION?

I find television very educational. Whenever anyone turns the TV on, I leave the room and go read a book.

—GROUCHO MARX

Saint Clare may have found it odd when she was proclaimed the patron saint of television; and she would have hated the fact that souvenir shops in Assisi sell plastic statues of her likeness that contain two holes in the back for a TV antenna, and a guarantee the statue will improve your TV reception. In 1958, during the early days of television, Pope Pius XII, seeing the power and potential of TV, proclaimed Saint Clare as the patroness of television. The reason for the choice can be traced back to an incident described in Chapter 18 of Thomas of Celano's life of Saint Clare. According to the legend, on Christmas Day near the end of Clare's life, all the sisters went to the church of St. Francis to join the friars in praying matins. Clare was bedridden and far too sick to attend. The thought of missing the service being held at the very hour of the birth of Christ deeply saddened Clare, and she cried out, "My Lord God, behold I am left alone."

Suddenly her room was filled with the inspiring sounds of the melodious singing coming from the church, which was a considerable distance away. Clare clearly heard the joyous psalmody of the friars, the harmony of the chants, and even the sound of the organ. Moreover, she had a vision which enabled her to see the Lord's manger in the church as well as the service. The following morning, the sisters came to see Clare and they anxiously told her about the beautiful service. She interrupted their report and said, "Blessed be my Lord Jesus Christ who did not abandon me even when you were all gone. By His grace I was allowed to participate in the entire service at the Church of San Francesco."

Miraculously, Clare was able to see an event at which she was not present. Today, thanks to the miracle of television, we can do the same, and so the pope blessed the new medium by making Saint Clare its patroness.

Given the sorry state of TV programming (at least in the United States) and its proclivity to pander to the lowest instincts in humanity, perhaps we need to start praying to Saint Clare before we turn on the TV. On second thought, a better alternative to praying before turning on the TV would be not to turn on the TV at all.

Nowhere to Be Seen

Avoid entertainments given by outsiders and by persons ignorant of philosophy. For you may rest assured that if a man's companion be dirty, the person who keeps close company with him must of necessity get a share of his dirt, even though he himself happens to be clean.

—*EPICTETUS*

This pilgrimage will unofficially come to end on September 16, 1997, when I attend the Eighth International Colloquium on Theology and Communication. The four-day conference is sponsored by the Pontifical Gregorian University and will be held in the Alban Hills, south of Rome. The theme of the conference is "Religion and Popular Culture," and I will be part of the fourth panel of speakers whose topic is: the perspective of critics and producers. From what I could gather from the material sent to me about the conference, it seems the participants feel a person can have an experience of God through the popular media, especially film and television. I wholeheartedly disagree with that premise. Here is an abridged version of the paper I will deliver, which I entitled, "Nowhere to Be Seen."

When I was informed that my participation in this conference should answer the question, "Did you ever think about religious sensibilities while producing *General Hospital*?" I thought about the question for a few seconds and my answer was very simple and direct: "No."

End of paper.

Suddenly, I was horrified at the thought of having to submit a twenty-five-page paper...after all, how could I possibly add anything to my simple and direct answer. Moreover, I felt a bit intimidated by the impressive academic credentials the other participants have in the fields of theology, communication arts, media history and social studies. Skipping college, I began my television career giving out tickets to the *Ed Sullivan Show* when I was only seventeen years old. Fifteen years later, I was the executive producer of a network soap opera.

So, I don't bring any academic credentials into this conference. I come, humbly, as an artist...an artist who has left the world of commercial television in order to dedicate myself completely to writing (mostly books, along with occasional works for television) about spirituality and my own personal encounter with transcendence. And so I have no grand theories about religion and popular culture to offer you; nor do I have any insightful analysis of the current state of affairs regarding religion and popular culture. All I have to offer are a few stories from my own personal experience of producing television shows at all three major commercial networks in the United States, and the results of an informal survey I conducted in which I asked a few friends who write or produce network television shows if they ever think about religious sensibilities as they are writing or producing their shows.

After stepping down from the job of running the CBS Television Network, former executive Howard Stringer implored those working in the television industry to take personal responsibility for what is aired, saying, "...if we separate, like church and state, our artistic values from our personal values, then we create programs for others we would not be willing to share with our own family and friends." It is my contention, based on practical experience, that people in the entertainment business do, on a regular basis and with relative ease, separate their spiritual beliefs from the business of creating and producing television programs and movies. They have a highly developed ability to compartmentalize their faith and their work. Of course, this is not universally true, and there are a few exceptions...but they are rare. Very rare.

God is everywhere...but don't try looking for him on commercial television. Why? Because the Creator and Sustainer of the universe doesn't generate ratings. God is great...but he isn't big box office. Please don't misunderstand: I do not consider any area of human activity, including mass media, to be indifferent or foreign to the affinity which exists between God and humans. But the television industry has banished God to the outer reaches of its universe, reducing him to a fringe figure who is either oversimplified or ridiculed. Occasionally, a show (usually one headed by a powerful or respected writer) tackles the subject of religion, and manages to do so in a dignified and thoughtful manner. Character-driven shows such as *NYPD Blue* and *Homicide: Life on the Streets* have explored the spiritual dimension of one of their characters, but in two cases which I can recall, those episodes addressed a character's inability to believe in God. The spiritual life of the vast majority of characters (if indeed they even have a spiritual life) presented on television is either ignored or unimportant.

Popular art, in its television expression, is at its core far more business than art. We do call it show business, and it has been my experience that if you ignore the "business" element, you do so at your own peril. Art and religion may in fact travel together in virtually all cultures, but they are rarely seen in the same company in studios where television programs are produced. And the reason is simple: studios are not producing art, they are producing commercial delivery systems. And if you think that assessment is harsh, then listen to the following true story from my life as a television producer.

Back in the early 1980's, I was the executive producer of a network soap opera. I was hired because the show's ratings were suffering from a steady decline and the network wanted me to infuse new life into the show. And with great enthusiasm, I set out to do just that. I brought in new directors, writers and actors, and dramatically changed the look, tone and direction of the show. In an effort to get each scene "just right," I frequently took more production time than was budgeted. One day, a vice president called me into his office in order to give me a lecture on cost control. He said, "Your problem is that you think of yourself as an artist...and you are. But, we don't want art. All we want from you is filler to keep the commercials from bumping into each other." My show, which I treated as a piece of art, was in fact nothing more than a vehicle that delivered commercials. And if the commercial revenue went into decline as a result of low ratings, then I was told to correct the problem by putting "a babe in a hot tub."

As an executive producer, my job could be boiled down to one word: God. I may not have been all-powerful, but I certainly wielded a great deal of power. I hired (or fired) the writers, the directors and the actors. I set the tone, pace and direction of the show. So, it should have been fairly easy for me to gently inject into a story line ideas or insights that reflected my religious beliefs, especially at Christmas and Thanksgiving, two occasions when God is a natural part of the fabric of a national holiday. (Soap operas are on five days a week, fifty-two weeks a year, and so they coincide with the seasons and holidays that are being experienced and celebrated in real life.)

One year, a very young Brooke Shields had a guest role on

one of my shows. She played the girlfriend of the son of one of the main characters. The show was in the middle of a story line in which a character was in the process of trying to stop smoking. Celebrities, including Tony Randall and Brooke Shields, were featured in numerous episodes in which they delivered an anti-smoking message. The episode in which Brooke Shields appeared took place on Thanksgiving Day. The entire family had joined together for a turkey dinner with all the trimmings. After the meal Brooke would catch her "boyfriend's father" smoking. When I read the first draft of the script, I thought that perhaps it would be good to start the meal with a simple prayer of thanksgiving...after all, all across America, people would be doing just that. I called the writer, who was a practicing Catholic, and she liked the idea. We agreed the prayer should be short and nondenominational. Because of her own rich prayer life, the writer had no problem scripting a simple yet meaningful prayer. Much to our surprise, both the actor and the network balked when they read the prayer. Essentially, their argument was that the character who delivered the prayer would never do such a thing...it was "out of character" for him to pray. After some heated discussions, a compromise was reached in which another character, a minor one, offered the prayer, which was shortened to the point where it hardly said any more than, "Thanks."

A few weeks later it was Christmas and, having not learned my lesson from the Thanksgiving prayer fiasco, I decided to have a minor character, a hospital orderly, mention during a staff Christmas party at the hospital that Christmas wasn't just about buying presents and that we shouldn't forget that the day was really about celebrating the birth of the Prince of Peace. The actor who played the character went ballistic in his vehement objection to my "injecting God into the show." I certainly wasn't injecting God into the show; I was merely saying Christmas was about Christ. Well, Christmas on that soap opera was about buying presents. Again, after enormous effort, a compromise was reached, but the result was so watered down that it was hardly worth the effort. Worse, I had to endure being labeled—behind my back—as "some kind of fundamentalist Christian."

While preparing my remarks for this conference, I told the Thanksgiving prayer story to a woman who is both a practicing Catholic and a very respected soap opera writer. A veteran of the genre, she recently was the co-head writer of a popular NBC soap opera. She pointed out something I failed to observe: "We all know about the pecking order among actors. Big stars who play leading roles know they have the power to influence a story, and we are used to dealing with them. But what is interesting about your story is that an actor playing such a small, inconsequential role felt secure enough to make a big stink over a line he had to deliver. The reason he felt comfortable voicing his objections to the line is that he knew he would find support all around him...because more than likely no other cast member would want to have said the line because none of them had any deep Christian commitment."

Then in an offhand but very revealing moment, she said, "It's easier to be gay." She was referring to the recent hoopla surrounding the lead character of the sitcom *Ellen* coming out of the closet and announcing she was a lesbian. She said that it is far easier to do stories on subjects like homosexuality than it is to get approval to do a story that has any spiritual or religious dimension. "My show," she said, "actually had more 'spiritual' story lines than most soaps, but it was never easy. The vice president of programming hated it when we had a character say a prayer or express some kind of religious belief. One character believed in angels. Surveys show most people do believe in angels, yet when we proposed a story about angels, the network balked. Why? Because the people in charge were uncomfortable with the subject. There is no conspiracy to keep God out of the shows. It's just that so many people in power do not believe in God or think that God is either too controversial a subject or not commercial enough."

When I heard the writer say, "Surveys show most people believe in angels," I didn't doubt her veracity, but I was a bit skeptical of the validity of surveys claiming most people in America believe in angels. A few days later, on June 17, 1997, the *Los Angeles Times* published the results of a poll conducted in the previous January by the Barna Research Group in which they telephoned a representative, random sample of 1,007 adults nationwide. More than seventy-five percent of those polled said they believe angels are real, and eighty-seven percent said their religious faith was important to them. While it is not germane to the subject at hand, I found the response to another question to be interesting enough to share. Amazingly, sixty-one percent said the Holy Spirit is merely a symbol of God's presence or power, but is not a living entity. Even more astounding, fifty-five percent of those who identified themselves as born-again Christians did not believe in the existence of the Holy Spirit. Ironically, those comments were published on the Vigil of Pentecost, and they reflect either gross ignorance or total rejection of one of the basic teachings of Christianity. In a similar vein, sixty-two percent said the devil was not real and was merely a symbol of evil.

A conversation I had with a vice president of a major film studio revealed that films dealing with themes that are devoid of any spiritual or moral value do not run into similar objections. The executive is in charge of production administration. He is a committed Christian and is very uncomfortable with many of the films his studio releases. Recently, the most morally reprehensible script he had ever read came across his desk. He said the film so openly and brazenly mocked Jesus that it would have offended even the most nominal of Christians. Yet the studio was close to giving the project a green light. Even though he wanted to stop the studio from making the film, he knew he couldn't just fly into a rage and condemn the film for religious or moral reasons. He had to keep his mouth shut and find a business-related reason to stop the film from being made. During the negotiations with the producer of the film, the vice president uncovered a major flaw in the budget. He presented the problem to the head of the studio and a decision was made not to make the film because of financial reasons. While the vice president took comfort in the fact the film was not going to be made at his studio, he knew that the producers would simply take the project to another studio and the film would eventually be made.

The soap opera writer had some very interesting observations about what it is like to be a Christian working in the entertainment business. She said, "You learn very quickly the unwritten, cardinal rule: don't make waves. And one of the ways you make waves is professing a belief in God. If you do, you run the risk of being branded as one of 'those people' or as 'some kind of religious fanatic' or, even worse, an 'enemy of art.' There is an enormous prejudice against religion. It's never stated openly. It's more of an attitude. Let's say a show is considering a story line that Christians would find offensive. A closet Christian on the production staff might raise the point by saying, 'It might offend believers' or 'It might offend them' (accentuating 'them' with a pejorative tone), but they would never say, 'It offends me,' because they don't want to be lumped in with 'those people' or 'those morons' who believe in God. In Hollywood, belief in God equals belief in flying saucers. It's a kiss of death because a believer is considered to be a nonrational person in the grips of superstition. Moreover, a believer is seen as not being an intellectual, and therefore not open-minded. I can't tell anybody that I go to daily Mass. It would be professional suicide. There are a few groups around town, people who are Catholics or evangelical Christians, who meet on a regular basis in order to help each other deal with working in an environment so hostile to spiritual beliefs. I went to one meeting, and I had to laugh because I felt as if I was part of some secret, underground society."

So...what is the relationship between popular art and religion?

My answer: None.

In early June, I called a woman who has written for many years for a number of New York City-based soap operas. I once worked with her on a show, and I knew she was (and still is) a devout Catholic. She said that she has gained a reputation as being "difficult," and not because she was strident in her espousal of Christian values. She earned the "difficult" reputation because she felt the stories she had to tell frequently forced her to make ethical and moral compromises. For instance, she recently had to write the script for an episode in which a doctor "pulled the plug" on a family member who was critically ill. "I just couldn't do it," she said, "I argued that they were treating the subject too flippantly and didn't carefully study or explore the ramifications of terminating a life. I just couldn't separate my moral convictions from what I was being asked to write, and so I resigned." She said she often found herself praying that she wouldn't be assigned the task of writing episodes that she found to be morally offensive.

A friend of mine is a screenwriter who has a development deal with a major film studio. He said, "This is a hard business, period. If you try to bring into it elements of your faith, then it becomes harder still. It is a little less difficult in the film world, because each script is its own universe, and far fewer people are involved in its creation. A script is either good or bad, funny or not; and because it sinks or swims on its own merit, a quality script that may have a spiritual dimension, such as *Dead Man Walking*, does occasionally get produced. It is much harder in television. Whenever I try to weave something spiritual into one of my scripts, I make sure I make it funny or interesting in order to lessen the chance that it will get cut. Still, I do not delude myself: My faith and the values that it engenders play a microscopic part in my work."

Another writer told me about a friend of hers who is a writer on a prime-time drama series. She said the writer always manages to infuse his own past struggles with Catholicism into his scripts. He does so because it is dramatic and adds an interesting color to the character's profile. It gives the character a certain wistfulness: I'd like to believe, but how can I—if only it was true. This "wishing he could believe" quality gives the character an existentially cool status which is perfectly acceptable because it subtly underscores the Hollywood belief that a belief in God is basically dumb.

The March 24, 1997, edition of *TV Guide* published an article entitled, "Prime Time's Search for God," which was written by Pulitzer Prize-winning author Jack Miles. Mr. Miles wrote: "God on prime-time television is like God in American culture: submerged most of the time, emerging only as a guest star whose appearance is rarely announced. Religion is a subject that Americans generally take pretty seriously. Television, though, may be most comfortable taking it lightly. It often glosses over the spiritual lives of characters—when was the last time anyone on *Drew Carey*, *Friends* or *Nash Bridges* went to church or synagogue?—or uses religion as a comedy element, as on *Seinfeld* when George considers converting to Latvian Orthodoxy for a woman he likes."

And the spiritual gap isn't restricted to entertainment programming on TV. Research conducted by the Media Research Center in April 1995, titled "Faith in a Box," reported that only one percent of network news stories dealt with religion. The same survey, turning its attention to entertainment programming, reported that there were 287 religious portrayals in more than 1800 hours of original programming. Commenting on those portrayals, the report made this observation: "The more seriously a person takes his faith, the more negative the depiction is likely to be."

A 1995 *New York Times* survey claimed that ninety-seven percent of all Americans want entertainment that concurs with their moral values. Yet, Hollywood continues to produce programming and movies containing excessive amounts of sex, violence and profanity. The Fall 1996 edition of *The Caucus Quarterly* published the Motion Picture Association of America ratings of films submitted over the past five years. Sixty-three percent of the films were given an "R" rating. In 1995, of the 697 films rated by the MPAA, 458 of them were rated "R" and 61 films received an "NC-17" rating; only 25 films were rated "G."

The reason why God makes so few appearances on TV and in the movies can certainly be attributed to the disbelief of so many writers and producers, but perhaps there is a more subtle reason. People turn on their TV's or go to the movies to be entertained...to escape for a few hours from the difficulties of life. God isn't into escapism; God is into transformation. Disregard for a few seconds the fact that a universally acceptable portrait of God in a multicultural and multireligious society that exists in America is not possible (even the wide variety of Christian expression precludes even the faintest hope of unity among the followers of Jesus). If a true portrait of God were presented on TV or in the movies, viewers would be forced to take a closer look at their lives instead of escaping the realities of their life. At the end of a long day, no one wants to take a close look at themselves, to see whether or not their day was lived in complete harmony with the God they say they believe in.

In his commentary on the Gospel of John, Saint Cyril of Alexandria, a bishop and Doctor of the Church who died in 444, wrote: "It can easily be shown from examples both in the Old Testament and the New that the Spirit changes those in whom he comes to dwell; he so transforms them that they begin to live a completely new kind of life." That's what God does...encourages us to abandon our old self-centered way of life and live a completely new life in him. And nobody wants that kind of radical change in their life. God doesn't fit the frivolous criterion for entertainment, which is why he makes so few appearances on TV. Or in churches.

The preliminary information I received about this colloquium indicated that one of the underlying questions we would address is: "Are there some forms of popular art that exclude the religious?"

Without hesitation or reservation, it is my considered opinion, based on a lifetime of working in the entertainment industry, that the television expression of popular art does exclude everything religious, with very, very few exceptions. As I have just learned firsthand, even those who make religious television programs are tempted to exclude much of their religious beliefs and convictions in order to reach a larger audience.

Here in Hollywood, at the fulcrum of popular culture, God is nowhere to be seen.

ONE FINAL EMBRACE

They discovered in each other the same luxury of God's presence and the same fire that consumed all the idols of their hearts, until they were ash.

—AUSPICIUS VAN CORSTANJE, O.F.M.

One of the frescos in the upper Basilica of St. Francis is called *The Mourning of the Poor Clares*. It depicts Saint Francis' body being carried through Assisi. The crowd in the funeral march is carrying branches and lighted candles. At San Damiano the procession is halted so that Clare and her sisters might view the sacred remains. Saint Clare is seen tenderly bending over Saint Francis for one final embrace.

Clare lived twenty-seven years after Francis' death, and during those years her community flourished and other convents were founded.

When Clare's mother was pregnant and praying for a happy delivery, a mysterious vision assured her that her child would be a light for many souls, and that was why she named her daughter Clare, from the Latin *clara*, a feminine form of *clarus*, meaning bright, clear, as in a shining light. Clare's mother's name was Ortolana, which means the gardener; Francis called Clare his "little plant," and fittingly she became the brightest flower of Franciscanism. After her husband's death, Ortolana followed her daughter's shining light and entered the convent at San Damiano.

The Roman Catholic Church celebrates Saint Clare's feast day on August 11th; and, Saint Francis' feast day is celebrated on October 4th. Also, 126 followers of Francis and Clare from all branches of the three Orders have been canonized saints by the Catholic Church.

Espresso and Saints

I met a priest from upstate New York in the piazza in front of the Basilica of St. Clare. He was traveling alone, on a quick one-day visit from Rome where he was attending some meetings. We decided to have an espresso together. Somehow the subject of the communion of saints came up, which led us to a discussion on prayer. During our chat, he related an insightful story involving Saint John Vianney (1786-1859), who is perhaps best known as the Curé of Ars and who is the patron saint of parish priests. One day, as the saint was sitting silently in his empty church, a woman entered and gingerly approached him. She told him that she had observed him day after day just sitting alone in the church. She asked, "Why? What are you doing?"

Saint John Vianney said, "I'm looking at God; God is looking at me."

After telling me the story, my espresso companion paused for a second and said, "Prayer is that simple."

The Communion of Saints

The Lord has placed us as patterns and mirrors, not only for the faithful...[but] for those who live in the world.

—SAINT CLARE OF ASSISI

When I was a child growing up in New York City in the 1950's, stories about the lives of the saints always fascinated me. Down through the centuries, the great saints were always larger than life, heroic figures whose dedication to and love of God knew no boundaries. The gospel was truly alive in them; their hearts, minds and actions reverberated with the spirit of Christ. But my childhood enthusiasm for these spiritual heroes did not survive my passage through puberty. Gradually, I came to see saints as quaint, pious remnants of the past, whose deep faith and dynamic lives had been reduced to lifeless statues of wood or plaster. When I was a teenager, their stories, filled with drama and miracles, began to recede for me into the realm of fairy tales, and the saints eventually took their place next to Santa Claus and the Easter Bunny, irrele-

vant and fanciful myths from my innocent childhood that had lost all meaning in the confusing world of teenage adolescence. By the time I reached my fortieth birthday, I was an atheist.

Now that I have reached my fifth decade, I clearly can see that the decline in my fascination with the lives of the saints came in direct proportion to the decline and eventual death of my faith. And, conversely, three years after the rather dramatic resurrection and renewal of my long-dormant faith, in March of 1995, my interest in saints has not only been fully restored, but also deepened and intensified. In order to love the saints one needs to believe in an infinitely supreme Being of immeasurable love, goodness and wisdom, with whom the core of our being is united by the act of creation.

As I began afresh reading the lives of the saints, I quickly realized saints were not saints. That is, that weren't born saints with halos firmly affixed over their heads, but became saints, overcoming doubts and intense struggles with temptations and their own human weaknesses. In Fire Within, Thomas Dubay, S.M., points out that saints "are weighed down with the same weak human nature we all have, and they experience the same temptations. The difference is that they say a complete 'yes' to the healing grace God offers to everyone, whereas most of us say 'maybe,' or 'somewhat,' or 'wait a while...not yet'" (page 15). Sainthood emerges from the depths of human frailty. The saints were one of us. They got mad, they were testy and impatient, they made mistakes, and they had firsthand knowledge of sin. Many, many saints, at one point in their lives, denied the existence of God. Most saints fought heroic battles as they transformed their natural urges toward selfishness and meanness into a desire for communion and a life of self-giving sharing. Saints represent the best we can be. While the saints were not perfect humans, they became, through hard work, truly authentic people...people who have demonstrated that the gospel can be lived.

As I struggle to live more and more the way Jesus taught us to live, the saints serve as irrefutable evidence that it really is possible to live the gospel ideal. The lives of the saints challenge us to hear—really hear—the message of Jesus and allow it to transform us. The saints show us how to take our lives in our hands and offer them to God, without knowing what will be asked of us in return. In the age of cynicism in which we live, the saints teach us how to trust. The saints show us what we might be, what we should be. Look into the heart of a saint, and you will see the heart of God.

We need to enter into the communion of saints, and allow the saints to become our friends, to hold our hands as we journey toward God.

THE SHINING LIGHT

And the light in the garden flamed high, the fire of its passion warming Assisi forever.
—MURRAY BODO, O.F.M., *CLARE: A LIGHT IN THE GARDEN*

As I came to the end of this part of the book, my mind drifted back to the beginning of my look at the life of Saint Clare, especially to my early stumbling and coming to grips with the long chauvinistic tradition of telling Clare's story as if her life was lived completely in the shadow of Francis. Sister Ingrid Peterson's insightful book truly opened my eyes. I wondered what Saint Francis would say to women today, women who are still treated as second-class citizens by the Church. Heck, I think women should be running the world...they can't do any worse than men have done down through the centuries. But I'm not Saint Francis, and I certainly don't know what he would say to women. Then by chance—*or was it grace?*—I picked up a book in which the author actually addressed today's women in words he imagined to have been spoken by Saint Francis.

The author was Carlo Carretto, whom I cited in writing about Francis in Part Two. Carretto's life had some interesting parallels to that of Saint Francis. Carretto was born in Alessandria, Italy, in 1910. He earned a degree in philosophy from the University of Turin and served as the National President of Catholic Youth in Italy from 1946 to 1952. At the age of forty-four, Carretto heard a voice telling him, "Leave everything, come with me into the desert. I don't want your action any longer. I want your prayer, your love." He had no idea what the voice meant, but he followed it anyway.

Without hesitation, he left his established and well-ordered life behind and traveled to North Africa where he joined the Little Brothers of Jesus of Charles de Foucauld without knowing anything about them or their founder. He then embarked upon a life of solitude and contemplation. His book, *Letters From the Desert*, was an instant success in Italy, where it went through more than twenty editions within ten years of its publication. It has subsequently been translated into countless other languages. During the last years of his life, he split his time between the Sahara Desert and the town of

Spello in the Umbrian hills near Assisi, where he lived as a hermit. He died in 1988.

In *I, Francis*, Carretto writes in the first person as Saint Francis. He ends the chapter entitled, "Clare, My Sister," by shifting from thirteenth-century Assisi and Clare's death to modern times, as Francis talks directly to the women of today. This is what Carretto's Francis said, first to the Church, then to women:

> Strange. I have asked myself many times how it is possible that, in spite of personages as remarkable as Clare, as Catherine, as Teresa, you in the Church are still so antifeminist?
>
> Yes, I have to say it, I, Francis. You are still antifeminist.
>
> I cannot understand!
>
> Have you fear of a woman because a woman endangers your virtue? Or do you consider her, without openly saying so, as belonging to an inferior race, unworthy to touch the holy things?
>
> But do you realize?
>
> Now and then you even forbid her to ascend to the altar, reverently to read to the assembly a text of Scripture. Any man goes first. All he has to do is be a man.
>
> Does this not seem to you to be exaggerating things?
>
> Are you still the slaves of ancient cultures, in which a woman was of no account, in which she was subjugated by male arrogance and destined to live behind a curtain like the women of the Muslims?
>
> One would say that you have no prophecy, that you have no truth to proclaim. Above all one would say that you are still living in the past.
>
> The past is the past and does not return.
>
> It has taken two thousand years for the Gospel to begin to enter the hard necks of men who are externally Christian but who are stuck back in circumcision. But now something is breaking through.
>
> The Council [Vatican II] has been a singular milestone in the transformation of the modern world, sweeping away a dead weight that burdened the Church.
>
> And it could be this because, after so much suffering, the Gospel has penetrated to the very tips of its veins.
>
> The political concept of the ancient theocratic state, in which we ourselves lived in the Middle Ages, where faith and culture, faith and politics, were one, is definitively superseded in the maturity of the Gospel, especially in these times of yours.

The juridicism of the ancients is submerged by the charity which conquers hearts.

The unconfessed racisms of caste have been reduced to dust by the sense of equality announced and effectuated by the building of the Kingdom.

There is something new for women, too. Read carefully.

Today, a woman must hear the words of Jesus as a man hears them; and if Jesus says, "Go and make disciples of all nations," it must no longer be that a man hears this one way and a woman in another.

How you must re-think everything!

And I would like to say to women of today, "Go!" with all the force of which my spirit is capable, and all my anxiety for the immense needs of a world athirst for the Gospel. This is an urgent invitation.

Transform your home into a convent—an ideal, spiritual one, as Saint Catherine did. Let prayer reign there, good counsel, and peace. Let your toil, whatever it is, be illuminated by the power of your calling—for you were made to love, to comfort, to serve.

Do not copy men. Be authentic. Seek, in your femaleness, the root that distinguishes you from them. It is unmistakable, for it has been willed and created by God himself. Repeat to yourselves every day: A man is not a woman.

Waste no time in approaching men in order somehow to resemble them. Rather seek to remove yourselves as far as possible from their model. It is not yours, and it is rather marred and muddled even so....

And one more thing.

Do not let yourselves be guided by men any longer just because they are men. If you let them lead you do so because they are saints, and do not disdain the help of persons like Clare—who, even though she was a woman, can tell you things of utility and power. (pages 39-40)

When Francis was alive, not everyone, including some of his own followers, agreed with everything he said. And so, too, today, not everyone will agree with everything expressed in those imagined words spoken by a fictional Francis. But the essence of the point Carlo Carretto makes is that Saint Francis had a deep respect for women, as he did for all living things, and he encouraged them in his day—as he would today—to be fully open to all the possibilities

God has for each human being. And women have far more possibilities today than they did in his day. Francis was fully aware that men and women are different, that they are endowed with different gifts and strengths, but he also recognized that women and men were equal.

Earlier in his chapter on Clare, Carretto tells the story of Francis cutting off Clare's hair and providing her with a sackcloth robe to wear. He concludes the story with this statement: "The ideal of poverty, accepted by woman, multiplied the strength of man, and rendered the beauty of the message universal."

Clare strengthened not only Francis but also his message of poverty and made it more universal. Francis never intended Clare to live in his shadow. He wanted her shining light to stand on its own for all the world to see.

Fittingly, I'll let "The Shining Light" have the final word:

Place your mind before the mirror of eternity!
Place your soul in the brilliance of glory!
Place your heart in the figure of the divine substance!
And transform your entire being into the image
of the Godhead Itself through contemplation.

—SAINT CLARE OF ASSISI,
FROM *THE THIRD LETTER TO BLESSED AGNES OF PRAGUE*

Giotto di Bondone
ST. FRANCIS MOURNED BY ST. CLARE
Late 13th century
Fresco, Basilica di San Francesco, Assisi

Part Four

GIOTTO

The Artist Who Loved Saint Francis

THE SAINT AND THE ARTIST

*A*rt *is the grandchild of God.*
— DANTE ALIGHIERI, *INFERNO*

You can't come to Assisi without running into the works of an artist named Giotto...his frescoes adorn the walls of Assisi's most famous church. A case can certainly be built to uphold the claim that Giotto is the grandfather of Italian art. During my second visit to the Basilica of St. Francis, I joined a tour being led by Brother Joseph Wood, O.F.M. Conv., and this gentle friar from America turned Giotto's frescoes in the upper church into a portal through which I came better to understand Francis. Brother Joseph skillfully blended the art of Giotto and the spirituality of Francis into a richly rewarding and deeply moving experience for all those on the tour.

Saint Francis of Assisi was truly a vessel of spiritual renewal within in the Catholic Church. By the time of his death in 1226, Francis had set Christian thinking on a new course. He opened windows which had been long closed; he let in fresh air and bright sunlight. Francis uprooted the gloom that pervaded Christianity, and supplanted it with joy. When Francis was a child, the faithful were taught their time on earth was brief and an insignificant prelude to eternity, and as they made their inexorable march toward this final reality, they did so alone. Saint Francis did not believe the prospect of the next world should cloud humanity's vision of this world. He saw a harmony between the spirit and the physical reality.

The effects of Saint Francis' teachings extended far into the future, touching the lives and actions of many people in many lands. In Italy itself, a few generations later, his legacy helped make possible the revolution in art wrought by Giotto—and, indeed, much of the creative effort that shaped the Renaissance. The gentle, yet zealous Francis was immortalized by countless artists.

Apart from Scripture, few sources of material have been more enthusiastically mined by painters, for the events of Saint Francis' life and legend seemed to lend themselves to their art. Two incidents in particular caught artists' attention, one miraculous, the other mundane: Francis receiving the stigmata and Francis preaching to the birds. The fascination Saint Francis held for medieval painters may itself have been a significant influence on art.

What drew Giotto and other painters to the life of Saint Francis? I believe it was his message, his view of this life. Listen to these insightful words of Sarel Eimerl, who is an art historian and a novelist:

> Francis preached the beauty of nature was God-given and therefore to be enjoyed; that all things of the world—animate and inanimate—were God's creations, and therefore kin: that all men were brothers. And since they were brothers, they must deal with one another as equals, as individuals, each with his own private hopes and agonies. In the relations between human beings the binding force was love—love born of the knowledge that Christ resided within all of them. The Christ described by Francis was not a terrifying ruler of the cosmos whose Word could be conveyed only through a priesthood. Rather, as Francis constantly reminded his listeners: "Your God is of your flesh, He lives in your nearest neighbor, in every man."

> This was the Christ whom Giotto, some decades later, would depict—a figure of familiar dimensions, as much of the earth as Giotto's farm-woman Madonna, a man to be loved, not feared. There was more that Giotto took from the preachings of Saint Francis: his compassion for humanity and his simplicity. No less important, Giotto followed Francis' injunction to behold and savor the world around him. (*The World of Giotto*, pages 14-15)

SO, WHO WAS GIOTTO?

Giotto di Bondone was born in 1267 in a small town in a valley north of Florence. (The exact date is not known. In fact, some historical sources date his birth as late as 1276, which modern scholarship finds doubtful.) His father was a peasant. By the time he was a teenager, Giotto was already a part of the Florentine artistic community. According to one legend, when Giotto was ten years old, his father gave him the job of watching his sheep in the field. Giotto did more than watch the sheep. He picked up a flat rock, and with another rock that had a pointed tip, he began to draw pictures of the sheep on the flat rock. One day the famous artist Cimabue happened to be crossing the field and he noticed the young boy working on depicting a sheep on a rock. Cimabue was so amazed that he asked the young Giotto if he would like to be an apprentice in his workshop.

THE SUMMIT

An artist, by his paintings, taught me to see the sunset. The Master, by his teachings, taught me to see the reality of every moment.

—ANTHONY DE MELLO, S.J.

And so Giotto went from drawing sheep in a field to working under the greatest and most influential painter in Florence. Giotto's training at the hand of the master took him to Pisa, Siena and Rome. Giotto was in his early twenties when he first climbed a scaffold in Assisi to begin work on the Old and New Testament cycles in the upper Basilica of St. Francis. Giotto died on January 8, 1337, in Florence.

More than a century after Giotto's death, the Renaissance paid tribute to the man regarded as the grandfather of Italian art by placing a commemorative medallion on the wall of the nave in the Cathedral of Florence, where Giotto was buried. Although Giotto's forte was painting, he is depicted in the painted stone medallion fitting a tile chip into a small mosaic of a head of Christ. Time has dulled the sheen of the stone and the blue of its painted backdrop. Giotto's face is rugged, his curly hair close-cropped. His body is

burly. To look at the artist in the act of creation, you see little pre-
tension and a great deal of strength and assurance...you see, clearly,
a man in command of his resources.

How true the likeness on the medallion is to the real Giotto is
uncertain. But there is no doubt about opinions expressed in Latin
in the inscription on the plaque below:

> I am he through whose merit the lost art of painting was
> revived; whose hand was faultless as it was compliant. What my
> art lacked nature itself lacked; to none other was it given to
> paint more or better.... But what need is there for words? I am
> Giotto, and my name alone tells more than a lengthy ode.
> (Eimerl, *The World of Giotto*, page 7)

Eimerl writes:

> Few artists anywhere, of any era, have evoked so awesome a
> tribute, and not the least remarkable part of it is the fact that it
> was written some 150 years after Giotto died, at a time when
> works more advanced than his in technique, more polished in
> execution, more spectacular in appearance, were pouring forth
> to herald the High Renaissance. The prime mover of that splen-
> did age, Lorenzo de' Medici himself, ordered this testimonial to
> Giotto; it was at his behest that Benedetto da Maiano, the sculp-
> tor who some believe guided the young Michelangelo's first
> ventures in marble, fashioned the medallion in 1490. And it
> was Lorenzo, a poet himself, who asked Angelo Poliziano, one
> of the best poets of the Renaissance, to compose the inscrip-
> tion. (page 7)

Giotto di Bondone may not be a household name, even among
artists, but in fact he is one of the most highly praised artists of all
time. From his day to ours, to speak of Giotto has been to speak in
superlatives. While Giotto was still alive, Dante acclaimed him by
name in the *Divine Comedy*, pronouncing him supreme in his field,
calling him "the summit" among painters. In the fifteenth century,
Lorenzo Ghiberti, creator of the *Gates of Paradise* of the Baptistery of
Florence, declared that "Giotto saw in art that which others failed to
perceive"; and Leonardo da Vinci observed, "After him art declined."

Down through the centuries, the freshness of Giotto's pictorial
language continued to inspire awe. In 1746, Voltaire wrote, "Giotto
painted pictures which still give pleasure." In 1908, Henri Matisse
wrote: "When I see Giotto's frescoes at Padua, I do not trouble to

find out which scene of the life of Christ is before me, for I understand at once the feeling which radiates from it, and which is instinct in line, the composition, the color. The title would only confirm my impression" (Eimerl, page 8).

In 1913, the great writer Marcel Proust, writing about the Giotto frescoes entitled *Allegories of the Virtues and Vices* in the Scrovegni Chapel in Padua, said, "Later I realized that the special quality that strikes one about these frescoes, their beauty, was due to the great part played in them by the symbol: the thought symbolized is not expressed; rather its reality as actually experienced or materially felt renders the meaning of the work more literal and more precise, conveying its admonition in terms which are peculiarly concrete and impressive" (found in *The Complete Paintings of Giotto*, page 13).

Eugene Delacroix, Johann Wolfgang von Goethe, John Ruskin, Vincent van Gogh and Bernard Berenson all sang Giotto's praise.

The famous Renaissance artist-biographer, Giorgio Vasari, writing 150 years after the death of Giotto, was moved to say of him: "Through the grace of Heaven, Giotto alone—though born at a time of incompetent masters—resurrected the dead body of art and raised it to such perfection that it could be called excellent. It was truly the greatest of miracles that so coarse and bungling an age could attain such skill...."

Vasari, like his contemporaries, saw little merit in the Byzantine style whose conventions Giotto transcended. However, contemporary critics are in agreement with Vasari when they, too, acknowledge the fact that Giotto gave a human, profoundly moving and highly personal aspect to art. His great fresco cycles in Padua, Florence and Assisi are a testament to a genius who endowed the divine with life and breath.

In the history of art, Giotto's significance is revolutionary. Giotto changed the course of European art by breaking away from the rigid stereotyped figures of the Byzantine and medieval traditions; his innovative genius gave the characters he depicted a natural movement and expression. In the preface to her definitive, exquisitely illustrated and very readable book, *Giotto*, professor Francesca Flores d'Arcais writes:

> Typical of Giotto is his groundbreaking intuition of the close relationship between light and color, particularly the innovative insight...in the cycle in the Scrovegni (or Arena) Chapel in Padua: that color changes in accordance with the variation of

light, not just in intensity, but also in quality....

[H]is extremely radical approach to everyday life, as seen in his diligent curiosity about ordinary objects, animals, plants, and the clothing of his characters. One could say that he looked at reality through a new, wide-open lens, intent on a new reading of the world, and he affectionately examined it in all aspects, from the most aristocratic and sacred to the most humble and poor, to set it before us within truthful landscapes and realistic architectonic spaces. And in this reappropriation of reality, beyond the traditional patterns, man, newly individualized, reappears as the true protagonist of painting, in the concreteness of daily life and the profundity of emotions. This was and is the most modern and revolutionary aspect of Giotto's language, still alive and just as gripping for viewers today. (page 7)

Giotto's frescoes depicting the life of Saint Francis are populated with three-dimensional characters who fully reflect their earthy humanity.

PILGRIMAGE DIARY 62

A Portal to the Soul

Art enables us to find ourselves and lose ourselves at the same time. The mind that responds to the intellectual and spiritual values that lie hidden in a poem, a painting, or a piece of music, discovers a spiritual vitality that lifts it above itself, takes it out of itself, and makes it present to itself on a level that it did not know it could achieve.

—*THOMAS MERTON*, NO MAN IS AN ISLAND

I once lived on the west side of Manhattan, on West 73rd Street, just off Central Park. Whenever I felt my spirit needed a lift, I simply would walk across the park to the Metropolitan Museum of Art. And I did so frequently. More often than not, I would only spend twenty or so minutes walking among the masterpieces of French impressionism and my spirit would be soaring. At that time of my life, a visit to the museum was like going to church for me.

The first time I walked into the upper church of the Basilica of St. Francis, it was a profound experience for me, far beyond anything I had ever experienced in any museum, including the great art museums of Paris and Amsterdam. The twenty-eight frescoes that comprise the life cycle of Saint Francis so thoroughly captivated my imagination that I became obsessed with learning everything I could about the artist. But this isn't about that; it's about Giotto's ability to make the story of Saint Francis come to life in a way that was completely refreshing for me. The books I had been reading about the life of Saint Francis were either too scholarly or too pious to really reach my soul. Giotto's vision of Francis didn't merely enter my soul, it invaded it. This is the power of art. Since that first encounter with the Francis of Giotto, I have spent dozens upon dozens of hours gazing at the walls of the upper church. Each time I visit, I see more.

I've heard people debate the merits of such a monumental building, rich with priceless art, commemorating the memory of a lover of poverty. I would be one who is inclined to think the basilica should never have been built, simply because Francis would have hated it. However, I wonder how many people over the centuries have been moved to a deeper understanding of their faith because of the art which graces the walls of both the lower and upper churches. I once asked Brother Joseph, a Conventual friar who lives in the Sacro Convento, if he ever gets bored with his job of continually conducting tours of the basilica. He said that he was aware of a number of young men who had been so moved by the connection of the spirituality and the art and the friars present during the tour that they have entered the Order. He said just knowing some young, impressionable man might respond to his faith and love of the art keeps him and his tours fresh. I'm glad the basilica is here, even if it wouldn't please the saint it honors. The art is a portal to the soul, wordlessly expressing the inexpressible.

As I look at the art of Giotto, and its power to inspire, I cannot help but think that the Church needs artists to communicate the message of Christ. We need to touch the modern, secularized, jaded soul with the message of love, and we need to do it in a new way. Let's encourage and support artists who love the Lord. If nothing else, let's pray for them...theirs is a lonely and difficult road.

THE ART OF GIOTTO

Every work of art is an open window onto the invisible.
—CHARLES DAMIAN BOULOGNE, O.P.

The thing that made Giotto's art so appealing was its austerity, the way he stripped away all but the bare dramatic essentials of the story he told with his paintbrush. He painted with directness and economy, which allowed the figures and actions he portrayed to be more easily appreciated, for they were uncluttered by unnecessary embellishments or stage trappings.

Sarel Eimerl writes, "The measure of an artist's effectiveness is his [or her] ability to make contact with the viewer.... Giotto's greatness lay in his recognition that a painting could be a shared experience. After six centuries of painters who have performed that feat, often brilliantly, such an accomplishment may seem less momentous. But, it was Giotto who led the way. In his hands, paintings for the first time projected people and emotions and situations which the onlooker could readily identify" (page 8). The people in Giotto's paintings had the down-to-earth solidity of peasants; their feet were unmistakably planted on the ground, and they had weight and roundness and three-dimensional believability. By the skillful distribution of light and shadow, Giotto gave his figures a depth which cut into the space around them. He then further defined the space by the clarity and logic with which he arranged his figures in relation to one another and to their setting.

Although the laws of perspective were not worked out with mathematical precision until the fifteenth century, decades before then, Giotto showed his intuitive grasp of the rational disposition of forms in space. Such technical prowess alone would have ensured Giotto's enduring fame. But he was also a master storyteller and a superb stage manager. And above all he had a gift for simplicity. He never yielded to the temptation to overdo. The hallmark of his work is economy and understatement...his truths required no embellishment.

In 1874, after visiting Giotto's frescoes in Florence, the great English critic John Ruskin exclaimed: "He painted the Madonna and St. Joseph and the Christ—yes, by all means, if you choose to call them so—but essentially, Mamma, Pappa, and the Baby." Giotto had single-handedly effected a fundamental breakthrough in art: he elevated painting from the service of symbolism and made it a mirror of humankind.

Again quoting from Eimerl:

For the most part, painting prior to Giotto had served two purposes: it was purely decorative or it was frankly dogmatic.
Wealthy Romans who had the interiors of their villas adorned
with imaginary vistas sought no more than sheer sensuous
delight of the eye. With the Christian era painting became a
means of propagating and strengthening the faith. From the
minuscule illustrations on the pages of manuscripts produced
in monasteries, as well as from the depictions of religious
themes on the walls and altars of churches, the viewer could
draw doctrinal guidance, a knowledge of Scripture and sacred
legend and, perhaps most important, a proper sense of reverence. Sometimes, indeed, the painting itself functioned as an
icon to be venerated.
   Giotto made no attempt to break with the tradition that art
must be the handmaiden of the Church. But he infused his art
with a new humanity. Instead of using the glittering gold backdrop which previous painters had employed to create an aura of
supernatural mystery, he placed his figures in settings of hills,
meadows and houses familiar to any Italian. Whereas previous
painters had disposed their figures with little regard for their
relationships, he arranged people in a meaningful, natural manner; moreover, he grouped them along the lower half of the picture, so that the viewer could look at, rather than up to, the
scene before him. The subtlety of these innovations was not
lost on Giotto's contemporaries; he was proclaiming his belief
that a man and his faith must meet on a comprehensible level.
(pages 8-9)

To put it simply and clearly, Giotto played a primary role in the
renewal of art.

Hang an Icon in Your Heart

You ask only for our wills, that our souls should be prepared as
wax to receive your seal.

—*SAINT TERESA OF AVILA*, THE INTERIOR CASTLE

*Life sometimes seems to be nothing more than an endless series of prob-
lems to be solved or resolved. Some problems eat away at us for months*

or years at a time, such as a boss who makes life miserable for us. Every day we are confronted with a string of decisions which must be made, some trivial, some serious. Problems, big and small, and decisions, major and minor, consume our days, often causing tension and unrest.

As I stand before this parade of problems and decisions, where is Christ? All too frequently, he is not in the picture. My first impulse is to solve the problem by or make the decision after consulting my reason. As I go about the mundane business of living, I easily lose sight of Christ's invitation to unite ourselves with him. He assures us that all our problems will be resolved if we are united with him. In the noise of the day, that assurance falls on deaf ears.

In the past year, I've stumbled upon a way that is proving helpful in bringing Christ into my problem-solving and decision-making process. The initial insight came during a reflection on the Gospel story of Peter walking on the water. As long as Peter keeps his eyes focused on Jesus and as long he continues going toward him, he has no difficulty walking on the stormy waters of the lake. But as soon as Peter becomes distracted by the wind and the waves, he takes his eyes off Jesus and suddenly fear pulls him down and he begins to sink. The dangers and temptations, along with the parade of problems and decisions, I encounter every day often cause me to lose sight of Jesus. All of my faults and failures have their origin in my turning my glance away from Jesus. To look into the face of Jesus is to be transformed. When you see Christ, you see the solution to problems through him.

O Lord, show me your face.

To help me remember to keep my eyes on Christ, I set aside a few minutes each day to sit and simply stare at an icon of the face of Christ. This practice has helped me realize that to be united with Christ, I need to carry within myself an intensely real image of the Savior. Creating this image, a vivid icon to hang on the wall of my heart, is the work of a lifetime. And I cannot paint the image myself; that would only be the work of my imagination. I can only hang the canvas of my soul on the wall of my heart, and wait in meekness and humility for Christ to imprint his image upon it. I firmly believe that as the portrait becomes clearer and clearer over time (and with the aid of prayer), it will become easier for me to take an inward gaze in times of trouble and have all my difficulties melt like snow in the sunlight of Christ's radiance.

The acknowledgment of my own weakness is the first step toward an acknowledgment of Christ's strength.

Slowly, I am learning that to embrace Jesus is to embrace the solu-tion to any problem I encounter.

THE MYSTERY

There is more to Giotto's story...there is also a mystery. The mystery is simple: Did Giotto paint the cycle of twenty-eight frescoes depicting the life of Saint Francis in the upper Basilica at Assisi, or are they the work of a number of other artists?

Unfortunately the mystery does not have a simple answer.

In 1228, only two years after the death of Saint Francis, construction began on a huge basilica in his honor. Pope Gregory IX laid the cornerstone for the church on July 17th, the day after a solemn canonization ceremony. Many of the saint's followers regarded the magnificence of the project to be a perversion of Francis' ideal of poverty, but, fortunately for art lovers, other minds prevailed. Amazingly, the whole structure was completed within eleven years. Artists then began the work of decorating the interior of the church with frescoes and stained-glass windows. Some of Italy's greatest masters, including Cimabue, Pietro Lorenzetti and Simone Martini, contributed their talents to creating a lasting memorial to Francis that would offer pleasure and inspiration to generations of pilgrims. The basilica was officially dedicated by Pope Innocent IV on May 24, 1253.

For hundreds of years, it was generally accepted that Giotto had painted at Assisi, specifically the twenty-eight frescoes in the upper church. But, in 1791, Guglielmo della Valle, a Franciscan priest and amateur art historian, noting certain stylistic discrepancies between the scenes, suggested Giotto had not painted all of them. In the next fifty years, other critics supported this view, adding the notion that Giotto did not paint anything at all in Assisi. Since then the controversy has flourished.

Unfortunately, no document exists to solve the mystery conclusively; for example, there are no ledgers or contract records to show Giotto was assigned to the work or was paid for it. Those who believe Giotto painted the Saint Francis cycle cite tradition and commentaries by later writers. Doubters rely on stylistic comparisons with known Giotto works.

I am neither an art critic nor an art historian, hence I am hardly qualified to render an opinion on the mystery. I can only say it is my sense that current scholarship leans toward supporting the idea that Giotto painted the frescoes and that the five distinctly different styles in the series are explainable. The explanation I find most plausible comes from James H. Stubblebine in *Assisi and the Rise of Vernacular Art*. The question of Giotto's authorship of the Assisi frescoes is not Stubblebine's central theme; rather, his primary concern is to offer a new understanding of how the frescoes reflected the needs and perceptions of the time and of the audience they were created for, and how the frescoes represented a new, popular, reality-based imagery intended to attract a large audience of the faithful.

The author writes:

> Gradually, there has come into being a general consensus that Giotto's was the mind behind the series but that he was helped to a greater or lesser degree by one or a number of assistants. This has proved to be a more acceptable position for the majority of art historians insofar as the individual could decide for himself the degree to which he thought Giotto had been assisted, without running athwart the broad consensus which saw the St. Francis Legend as being in fundamental ways a Giottoesque work.

A Gush of Fresh Air

I find myself greatly attracted to Giotto. As a secular Franciscan, Giotto had a great love for the Church, which was just beginning to reach out to the common people. He wanted to bring the Church closer to the people through his art. But Giotto was born into an artistic tradition that resisted change. The rigid Byzantine style left absolutely no room for individuality or the warmth of humanity; depictions of people were lifeless and indistinct, part of a faceless mass, portrayed in traditional, flat, two-dimensional ways, which were hard to relate to. Giotto wanted to bring the spirit of Saint Francis to his art. The people in his frescoes had expressions, feelings and emotions; they were real, alive and fully human, and far removed from the idealized archetypes seen in Byzantine art. Even the Madonna became a woman. The real world in which we live was all but absent in Byzantine art, which stressed divinity and the otherworldliness of Christ and the saints. Giotto wanted no part of that tradition, and so he set his scenes in easily recognizable places. The world as it actually existed entered into sacred art for the first time in the history of art. There were buildings and mountains in Giotto's frescoes. There was perspective instead of flat planes. Human figures were rounded in sculpted forms. Giotto placed an emphasis on the real, as well as on the divine. For nearly 700 years, his art has touched those who see it. With a gush of fresh air, Giotto explored the natural world, reflecting its beauty. Giotto was truly a great artist whose art formed a bridge between the medieval world and the age of the Renaissance.

THE ART OF FRESCO PAINTING

The image is the starting point of our knowledge. It is that from which our intellectual activity begins, not as a passing stimulus, but an enduring foundation.

—SAINT THOMAS AQUINAS

Bruce Cole's fine book on Giotto's exquisite work in the Scrovegni Chapel in Padua devotes a few pages to describing in detail the intricate process of fresco painting. After reading Cole's excellent description of how a fresco is actually painted, I was filled with even more awe for Giotto and what he accomplished. To begin with, fresco painting is more difficult than I ever imagined. Fresco painting required extensive training and a wide range of skills beyond the art of composition and color. The artist had to be a master plasterer, as well. Painting a fresco required a great deal of preplanning, tremendous patience, some scientific knowledge and the ability to work fast. And work with eggs also. I'll get to that later. "In essence," writes Bruce Cole, "fresco painting is the application of pigment by brush to wet plaster spread on a wall. Once the plaster dries the paint brushed onto the wall's surface bonds to it by means of a chemical reaction" (page 19).

Though the task was a difficult one to perform, fresco painting was popular because it used inexpensive materials and could cover large areas cheaply. And if the frescoes were properly protected they would last a very long time.

Here is an excerpt from Bruce Cole's *Giotto*, in which the author describes the process of painting a fresco.

The fresco painter would begin by laying down a coat of rough plaster, called *arriccio*, both to smooth out the wall to be painted (which was usually made of brick or stone) and to provide a moisture barrier between the wall and the final painting. When the plaster had dried, the painter rolled strings in charcoal or wet paint and snapped them against the wall, making vertical and horizontal guidelines [to] help him find the exact center of the area to be painted, so that he could then center the composition and correctly align the forms he was about to paint.

Next, with a charcoal stick he would work up a full-scale preparatory drawing of his subject on the plaster (after 1450, this practice would be replaced by the use of paper cartoons, stencil-like drawings that allowed the artist to make preparatory drawings in his studio). The charcoal drawing on plaster would be corrected and adjusted until the artist, and often his patron, were satisfied. Then, with a brush dipped in water and sinopia (a red iron oxide pigment named after its source in Sinope in Asia Minor), the artist retraced the preparatory charcoal drawing. When the sinopia was dry, the underlying charcoal drawing, which might possibly stain the final painting, was brushed off with a bunch of feathers. Now the artist was able to begin the actual painting of the fresco.

This painting was done on a second coat of finer plaster called the *intonaco*, which was troweled over the *arriccio*. Because the pigment (which was mixed with water) would bond only with plaster that was still wet, it was necessary to replaster an area only as large as the painter could paint before it dried. To do this, the second coat of plaster was applied in patches, sometimes called *giornante*, an Italian term meaning "tasks done daily," and not necessarily, as is sometimes stated, "one day's work." The painter would start putting in his patches at the top and work downward so that any drips would fall on the *arriccio* that was being covered and not on the new plaster. During this process, the sinopia drawing, which would gradually be covered, acted as an indispensable guide to proportion, scale, and subject for what was being painted on the patches. Without the sinopia drawing, the artist would have to invent and proportion the scene as he painted it on the second coat of plaster, a difficult, if not impossible task.

The painting of the second coat of plaster presented many difficult technical problems. For instance, the degree of wetness or dryness of the plaster when the pigment was applied could ultimately affect the value (the darkness or lightness), and sometimes the color, of that pigment after the plaster had dried. To keep color consistent throughout the fresco, the pigment had to be applied during the brief amount of time when the plaster was just right for painting. Thus, it was necessary for the artist to understand how plaster dried under all sorts of atmospheric conditions and to be able to paint rapidly enough to cover the whole patch while it was in the optimal condition to receive pigments. If the plaster dried too fast or too slowly and the colors changed drastically from patch to patch, it was necessary to chip out the plaster and begin again, a laborious process indeed. Fresco painting is a very unforgiving medium: once the pigment is brushed into the wet plaster it is absorbed immediately and cannot be erased or easily altered.

Fresco painting is always a race against time, a race to finish before the plaster dries. One can imagine the need for careful planning and organization as the painter and his apprentices, surrounded by buckets of water and pots of pigment, stood on scaffolds high above the floor, feverishly applying paint to the rapidly drying surface. This process of fresco painting conditioned the way artists approached their work. To achieve the necessary speed, the design of most frescos, especially the early ones done with sinopia drawings, is ample and bold in conception and short of much time-consuming detail. Crisp detail is, in any case, hard to achieve in the wet, blurring pigment and absorbent plaster of fresco; the detail that is found on most fresco is often applied with pigments mixed with egg yolks or glue after the plaster has dried. (pages 19-22)

I'm exhausted just reading how to paint a fresco.

Besides patience and a knowledge of art and science, the painter also had to conquer any fear of heights! Knowing what went into painting a fresco helped me better appreciate the magnificent works that adorn the walls of the upper church of the Basilica of St. Francis. Looking at Cole's lavishly illustrated book on Giotto's frescoes from the Scrovegni Chapel, I'm ready to hop on a train to Padua to see them in person. But first, I'd like to take you on a tour...of some churches in Assisi.

Before we rush off, I'd like to leave you with a few poetic words from Murray Bodo, O.F.M., words which are a meditation on Francis and the frescoes which portray him:

The image I have of the medieval Church immediately before Francis is that of a fresco that has faded back into the bare outlines of its own cartoon, and there is no one to bring back the freshness and color of the original image.

Then along comes Francis of Assisi and his followers, and the fresco begins to take on color and life and move through the countryside like a fluid painting. And it is authentic to everyone who views it, because it restores precisely what has faded out in the original: the features of the the icon of the Father, Jesus Christ.

Francis, icon of the Savior. Francis and his followers, frescoes of the true Church. It is not what Francis did in the Church, then, that is so important, but the image that Francis and his followers became. They imaged what the Church and each individual Christian can be. He held up an icon that people recognized as a mirror both of Christ and of themselves, provided they were indeed what they were meant to be. And the more Francis lived the Gospel literally, the clearer the picture became. (*Tales of St. Francis*, page 180)

Fill in the Blank

Father Bodo's last paragraph begins with the statement: "Francis, icon of the Savior." When I read that, an idea flashed across my mind: make a similar statement about myself.

Gerry, icon of _____.

I wasn't happy with the way I had to fill in the blank.

I'm still a cartoon of what I hope to become, what I was meant to be.

PILGRIMAGE DIARY 63

Heart of Stone

On the tree of the Cross, the Heart of Jesus beheld your heart and loved it.

—*SAINT FRANCIS DE SALES*

*N*ear the end of Part One of this book, I mentioned being especially moved one day during morning prayer at Sant' Isidoro upon hearing the words from Ezekiel, when the Lord promises to give the people a new heart in place of their "heart of stone." Today's reading from the Liturgy of the Hours included a portion of one of the medieval treatises of Baldwin of Canterbury.

The reading ended with:

> Lord, take away from me the heart of stone, a heart shrunken and uncircumcised—take it away and give me a new heart, a heart of flesh, a clean heart. You cleanse our heart and love the heart that is clean—possess my heart and dwell in it, both holding it and filling it. You surpass what is highest in me, and yet are within my inmost self! [I love that sentence.] Pattern of beauty and seal of holiness, mold my heart in your likeness: mold my heart under your mercy, God of my heart and God my portion for ever. Amen.

In March of 1995, during my first visit to the Collegio Sant' Isidoro, the same reading from Ezekiel caught my attention...and for good reason: my heart was changing. I even managed to work a verse from Ezekiel into my novel, The Canvas of the Soul:

> Day Seven. I arose early today and attended morning prayer with the friars.... As I thumbed through the Liturgy of the Hours, my attention was arrested by a canticle from the Book of Ezekiel, Chapter 36:
>
> > A new heart I will give you,
> > a new spirit I will put in you;
> > and I will take out of your flesh the heart of stone
> > and give you a heart of flesh. (25-27)
>
> A new heart and a new spirit. Sounds good.... My heart has not turned to stone, but it has grown weary and cold. And sad. As the voices united in songs of prayer echoed through the church, my heart and spirit were cloaked in serenity.

Later in the day, Jim and Bernie tour Rome and visit the crown jewel of Jesuit churches, the Gesu:

> The Church of Il Gesu was built in the late sixteenth century as the Mother Church of the Jesuit Order. ...Pierre Teilhard de Chardin summed it up best in a letter written in 1948: "...despite its orgy of marbles and mouldings...one feels [in the Gesu]...the security of a faith that will not be sidetracked." I did not feel the security of faith, but I certainly noticed the orgy of marbles and mouldings.
>
> The effusiveness of Gian Battista Gaulli's ceiling painting entitled the Adoration of the Name Jesus caught the literary eyes of the De Goncourt brothers. In their novel *Madame*

Gervaisais (1869), the protagonist "loved the vault over her head which resembled a golden arch, bedecked with ornaments, with coffers and arabesques, illuminated by windows where saints burst forth into the sunlight. She loved the blazing festivity of the ceiling where, in Gaulli's glorious colours, the apotheosis of the Elect triumphs over vaporous clouds that seem like incense and which, garnished with flowers, overflows their borders. All poured forth, glimpses of sky and veritable clouds suspended from the vault where angels swirled with much thrashing of legs and beating of wings." In other words, Gaulli went for baroque in this fresco. The glorious colors have faded over the years, and much of the church's busy decoration in stone, paint, and plaster seems overdue for restoration.

In the left transept, under a panoply of marble, gold and bronze, is the tomb of St. Ignatius of Loyola (1491-1556), the founder of the Society of Jesus, known as the Jesuits. Above the altar is a large statue of the saint, which stands under a sculptural representation of the Trinity including a globe made of the largest piece of lapis lazuli ever found on earth. The original statue was melted down in the French Revolution. Every inch of the walls of this small chapel is covered with paintings, statues of angels and biblical figures, and gold trimming.

After a short discussion on art and faith, Jim and Bernie walk around the church...back to the novel:

We headed for the other side of the church and entered the Chapel of the Sacred Heart. While I paused to look at a painting of Jesus which hung over the altar, Bernie wandered off. The painting caught my attention because it reminded me of the old-fashioned piety that infused the Church during my grandmother's time. Jesus, looking tender and angelic in his long, flowing brown hair, was holding his own heart in his hand, as if extending it to whomever was looking. A golden glow surrounded the heart. I thought of my grandmother's simple faith. The Feast of the Sacred Heart of Jesus was one of Gram's favorite feast days. On one occasion she told me she prayed I would "experience the sweetness of the tender Heart of Jesus." The canticle from Ezekiel I had read that morning echoed in my mind: I will give you a new heart.

I knelt down, and prayed, "Dear Jesus, your heart loves so deeply, while mine loves so weakly. Help me grow in love...of you and all whom I encounter. Help me know the sweetness of your heart."

I stood up, and as I turned to leave the chapel, I noticed a painting of St. Francis of Assisi on the side wall. Francis was preaching to the birds. Instantly, I knew his secret: it was the purity of his heart. I was then surprised to notice that all the paintings—seven in all—on the side and back walls of the Chapel of the Sacred Heart were of St. Francis of Assisi, each painting depicting a scene from his life. How fitting, I thought, for the heart of Francis came the closest to resembling the heart of Jesus. I couldn't wait to get to Assisi.

A couple of weeks later, Jim and Bernie are traveling on a night train to Amsterdam. Bernie is asleep. Jim pulls out his notebook and pens this prayer:

A Prayer for a More Loving Heart

O Most Sacred Heart of Jesus
create in me a pure heart,
a heart that doesn't lust or hate,
a heart that isn't proud or envious.

O Most Sacred Heart of Jesus
help me purify my polluted heart,
help me soften my hardened heart,
help me warm my frigid heart.

O Most Sacred Heart of Jesus
help me transform my heart
into a heart that beats
more in rhythm with your Sacred Heart.

Jesus my Lord, you are the source
of every blessing and I ask only this:
Let my contrite heart beat with love,
the way your Most Sacred Heart does.

Composed by James Francis Howard
on April 26, 1995
on board train # 283,
from Paris to Amsterdam.

After writing that prayer, I must confess that I forgot about it...that is to say I personally never prayed it. It was fiction.

After reading Baldwin of Canterbury, I dug out my novel (which I had brought with me) and took a look at that prayer. Thinking about it, I realized that the Lord isn't into heart transplants—removing a heart of stone and replacing it with a heart of flesh. No...the new heart comes as we gradually conform our hearts of stone to the Sacred Heart of Jesus.

God will give us a new spirit, a new heart—when we surrender our old spirit, our old heart.

It's the surrender that takes time, each day giving up a little more of the self and everything that is not of God.

I think I'll start praying that prayer.

The Liturgy of the Hours

A reading from the letters of Saint Margaret Mary Alacoque:

I believe the reason behind our Lord's great desire that especial honour should be paid to his sacred heart is his wish to renew in our souls the effects of our redemption. For his sacred heart is an inexhaustible spring which has no other purpose than to overflow into the hearts which are humble, so that they may be ready and willing to devote their lives to his goodwill and pleasure.

Out of this divine heart three streams gush forth uninterruptedly. The first is one of mercy for sinners whom it brings in its flow the spirit of contrition and penance. The second stream is one of charity which flows to bring help to all those who are labouring under difficulties and especially to those who are aspiring after perfection, that all may find support in overcoming difficulties. But the third stream flows with love and light to those who are Christ's perfect friends, whom he wishes to bring to complete union with himself, to share with them his own knowledge and commandments, so that they may give themselves up entirely, each in his own way, to enhancing Christ's glory....

This divine heart is an ocean full of all good things wherein our poor souls can cast all their needs; it is an ocean full of

joy to drown all our sadness, an ocean of humility to over-
whelm our folly, an ocean of mercy for those in distress, an
ocean of love in which to submerge our poverty.

Unite yourself, therefore, to the heart of Jesus Christ.... Do
you find that you are making no progress in prayer? Let it be
enough for you to offer to God the prayer which our Savior
makes for us in the most holy sacrament of the altar, using fervent offering to make reparation for your lukewarmness. And
whenever you do anything, pray this way: "My God, I am
going to do this or endure that in the sacred heart of your
divine Son and according to his holy intentions which I offer
you to make reparation for whatever evil or imperfections
there may be in my own deeds." Continue in this way in all
circumstances of life. And whenever anything happens to you
that is painful, hard to bear or mortifying, tell yourself this:
"Accept what the Sacred Heart of Jesus sends you in order to
unite you to himself."

But above all things maintain peace of heart which surpasses every treasure. For maintaining this peace nothing is
more effective than to renounce one's own will and set in its
place the will of the Sacred Heart, so that he may do for us
whatever redounds to his glory and we may joyfully submit to
him and place in him our full confidence.

The Synthesis of Love and Matter

The Sacred Heart is the Center of Christ, who centers all on
himself.

—*PIERRE TEILHARD DE CHARDIN, S.J.*

*Pierre Teilhard de Chardin believed that the conjunction of God and the
world took place in the heart of Christ. Fellow Jesuit Robert Faricy, a professor of spiritual theology at the Pontifical Gregorian University in
Rome, discovered in a desk drawer located in a Jesuit house in Chantilly,
just north of Paris, unpublished notes penned by de Chardin which contain some of his thoughts on prayer. In Father Faricy's book* Praying, *he*

includes the following entry, written by de Chardin on the seventh day of an eight-day retreat:

First Friday (December 1, 1939)

The Sacred Heart: Instinctively and mysteriously for me, since my infancy: the *synthesis* of Love and Matter, of Person and Energy. From this there has gradually evolved in me the perception of Christ uniting all things in a universal cohesion. I would like to spread the vision (I do not say "devotion," much too sentimental and too weak) of the universal Christ, of the *true* heart of Jesus.

Faricy offers this commentary:

Teilhard's attachment to the heart of Jesus had none of the sentimental narrowness often found in the traditional devotion that began in seventeenth-century France. On the contrary, it freed him because it enabled him to see a unity and consistency in all of reality, because it showed him the absolute Center of a changing world. Through the symbol of Jesus' heart the Divine took on for Teilhard the properties, the form, and the qualities of a Fire capable of transforming anything and everything through the power of its love. "Christ, his Heart, a Fire, capable of penetrating everything—and which, little by little, spreads everywhere." (pages 81-82)

Sacred Heart of Jesus, sacred temple of God,
  have mercy on me.
Sacred Heart of Jesus, full of goodness and love,
  have mercy on me.
Sacred Heart of Jesus, King and center of all hearts,
  have mercy on me.

Sacred Heart of Jesus, help me to complete a silent oblation of my self,
  and surrender this meek and humble offering completely to God.

Sacred Heart of Jesus, guide me to my own center,
  and from there help me pass into God.

Paolo Grimaldi
Cielo d'Oro su Assisi
1997
Oil, tempera and gold leaf on panel

Part Five

ASSISI

The Holy City on a Hill

PRELUDE

*T*here is something about Assisi—the town—that defies description. Something intangible, a mystical aura that blankets the entire hillside upon which the town sits. Evelyn Underhill claimed, "Its soul is more manifest than any other city I know." Down through the ages, few visitors have escaped sensing this feeling. Some notable exceptions are Wolfgang von Goethe, Nathaniel Hawthorne, John Ruskin, Henry James and Theodore Dreiser. Goethe visited Assisi in 1786 and the only thing that caught his fancy was the classic Roman temple of Minerva. Nathaniel Hawthorne couldn't see past what he considered the "decay" of a "fossilized city" during his visit in 1858. John Ruskin found the bells annoying during his visit in 1873. Henry James found Assisi "very hot" and Theodore Dreiser found it disappointing and "very poor." But there is scant other evidence from the pens of writers and artists who have come to Assisi and not been charmed by its mystical lure.

Shortly after I returned home from my first visit to Assisi, I met a woman who was so thoroughly captivated by Assisi she vowed to return within a year for a longer stay. She had stumbled upon Assisi during an unplanned stop and knew from just a short one-night stay that she had to return. And so she did. Upon her return home from the second visit, which lasted a full ten days, she began to make plans to move to Assisi. The birthplace of Francis and Clare can have that kind of magnetic attraction for many people. My dream is to live there one day, too.

A great deal of this mystical aura that most visitors sense in Assisi seems to emanate from the town's numerous churches and shrines. Before we begin our tour of these holy places, I would like to share an extended quotation from Raphael Brown's excellent book, *True Joy from Assisi*. The quotation forms the entire short chapter entitled, "Mystery: Encounter with Christ."

> The Assisi experience might be termed almost a mystical or proto-mystical experience, in the broad sense that not a few visitors described how the cumulative effect of the beauty, light, peace, joy, and the living presence of the Saint, culminating in a kind of foretaste of heaven, has raised their consciousness to a new and higher perception of spiritual truth and the reality and presence of God.
>
> So Assisi can also be a theophany, an epiphany, an encounter with God in which He reveals Himself to us.
>
> ...[A]ccording to the perceptive Romano Guardini, "our soul is stirred by the mystery of this town, a mystery that is radiance."
>
> Reinhold Schneider goes further into this mystery: "As Pascal said, all things are veils behind which is hidden a mystery. The mystery is God. And God manifests Himself in Assisi, beneath the veil of beauty, with overwhelming gravity.... If there is in that city something eternal...it is founded on the way in which St. Francis...in a sense brought Christ back to earth.... For those who have perceived in Assisi this fusion...of the mourning at Calvary and the hymn of the blessed, this city of a Saint will be the hallowed threshold of the city of God."
>
> Francois Mauriac contributes this profound insight into Assisi's mystery of God's Self-revelation through the spirit and presence of Christ's most perfect follower: "A soul has been there for the last eight centuries...but that soul withdraws before a new Presence. The steep walls of Assisi bear an imprint still deeper than the one left there by the passing of a saint: superimposed on the land of Umbria appears the face of Christ."
>
> Here we find a modern echo of that traditional Franciscan theme of the conformity of the Saint with his Divine Model— of course, with all due theological reservations and distinctions

between God and man. This theme was boldly proclaimed in the opening sentence of the *Fioretti*: "First it should be known that the glorious St. Francis was conformed to Christ in all acts of his life." In 1399 Friar Bartholomew of Pisa's monumental compendium *The Book of Conformities* exhaustively document- ed no fewer than forty major points of resemblance. Earlier in the fourteenth century, Giotto and his pupils enshrined the theme by painting on the facing walls of the Upper Church of San Francesco twin series from the lives of Christ and St. Francis.

The profound and lasting truth of the theme—always with- in proper theological limits—lies in the two complementary imperatives of Christian spirituality: the deliberate, faithful "imitation of Christ" by His disciples and followers (no matter what their particular vocation may be), and, as a consequence, their progressive "deification" by Him in growth in mystical union with Him, by means of the inner trauma of His pattern of Self-sacrifice. This is the deepest meaning of the inner suffer- ings and the outer wounds of St. Francis of Assisi.

Thus our encounter with Francis—in Assisi or anywhere, but especially potently in Assisi—becomes necessarily an encounter with his Model and Pattern, Jesus Christ.

And, depending on our response, not just a passing encounter, but a life and gradual fusion, through growth in inner transforming union. (pages 135-137)

Well, put on your walking shoes and let's tour the churches of Assisi, remembering as you walk that to walk in the footsteps of Francis is to walk in the footsteps of Christ.

Walk slowly, walk prayerfully.

Take the time to listen to the silence.

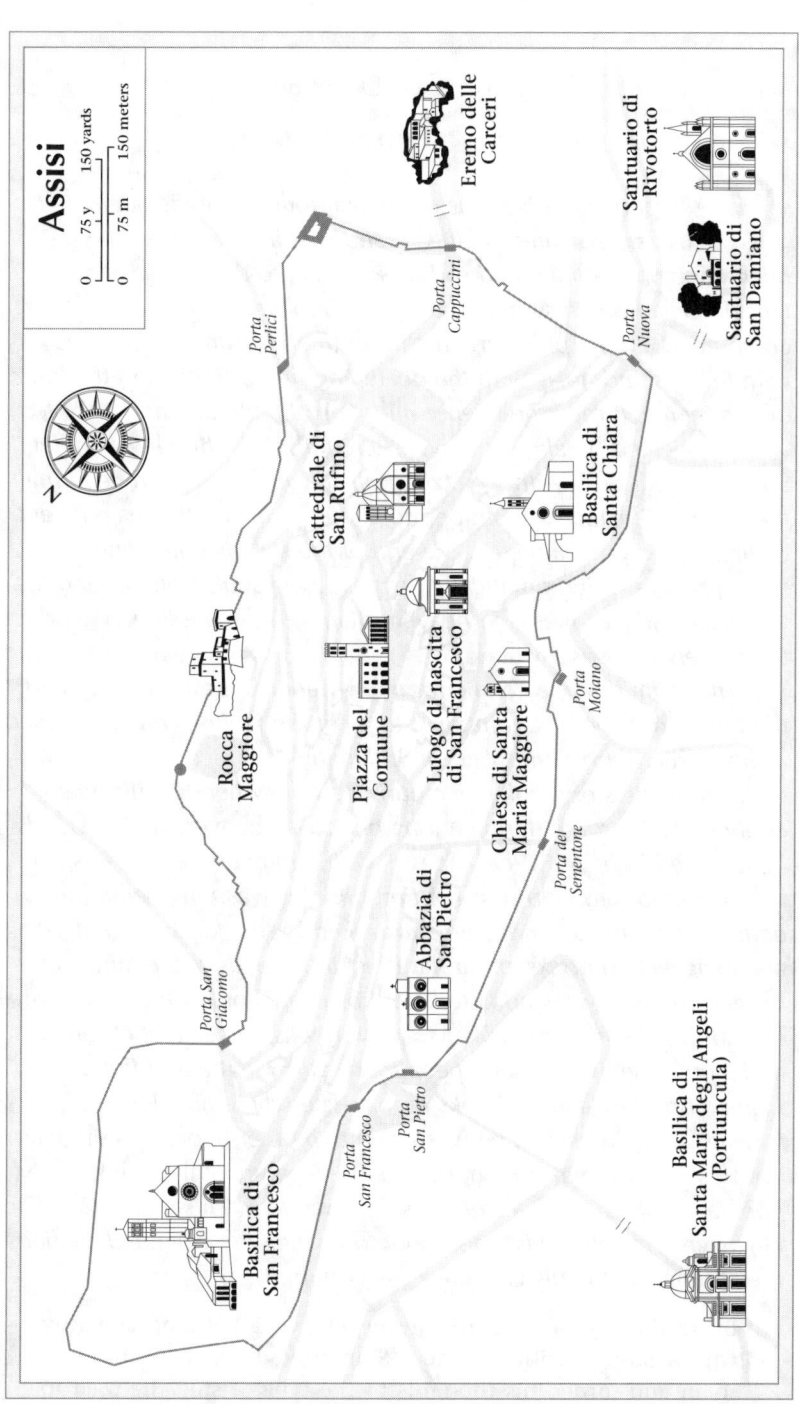

Assisi

0   75 y   150 yards

0   75 m   150 meters

N

Porta Perlici

Porta Cappuccini

Porta Nuova

Eremo delle Carceri

Santuario di Rivotorto

Santuario di San Damiano

Cattedrale di San Rufino

Basilica di Santa Chiara

Rocca Maggiore

Piazza del Comune

Luogo di nascita di San Francesco

Chiesa di Santa Maria Maggiore

Porta Moiano

Porta San Giacomo

Abbazia di San Pietro

Porta del Sementone

Porta San Francesco

Porta San Pietro

Basilica di San Francesco

Basilica di Santa Maria degli Angeli (Portiuncula)

PILGRIMAGE DIARY 64

Time

*T*he feast of Saint Ignatius of Loyola, founder of the Society of Jesus, is celebrated on July 31st. I was in Rome after the pilgrimage on that date and so I took a walk to the Chiesa Sant' Ignazio. The Roman summer heat was suffocating. The heat, combined with the pulsating rhythm of the busy streets, crowded with tourists and noisy with the deafening din of traffic and the buzz of commerce, turned the twenty-minute walk into an endurance test, which I seemed barely to survive. Mercifully, the church was quiet and cool...but busy with a dazzling display of baroque art covering the ceiling. Bursting with color and exquisite detail, the magnificent ceiling fresco was painted at the end of the seventeenth century by a Jesuit priest, and it dramatically depicts saved souls from around the world ascending to Jesus in heaven, thanks to the missionary work of the Society of Jesus.

After admiring the ceiling for a few minutes, I sat down to read the Office of Readings from the Liturgy of the Hours, which included a short excerpt from the "Acts of St. Ignatius" as recorded by Luis Gonzalez. The story took place during a time when Ignatius was confined to his room during a long period of recovery from wounds he received in battle. When he was well enough to read, he asked for some books to help pass the time. As this was long before he dedicated his life to Christ, Ignatius asked for the kind of "aimless and exaggerated books about the illustrious deeds of the famous," because he was "very addicted" to those kinds of books. (People are still addicted to those kinds of shallow books, books that chronicle and glorify the lives of such people as Frank Sinatra and Princess Diana.) But they had no books of that type where Ignatius was staying; and so, instead, he was given two other books: The Imitation of Christ, *by Thomas à Kempis, and* The Flowers of the Saints, *a popular book on the lives of the saints, written in his native Castilian language. This plot twist was about to change the wounded soldier's life. According to Luis Gonzalez's account:*

> By reading these regularly he developed a certain sympathy with what was written in them. Sometimes he took his mind off them and turned his thoughts to the type of story he used to

read earlier on; sometimes, according as it occurred to him, he thought about those idle inclinations and things of that nature, such as he used to think about formerly.

But divine mercy was at hand and, in place of these thoughts, it used to substitute others from what he had recently read. For when he had read the lives of Christ our Lord and the saints he would think to himself and ponder, "What if I were to do what blessed Francis did or what blessed Dominic did?" And he used to meditate a good deal in this manner. This way of thinking lasted for some time, but then other things intervened, and he resumed his idle and worldly thoughts, and these persisted for a long time. He was involved in that succession of changes of mind for a considerable time.

But there was a difference in his two types of subject for thought. When he was intent on his worldly interests he got great pleasure at the time, but whenever he wearied of them and gave them up, he felt dejected and empty. On the other hand, when he thought about the austerities which he found that holy men practiced, not only did he find joy in the account of them, but when he stopped thinking of them his joy remained unabated. However, he never noticed the difference or thought about it, until one day it dawned on him, and he began to wonder at it. He understood from experience that the one subject of thought left him dejection, while the other left him joy. This was the first conclusion which he reached concerning things of a supernatural nature. Afterwards, however, when he had undertaken spiritual exercises, this experience was the starting point for teaching his followers the discernment of spirits. (The Liturgy of the Hours, Vol. III)

Two things strike me about that story, and they both concern the same topic: time.

First, Saint Ignatius was forced, by his injury, to spend time, lots of time, alone with nothing to do. He was forced to sit still, not moving about busying himself with...life. (In a similar fashion, Francis was confined to bed for many weeks after becoming ill during his year in prison in Perugia; it was a time of solitude, silence and deep reflection.) Had Ignatius not had the time "to kill," he would never have read the spiritual books that opened his mind to the deeper mysteries of God, nor would he have had the time to ponder them. Second, once those mysteries began to penetrate his mind, and he slowly began to notice how he felt better after reading and thinking about spiritual matters than after devoting his time to reading "aimless" books, it still took the future saint a long time to gradually overcome his addiction to things not of God and to turn fully to living his life for God.

We want quick results, instantaneous salvation. It doesn't happen. Saint Francis of Assisi needed a lot of time before he reached the point where he could hear God speak to him as he knelt at the foot of the cross at San Damiano. Neither Francis nor Ignatius instantly transformed themselves from soldiers to saints. For both men, it was a gradual, lengthy process along a path strewn with doubts and setbacks. The way of the cross is neither easy nor short.

I was struck by the reality of God in a transforming moment of time which transcended time. But that moment, that precious and wondrous moment, was only the first tick of the clock that would mark my reborn spiritual life. Even though shortly after that moment I began reading more deeply about Saint Francis and was moved by his life and his profound love of Christ, until very recently I still preferred reading about the New York Yankees or the latest film by Woody Allen. Grace is imperative; without it we would wither on the vine of life. But time, time for the seed planted by grace to mature and bear fruit is equally important. And the true harvest comes at the end of the time we are given.

And how have we used that time? I've used it badly. The lives of these two great saints teach me that I can't afford to waste time. Moreover, my spiritual growth is going to require more than the brief amount of time (hardly ever more than a half hour a day) I give to prayer and reflection. Francis spent half of his converted life in solitary prayer. The friars and sisters on the pilgrimage were acutely aware of the huge effort they must make just to squeeze a one-week retreat into their yearly schedules. Young people look at priests and sisters and at times see exhausted people on the verge of burnout. That is not an attractive picture of religious life: No wonder vocations are dwindling. But that's another subject.

Time...we have so little of it and we need so much of it.

In truth, I believe God gives us the time we need. For me, I need to learn how to use it wisely.

BASILICA DI SAN FRANCESCO

The Basilica of St. Francis is a monumental building complex consisting of a lower and upper church, the tomb of Saint Francis, located in a chapel beneath the lower church, and the huge Sacro Convento which houses the friars. The massive double basilica, one church superimposed on top of another, is the most easily recognized building in Assisi. Built of pink and white stone on the side of a hill which once served as the burial ground for criminals, outcasts and the poor, the basilica serves as an elaborate headstone for the tomb of Saint Francis, his bodily remains solemnly resting in a small crypt below the two churches, even though the saint may have preferred an unmarked grave amongst the kinds of marginal people he loved so dearly.

The basilica also houses a treasure trove of magnificent paintings, frescoes and mosaics. It is not an exaggeration to say the church is one of the richest art galleries in Italy. I think of it as the world's largest and most beautiful picture book. In fact, you cannot open any illustrated book on art without coming across reproductions of the frescoes that cover the walls of the lower and upper churches, works painted by the masters of early Renaissance art. Sir Kenneth Clark, in his 1969 book *Civilization*, wrote: "Two years after his [Francis'] death he was canonized and almost immediately his followers began to build a great basilica in his memory. With its upper and lower churches, jammed onto the side of a steep hill, it is both an extraordinary feat of engineering and a masterpiece of gothic architecture. It was decorated by all the chief Italian painters of the thirteenth and fourteenth centuries, from Cimabue onward, so that it became the richest and most evocative church in Italy" (page 77). In the last dozen years, at least half a dozen books dealing solely with the basilica's architecture have been published; the number of books devoted to the art on the walls of the basilica are too numerous to count.

The basilica is a magnificent synthesis of architecture, painting and spirituality. Attracted by the art and spirit within its massive walls, every day of the year people from around the world pour into Assisi by the busload in order to visit the Basilica of St. Francis. They enter this sacred space to marvel at the art and to kneel at the tomb of Saint Francis. Art and holiness combine to forge an unforgettable experience. Nearly a hundred years ago, novelist Henry James recorded his impression of the paired basilica in *Italian Hours*: "This twofold temple of St. Francis is one of the very sacred places of Italy, and it would be hard to breathe anywhere an air more heavy with holiness."

The Basilica of St. Francis is a place where creativity and spirituality converge. It is a holy and artful place. The art on the walls pulls you in; the spirit within the walls lifts you up.

The Lower Church

For reasons I'll explain later, I think it's best to enter the lower church first.

The square adjacent to the entrance of the lower church is surrounded by a portico that dates back to the fifteenth century. The arched arcade provided shade for pilgrims, who tied their donkeys and horses to rings embedded in the columns and walls.

Over the twin doors leading into the lower church is a small rose window whose richly sculptured motifs caused one art critic to call it "the most beautiful church's eye in the world." Just beneath the rose window is a small mosaic of Saint Francis blessing all who enter. The large wooden door on the left contains carved scenes from the lives of Saint Francis and Saint Clare; the door on the right depicts scenes from the lives of Saint Anthony and Saint Louis of Anjou. The magnificent portal surrounding the double doors and the rose window was carved shortly after 1300. You enter into a transept running across the rear of the church, only the middle section of which dates back to the original church; the other two sections were added in 1271. On the left wall as you enter is the small chapel of Saint Sebastian.

The lower church consists of a single, low-ceilinged nave, divided into four bays by rounded arches, each with elaborate crossvaulting. Solid, massive pillars support the vault and, combined with the thick walls and small windows, they give the church a somber feeling which puts you in touch with the mystery and peace of God. Your attention is immediately drawn to the high altar. The tomb of Saint Francis is located in a crypt directly below the altar. Consecrated by Pope Innocent IV in 1253, the gothic altar is adorned by lavish mosaic decorations, calling to mind Francis' deep devotion to the Eucharist. Francis, a lover of poverty, wanted to spare no expense for chalices and other items required for the celebration of the Eucharist. The vault of the altar is divided into four sections, each featuring allegorical paintings depicting the exaltation of the glory of Saint Francis through his three vows of poverty, chastity and obedience. Magnificently carved wooden choir stalls dating back to 1468 line the wall behind the altar. The stalls consist of two tiers, the upper containing thirty-one seats and the lower, twenty seats. The choir stalls are enclosed by a balustrade of columns and supporting interlacing inlaid arches. The Romanesque architectural style of the lower church creates a prayerful atmosphere.

It seems as if every inch of the walls in the lower church is covered with frescoes created by the masters of the Florentine and Sienese schools of art. The greatest painters of the time poured into Assisi to help with the pictorial decoration of the church. Among the giants of Italian art who helped honor the little man of Assisi were Cimabue, Giotto, Simone Martini and Pietro Lorenzetti, whose combined work organically depicts and celebrates the life of Saint Francis. Entire books have been filled detailing and describing the art. Cimabue journeyed to Assisi in 1280 and set to work creating a masterpiece in the right transept of the lower church depicting a wonderfully sweet Madonna sitting on a royal throne flanked by four angels. Cimabue also painted the most famous depiction of Saint Francis, which can be found in the right transept. The right transept also features a number of scenes from the life of Christ, including the nativity and the crucifixion painted by Giotto. I lack the fluency to describe adequately the frescoes depicting scenes from the Gospels and parallel themes from the life of Saint Francis, but I can say they brought the Middle Ages alive in my imagination. The colorful costumes, musical instruments, such as flutes and guitars, the drama, the heroic nobility, the humble peasants, the minstrels and singers were all there surrounding the saintly Francis. Perhaps my favorite is a portrait of Saint Francis preaching to the birds, which can be found on the left wall of the nave. (The subject is also represented in the upper church.) The tenderness and austerity of this fresco are captivating.

Some of the oldest frescoes on the side walls were partially destroyed in the early 1300's when side chapels were added to accommodate the throngs of pilgrims visiting the basilica. For instance, all that remains of a fresco depicting Christ being stripped of his garments during the crucifixion are remnants of the Savior's clothes. On the opposite wall, as a mirror image of the Gospel scene is a scene from the life of Francis in which he strips his clothes off in the square in front of the bishop. Five entrance arches were constructed in the walls leading to a series of eight interconnecting chapels. Two of the chapels on the left are dedicated to Saint Martin of Tours and Saint Andrew, and between them is a small, irregularly shaped chapel featuring a multicolored wooden seventeenth-century statue of the Madonna. The Chapel of Saint Martin features exquisite frescoes, painted by Simone Martini in 1329, depicting with grace and delicacy ten episodes from the life of Saint Martin. The five chapels on the right are dedicated to Saints Louis, Stephen, Valentine, Anthony of Padua and to Mary Magdalene. Each of the chapels is elaborately decorated with frescoes and stunning stained-glass windows. Frescoes painted by Giotto in the Chapel of St. Mary Magdalene depict her in such scenes as at dinner with a Pharisee and at the resurrection of Lazarus. The lower church also contains three additional chapels. In the left transept is the Chapel of St. John the Baptist, and in the right transept the Chapel of St. Nicholas. At the end of the entrance bay there is the Chapel of St. Catherine of Alexandria.

A door in the right wing of the transept leads to a room known as the Chapel of the Relics, originally the Chapter Room. Here are housed priceless treasures from the life of Saint Francis, including his tattered, worn tunic and an ivory horn given to Francis by the Sultan of Egypt, Malek el Kamel. The room also contains two other items of great importance to Franciscans: the handwritten Rule of 1223, and the blessing penned by Francis and given to Brother Leo.

Along the right wall of the nave, there are stairs leading down to the heart and soul of the basilica, the tomb of Saint Francis. After his death, Francis was entombed in the Church of St. George. Four years later, the mortal remains of the saint were moved and placed under the high altar of the lower church of the new basilica. Access to the tomb was restricted. Those permitted to enter gained access through a tunnel leading from the choir to a small sepulcher chamber. In 1442, an invading force from Perugia stormed Assisi and tried to steal the relics of Saint Francis. After the failed attempt, Pope Eugene IV ordered the entrance to the tomb sealed in order to safeguard the body of Saint Francis. In those highly superstitious times, holy relics were thought to be the key to ensuring God's favor and help in winning battles and improving the economic status of a city. So, for security reasons, the tomb of Saint Francis remained unseen for 342 years following the last papal visit.

In 1818, Pope Pius VII ordered access to the tomb to be opened. The careful excavation work was done in secret at night, taking fifty-two nights to complete. A stone sarcophagus surrounded by an iron gate was imbedded in living rock, which in turn was protected by layers of concrete. No one was ever going to steal the body of Saint Francis. The well-preserved skeletal remains of the saint were inspected by a special commission of experts and bishops. The body was removed while workers completed the task of making a suitable entrance to a more beautiful chapel to house the sarcophagus. The neo-classic crypt which was constructed did not win any accolades, and in 1926 construction began on the more simple and austere chapel which we can freely visit today. In 1978, Pope Paul VI authorized the removal of the saint's body from the tomb so that the remains could be studied and replaced in an improved coffin that would ensure their preservation. The bones were placed in a small acrylic casket, and returned to the metal casket of 1820, which in turn was placed in the original stone coffin in which the body was placed in the thirteenth century. Over the altar in the chapel, we can see part of that stone coffin inside the roughly hewn stone sarcophagus, which rises from the floor to the ceiling.

The chapel is dignified and solemn, and completely unadorned. The undecorated walls and ceiling are made of heavy stone. It is a place of silence and prayer. Buried in the walls surrounding the tomb of Saint Francis are the remains of four of his early companions: Masseo, Angelo, Rufino and Leone. At the foot of the stairs in the back of the chapel the remains of "Brother Jacoba" rest in a small urn. A votive candle hanging in front of the tomb of Saint Francis was a gift of the communes of Italy. It burns night and day. Each year, a different commune offers a supply of oil on the Feast of Saint Francis to ensure the candle always remains lit, as a symbol of Italy's love for the saint.

After prayer at the tomb of Francis, it is time to ascend to the majestically adorned upper church. As you pass through the lower church, observe the darkness created by the low ceiling, thick walls and small windows. Even the vivid frescoes can't dislodge the dimness that envelops the nave. The darkness of the lower church suggests to me our struggle to move toward illumination. We pass through the purgatorial gloom of the lower church and ascend into the heavenly brilliance of the upper church. This movement from darkness into light is the reason I prefer beginning a tour of the basilica in the lower church. Also, the lower church is a place to meditate on the life of Saint Francis, while the upper church is suited to celebrating the life of the saint.

The Upper Church

The upper church is a visual symphony of color and shapes where the Franciscan motto of "poverty and joy" are perfectly reflected. The poverty resides in the simplicity of the architecture, devoid of all flowering embellishments. The joy exudes from the vivid frescoes adorning the flat walls. While the lower church is cramped and womb-like, the upper church is luxurious in the freedom of space beneath the high cross vaults. The structural lines create a joyful upsurge, forcing attention heavenward toward the majestic ceiling. The paintings on the ceiling sum up all the stories and spirituality expressed by the art on the side walls. The message is simple and clear: Christ is everything, the beginning and the end, and Francis' life was dedicated to imitating his Savior.

The nave is divided into four bays covered by quadripartite cross vaults, which are each supported by clusters of three piers. Large, lance-shaped, stained-glass windows in the center of each bay allow bands of colored light to flood into the cavernous space, designed to resemble a covered piazza without the hindrance of lateral aisles. The upper basilica is an extremely tall and large Gothic church; in fact, it was the first large Gothic church in Italy. The transept is crowned with a polygonal apse. In the middle of the apse there is a large marble throne for use by the pope—a subtle reminder that the church was originally conceived as a papal chapel. The facade features a magnificent rose window, which also splashes joyful light onto the walls and floor. More light floods in through two large windows on either end of the transept, plus the enormous stained-glass windows along the back wall of the apse.

For more than twenty-five years after the construction was completed, the walls of both the lower and upper churches remained undecorated. By the time the painters finished with the upper church, virtually every inch of it was covered in frescoes, including the ribs of the vaults and the clustered piers of the walls. An ocean of ink has been used to describe the decoration of the upper church. Painted over a long period of time, some of the art reflects the power struggle within the Order between the Conventuals and the Spirituals, even though neither group had the final word, because the church was under the jurisdiction of the Holy See. Cimabue was given the task of decorating the transept by Pope Nicholas III, sometime between 1277 and 1280, although it is not certain when the work was actually done.

The art which graces the walls of the upper church had an important function that went far beyond merely being decorative. Eschewing words, the art told stories through images. Many of the peasants and pilgrims who visited the church were illiterate, and so the art visually told them two important stories: the story of Francis and the story of faith. All of the art is interconnected, and together tells an organic and unified story of salvation. For instance, throughout the whole church the vaults follow a homogeneous design, in which areas covered by a starry blue patch alternate with areas with images of Doctors of the Church in one vault (in the first bay, painted by Giotto and his school), the saints in another (the third bay, painted by Jacopo Torriti, commissioned by Pope Nicholas IV, the first Franciscan pope), and the evangelists in a third (the cross vault, painted by Cimabue and his school). Each of the three triangular figural vaults are framed by wide decorative borders. The key to the story is found in the third cross vault, in which Saint Francis is depicted as an intermediary between God and humanity.

The unified story presented, painted over many years by a variety of artists, is divided into four themes. The story begins on the walls of the presbytery. The right transept displays the stories of the apostles. The frescoes in the left transept depict the Apocalypse. In the choir, scenes from the life of the Virgin Mary are arrayed. And high in the central vault, the evangelists are introduced. In the upper parts of the side walls in the nave, facing one another, are stories from the Old and New Testaments, which symbolize God the Father's breaking into human history and God the Son's redeeming it. (Flanking the stained-glass window in each bay are four biblical scenes. Sadly, many of these scenes in the upper parts of the nave have been partially erased by the hands of time.) The lower parts of the wall tell the story of Saint Francis' life and his ascent to God. The life cycle of Francis is a visual interpretation of Saint Bonaventure's masterpiece, *Itinerarium Mentis in Deum—The Soul's Journey Into God.* The stigmata proved that Francis reached the highest level of a mystical journey toward God, and his life reminds us of our need to more closely imitate the life of Christ. Like chapters in a book, each window bay in the nave presents theologically significant episodes from the lives of Christ and Francis which progressively unfold the story of salvation.

The frescoes on the upper walls of the right (north) transept have suffered badly over the course of time, and many parts of them are missing. Likewise, Cimabue's masterpieces in the left (south) transept, as well as those on the lower part of the walls in the right transept, are in a very poor state of preservation due to the oxidation of the white lead. The pigment has turned black and caused an over-all darkening of the paint, creating an effect which looks somewhat like a photographic negative.

The Life Cycle of St. Francis

My focus here will be on the revolutionary *Life Cycle of St. Francis* painted by Giotto and his workshop. These twenty-eight frescoes have survived the centuries in relatively good condition. The frescoes are divided into eight window bays, six containing three scenes and two containing four scenes, and one bay on the facade wall surrounding the main entrance comprised of two scenes, one on either side of the doors. All the frescoes are 2.7 by 2.3 meters in size, except for the two frescoes on either side of the entrance, which are slightly smaller, measuring 2.7 by 2.0 meters each.

First Bay: We begin our pictorial journey through Francis' life with three scenes showing the conversion of the saint from seeking honor and pleasure to seeking God. On the right (north) wall of the nave, close to the altar, the first fresco is *Francis Receiving the Homage of a Simple Man*. Here, Francis, not yet twenty-four years old, is seen wearing the refined clothes of a wealthy man. In front of the Temple Minerva he encounters a poor man, who somehow recognizes the future greatness within the young Francis, and spreads his cloak out on the ground, covering a puddle of water, in front of Francis. During Francis' time, part of the Temple Minerva was used as a prison. The choice of setting is perhaps meant to suggest that Francis was still imprisoned by his own selfishness. While it is clear that the building is the Temple Minerva, the artist added something to the building which did not in fact exist: a rose window on the pediment, symbolizing the eye of God watching over Francis.

The second fresco is *The Gift of the Cloak*. After his release from prison in Perugia, Francis was riding through the countryside when he encountered a brave but fallen and destitute knight who was very poorly dressed. In an act of chivalry, Francis exchanged his fine cloak for the old one worn by the knight. Symbolically, Francis was taking off the "old man" of his former self, and putting on a "new man" in Christ. The setting is in front of two rocky hills. Atop the peak of one hill are city buildings, representing the world of commerce. Atop the other peak rests a monastery, representing the spiritual world. The descending slopes of each hill converge behind the saint, drawing our attention to him. This fresco holds the first indication that Francis, standing between the worlds of commerce and prayer, will decide to lead a life of secluded poverty and preaching in the city squares. I love this fresco. I like the docility of the horse and the youthful goodness that can be seen in Francis' face, highlighted by his innocent eyes.

The third fresco is the *Vision of a Palace*. As another crusade is being mounted, Francis the soldier succumbs to the allure of military glory and honor. Francis is shown reclining in sleep, as Christ appears to him, showing Francis a palace filled with military arms. While Giotto is wonderful in capturing moments of action, he seems to have trouble portraying people lying down, and this is one of the least successful frescoes. In the foreground on the left is the room where Francis lies, with Christ standing next to him, his right hand and supple fingers pointing to a symbolic palace on the right side of the painting, on a slightly retreating plane.

The unified story this bay tells presents a prediction of future sanctity, Francis' generosity and a reward.

Second Bay: The three frescoes in this bay show Francis growing in trust and commitment. In the first fresco (#4), *St. Francis and the Crucifix in San Damiano*, Francis is in the silence and darkness of a half-ruined church, kneeling before the painted crucifix, his arms raised more in fright than praise. Francis' reaction offers us a more poignant understanding of the episode. The saint's hands appear to be almost shaking as he undergoes his first mystical experience. Giotto effectively uses gaze and gesture to illustrate Francis' surprise and concern over what was happening. Unfortunately, this fresco has faded over the years, and small sections of it have actually peeled away, which, oddly enough, enhances the texture of the dilapidated church.

The second fresco (#5) in this bay is *Renunciation of Worldly Goods*. In this famous scene, Francis' father appears before the bishop and accuses his son of stealing and squandering his fortune. Pink houses on either side of the picture remind us that we are outside the bishop's palace in the piazza S. Maria Maggiore. Francis dramatically responds to the charge by removing his clothes and returning them to his father. The father is furious, as he watches his son looking up to his Father in heaven. Pietro is being restrained from throwing a punch by a citizen whose ermine-lined cloak and tippet tell us he is a man of some distinction. Standing behind the father are two small children clutching their garments, which contain rocks they intend to throw at Francis. The disconcerted bishop covers Francis' naked body with his cloak. The public repudiation of his father is a decisive step in the saint's life. Giotto illustrates the sensational public split by aligning two groups of people on opposite sides. The buildings further reinforce the gulf between Francis and his father, and between the Church and the world. The confrontation between the bourgeois world in which Francis was raised and the spiritual world he is about to enter is clear. The focus of the picture is Francis' concentrated gaze at the hand of God, poking out of the clouds, imparting a blessing on the future saint.

In *The Dream of Innocent III*, the third fresco (#6), we see the pope during a dream vision. Innocent III was a powerful man, renowned for his political mind and his mystical spirituality. In his dream we see the seat of his power, the Church of St. John Lateran, crumbling to the ground due to the corruption of leadership with the Church. All that is protecting it from complete collapse is a poor man dressed in rags who is holding it up. The next day after this vision, the pope recognizes Francis as the beggar in his dream and confirms Francis' rule of life for his new brotherhood. Francis wants to heal the Church, to rebuild it, rather than attack it and tear it down. For the first time, Francis is shown wearing a habit.

Third Bay: The first fresco (#7) is the *Approval of the Franciscan Rule*. This wonderful fresco illustrating Pope Innocent III confirming the rule of the new community of brothers is set in the first perfectly unified internal space ever seen in Italian painting. In a magnificent interior, constructed in perspective, the pope blesses Francis, who is holding a parchment on which the rule is written. Francis' companions and leaders of the Church follow the action with expressions of concentration, clearly demonstrating the consequences and importance of what is taking place. Each observer vividly reacts in a different manner, from quiet contemplation to rapt attention to skeptical deferment, as Giotto brilliantly displays his keen understanding of human nature. It is interesting to note the placement of the figures, which are graded in depth one behind the other rather than being placed side by side. As Francis humbly kneels at the feet of the sovereign ruler, you can sense the saint's love and faith, and his knowledge of the righteousness of his mission.

In the second fresco (#8), the *Vision of the Fiery Chariot*, we see several brothers sleeping in a cramped shelter at Rivotorto and others standing outside the building. Those standing gesticulate excitedly at the curious manifestations in the heavens, while Francis, surrounded by a mandorla of golden rays, rides in a Roman chariot through the skies. The scene demonstrates that Francis is a new leader, not only of his companions, but also of the Church. Giotto distinguishes the spheres of heaven and earth clearly through the use of color. The meaning of this episode is that the friars were to follow Francis' leadership, just as the Israelites had followed the guidance of Elijah. It is difficult to see the saint's face because that part of the fresco has faded.

The third fresco (#9) is the *Vision of the Thrones*. A friar, Brother Pacifico, was praying fervently in an empty church when he fell into a state of ecstasy during which he had a vision of many thrones in heaven. One throne was larger than the rest and was brightly adorned with precious stones, causing the brother to wonder for whom it was reserved. A voice informed him that the chair was once the throne of a fallen angel, but it is now reserved for the humble Francis. Francis is seen in the scene devoutly praying on the steps of an altar. Nothing can exceed the grace in which Giotto depicts the wide-winged angel floating down to earth to acknowledge the humility of Francis; the angel's garments appear to be slightly spread by his movement through the air.

Fourth Bay: This bay at the rear of the church is the first of the two bays containing four frescoes. The first fresco (#10), the *Driving Out the Demons From Arezzo*, is very interesting and complex. During a civil war in Arezzo, Saint Francis saw demons over the city and asked Brother Sylvester, a priest, to pray and drive them out. The scene of the fresco is dominated by the architecture of the walled city on one side, divided from the rest of the world by a deep fissure in the earth, and, on the other side, by a towering church building. Francis is portrayed kneeling in intense prayer in front of the church. His prayers seem to animate Sylvester, who raises his hands skyward as he commands the demons to flee. The scene captures the fleeing demons and the citizens returning in peace. Francis had been summoned to Arezzo to intercede between rich and poor Christians who had been feuding, and is portrayed as a mediator between God and humanity, as his prayers were able to cast out the evil from the hearts of the people.

The second fresco here (#11) is *St. Francis Before the Sultan*. In order to convert the sultan, Francis is willing to walk through a fire. Here the saint stands at the center of the picture, in the midst of the royal architecture, surrounded by Islamic holy men and aides to the sultan, who is seated on his ornate throne. Giotto creates a humble Francis who nonetheless holds the secret power of faith which so impresses the sultan. As Francis points to the fire, he turns to the sultan, who appears surprised at Francis' proposal of a test of faith and annoyed at his priests who are fleeing the challenge. Giotto vividly depicts the anxious priests and the suddenly powerless sultan. While Francis is, of course, the central figure, Giotto subtly draws our attention to the sultan, portrayed not as an ignorant heathen, but as a noble, dignified leader.

The third fresco (#12), *Francis in Ecstasy*, depicts a scene from a story not in the writings of Bonaventure or Celano. It comes from an oral tradition which told how one day while Francis was in divine communion with God, he became rapt in ecstasy and his companions saw him rise up off the ground in a cloud. The friars on the ground appear human and real in their astonishment, but Francis in the cloud is less convincing. It is thought that the composition of the scene, as well as the architectural form on the left, were done by Giotto, but the execution of much of the painting was done by his assistants.

The fourth fresco (#13) is *The Crib at Greccio*. The thrill of the Christmas celebration in which Francis dramatically arranged a Nativity scene is fully felt in this stunning fresco. Giotto employed his artistic license by setting this scene inside a church. Francis is shown wearing deacon's robes. As the solemnities of the Mass are celebrated beside the manger, Francis lovingly holds the Christ child in his arms.

Fifth Bay: *The Miracle of the Spring* (#14), the first fresco here, is located on the back wall, to the left of the main door. La Verna is the setting for this scene, and the mountain itself becomes the protagonist of the story. The farmer who lent the brothers his mule to carry Francis up the mountain had become desperately thirsty. Francis, having gotten off the mule, kneels in fervent prayer on the arid mountainside, surrounded by stunted trees. In response to the prayer, water bubbles up from the rocks. The farmer kneels on the ground, greedily gulping up the water. Two brothers stand near the mule, offering silent commentary on the action with an eloquent exchange of glances. The rising sweep of the rocky mountain enhances the saint's petition to heaven for water.

The second fresco (#15), the *Sermon to the Birds*, also located on the entrance wall to the right of the door as you leave the church, is my favorite fresco, and the most poetic painting in the entire cycle. In this beautiful nature scene, Francis stands between two trees gently preaching to a flock of wild birds. His left hand extends downward toward the birds surrounding him on the ground. His right hand is slightly raised as he blesses the birds. Standing behind Francis is a friar, whom Giotto uses to demonstrate the extraordinary nature of the event. The brother's expression and body language clearly show his astonishment at the birds' response to Francis. Sadly, the upper layer of paint has faded over the centuries, and some of the birds are partly effaced. The delicacy and dignity of this fresco suggest Giotto believed the story of Francis' preaching to the birds to be true.

Sixth Bay: This is the second bay containing four frescoes and is on the rear wall opposite the fourth bay. The first fresco (#16), *Death of the Knight of Celano*, on the side wall adjacent to the sixth bay, requires a bit of background to set the context. Francis had been invited to dine at a knight's home. Before the meal, Francis led those assembled in prayer. After the prayer, he took the knight aside and told him that he would soon be partaking of a heavenly banquet and that he had better prepare himself by going to confession with a truly repentant heart. The knight heeded the saint's advice and immediately prepared himself for death. As the household and the guests sat down at the table for dinner, the knight collapsed and died. All of Giotto's dramatic story-telling ability, unique at the time, shines forth in this amazing fresco. Giotto's brush gently touches upon human sorrow with simplicity, truth and restraint. He does not employ exaggerated gestures of grief or feigned expressions of surprise at the sudden death of the knight. The fresco contains not a single false note. The movement of the sorrowful people, gazing down on the dead knight, some weeping, vividly conveys the awful grief gripping their hearts. The suddenness of the knight's death is captured by a friar still seated at the table, holding his fork. Saint Francis has just risen to go to the knight's side. A man turns to Francis, and from the gesture of his hand, seems ready to say that the prophecy came too quickly.

Next is *Francis Preaching Before Pope Honorius III* (#17), the second fresco in this bay. The plan was simple: Francis would deliver a well-planned sermon to the pope. But, as he approached the pontiff, the memorized words flew out of his mind. Francis had no other choice but to improvise, speaking directly from his heart, relying completely on the inspiration of the Spirit. The eloquence of the sermon captivated everyone, convincing them Francis truly was a man of God. The Gothic hall in which the scene is set emphasizes the dignity and majesty of the pope. Each of the figures listening to Francis' inspired words reacts with lively facial expressions. The stern and earnest pope, deep in thought, is leaning his chin on his hand, perhaps perplexed by the dusty, poorly clad man before him. A cardinal in orange-tinted robes seems absorbed by the saint's words, while another man gazes critically at the saint, perhaps annoyed at Francis' suggestion that the leaders of the Church have grown far too comfortable. This fresco has suffered from heavy restoration.

In the third fresco (#18), *The Apparition at Arles*, Saint Anthony of Padua preaches to a number of brothers meeting in a cloister at Arles, in the south of France. As Saint Anthony speaks of Christ, Francis appears, arms outstretched, suggesting his Christlike life. Only Anthony and one of the brothers notices the apparition. All the others are listening with full attention to Anthony. It is believed that Giotto conceived this fresco but painted only the figure of Saint Anthony.

In *The Stigmata* (#19), the fourth fresco, high atop an isolated peak of Mount La Verna, Francis is shown on his knees before a vision of Christ wrapped in an angel's wings hovering in the sky. Fine golden rays lead from the wounds of Christ to Francis' feet, hands and side, marking on his body the wounds of the Savior.

Seventh Bay: The nine frescoes in the last three bays show Francis' death and the miracles that followed it. These frescoes, believed to have been created several years after the others, are less well-known and in worse condition than the others.

In the first of these, *The Death of St. Francis* (#20), Francis is shown on his deathbed, surrounded by a number of his brothers, who are profoundly sad over the impending death of their founder. The scene, surrounded by a number of priests and people of Assisi, suggests the solemnity of a requiem Mass, as the saint's soul ascends to heaven, escorted by a chorus of angels. This fresco is located beneath the fresco in the upper portions of the wall, depicting the Crucifixion of Christ, thereby connecting, through their proximity,

Francis' complete conformity to the life of Christ.

The second fresco (#21) is the *Apparition to Brother Agostino and Bishop Guido*. Agostino was the minister at Lavoro, and was known for his holiness. During a prolonged illness, he had lost his ability to speak. As he approached his death, he had a vision of Saint Francis, during which he cried out, "Wait for me, Father, wait for me; I am coming with you...." On the same night Francis appeared to Augustino, he also appeared to the Bishop of Assisi, who was on a pilgrimage to the Church of St. Michael, on Mount Gargano. In the vision, Francis told his friend the bishop that he had left earth and had gone to heaven. Saint Francis does not appear in the fresco, and without knowing the story from Saint Bonaventure, it would be impossible to understand the reaction of the bishop.

The *Verification of the Stigmata* (#22) is the third fresco. After Francis' death, his body was displayed so that the people of Assisi could see it and kiss the sacred stigmata. Among those who came to honor the saint was Jerome, a soldier who doubted the miracle of the stigmata. In an episode reminiscent of the apostle Thomas who doubted the appearance of the resurrected Jesus, the soldier touched the wounds on Francis' body and his doubts vanished. This fresco is badly damaged, making it difficult to enjoy it as a whole, while some of the figures of the young acolytes holding lighted torches, and the priests reading prayers and sprinkling the body with holy water, are very lifelike. This fresco is artistically interesting, because all the characters are portrayed in profile. Even more daring, one figure has his back to the viewer, an idea that would have been unthinkable in the more formal Byzantine tradition.

Eighth Bay: The first fresco (#23), the *Mourning of the Poor Clares*, is, to me, the loveliest of the last nine frescoes, though the tragic dimension of Clare and her sisters' final farewell to Francis is somewhat restrained. The fresco radiates with graceful charm as the sisters hurry out of San Damiano, whose humble facade of stone has been transformed by the artist into marble and mosaic, and richly decorated with niches and an eagle atop the gable. Saint Clare, a halo surrounding her veiled head, bends over to kiss the saint goodbye as the citizens and priests of Assisi sing hymns of praise. In a delightful touch, a child climbs a tree and tears down a branch, presumably to place on the road in front of the passing bier.

Next is the *Canonization of St. Francis* (#24) depicting Pope Gregory IX's visit to Assisi in order to canonize Francis. The fresco is badly damaged, rendering it impossible to judge or appreciate its composition.

The third fresco (#25) is the *Dream of Gregory IX*. One night while staying in Perugia, the pope was visited by Francis during a dream. Francis knew the pope had reservations about the authenticity of the stigmata, and so he pulled back his tunic and showed the pope the wound in his side. In the dream, the pope handed Francis a cup, which Francis filled with blood streaming from his wound. It is known that Giotto did not have a hand in the execution of this fresco.

Ninth Bay: The first fresco (#26) is *The Healing of the Man at Lerida*. The man at Lerida was devoted to Saint Francis. One day he was ambushed by some thugs who nearly beat him to death, stabbing him numerous times. As he lay alone, mortally wounded, the man repeatedly called out Francis' name, imploring the saint to help him. Because of his trust, he was miraculously healed.

The *Confession of the Woman of Benevento* (#27) depicts another miraculous event. A woman who had a special devotion to Saint Francis had died. As her corpse was surrounded by priests keeping the accustomed vigil and offering prayers, the dead woman suddenly stood up. As the astonished priests listened, she told them that following her death her spirit was sent to a dreadful dungeon because of her failure to confess a certain sin. But Saint Francis prayed that she would be allowed to return to life in order to have the chance to confess. After confessing the sin to a trembling priest, the woman was given absolution and quietly lay down on the bier and fell peacefully asleep in the Lord. The fresco tenderly captures the sadness and solemnity of the scene. In the upper left corner of the fresco, in the sky above the building, Francis is seen kneeling before Christ, interceding on behalf of the woman.

The third fresco in this bay (#28), and the last in the series, is the *Liberation of Pietro the Heretic*. A heretic who had been bound in chains and imprisoned by order of Pope Gregory IX prayed fervently to Francis, imploring the saint to help him gain his release. On the vigil of the feast of Saint Francis, the saint made a twilight visit to the prison cell and told the heretic to get up. As the man stood, the chains that bound him fell off and the doors of the cell were unlocked without any human aid. As the man emerges from his cell, the Bishop of Tivoli, who was given charge of the prisoner, falls to his knees and Saint Francis is seen ascending back to heaven.

In Giotto's Hands

In Giotto's hands, humanity becomes eternal. Giotto overcame convention and bequeathed to us dynamic, living, breathing imagery. He strips away the formal sacerdotal detachment of the Byzantines and gives biblical scenes the appearance of an event happening right before our eyes. He gives us real people, people we know, showing us their hopes and anxieties. He gives us a flesh-and-blood, human Saint Francis, who is both profound and poetic. Francis, in Giotto's hands, is not a remote transcendental soul steeped in unfathomable mysticism, but a fully human being who experiences the full sweep of emotions from joy to despair. The peasants, in Giotto's hands, are rough-and-tumble; the women are graceful. And he garbs them in familiar garments; moreover, he places them in the everyday settings of a town or the countryside. Giotto's paintings seemed to live in the present moment. His subjects are full of life and seem to be in motion...and filled with emotion. They gesture and they have passion. And in his paintings, we see grass and trees and birds, common things, everyday things. In the naturalistic climate Giotto created, he found a balance between the abstract ideal and essence of divinity, and the concrete reality of humanity.

In the Old Testament stories of Isaac painted on the upper walls of the second bay, Giotto introduced, for the first time, a natural, three-dimensional presence of individual objects, people and settings on the flat surface of a wall. Giotto's art surpasses the limits of time and space. Every practical necessity disappears in order to create a new transcendent reality in which the ideal and the real are mutually complementary. The simplicity of his composition, combined with the economy of means used in its execution, created a grandiose effect. Every element of the composition reinforces the main event being depicted. Architecture and landscape forms are small in relationship to the figures, who, in turn, are monumentalized, made bigger than life. The perspective is psychological rather than linear. Secondary figures buttress the main figures by means of a glance, pose or gesture. He introduced a touch of elegance to his scenes by merely including charming pieces of architecture.

A great artist like Giotto did not merely reproduce nature; instead, he used his imagination to express the deepest sensations his subject had upon him. Giotto did not paint the surface of things; rather, he used the surface appearance as a tool to expose the undercurrent of life. He did not merely illustrate an event (any good craftsman could do that), he plumbed the depths of his intense humanity and artfully interpreted the event. Francis entered fully into the poverty, nakedness, humiliation and abandonment of the Lord, and Giotto takes us with the saint on his journey to God in a way we can understand. Giotto's vision was not hampered by tradition or rules of painting. His guiding force was his own personal integrity as an artist. Giotto strikes the imagination, as he sings a sublime hymn to the Christian faith. And it is a colorful tune.

In the Basilica of St. Francis, I learned a lot about art and spirituality. The greatest lesson I learned is that advancement in either discipline takes time, dedication and persistence. Sadly, that troika is lacking in many modern lives...at least it was for most of my life.

PILGRIMAGE DIARY 65

The Actual Sun and Moon Over Assisi

One thing I grasped very soon after my conversion to the Gospel. It was the power of signs. I had joyfully realized that everything around me was a sign of God, his token, and I could no longer look at anything without thinking of him, my most High and good Lord.

—CARLO CARRETTO, I, FRANCIS

Near the end of cena (supper) on Wednesday, July 9th, word spread through the dining room at Casa Papa Giovanni that there would be a free concert featuring the Boys Choir of Westminster Under School that evening at 9 p.m. at the Basilica di San Francesco. Two nights earlier, I had attended a beautiful concert given by another English choir—The Uppingham Choir—at the Chiesa di Santa Maria Maggiore, and so my first inclination was to pass on this second concert. Then I heard one of the team members mention that concerts in the Basilica of St. Francis were special treats because they are the only times all the lights in the upper church are turned on, fully illuminating, with great effect, the church and Giotto's frescoes. I instantly changed my mind and shortly after dinner I began a slow walk to the basilica.

As I walked, my mind drifted to thoughts of the crucifix of San Damiano. Just before dinner we had watched a half-hour slide presentation on the crucifix in preparation for the next morning's *liturgy, which would be celebrated in the small chapel in the Basilica of Santa Chiara where the crucifix now hangs. After the liturgy we would be going to the tiny church of San Damiano, where long ago Francis heard a voice from the crucifix tell him to repair the church.*

I wished I could hear a voice, get some clear direction from God. The direction I was wishing for as I walked pertained to this book. For a few days prior to that night, my mind began entertaining doubts about this book. The more I learned during this pilgrimage about the depths of Franciscan spirituality—as well as the Christian faith—the more inadequate I felt to the task of presenting another look at the lives of Francis and Clare. The more I learned, the more I realized how much I didn't know, and consequently how much more work still needed to be done to complete it.

Why me? Why should I be writing a book on Saint Francis? I'm surrounded by people who know him—and Clare—better and love them more. That very afternoon I spent a few hours in the library of the Conventual convento where I'm staying because there wasn't enough room at the pensione. So many books. Well-written books. What could I possibly add? "Not much," was my feeling as I walked to the basilica. All I had was my burning passion, my unbridled enthusiasm. Was that enough? I wasn't sure. Should I stop now, abandon the project? I didn't know. If I did abandon it, would I have wasted the last two years? So many questions. So few answers.

Was Francis plagued by questions? Did Clare have any second thoughts as she approached the gates of the city on that Palm Sunday night when she turned her back on her family and her future and raced in the darkness toward Francis and the friars?

I wanted to hear a voice. But I didn't think I would.

I was just a few minutes from the basilica when something happened. Something unexpected. Something breathtaking. God spoke to me. Not in words or an audible fashion, but in a symbol...a symbol I could clearly understand.

Near the end of the long, narrow street leading to the basilica, the road curves and reveals a wide open vista. Before me was the grassy knoll in front of the basilica. The basilica was framed by a wide panoramic view of the valley below. To the right of the basilica, the sun was just minutes away from setting. The entire scene was bathed in a golden glow. Then, off to the left of the massive building, high in the sky, I saw the moon. Right there, framed before me, right

at that very moment, were

The Sun and Moon Over Assisi

My heart leaped...and danced in joy.

In a place I wouldn't have been had I not overheard something that caught my ear, I saw something that seemed meant for me.

A coincidence? I no longer believe in coincidences. Coincidences didn't bring me to Assisi.

A few minutes later, a Franciscan sister who is on the pilgrimage came around the corner. I excitedly ran up to her. "Look," I said, just seconds before the sun would slip behind the distant mountain, "the sun and moon...over Assisi!"

She smiled. Broadly. She knew the title of my book. I told her about my doubts, and how the sight of sun and moon had just excited me and filled me with confidence. I said, "Is it a sign from God? Or is that silly?"

"No, it's not silly," she said. "God is speaking to you."

As I sat in my room a few hours later, I realized God didn't speak to me the way God spoke to Francis. God spoke to me the way I could best hear the Voice. God speaks in unexpected ways, in unexpected moments. Each moment of our lives is pregnant with possibilities for the connection with the divine. Each moment holds the potential to dramatically alter every subsequent moment. Saint Catherine of Genoa said it best: "We must not wish for anything other than what happens from moment to moment."

A few days later, I came across this quotation from Saint Irenaeus (c.125-c.203): "With God nothing is empty of meaning, nothing without symbolism."

Even a sunset.

BASILICA DI SANTA CHIARA

In comparison to the beauty of the Basilica of St. Francis, the basilica built to honor Saint Clare can't hold a candle, even though it is a smaller replica of the upper church of San Francesco. However, what the Basilica di Santa Chiara lacks in aesthetics, it more than makes up for in spirit and grace. The interior of the basilica has a humble feel. The fine frescoes painted by followers of Giotto have suffered badly from the effects of time and temperature, and only fragments of them remain. Yet, I found the faded, partial works of art to be mysteriously beautiful and intriguing.

The basilica is just a short walk from the Piazza del Comune by way of Corso Mazzini, a charming street dotted with bakeries, ice-cream shops, first-class restaurants, art galleries and upscale souvenir shops. At the end of the street, just before the large piazza in front the basilica, there is an international newspaper stand that sells porno magazines and postcards of the basilica.

Construction began in 1257, and the basilica was consecrated in 1265. It was built on the site of the ancient church of San Giorgio. As a young man, Francis learned to read in the Church of San Giorgio, and, after his conversion, he preached his first sermon there. After his death, his body rested in the church from 1226 to 1230 awaiting the completion of his final resting place, the Basilica di San Francesco. San Giorgio was also the site of Francis' canonization by Pope Gregory IX in 1228. The southern wall of the old church remains and forms the side wall of the Cappella di San Giorgio, which has been divided into two smaller chapels that are on the right side of the basilica.

And it was those two chapels that captivated me. The larger of the two is the Oratorio del Crocifisso, which contains the famous Crucifix of San Damiano that spoke to St. Francis in 1206, commanding him to "rebuild my church." I knelt before the cross and prayed the prayer Francis prayed:

> Most high,
> glorious God,
> enlighten the darkness of my heart
> and give me, Lord,
> a correct faith,
> a firm hope,
> a perfect charity,
> with wisdom and perception,
> so that I may do
> what is truly your most holy will.

What a beautiful—and perhaps perfect—prayer. I wished the crucifix would talk to me. The crucifix remained silent.

At the far end of the Oratorio is an iron gate, behind which a number of precious relics are on display, including a breviary used by Saint Francis, and a deacon's alb embroidered by Saint Clare. A glass partition separates the Oratorio from the Cappella del

Santissimo Sacramento, or Chapel of the Blessed Sacrament. The wall behind the altar of this smaller chapel contains fragments of frescoes painted in the thirteenth and fourteenth centuries. A curtain behind the altar conceals a choir room where the Poor Clares assemble so they may participate in liturgies offered in the chapel. If you are lucky, you may be seated in the chapel during the times of the day when the nuns gather in the room behind the curtain to chant the Liturgy of the Hours. The sound of heavenly voices gently fills the chapel.

The Chapel of the Blessed Sacrament is one of my favorite places in Assisi to just sit and be still. One night I was sitting in the darkened chapel. It was about 6:30, and the only light came from two candles burning on the altar. The nuns began chanting the Hours in Latin, accompanied by a solo organ. I prayed the rosary as I listened. As I gazed at the fragment of one of the frescoes, I suddenly recalled my first visit to this chapel, back in March of 1995, shortly after the rebirth of my faith. The fresco featured the upper torso and heads of three figures. Time had erased their bodies from just below their shoulders. As I stared at the fresco fragment, the words "mostly heads" came into my mind. The words meant nothing to me. Then a question popped into my mind: What's missing? Instantly, I knew the novel I was writing came mostly from my head. As I took a deep breath, I was filled with the conviction that the book would die unless I began to write from the heart.

The Chapel of the Blessed Sacrament serves as a reminder of Clare's love of the Eucharist. Clare's heart and mind were always focused on Christ. The inner love she had for the Lord drew her often to a physical encounter with the Real Presence of Christ through devotion to and reception of the Blessed Sacrament. In her time, devotion to the Exposition of the Eucharist was becoming increasingly popular among the faithful. This led to Pope Urban IV's creating the Feast of Corpus Christi in 1264. Clare's day included frequent visits to the Blessed Sacrament. Also, in that time, frequent reception of the Eucharist was beginning to be promoted by the Church. And Clare, according to testimony of the sisters during the process of canonization, often received Holy Communion. It was said that she approached the altar with awe.

The depth of Clare's devotion to the Eucharist was clearly revealed when Muslim soldiers invaded Assisi in 1240. When the Saracens approached San Damiano, the sisters were terrified. Clare calmly had the chaplain bring out a small ivory-bound silver box containing the Sacrament of the Body of Christ to the door and prayed that Christ would guard and protect his humble servants. Clare heard a sweet voice promising protection for the convent and sisters. Clare then immediately thought of the people of Assisi, and prayed, "Lord, be pleased also to defend this city."

The nave of the Gothic-styled basilica is divided into four bays and covered with a cross vault. The floor plan is similar to the upper church of the Basilica of St. Francis. The frescoes which once decorated the side walls were covered with plaster in the seventeenth century, and suffered severe damage during the disastrous earthquake of 1832. The nave frescoes are completely lost, except for the votive paintings on the left wall featuring the Madonna of Mercy and the Holy Face, painted in 1391 by Maestro dello Stendardo di San Leonardo. Now, lights shining through the stained-glass windows dance on the barren walls. Mercifully, the frescoes adorning the transept have survived. They depict stories from the Old Testament and from the life of Christ, as well as episodes from the life of Saint Clare. It is believed that these frescoes, which display the great expressive abilities of the painter, were painted by a student of Giotto's in the early fourteenth century. Hanging above the main altar is a large Byzantine icon of the crucified Christ; Francis and Clare are kissing the Lord's feet.

Above the altar in the right transept is a magnificent wooden icon featuring scenes from the life of Saint Clare. Clare stands gracefully in the center of the wooden panel. To her left are small depictions of her receiving the palm from Bishop Guido, being welcomed at the Portiuncula by Francis, having her hair cut by Francis and clinging to the altar resisting her father's attempt to take her home. To the right of Clare is a depiction of Agnes, Clare's sister, resisting her relatives' attempt to remove her from the convent, the miracle of the loaves in the presence of Pope Gregory IX, the Virgin Mary appearing to Clare on her deathbed and her funeral, celebrated by Pope Innocent IV in 1253. The icon was painted in 1283, just thirty years after the saint's death.

On the left side of the nave is the charming fourteenth-century Cappella di Sant' Agnese, the Chapel of St. Agnes, containing many fine works of art and featuring a pentagonal floor plan and a ribbed vault. A beautiful wrought-iron gate stretches across the entrance and relics of Saint Agnes are under the altar.

In the nave, just to the right of the entrance to Oratorio del Crocifisso, is a staircase leading to the crypt housing the tomb of

Saint Clare. After her death, Clare's body was buried within the Church of San Giorgio. In early October of 1260, the body was transferred to a burial vault under the newly completed basilica, authorized by Pope Alexander IV and built to honor her memory after her canonization in 1255. Her mortal remains were held under the altar for nearly six centuries. The body was removed and examined in September of 1850, and found to be intact. One hand lay across her breast, the other arm was at her side. Rather than return the body to the inaccessible vault, a crypt chapel was constructed, enabling pilgrims to view her remains. Once the body was placed in the crypt and on public display, it began to deteriorate. Her body was then encased in a ceramic mold. The mold, dressed in a habit, now rests in a glass coffin. Clare's head rests on an olive-wood pillow. In the center of the crypt, a spiral staircase leads to a platform where you can view the vault where the saint's body rested for centuries; the original sarcophagus is displayed in the vault.

Next to the church is the monumental Protomonastero (convent) di Santa Chiara, where the Poor Clares have resided for more than seven centuries. The oldest part of the convent is located to the right of the facade of the basilica. Between the fourteenth and sixteenth centuries, the Convento was expanded many times.

The piazza in front of the basilica is perhaps the most charming in all of Assisi. The low wall along the right side of the piazza offers a spectacular panoramic view of the valley below. It is a favorite spot to sit and watch the sunset. As you look out, the apse of the Chiesa di Santa Maria Maggiore graces the foreground to the right. The piazza also offers a great view of the Rocco, looming over the city, high atop a hill. In the center of the piazza is a delightful polygonal fountain that was constructed in 1872.

The facade of the basilica, with its rows of white and pink stone, casts a watching eye over the piazza. Atop the facade rests a large triangular tympanum with a circular window. Below that small window is a very large rose window with four concentric circles. The basilica's most notable exterior features are the three large flying buttresses along the left side of the church supporting the vault. They were added in 1351. The right side also has three flying buttresses, but they are hidden inside the oldest part of the convent. To the right of the basilica's apse rises a wonderful campanile (bell tower), the tallest in Assisi.

CATTEDRALE DI SAN RUFINO

The Cathedral of San Rufino, besides being rich in Franciscan history, is the Mother Church of the Diocese of Assisi. Construction on the cathedral began in 1140, slightly more than forty years before Francis was born. The church was built on the site of a Roman cistern, which can still be seen today. Incorporated into the design is a small oratory built in the fifth century to house the relics of Saint Rufino, a martyr drowned in the Chiascio River in 238.

At the time of Francis' birth, construction on the cathedral was far from completed; in fact, it wasn't fully complete until the middle of the thirteenth century. Nonetheless, it is possible that Francis was baptized in the church. It is certain, however, that the baptismal font in the church, originally in Santa Maria Maggiore, is the very one used for the baptism of both Francis and Clare. Emperor Frederick II, who was born in the nearby town of Jesi, was also baptized in the font. The house where Clare was born and raised was located off the piazza next to the cathedral, but sadly nothing remains of it. We know where it stood, because in 1148, Clare's grandfather signed a notarized document in which he promised not to enlarge his house so as not to distract from the harmony of the new cathedral.

When you enter the Piazza Santo Rufino, you are immediately captivated by its charm and grace. The first thing that catches your attention is the large, square, stone bell tower to the left of the church, towering over the cathedral and the plaza like a gentle yet strong giant. The Romanesque-style facade, with its three portals and three rose windows, richly decorated with carvings of animals and saints, is equally impressive.

For structural reasons, the interior of the church was radically redesigned in the early 1570's, and in the process lost its original Romanesque charm.

The nave is divided into five bays. The center nave has a barrel vault with large reinforcement arches, while the lateral bays have simple cross vaults. A polygonal dome floats over the presbytery. Along the side aisles, corresponding to the bays, there are ten altars. The walls behind the altars are adorned with paintings by noted artists. Jutting out from the right wall is the Cappella del Santissimo Sacramento (the Chapel of the Blessed Sacrament), which was built in 1663 and is the most perfect example of the highly ornate Baroque style in Assisi. This large chapel contains numerous exquisite paintings, as well as frescoes by Giorgetti, Carboni and Ciro Ferri. A wooden Pieta carved in Germany during the fifteenth century is haunting. The altar is made of polychrome marble and dates back to 1764. On either side of the altar are two Baroque angels in gilded wood. The chapel is a visual feast. Also along the right side of the church is the entrance to the cathedral museum, which contains priceless works of art.

It was in this church that Saint Clare heard Saint Francis preach for the first time. This is a perfect place to sit and reflect on the first time the life and spirituality of Saint Francis truly entered your heart, and how you have responded to it. The baptismal font where the two saints were baptized calls to mind the importance of that central moment in our Christian journey. Also, it was in this church that Saint Francis openly admitted his weaknesses, and it is a good place to think about ours.

One day Francis was preaching in the piazza in front of the church. After he completed his sermon, he asked the people not to leave until he returned. He went into the church, removed his tunic and had one of the brothers tie the cord from his habit around his neck and lead him naked back into the square. In front of everyone, he confessed to having eaten meat during a recent illness and saying that he was not as holy as they thought, and that he had failed in his efforts to renounce the world. After he had finished his public confession, he had another brother sprinkle ashes on the spot where he had delivered his sermon before this graphic display of humility. As the people stood in the cold morning air, they were touched by the humility of the holy man, and forced to confront their own failures to live a more pure spiritual life. This story can be found in Chapter 61 of *The Mirror of Perfection*, and in Chapter 39 of the *Legend of Perugia*.

This church has a special meaning for me because a true hero whom I had the good fortune of meeting and befriending, a priest named Don Aldo Brunacci, was also baptized in this church.

PILGRIMAGE DIARY 66

The Assisi Underground

*T*hese pages have already presented two horrific accounts of atrocities committed by Nazis during World War II. When I began work on this book, I never could have predicted it would contain one Nazi-related story, let alone two of them. And now this pilgrimage has brought me face-to-face with yet another Nazi story...as well as a real-life hero who played a pivotal role in the story. Thankfully, this third Nazi story features hope and mercy, not brutality and atrocities.

Coming up the road from Santa Maria Degli Angeli, as you approach the city wall of Assisi, you will see a memorial plaque honoring the memory of a German medical colonel, Dr. Valentin Mueller. The brass plaque was mounted on the wall by the citizens of Assisi. Il Colonnello, as Dr. Mueller was called by the people of Assisi, was the commander of Assisi from February 1944, through June 16, 1944, when the German army retreated from the area. Why would the citizens of Assisi honor their former Nazi occupier? Because he protected and saved the city from being bombed and also from being plundered by the retreating German forces. During the war, the citizens of Assisi liked to claim that they had three protectors shielding them, the city and its treasured churches from harm: God, Saint Francis and Colonnello Mueller.

Living in Assisi today, there is an eighty-three-year-old man who knows a lot about the city's three protectors. He is Don (Father) Aldo Brunacci, a priest and the Prior of Canons of the Cathedral of San Rufino. He is also an authentic hero, who risked his life by hiding Jews during the war.

On September 4, 1997, I caught an early morning train from Rome to Assisi, and later that afternoon I had the privilege of spending a few hours with Don Aldo, who graciously agreed to be interviewed, through an interpreter, so his story could be included in this book. But first, I'll set the stage by telling Colonel Mueller's story.

Valentin Mueller was a medical student when World War I began, and he was drafted into service. He served with distinction, risking his life in order to save some injured soldiers at the front line. His bravery earned him the Bavarian Silver medal.

At the beginning of World War II, Mueller was a surgeon living and working in Eichstatt. Due to problems he had with local Nazi authorities in Munich, Mueller was forced to move to Eichstatt, seventy-five miles north of Munich, in 1933. In 1937, he bought a house from a Jewish family, paying for it in cash, so the family would have the means to immediately flee Germany. In 1939, he again was pressed into military service. As a surgeon he was given the rank of captain and served in Poland, Russia and France. In 1943, he was sent to Italy. Later that year he heard about plans to establish a hospital in Assisi, and he managed to get himself appointed commander of the city. Arriving in Assisi in February of 1944, the energetic Dr. Mueller quickly established a hospital that treated more than two thousand sick and injured people. His hard work was rewarded with a promotion to the rank of colonel.

When Mueller arrived in Assisi, the Allied forces were occupying Anzio, just one hundred ten miles away. Assisi was in extreme danger of being destroyed because of its strategic position near airports at Perugia and Foligno. The city's cultural, historical and ecclesiastical importance was of no significance in the heat of battle. The magnificent Benedictine Abbey of Monte Casino had already been reduced to rubble by Allied bombs. The Allied forces wanted to declare Assisi a hospital city, thereby protecting it from any military harm, but the German army didn't go along with the proposed plan. Dr. Mueller knew that if Assisi had the status of a hospital city, no fighting forces, even the German army, could enter the city, according to the Geneva Convention of the Red Cross. Mueller's efforts to get German headquarters in Berlin to approve the plan met with reluctance because it would put the German army at a tactical disadvantage. But Mueller wouldn't take no for an answer. Without having the authority to do so, he ordered the German troops out of the city, locked the gates and placed guards around the walls to prevent withdrawing German soldiers from entering the city. His actions put Mueller at great risk, but eventually the German ambassador to the Vatican declared Assisi a hospital city.

Inside the gates, freed from the fear of German soldiers, the citizens had great respect for Mueller. And he loved them. He visited the friars. He visited the sick in their homes. He treated everyone with respect and always took time to listen to their problems. Everyone knew his phone number—210—and they didn't hesitate to call him if there was a problem. If a German soldier stole something from a citizen, Mueller would offer the person reparation. One day, two German soldiers, claiming there was an emergency, drove off with a taxi. The owner called Mueller, who set out on his motorcycle, found the soldiers in Perugia and ordered them to return the taxi. One night, drunken soldiers were harassing a woman and her two young children and Mueller intervened and escorted her home.

Il Colonnello treated, free of charge, the poor and the sick in the army hospital. He was on good terms with the bishop, Giuseppe Nicolini, and the mayor, Arnaldo Fortini (a biographer of Francis). As the German army withdrew, Mueller ordered that all medical equipment and supplies be left to the bishop for distribution.

Dr. Mueller returned to Assisi in 1950, as a private citizen, and he was given a hero's welcome. People placed flowers at his hotel entrance, which served as his headquarters when he was commander of the city. During his return visit, he was a guest of the Hotel Subasio. He visited homes, walked the streets and everywhere he went, people embraced him.

Mueller died soon afterward, on July 31, 1951. He was sixty years old. On July 31, 1990, Don Aldo Brunacci celebrated Eucharist in the chapel of his guest house, Casa Papa Giovanni, in memory of Il Colonnello. All the senior citizens of Assisi gathered to remember him.

Don Aldo told me that Dr. Mueller was a prayerful Catholic, and that he often prayed at the tomb of Saint Francis. He said the doctor was forced into military service and he, from the inside, did his best to subvert the Nazi atrocities he hated. The priest said the colonel was the last soldier to leave the city and the citizens escorted him to make sure he was unharmed during his departure. Don Aldo said Mueller was acutely aware of the danger that he could have been severely punished for aiding the enemy. He loved people, all people, including Jews. Mueller knew Jews were being hidden in monasteries and private homes...and he chose to ignore it.

Don Aldo said the real danger came from Italian Fascists who kept a tight surveillance on the town, photographing people they suspected of harboring Jews. Father Brunacci said that before Mueller arrived in the city more than three hundred Jews had sought refuge there. "They began arriving in September of 1943, after the German occupation. Many of them came from the north. I often asked them why they came to Assisi for refuge when the city had no record of Jewish citizens. Nearly always I received the same answer: they felt drawn to Assisi by Saint Francis, thinking and hoping he would protect them. They trusted Saint Francis." And they trusted Don Aldo. He once escorted a Jewish mother and her sick child to the tomb of

Saint Francis, where they prayed. He hid Jews in monasteries, in private homes and in the bishop's house. So many were hidden in Bishop Nicolini's residence that the bishop gave up his own room to make space for one more family to hide there.

Though many Italian refugees from bombed cities throughout Italy were being sheltered in Assisi, still the presence of three hundred Jews in such a small city was bound to be noticed. That was just one of the problems Don Aldo faced. First he had to get them false identification papers and teach them the cultural customs of the city so they could move about without being detected.

"We felt that our Jewish friends as well as their hosts had to be protected, and the most practical plan was to provide them with false identity cards and to pass them off as refugees from places already occupied by the Allies." Don Aldo told me he often had to bicycle to Perugia to have the papers printed, and also have official rubber stamps forged so they could authenticate the papers.

When Jewish refugees arrived in Assisi, they were initially led to the bishop's house, which functioned as the center of operations for the hiding of Jews. Don Aldo worked directly for Bishop Nicolini. While the documents were being prepared, the Jews needed to be carefully hidden. "Our chief center was the convent at San Quirico, where most of our Jewish friends stayed until we could get them new ration books and all the papers they would need to live unmolested. With the documents, many were able to live in a hotel." Don Aldo and his trusted friends would then teach the refugees "the geography of their new home. We primed them with every detail we could collect about local habits, personalities and even local gossip. The hard part was teaching them to speak with the right accent and intonation. But somehow, we did. The Lord was very kind to us." Don Aldo also said they took great care to hide the refugees' sacred books and personal papers in the basement of the bishop's home.

Some of the Jewish refugees endured great hardships just getting to Assisi. "One evening a father, mother and son arrived. They had escaped from a concentration camp in France. They crossed the Alps on foot! Thanks to the help they received from the curia in Genoa, they made it to Florence and then to Assisi."

One old Jewish woman from Vienna died while in hiding. "That was a difficult case, because we had to bury her without a Catholic funeral and yet not arouse suspicion. We managed to do it and

Madame Weiss now rests in the cemetery of Assisi under the name
Signora Bianchi." "Weiss" and "Bianchi" both mean "White" in their
respective languages.

The people of Assisi, under the guidance of the Bishop and Don
Aldo, also tried to provide the young Jewish boys and girls with some
basic education. "We didn't want them to be wasting their time."
They treated their guests with great dignity and tried to provide them
with the space to practice their faith. "In the quiet of the Assisi
convents, the Jews were naturally free to join together for their
devotions, and it often happened that while the nuns were praying,
close at hand, under the same roof, the Jews, too, were imploring the
Divine mercy and asking God for justice and peace. I remember
how, just after the Jews began to arrive in Assisi on October 8, 1943,
they were celebrating their Feast of Tabernacles in the Convent of
San Quirico, a quiet, hidden celebration of refugees. The sisters,
however, had the happy inspiration of decorating the refectory and
tables with flowers for a feast. When their guests sat down to the first
meal after a long, ritual fast and looked around, they no longer felt
like strangers and understood that in the bond of charity we are all
brothers and sisters."

Don Aldo said there were many moments of great anxiety as he
and his friends tried to "help those whom Providence sent us during
those hard years." One of those anxious moments filled Father
Brunacci's heart on May 15, 1944. He was ascending the stairs to his
apartment at Number 7 Via San Francesco when he was approached
from behind by German soldiers who wanted to question him.
Hiding in his apartment was a Jewish family. Don Aldo knew if he
entered the apartment for any of his personal effects or papers the
family would have been detected and arrested. Remaining calm, Don
Aldo simply walked back down the stairs, essentially giving himself
up rather than risk being interrogated in his apartment. Don Aldo
was arrested and taken to jail. The family was not detected. Shortly
before the Allies entered Rome and liberated Italy on June 4th, Don
Aldo escaped the jail and headed back to Assisi in order to help
more Jews. But his help was no longer needed. "In all, about three
hundred Jews had been entrusted to us by Divine Providence; with
God's help and through the intercession of Saint Francis, not one of
them fell into the hands of their persecutors."

Don Aldo told me that shortly after the war, he received a letter from the woman he prayed with at the tomb of Saint Francis...she wrote, "Our Lady and Saint Francis saved my son in Assisi."

In 1977, the State of Israel honored Don Aldo for helping to save Jewish refugees by presenting him with the "Medal of Righteous Gentile," a prestigious award given to a non-Jew who risked his or her life to save Jews. The medal bears a Talmudic inscription: "Whoever saves a single soul, it is as if he had saved the whole world." Don Aldo is also immortalized in the Holocaust Museum in Washington, D.C.

Don Aldo was born in Assisi in 1914, and has lived in Assisi all his life, except for his seminary years in Rome. As a young boy, he told me his hair was long, and one day his mother told him to "go to the barber shop, you look like Sabatier." That's Paul Sabatier, the famous biographer of Saint Francis. Don Aldo was too young to know Sabatier, but he did become friends with Johannes Jörgensen. He told me Jörgensen's conversion was very gradual, and his faith deepened as he, over the years, visited and spent time in all the hermitages where Francis spent time in prayer. He said Jörgensen was a great poet, but most of his literary friends in Norway broke their relationship with him when he became Catholic.

I ended the interview by asking Don Aldo how Assisi has changed over the years. The pained look on his face told me the answer before he spoke. "Assisi has changed a lot, especially in these last few years. Assisi had been a great call to deep souls. People came here searching for something deeper in life. Many found faith through Saint Francis. Today...too many tourists who seem to be only interested in shopping. And they come dressed for the beach. Very disturbing." His words trailed off as he shook his head. Then a smile began to cross his face. "Francis is still talking through the stones. I ask the young children, 'Did you meet Francis?' And then I tell them, 'If you listen, for sure you will meet him.'"

Don Aldo listened. Don Aldo met Francis.

"Francis," he said, "opened the Gospels—they had been closed in his day—and he preached it with his life."

As I stood to leave, he told me to wait a minute, and he disappeared into his office. A few minutes later, he came out and gave me a large photograph of Johannes Jörgensen, saying, "Keep writing. Keep praying."

BASILICA DI SANTA MARIA DEGLI ANGELI

In 1937 I had two marvelous days in Assisi. There, alone in the
12th-century Romanesque chapel of Santa Maria degli Angeli, an
incomparable marvel of purity where St. Francis used [to] often
pray, something stronger than I was compelled me for the first
time in my life to go down on my knees.

—SIMONE WEIL

What draws people to St. Mary of the Angels has nothing do with its impressive size or architecture, but what is housed inside the church. The grandiose church functions as a womb for the humblest shrines connected to the life and death of Saint Francis.

A visit to the church requires a short bus ride down to the valley. The huge Basilica di Santa Maria degli Angeli, which can clearly be seen from Assisi, is located just a few blocks from the train station and dominates the valley's landscape.

On my first visit to the church, the day was bright and beautiful. The deep blue sky was clear, with only a few puffy cottontail clouds snuggling together at the top of Mount Subasio. The sun bathed Santa Maria degli Angeli, causing it to shimmer in the distance. The bus slowly wound its way down the hillside, lazily traversing the five-kilometer distance to the church.

Construction began in 1569 on the huge new church that would replace two older and smaller churches that each housed very sacred Franciscan shrines: the little field chapel known as the Portiuncula— often referred to as the Porziuncola—the first permanent home for Francis and his first followers, and the Chapel of the Transitus, where Francis died.

In Francis' time, the area surrounding the basilica was heavily wooded. A simple footpath through the forest led to a small plot of cleared land where there stood an ancient chapel, built in 352 by hermits returning from the Holy Land. Until well into the tenth century, pilgrims traveling to and from the Holy Land often stopped in the small, rustic chapel, originally named St. Mary of Josaphat, because enshrined within the chapel was a fragment of the Blessed Virgin's tomb, given to the builders of the church by Saint Cyril.

In time, the chapel became known as Saint Mary of the Angels, because angelic songs were supposedly heard there, and even occasional angelic apparitions had been reported. The change in the name might also be more realistically traced back to a very old painting on the wall behind the altar which depicts the Assumption of the Blessed Virgin. In the painting, Mary is surrounded by a bevy of floating angels...hence, the peasants, most of whom were illiterate, probably began referring to the church as St. Mary of the Angels. Eventually, the church became known simply as the *Portiuncula*, a word which means "little portion of earth." That designation was originated by the Benedictines who lived on Mount Subasio. In 576, the chapel was given to them. By 1075, it had fallen into such a state of ruin, the Benedictines abandoned the property even though they still retained the rights to it. More than a century later, Francis, of course, would see beauty in the ruins and restore the church.

Many years later, when Francis was dying, he asked to be taken to his favorite spot on earth...the Portiuncula. He was placed in a small infirmary, little more than a cell, near the Portiuncula, where he died on the evening of October 3, 1226. The infirmary was converted into the Chapel of the Transitus (Cappella del Transito), so named because it was from there that Francis embraced Sister Death and made the transition (*transito* [Italian] or *transitus* [Latin]) from this life to eternal life.

Today, both the Portiuncula and the Chapel of the Transitus, containing an enameled terracotta statue of Francis by Andrea della Robbia, stand just a few feet apart under the great dome of the basilica.

The exterior of the majestic church is powerfully beautiful, a balanced blend of columns and arches crowned by a gold statue of Mary. The golden Mary looks down on the piazza, usually filled with tourists taking pictures or eating picnic lunches, vendors selling statues and postcards, and local kids kicking a soccer ball.

With the approval of Pope Pius V, the first stone was laid by the bishop of Assisi on March 25, 1569. Following the design of the renowned Umbrian architect, Galeazzo Alessi of Perugia, construction of the massive church took more than a hundred years to complete. In 1832 an earthquake seriously damaged the building, but fortunately, the dome over the Portiuncula resisted the tremors and no harm came to the tiny chapel. The nave was quickly rebuilt following the original plans. The facade was temporarily fixed. Between 1924 and 1930, the temporary facade was dismantled and the modern facade designed in a neo-baroque style was erected.

The most notable feature of the basilica is the elegant dome which majestically towers over the highest point of the tympanum atop the facade. The dome is capped by an octagonal cylinder in which there are large windows with alternating lunettes and tympanums divided by Corinthian pillars. To the right of the apse is a bell tower. The facade of travertine and bricks is decorated with massive angels. In two niches on either side of the facade are statues of Francis and Clare. Atop the tympanum is a colossal, gold-plated statue of the Madonna, measuring over twenty-one feet tall.

While the church houses a rich heritage of artwork, including a stunning crucifix painted by Giunta Pisano in 1236, your attention nonetheless is immediately drawn to the Portiuncula. The first impression that hit me as I entered the church was that I had stepped into a magnificent tabernacle housing the humblest of guests, in much the same way as ornate, draped, cabinet-like shrines on altars house consecrated pieces of bread mysteriously containing the essence of Christ. The small, simple, stone chapel, once surrounded by trees and birds and crickets, contains the essence of Saint Francis.

Inside this chapel Francis prayed, cried, sang, heard the voice of God and nurtured his disciples. The dense, green forest is long gone, replaced by a concrete grove, a towering marvel of art and architecture. In 1829, a beautiful fresco entitled *The Great Pardon* painted by G. F. Overbeck was added to the tiny facade of the Portiuncula. The Portiuncula is a rectangular building made of stone from Mount Subasio. It has a gable and a portal with a semicircular arch. When I passed through the arched entrance of the chapel Francis loved, I sensed I was entering into the heart of the Franciscan spirit...*simplicity, serenity, sincerity, silence, song.* I smiled, thinking of Brother Francis humbly walking into the chapel with a broom in his hand, and quietly sweeping God's house. A swell of emotion swept over me as I knelt down.

Except for the rear wall behind the altar, the interior is undecorated. The barren, rustic simplicity invites prayer and contemplation. The apsed room is covered by a stonework vault. Single kneelers line either wall. The altar wall is entirely covered with a splendid painted wooden panel created in 1393. The center of the panel features a gentle rendition of the Annunciation, which is surrounded by depictions of several episodes from the life of Saint Francis.

The enormous basilica, one of the largest in the world, contains sixteen small chapels along the side walls, each containing a number of fine paintings and frescoes. On the right side of the apse, there is an entrance to a rose garden. Just beyond the garden is the tiny Cappella delle Rose, Chapel of the Roses. The oldest part of this chapel was built by Saint Bonaventure on a spot where the hut used by Saint Francis once stood. Saint Bernardine of Siena enlarged the chapel in the early part of the fifteenth century. Along the corridor leading to the chapel is a statue of Saint Francis, and living doves are always sitting in his outstretched hands.

SANTUARIO DI DAMIANO

On the hillside below Assisi quietly sits the cradle of the Franciscan movement, the little Church of San Damiano, whose history, poetry and simplicity loom large. If Francis and Clare were to walk down the hill to San Damiano today, they would have no trouble recognizing the place where Francis heard Christ speak to him from the crucifix, where Clare lived for forty years, where Francis wrote *The Canticle of the Creatures*, because despite the repairs and improvements made over the centuries, San Damiano remains today essentially the way it looked in their time.

The best way to visit San Damiano is to begin at the Basilica di Santa Chiara. Kneel in front of the Crucifix of San Damiano for a few minutes, and allow your mind to wander back nearly eight hundred years, to the time when the crucifix hung unobserved in the neglected little church of San Damiano. Imagine a young man so hungry for God he turned his back on everything he knew in order to experience something beyond knowledge. He was all alone in his quest, a lowly beggar dressed in rags bent on feasting at the bountiful banquet of the Lord of Lords. One day, as he walked on the hillside below the city walls, he felt compelled to enter the church and pray. Picture it...a lonely outcast and an empty church, the man and the building both looking neglected and hopeless. Yet something far, far beyond anyone's wildest imagination happens inside the church...and inside the man. What happened, no one can say for sure...except the course of history changed in the silence surrounding the Crucifix of San Damiano. And now you are about to walk back into history, open to a change within you.

A short walk down Via Borgo Artenio from Santa Chiara brings you to Porta Nuova, where you begin the descent. An escalator takes you down to the parking lot filled with cars and giant buses, and ringed with souvenir stalls. Francis and Clare wouldn't recognize this site. Within minutes you are on the narrow, paved path that gently winds its way down the hill. The path is bordered by fields, vineyards, cypress trees and olive groves. Along the way, you will pass the ruins of a Roman tomb. The valley below is spread out before you in all its splendor. The city sounds gradually give way to Sister Cricket's singing. The downward slope of the path soon becomes steeper. You can't help but notice how pilgrims walking back to the city are struggling, huffing and puffing their way up the steep grade. Free advice: Think about the miracle of San Damiano, not the walk back up the hill.

After a walk of about fifteen minutes, you reach the small square in front of San Damiano. The square is bordered on three sides by a charming portico with segmental arches. The church itself is, fittingly, unassuming, even humble. The facade is simple, built with irregular stones, whose most notable feature is a large, round rose window. The window has a curious quality. First, it is off-center, which I imagine can be attributed to an expansion added along the right side of the building. Second, there is a door that almost touches the circumference of the circular window, at what would be about 10 o'clock if the window were a watch. One immediately wonders what a door, without any steps leading to it, is doing so high off the ground. The answer helps you better understand the tenor of the times when Saint Clare lived here. One of the scourges of life in the Middle Ages was the state of chronic insecurity that rippled through everyday life. In Clare's time, there would have been a wooden stairway leading to the second floor and the sisters' dormitory; at night, for security reasons, the stairway, which was suspended on chains, would have been raised. A careful look at the facade reveals what the building looked like in Francis' time. In fact, marks in the bricks give evidence of where Francis restored the wall.

The exact date of construction of the original church is unknown. It is possible that it could have been built as early as the eighth century. Ancient documents clearly show the church was a Benedictine priorate from the year 1030. Early in the twelfth century the Benedictines handed control of San Damiano to the church of San Rufino. But from ancient times, long before the church was built, the actual site itself was considered sacred ground. Below the refectory is a subterranean grotto, which scholars think was used for some kind of cultic rite. Francis had discovered this pre-Christian, underground cave and at times found solace in its darkened silence. After Clare and her sister moved into San Damiano in 1212, a dormitory above the nave was added. In 1260, seven years after Clare's death, the Poor Clares left San Damiano and moved within the walls of the city, settling in the Chiesa di San Giorgio. The friars returned to San Damiano and remained there until 1860, when the abolition of ecclesiastical property resulted in the sale of San Damiano to an English Lord, whose heirs donated the property back to the friars in 1983. In the sixteenth century, the friars added a cloister and enlarged the convent. Today, San Damiano houses a small community of Friars Minor who oversee the property and run a novitiate, where novices from around the world spend a year studying Franciscan spirituality.

To the right of the main entrance of the church, there is a door leading to a small side chapel and this is where the pilgrim enters to begin his or her visit to San Damiano. The Cappella di San Girolamo (Chapel of St. Jerome) is adjacent to the main church. It is believed that this little chapel originally was the primitive home (convento) of the friars to whom Francis had given the task of assisting the Poor Clares. In the lunette at the far end is a fresco painted in 1517 by Tiberio d'Assisi depicting the Madonna with Child seated on a throne surrounded by adoring angels and Saints Jerome, Bernardine, Francis and Clare, and a nun in adoration.

You next come to the Cappella del Crocifisso, the Crucifix Chapel, so named because it houses a venerated wooden crucifix carved in 1637 by Brother Innocent of Palermo. While art critics might tend to dismiss the crucifix, its tragic realism has touched the hearts of countless pilgrims who have knelt before it over the centuries. The intense agony on the face of Jesus is a fitting portal through which to enter into a meditation on the mystery and gift of salvation, keeping in mind that the crucifix was central to the life and spirituality of Saint Francis. The renowned English mystic Walter Hilton, who was a Canon Regular of Saint Augustine and who died in 1395, began his monumental book on contemplation and prayer, *The Ladder of Perfection*, with an epigraph taken from the writings of Saint Francis: "Lord Jesus Christ, I pray that the fiery and honey-sweet power of Thy love may detach my soul from everything under heaven, so that I may die from love of Thy love, who out of love for Thy people did die upon the tree of the Cross." As I kneel in front of Brother Innocent's crucifix, I can think of no finer prayer to utter. From this small, side chapel you can enter the main church.

You are immediately drawn into the rustic simplicity of the church.

The semicircular apse is surrounded by wooden choir stalls dating from 1504. Above the stalls is an opening through which the cloistered nuns received the Eucharist. The apse vault is decorated with a fresco of the Madonna with Child, flanked by Saint Rufino and Saint Damian. Above the arch of the apse is a modern replica of the original crucifix of San Damiano which spoke to Francis. On the right wall near the front door is a niche known as "the window of the money," because it is where Francis threw his purse containing the money that had been offered to the priest after he had rejected it.

A small door on the right near the apse leads to the Sepolcreto where the first Poor Clares are buried. Close by is a small chapel with simple stalls and a lectern from Saint Clare's time. Continuing, you come to a narrow staircase leading to a small, terraced garden where it is believed Saint Francis composed his hymn to the universe, *The Canticle of the Creatures*. Further up the stairs, you come to a small room known as the Oratory of St. Clare. Frescoes on the vault of the little chapel have been partially restored. The Blessed Sacrament was kept in a small niche on the left of the altar. Clare and her sisters often worshiped the Divine Presence in this chapel.

Up three steps from the oratory is the dormitory of the Poor Clares. It is a large barren room with a trussed rock and brick floor. It was in this room that Saint Clare died, on the evening of August 11, 1253.

As the pilgrim leaves this profoundly moving room, he or she descends to the cloister which dates from the sixteenth century. Along one side of the cloister is the Refrettorio, or refectory, where Clare and her sisters took their simple meals. It is a dark, rectangular room covered by low cross vaults. The benches are the original benches used by Clare. At the end of one of the narrow tables lining the side wall is a vase of flowers, which marks the place where Saint Clare customarily sat. On the back wall is a large fresco depicting the crucifixion with Saint Francis kneeling in adoration.

San Damiano is a place of prayer. And it is a powerful symbol of the virtue of poverty which Saint Clare so strenuously upheld.

CHIESA DI SANTA MARIA MAGGIORE

This is the church where Saint Francis was baptized. Chiesa di Santa Maria Maggiore was a cathedral until that honor was transferred to San Rufino in 1035; however, the church has remained the episcopal seat of the bishop whose residence is just a short distance from the church. It was in the plaza in front of the bishop's residence that Francis renounced his father by removing all his clothes in front of

Bishop Guido. Francis spent the last days of his life in the bishop's residence before being carried down to the Portiuncula, where he died; but nothing remains of the original residence, which was rebuilt and enlarged in 1612.

The church was restructured during the twelfth century, after a fire had badly damaged the original structure. At the time, the church interior was adorned with frescoes, but today only faded fragments remain. The interior is composed of a nave and two side aisles. The facade, which has two entrances, is made of blocks of ashlar stone and is very plain; its most notable feature is a charming central rose window, added in 1162. The bell tower was added in the fourteenth century. Ruins of a Roman temple can be seen in the crypt.

The simplicity of this church is a major part of its charm.

PILGRIMAGE DIARY 67

Sleaze in Assisi

I was on my way to Santa Maria Maggiore, taking a leisurely stroll down Via Giorgetti, a narrow, quiet street in a residential section between the Basilica di San Francesco and the Piazza del Comune. After a few blocks the street twists to the right and descends to Via Fontebella, where it ends. I turned left on Via Fontebella, a wider street lined with small businesses and hotels. The shops all had apartments over them, each with three or four floors. One shop sold newspapers, postcards and tourist books. I went in to buy a newspaper. In the rear of the store, right next to books about Saint Francis, was a display of a wide assortment of triple-X-rated porno magazines and videos, all featuring provocatively posed nude women on the covers.

Walking past the young woman at the cash register, I left the store without buying the paper. Outside, I took a closer look at the building. Above the ground floor business were three floors of apartments, each with shuttered windows. Inlaid in the exterior stone wall of the second-floor apartment was a brightly-painted porcelain plaque featuring the Madonna and child, under which the words "Ave Maria" were inscribed. Directly below the Madonna was the brick archway entrance to the business. There was no hint that they *sold such filth...next to books about Saint Francis and under the watchful eye of the Virgin Mary holding the Infant Jesus.*

Was there a market for this kind of sleaze in Assisi? It wouldn't be there if there weren't. In my humanist/atheist days, I bought the lie that pornography was a victimless business. Not so! It degrades women and fills men with lust. Those who make it, distribute it, sell it and buy it are all tainted by its corrupting influence. I know about pornography; its lure has attracted me many times in my life. I'm only drawn to pornography when I feel worthless or useless or hopeless. Pornography preys on the weak, offering momentary relief or escape.

In a letter to Ermentrude of Bruges, who had founded several monasteries in Flanders where the sisters sought to live according to the way of the Poor Ladies of San Damiano, Saint Clare wrote:

> Our labor here is brief,
> the reward eternal;
> may the excitements of the world,
> fleeing like a shadow,
> not disturb you.
> May the false delights of the deceptive world
> not deceive you.
> Close your ears to the whisperings of hell
> and bravely oppose its onslaughts.
> (Clare of Assisi: *Early Documents*, page 52)

Of course, Clare was not talking about pornography. Still, "the whisperings of hell" could be heard in that small shop. And how do we "oppose its onslaughts?" I have no idea. I would not be comfortable opposing the right of free speech by trying to legally ban such material. The fact is that we live in a secular world where Christianity is just one voice (and fractured, at that) among many, and it is not even the dominant voice. And in the secular world, we are asked to be tolerant of all religious beliefs as well as the unbelief of the atheist.

The unexpected sight of such filth in this holy city deeply disturbed me.

ABBAZIA DI SAN PIETRO

This church has a beautiful yet simple facade, which reflects its origins as a Benedictine abbey church. The church was built at the end of the tenth century in a Romanesque style with Gothic influences. At the time, it was just outside the wall of the city. Early in the fourteenth century, a newly constructed city wall was built around the church, making it a part of the city. During the middle of the thirteenth century, the church was restructured and enlarged. The vaulting of the nave and the dome with its architecturally interesting concentric rows of bricks date back to this period. The present church was dedicated by Pope Innocent IV in 1253. The soberly decorated, rectangular facade was completed in 1268. The facade originally was topped off with a tympanum, which was badly damaged in an earthquake in 1832 and had to be torn down. Running across the top and midpoint of the facade are lovely cornices embellished with small arches. Between the cornices are three elegant rose windows, of which the middle one is much larger than the other two. The large main entrance, guarded by two stone lions, is flanked by two smaller doors. The roof is crowned with a bell tower.

The stark and austere interior of the church reflects its Benedictine origins. The church has a feel of great solemnity. The large interior is composed of a nave and two side aisles. There is an interesting funnel-shaped cupola over the elevated sanctuary. The interior was restored in 1954, but traces of fragmentary frescoes dating back to the thirteenth through sixteenth centuries remain. In the chapel of the left transept is a magnificent triptych painted on wood by Matteo da Gualdo depicting the Madonna and Child, with Saint Peter and Saint Vittorino on either side.

PILGRIMAGE DIARY 68

Benedict and Francis

*T*he Church of St. Peter is special for me because it symbolizes the friendship between the Benedictines and the Franciscans. Despite the fact that Francis rejected the monastic style of life founded by Saint Benedict, his spirituality has much in common with that of Benedict. Both Benedict (who died around 547) and Francis were determined not to live as everyone else did, and decided to dedicate their lives in full accordance to the gospel. They gave up possessions and took up prayer. They both embraced community and humility. And both saw the importance of contemplation and solitude. The very first word of The Rule of St. Benedict is "listen." But an important difference is that Francis broke from the monastic way of life established by Benedict, and, for him, the world was his cloister.

While teaching at the Gregorian, I was able to take a weekend trip with one of the students to Subiaco, which is about seventy kilometers east of Rome. Saint Benedict lived in Subiaco for twenty years, the first three of which were spent alone as a hermit in a cave. Today, the cave, carved into the side of a stony mountain, is known as the Sacro Speco (Holy Grotto) and is honored as the birthplace of western monasticism. The cave is now surrounded by a shrine which includes two churches, one above the other, and several chapels in an irregular arrangement of walls, vaults and steps built into the mountainside. Every wall not made of natural stone is covered with frescoes. The student took me to Subiaco because of its connection to Saint Francis. Near the lower church, in the little chapel of Saint Gregory, there is a famous fresco of Saint Francis of Assisi, who visited the Sacro Speco sometime before 1224. What makes the fresco so famous is that it was painted while the saint was still alive. Francis is depicted without a halo and without the stigmata. Moreover, the inscription identifies him as Father Franciscus.

I spent some time standing in silence before the painting, struck by its magnificent simplicity. Here, in this earliest known portrait of Francis, his humility and serene spirit are vividly depicted.

The visit sparked within me an interest in the life of Saint Benedict, whom I've come to greatly admire. Benedict said, "If a man wants to pray, let him go and pray." Prayer is that simple. I made it too complicated, searching for ways to pray. For Benedict, life was a continual dialogue with God. For Benedict, solitude leads to communion, and silence leads to dialogue.

Benedict and Francis have much to teach us.

CHIESA DI SAN STEFANO

The tiny, humble Chiesa di Santo Stefano is surrounded by a cluster of medieval Roman houses. Construction on the church began in 1166, using pink stones from Mount Subasio. It has small narrow windows and a tiny, semicircular apse. The nave of the church is covered by wooden beams supported by four brick arches. The faded fragments of frescoes on the left wall date back to the early 1400's. The bare simplicity of the church makes it a perfect spot for quiet prayer. Local legend has it the bells of Santo Stefano's small, vaulted bell tower began ringing on their own upon the death of Saint Francis.

Pilgrimage Diary 69

In the Silence of San Stefano

> Temporary solitude from all things in life, the meditation within yourself about the divine, is food as necessary for your soul as material food is for your body.
> —*LEO TOLSTOY*, A CALENDAR OF WISDOM

Today is Wednesday, September 3, the feast of Saint Gregory the Great, pope and Doctor of the Church, who died in 604, and who once said, "I do not preach as I should nor does my life follow the principles I preach so inadequately." In that regard, I have a great deal in common with Gregory the Great.

Yesterday, I interviewed Don Aldo Brunacci. Tomorrow I go up to the Carceri for a four-day silent retreat. Today was wide open and free...no plans, no agenda. I thought I would start the day with Mass at the Basilica di San Francesco. Well, not exactly start it—the day starts with two cups of cappuccino in the Piazza del Comune. One must wake up before one starts anything. Seeing as I woke up too late to make it to the 9 a.m. Mass, I decided to sit in the silence of Chiesa di Santo Stefano and read the morning prayers from the Divine Office.

In a city crammed with churches, including two containing the tombs of the city's two saints, Santo Stefano is my favorite church. Perhaps what I love is its simplicity. Or its silence...few people stop here, it's off the beaten path and inconsequential: other than centuries of prayer, nothing much happened here to draw the spotlight of tourists' attention. The church was empty when I arrived. The morning light, soft and bright, was streaming in the small windows behind the altar, gently illuminating the stone sanctuary and the vases of yellow flowers that cheered the tabernacle, the altar and a wooden statue of Mary. I couldn't help but think of the contrast between the silent church and the hustle-bustle of the coffee bar. I sat, quietly absorbing the simplicity, beauty and harmony of this sacred space, my mind playing with the notion of a young Francis sitting alone in this church, thinking, wondering, praying.

My daydream was interrupted when a young nun emerged from the sacristy. She genuflected in front of the tabernacle, which is located to the left of the altar. On the altar, a large book of Scripture was sitting open on a wooden stand, facing the wooden chairs and kneelers. On either side of the word of God were candles. The nun lighted them. She again genuflected and went back into the sacristy. A few minutes later, she came out again, this time accompanied by two other sisters. They sat down on small benches placed in a semi-circle around the front of the altar. One of the sisters motioned for me to join them in prayer. I did. As they sang and read the psalms—in German—from their prayer books, I silently read the psalms from morning prayer. Their singing was heavenly. One of the sisters read a passage from Scripture and then they sat in silence for several minutes. After a closing song, one of the sisters, speaking in perfect English, thanked me for joining them in prayer, and then she invited me to sit in their garden and have a drink of water.

We had a delightful conversation. I told her about my writing. She told me that she and the other two sisters were from Germany. One worked in a soup kitchen, one in a hospital, and she was a teacher in a small village. They were in Assisi for a few weeks of prayer and reflection. Santo Stefano is no longer a parish church, she told me. It is administered by Santa Maria Maggiore and is used for weddings and for services held by various groups that come to Assisi. Franciscans from Germany rent the garden area and the rectory during the summer as a center for German priests, brothers and sisters to come and pray and study.

After our chat, I returned to the church and sat in silence for a few minutes. I was touched by the young nun's faith. Her name was Gratias, meaning (in Latin) besides thanksgiving, grace. It was a *grace-filled morning. As I gazed upon the small cross hanging over the altar, I thought about the way each of the sisters reverently genuflected in front of the tabernacle, gracefully acknowledging God in Jesus, Jesus in the Eucharist and the Eucharist in them...and also acknowledging that God is in control, God holds sway in their lives.*

SANTUARIO DI RIVOTORTO

In the early days of the Order, when Francis began to have followers, he lived with them at Rivotorto.
—THE LEGEND OF PERUGIA

Along the main road from Assisi to Spello and Rome, a few miles from Santa Maria degli Angeli, is the Church of St. Mary of Rivotorto. The church takes its name from the nearby brook which runs along the left side of the building. It was here that Francis and his first followers set up camp, and so the spot is considered to be the cornerstone of the Franciscan Order. Inside the church is a replica of the humble *tugurio* (or hut) where Francis and the friars lived from 1209 to 1211. It was at Rivotorto that Francis wrote the first Rule which was given oral approval by Pope Innocent III.

The original hut was turned into a chapel in 1455, and a church dedicated to the Madonna was built around it. In 1586, Pope Sixtus V initiated construction of a large church to protect the primitive hut. Construction of the new church was completed around 1640. A devastating earthquake in 1853 destroyed much of the church. Shortly afterward, reconstruction began, converting it into a magnificent neo-Gothic church. In 1926, the hut was completely restored to the way it looked in the fourteenth century.

The tugurio is a fitting witness to the simple and poor life of the original friars. The beauty of the new church merits a visit in its own right.

CHIESA DI SAN GIACOMO DI MURO RUPTO

Tucked away on Via Metastasio, just a short uphill walk from the Basilica of St. Francis, is one of Assisi's hidden jewels, Chiesa di Santo Giacomo de Muro Rupto. *Muro rupto* is Italian for "broken wall," and the church takes its name from the fact that it is built next to the ruins of the ancient town wall. The tiny eleventh-century church is now part of a convent of German nuns, and you must ring their bell to gain access to the church, which consists of a nave, divided into three bays with cross vaults and supporting arches, and a transept. The apse has one small window to allow light to shine in; on the arch of the apse hangs a beautiful seventeenth-century crucifix. With the exception of a faded fresco of the Madonna and Child on the left wall, the interior of the Romanesque church has no decorations. There are no stained-glass windows. All is bare and gray, except for the coloring rendered by the sunlight that falls on the old stones, giving them new life. The church is a silent hymn to the richness of poverty, simplicity and humility. The sacristy contains a votive fresco from 1536 depicting a nursing Madonna and Saints Clare, Rufino, Francis and Benedict. For a short time during the thirteenth century, the monastery was occupied by Benedictine nuns. A door in the left transept leads to a peaceful garden and part of the remains of the original Roman wall.

This is a wonderful place to sit and listen.

EREMO DELLE CARCERI

So greatly burned in such a heat
my heart could find no sure retreat,
but step by step my eager feet
to the tree-top must carry me.
—JACOPONE DA TODI, *TREE OF LIFE*

Near the top of Mount Subasio, built into the cliffs at the back of a ravine and surrounded by a thick forest, quietly sits a hermitage known as the Carceri, an isolated spot where Francis went for solitude. The friars lived in individual caves which they called cells. The word *carceri* means *prison*. However, when the word is applied to the mountaintop dwelling used by Francis, it is not used in the sense of a jail, but rather in harmony with the religious concept of seclusion. For Francis, *carceri* meant *solitary*, a private hermitage where he could be alone with God. The Carceri is located about four kilometers from Assisi. The steep road leading to the Eremo delle Carceri begins at the Porta del Cappuccini (the Capuchin Gate).

At first, the incline is gentle and the road gradually ascends through olive groves. But quickly, the slope becomes steeper and the olive trees give way to the thick vegetation of small bushes, yellow broom flowers and small bay oak trees. As the road twists and winds its way to the summit, it graciously offers arresting views of the valley below. Off in the distance you can see Santa Maria degli Angeli and the towns of Bastia and Cannara. And far to the east, you can see Foligno. Some locations along the road offer beautiful views of the Rocca Maggiore and Assisi. These vistas are paid for with the sweat and strain of the climb. At the end of the hour-long walk, you realize the hermitage sits atop a deep gorge just below the summit, and is hidden by a dense forest of tall oak trees. This is isolation. Far from the sound of any voice, Francis would come to the Carceri to live in isolated communion with God.

Creating Something Out of Nothing

Whenever I climbed Mount Subasio in the sunshine I had the feeling that my whole body was penetrated by light and, with the light, by joy.

—CARLO CARRETTO, I, FRANCIS

The arduous hike up to the Carceri is rewarded with a spectacular view of the valley of Spoleto and the hills upon which Assisi sits. As I climbed higher and higher, my appreciation for the beauty spread out before me rose steadily. A thought expressed by the nineteenth-century Jesuit poet Gerard Manley Hopkins suddenly became electrified with meaning: "The world is charged with the grandeur of God."

The first time I made the exhausting climb up to the Carceri, I felt God's presence in the beauty of the natural wonders before me...and it had nothing to do with the design argument for God's existence expressed by some philosophers. The feeling was more poetic than philosophical.

However, as my spirit danced before the grandeur, my mind recalled something penned by Marcel Proust, which voiced a totally different reaction to the same beauty: "It has been said that the highest praise of God consists in the denial of Him by the atheist, who finds creation so perfect that he [or she] can dispense with a creator."

I couldn't see God's fingerprints on the natural wonders before me. James Joyce wrote, "The artist, like the God of creation, remains within or behind or beyond or above his handiwork, invisible, refined out of existence, indifferent, paring his fingernails."

I smiled as I looked over the lush valley, imagining God, the Supreme Artist, casually looking down on his flawless creation as he pares his fingernails.

In the brightness of the day, questions about how all this came into being seemed irrelevant. In the beginning...who knows? Who knows from where it has come and how it happened? It is the riddle of all riddles. Questions about what God did before creation or how God created the world without using any raw materials or why, if God was perfect and complete, within the Divine Being did the need and will to create arise in God have no convincing answers.

Hindus offer a dazzling variety of answers to the riddle, all of which include a wide assortment of gods and mythologies, but ultimately they are more content with doubt than dogma. Buddhists offer no answers to the riddle. Jews, Christians and Muslims offer rigid answers provided by One Book authored by their One God. Many thoughtful people, such as the followers of Confucius, are indifferent to the riddle of creation and don't trouble themselves with thinking about it. The scientifically-minded among us can't agree on one theory that explains it all. Saint Augustine said, "There is but one miracle, and that miracle is creation." Bernard of Clairvoux said, "What I know of the Divine Sciences and Holy Scripture, I have learnt in the woods and fields. I have had no other Masters than the beeches and the oaks." We have become deaf to the preaching of the trees.

As I looked over the vast valley pulsating with life, I pledged to rejoice in creation instead of trying to explain it.

Francis was so inspired by the beauty of creation that he too created something beautiful out of nothing...himself!

PILGRIMAGE DIARY 70

Forgetful

*L*ooking out over the Valley of Spoleto, I can't help but recall how forgetful I am. I forget that God clothes the lilies of the field below. I forget God feeds the birds in the sky overhead. I forget that God leads the lambs to water. It is amazing how utterly forgetful I am of God, the Divine Parent who loves me beyond all measure.

God, forgive me my forgetfulness, forgive me my neglect in responding to your bountiful love.

Praise God from whom all blessings flow.

THE END OF THE ROAD

With each step along the steep road leading to the Carceri, you can feel the air becoming lighter and cooler. Poet Susan Saint Sing nicely captured that feeling in her beautiful book, *St. Francis, Poet of Creation*:

> Assisi is a place of wind. Perched on a knoll, half way up the side of Mount Subasio, the city lies suspended midway between the breaths of the mountain's coolness and the valley's heat. Near the forest of the Carceri, where Francis lived with his brothers in craggy rocks and caves, there is a great bluff. The afternoon wind rushes up its face, releasing the hot Umbrian air to this cooler altitude, mixing updrafts and currents into a playful aerial intersection for larks, swallows, insects, and gossamers of all sorts. (page 59)

Eventually you reach the end of the road, and the beginning of a trip back in time, to the heart of the Franciscan charism of solitude. At the road's end, there is a small stand selling cold drinks and postcards...it is the beginning and the end of commercialism at the Carceri, thankfully. Once inside, there is nothing to buy, no gift shops to visit. You enter through iron gates which are open from seven in the morning until seven at night. A dirt path with a slight incline leads through the forest, along the edge of a steep ravine. Through the trees, the stone complex soon begins to appear.

At the end of the path, you descend stone steps to a large vault, and passing through it you enter a small, triangular terrace known as *chiostrino dei frati*, or "friars' small cloister." There is a low wall along the section of the terrace that does not border a building. Looking over the wall, you begin to get the sense of how the convento is built at the top of and into the side of a steep ravine. When Francis and the first friars came here, they found natural caves in the facing wall of the cliff. Looking across the ravine you see a thick forest. Looking out of the ravine, you can see the Valley of Spoleto at the base of Mount Subasio.

On the left side of the terrace, as you enter it, is a door leading to the refectory built by Saint Bernardine of Siena in 1426. On the floor above the refectory is a dormitory where the friars' cells are built against the bedrock of the mountain. This part of the convento is closed to the public. Across the chiostrino from the vault is the entrance to the Cappella di San Bernardino—or the Chapel of St. Bernardine of Siena. The room is very small. And dark. The chapel's one window is a small stained-glass depiction of the Madonna with Child; it was brought from Lyons, France, and was made near the end of the thirteenth century. The low vaulted ceiling has been darkened over the centuries by burning candles and incense. To the left as you enter is a simple stone altar. The wall behind the altar is decorated by a fresco of the crucifixion, with Saint Francis kneeling at the feet of Christ as he hangs on the cross. Angels are holding chalices, which are being filled with the precious blood of Christ as it spills from the wounds in his hands and on his side. Mary the mother of Jesus, standing behind the kneeling Francis, is depicted with such a pained look on her face that she is forced to turn away from looking at the agony being endured by her son, vividly illustrating the words of Saint Bonaventure in his *Tree of Life*:

> What tongue can tell,
> What intellect grasp
> the heavy weight of your desolation,
> Blessed Virgin?

The cross was central to Francis' spirituality. And Clare's, too. In a letter to Ermentrude of Bruges, Clare wrote, "Meditate constantly on the mysteries of the cross and the agonies of His mother standing at the foot of the cross." Along the back wall of the Chapel of Saint Bernardine there is a wooden choir stall with five seats. High on the side and back walls are fourteen small, framed lithographs depicting the Stations of the Cross.

PILGRIMAGE DIARY 71

Two Thoughts

*W*hile sitting alone in the Chapel of San Bernardino one night, *I found myself pondering two thoughts expressed by Hans Urs von Balthasar in* The Last Grain of Wheat:

God gives us many things only so we will sacrifice them to him. He himself assumed a body only in order to sacrifice it on the Cross and nourish us with it.... (page 46)

The real essence of Christ's passion consisted in two things we least like to bear and suffer: fear and disgrace. (page 69)

As I pondered, I realized I must dig deeper, much deeper.

A STONE BED AND A WOODEN PILLOW

The distractions of the daily preoccupations of living with others were stripped away [at the Carceri], and you lived alone with Jesus in the purity and rigor of the mountain. The stone Francis slept on in the hermitage seemed softer by far than the bed he had slept upon in his father's house.

—MURRAY BODO, FRANCIS: *THE JOURNEY AND THE DREAM*

Directly across from the entry to the chapel is a small archway leading to the simple Cappella di Santa Maria delle Carceri, a very small room partly dug into the bedrock. No more than five or six people can stand in it at a time. On the back wall, facing you as you enter, is a faded fresco of the Madonna with Child and Saint Francis painted by Tiberio d'Assisi in 1506. The fresco has suffered badly over time, and only part of it has survived. The missing sections reveal that the Madonna was frescoed over a crucifix fresco from the end of the thirteenth century. The frescoes on the side walls and the curved ceiling are badly faded and virtually unrecognizable. Along the left wall there are steps leading up to an old wooden door that leads into the convento, which is closed to the public. On the other side of the door is a small room where, for centuries, the friars have prayed the Office.

On the right is a low, narrow passageway leading to a small landing, illuminated by a very small window, looking out over the ravine. Tucked into the corner of the landing is a very old, wooden confessional consisting of a bench for the priest, a partition and a kneeler for the penitent. On the left side of the landing, there is a steep flight of stone steps leading down to the grotto of Saint Francis. Three quarters of the way down to the lower level of the complex is a tiny platform where you must turn right, squeeze through a very narrow doorway, turn right again and proceed down an additional three steps. High on the wall at the end of the initial descending stairs are the faded remains of a fifteenth-century fresco depicting the Pieta. At the base of the second short flight of steps is another small landing. The stone steps leading to the lower level have been worn to a smooth and shiny finish over the centuries by pilgrims coming to the place where Francis entered into mystical communion with God. At the end of this lower landing there is a small door on the right wall. Just opposite the door there is a small window, which is usually open...stick your head out and you'll get a clear sense of how high up the cliff the original cave was. After squeezing through the doorway, you are at the heart and soul of the Eremo delle Carceri: the Grotto of Saint Francis.

The grotto is divided into two rooms, one where Francis slept, the other, where he prayed. The first room, actually a cave, features the "bed" where Francis slept. The bed is a low, flat section of the bedrock which was exactly the right size to accommodate Francis' small frame as he lay in recline. Legend has it that Francis rested his head on a log when he slept on this slab of rock.

A stone bed and a wooden pillow—this was not the Ramada Inn. One cannot minimize the degree of physical deprivation Francis imposed on his body. If I decided to spend time in a cave seeking God, I'd bring an air mattress, a down sleeping bag, a lantern, a gas stove and a supply of food. Francis wasn't camping, wasn't spending time in nature—he was transforming his nature. And when he rested from that hard work, he rested on hard rock. We can only imagine...no, we can't. Life in this cave is beyond our imagination. Or at least mine.

The second room is a small chapel built to commemorate the place where Francis meditated. The archway between the grotto and the chapel (built in the twelfth century) was too narrow for my frame; in order to squeeze through, I had to bend down and step through sideways.

The chapel is made of white stone and is only four or five feet wide and perhaps six or seven feet high. It contains only a modest stone altar and a crucifix. There were a handful of dried flowers humbly lying on the altar in front of the crucifix. The air was cool and dry. During my first visit, in 1995—on my birthday, March 31st—I stood in silence before the altar for a few minutes, almost feeling Francis' presence. I could hear the sound of a large fly buzzing. I could only imagine the kind of complete and uninterrupted silence Francis enjoyed in this cave-like chapel. I stood in front of the altar and silently prayed Francis' prayer before a crucifix.

The simple, rustic character of the grotto and chapel was forever preserved when Saint Bernardine of Siena had a small friary built over and around the original shrine in the fourteenth century. In the cloister of the friary there is a well which, according to tradition, began to yield water after Saint Francis prayed that it would. In the woods surrounding the friary are other cave-like grottos used by the disciples of Francis. The forest hermitage, given to Francis by the Benedictine Monks of Mount Subasio as a place for contemplation and recollection, is more in the spirit of the saint than the great art-filled basilicas. His humble bed hollowed from the rock in the grotto where he prayed and slept is all the memorial he needed.

Note: All the historical and descriptive material on the Carceri, as well as the reflections, were written before I went on the pilgrimage. I had planned to write one short pilgrimage diary based on the study pilgrimage's visit to the hermitage. However, as you will read, I was given the opportunity to spend four days living with the friars in the Carceri in early September. Those four days, with their ups and downs, were chronicled in a series of pilgrimage diaries. I point this out because the first-person narrative of the descriptive material and reflections are based on two short visits to the Carceri in the spring and fall of 1995; and the first-person narrative of the pilgrimage diaries is based solely on my four-day stay in the fall of 1997. I hope, with this in mind, the reader will not be jarred by my jumps and apparent lapses in continuity.

PILGRIMAGE DIARY 72

Cella Frate Fuco

Only silence is great; all else is weakness.
—*ALFRED DE VIGNEY* (1797-1863), LA MORT DU LOUP

*A*s I put my pen to paper, it is 2:45 p.m. on Thursday, September 4th. I'm in my room. At the Carceri! Actually, it's a cell. Very small. And very spartan. There's a bed, a small writing table and wicker chair, and a sink whose one faucet dispenses only cold water. That's it. Three hooks on one wall serve as a closet. The floor is made of large bricks, faded red in color. There is hardly enough floor space to put my suitcase down. My large, heavy suitcase. The white walls are bare except for a small crucifix over the desk, and a small icon of the Blessed Virgin Mary over the bed. Three very old wooden beams cross the white ceiling. There is one small window which looks out on the chiostrano dei frati and the entrance to the santuario. At the moment, I'm sharing this space with three large— and very noisy—flies. A wave of bewilderment washes over me.

What am I doing here?

Perhaps I should tell you how I got here. I took a taxi. Seriously, my stay here was arranged when the study pilgrimage visited the Carceri last July. It was my third trip up the mountain to this holy hermitage. My previous two visits were short. The hike up and down the mountain is so tiring and time-consuming, it leaves little energy or time for a long or prayerful visit. Even the day with the pilgrimage was hurried; in fact, we spent only three hours at the Carceri, including a liturgy celebrated in an outdoor shrine. And so, I've always had this longing to spend more time here, to try to enter into the spirit of prayer and contemplation which is a natural part of life in a hermitage. But an extended stay here was not possible for two reasons. First, they have only a few rooms reserved for guests, and those are usually occupied by friars spending a week or month or even a year on retreat. Second, the friars living here speak only Italian, and so making arrangements would be impossible, and, in addition, they prefer guests who can speak at least enough Italian to understand the basic rules and schedule.

During our visit in July, I heard an Irish accent. I turned and spotted a seminarian whom I knew from Collegio Sant' Isidoro. He took me on a short private tour of the parts of the convento that are not open to the public. When he showed me one of the guest rooms, the one he was staying in during his month at the Carceri (giving tours in English), I asked if there was any way I could spend a few days here. He took me to the friar in charge, and initially he was not receptive to the idea, stating, in part, that I wouldn't be able to talk with anyone. I said, "Great! I don't want to talk with anyone." When my words were translated, the friar smiled. The seminarian told him I was writing a book on Francis and Clare, and a few days of solitude would be helpful. Bingo...I was in.

I've been here only a few hours, and everything inside of me is screaming—"I want out."

Why?

I don't know. I was about to be bathed in the silence and solitude I had been seeking, yet I was suddenly filled with intense loneliness.

The taxi let me off just outside the main entrance to the hermitage. I had one suitcase and my briefcase containing my manuscript and a few books. I have too much stuff, and so I had a difficult time lugging it up the dirt and pebble path leading to the convento. "Up" is the key word. By the time I completed the ten-minute walk I was out of breath and perspiring badly. Did I need two pairs of pants and six shirts to spend four days in silent reflection and prayer in the woods?

I entered a small office and tried to tell a young friar sitting at the desk who I was and why I was here. He looked at me as if I were from Mars. After a few minutes of my speaking English and his speaking Italian, words of both of us falling on deaf ears, I began to worry that my reservation may have been lost. The friar motioned for me to sit down and he left the office. He reappeared ten minutes later with the friar who had taken my reservation in July and instantly everything was OK. "Gerry," he said. Never before had the sound of my name sounded so good. He led me to my room.

After crossing the small courtyard, we entered the convento. We walked through the refectory of Saint Bernardine of Siena (1380-1444), a long, stone room shaped like a tunnel. It had a low, curved ceiling, partially covered with faded frescos. The small windows along the outer wall did little to relieve the darkness of the room, which was also damp and cold. What seemed enchanting in July suddenly looked foreboding. A fresco of the Last Supper, painted in 1595, adorns the back wall, but it is hardly visible in the dim light. Running along each of the side walls were long wooden tables dating back to the early fifteenth century, where friars once ate. This part of the convento was completed in 1426 when Saint Bernardine of Siena enlarged the original complex. At the end of the table, under the windows was a vase of fresh flowers. Light from the third window bathed the flowers which marked the spot where Saint Bernardine sat. We quickly passed through the room as I struggled with my bags.

As we exited the back door of the refectory, we entered a small, long, dark corridor. I felt as if we were entering a cave. And we were! Sort of. The left wall of the corridor is cut out of the stone mountainside. This section of the building dates back to the thirteenth century. A room on the right wall served as a small, primitive chapel, once used to pray the Divine Office. It contains wooden choir stalls along three of the walls and in the center is a large stand on which rests a very large book of psalms. Along the left wall, in this cloistered section of the building, was a steep flight of stone steps leading up to the second floor. The friar graciously asked to carry one of my bags. I gave him the smaller one. Again, the inner wall of the second floor was the actual bedrock of the mountain. Along the outer wall of the narrow dark corridor there were eight small cells. The arched doorway was barely big enough to squeeze through. The wooden doors were centuries old. My cell was the last one.

When we arrived at my door, the friar pointed to a sign on the door and said something in Italian. I gave him a blank stare. He said something like "fire," and I thought he was talking about a fire alarm, but I really didn't have a clue as to what he was saying. After he left, I got out my Italian/English dictionary and looked more closely at the sign. And smiled. It said, "The Cell of Brother Fire." I looked at the other doors and each cell was named for one of the elements—sun, moon, water, wind, etc.—featured in The Canticle of the Creatures. Frate Fuco—it's fitting, I guess, because it was my fire for Francis that brought me to this room.

But now I am scared. And alone.

Making do on less sounds good in theory, but when you suddenly find yourself with less, what sounded good looks bad. There was no lamp on the desk...would the ceiling light be good enough for me to work at night? The toilet and the shower are at the far end of that long, narrow, dark corridor...God knows what it looks like. I was alone in the room for about ten minutes—trying to figure out where to put my stuff—when I was hit with panic: This was a big mistake, I should have stayed in Rome.

I went to the midday prayer. As the friars read the psalms from the Office in Italian, I followed along in my English edition of the Divine Office, which I purchased in Rome before leaving because I didn't want to get out of the rhythm of saying the Office each day. After prayer, I followed the friars to their small refectory, which is adjacent to the San Bernardino refectory. In fact, the friars' refectory looks as if it once served as the kitchen for the larger refectory. This small refectory is actually a cave, as rock forms three of the four walls and most of the ceiling. At the back of the room, cut into the stone, is a large, rounded, brick hearth. In truth, the room is delightfully charming. The two tables are adequate for the five friars and me, their sole guest. I ate in silence as the friars chattered away in Italian. I said, "Grazie," each time I was given pasta, salad, chicken, bread, wine or fresh fruit.

Why am I here? What am I supposed to be doing?

Oh, the angst of those existential questions!

The good news is that I now have answers to some of those questions, though at times the answers are slow in coming or hard to accept. Years ago, I was so tormented by the fact that I couldn't find any reason or explanation for my own existence, that I saw little reason for living. God had died and had left a terrible void, leaving my life dangling over a precipice of unfathomable nothingness. That was true angst. What I was feeling now was a bad case of doubt and disequilibrium.

I had everything I needed in Rome. The library and the companionship of Sant' Isidoro lacked nothing. When I got tired or bored, I had all of Rome outside the gates with endless sights to explore. And I had coffee bars and bookstores galore. Now I'm in this tiny room. On top of a mountain. The place is locked up at seven o'clock at night. As for silence, tourists are still pouring in, most of them ignoring the silenzio signs. As I walked up one path leading to the caves of Francis and his early companions, I heard a cell phone ring. Why come to a hermitage and bring a cell phone? Silence is impossible for most people. Composer John Cage was right on the money when he said (in his book Silence): "Try as we may to make a silence, we cannot."

I'm not really alone...just set apart, isolated by language. And I suppose jolted by the transition from the excess of urban Rome to the starkness of rustic solitude.

Humans are creatures of habit and we hate having our comfortable routines interrupted. We are also uncomfortable with the unfamiliar. My being out of sorts is natural. I've got to relax, got to trust my instincts. That's the way it's been for the past two years of working on this book. This place was an important part of Francis' life. I need to calm down and settle into the spirit of the place, a

spirit of silence and prayer.
I think I'll go for a walk...into the woods.

Space for Silence

Come now, disciple of Christ, search into the secrets of solitude
with your loving teacher, so that...you may become an imitator
and sharer of his hidden silence....

—*SAINT BONAVENTURE*, THE TREE OF LIFE

From the very beginning of his new life in Christ, Francis wanted to know
what he should do. He was drawn both to solitary prayer and to a com-
bination of doing good works and proclaiming the Good News. But before
Francis could actually "do" anything, he had to "become" something,
because "being" must come before "doing." Thomas Merton, in
Contemplation in a World of Action, *expressed this principle well: "He*
who attempts to act and do for others or for the world without deepening
his own self-understanding, freedom, integrity and capacity to love, will
not have anything to give others. He will communicate to them nothing
but the contagion of his own obsessions, his aggressivity, his egocentered
ambitions, his delusions about ends and means, his doctrinaire preju-
dices and ideas" (pages 160-161).

I read somewhere that Saint Francis spent half his life alone in seclu-
sion. During that time, Francis became something.

In his journals, Gandhi made a reference to his practice of reserving
one day a week for total silence: "A periodic decree of silence is not a tor-
ture but a blessing."

Modern life leaves little space for silence.

Silence gives us space for receptivity; it allows us to hear the speech-
less language of God and to respond with our hearts.

The seventh-century saint of the Eastern Church John Climacus
wrote in his The Ladder of Divine Ascent: *"The friend of silence comes*
close to God. In secret he converses with him and receives his light."

Silence's partner in prayer is humility, and together they are internal
manifestations of the external acts of renunciation and poverty.

The Liturgy of the Hours

For even though the fig does not blossom,
nor fruit grow on the vine,
even though the olive crop fail,
and the fields produce no harvest,
even though flocks vanish from the folds
and stalls stand empty of cattle,

Yet I will rejoice in the Lord
and exalt in God my savior.
The Lord my God is my savior.
He makes me leap like deer,
he guides me to the high places.
(Habakkuk 3:17-19)

VIALE DI SAN FRANCESCO

Without comfort or glamour, this life did not permit any disguise.
There one was compelled to face one's own self.
—ELOI LECLERC, O.F.M., *THE WISDOM OF THE POOR ONE OF ASSISI*

You exit the chapel portion of the Grotto of St. Francis through a tiny doorway (no more than four feet high) that leads to a small portico, which extends out over the ravine. On the exterior wall above the door is a faded, poorly preserved, fifteenth-century fresco of Francis preaching to the birds. On the floor directly in front of the door, there is a small hole in the stone. If you bend over, you can look through the hole and see the basin of the ravine far below. The ground is covered with coins visitors drop in the hole. There is a legend attached to this hole: The hole was made by the devil when he was driven away by Brother Rufino, whom the devil had been severely tempting. The story can be found in the twenty-ninth chapter of the *Fioretti*. Looking out from the low wall of the portico, you can see to the other side of the ravine.

A long flight of stairs from the portico brings you back up to the main level of the hermitage. At the top of the stairs, to the left, is a small stone chapel, a building which is independent from the convento, and contains the tomb of Blessed Barnabas Manassei of Terni, a friar who died in 1474. Barnabas, along with another friar, established a type of pawnshop system known as *Monti di Pieta*—or "Deposit of Charity." In times of pressing need, the poor could entrust some object of value with the friars in exchange for an interest-free loan.

Off to the left from the stairs leading up from the Grotto of St. Francis is a dirt path which heads over a bridge and around to the other side of the ravine. The path, known as Viale di San Francesco, is bordered on the left by a six-foot-high wall of stone, part of the bedrock of the mountain. At the top of the wall, the tree-covered mountain continues up to the summit. On the right side of the path is a rustic wooden fence, beyond which is the steep descent of the wooded ravine. The path is naturally secluded and peaceful.

A little way up the path, there is a smaller path leading down to the cave of Brother Leo. Continuing along the main path, a little farther along is a stone altar used by groups for liturgical celebrations. Behind the altar is a natural amphitheater with rows of seats naturally formed into the rock. A tree stump has been carved into a lectern. At the end of the main path, there is another altar inside a little three-sided chapel honoring the Blessed Mother. All along the main path from the convento there are numerous narrow paths leading down the ravine or up the mountain. Along the narrower paths there are many spots to sit—on large rocks, logs or benches—and reflect. One path leads to the other side of the ravine and grottos once used by Bernard of Quintavalle, Giles, Silvestro and Andrea da Spello. Also from the tomb of Barnabas Manassei there is a path leading farther up the ravine to the grottos (or caves) of Blessed Rufino and Blessed Masseo.

PILGRIMAGE DIARY 73

The Dinner Bell

Listen to God's speech in his wondrous, terrible, gentle, loving, all-embracing silence.

—*CATHERINE DE HUECK DOHERTY*

*A*t six p.m., an hour of prayer began with the exposition of the Blessed Sacrament. Everyone knelt on the stone floor of the new chapel (built in 1970 for liturgical celebrations) as the priest incensed the gold monstrance containing a large sacred host, the consecrated Body of Christ. One by one, the friars, sisters and laypeople in attendance sat down for a thirty-minute period of silent adoration and meditation. I knelt for several minutes, most of that time thinking about the physical discomfort suffered by the seraphic saint in his attempt to purify himself and become fully united with God. The endless hours in those cold, damp caves, kneeling, sitting and sleeping on stone. My knees could only endure ten minutes and I had to sit down.

Despite my calming walk in the woods, my mind was like a monkey in a cage, jumping from side to side, swinging from one thought to the next, most of them trivial and jejune. I managed to slow my mind down by attentively praying the Jesus Prayer—"Lord Jesus Christ, have mercy on me, a sinner." Gradually, stillness came. I also almost nodded off.

I feel better. This is good. It's good to be here.

I offered a silent prayer: Lord, I long to hear your voice during the next few days.

Staring at the monstrance brought back memories. I remembered going to services like this as a kid. We've thrown a lot of good stuff out.

Going from thoughts of my wife, whom I missed greatly, to thinking about something Saint Gregory the Great, pope and doctor of the Church, wrote in the sixth century clearly demonstrated the kind of mental gymnastics of which my mind is capable. In a homily on Ezekiel, featured in yesterday's readings from the Office, the pope talked about his shortcomings in preaching and prayer. About his poor prayer life, Gregory offered an excuse, one most of us can understand: "When I lived in a monastic community I was able to

keep my tongue from idle topics and devote my mind almost
continually to the discipline of prayer. Since taking on my shoulders
the burden of pastoral care, I have been unable to keep steadily
recollected because my mind is distracted by many responsibilities."

Francis knew about distractions...that's why he spent so much
time in the Carceri—to escape them. Pope Gregory lamented that his
position compelled him diplomatically to "listen patiently" to
"aimless chatter," adding that his own weakness drew him "gradually
into idle talk and...saying the kinds of things that" beforehand he
"didn't even care to listen to." And he didn't own a TV! Saint
Gregory the Great also said, "My mind is sundered and torn to
pieces by the many and serious things I have to think about," thereby
making it difficult to effectively preach or pray.

The pope's comments came to mind because I was thinking how
difficult it is to stop thinking, to be still, really still, before the Lord.
Today I overheard an English-speaking friar talking to a group of
pilgrims. He was saying how difficult it was for him to even say the
Our Father without his mind disengaging from the words of the
prayer Jesus taught us. "I have to say it slowly, forcing myself to think
about each word, and even then I sometimes only make it halfway
through and my mind is thinking about something else; and when
that happens, I stop and start over." The priest was trying his best to
tell his audience just how far removed he and they were from the
kind of deep, all-consuming prayer that Francis entered into in these
woods.

My walk in the woods helped me to relax, but on the two or
three occasions I sat down to be still and to pray, my mind would
have no part of it. Do you think that taxi driver understood to pick
me up on Monday? *Lunedi* does mean "Monday," doesn't it?

At 6:30 p.m., the silent meditation before the Blessed Sacrament
came to an end and we began reciting evening prayer from the
Office. Rather, they began singing it, as I quietly followed by reading
it in English to myself. The opening hymn contained this verse:

> Lord, we thy presence seek;
> may ours this blessing be;
> give us a pure and lowly heart,
> a temple fit for thee.

Yes, Jesus...come, let me hear your voice.

I looked out the window, which was wide open. The trees, huddled together, swayed in the breeze. Rabindranath Tagore, the Bengali poet and mystic, once whispered: "Be still, my heart, these trees are prayers." Amen. Trees are silent priests. I saw a gray cat curled up asleep on a wall...two feet away from the cat sat a bird, fearless of the sleeping terror. As I gazed at the beauty of the ravine, the congregation finished reading the psalms.

A friar stood up and read the Scripture, from the first letter of Peter:

> You have been obedient to the truth and purified your souls until loved like brothers, in sincerity; let your love for each other be real and from a pure heart—your new birth was not from any mortal seed but from the everlasting word of the living God. (1:22-23)

After the conclusion of evening prayer, the priest blessed the people by making the sign of the cross with the monstrance. He then removed the sacred host and placed it in the tabernacle. Good night, Jesus.

Peaceful hour.

Afterward, all the visitors had to leave, and the gates were locked. I was inside and glad. I sat in the now-silent triangular courtyard. A friar fed the gray cat, saying as he placed the dish on the ground, "Mangia" ("eat"). After eating, the cat jumped up on me, looking to have its head rubbed. I obliged.

At 7:30 p.m., I took a stroll along the path leading to the caves. The rustle of the leaves playing in the wind and the crunch from my sandals on the pebbles below my feet were the only sounds I heard as night slowly descended on the mountain. The fading light from the golden glow of the setting sun, lightly veiled in fine misty clouds, was barely squeezing through the thicket of trees. Coolness came faster than darkness. I'm glad I brought a jacket. As I passed two friars dressed in their habits and sandals and walking back toward the convento, they reminded me that dinner was at eight p.m. I walked a little farther and then headed back. As I walked, it was easy to imagine the ideal of Franciscan spirituality and the mystic rapture evoked in the Fioretti.

This is good. The quiet. Being apart. Praying. Looking in. Listening...for the dinner bell, which rang at eight p.m.

> *The convento fig trees had blossomed, and gifted us with a delicious dessert.*
>
> *Thought: Francis bloomed in the fertile ground of stillness.*
>
> *I'll end with the poetry of T. S. Eliot, taken from "Choruses from 'The Rock'":*

> The endless cycle of idea and action,
> Endless invention, endless experiment,
> Brings knowledge of motion, but not of stillness;
> Knowledge of speech, but not of silence;
> Knowledge of words, but ignorance of the Word.
> ...
>
> Where is the Life we have lost in living?
> Where is the wisdom we have lost in knowledge?
> Where is the knowledge we have lost in information?

Where is the information superhighway headed...without God?

THE GROTTO OF BROTHER GILES

One of the paths off the Viale di San Francesco leads to the Grotto of Brother Giles. The path is steep and it winds and twists its way down one side of the ravine and up the other. On my way to Giles' cave, I nearly stepped on a snake—it scared the living daylights out of me. And it reminded me just how untamed these woods were in the days when Francis and his pals hung out here. The sight of the snake almost had me running back to Assisi. Not long after my close encounter with the snake, I came upon the hermitage of Bernard of Quintavalle. It was located far below the convento complex on a ledge above the basin of the ravine. Very secluded, almost hidden. The hermitage was built of stone, with the bedrock of the mountain forming part of the roof and all of the back wall.

A little farther along the ledge is a second hermitage; this one, according to a sign posted in 1860, belonged to Giles. It was similar to Bernard's except the rockbed had formed a natural hollowed-out space to which Giles simply added a stone wall to create a cave-like effect and give him some protection from the cold and rain. A little farther along the ledge was another small hermitage built in the rock. But this one was occupied by a young couple...and they weren't praying. I discreetly returned to Giles's hermitage, without ever finding out which of the early companions occupied the lovers' hermitage.

Giles was at Francis' side from the very beginning. In the spring of 1209, when he was only eighteen years old, Giles became the third person to join Francis. (Bernard of Quintavalle and Peter Catanii were the first two.) When the four men set out on their first missionary journey, Francis was paired with Giles and they headed for the Marches of Ancona, while Bernard and Peter took another direction. Giles, who was a native of Assisi, was illiterate and a simple man, the son of a peasant couple, yet Francis loved him dearly. While he may have lacked riches and education, Giles had a noble mind which was capable of shrewd judgment and quick wit. During the later years of his life, Giles was highly respected for his piercing common sense and spiritual insight, and learned people sought him out in order to obtain some pithy word of wisdom.

Brother Giles went on pilgrimages to Santiago de Compostela (in Spain) and Jerusalem. For a time he lived as a hermit in a grotto at the Carceri atop Mount Subasio. Francis praised Giles's spirit of contemplation. Giles was present at Saint Francis' death in 1226; he was also present at Bernard's death in 1241. Giles deplored what he saw as the relaxation of spirituality in the Order after the death of Francis. During the last twenty years of his life, he lived as a hermit near Perugia, where he was visited by Pope Gregory IX, Saint Bonaventure and many cardinals. Giles died on April 22, 1262. (On that date, 712 years later, my daughter, Adrienne Frances Straub, was born.)

During the past hundred years, the most widely read book on the life of Saint Francis has been *The Little Flowers*, which was written by an Italian Franciscan, Brother Ugolino di Monte Santa Maria, who lived a century after the death of Francis. Raphael Brown's modern English translation of the book appeared in 1958, and nearly fifty pages of that expanded edition of *The Little Flowers* is devoted to Giles. Part Four covers his life, as written by Brother Leo, and Part Five is devoted to "The Sayings of Brother Giles." It seems the illiterate Giles had a lot to say...and here is some of it, from Part Five of *The Little Flowers*:

> He who does not see great things thinks that small things are great.
> Grace attracts grace. One vice connects with other vices.
> Humility sets the mind at rest because it produces patience.

That man is happy who does not wish to seem different, either in word or character, from the manner in which God shaped him.

That man is happy who avoids thinking, saying, or doing anything that calls for rebuke.

A man should never give way to the desire to see, hear, or discuss anything useless to his soul. He should always stick to this rule.

Those five aphoristic pieces of sage advice form a solid foundation upon which any person can build a moral, ethical and godly life. I'm particularly struck by the bluntness of the last dictum, which, if I assiduously followed it, would pretty much rule out my involvement with much of modern life...or at least cause me to stop watching David Letterman or any movie featuring Arnold Schwarzenegger.

PILGRIMAGE DIARY 74

Wake Up

His safest haven was prayer; not prayer of a single moment, or idle or presumptuous prayer, but prayer of long duration, full of devotion, serene in humility. If he began late he would scarcely finish before morning. Walking, sitting, eating, or drinking, he was always intent upon prayer. He would go alone to pray at night in churches abandoned and located in deserted places.

—*THOMAS OF CELANO*, FIRST LIFE

*M*y first night in my cell went well. I did a little writing, and some reading, but I tired early and turned the light out by 10 p.m. It was very dark and very quiet on top of the mountain. I cannot recall hearing a sound the entire night. But the silence—and my sleep—was shattered at 6:15 a.m. by the ringing of the rooftop bell. It was so loud, it sounded as if it were right outside my window.

Morning prayer began at 6:45 a.m. And it's done a little differently than at Sant' Isidoro. Here, they begin with the Office of Readings, which are read in private at Sant' Isidoro. They sing two psalms and then a friar reads the longer passages. When this "extra" part of the Office is completed, at 7:00, they then begin a half-hour period of silent meditation. At 7:30, they recite morning prayer, *which is immediately followed by the celebration of the liturgy, including a full homily.*

The Office of Readings, meditation, morning prayer and Mass take a full hour and a half. And they do it every day. I enjoyed it, although once during the meditation my mind drifted off to a coffee bar in Assisi and a hot cup of cappuccino.

THE CAVE OF BROTHER LEO

The cave of Brother Leo is reached along a path that is shorter and less steep than the one going to Brother Giles's cave. As I stood silently in front of Brother Leo's cave, I recalled a passage from Nikos Kazantzakis's *Saint Francis*, in which the novelist writes as Brother Leo.

> And while I was mulling all this in my mind, my body trembling, Francis suddenly emerged from the cave. He was radiant—a gleaming cinder. Prayer had eaten away his flesh again but what remained shone like pure soul. He held out his hand to me. A peculiar expression of joy was promenading over his face.
>
> "Well, Brother Leo, are you ready?" he called....
>
> He seemed delirious. His eyes were inflamed and as he came closer I descried angels and phantoms within the pupils. I was terrified. Could he have taken leave of his senses?
>
> He understood, and laughed. But his fire did not subside.
>
> "People have enumerated many terms of praise for the Lord up to now," he said. "But I shall enumerate still more. Listen to what I shall call Him: the Bottomless Abyss, the Insatiable, the Merciless, the Indefatigable, the Unsatisfied. He who never once has said to poor, unfortunate mankind: 'Enough!'"
>
> Coming still closer, he placed his lips next to my ear and cried in a thunderous voice:
>
> "'Not enough!' That is what He screamed at me. If you ask, Brother Leo, what God commands without respite, I can tell you, for I learned it these past three days and nights in the cave. Listen! 'Not enough! Not enough.' That's what He shouts each day, each hour to poor, miserable man. 'Not enough! Not enough!' 'I can't go further,' whines man. 'You can!' the Lord replies. 'I shall break in two,' man whines again. 'Break!' the Lord replies."

Francis' voice had begun to crack. A large tear rolled down his cheek. I felt overwhelming compassion for Francis.

I became angry: an injustice was being done. I felt overwhelming compassion for Francis.

"What more does He expect from you?" I asked. "Didn't you restore San Damiano's?"

"Not enough!"

"Didn't you abandon your mother and father?"

"Not enough!"

"Didn't you kiss the leper?"

"Not enough! ...We're dealing with God, and from Him there is no escape!" (pages 118-119)

In that scene Kazantzakis dramatically expressed the way mystics seem to experience God as an abyss that attracts and captivates, and that the attraction and captivation increases in intensity as the mystic gets closer to God. Saint Catherine of Siena expressed that reality in her *Dialogues*:

O eternal Trinity! You are a bottomless sea into which, the more I sink, the more I find You; and the more I find you, the more still I search for You. Of you I could never say "enough." The soul which fulfills itself in Your depths, longs unceasingly for You because it is always hungering for You; it is always desirous of seeing its light in Your light. Could you give me anything more than Your own self? You are the fire, always burning and never consumed. You are the fire which consumes all selfish love of the soul; You are the light beyond all light. You, the cloak which covers all nakedness, food, that with its sweetness makes all who are hungry happy.

Clothe me, eternal Trinity, clothe me with Yourself that I may live this life in true obedience and in the light of faith with which you have inebriated my soul.

In the darkness of this cave, an earthly womb that nurtured a reconnection to the divinity within him, Brother Leo experienced the light of faith that inebriated his stout soul. We can only imagine.

PILGRIMAGE DIARY 75

Il Sole e la Luna Sopra Assisi

God is a friend of silence. Trees, flowers, grass grow in silence.
See the stars, moon, and sun, how they move in silence.
—*MOTHER TERESA*

*A*fter evening prayer on my second day at the Carceri, I once
again rushed off to enjoy the primitive chapels, and the
outdoor grottos in the splendor of silence. As I walked back from
Brother Leo's cave, I could hear organ music off in the distance. One
of the friars must have been practicing. An owl and some birds
formed a chorus and added to the music. Before entering the
convento, I decided to walk down the stone pathway to the Grotto of
St. Francis and say a prayer where he used to meditate. During the
day, the door to the grotto is an exit, but now, with the hermitage
closed to the public, I was free to enter the exit. After a few minutes
of quiet time, I started back to the convento. When I emerged
through the small doorway, the sun was just seconds from setting.
High in the quickly darkening sky was the faint trace of a quarter
moon, surrounded by a few bright stars. Off in the distance below,
beyond the trees of the ravine, I could see lights twinkling in the
valley. It was a magnificent picture, one the author of The Canticle of
the Creatures, whose rock bed was only a few feet away, had seen
many times.

The next morning when I read the following verses from Psalm
8, that picture danced across my mind:

> When I see the heavens, the work of your hands,
> the moon and the stars which you arranged,
> what is man that you should keep him in mind,
> mortal man that you care for him?
>
> Yet you have made him little less than a god;
> with glory and honor you crowned him,
> gave him power over the works of your hand,
> put all things under his feet. (4-7)

*As beautiful as that picture was, that brief moment in time, it could
not compare to what Francis saw in the darkness of his cave, now a
shrine, when he looked deeply within himself. As Origen said in*

Hexapla, "Thou art a second world in miniature, the sun and moon are within thee, and also the stars."

Oh, Lord Jesus, help me discover my own inner beauty,
so that I may then see more fully the beauty of my Creator.

The Liturgy of the Hours

Praise him, sun and moon,
praise him, shining stars.
Praise him, highest heavens
and the waters above the heavens.
(Psalm 148:3-4)

PILGRIMAGE DIARY 76

Preghiera

To pray is to surrender our whole being to God, letting him take
over the rudder of our existence.

—*JEAN VANIER*, COMMUNITY AND GROWTH

*Preghiera means "prayer"...and the community of friars and
sisters living at the Carceri do pray. Each day, they spend two
hours and forty-five minutes in public, communal prayer. That's a bit
more than ten percent of each day...given to the Lord.*

*Praying is hard for me; it is often an arid, lifeless ritual that seems
forced. I suppose my biggest shortcoming in my prayer life is that I
fail to give it enough time. Saint Francis de Sales wisely pointed out,
"We seldom do well what we only do seldom." Evelyn Underhill
called prayer a "difficult art." I know the most important ingredient
in advancing in the arts is a single-minded dedication to mastering*

the laws and traditions of your chosen field of expression. Great
saints and great artists are alike in their willingness to sacrifice
anything and everything—including family and friends—in pursuit of
the object of their affection, either their God or their art. Writing of
this similarity between saints and artists in The Essentials of
Mysticism, *Underhill said, "The vitality which we diffuse amongst*
many interests and loves, these [saints and artists] must concentrate
on the object of their quest. Hence St. Francis himself flung his
family aside without scruple when it came to a parting of the ways.
Hence Jacopone da Todi was warned that even spiritual friendships
must be held lightly by the pilgrim on the way of the cross" (page
170).

Here in the Carceri where contemplative prayer is part of the
fabric of daily life and the fruit of that life is so abundantly rich, I
can't help but wonder why so many—including myself—find it
difficult to enter into a more contemplative prayer life. Actually there
is no reason to wonder, for the reason is obvious: It takes sacrifice.
That reason became obvious to me when I read the following from
Chapter 31 of the third book of The Imitation of Christ:

> Lord, I am greatly in need of yet more grace if I am to reach that
> state where no creature can impede my progress. For as long as
> anything holds me back, I cannot come freely to You.... Who is
> more free than he who desires nothing upon earth? Rapt in
> spirit, a man must rise above all created [that is, perishable]
> things, and perfectly forsaking himself, see clearly that nothing
> in creation can compare with the Creator. But unless a man is
> freed from dependence on creatures, he cannot turn freely to
> the things of God. This is the reason why there are so few con-
> templatives, for there are few who can free themselves entirely
> from transitory things.

In fact, Saint John of the Cross felt few are willing to pay the full
price of renunciation at which alone the mystic experience can be
purchased; indeed, rare is the person willing to make the Ascent of
Mount Carmel with him.

Am I willing to give up all—or even much—of what I cherish?
Or, more basically, can I relegate all the things and people whom I
consider important in my life to second place, so that God alone
occupies the throne of my heart and mind?

Before any progress is made along the spiritual path, it seems essential that we consider exactly where our affections really lie. The Carceri is a good place to do that.

The Liturgy of the Hours

An excerpt from a sermon of Pope Saint Leo the Great on the Beatitudes:

The blessedness of seeing God is rightly promised to those who are pure of heart. For the eye that is filled with dirt cannot see the brightness of true light; what is joy to the clear, shining mind is punishment for the mind that is stained. Let the darkness of the empty things of this world be set aside and the eyes of the soul be cleansed of all the filth of sin so that the inward sight may enjoy the wonderful vision of God.

PILGRIMAGE DIARY 77

Empty Things

God is ready to give great things when we are ready...to give up everything.

—*MEISTER ECKHART*

The real reason prayer is hard for me is that I'm still far too attracted to the empty things of the world. I am a sinner. The real reason the presence of porno magazines in Assisi bothered me so much is that a few weeks ago in Rome...I bought one.

A Tiny Seed

Prayer means turning to Reality, taking our part, however humble, tentative and half-understood, in the continual conversation, the communion, of our spirits with the Eternal Spirit....
—*EVELYN UNDERHILL*, THE SPIRITUAL LIFE

I tried to ignore God, to forget God and even to deny God. Yet, somewhere deep within me there was this unexplainable longing for God. Most of the time, the grind of daily life was able to still this vague yearning, to muffle its soft voice. In those rare, brief and quiet moments when I did feel its dim presence, I wasn't sure what it was. I just felt something was missing. I thought of it as a faint wish that God was real, and that an encounter with the Eternal was possible. This longing for completion, for God, was a tiny seed buried within my human imperfection that longed to grow into divine perfection. That seed is buried within each of us. The seed grows when it is watered by prayer and recognizes its dependency on God. The tiny seed slowly blossoms as God increasingly becomes the center of our lives.

I think Saint Francis saw a connection between prayer and poverty. The image of Jesus lying helplessly in a manger and the image of Jesus naked and exposed, hanging on the cross, were central to Francis' spirituality. Christ was poor and fully open to the will of God. And so Francis believed Christ sought the same poverty from his followers, who should be free of all ties to earthly goods, living without any concern for them, dependence on them, or desire for them, so that they would belong fully and exclusively to God.

PILGRIMAGE DIARY 78

Unmended Flaws

My faults and flaws are ever before me, masked but unmended. My only hope is knowing that you see me as I am and forgive me without hesitation or question. In your kindness, God, have mercy on me, a sinner.

The Liturgy of the Hours

A reading from the sermons of Saint Bernard.

The whole of the spiritual life turns on these two things: we are troubled when we contemplate ourselves and our sorrow brings salvation; when we contemplate God we are restored, so that we receive consolation from the joy of the Holy Spirit. From the contemplation of ourselves we gain fear and humility; but from the contemplation of God, hope and love.

PILGRIMAGE DIARY 79

A Joke

I f I had a phone in my room, I could call it a cell phone.

PILGRIMAGE DIARY 80

A Prayer

*Help me, dear lord,
to turn my loneliness
into a love of solitude.*

*Help me, dear Lord,
transform my inner hostility
into generous hospitality.*

*Help me, dear Lord,
to convert my illusions
into faithful prayers.*

The Big Room

*O*n my first day at the Eremo delle Carceri, I commented, ruefully, on the size of my room, noting how small it was. Well, today I found out that I had the "big" room. Not only are the other cells slightly smaller, but most do not even have a writing table and only one other room has a sink.

Suddenly, this small room seems like a suite. By the way, it's more than enough space.

We each need to create a little space for ourselves, a space to be alone. Thomas Merton writes:

> There should be at least a room or some corner where no one will find you and disturb you or notice you. You should be free to untether yourself from the world and set yourself free, loosing all the fine strings and strands of tension that bind you, by sight, by sound, by thought, to the pressure of other men.... Once you have found a place, be content with it, and do not be disturbed if a good reason takes you out of it. Love it, and return to it as soon as you can. (*New Seeds of Contemplation*, pages 81-82)

Long before Merton's pen ever touched paper, the American novelist Louisa May Alcott had discovered the wisdom of having a space all her own: "I have at last got that little room I have wanted so long, and I am very happy about it. It does me good to be alone."

Going Beyond Meaning

> Without silence around us, the inward stillness in which God educates and molds us is impossible.
> —*EVELYN UNDERHILL*, THE WAYS OF THE SPIRIT

I find myself thinking about all the years I spent searching for some meaning to life. Every path I followed was a dead end. Ironically, the meaning was right before my eyes, if I had just looked within, where the meaning is buried in a place beyond meaning.

The Carceri is a place of inspiration, a place where human

consciousness can be temporarily set free so it can, with the help of grace, catch a glimpse of the wholeness of God mysteriously hidden within us...and also all around us.

Silence produces an inner restfulness that helps the soul to soar. The greatest malady of our time is the absence of stillness and silence.

The Essence of a Full Life

The Divine Presence has always been with us, but we think it absent. That thought is the monumental illusion of the human condition. The spiritual journey is designed to heal it.

—*THOMAS KEATING*, INVITATION TO LOVE

Here is a guest reflection from Evelyn Underhill, taken from her book The Ways of the Spirit*:*

Christ's idea of love is not a sentimental one. It requires the consecration of all our intelligence and all our energy as well as our feeling, for it involves the gift of the whole personality to God. It means turning in prayer to God Himself, attending to Him, entering by self-forgetfulness into His very life. This is not an easy thing to do, nor is it an especially emotional thing to do. There is nothing effusive about it, but it is the essence of full life.

Religious emotion and sanctity are not the same thing. Sometimes they appear to be mutually exclusive. But pure love or charity, that utter self-giving of the creature which is the human reply to the love of God, that is the same as sanctity.

What is pure love? It is that which gives and gives and never demands. It is steady, orderly, and without feverishness. (page 61)

Oh Lord, your love is the cure for my sinfulness. Lord, I beg you, please help me not to forget that your love is ceaselessly present in me, constantly molding me, and always inviting me to grow into greater love, and into a deeper reality of you.

The Liturgy of the Hours

O Lord, you search me and you know me,
...
You mark when I walk or lie down,
all my ways lie open to you.

Before ever a word is on my tongue
you know it, O Lord, through and
through.
...
O where can I go from your spirit,
or where can I flee from your face?
(Psalm 139:1,3-4,7)

PILGRIMAGE DIARY 83

Alone in a Cave

Heaven and hell are separated only by our ego. If we abandon
the ego, we enter the kingdom of God. There are no magical rituals that take us there, only the dying of our false ego. Only
love gives us the power to abandon everything so as to enter
into this new order of being.

—*WILLIGIS JAGER*, SEARCH FOR THE MEANING OF LIFE

*I*t is, of course, abundantly clear to me just how important
solitude was in the life of Saint Francis. Still, his penchant for
solitude struck me with new force today, when I sat alone in a cave
and read the following passage from Celano's First Life:

He made himself insensible to all unnecessary external noise;
he constantly strove to master his exterior senses and dominate

his lower inclinations in order to occupy himself with God alone. The cleft of the rock was his preferred nesting place, between two panels of the wall of a hut the abode of his choice. His contemplative soul was happy to find a cabin in complete solitude during his various journeys; he would remain there a long time and would annihilate himself then in the contemplation of the wounds of the Lord. He therefore frequently chose to withdraw into solitary places in order to occupy himself directly with God. (71)

The cave has always been a symbol of the unconscious and a place for encounters with God. If you follow the inner path, you eventually come to the cave of your heart, where you will encounter the wilderness and darkness of isolation, shut off from thoughts, feelings and ideas, in order to be open to a visit from God. Everything must be left behind, including the ego, before entering the cave if we hope to emerge transformed.

Pilgrimage Diary 84

Cold Shower

Scripture exhorts us to praise God in everything...the good and the bad alike. But it's hard to praise God when things don't go our way. This morning when I turned on the shower, I waited and waited for it to get hot. Eventually I noticed that someone had unplugged the little water heater which is mounted high on the wall.

Never once during my cold shower did I praise God.

Pilgrimage Diary 85

No Wedding Bells in Brother Masseo's Cave

Love is not ruled by what must be nor by what is possible. Love knows nothing of this law; it has no rule, it knows no bounds.
—*SAINT PETER CHRYSOLOGUS* (406-c.450)

It is five o'clock in the afternoon on Saturday, September 6th. I'm sitting alone in Brother Masseo's cave, located at the far end of the ravine; but my heart is in Albany, New York, where it is eleven o'clock in the morning, and my nephew (and godson) Brian's wedding is about to begin.

I should be there, taking pictures for him and his lovely bride, LeAnn.

Everyone else is there. My daughter, Adrienne. My brother, Bill, and his wife, Norma. My sister Terry and her husband, Joe. All the cousins are there: Susan (and her husband and two kids), Nancy, Billy (and his wife), Donna, Carolyn, Kevin, Craig and Keith. And, of course, Brian's brothers, David and Gregory (and his wife), are there. My sister Regina and her husband, Ron, have planned a wonderful day for the second of their three sons.

And I should be there.

But I should be here, in this cave, too.

The ability to bilocate would be handy today. Most days, being in one place is tough enough, but today I'd be happy to be in two places at once. I cried earlier today because of the remorse I felt at not being at Brian's wedding. An hour-long phone conversation I had with him last weekend was of some solace. Brian holds a special place in my heart. He knows how much I want to be there, and he loves me enough to be glad I'm where I need to be.

Perhaps from this cave I can tell Brian what I wouldn't be able to say to him during a festive wedding reception.

Years ago, I told Brian I was a mystic agnostic. It was my way of saying I was attracted to spirituality, yet I couldn't believe in the Source of spirituality. We often talked about our "difficulties" with this "God stuff." I wish Brian could be sitting in this cave with me and I could open my heart and show him how much God means to me today. In our phone conversation last weekend, I shared with him my thoughts on marital love—in which a couple does not try to possess or change each other but instead gives each other the freedom to be who they are and all they can be—but I wish instead I could have told him how my love for God had renewed and intensified my love for my wife. Loving God, who is the Source of love, has taught me how truly to love my wife, and shows me how I can be a channel of God's love for her.

The alarmingly high number of failed marriages—including my own first marriage—reflects our failed relationship with God. As selfless, unceasing and unconditional as God's love is for us, so, too, should our love be for our spouses. It's a love that puts the needs of the other first...a love which was beautifully expressed by Hans Urs von Balthasar: "To live with another within the compass of one heart: I must move to the side, must make myself small, so that the other has space and does not feel crowded" (The Last Grain of Wheat, page 9). This kind of love is far different from the romantic love we seem to crave. One does not "fall" in love. The idea of "falling" in love contains the opposite possibility, that is, we can "fall" out of love. Love is a choice. It takes commitment, dedication and work and has nothing to do with the romantic fairy tales manufactured by the Hollywood dream machine, which tell us that our happiness can be found only in the perfect "other." There is no perfect other, other than God. Moreover, before you can find happiness in another, or the Other, you need to find it within yourself. The mystery is that in discovering your own inner self, you discover God, who is the One and only source of love and true happiness. And true happiness does not mean, as Hollywood suggests, a life without pain, suffering and death. True happiness is the ability to see God in these unpleasant facets of human life.

If Brian were here in this cave, I'd tell him the best way he could love LeAnn is to love God. And the best way to love God is to strip himself as bare as this cave, and to stand naked and empty before God who wants only to clothe him and fill him with love.

As much as I love Brian and wanted to be with him and the entire family on this day...this cave is where I need to be because the cave is showing me that I still haven't stood completely naked and empty before God.

May God bless Brian and LeAnn, and grant them a lifetime of mutual love.

DETACHMENT AND RENUNCIATION

Sitting alone in Brother Masseo's cave quite naturally led me to thoughts of detachment and renunciation and, of course, to Lady Poverty. A few days earlier I had found in the library of Sant' Isidoro a charming little book published in London in 1901—*The Lady Poverty: A XIII Century Allegory*. The book was a new translation (by Montgomery Carmichael) of the *Sacrum Commercium Beati Francisci cum Paupertate*. Part of the book's charm came from its delicate design and layout. And the translator had inscribed a personal note to the "Vicar General of the Order of Friars Minor" which was dated Christmas 1901.

Of course, the *Sacrum Commercium* is an allegory, simple in form and charming in conception, telling how Francis wooed and won the heart of Lady Poverty. But what I liked about this particular publication was the inclusion of a chapter titled "The Spiritual Significance of Evangelical Poverty," written by Father Cuthbert, a respected biographer of the saint. In the first part of his essay, Father Cuthbert writes:

> Artificial stimulus and transient excitement could add nought to the Joy that was his. To him the sky and the earth, the sun and the flowers, the fields and all living things, spoke with articulate speech of the life that is in them. As for his fellow-men, their life was his life. He had come to pass beyond the bounds of his own personality, and to enter into that spiritual communion with all living things, whereby man escapes from his own limitations, and the world lives in him as he in the world. And above all, and yet in all, he beheld the ever blessed God, that author of all life that is. To Francis, God was ever present in the Creation, the Life behind all life.... The intimate relationship binding creation to its Creator was to him an abiding perception; he could not think of Earth apart from Heaven, nor of finite man apart from Infinite God. Whatever was good and beautiful was to him an indication of the Divine Goodness and Beauty, a portal of the Eternal Kingdom; and with keen spiritual intuition he discovered the good and the beautiful, where men of lesser sensibility would only find the commonplace and the material.

Father Cuthbert goes on to discuss the role of detachment and renunciation in the spiritual life of Saint Francis. The excerpts that follow are his closing remarks.

> Here it may be as well to take note how alien is the poverty of St. Francis from the vulgarity and squalor, the idleness and discontent, which mark too frequently the life of the poor. No greater misconception of Franciscan poverty could there be than to conceive it as sanctioning or condoning any condition that detracts from the proper native dignity of man....
>
>   The poverty of our city slums where hearts break in discontent, and souls are starved for lack of spiritual intelligence—

such was not the poverty of Francis' dream. To use his own manner of speech, this is poverty in slavery, degraded and dishonoured by the vice and selfishness of man. With a full heart would he have set himself to rescue his Ideal from her modern degradation and restore her to her place of honor upon the earth. Knight-errant as he was, he would not have rested until poverty was made honourable amongst men. To rescue the poor from conditions which have so effectually demoralised them during the past two or three centuries of unheeding individualism, would undoubtedly have been to Francis a first and urgent duty were he with us today. Even in his own time he regarded with anxiety the conditions which debased the poor; even then he considered himself the knight-errant sent to rescue the comely maiden Poverty from the neglect and heartless scorn of the world. But was ever Italian peasant so utterly degraded as are many of the victims of modern industrialism? Poverty with Francis was the mother of spiritual freedom; poverty in the London slum is synonymous with hard materialism and irreligion. Was ever contrast greater? And yet Francis has made evident to us that beneath the squalor and degradation of the modern city, there is a spiritual possibility, if only it can be recovered....

Assuredly to us who live our lives upon the pulse of a great industrial empire, this message of the Poverello comes with a distinctness not to be passed unheeded. As a race we are a prosperous people, and money-making is our first preoccupation. Luxuries are easily within our grasp; cheap luxuries, perhaps, which is all the worse, for that very cheapness is a snare blinding us to the fact that what we indulge in is a luxury. In money-making and luxury lie the elemental dangers to our spiritual life.... To all who revolt against the vulgar materialism which dominates so much of our present life, Francis of Assisi is a prophet sent by God. Standing against the dark background of Avarice and Luxury which has already infested the growing commercial centres of the mediaeval world, he throws the light of his own clear personality into the dark corners of our life.

We yearn, many of us, for a deeper spiritual life, we sorrow because the joy of life seems flitting even further and further away from this complex social organism of ours. We seek direction, and the Poverello is here to lead us; and the way he leads is that of detachment and renunciation. But his own personality and life are an assurance to us that the renunciation he preaches, leads to richer gain; he leads us through death, only that we may find life even here, in some measure, upon the earth, and in the fullness of the spirit hereafter. Thus and not otherwise does he interpret to us the Poverty of Christ.

One hundred years later, things are still the same.

PILGRIMAGE DIARY 86

Not a Sound

Silence is God's first language; everything else is a poor translation. In order to hear that language, we must learn to be still and to rest in God.

—*THOMAS KEATING*, INVITATION TO LOVE

After evening prayer, one of the friars was about to lock the door to the Cappella di San Bernardino, when he noticed me standing nearby. Graciously, through simple gestures, he asked if I wanted to go in. I nodded yes. "Dopo," he said, holding up the key, indicating he would lock it later.

For one hour, I was alone in the two upper chapels and the lower, two-room grotto of Saint Francis. I was able to take an unhurried, quiet look at all the details of the art and design, and jot down notes for use in enhancing my manuscript. After about forty minutes, I put down my pen and notebook.

Alone in the tiny chapel commemorating the place where Francis meditated and prayed, I stood in front of the crucifix, in silence, my eyes shut, my hands raised, for fifteen minutes.

Not a sound.

Peace.

In The Ladder of Divine Ascent, *Saint John Climacus writes, "The friend of silence comes close to God. In secret he converses with Him and receives His light."*

PILGRIMAGE DIARY 87

You Are

*You are
who
you are
when
you are
alone.*

PILGRIMAGE DIARY 88

Nocturnal Adoration

Jesus went into the hills to pray; and he spent the whole night in prayer to God.

—*LUKE 6:12*

O n Saturday night and Sunday morning, the schedule varies slightly. You get to sleep fifteen minutes longer on Saturday night, because morning prayer on Sunday begins at seven instead of 6:45. And morning prayer begins not with the office of the readings, but with a half hour of silent meditation. The Office of the Readings for Sunday is read on Saturday night at 9:30.

Following the fifteen-minute service on Saturday night, I was standing near the wall in the small cloister, enjoying the starry night and the twinkling lights of the valley below, when a young Italian seminarian came up to speak with me. Five young men, all about to enter a diocesan seminary in a few weeks, were spending a few days on a silent retreat at the Carceri. They were staying in a little guest house that is not connected to the friary. Two of the young men spoke a little English and I had spoken briefly to them two or three times during my first three days at the hermitage. The young man wanted to tell me that they were going to have an all-night vigil of adoration of the Blessed Sacrament in the crypt. Crypt? I didn't know there was a crypt, so I naturally wanted to see it.

I followed the young man back into the new church. We descended a flight of stairs to a lower level where there was a small chapel made completely of rustic, earth-tone bricks. The low vaulted ceiling and the walls were free of adornment, except for a sculpted crucifix mounted on the front wall behind the small stone altar. Along the back wall, there was a beautifully carved wooden statue of Mary. Simple wicker stools lined the side walls.

When we entered the crypt, the four other seminarians were already there. They had been joined by the three nuns who work in the kitchen, and one young Italian woman who would be entering the Order in the fall. One of the sisters was an elderly Italian woman, another a young woman from India, and the third a young Italian woman. The sisters always wore their Franciscan habits, which were similar to the friars' habits, including the white cord around the waist; the habit included a simple, white veil, which covered all but a small portion of their hair.

Within minutes of our arrival, Father Sergio entered, carrying a small, simple monstrance housing the consecrated host. As he entered, everyone knelt on the stone floor. After saying a few prayers, the friar left the crypt. We all remained on our knees. In silence.

Adoration is the oxygen of spiritual life; but, sadly, in our time we've forgotten how to renew ourselves by breathing deeply the pure divine glory of Life itself.

I was the first to sit down. The old sister was the last. I stayed in the chapel for about an hour. The young men were going to spend the entire night, until morning prayer, continually praying in shifts. At least one guy would be in the crypt until morning.

Imagine...five young, virile, good-looking guys spending an entire Saturday night worshiping Christ in the Blessed Sacrament. I was deeply moved by the faith of the seminarians and the sisters. Before leaving, I looked at their faces as their attention was fixed on the host on the altar. Their faces displayed a serenity and contentment that is rarely, if ever, seen in daily life. From my contact with the sisters and seminarians (and the friars also), I found them to be real people. Gentle, kind, caring...and bright. They weren't religious fanatics. They didn't exude some false or plastic piety...or spiritual pride. They were real people who have found peace in Christ and have dedicated their lives to prayer and service.

The beauty of the Franciscan charism is that it has room for a contemplative expression, as well as a more active life, such as the friars in Philadelphia lead, busy in service to the poor, yet rooted in *prayer, living simply so others can simply live. The peace I saw on the faces of the sisters and seminarians in this tiny, mountaintop chapel I also saw on the faces of the friars, nuns and laypeople working in the slums of Philadelphia.*

The peace was within them.

PILGRIMAGE DIARY 89

Morning Offering

O Jesus, through the Immaculate Heart of Mary, I offer Thee the prayers, works, sufferings and joys of this day for all the intentions of Thy divine Heart in the Holy Mass.

The Liturgy of the Hours

The Lord is good to those who trust in him,
to the soul that searches for him.
It is good to wait in silence.
(Lamentations 3:25-26)

PILGRIMAGE DIARY 90

Time Apart

Every solitary hour that is truly such contains a challenge. That is why there is so little real solitude. Although we pretend to long for it, we avoid it and start up a noise within ourselves.

—*HANS URS VON BALTHASAR, THE LAST GRAIN OF WHEAT*

*O*ne of the things I've learned about the spiritual life during the past few years, which was made clearer during the pilgrimage, is the importance of silence—and its most supportive companion, solitude. But silence and solitude alone are not enough. My time here at the Carceri has made me more keenly aware of the importance of time, that is, of giving plenty of quality time to spiritual pursuits.

This is my fourth visit to the Carceri, but, as I mentioned, the first three visits were very short. With the luxury of time, this extended visit is yielding better fruit. Each day, I see more, understand more. I am able to enter into the flow and rhythm of life here. The friars and sisters give almost three hours each day to prayer. I have this hunger for a deeper and more contemplative prayer life, yet I have not allocated the time for it to develop. I wish I could have spent four weeks here instead of four days.

But even four weeks wouldn't have done much good if my attention was focused on writing a book. I've been very busy these days. Oh, they've been silent and I've spent most of my time in the solitude of my cell, yet these have been a very active three days. My mind has been on this book. And that's OK...the book is the reason I'm here. What I need, whether here or in Los Angeles, is to spend time apart...with nothing on my mind, with no agenda other than being still...and listening.

I wanted to hear the Lord's voice during my time at this holy hermitage. But I didn't take the time to listen. And it takes time, real time, and not just a few minutes here, a few minutes there, haphazard or stolen moments grabbed from a full day.

The two primary ingredients for advancing in the spiritual life—silence and time—are the two hardest commodities for the modern person to find. When I go back to Rome, even the relative quiet of Sant' Isidoro is going to feel very loud and busy. And when I return to Los Angeles in mid-October...life is going to be full and fast.

Sadly, most of the visitors to the Eremo delle Carceri are in and out of here in under forty-five minutes (unless they are slowed down by a couple of calls on their cell phones), barely pausing long enough to breathe in the air once breathed by Francis.

PILGRIMAGE DIARY 91

The Cave of Brother Rufino

*T*oday I spent time sitting alone in the snug little cave of Brother Rufino. I spent the first few minutes reading from Bonaventure's Life of St. Francis. I randomly opened Ewert Cousins's translation to this passage: "No one can be said to have perfectly renounced the world if he still keeps the purse of his own opinion in the hidden recesses of his heart."

I took a deep breath, closed the book and thought about that sentence for a while. That is the height of poverty, to renounce your own ideas, along with the wisdom of the world. Francis wanted his friars to live among the poor as pilgrims and strangers. Bonaventure says, "Sometimes he ordered the friars to tear down a house they had built or to move out of it if he noticed something contrary to the Gospel poverty either because they had appropriated it as their possessions or because it was too sumptuous" (Bonaventure, page 241).

There is nothing sumptuous about Brother Rufino's cave. As I look around it, I can't help but think of all the things in my "cave" which I consider to be essential. Poverty quickly helps you distinguish between what truly is essential and what is essentially frivolous.

I need to give up my worthless ideas about life, which I cling to as if they were priceless pearls of wisdom. I once was able to say with rather firm conviction that God did not exist. I need to replace my faulty thinking with the wisdom of God.

THE RULE FOR HERMITAGES

The real wilderness of the hermit is the wilderness of the human spirit which is at once his and everyone else's. What he seeks in the wilderness is not himself, not human company and consolation, but God.

—THOMAS MERTON, "SOLITUDE," IN *SPIRITUAL LIFE*

Amid the oldest manuscript collection of the writings of Saint Francis, there is a very short, simple document composed of only four paragraphs which sets down a Rule for hermitages. Francis wrote the Rule sometime between 1217 and 1221. Francis was keenly aware of the need for the brothers occasionally to interrupt their preaching and their work among the poor and withdraw into solitude for a period of time. In the peace of a cave or austere hut, they could strengthen their souls for the apostolic work that had been entrusted to them. A hermitage was little more than a collection of huts in an isolated area, usually high atop a mountain. The hermitages were places of spiritual respite, where the focus was on prayer and renewal.

Occasionally, a brother desired to spend longer periods of time in isolation. Francis wrote a Rule governing life in a hermitage, which cleverly allowed some brothers to live entirely in silence as children being served and protected by other friars acting as loving mothers. Francis said a hermitage should consist of three or four brothers. Two brothers should act as mothers, following the example of Martha, caring for and serving the other one or two friars who are living a life of Mary. The brothers who are mothers must not permit anyone to disturb their sons or allow anyone to talk with them. The sons should spend their time alone in their enclosed space. Both the mothers and the sons should pray the Office. After a time, the friars should switch roles. It is as simple as Martha, Mary and Jesus.

That was it, not long on rules and regulations, but shimmering with grace and simplicity. Francis had a wonderful knack for applying Gospel stories to the life he lived.

The Rule reflects the maternal instinct within Francis, whose tireless tenderness was always at the service of all in his care. The short Rule uses the word "mother" six times, as he instructs the brothers to be mothers to each other.

Essentially, a hermitage is a place of silence. The silence of the hermitage taught the brothers how to speak in the noisy streets of the city.

Eremitical solitude is an essential part of Francis' spirituality. He did not consider solitary adoration as an optional extra. Francis founded at least twenty mountain hermitages. They were primitive, poor and simple. Saint Bonaventure was washing dishes in a hermitage when he received the news he had been made a cardinal. While Francis and his followers were deeply involved in evangelization, they recognized the importance of maintaining a certain distance and perspective from society. The hermitage experience kept them from becoming too deeply submerged in active cares, and also safeguarded them from becoming physically and spiritually drained by the demands of their exhausting work of caring for the poor and preaching the Good News. Prayer does not flourish without help, and the hermitage helps revitalize prayer by providing it with time and space.

We all need time in a hermitage.

PILGRIMAGE DIARY 92

The Golden Caterpillar

The Christian of tomorrow will be a mystic, one who has experienced something, or he will be nothing.

—KARL RAHNER

*A*round 10 p.m. Sunday night, my last night in the Carceri, I went out to the friars' small cloister. I had just finished packing and I wanted simply to breathe in the air before going to bed. The evening was overcast, but still, and some stars were visible. I listened to the night noises. Twigs snapping under the weight of some small creature. Crickets singing, owls hooting, birds chirping. Gentle sounds. As I looked out over the V-shaped ravine, I could see the lights of the valley far below. Not many lights...nothing compared to Los Angeles at night as seen from the Santa Monica Mountains on Mulholland Drive. Here you see just a few scattered lights. As I looked out, I spotted a train, just four cars long, slowly making its way across the valley on the way to Perugia. From this distance, some eight hundred meters above the valley floor, the train looked like a golden caterpillar crawling along the ground. I then realized that in exactly twelve hours, I would be boarding a train going the opposite direction, toward Foligno and Rome.

And I became sad. I like it here. This has been the best four days of the trip. And I'm not sure I could explain why. I could tell you why I loved my day in Cortona, or why I loved my day in Bagnoreggio and Narni with Father Liam. But this was different. Earlier this evening, I knelt in front of the crucifix in the chapel of St. Francis and rededicated my life to Christ. It was a time of sweet communion. Nothing exceptional happened. There was no profound mystical experience. The cross didn't speak to me or anything. It was *just a quiet, peaceful time of recognizing where I've come from and where I need to be going. I committed myself—to myself and to Christ—to deepen my prayer life. This entire pilgrimage has been pointing me in that direction.*

I want to move forward, and I'm very aware of how easy it is to slip backwards. I've been where backwards is going. It's going nowhere.

I've got to carve into the bedrock of my life, amid the forest of things I must do, time and space for silence and solitude. I have to create my own Carceri within me.

PILGRIMAGE DIARY 93

Happy Birthday

Our deepest contacts with God are so gentle because this is all we can bear.

—EVELYN UNDERHILL

*M*y last morning. And on this day—September 8th—the Church is celebrating the birthday of the Blessed Virgin Mary. And the feast day is celebrated with special readings and prayers. Additionally, the psalms and canticles from morning prayer are taken from Sunday of Week One, instead of the ones designed for Monday of Week Three. And so the first psalm we read was Psalm 62, which begins with this verse:*

Oh God, you are my God, and for you I long;
for you my soul is thirsting.
My body pines for you
like a dry, weary land without water.
So I gaze on you in the sanctuary
to see your strength and your glory. (1-2)

Tears came to my eyes. Almost two and a half years ago—on March 16, 1995—I read that psalm for the first time. I was alone in the empty church of Collegio Sant' Isidoro. I was an atheist. But something happened while reading that psalm...something that changed my life, and set me on a new course, a course that led me to these four days of near-silence. Reading that psalm as I was about to travel to Rome and the Collegio Sant' Isidoro filled my heart with awe as I considered how drastically my life had changed since I first read it. And during these four days, it was as if Lord were saying, "Nice job, well done. But there is much more to be done. You've only just begun to taste the sweetness of my love."

Of course, I "heard" no such words.

Those words are just my expression of how I felt during morning prayer. Nothing happens without prayer, and I can no longer be content to just attend daily Mass—said, usually, in about twenty minutes—and expect to know the heart of God. It takes more than that.

My taxi arrived at the appointed hour. It was a Mercedes-Benz...I smiled thinking about how I began this journey in a limo in Los Angeles for a ride to the airport, and now seventy-eight days later, I'm getting into another expensive car for a ride to the train station. It felt odd leaving this humble hermitage in such royal style. I was immediately jolted out of the slow pace of life at the Carceri, as the taxi driver hit speeds of over a hundred kilometers per hour along narrow, farm roads of the Spoleto Valley. In less time than it takes to say a rosary, I was deposited at the train station, which is just a few blocks from the Basilica di Santa Maria degli Angeli.

I bought the Herald Tribune for the first time in six days. It contained these headlines:

Scores More Slain in Algerian Town
30 in India Killed in Maoist Raid on Rivals
Ulster Stalked by a Renewal of Violence

I also read that a few days earlier, another suicide bomb exploded in Jerusalem, this time in a mall, killing five, including three young girls.

I felt like taking a taxi back to the Eremo....

PILGRIMAGE DIARY 94

Thoughts Scribbled While Walking

*G*od is far beyond us and deep within us.
Prayer is the breath of life.
Without solitude and silence, I easily lose my self. And God.

Prayer acknowledges our dependency on God.
Our greatest violation of poverty is to hold the good God gives—
    goodness has to flow.
Solitude is a presence, not an absence.
Prayer helps us become more aware of God's presence. The goal
    of prayer is communion with God.
Silence is the soul of simplicity.
Simplicity is the sister of purity.
All life is a cry to God.
I am a child of God. Do I act like it?
Without voice, God silently speaks in and through everything.

As I look back over all thoughts scribbled down while walking, I realize that I have learned more in solitude than I have anywhere else. Here is a bumper sticker worth putting on my car: Make room for solitude.

[Note: the following reflection was written following my second visit to the Carceri, in October of 1995.]

Sounds of Silence

> Whoever wishes to listen well to divine speech must enclose himself in great silence.
>
> —SAINT UMILTA OF FAENZA, SERMONS

In the silence of the Carceri I felt as if I could hear, ever so faintly, the collective song of humanity of which Thomas Merton writes in Seasons of Celebration:

> Now each man's individual song, that he sings in secret with the Spirit of God, blends also in secret with the unheard notes of every other individual song...these voices all form a great choir whose music is heard only in the depths of silence, because it is more silent than the silence itself. (page 215)

For nearly an hour, though it seemed much longer, I sat alone listening to the vibrant, pulsating sound of the great choir of silence singing the har-

mony between mankind and God.

As I walked down the mountain, I held the stillness of the summit in my heart until I began to lament wasting so many years of my life engaged in feverish and pointless activity. And then, with each step of the descent, the heavenly symphony of silence gradually succumbed to the loud "boom box" of noise and chaos that plagues modern life.

Saint Francis, help me hear the sounds of silence, help me recall the summit as I wander through the valley of life. Amen.

PILGRIMAGE DIARY 95

Home

The mystical lives in the field of daily action.
—*DIANE M. CONNELLY,* ALL SICKNESS IS HOMESICKNESS

I' m "home." Safely back from the mountaintop above Assisi to the hill atop Piazza Barberini...and the Collegio Sant' Isidoro. Slipped under my door during my absence were two letters, a fax and a message to "immediately" return a phone call. My first night back, I had dinner at a Chinese restaurant with two Jesuit priests. We discussed the upcoming colloquium on religion and popular culture sponsored by the Pontifical Gregorian University and being held near Castel Gandolfo, the summer home of the pope. I will be addressing the conference and my remarks (which I've already recorded here) will focus on the religious sensibilities of Hollywood television producers. After dinner I was handed a large envelope stuffed with advance copies of the remarks that will be delivered by scholars in the fields of communication and theology. I had to read them. We also talked about the three-week course I will be teaching at the Gregorian, a course that begins the day after the conference ends. My remaining time in Rome will be full and fast.

When I got back to my room shortly after 11 p.m., I closed the door...and wished I was back at the Carceri.

On the train to Rome today, I had this thought: Christianity is a mystical religion practiced by non-mystics...no wonder it is so unattractive to so many.

Singing the Praises of Solitude

The truest solitude is not something outside you, not an absence of men or of sound around you: it is an abyss opening up in the center of your own soul.

—*THOMAS MERTON*, SEEDS OF CONTEMPLATION

While writing this book, I was forced to come to grips with the roles of prayer, poverty, silence and solitude in my own life. Before I began work on the book, I had already understood, at least marginally, the importance of solitude. Creative artists down through the ages have always valued solitude and understood its vital role in the creative process. Poets and painters are solitary creatures. That solitude promotes insight as well as change has been recognized by great religious leaders, who have usually retreated from the world before returning to it to share what has been revealed to them. Many of the great movements within all faiths began in the desert or on top of a mountain. But spending time alone with Francis and Clare has deepened my appreciation of thoughtful solitude, and also heightened my awareness of how much the world and contemporary society devalue solitary time.

Henry David Thoreau tells us that solitude brings us face-to-face with "the essential facts of life." Solitude is a meeting place...a place to meet ourselves and God. Solitude is a place where we can change and grow, a place where we can set new priorities. It is a place of new beginnings, and also a great place to cure self-deception and put to death bad habits. Solitude is also a school, a place where we can learn sensitivity, compassion and empathy...and truth. Solitude is ideal for reflection, self-examination, creation, purification, penitence and prayer. For this reason, Thomas Merton writes, "Solitude is as necessary for society as silence is for language and air for the lungs and food for the body."

Artists and monks, as people who have plumbed the depths of inner life, have much to teach us regarding the essential importance of solitude as a tool for helping us bring contemplation and silence back into our busy lives.

A warning: Without reservation, solitude is important to the creative artist. But for those who enter into solitude for spiritual reasons, a caveat is in order. Thomas Merton states categorically, "You will never find interior solitude unless you make some conscious effort to deliver yourself from the desires and the cares and the attachments of an existence in time and in the world" (Seeds of Contemplation, *page 60). As Richard Anthony Cashen points out in* Solitude in the Thought of Thomas Merton, *"This is by no means a retreat into the ego-self, which Merton called a fake interiorization. He characterizes as an eccentric and regressive solitude any withdrawal into self for the purpose of focusing 'more pleasurably and more intently' on one's self, for a heightening of self consciousness. What this amounts to is the substitution of one's own idols and illusions for those of society" (page 70). This kind of egocentric solitude only fills one with emptiness. It is more an act of introversion than true solitude, which emphasizes pure detachment that results in emptying one's heart. In* New Seeds of Contemplation, *Thomas Merton warns that "solitude is not and can never be a narcissistic dialogue of the ego with itself."*

Entering into solitude with the idea of affirming ourselves, or separating oneself from others, even interiorly, in order to be different, or by intensifying one's individual self-awareness is not in harmony with the purity required for spiritual growth. For the Christian, pure solitude is a place of self-emptying in order to experience union with Christ; in the interior abyss of inner solitude we become detached from our petty false self and open ourselves up to the vastness of the Infinite.

PILGRIMAGE DIARY 96

A Mystery

*T*his morning, as I sat in the silence of the church at Sant' Isidoro, I thought about my life prior to my first visit here. Back then, I had a fairly large portfolio of accepted truths, things about which I was absolutely certain. Certainty gives a person a sense of strength. Certainty is a safe refuge in a confusing world. Today, that portfolio is practically empty. It contains only one item: God is love.

To enter into a relationship with God is to enter into a mystery. And the mystery, far from being comforting, is very often disquieting, as it forces you to ponder thorny issues and ultimately to abandon your cherished security blanket of certainties. The mystery has compelled me to live without certainties, except for one: God loves me...no matter what I do, no matter how frequently I fail to return that love.

PILGRIMAGE DIARY 97

The Tip of My Pen

[God] is in some sort at the tip of my pen, my spade, my brush, my needle—of my heart and of my thought.

—*PIERRE TEILHARD DE CHARDIN, S.J.*

As the tip of my pen glides across this page of my notebook, a friar is playing the organ in the empty church. My little hermitage, attached to the church, is vibrating with heavenly sounds as I struggle with thoughts of contemplation and action.

In Bread in the Wilderness, *Thomas Merton wrote, "The secret of contemplation is the gift of ourselves to God."*

It is hard to consider myself a gift, much less give myself to God. This thought just crossed my mind: Relinquishing the possessions of the ego we all amass inside ourselves is the most demanding form of poverty.

AN ETERNAL SHRINE

Pope John XXIII was in Assisi on October 4, 1962, in order to celebrate the feast of Saint Francis. On that occasion, he said:

> It may be asked: why God lavished on Assisi such enchanting surroundings, such a wealth of art, such a fascination for holiness which seems to hover in the air and which pilgrims subconsciously sense? The answer is simple: so that we, through a common, universal language, might learn to know our Creator and to feel ourselves in solidarity with one another.... (Pasqual Magro, O.F.M. Conv., *Assisi*, page 22)

In Assisi, I came to know the Creator and truly did feel in solidarity with all of humanity. And that knowledge and feeling stayed with me after I left the holy little city that sits on a hill. It burns within me. But I must keep it burning. Each day, as best I can, I try to stoke the flames within me, the flames of the spirit of the eternal shrine that is Assisi.

All praise be yours, my Lord,
through all that you have made....

Il Terremoto Uccide

*T*his book should have ended with the above phrase from The Canticle of Brother Sun. *And it would have, had it not been for the tragic events of September 26, 1997, the day when Assisi was mortally injured.* Il terremoto *is the Italian for earthquake, and the headline of the newspaper* Il Tempo *said it all:* Il terremoto uccide...*the killer earthquake. Below the big, bold headline was a photo taken from inside the Basilica of St. Francis as the collapsing ceiling came crashing to the floor in a huge cloud of dust that quickly enveloped the entire church.*

It was a nightmare.

THE DAMAGE

The nightmare began in the middle of the night. Beginning at 2:33 a.m. on Friday, September 26, a series of earthquakes struck Assisi and, by the time they subsided, the region was plunged into mourning over the tragic loss of life and art. The epicenter, in spirit if not fact, was the Basilica of St. Francis. The first quake measured 5.5 on the Richter scale. Lighter tremors were felt throughout the night into dawn. But they did not cause any major damage. Mostly, they rattled nerves. A photographer who had been working at night photographing all the art in the basilica had just finished his night's work when the quake struck. He entered the church and noticed some menacing cracks in the vault. He noticed a white fissure in the archivault of the interior facade cutting diagonally across a fresco of Saint Francis and Saint Clare. He shined his flashlight on the great stained-glass window, and noticed a segment missing. The friars from the Sacro Convento were busy dealing with the water gushing out of a broken pipe. When they finally entered the darkened upper basilica and the photographer showed them the damage, they were horrified. But the bad news would soon get worse. As they gathered up small fragments of fresco-covered plaster, smaller tremors foretold more horror.

Later in the day, as friars and an expert team of art restorers and technical experts were inspecting the upper basilica, a slightly stronger quake jolted the area. It was 11:42 a.m., and time was about to stop. Measuring 5.7 on the Richter scale, this tremor brought down two large 360-square-foot sections of the fresco-covered vaulted ceilings. It happened so fast. The thundering noise was deafening as chunks of the concrete ceiling crashed to the floor. Scaffolding the experts had been using to examine the damage from the first quake rattled and jumped. A worker still on the scaffold held on in terror as the massive building swayed. Within seconds, the entire cavernous space was filled with a thick cloud of dust. About twenty people were inside. Screams echoed through the building. As they fled for their lives, the plaster dust was so thick they could hardly see. Some feared choking to death on the thick dust. The main entrance was blocked by a mountain of rubble. Not everyone managed to escape the terror. Some people were buried for hours before workers were able to plow through the ruins of shattered masonry to free them. One survivor said the rubble was up to his hips. Four people, two friars and two government workers, were crushed to death, their battered bodies discovered late in the day.

It was later learned that the second midday quake was actually two quakes in rapid succession. The first one created an undulating effect; the second, a vertical shaking one. The result of the combination of the two quakes, perhaps a minute apart, was that buildings were literally twisted, leaving many smaller structures in the area in a slightly different position.

Initial reports indicated that as many as seventy percent of the buildings in Assisi were evacuated because of safety fears. The Basilica of St. Clare and the Cathedral of St. Rufino were very badly damaged. Since the 1300's, twenty-three major earthquakes have rocked the region. One quake during the eighteenth century destroyed much of Assisi. Before now, the Basilica of St. Francis had avoided any mortal blows. Now death had come to the place where Italian painting was born. Some blame the collapse of the ceiling on faulty restoration techniques used in the 1950's, when wooden beams over the vault were replaced by reinforced concrete supports which did not "give" during the second quake. Besides the damage to the art, the basilica also suffered some structural damage. The tympanum (the large triangular apex) of the left transept of the upper church partially collapsed. (On October 7th, a 4.9 aftershock caused even further damage to the tympanum.) In addition, the bell tower sustained damage in its upper section. The Sacro Convento, which is home to the Conventual friars and is attached to the basilica, was heavily damaged. The vault in the Papal Hall collapsed. The museum was considered so unsafe that the precious art it held had to be removed. The large refectory received extensive damage. And the Cloister of Pope Sixtus IV, who once lived here, was also badly damaged; the wall on the lower side became detached.

The earthquakes rocked the entire region, causing extensive damage in the villages strung along the hills of the rugged Apennines. In neighboring Norcea Umbra, the bell tower of the cathedral, built in the Middle Ages, collapsed. The thirteenth-century cathedral in Bevagna sustained major damage. The main facade of the Church of San Biagio e Romualdo was destroyed. In Orvieto, the magnificent Romanesque-Gothic Duomo was also damaged. And the fifteenth-century Church of St. Nicholas in Tolentino was badly damaged. Besides the four deaths in the Basilica of St. Francis, seven other people in the region were killed, including two elderly couples from the mountain villages of Collecurti and Cesi. Structural damage was far greater in other towns than it was in Assisi. Dozens of people were pulled out alive from under piles of debris, including a seven-year-old boy. As the autumn chill approached, the quakes left at least five thousand Umbrians homeless, forced to live in pup tents issued by the Italian government. Tens of thousands of residents of the area chose to sleep outside their homes, fearing further quakes. The continuing tremors frayed nerves beyond measure. Within a week of the quake, inspectors examined over thirty-five hundred homes in the region, and found forty-one percent of them to be uninhabitable. In some small villages, the percentage was even higher.

Shortly after the quake, which could be felt in Rome, one of the friars living at Sant' Isidoro rushed up to Assisi. Davide Marzaroli was born in the area and is a member of the Assisi Province. He had to go home to check on his family and friends, and to see the damage for himself. Late Sunday night, I heard his car drive up the stone-covered path to the friary. I rushed down to greet him and to get a firsthand report of the damage. In those early hours after the quake, details of the damage appearing on TV and in the papers were often contradictory. Rumors about the damage to the art claimed the same fresco was both destroyed and unharmed. Davide's face told me how bad the situation was before he had said a word. He began his account of the weekend with these haunting words: "It is a dead city."

The damage to the art in the Basilica of St. Francis was incalculable and irreplaceable. The earthquakes destroyed—actually completely obliterated—two ceiling frescoes, one of Saint Matthew by

Cimabue and the other an early work by Giotto depicting Saint Jerome instructing a monk. The Saint Jerome fresco was one of four frescoes that comprised the vault of the Doctors of the Church; likewise, the Saint Matthew fresco was one of a cluster of four frescoes that depicted the four evangelists located high above the main altar. The two sections of the vault which collapsed fell twenty-two meters and hit the marble floor with such a force that it not only pulverized the frescoes, it also caved in some of the floor. Lost also were frescoes of Francis and Clare from the archivault over the main entrance. Workers later found a portion of Francis' eye and a tiny sliver from his mouth. Facing the archivault, the fresco lower and to the left of Francis and Clare was of Saint Anthony and Saint Benedict. It also collapsed, shattered into little pieces. To the right of Francis and Clare, two additional panels, one depicting Saint Victorinus and Saint Rufinus and the other Saint Peter and Saint Dominic, were also destroyed. The main altar of the upper basilica was crushed and completely demolished. Within a day of the quake, workers began gingerly to remove the tiny fragments of the frescoes, placing them under tents outside the main entrance. Two hundred volunteer restorers sifted through the rubble, hoping to be able to restore some of the art. Wearing white cotton gloves, they carefully classified thousands of tiny fresco chips.

The twenty-eight-fresco life cycle of Saint Francis covering the walls survived, with two panels sustaining jagged cracks. Some old cracks, which had been restored, reopened. Amazingly, the lower church sustained only minor damage. Frescoes in the Chapel of St. John became partially separated from the wall. Mercifully, the most sacred spot in the basilica, the tomb of Saint Francis, was unharmed.

One of the two friars killed in the earthquake was Father Angelo Api, O.F.M. Conv. He was forty-eight years old. The other friar was a twenty-two-year-old postulant named Zdizlaw Borowiec; he had arrived in Assisi from Poland only a week before the earthquake. Another friar said that eyewitnesses had seen Father Angelo pull the young postulant close to him as the ceiling began to fall, protecting his charge until the last second. Their sudden and violent deaths remind us of the uncertainty of life. In this uncertain world, where violence is always looming, the Basilica of St. Francis has been through the centuries a symbol of pilgrimage, prayer and peace, and while lives have been lost and art destroyed, the spirit of the basilica will continue to live and touch the hearts and souls of everyone who enters it when it is once again safe to visit. [The Basilica reopened in the fall of 1999.] It is the spirit of Saint Francis which draws people of all faiths to Assisi. The experience of being in Assisi and praying at the tomb of Saint Francis is profoundly deep, not because of the buildings and frescoes but because of the life of Francis who attached no importance to bricks and mortar. We are touched by the life of a man who loved Christ so passionately that he eagerly gave up everything to follow him.

PILGRIMAGE DIARY 99

A Somber Celebration

*O*n the morning of October 4th, just eight days after the earthquake, I caught an early morning train from Rome and traveled to Assisi to celebrate the feast of Saint Francis.

I wondered if a celebration was possible in such a mortally wounded city. The day before, on Friday, another series of aftershocks caused new damage. The strongest struck at 10:55 a.m. and registered 4.8 on the Richter scale. Six people were hurt. At 1:04 p.m. a tremor with a magnitude of 3.5 hit, followed forty minutes later by another aftershock almost as strong. Rumors said part of the bell tower at the Basilica of St. Francis collapsed during the morning tremor. Word reached Sant' Isidoro late Friday afternoon that the Carceri had to be evacuated due to new damage. What is happening? As the community gathered to celebrate the Transitus of St. Francis that evening, a sadness hung in the air. As I watched the burning incense rise in the darkened church I could not help but wonder why Assisi is being tortured.

I would later learn that my friend Father André Cirino, O.F.M., was celebrating Mass in the little Church of San Stefano for a new group of Franciscans on a pilgrimage when the Friday morning aftershock struck. A brick from the ceiling was jarred loose and fell, glancing Father André as he stood at the altar. He was fortunate to sustain only a minor injury. The week had been so stressful because of all the aftershocks, that Friday's tremors convinced André it was no longer safe to stay in Assisi, and he and the pilgrims he was guiding were forced to leave.

Before today, I've taken the train from Rome to Assisi four or five times. I clearly remember the first time, back in March of 1995. I was

filled with a heightened sense of anticipation. My first glimpse of
Assisi from the train, the city sitting majestically on the hill, stirred
wonder and hope in my heart. Every subsequent train trip had the
same impact. Today was different. The anticipation was there, but it
was tinged with anxiety. I wondered what I would see, how bad the
damage really was, and if there would be another strong aftershock.
The morning paper carried the news that St. Mary of the Angels, the
home of the Portiuncula, also suffered new damages in Friday's
tremors. In the Marches, northwest of Assisi, it was reported that 134
churches sustained severe damage yesterday. A woman, who had
been forced to live in a tent after her house was destroyed, died of a
heart attack. Panic swept the region. Cries of anguish could be
heard, "It's not over yet."

Between Foligno and Assisi, the normally pastoral landscape was
dotted with blue tents. It was the first sign of the trouble that lay
ahead. As the train rumbled down the tracks to Assisi, I noticed a
Franciscan sister sitting alone. As she stared out the window, I saw
tears in her eyes. I knew what she was thinking.

As I left the train station in Assisi, I spotted a taxi driver I knew, a
wonderful man named Marcello. It was good to see a familiar face. I
ran over to him. We hugged. He told me that Casa Papa Giovanni
was not damaged, and that Don Aldo was doing fine. I was greatly
relieved by the news. He told me about Father André's being forced
to leave. I was saddened by the news that the St. Anthony Guest
House, the place where I stayed during my first visit to Assisi, was
badly damaged, and that the sisters had evacuated the building.
Marcello told me that Mass would be celebrated in the large piazza
in front of St. Mary of the Angels. We made plans to meet after Mass
so he could drive me up the hill to Assisi.

About five thousand people assembled in the piazza for Mass.
The liturgy was broadcast live via RAI television. The piazza was
about three-quarters filled when the service began. Despite the
military guard and the banners, the mood seemed very subdued. Yet,
as the procession began, there was a hint of joy and hope in the air
because we were focusing our attention on the person of Francis,
and not on the destruction of buildings which honor him. With
incense burning and rising into the sun-drenched sky, dozens upon
dozens of priests, including seven bishops and a cardinal, walked
down the middle of the piazza to the altar, which was set up at the

end of the piazza directly in front of the facade of the church. Looking up, I saw the statue of Mary on top of the church. I prayed that there would not be an earthquake during the liturgy. The service began with the reading of a message from Pope John Paul II. The homily, delivered in Italian, was longer than the Omnibus of Sources. As the sun burned off the morning chill, so, too, the voices of the choir lifted the downcast spirits.

After Mass, Marcello drove me to the St. Francis Gate (Porta San Francesco) in Assisi. At first glance, as I walked through the gate, things looked—at least on the surface—fairly normal. As I walked towards the Basilica of St. Francis, I noticed piles of bricks and large stones at regular intervals. I saw numerous broken windows, and buildings with large cracks in them. It felt like a ghost town. A silence had fallen over the city. Francis would have liked that. No bells rang. Except for a few vendors, no one was hawking tacky souvenirs. Few people walked in the streets, and those who did looked more like residents than tourists. Except for police vehicles, there were no cars zipping up and down the narrow streets. The plazas were nearly empty. Loose bricks cluttered the streets. At the Sacro Convento, instead of friars greeting pilgrims, soldiers guarded the entrance. The piazza in front of the upper basilica was fenced off. Debris from the collapsed ceiling was piled high outside the front doors. Five of the six medieval gates that encircle the town were damaged and had to be closed.

I walked the near-empty streets to Santa Chiara. The severity of the structural damage to the building was apparent even to an untrained eye. A large crack on the left side of the building, facing the street, ran from the roof to about three-fourths of the way to the ground. Piles of mortar and debris surrounded the building. The facade looked as if it was about to come loose from the building. The facade itself had two large cracks running from just below the base of the stained-glass window to just above the frame of the door. Someone in the piazza told me the Poor Clares had to evacuate the large monastery attached to the church, and that a few of the nuns were living in tents on the grounds in order to guard the remains of Saint Clare.

Father Davide was right, I thought: This is a dead city. But the promise of resurrection was in our hearts, even though our minds struggled to make sense of all the destruction and death.

The few people I encountered as I walked around the town seemed to be trying to grapple with what all this meant. I overheard a priest, who sounded as if he were an American, say, "Before the quake, Assisi no longer reflected the spirit of Francis. It exhibited the spirit of Pietro, the spirit of commerce. Many people came to shop, not pray. Maybe the earthquake will change this trend." But was the death of four people, including two friars, necessary to accomplish such a change? I didn't mean to question the wisdom of God, but why not destroy businesses instead of basilicas? Moments later, I felt one of the many slight tremors that gently shook the area that day.

I sat near a fountain and read the Liturgy of the Hours, which included a reading from Saint Francis' Letter to the Faithful: "We should not be wise and prudent according to worldly standards, but rather we should be simple, humble and pure." The earthquake made the practice of humility a little easier.

I ran into a friend, Sister Clare, a Franciscan Missionary Sister of the Child Jesus—Suore Francescane Missionarie di Gesu' Bambino. Her order's motherhouse is in Assisi, and she told me of the damage to it. Born in Italy, Sister Clare has worked for many years in the United States. She, too, was wondering why this was happening to her city. "What is God telling us?" she asked. Jokingly, I said, "Don't live in old buildings." She lovingly slapped me on the arm, saying, "Don't be silly." She suggested that perhaps Saint Francis is praying for us, not to simply rebuild the building which honors him, but to rebuild the spiritual heritage he left us. That wasn't a silly idea. Sister Clare told me that there was going to be a procession later in the afternoon. All the people of Assisi were prayerfully to walk from the Porta San Francesco to the Basilica di Santa Maria degli Angeli.

The procession was to begin at four in the afternoon. I arrived about a half hour early. The crowd was forming. A television news crew was there, about to interview the bishop of Assisi, who was to lead the procession from the city where Francis was born to the place where he died, the tiny chapel of the Portiuncula. The bishop was surrounded by a few reporters. One journalist asked, "Is this the first time the feast of Saint Francis was celebrated in the spirit of Saint Francis?" Ouch. What a poignant question. I was unable to understand the answer, which the bishop delivered in Italian. I could not help but think that we were going to be walking in a spirit of need, a spirit of true poverty, acknowledging our dependency on

God...Saint Francis would like that.

It seemed as if everyone who lives in Assisi was present. They carried statues, banners and crosses. Different groups wore special clothing designating their affiliation with a particular fraternity. A friar carrying a large cross led the way down the hill. In a very orderly, reverential way, two single lines were formed as we walked into the bright sun. A friar with a loudspeaker led the people in prayer and singing the psalms. After walking for some time, I turned and looked back. It was an amazing sight. Two long lines of humanity, reverently walking and praying as the sun drenched the city on the hill behind them. There were young people, old people, people from around the world, all walking together with scores of friars and sisters, singing and praying.

We walked past small buildings visibly scarred by the earthquake, roofs and walls collapsed. The recently turned fields awaiting seeding were now dotted with tents. Normally, the feast of Saint Francis is the busiest day of the year for the local citizens who operate the gift shops and restaurants. Today, they had time to pray. The friar leading the prayers said a litany of some sort, and the people responded with the Italian words for "pray for us." I walked with a group of Conventual friars from the Franciscan Center for Ecumenism and Inter-Religious Dialogue, where I had once stayed as their guest.

As the prayers shifted to a repetition of the words "Lord, have mercy," we passed a field of grapevines. About halfway down the hill, there is a small house—number 157—with a plaque commemorating the spot where Francis, carried on a stretcher because he was too sick to walk, asked the friars carrying him to pause and turn the stretcher around so he could have one final look at his beloved city. Francis blessed the city, and the friars continued carrying him to the Portiuncula. The procession stopped at that very spot. Everyone turned back toward Assisi, knelt down and prayed for God's blessing on the town. After asking God to forgive them their sins, everyone stood up, turned toward St. Mary of the Angels and continued walking. It was one of the most moving events I have ever experienced.

As we walked, I thought about the words Francis heard so long ago in San Damiano: "Rebuild my church." Those words were in the air. People knew the city would be rebuilt, that the damaged churches would be restored, but they also knew in their hearts that their lives had to be rebuilt...rebuilt on a firmer foundation, a foundation of prayer, not commerce.

Shortly after we arrived at the piazza in front of St. Mary of the Angels, about 5:15 p.m., there was another strong aftershock. You could hear the fear in people's muted voices. Another liturgy began at six. Fifteen minutes later, another strong aftershock rattled the piazza. Some said they could see the golden statue of Mary wobble.

I caught a train back to Rome. It was a day of somber celebration, and I was thankful for having been a part of it.

I was ready to go home. The pilgrimage was nearly over. My flight was to leave in a few days.

PILGRIMAGE DIARY 100

Ground Speed

To attain union with God, a person should advance neither by understanding nor by the support of his own experience, nor be feeling or imagination, but by belief in God's being.
—*SAINT JOHN OF THE CROSS*, COLLECTED WORKS

I'm on a plane heading home.

One hundred eleven days...it's been a long trip. While I'm sad to leave, I'm glad—really glad—to be going home. In the early morning hours, as I struggled to fall asleep in my little hermitage, I felt a slight tremor. This morning's paper carried the news that a 4.9 aftershock struck central Italy at 1:34 a.m. The jolt caused a wave of panic among the fifty thousand displaced people sleeping in tents. It also caused more stones to fall from the fragile tympanum of the south transept of the Basilica of St. Francis. The medieval bell tower of the town hall in Foligno was severely damaged and was about to collapse.

As I stare out the window, my mind naturally flies to Francis. I've come to know him better during these three and a half months. As I look at the splendor below me, spread out on the huge, varied and endless canvas of earth, I think about The Canticle of the Creatures. Francis would have marveled at this sky-high view of creation. He praised the making of the sun and all creatures because he was *in love with the Maker.*

When I land, I pray I am able to walk more closely in the footsteps of Saint Francis of Assisi, and that I am able to put into practice at least some of what he has taught me. I want to approach each day with the humility of a student ready to learn from God.

ONE YEAR LATER

On September 9, 1998, I returned to Rome to teach my annual course at the Pontifical Gregorian University. I was anxious to see firsthand how Assisi was recovering from the earthquake, so as soon as I could, I dashed up to Assisi for a quick three-day visit before the course began. I planned to spend a full week in Francis and Clare's hometown after the conclusion of the course.

PILGRIMAGE DIARY 101

The Wounded City

*O*n Saturday, September 11, as I boarded the train it began to *drizzle. As the train made its way to Umbria, the skies became increasingly dark and the rain heavy. When the train pulled into the station at Assisi, we were greeted by a full-fledged deluge, accompanied by thunder and lightning. The miserable weather added to my anticipated gloom at visiting the wounded city whose recovery has been slow and painful. The bus that wound its way up Mount Subasio was full, yet the wet tourists and pilgrims were orderly and polite. Most got off at the first stop, Porta San Francesco. As an experienced veteran at arriving at Assisi, I knowingly smiled at their rookie mistake. It is much more prudent to stay on the bus a bit longer and get off at either Porta Nuova or Piazza Matteotti, which are at higher elevations, because it is easier to walk down the steep streets of Assisi than walk up them, especially if you are lugging heavy suitcases.*

As I got off the bus, the rain seemed to have intensified, made worse by strong gusts of wind. During many of my previous visits to Assisi, I had noticed a delightful-looking little hotel that sat on the outskirts of the upper city, surrounded by a pretty garden that offered a spectacular view of the city and the valley below. Using the rain for an excuse to justify such lavish digs instead of staying, as I usually do, in one of the guest houses catering to pilgrims, I stopped in and asked the price. After being told, I paused, trying to calculate the cost in American dollars; the owner quickly offered me a "discount" of fifteen thousand lire, just under ten dollars. Realizing that the price was actually reasonable before the discount, I checked in. The instant discount was an indication that business was still slow in the wounded city.

After taking my bags to my room, and borrowing an umbrella from the hotel's owner, I walked to Casa Papa Giovanni in hopes of running into Don Aldo Brunacci. Don Aldo was alone in the chapel, having just finished saying noon Mass. He asked, in his halting English, about the book. I told him it hadn't yet been published, but that the manuscript was in my hotel room. Just as I thought he hadn't understood what I had said, he asked if he could see the manuscript. He had to leave soon, so he wanted to know if I could be back with the manuscript in twenty minutes. I said I could. I huffed and puffed my way up the hill as fast as I could. I stuffed the fat manuscript— almost 500 single-spaced pages—into my briefcase and started back down the hill. It didn't seem possible, but it began raining even harder. And the wind rendered the umbrella almost useless. As I traversed the Piazza del Comune, it was impossible for me to avoid the pools of water that dotted the pavement. I briefly joined a large group of tourists who were taking refuge under the covered portico of the Temple Minerva. I noticed that from below my knees, my trousers, as well as my shoes and socks, were completely and thoroughly soaked.

Minutes later, the old priest greeted me at the front door of Casa Papa Giovanni and led me to a small room off the vestibule, where we sat side by side on a small couch. He held the manuscript in his hands, gesturing his surprise at its bulk. He opened it, and looked for the index. I tried to explain that there was none, because I was trying to avoid giving the impression that the book was a scholarly tome. I took the manuscript from him and opened it to Pilgrimage Diary 66, "The Assisi Underground," and handed the manuscript back to him. He began to read the text, his index finger slowly moving across the page under each word. Occasionally he gave a sign of approval with a gentle smile, sometimes accompanied by the words, "bene,

bene"..."good, good." As I sat there next to him on the small couch, puddles forming at my feet from my soaked pants and shoes, I felt honored that this noble man seemed to be enjoying reading what I had written about him.

After returning the manuscript to my hotel room, I took a walk to the other end of the city and visited the Basilica of St. Francis. The rain had stopped, except for an occasional brief shower. The sight of the basilica filled me with sadness. Much of the beautiful exterior was covered with scaffolding. A wooden fence surrounded the upper church, blocking all the entrances.

The entrance to the large Sacro Convento occupied by the Conventual Friars was also girdled by scaffolding. The Sacro Convento had been heavily damaged and the normally high level of foot traffic going in and out was reduced to a trickle. Before the quake, more than seventy-five friars lived here; today only fifteen remain. There are still lots of tourists, but nowhere near the normal numbers. Before the quake, this piazza would have been filled with tour guides and friars preparing groups for a tour of the church.

I entered the lower church, and was relieved to see that neither the lower church nor the tomb of Saint Francis gave any indication of the catastrophic damage sustained by the upper church. I always loved visiting the lower church and the tomb of Francis. The lower church, with its Romanesque design, its low ceilings, rounded arches, thick walls and small windows, is like a dimly lit womb containing the peace and mystery of God. The tomb is a place for prayer and contemplation. After a solemn visit to the tomb and the lower church I loved climbing the stairs and relishing the joyous exultation of the upper church, taking great delight in Giotto's frescoes. But that would not be possible for more than two more years.

I sat in the tomb of Saint Francis for some time. There was a steady stream of visitors, but a trickle compared to the normal numbers before the quake. In the hushed silence of the tomb, I felt sad that the magnificent art that graces the walls of the upper church would go unseen by these visitors. However, the spirit of Francis, the true essence of his life, is better captured here at his final resting place than in the upper church. The starkness and simplicity of the tomb symbolizes the saint's quiet inner life. The dazzling art of the upper church communicates action. Unable to see those external displays of the life and spirituality of Saint Francis, we are perhaps given the hidden blessing of looking more seriously at the inner beauty of Francis' soul.

Resting in a Pause

This book sprang from a tiny seed of interest in the life and art of Vincent van Gogh and evolved over time into an exploration of the life and faith of Francis of Assisi. What drew me to both men was the connection between creativity and spirituality, between art and faith. After all this time, I am still learning about that connection and I'm hardly qualified to comment in any depth on it, but as this book draws to a close I would like to share two aspects of the correlation between art and faith that have become crystal clear to me and are essential for growth in each: the need for detachment and dedication, and the need for developing a sense of mindfulness.

It is a commonly held belief that to undertake a life of letters, a life of art, or a life of research requires a person's full concentration. Every fiber of one's being must be applied to each of these undertakings. Unless you are a genius of the highest order, you cannot delve into writing, art or scientific research on a sporadic basis and hope to be successful. These undertakings demand the entire being. In the spiritual life, if one wants to advance in the art of contemplation, one must make that the focus of one's life. Contemplation spills out into every aspect of your life. It is not turned on and off. We must give it our whole heart, our whole mind, our whole life if we are to attain great ends. We cannot compartmentalize art and faith; they must permeate our entire existence. Or else they are merely hobbies.

This, of course, does not mean that every second of every day is dedicated fully to, and completely engrossed by, the pursuit of art or faith. Ceaseless preoccupation would not be wholesome, even if it were possible. Intermission is part of the mission. If we looked exclusively at only one thing, we would soon lose sight of everything. What is important is that our sense of purpose—the pursuit of art or faith—must always be with us. Our "vocation" is never on vacation, even when we are doing something else.

If you think of God now and then, if your heart is filled with the love of art now and then, you will never reach the same degree of perfection as someone whose heart and mind are often and deeply beating and thinking about the object of their desire. To scale the heights of creativity and spirituality requires vigilant dedication.

Detachment brings our inner longings in line with our external, temporal life. Detachment translates our inner values into an external reality. Detachment does not require cutting ourselves off from everything, from all material interests. Detachment does not demand absolute isolation. It is merely a way of expressing our attachment to God or art. Many people who walk the spiritual path hit a dead end because they turn toward God without turning from themselves. Vincent and Francis taught me that it takes dedication and detachment to turn away from everything that stands between us and entering fully into a life of art or a life with God.

Mindfulness is stopping time. Time is pain. Time ticks with our regrets and our fears. Time watches over all we strive for and all from which we try to escape. Faith and art stop time and liberate us from suffering. Vincent van Gogh stopped time for a moment in a still life of a sunflower. Time dissolved, purity emerged. On his knees in an abandoned church and in the dark stillness of a cave, Francis stopped time. Time evaporated, God appeared.

The mindfulness of Vincent and Francis linked both of them to the eternal moment of the poet, as "sometimes we see not with our eyes, but with our thoughts/ time resting in a pause" (Octavio Paz, "Response and Reconciliation"). For one brief moment, in an empty church in Rome, I rested in a pause. And a new reality opened up for me.

Mindfulness is awareness of the reality that surrounds us. It creates a sense of reverence...for the flower and the flower-maker. Sadly, life in our global village has shoved mindfulness off the stage, replacing it with nonstop noise, a mindless acceleration which demands that everything from computers to cars be faster and faster, and a frenetic consumerism which is creating a huge gulf between the rich and the poor.

Art and faith require mindfulness. And dedication and detachment. Which is why today we do not see any Vincent van Goghs or Francis of Assisis. We're too busy.

Path of Hope

*T*oday is Sunday, Day Two of my quick three-day visit to Assisi. I paid an early morning visit to the Cathedral of San Rufino. As I stood in the piazza in front of the church, I was saddened to see the cathedral's beautiful face covered by a veil of wood and iron scaffolding. Entrance to the church was restricted to the small door on the right. Once inside, I could see why. The entire church is filled with scaffolding. Only the right aisle is open, to allow access to two side chapels. I can hardly see any of the church's beauty. The ugly iron scaffolding rises from the floor all the way to the ceiling. I felt the way I did when I once visited a lifeless, mortally wounded friend who was hooked up to life-support systems. Very sad. There were long, deep cracks—gashes, actually—in the cathedral's high, majestic ceiling. The baptismal font of Francis and Clare, just inside the right front door, guarded by six of Francis' early companions, provided the only measure of comfort for visitors.

I stood in front of the baptismal font, and silently asked Francis and Clare to baptize me spiritually, renewing the sacramental graces of my own Baptism. I lit a candle for Don Aldo and the church, and left with a saddened heart that nonetheless was hopeful for a full recovery for the noble church. Yesterday Don Aldo said, "Before I die, I want to see San Rufino rebuilt." I sincerely hope his wish is fulfilled.

Afterward, I spotted Don Aldo, wearing his unmistakable beret and broad smile, near the Piazza del Comune. He was on his way to celebrate Mass in the cathedral's temporary home. Together, we walked slowly up the steep hill, walking under wooden tunnels supporting some of the buildings that line the narrow street. Behind the cathedral, in a garden, the parishioners constructed a small, simple, prefabricated metal structure for liturgical celebrations. Towering over the one-story building was the huge, wounded cathedral. We entered the building. The walls were painted white. Behind the altar, slightly to the left was an icon of the Blessed Mother. To the right, a reproduction of the cross of San Damiano. Between them, on a small table, was a very old, wooden tabernacle, a humble home for the Lord of all. The contrast between this temporary warehouse of worship and the glorious splendor of the cathedral was startling. Yet the life of a church does not reside in a building, but in the spirit of the people. And the temporary church was filling up with the faithful, many of whom were elderly women, longtime inhabitants of Assisi. A beautiful young girl, flanked by two young nuns, led the choir. It was a beautiful celebration.

Before Mass, Don Aldo sat alone in a corner, praying the Liturgy of the Hours. As I watched him, I thought about my struggles with prayer...and realized again, yet for the first time, clearly the importance of perseverance. Don Aldo has been praying the Office for far more than sixty years. He must have it memorized by now. His faithfulness to prayer is the source of his inner richness and peace. Prayer, without a doubt, is the rudder of his life.

After Mass, he told me he would make arrangements for me to have a private visit to the upper Basilica of St. Francis when I return to Assisi in four weeks, after I finish my course at the Gregorian. He also said he would give me a tour of the archives below the Cathedral of San Rufino. The archives are always closed to the public, so I was excited about seeing some of its treasures.

I then visited another mortally wounded church, the Basilica of St. Clare. Because of my love for this church, the pain I felt over its injuries was very intense. Because of the damage to the front facade, which was also covered by a web of scaffolding, access to the church was restricted to a small side door. To even get to the door, I had to walk through a wooden tunnel, which offers protection from repair work to the cracks on the side of the building. Inside, access was limited to the small chapel housing the Cross of San Damiano. There was a wooden barrier erected near the front of the church, blocking off access to the severely damaged facade. On the wall was a display of photos and text, telling the story of the destruction and the displacement of the Poor Clares. As bad as the damage to the church was, much more serious damage was inflicted on the large monastery attached to the church. Pictures of the small, simple bedrooms used by the nuns showed huge chunks of concrete resting on beds, deep cracks in the walls and ceilings. The photos made clear how horrific the damage was. Rooms were littered with mounds of brick and mortar. For the first time in 700 years, the cloistered Poor Clare sisters were forced from their home. They are staying at the friary of San Francesco del Monte in Perugia, where they are the guests of the Friars Minor. A few sisters remain here so that it will continue to be a place of uninterrupted prayer and in order to keep watch over their severely damaged monastic home until it can be repaired. The Poor Clares had this message for all who visit: "With the intimate certainty that even now the words of our Blessed Lord addressed to Saint Clare in a moment of danger—'I will watch over you always!'—are being accomplished, we abandon ourselves to God's providence, guided by His wise and loving will, which would have us set our footsteps on its path of hope."

PILGRIMAGE DIARY 103

The Feast of the Exaltation of the Cross

*T*oday is Monday, and it is the Feast of the Exaltation of the Cross. A slight tremor, about 3.3 on the Richter scale, gently woke everyone up today, rattling some china and reminding everyone of the unseen danger. I was glad to be up early. In honor of the feast, I wanted to spend a few quiet minutes in front of the Cross of San Damiano, and then walk down the hill and visit the former home of the Poor Clares. By mid-afternoon I must catch a train back to Rome and start to prepare for the classes.

Last night I attended another Mass celebrated by Don Aldo. It was held in the small crypt under the Cathedral of San Rufino. I didn't understand a word of his sermon; still his tone and mannerism made it seem very heartfelt. People seemed to be actually listening. Afterward, I walked him down the hill to the Piazza del Comune and up the hill to Casa Papa Giovanni. As we walked under the stars, we exchanged very few words; it was nonetheless a time of deep communion.

After I returned to my room in the Hotel Ideale, I turned on the TV. Teleumbria, the main station in the area, was broadcasting a commercially sponsored soft-core film...lots of nudity and guns. I turned the TV off and read Saint Bonaventure's The Tree of Life, which is a simple meditation on the life of Jesus.

> Come now, disciple of Christ,
> search into the secrets of solitude
> with your loving teacher,
> so that having become a companion of wild beasts,
> you may become an imitator and sharer of

the hidden silence, the devout prayer, the daylong fasting
and the three encounters with the clever enemy.
And so you will learn
to have recourse to him
in every crisis of temptation
because we do not have a high priest
who cannot have compassion on our infirmities,
but one tried
in all things as we are,
except sin. (*Bonaventure*, page 134)

*I entered Santa Chiara at 9:15 a.m., and went directly to the chapel
and knelt in front of the Cross of San Damiano. Within five or six
minutes, the four people, including one nun, who were in the chapel
when I arrived left. I was alone for nearly ten minutes before a
woman entered, knelt down before the cross and prayed. As she
prayed, a couple entered. The man videotaped the cross for a few
seconds, and they quickly departed, perhaps not even realizing what
they had seen. Prior to last year's earthquake, fifteen minutes of
virtual solitude before the cross would have been impossible. As I
write these words, a large group of German tourists have entered the
chapel.*

*Walking down the steep grade to San Damiano, I thought about
the notion of poverty. A year after my pilgrimage, I still wrestle with
the ideal of Saint Francis...I guess I am a Franciscan, the issue will
not go away. As I sat in front of the Cross of San Damiano this
morning, I imagined all the replicas of the cross on sale in the shops.
They come in all sizes and prices. The mix of commerce and
spirituality still confuses me. Without money, I wouldn't be in Assisi.
Just yesterday, I bought an 1886 sketch of the Temple Minerva,
artfully encased in a fine antique frame. Just moments ago, I was
sitting in a side chapel in the Church of San Damiano, gazing at the
graphic image of the crucified Christ hanging on a large cross.
Battered, bruised and bloodied, a gash in his side, wearing a crown
of thorns. This is poverty, complete and absolute. We are far too
pampered to be able to grasp even remotely Francis' ideal of poverty.
We can only compromise, make modern adjustments to an ancient
concept that has lost all viability for us, even among the poor. If I
gave all away and walked about as a beggar, I would be scorned or
ignored. I have too much to lose.*

A Rich Harvest

Spiritual reading is a regular, essential part of the life of prayer, and particularly is it the support of adoring prayer. It is important to increase our sense of God's richness and wonder by reading what His great lovers have said about him. Left to ourselves, our thoughts of Him soon get formal and poverty stricken.

—*EVELYN UNDERHILL*, THE WAYS OF THE SPIRIT

Since March of 1995, my inner life has been nourished by spiritual reading. Since so few of the people I knew felt like talking about God or spiritual matters, I found myself taking refuge in books written by people who had a thirst for God, and these authors became my friends with whom I spent most of my free time. Reading helped satisfy my deep hunger for communion with God. While reading the words of the great Christian writers whose insights have inspired so many over the centuries, my mind became more easily attuned to God. However, I must confess, in the beginning of my new life of faith, I read far more than I prayed...and this is a danger.

Reading and speaking too much of God can create a facile habit for such things. Additionally, reading is a work of the mind, which falls easily into pride, and it can predispose a person to a false sense of self-esteem which can very easily temper the need for more practical efforts, such as prayer and good works. The danger is clear: by flattering ourselves with our success in such a mental activity as reading, we may hinder real progress in approaching the fullness of God. Moreover, a person can actually become so attached to reading that the attachment can create a wall between the heart and God. I suppose it all comes down to a matter of balance. Spiritual reading is good and helpful, but only in proportion to prayer and contemplation. For me, reading the works of such great saints as Benedict, Bernard of Clairvaux, Bonaventure, Ignatius of Loyola, Catherine of Siena, Teresa of Avila, Thérèse of Lisieux, to name just a few, became a social act, as it allowed me to have real intercourse with great souls who truly loved God; it was a way for me to enter into and experience the communion of saints. And the saints all speak of the primacy of prayer.

PILGRIMAGE DIARY 104

'Was that Jesus?'

[W]e do not fully welcome Christ if we are not ready to welcome the poor person with whom He identified Himself.
                              —*RANIERO CANTALAMESSA, O.F.M. CAP.*

*A*s I mentioned, I'm still struggling with poverty and how to
respond to it.

*During the past week, in the midst of two pleasant strolls through
the heart of Rome, I witnessed two startling and very distressing
sights, one involving an elderly woman, the other a young girl.*

*The first incident took place a few blocks from Sant' Isidoro. I
had just purchased a train ticket to Assisi and was walking back to
the friary. As I reached the corner of Via L. Bissolati and Via Santo
Basilio, I looked to the right and was jarred by the sight of an old,
homeless woman defecating on the sidewalk. It was obvious that she
was suffering from diarrhea. Not to mention embarrassment. She was
holding her worn, tattered skirt tightly around her waist, leaving her
exposed—totally naked—from the waist down. Her legs were slightly
spread apart, helplessly waiting for the attack of diarrhea to end. I
took in this sickening sight in a flash, then quickly turned my head
away and crossed the street.*

*When I reached the opposite curb, safely away from this
suffering soul, I stopped and looked back. It was beyond sad. I didn't
know what to think or feel. The situation was made worse by three
young men who walked by and taunted her...laughing at her
deplorable situation. Within two minutes, she was able to move on.
But before doing so, she gingerly walked to a nearby trash can, still
clutching her skirt about her waist, and rummaged through the can
for a piece of newspaper, which she used to awkwardly wipe herself
off.*

*I was overwhelmed and confused by what I had seen. I stood
motionless as she walked away and slowly disappeared in the urban
landscape.*

Was that Jesus?

*A few days later, I was walking across Piazza della Pilotta, on my
way from the Pontifical Gregorian University to the Basilica dei Santi
Dodici Apostoli (a church run by Conventual friars). As I walked*

alongside cars parked on the left side of the piazza, my attention was arrested by a rustling sound, which I initially assumed was a discarded newspaper being jostled by a breeze. As I reached the back of one of the cars, the rustling sound again caught my attention. Perhaps it was a cat. As I turned to look down the narrow space between the parked car and the wall, I saw a young girl, perhaps eight or nine years old, squatting and urinating, using the car and the wall for a small degree of privacy. Having spotted me, she quickly emerged from the shadow of the car and ran towards the closed end of the piazza and the narrow street leading to Piazza Santos Apostoli. As she ran, she was pulling up her panties and lowering her oversized skirt. A few feet down the narrow, cobblestone street, her mother waited for her. When the little girl reached her mother, they both quickly walked away.

Was the little girl Jesus?

A few minutes later, I found myself sitting in the Basilica...wondering, thinking, praying. Oh, how we long to find God in some moment of spiritual ecstasy, looking for the Divine in some spectacular or extraordinary event. Yet God comes to us, if we are to believe—fully believe—what Scripture says, in a humble disguise, in unexpected places. God comes to us poor, hungry, thirsty, diseased, imprisoned, alone and lonely. God comes to us in an old woman and a young girl forced to use a public street for a toilet. God comes to us in people, places and ways that make it difficult for us to see him or receive him. We don't find God where we expect or want to find him.

Lord, I have often prayed to be able to see you, hear you, touch you and know you where you really are, yet when I do see you in a lowly, dirty, perhaps crazy person living on the street, I don't know how to respond. Teach me, I beg you, what to do. Knowing you are in the poor is one thing; knowing how to embrace you in the poor is a much more difficult matter. I don't want to be indifferent to the suffering I see each day, but I don't know how to make a difference. A few coins in an outstretched hand doesn't seem enough, yet what more can I do?

You, my Lord, opened my eyes and I did see you. Now open my heart to know how to respond the next time I see you defecating or urinating on the street. Help me share the wonders of your love...in the squalor of life.

PILGRIMAGE DIARY 105

Saint Vincent de Paul

A few days after the events described in the previous diary, "Was That Jesus?", the Church celebrated the Feast of Saint Vincent de Paul (September 27). The day has special meaning for me because Vincent de Paul founded a religious order of priests and brothers called the Congregation of the Mission, or Vincentians. As a teenager, I entered a Vincentian minor seminary in Princeton, New Jersey, the first step on a long road (twelve years) to ordination as a priest. I didn't get very far down the road. I only lasted six months. Nonetheless, Saint Vincent de Paul still holds a special place in my heart.

Here is a short excerpt from the writings of Saint Vincent, taken from the Liturgy of the Hours: "The service of the poor is to be preferred to all else, and to be performed without delay. If at a time set aside for prayer, medicine or help has to be brought to some poor man, go and do what has to be done with an easy mind, offering it up to God as a prayer" (Vol. III, page 283).

PILGRIMAGE DIARY 106

Thoughts Scribbled While Walking

E very day, God asks the same question: Are you willing? Self-absorption makes me forget the reality of God. Humility frees me from absorption in myself.

Hope is the fruit of charity.

To be human is to be poor.

God loves me because I am weak and powerless, not in spite of those qualities. I am poor and needy, and God lifts me up.

Without self-denial and sacrifice, my prayer life will wither on the vine.

Don't allow luxuries to become necessities.

Humility, in all her lowliness, is the highest of all virtues.

Silence is an expression of love and strength.

Following your deepest aspirations makes life meaningful.

Solitude gives you the ability to hear an inner voice longing to tell you the truth about yourself.

PILGRIMAGE DIARY 107

On the Steps of the Gregorian University

The most deadly poison of our time is indifference.

—*SAINT MAXIMILIAN KOLBE*

*O*n my first day of class in the fall of 1998, I noticed a homeless man sitting on the steps of the Pontifical Gregorian University. Like everyone else, I walked by him without pausing or acknowledging his presence. He passively sat there with his right hand stretched out in hopes someone would give him a coin. No one did. Everyone, students and faculty, laypeople and priests, sisters in habits, all walked by without even acknowledging his existence. On the second day, he was still there; likewise, the third day. On those latter two days, I slowed down enough to see he was perhaps fifty years old. His long coat, though soiled and frayed, looked as if it might provide adequate protection against the now chilly nights. He had a long, thick, bushy, brown beard. He was dirty. On the third day, I managed fleeting eye contact with him, as I gave a faint shrug indicating that I had nothing to give. He was expressionless, which is understandable, considering that virtually no one responded to his presence. He might as well have been another statue, just a lifeless part of the historic cityscape of Rome.

On the fourth day, I once again walked past him, only I was becoming increasingly aware of his presence, as well as of the apathy of all those who walked past him as they entered the hallowed halls of this prestigious Catholic university, where they would study theology, missiology, philosophy and biblical exegesis. They may even hear a professor, more than likely a Jesuit priest, say, "The poor are a living tabernacle humbly housing the Lord of Lords." In my class that day, a student from Kenya read aloud the premise for her screenplay. She eloquently spoke about the evil of indifference. When she finished, I asked, "What did you do as you passed that homeless man sitting on the steps on your way into the building?"

"What homeless man?" she responded.

"The guy who sits every day on the top step in front of the main door."

"I didn't notice him. Perhaps he had left by the time I arrived."

At that point, it was time for our scheduled break. On our way to the snack bar off the main lobby, I asked her to come with me to the front door. The man was still there. I said, "He was there when you came in, and you didn't notice him. He is there every day. I don't think you are ready to write about the evils of indifference."

On the fifth day of the course, it was now impossible for me to be indifferent. I gave him a two-hundred-lire coin...worth about twelve cents in American money. Big deal! I guess my comments upset the student because she came up to me before the class began and told me that beggars like the guy on the front step probably make about fifty thousand lire a day (about thirty-two dollars), which is more than she makes in her part-time job. Her point being: she needs her spare change more than the beggar. Which, of course, is understandable.

During the weekend, the man on the steps of the Gregorian University was on my mind. On Saturday, I attended a lecture given by a Franciscan theologian from the Netherlands, who spoke about the three dimensions of Franciscan spirituality: poverty, love and humility. Afterward, I spoke with the friar and told him about the man on the steps, and also about the woman and the little girl I had seen relieving themselves in the street. I asked, "If, by grace, our eyes are opened to the poor and we are able to see Christ in them, then what do we do?"

He seemed caught off-guard by the question. Before he could respond, I said, "If I see Christ in a homeless person and just walk by, it is worse than not seeing Christ in the person. It is not enough to see Christ in the homeless; we need to embrace them. How do we, in practical terms, do that?"

We talked about it for a while, but there was no clear answer...just the usual dodges and rationalizations.

On Monday morning, the man on the steps was there as I entered the university. We made eye contact. I gestured to him that I didn't have any change. He said, shrugging, "Don't cry for me."

"You speak English," I responded in surprise.

"A little," he said.

I then reached into my pocket and pulled out a five-hundred-lire coin, which I handed to him, saying, "This is all I have."

He said, "A little is better than nothing."

I nodded and disappeared into the massive building.

The next day, he was once again sitting on the steps when I arrived for class. I said, "Good morning."

He said, "Hi."

I then asked, "Where are you from?"

He looked puzzled, perhaps not expecting a conversation or a question. "Home," I said, "where is your home?"

"I'm ex-Russian."

"Russian?"

"Yes. And you...are you an American?"

"Yes." I then asked another question: "What did you do?"

No response. I asked the question again, differently: "What kind of work did you do in Russia?"

"I was in the navy," he responded.

A few silent seconds slipped by, and then I said, "It's tough, hey."

"Yes," he said.

I gave him a thousand-lire bill (sixty cents), and entered the university.

We had connected. From the little he told me, I could begin to imagine some of his history, which more than likely included the collapse of the Soviet Union, which left him with no pay, no benefits, nothing. As I walked to the classroom I wondered how he got from Russia to the steps of the Gregorian University.

The next day, Wednesday, I asked him his name.

"Joseph...Guiseppe here."

"My name is Gerry."

He nodded, as if he were glad to know it.

I handed him some money, patted him on the shoulder and said, "Try to have a good day, Joseph."

"Thanks, Gerry."

That night, there was an intense thunderstorm. Flashes of lightning lit up my little hermitage. The rain pounded against the window. As I lay snugly under the warmth of the covers, I wondered about Joseph...where was he?...was he dry?

The next morning, his spot on the steps was vacant. Not far from where he usually sat, another homeless man was lying across the bottom step. His clothes were damp and his body was twitching as

he slept. As I walked past him, a sentence from William McNamara's
Earthly Mysticism *echoed through my mind: "We must not dare ever*
come into God's presence alone. God will say, 'Where are the
others? Where is my broken world?'"

I left them on the steps of the Gregorian University, Lord.

I entered the classroom where I would teach priests and sisters
how to use the medium of television and films to better
communicate the gospel. I felt like a hypocrite.

Contemplation and Action

Interior experience is geared to action. It is designed to soften
up our self-centered dispositions, to deliver us from what is
compulsive in our motivation, and to open us up completely to
God and the genuine service of others.

—*THOMAS KEATING,* THE HEART OF THE WORLD

I *struggle with the question of what to do when I encounter a*
homeless person. The reason I don't know what to do is that I
haven't spent enough time listening to God in order to find out what
he would like me to do.

This insight came today—on the Feast of Saint Francis—during
Father Liam's homily. Father Liam reminded us that Francis spent half
his life in prayer, in order to find out what he should do. He left the
busy, noisy marketplaces and ascended the mountains in search of
silence and solitude, where he could better hear the voice of God by
deepening the vast reservoir of his prayer life. "I have done what was
mine to do," the saint said. "Pray that God shows you what is yours
to do."

I don't have the ability or the freedom to help every homeless
person I encounter on the streets. However, if my life is sufficiently
grounded in prayer, then—and only then—I will be receptive to
promptings from the Lord on how best to respond to a particular
situation. Perhaps it might be to give a little money. Perhaps it might
be to offer a silent prayer or a reassuring smile. I truly felt something
deep inside me urging me to talk with the man on the steps of the
Gregorian University. Perhaps God might be asking me to volunteer

some time in a soup kitchen when I get home. The point is, only through prayer will I find "what is mine to do" in relationship to the poor.

Francis was unique. He was a mystic and a man of action. His actions flowed out of his contemplation, out of his longing glance at what is real. The word "contemplation" actually means to witness and respond. Thomas Merton, in Bread in the Wilderness, reminds us that "the secret of contemplation is the gift of ourselves to God." And when we give ourselves to God in prayer, we begin to experience the richness of divine love and mercy, and are better able to share that love and mercy with others.

In prayer, Francis was freed from the complexities of thought (and figuring out what to do) and he discovered the simplicity of his own heart.

A simple heart is a heart where God is. A simple heart is a pure heart, a heart always willing to surrender itself to the will of God.

Lord, show me what is mine to do.

Beato Solitudo

Meister Eckhart claimed God doesn't require long vigils, fasting, prayer and mortification from us. But he does demand tranquillity. Eckhart urges us to flee and hide from the storm of inner thoughts. Today, he would tell us to also flee the inferno of noise that engulfs modern life. We need unruffled calmness to encounter God.

Here are two random suppositions which I think are somehow connected:

1) It has been calculated that the average American spends fifteen years of his or her life in front of a television.

2) Consumerism has killed the spirit of mysticism. The rise in an interest in Tao and Zen demonstrates people are hungry for the fruit of mysticism.

The key to being a pilgrim is to remain still interiorly as you journey...otherwise you are just a wanderer.

PILGRIMAGE DIARY 109

The Man on the Steps

He sits, staring off
　　into the piazza
　　as we pass him by.
Day after day, nothing
　　but sitting,
　　"waiting
　　yet
　　not waiting
　　or he has lost hope,"
as Jean Vanier would say.

Joseph knows the worthlessness
　　of his days, his life.
Jean Vanier spoke of this
　　in Tears of Silence:

"his misery is the awareness of his misery
　　'i remain in the vomit of my worthlessness.....'

he knows this worthlessness
　　and has lost hope
the man in misery is not ignorant
only lacking in strength...vitality
that which springs from hope
　　and he has no hope......
his misery is greater because of his awareness
　　therein lies his despair
　　he cannot rise
　　not feeling worthy to rise

the person in misery does not need a look that
　　judges and criticizes
but a comforting presence
　　that brings peace and hope and life
　　and says:
　　　　'you are a human person
　　　　important
　　　　mysterious

infinitely precious
what you have to say
is important
because it flows
from a human person
in you there are those seeds
of the infinite
those germs of love...of beauty
which must rise from the earth
of your misery
so humanity be fulfilled.
if you do not rise
then something will be missing
if you are not fulfilled
it is terrible
you must rise again
on the third day.....
rise again because we all need
you
for you are a child of God....'" (pages 26-28)

you, Joseph
my brother
be loved
beloved
for you are
a child
of God.

PILGRIMAGE DIARY 110

Pastry for the Man on the Steps

*T*oday as I walked to the university to begin my third and final week of teaching, I passed a pastry shop on Via Purificazione. Suddenly, I was hit with the impulse to go in and buy something for Joseph. Spare change seemed so impersonal.

I went in and bought three lovely pieces of pastry. When I arrived at the university, Joseph was sitting on the steps. I handed *him the bag. As he took it, he gave me a slightly puzzled look. He opened the bag and looked inside it. The sight of the pastry brought a gentle smile to his sullied face. He looked at me. Our eyes connected. His eyes said "thank you." My eyes said "you're welcome." No words, no gestures. Just a moment of grace where love broke through the pain of life.*

Stop Talking, Start Walking

Francis experienced God through the recognition of the supernatural within him. He wasn't converted by theological ideas. Once he had awakened to the reality of God, he simply followed the gospel in purity and wholeness, transforming it from an ideal into a way of life. And he gave the gift he was given to others. As others followed him in this new way of life, he was unable to give a clear rule or code to live by, other than presenting to them the words of Christ.

His simplicity and firmness about living in full compliance to the gospel was perplexing and troublesome to many of his early followers. It was all so simple for Francis: repent and live the gospel in simplicity and fullness, period. No need for embellishments or refinements, and certainly no need for altering or discounting anything that Christ asks. His idealism was uncompromising. Francis wanted for himself and his friars nothing but complete compliance to the gospel, giving your highest and utmost to God and eliminating everything else from your life.

Few could follow his ideal of perfect living, whose foundation was a poverty so absolute it required living totally for God without any concern for anything beyond God. Francis saw in the Church and in the religious orders a material avarice and spiritual corruption so profound that only a strict and literal adherence to the gospel could remedy the situation.

His solution was so simple, yet so impossible.

The simple part appeals to me. The impossible part leaves me feeling frustrated and hopeless. And at a crossroads.

After spending more than four years submersed in the world of Saint Francis, I am left with the prospect of facing an extreme challenge: How do I incorporate his ideals into my world? In his Sixth Admonition, Francis wrote: "It is a great shame for us, the servants of God, that the saints have accomplished great things and we want only to receive glory and honor by recounting them."

Francis' life was about imitating Christ. What is my life about? I talk about imitating Christ. I aspire to imitate Christ. But I have yet to convert my aspiration and talk into action. This is my challenge. Francis has pointed the way. I must now start walking.

PILGRIMAGE DIARY 111

Thoughts Scribbled While Walking

*Poverty of spirit frees us from the tyranny of wealth.
   Littleness is a big part of holiness.
Holiness is wholeness.
Give your incapacity to God.
Christ shows us that mercy is more than compassion or justice.
   Mercy requires us to become one with the poor and hurting, to
   live their misery as though it was our own. Christ took his place
   with the condemned, an innocent deliberately allowing himself
   to be arrested. God's love gives everything, always.
My anguish, my fear, my temptations can become a path to God if
   I acknowledge my littleness, my weakness and transform them
   into a trust that God alone can bring light into my darkness if I
   abandon myself completely and take refuge in God's love.
Poverty of spirit is a means of maintaining a continual attitude of
   dying to self without succumbing to self-hatred or causing a
   lack of self-esteem. We need to die to self because it is the only
   way to be fully alive to God.
Grace is the breath of Love.
Acts of charity are the wings of Love.
Submit to God the imperfections of your self-love.
Strive to live the present moment as it truly is: a present from God.*

PILGRIMAGE DIARY 112

'Down and Out on the Via Veneto'

After five days of near-constant rain, it was a clear, crisp, dry night. I was walking up the Via Veneto with one of my students, a young woman from Kenya who works at Vatican Radio.

We were on our way to dinner with a Maryknoll missionary from Massachusetts who has spent most of his adult life working in Tanzania. As we strolled past the elegant shops and expensive restaurants, past scores of smartly dressed people enjoying an evening walk, I caught out of the corner of my eye a homeless woman sitting on a box, her back against the face of the building. She was partly obscured by the shadow that lingered between two shops. I motioned to the student to look. Just the day before we had watched my film, We Have a Table for Four Ready, *and so the homeless issue was on our minds. As the student and I turned our gaze toward the woman, the poor soul did something totally unexpected. And disturbing. She removed her shirt by pulling it up and over her head, revealing her breasts. There she sat, on the box, in the shadows, naked from the waist up, as she calmly folded the shirt, put it in a bag, and then removed another shirt from a different bag. In one continuous, unhurried motion, she unfolded the second T-shirt and slipped it over her head and pulled it down. She gave no hint of embarrassment or even awareness of people walking by as she casually changed her clothing as if she were in the privacy of her own home.*

The student and I looked at each other in disbelief—not knowing what to say. After dinner, we sat in a parlor at Collegio Maryknoll on Via Sardegna and spoke with the priest about the brutality of the ethnic violence in Africa, and also about the work of a Maryknoll brother who compassionately cares for the needs of those dying of AIDS.

The homeless woman and the sad stories that permeated our conversation left me feeling far from la dolce vita.

Letting God In

For a long time, I had a set morning routine that seemed harmless. As soon as I got up, I brewed a pot of coffee, poked my head outside the front door and collected the two papers I have delivered, the Los Angeles Times and The New York Times. While sipping the coffee, I read all that passes for news from the previous day. Without realizing it, I was a prisoner of my routine. Moreover, the seemingly harmless practice was in fact having a serious negative impact on my life and was blocking my *progress in the two most essential components of my life: writing and praying.*

I recall once reading that a person reading a paper such as The New York Times *will process more information in the time it takes to read the paper than an average person living as recently as 200 years ago would process in his or her lifetime. The tangle of human affairs from around the world, steeped in complexity, is spread out before us each day. Crime, violence, corruption, scandals and wars from every continent are report-ed in gritty detail. The intricacies of local, national and international politics are reported and analyzed. Sections of the paper are devoted to the worlds of business, finance, science, technology, publishing, medicine, religion, sports and entertainment. We learn about hot stocks, hot films and books, the hottest fashions and cars, the newest diet craze or med-ical scare, and the latest baseball player to sign a contract for ten million dollars for what is essentially a summer job. The editorial pages pepper us with a barrage of diverse opinions. We read about murders and geno-cide, famines and floods, plane crashes and earthquakes, celebrity gossip and presidential peccadilloes.*

Without realizing it, I was exhausted after forty-five minutes of read-ing the papers. My mind was scattered in dozens of different directions. My emotions had been taken on a roller-coaster ride. I was angered by political, racial or religious violence from every corner of the world. I was saddened by deaths caused by natural disasters. Some stories left me with a sense of bewilderment, others filled me with a sense of utter confusion. After reading the paper, I would go to my office and sit down to write. As I faced the blank white sheet of paper, my mind was scattered and I had a difficult time focusing on the task before me. And so I fiddled, content that this was a normal part of the writing process.

One day, I decided that I would devote some time to praying before I started writing. But this time of prayer didn't seem to yield much fruit. Again, my mind was too scattered. I tried reading Scripture, reading spir-itual books, meditating, but it was all too mechanical, just doing it for the sake of doing it. I really didn't know what was wrong, or even how I could change the situation.

As I studied the life of Saint Francis, the thing that constantly impressed me was how he focused his entire being on God. One day, it hit me...God is not the first thing I think about when I get up. Out of sheer habit, before I actually thought about anything, I grabbed the paper and started reading. Saint John of the Cross, the Spanish mystic and giant of

Carmelite spirituality, suggested that we not feed our spirits on anything apart from God. Yet, I was beginning my day by feeding on the news, which effectively was a recollection of the previous day's manifestations of human frailty. In essence, I greeted the good news of a new day with the bad news from yesterday. It was so obvious that I did not see it...until I saw it. Then I decided to restructure my day, which amounted to establishing clear priorities. I wanted to emulate Francis as much as possible, and so my day would begin by focusing attention on God.

I would take fifteen minutes to wake up, silently and thoughtlessly brewing some coffee. Then I would spend thirty minutes in prayer. I noticed results almost immediately. At first, it was tough breaking the newspaper habit. And it wasn't easy just sitting still for a half hour. I felt as if I wanted "to do" something. I tried to give the time some structure. I began by reading the Liturgy of the Hours. Afterward, I would either simply sit still, reflecting on what I had read, or I would try not to think about anything, just allowing a thought to flow into me. The entire tone of my day changed. It now began in tranquillity and renewal. My ability to worship God increased. Within a short period of time, I went from figuring out how to squeeze time from the day to pray, to squeezing time from the day to read the paper. My priorities were now in order, and in harmony with the desires I had for my life.

After my period of morning prayer, I sat down to write. And instantly my writing became more productive, because I was bringing a calm, refreshed mind to it.

Putting God first in my day led me to a deeper reality of the various ways in which we let God into our lives. Prayer takes many forms, and I wanted to become familiar with as many as possible, in order to find the most effective form for me. Gradually, I learned that there are two primary approaches to prayer. One approach emphasizes words and images, and the other stresses mystery and experience. The former acknowledges that God can be discovered through Scripture and through images and symbols. The latter accentuates the transcendent, unfathomable mystery of God, who is best approached by self-emptying and letting go of all preconceived images and ideas of God in order to enter into an authentic experience of God as pure love. One approach sees God in everything; the other abandons everything to experience God in a darkened void. My hunch is that a healthy balance between the two distinctive approaches is ideal. As I experimented with the various forms of prayer associated with these two traditions, I learned to approach God with open hands, a *searching mind and a loving heart. Saint Francis would remind us that enhancing our relationship with God requires growth in humility, simplicity and poverty.*

PILGRIMAGE DIARY 113

A Gift of Love

If we neglect prayer we are like the unweaned child taken from its mother's breast and given no substitute.

—*RUTH BURROWS*, INTERIOR CASTLE EXPLORED

*T*he end of isolation is found in prayer. Through prayer, we become aware that God is ever present. Through prayer, we are made to feel at home with the living presence with whom we can share everything. When we enter into the living presence, we become aware of our complete dependence on the Creator. Prayer fosters within us a spirit of humility and the realization that we cannot truly live without God.

Prayer is a gift of Love, and a means of living our whole life in communion with the Lord, who, through the Incarnation, came to share in our humble condition. As we encounter God in the depths of ourselves, we are no longer astonished by the darkness of God's mystery, but we merely accept it. We now live by faith. We no longer belong to ourselves but to Love, the giver of the gift. When we enter fully into the living presence, we experience spontaneous joy...even in the midst of trials, hardships and suffering. When we are weak, empty and hurting, we know the Lord is present. Trusting in this presence, we are compelled to accept everything as coming from God.

PILGRIMAGE DIARY 114

Farewell to Assisi

*M*y class at the Gregorian ended on Friday, October 9th, and early the next morning I traveled via train back to Assisi for a week of reflection and a closer look at damage to the churches *there caused by the earthquake. I was filled with anticipation about seeing the interior of the upper Basilica of St. Francis. Don Aldo was making arrangements for me to get a special tour of the repair work.*

I met Don Aldo at Papa Casa Giovanni at five Saturday evening. He told me that he was unable to reach the only friar who could authorize a private visit, adding that entrance to the closed upper church is very rarely granted. He suggested we go to the basilica and try to find the friar, who was our only hope.

As we walked along Via Metastasio we enjoyed the cool breeze which accompanied the splendid view of the valley offered by the street. The valley was drenched in sunlight, except for far off on the distant horizon where clouds allowed only a few rays to peek dramatically through. We walked in silence, our pace reflecting the priest's advanced age. I wondered how many times during his long life he has made this same walk—did he ever tire of the spectacular view? I doubt it. I became sad at the thought of seeing the damage the earthquake inflicted on the upper church. Don Aldo said he hadn't been in the basilica since the quake. I guess the treasured memory of its beauty outweighed his curiosity at seeing how it had been marred, for he also appeared to be sad.

When we arrived at the basilica, we were unable to find the friar with the clout to get us in. It was hard for me to believe a legend like Don Aldo could be denied entrance into anything in Assisi, but the basilica appeared harder to breach than Fort Knox. On our walk back to Casa Papa Giovanni, Don Aldo showed me the house where he lived as a little boy. Even though our short outing did not yield the results I had hoped for, spending time with Don Aldo was reward enough.

Once again I was staying at the Hotel Ideale. Early Sunday morning, I sat on the terrace and soaked in the peaceful ambience of the waking city. Only church bells and barking dogs interrupted the silence. As I looked over the tranquil city, the back of the Cathedral of San Rufino loomed in the foreground. Scores of birds danced over its roof. Atop the mountain overlooking the town hovered the Rocca Maggiore, whose defiant sturdiness seemed to proclaim that it was the king of the hill. The valley below was hidden beneath a thick cover of early morning mist, fog and low clouds...creating an illusion that the town of Assisi was an island floating in a sea of mystical mist. A lizard poked his head out of a crack in the wall surrounding the patio. "Good morning, Mr. Lizard." Perhaps it was too early for a chat, so he ignored me and darted away. Off in the distance, I saw the faint outline of the moon. I turned and looked behind me and saw the rising sun. The sun and moon over Assisi...again.

Suddenly, my morning meditation was interrupted by the sound of distant drums beating, coming closer and closer. The sound drew me down to the plaza in front of San Rufino, where, much to my delight, I saw a parade in progress. The marchers comprised a colorful display of medieval pageantry, with some people dressed as nobility, some as peasants. Many carried crossbows and flags. Assisi seemed alive and ancient. It was wonderful. And in the crowd of onlookers, I spotted Don Aldo. He told me he was sorry we couldn't get into the upper basilica, but that he hadn't given up trying to contact the friar. Meanwhile, he offered to give me a tour of the archives below the Cathedral of San Rufino, a room rarely seen by visitors, mostly because few people know of its existence and even fewer people have a key to it.

For me, the cathedral archives was an orgy of historical treats. Using large skeleton keys, we entered a series of outer rooms far below the cathedral before we arrived at our destination. Don Aldo removed a gigantic book from one of the shelves. It had to be two feet tall. He gently placed it on a desk and opened it. It was a hand-printed book used for the celebration of the liturgy. The only word I understood on the cover page was messe—the plural of the Italian word for Mass. Slowly turning the pages, each a masterpiece, Don Aldo said the liturgical book was from the year 1200. I marveled at the gold lettering, and the artistry that created a book that would only be seen by a priest saying Mass. I imagined that Francis might have seen—or even touched—the book.

Next, Don Aldo removed a missal that would have been used by a parishioner while Saint Francis was alive. It, too, was hand-printed and contained elaborate and colorful artwork, including a full-page painting of Christ crucified. A closer look revealed light pencil lines used to keep the lettering straight. The book was about six hundred pages in length, and contained many pages of hymns. I could actually follow the flow of the liturgy, noticing the selection of Gospel readings. I was overwhelmed by the sense of tradition within the Catholic Church. After centuries of changes and modifications to the liturgy, it remains essentially the same.

Opening a drawer, Don Aldo removed a piece of parchment, an official document dated in the year 963, making it one thousand thirty-five years old. Don Aldo said the document had something to do with the ancestors of Saint Clare. Two more parchments, one dated 980 and the other January 1000, were removed from the drawer, one having something to do with the marriage of a noblewoman, which had taken place in the Rocca Maggiore. The last document Don Aldo showed me was a letter written by Pope Alexander IV, dated December 3, 1257, concerning the church of San Giacomo de Muro Rupto.

Some of the large books Don Aldo removed from the shelf were so heavy I had to help him carry them to the desk. The dusty room contained administrative records from the cathedral dating back to 1455. They were stored in large binders, with labels indicating the years. I jotted down a few years from the bulging files: 1455-1500, 1506-1515, 1561-1572, 1580-1585, 1750-1804. There were copies of Missale Romanun—the Roman Missal—in all sizes and from all centuries. I still have a Roman Missal, St. Joseph's Edition, that was given to me by my godmother when I was a child. And I thought that was old. The last thing Don Aldo showed me was a map of Assisi dated 1599. He pointed out the Piazza del Comune and the Cathedral of San Rufino.

Leaving the archives, Don Aldo took me on a quick tour of the ancient ruins of the crypt from the fifth-century church buried beneath the cathedral. For me, after the archives, it was a case of sensory overload, and I think I only saw half of what he showed me. I can only recall a very ornate Roman sarcophagus dating back to the third century.

The tour ended around noon. After we parted company, my head was so filled with history, I decided to take a long, slow walk up to the Carceri. Father Sergio smiled when he saw me. We managed to exchange a few words in our limited vocabulary of English and Italian. I walked to Brother Masseo's cave and said a short prayer for my nephew Brian and his wife LeAnn.

I sat in silence for some time in the tiny chapel next to the Grotto of St. Francis. Before leaving, I stood in front of the cross, reflecting on the past year, wondering about the future. Should I write another book? Should I make another documentary film? Then I realized it doesn't matter whether I write a book or direct a film...either is fine as long as I love. I prayed that I would be able to surrender more and more of myself, until "I" disappeared. "Lord, teach me to die to myself, to nail everything that is not of you to the cross, so the 'me' that remains is the little boy who once only loved you."

Before I left for the trip, a Poor Clare nun from Ireland staying at Sant' Isidoro told me to "find the little boy" within me and he would tell me what I should do in the future. I was beginning to understand her wise advice. By finding the child I was, the little boy in his innocence and uniqueness would reveal to me what I had been called to do with my life. I lost my innocence before I knew who I was and what I was meant to be.

I knelt down to offer one final prayer before descending the mountain. As I knelt in silent adoration, I "heard" these words: "The pilgrimage has just begun." There was a pause. Then I sensed these words being directed to me: "Walk in humility, silence, awe and love. Give as I ask."

The pilgrimage was not over. It never ends. Our entire life is a pilgrimage.

Learning How God Makes Movies

The desire is a pledge of the fulfillment of the desire.
—*SAINT BERNARD OF CLAIRVAUX*

I brought with me to Assisi a book entitled When the Well Runs Dry *by Thomas Green, an American Jesuit priest. This book served me as a silent retreat master, and I would like to share what it taught me.*

In the beginning of our lifelong pilgrimage of prayer, the main focus is deepening our initial encounter with God. We do so by getting to know God through spending time in prayer, meditation and contemplation. This is a time of quiet, spending time in the desert discovering the depths, heights and majesty of God. This part of our pilgrimage affords us the opportunity to recognize and to begin ridding ourselves of anything that blocks the blossoming of love in our souls and hearts. Some say this beginning stage can last several years, but, in a sense, no matter how far we advance in the spiritual life, we are always only at the beginning in comparison to the infinite and inexhaustible goodness and grandeur of

God. Saint Bonaventure suggests that instead of increasing our knowledge of the Lord, we should, in time, be more concerned with increasing our love for the Lord. Prayer is essentially loving God, which is why we need to deepen our prayer life in order to deepen our love.

While the first stage is concerned with getting to know God, the emphasis in the second stage moves from the head to the heart. Saint Teresa of Avila uses the the metaphor of a garden: The flowers are virtues and the water which nourishes them is prayer. In this stage, God moves from an image to a feeling. God becomes transcendent, all-holy and completely beyond our rational or sensible grasp. Imagine a painting or statue of Christ giving way to the essence depicted, and you will get an idea of what is happening at this stage. Along this portion of the pilgrimage road, we are visited by wonderful spiritual consolations. Prayer moves from being plodding to being joyful. But we eventually run out of water and our prayer renders no consolations. The pilgrimage to God has taken us to the dry well of Saint Teresa of Avila and to the dark night of Saint John of the Cross.

Prayer becomes a dry, barren wasteland. And God seems to have disappeared, vanished from our intellect, our feelings. We are in nada land. It is here that we learn that God is in control. And in this void, this emptiness, this feeling of abandonment, we must tenaciously cling to God. Saint Teresa found this period so perilous and so difficult, she told God that it comes as no surprise to her that he has so few friends, because look how badly he treats the few he has. Instead of "watering" Saint Teresa and the other great saints, God chose to inflict them with severe drought. But, in this drought, in this dark night, Teresa and the saints discovered genuine love. And this new love transformed their old self-gratifying love, which sought its own delights, into a self-sacrificing love which happily dies to its self in order to serve the other.

This is poverty, the poverty that can proclaim: Blessed are the poor in spirit, for theirs is the kingdom of heaven. On our pilgrimage we become the anawim, the poorly disposed of Israel, whose wealth is not material but of their love of the Lord. Thomas Green writes, "It is not what we possess but what we are attached to—what possesses us—which makes us unfit for, incapable of inheriting the kingdom of God."

Francis of Assisi reminds us that Jesus is always calling us to detachment, and not simply material or monetary poverty. Francis knew that material poverty was a great help to our efforts of purifying our souls and hearts. He knew how easily money and possession can ensnare our hearts. For Francis, his external and material poverty symbolized his inner and spiritual poverty. Father Green suggests that "poverty of spirit means to have no will of my own." And that is the kind of surrender God seeks. We must even surrender our will to be holy. We begin by surrendering things. Then we move to surrendering our attachment to things. And finally we surrender our wills. As a TV producer and director, I realize this essentially means that I must not be the producer and director of my own life. Francis' life tells me I do not need to be always doing something, or trying to control events. I simply need to dispose myself to God and respond to God's prompting. It is not a matter of simply going with the flow. It is about going with the flow of God. Mystics call this passive purification. Francis allowed his will to dissolve into the will of God. It was his extreme poverty of spirit, the total submersion of his will into the will of God, that gave Francis his amazing energy, drive and convictions. Francis did not change himself and his world by the power of his own will; that would have gotten him nowhere. He changed himself and his world by harnessing his will with God's, and that made all the difference in the world.

I'm still reading Father Green's book. I'm still walking along the pilgrimage road. And I am still producing and directing my own life...but I am ready to give the job to God. In time, God might make me a co-producer. Meanwhile, I am happy to be an intern, learning how God makes movies.

For God Alone

This book has been rich in words and thoughts on poverty. Do I dare add a few more? Just a few.

Francis' poverty was his highest wealth; he was poor in order to possess the whole fullness of God and to lavish it in love on all creation and every creature whom God allowed to cross his path. How weightless are his wings of poverty which flew his soul into the sunshine of true freedom. Francis, having nothing anywhere, found God everywhere. He was completely indifferent to temporal things. Yet his material poverty was nothing in comparison to his poverty of spirit. Nothing distracted him from prayer, and nothing diverted his love from God. His detachment was so great, his heart was completely emptied, leaving it undivided and available for God alone.

Out of the Cloud of Dust, a Ray of Hope

*T*wo days later, Don Aldo and I returned to the Basilica of St. Francis. This time, everything was set. Or so we thought. When we arrived at the basilica, we were greeted by Father Nicola Giandomenico, O.F.M. Conv., who had been inside the upper basilica when the ceiling collapsed. He and Don Aldo exchanged warm salutations in Italian. It soon became clear that the friar had only agreed to talk with me, out of deference to Don Aldo, but that he had no intention of allowing me into the closed upper church. Fortunately, he spoke fairly fluent English. He wanted to know why I wanted to see the damaged church. I told him about the book I was writing, and how the "pilgrimage diaries" ended on the feast of Saint Francis, just days after the earthquake. He seemed unimpressed. He mentioned something about the danger, and also about his concern over bad press, which has left people around the world thinking Assisi was a disaster area, and that the beauty of the upper church was permanently marred. I told him of my love of the saint, his Order, the basilica and the city, and that I would never do anything to harm any of them. Again, he seemed unimpressed. I then told him I was friends with an American Conventual friar who once lived in the Sacro Convento attached to the basilica. Again, he was unimpressed. Every so often, he spoke Italian with Don Aldo, as if trying to explain to him that it was not possible to enter the upper church.

Just as I was about to give up my efforts, because I could see the friar was becoming upset with my persistence, I was moved to say, "I need to see it for my soul." He looked right at me. Suddenly, I had his attention. "The art in the church was an integral part of my conversion. I had written about it with great love in my book before the earthquake. I love the church. Seeing it will help me heal the pain I have felt for more than a year because of the wounds it has suffered. I need to see the damage for myself, so I can write with hope for its recovery."

There was a silent pause in which I detected a slight smile on his face which seemed to say, "Why didn't you say that in the first place?" Having seen my heart and the purity of my intentions, he waved his arm indicating Don Aldo and I should follow him. He removed a key from his pocket and unlocked the gate on the chain-link fence surrounding the church.

When we entered, I was horrified and shocked. The last time I was in this church, just a week before the earthquake, it was radiant with beauty and intoxicated my being. Now, it looked like a construction site. Ugly. Dark. Ominous. The walls were draped with scaffolding. A long chorus line of silver pipes stretched from the floor to the ceiling far overhead. I had to look between the pipes to see the frescoes which adorned the side walls. As I strained to see them, the pain intensified. The once bright, vivid frescoes, lovingly painted by Giotto, had lost their luster. It was as if they were covered by a veil. Father Nicola saw the concern on my face. "The frescoes," he said, "are covered with dust."

Pictures caught live on TV captured the vault over the altar collapsing, creating an explosion—a mushroom cloud—of dust that filled the church within seconds of the ceiling's hitting the floor. The second section of the ceiling which collapsed seconds later, and killed the two friars, added even more dust and debris to the already heavily polluted air. The dust covered and clung to the walls. Not dust like you would find on a tabletop and easily wipe off. The dust I saw consisted of thick particles of concrete, plaster and stone caked into the walls by the force of the explosion. The dust was imbedded in the pores of the wall. Father Nicola showed me two frescoes on the south wall where workers tested a small area to see if they could remove the dust without harming the frescoes. The tests were more than hopeful.

The entire floor of the church was covered with thick planks of wood, completely obscuring the beautiful marble floor. We walked to the area where the main altar had stood for centuries until those few seconds a year ago when it was reduced to rubble. The friar explained some of the things being done to repair the damage and to safeguard the building from further disasters, but for most of our short time inside the church, we exchanged few words. What we were looking at said it all.

Despite the deep heartbreak I felt as I looked around the church, I also felt a sense of hope. The art that was lost is without question a major tragedy, albeit minor in comparison to the four lives snuffed out under the mound of rubble. But I was given the grace to look at all the art that was not damaged, which is most of it. True, some of the frescoes will have cracks, but the church will reopen* and the art that survived will still be able to touch souls with the timeless message of the gospel and Saint Francis of Assisi. And, perhaps, the terrible, devastating earthquake that rocked the church might remind us of our own fragility and vulnerability. It might also remind us the art on the walls means nothing if we do not carry the message it conveys in our hearts.

* Note: The basilica did indeed reopen in December 1999.

PILGRIMAGE DIARY 116
Fides et Ratio

*F*aith and reason are archenemies. Or so I thought for most of my adult life. I allowed reason to strangle my faith. After the death of my faith, reason alone was of no comfort to me. But today, the pope said faith and reason not only can coexist but also must be on friendly terms with each other. I can think of no more fitting way to end my long pilgrimage back to faith than by sinking my teeth into the powerful new encyclical from the pen of John Paul II, released today, just days before his twentieth anniversary as pope. The 150-page encyclical, entitled Faith and Reason, the thirteenth of his pontificate, spans the history of thought from Sophocles to Buddha and beyond, as it argues that philosophy needs God and the Church needs philosophy if either is going to survive the frenetic pace and intellectual fragmentation of society at the end of the millennium. Written to the bishops of the Catholic Church, the decree says these two venerable strains of human endeavor need not exclude each other in pursuit of truth.

The pope begins his encyclical by saying, "Faith and reason are like two wings on which the human spirit rises to the contemplation of truth; and God has placed in the human heart a desire to know the truth—in a word, to know himself—so that, by knowing and loving God, men and women may also come to the fullness of truth about themselves." The pope laments the despair created during the twentieth century by such philosophies as Marxism and postmodern nihilism, which have given rise to a "fateful separation" of faith and reason, and have spawned a reliance on "exaggerated rationalism." We are living in a time when many philosophers have grave doubts *about humanity's ability to know anything for certain, and many theologians fear that reason leads to doubt. This climate of thought "has given rise to different forms of agnosticism and relativism." I traveled down that road and quickly got stuck in the underbrush of skepticism. We all have our own opinions, and are happy with "partial and provisional truths, no longer seeking to ask radical questions about the meaning and ultimate foundation of human, personal and social existence." The "philosophy of nothing" is leading us nowhere. Most people I know, even Christians, are very reluctant to make any claim to universal or abiding truth. Many of my friends proudly cling to autonomous reason as an alternative to faith. The pope is saying that faith is not a substitute for reason, nor is it the enemy of reason.*

Life is a journey of discovery, and a most important goal of the quest is to know yourself. The ability to speculate is a part of our human intellect. God made us thinkers. We need to strive to discover universal elements of knowledge, yet, today, many neglect the search for the ultimate truth which transcends our understanding of our humanity. The pope says reason "has lost the capacity to lift its gaze to the heights, not daring to rise to the truth of Being." Obviously, the pope hails Christianity as "the path of truth" that allows men and women to take "full possession of their lives." Experience has taught me to agree with him, which, considering the way I lampooned him in my first book, is an astounding turn of events. Even though Pope John Paul II talks about the truth of Christianity, he acknowledges the rich religious and philosophical traditions of the East, singling out the ancient metaphysical traditions of India.

In this age of doubt, when so many people "stumble through life to the very edge of the abyss without knowing where they are going," the pope is asking philosophy to consider the meaning of life, not simply the meaning of words, and he argues that the Christian faith cannot be ignored in the quest for truth.

I must have confidence in the objective validity of the Christian revelation which, by grace, has been bequeathed to me. Nonetheless, my faith, for its own health and vitality, must stay friends with reason to ensure that my spiritual path does not wander off into myth or superstition. Perhaps authentic truth resides at the point where faith and reason intersect.

PILGRIMAGE DIARY 117

Sante Messa

*I*t is Sunday afternoon, October 18, 1998. I'm in my little
hermitage at Sant' Isidoro. I'm packing my stuff, getting ready for
my flight home. I leave early tomorrow morning. Today was a fitting
end to this book, which has chronicled my own personal pilgrimage
that began in March of 1995, just beyond the wall of this room, in
the darkened church with Father Liam. A friend at Vatican Radio
gave me a ticket for this morning's celebration of a Mass in St. Peter's
Square commemorating of the twentieth anniversary of John Paul II's
pontificate.

I left the friary just before seven o'clock and walked to the
Vatican. I enjoy the streets of Rome in the early-morning quiet. I
arrived at the Vatican about 7:45 a.m. and presented my ticket at the
Portone di bronzo, the bronze gate. Already, the square was filling
up quickly for the ten o'clock Mass. People sat in the sun for more
than two hours, just to get a closer look at the pope. They came from
every nation. There were young and old, lay and religious. The
square was filled to overflowing as the procession of hundreds of
priests entered. Cardinals and bishops from around the world
surrounded the pope. It was truly a glorious celebration.

The pope looked weak, his steps slow and feeble, but he seemed
truly humbled by and appreciative of the sea of love which engulfed
him. After the Mass, the pope was driven though the throngs
gathered to honor him. I was fortunate enough to be sitting in an
aisle seat, which gave me a very close look at him, as the car slowly
drove by. As he blessed the people, they responded with an
overwhelming outpouring of love and emotion. I blessed myself, and
thanked God for giving me the opportunity to end my pilgrimage at
such a magnificent event.

As our journey together in these pages comes to a conclusion,
may we say with Saint Catherine of Siena:

> We are pilgrims.... [The Word Incarnate] has accompanied us on
> our pilgrimage and given himself to us as food to make us run
> bravely,....reaching the goal of death we rest in bed, in the
> peaceful sea of the Divine Essence, where we receive the eternal
> vision of God.

PILGRIMAGE DIARY 118

Dear Reader, Let Us Pray

*W*ow...the book is finished. It has been an amazing journey for me. Writing this book has become such a part of my life that I find it hard to end it. I have been lugging this thick manuscript around with me for more than three years. It has been all over Italy, upstate New York and the state of Washington. The evolution of the book is interesting. When I began in early 1994, I merely wanted to tell the story of Saint Francis in a simple, unvarnished way that reflected the character of Francis. I was not a biographer, nor did I aspire to be one. I found the story of Francis' life inflamed my imagination. Writing about him, in truth, was a way for me to get to know him better. And I didn't realize it, but it was also a way for me to get to know God better. After my experience at Sant' Isidoro in March of 1995, I had this hunger to understand God—beyond the realm of possibility, of course. What I really wanted was to fall in love with God. The attraction was there, I just did not know how to proceed. Francis became my guide, showing me the way.

I chuckle to myself now when I think about just how naive I was when I began this project. I knew nothing about the miles upon miles of books that had already been written about Saint Francis. I was totally unaware of a century's worth of scholarship that had already dissected every aspect of the saint's life. I had no idea of poverty, be it literal or symbolic. I couldn't tell you the difference between a Conventual friar and a Capucin friar. I was totally untrained in theology. I had perhaps less then a rudimentary knowledge of Church history, except for all the bad stuff, like the Inquisition and popes with mistresses and illegitimate children. All I had was a saint who died more than 750 years ago and my thirst for God.

When this book evolved from a novel exploring the connection between creativity and spirituality, I had already sketched a rough outline of the saint's life. But the material I had written amounted to little more than a long essay. For one year, I sat alone in my study reading about Saint Francis. I accumulated dozens upon dozens of books which I purchased in used-book stores. In truth, I had no way to evaluate whether they were—from a scholarly point of view— good or bad. I found most to be either overly intellectual or overly pious. Still, I read everything I could get my hands on. As I read and *wrote my own account of Francis' life, the material began to rub up against my life. While examining Francis' life, I was forced to take a very close look at my own.*

I was a sinner. That was a tough reality to deal with, because it required me either to downplay what that meant or change my behavior. I am still a sinner. Perhaps a bigger one than when I began this book...because now I know better, and am more acutely aware of my faults. My many faults. And this awareness is not an unhealthy or a bad thing. Shining a spotlight on the ugliness within myself may appear to be a a negative thing, but it is not. It is incredibly positive, because by confronting it, I can transform it, with God's help and grace, into something beautiful.

I spent almost all of 1996 and the early part of 1997 working on the book. And working on myself. Still, I was mostly flailing around in the dark. My solitary efforts lacked feedback and exchange with people who had an understanding or appreciation of what I was doing. I wasn't even sure what I was doing myself. That began to change in June of 1997 when I went on the pilgrimage and spent three full months dedicated to nothing else but studying the life of Francis in the land of Saint Francis. Every day provided me with an opportunity for solitude and a chance to discuss Saint Francis with people who dedicated their lives to following the saint. André Cirino, O.F.M., was especially helpful. It was during those months that an approach to the book began to crystallize. Rather than its being just another book on Francis, which I was unqualified to write, it evolved into a book that not only told the story of Francis—and by now Clare also, because she, too, excited me—but also told how a modern person, someone with a naturally skeptical outlook, could respond to an ancient message. The story of the two saints from Assisi became the backdrop of the story of my own spiritual odyssey. The essays and diaries became equally as important as the historical sketches.

Work on the book slowed down in 1998 and early 1999, because my focus was split between writing the book and making a documentary film on a L'Arche community in Tacoma, Washington, which in itself was another incredible life lesson. Saint Francis would have loved L'Arche, and its emphasis on littleness and listening. My encounter with L'Arche had a profound impact on the growth of my faith. I also made a film in Albany, New York, telling the story of a seventy-year-old priest who ministered to the profound needs of drug addicts, alcoholics and ex-convicts. The making of this film also deepened my understanding of my faith. When it came to human weakness and the need for forgiveness and rehabilitation, I was no better than any of the drug addicts and criminals I met. Their fight to change their lives taught me about real courage.

OK...so why am I telling you, dear reader, all of this?

In early 1999, St. Anthony Messenger Press agreed to publish the book, which was still unfinished. During the past four months, I have dedicated all my time and energy to finishing the book. As I worked on the book, I was amazed by the journey I had taken. As I read all the essays and pilgrimage diaries I had written, I was able to take a closer look at my struggles with sin and prayer...and my response to the message of Saint Francis of Assisi. These past four months of complete submersion in the material have left me feeling very humble. The reason behind this final entry is to tell you that I still have a long way to go, that I have not fully integrated the lessons I have learned and written about into my own life.

Being alone with the book for the past four months has made it clear to me how disordered modern life is. We have greatly distanced ourselves from the gospel. I have fallen way short. I see more clearly now how I must put God first...from moment to moment.

Today is July 15, 1999. It is the Feast of Saint Bonaventure. I have about six weeks left to proofread and fine-tune the manuscript before delivering it to the publisher and then heading for Rome and my annual course at the Gregorian. I can't imagine what life will be like without the book as an active part of my life. I will have the rest of my life to try to implement all that Saint Francis and Saint Clare have taught me. It is time for me to shut up and start living what I have written. Pray for me.

I want to end with a sentence from Saint Bonaventure. He used it to end a treatise he wrote entitled Disputed Questions on the Knowledge of Christ—or for you Latin buffs, De Scientia Christi:

be granted the experience of that about which we have spoken.

May your journey with Francis and Clare enrich your life. May God give you peace.

Pace e Bene

Maestro di S. Chiara
CLARE ARRIVES AT THE PORTIUNCULA, detail
from ST. CLARE AND EIGHT EPISODES FROM HER LIFE
13th century
Painting on wood, Basilica di Santa Chiara, Assisi

BIBLIOGRAPHY

Many of the following works are out of print, but may be found in libraries and used-book stores.

Allen, Paul M. and Joan deRis. *Francis of Assisi's Canticle of the Creatures*. New York: Continuum Publishing Co., 1996.

Almedingen, E. M. *St. Francis of Assisi*. New York: A.A. Knopf, 1967.

Armstrong, Edward R. *Saint Francis: Nature Mystic*. Berkeley, Cal.: University of California Press, 1973.

The Art of Prayer: An Orthodox Anthology. London and Boston: Faber and Faber, 1977.

Au, Wilkie, S.J. *By Way of the Heart*. Mahwah, N.J.: Paulist Press, 1989.

Augustine, Father, O.F.M. Cap. *Some Loves of the Seraphic Saint*. Chicago: Franciscan Herald Press, 1979.

Augustine, Saint. *Confessions*, Henry Chadwick, trans. Oxford: Oxford University Press, 1992.

Bartoli, Marco. *Clare of Assisi*. London: Darton, Longman and Todd Ltd., 1993.

Bazin, René. *Redemption*. New York: Scribner's, 1908.

Bishop, Morris. *St. Francis of Assisi*. Boston: Little, Brown and Company, 1974.

Blake, William. *The Portable Blake*. New York: Viking, 1953.

Boase, T.S.R. *St. Francis of Assisi*. London: Thames and Hudson, 1968.

Bodo, Murray, O.F.M. *Francis: The Journey and the Dream*. Cincinnati: St. Anthony Messenger Press, 1988.

_____ *Clare: A Light in the Garden*. Cincinnati: St. Anthony Messenger Press, 1992.

____ *Tales of St. Francis: Ancient Stories for Contemporary Times.* Cincinnati: St. Anthony Messenger Press, 1992.

____ *Through the Year With Francis of Assisi: Daily Meditations From His Words and Life.* Cincinnati: St. Anthony Messenger Press, 1993.

____ *The Way of St. Francis: The Challenge of Franciscan Spirituality for Everyone.* Cincinnati: St. Anthony Messenger Press, 1995.

Boff, Leonardo. *St. Francis: A Model for Human Liberation.* London: SCM Press Ltd., 1985.

Bonaventure. *The Disciple and the Master: St. Bonaventure's Sermons on St. Francis of Assisi*, Eric Doyle, O.F.M., trans. and ed. Chicago: Franciscan Herald Press, 1983.

____ *The Holiness of Life.* Laurence Costello, O.F.M., trans. London: B. Herder Book Co., 1928.

____ *Major Life*, Regis Armstrong, O.F.M. Cap., trans., in *Omnibus of the Sources for the Life of St. Francis*, Marion A. Habig, ed. Chicago: Franciscan Herald Press, 1972.

Bonaventure: The Soul's Journey Into God, The Tree of Life, The Life of St. Francis, Ewert Cousins, ed. and trans. Classics of Western Spirituality Series. Mahwah, N.J.: Paulist Press, 1978.

Brown, Raphael. *True Joy From Assisi.* Chicago: Franciscan Herald Press, 1978.

Brunette, Pierre. *Francis of Assisi and His Conversions*, Paul Lachance, O.F.M., and Kathryn Krug, trans. Quincy, Ill.: Franciscan Press, 1997.

Burrows, Ruth. *Before the Living God.* London: Sheed & Ward, 1975.

____ *Interior Castle Explored.* London: Sheed & Ward, 1981.

____ *To Believe in Jesus.* London: Sheed & Ward, 1978.

Cantalamessa, Raniero, O.F.M. Cap. *Poverty.* New York: Alba House, 1997.

Carney, Margaret, O.S.F. *The First Franciscan Woman: Clare of Assisi and Her Form of Life.* Quincy, Ill.: Franciscan Press, 1993.

Carretto, Carlo. *I, Francis.* Maryknoll, N.Y.: Orbis Books, 1982.

Cashen, Richard Anthony. *Solitude in the Thought of Thomas Merton.* Kalamazoo, Mich.: Cistercian Publications, 1981.

Catherine of Siena, Saint. *The Dialogues of St. Catherine of Siena*, Algar Thorold, trans. Rockford, Ill.: TAN Books, 1976.

Chesterton, G. K. *Saint Francis of Assisi*. New York: Image Books, 1990.

Christian Spirituality: High Middle Ages and Reformation, Jill Raitt, ed. New York: The Crossroad Publishing Co., 1988.

Clare of Assisi: Early Documents. Regis J. Armstrong, O.F.M. Cap., ed., trans. Mahwah, N.J.: Paulist Press, 1988.

Clark, Kenneth. *Civilization*. New York: Harper & Row, 1969.

The Cloud of Unknowing, William Johnson, ed. New York: Doubleday Image Books, 1996.

Cole, Bruce. *Giotto*. New York: George Braziller, 1993.

Complete Paintings of Giotto, Edi Baccheschi, notes. New York: Harry N. Abrams, Inc., 1966.

Concilium, number 149, 1981. (Entire issue devoted to writings about Saint Francis.)

Cook, William R. *Francis of Assisi: The Way of Poverty and Humility*. Collegeville, Minn.: The Liturgical Press, 1991.

Coultan, G. G. *From Francis to Dante*. London: David Nutt, 1906.

Craine, Renate. *Hildegard, Prophet of the Cosmic Christ*. New York: The Crossroad Publishing Co., 1977.

Cunningham, Lawrence S. *Brother Francis: An Anthology of Writings by and About Saint Francis of Assisi*. San Francisco: Harper & Row, 1972.

_____ *Saint Francis of Assisi*, Dennis Stock, photographs. San Francisco: Harper & Row, 1981.

Cuthbert, Father, O.S.F.G. *The Life of St. Francis*. London: Longmans, 1935.

Dante Alighieri. "Paradiso," Canto XI, *The Divine Comedy*. D. L. Sayers and B. Reynolds, trans. New York: Penguin Books 1962.

d'Arcais, Francesca Flores. *Giotto*. New York: Abbeville Press Publishers, 1995.

da Todi, Jacopone. *The Lauds*, Serge Hughes, trans. New York: Paulist Press, 1982.

de Aspurz, Lazaro Iríart, O.F.M. Cap. *The Franciscan Calling*, Carole Marie Kelly, O.S.F., trans. Chicago: Franciscan Herald Press, 1974.

de Beer, Francis. "St. Francis and Islam," *Concilium*, no. 149, 1981.

de Caussade, Jean-Pierre. *The Sacrament of the Present Moment*, Kitty Muggeridge, trans. Glasgow: William Collins Sons & Co. Ltd., 1981.

de Chardin, Pierre Teilhard, S.J. *The Divine Milieu*. New York: Harper & Bros., 1960.

____ *The Phenomenon of Man*. New York: HarperCollins, 1980.

de Malan, Emilius Chavin. *The Life of St. Francis of Assisium*. J. B. Murphy, O.S.F., trans. Dublin: James Duffy, 1848.

de Mello, Anthony, S.J. *Awareness*. New York: Doubleday, 1990.

____ *The Song of the Bird*. New York: Image Books, 1984.

Dennis, Marie, Joseph Nangle, O.F.M., Cynthia Moe-Lobeda, Stuart Taylor. *St. Francis and the Foolishness of God*. Maryknoll, N.Y.: Orbis Books, 1993.

de Paris, Gratien, O.F.M. Cap. *I Know Christ: The Personality and Spirituality of St. Francis of Assisi*. Paul J. Oligny, O.F.M., trans. St. Bonaventure, N.Y.: The Franciscan Institute, 1957.

de Robeck, Nesta. *St. Francis of Assisi, His Holy Life and Love of Poverty*. Chicago: Franciscan Herald Press, 1964.

____ *St. Clare of Assisi*. Chicago: Franciscan Herald Press, 1980.

Doyle, Eric, O.F.M. *Song of Brotherhood*. St. Bonaventure, N.Y.: Franciscan Institute Publications, 1997.

____ and Damian McElrath. "St. Francis of Assisi and the Christocentric Character of Franciscan Life and Doctrine," in *Franciscan Christology*. Damian McElrath, ed. St. Bonaventure, N.Y.: Franciscan Institute Publications, 1980.

Dubay, Thomas, S.M. *The Fire Within*. San Francisco: Ignatius Press, 1989.

Eckhart, John (Meister). *Meister Eckhart*. Franz Pfeifer, ed., C. de B. Evans, trans. London: John M. Watkins, 1947.

Eimerl, Sarel. *The World of Giotto*. New York: Time-Life Books, 1967.

Elizondo, Virgilio. "Pilgrimage: An Enduring Ritual of Humanity," in *Concilium* (1996/4). London: SCIM Press/ Maryknoll, N.Y.: Orbis Books, 1996.

Englebert, Omer. *Saint Francis of Assisi, a Biography*, Eve Marie Cooper, trans. Chicago: Franciscan Herald Press, 1966.

Esser, Cajetan, O.F.M., and Engelbert Grau, O.F.M. *Love's Reply*. Ignatius Brady, O.F.M., trans. Chicago: Franciscan Herald Press, 1963.

Faricy, Robert. *Praying*. London: SCM Press Ltd., 1983.

Farnetani, Bernardino, O.F.M. Conv. *St. Francis of Assisi*. Assisi: Casa Editrice Francescana, 1984.

Fenelon, François. *Christian Perfection*. New York: Harper & Brothers, 1947.

Finley, James. *Merton's Palace of Nowhere: A Search for God Through Awareness of the True Self*. Notre Dame, Ind.: Ave Maria Press, 1978.

Flinders, Carol Lee. *Enduring Grace*. San Francisco: HarperSanFrancisco, 1993.

Forristal, Desmond. *Maximilian of Auschwitz*. Dublin: Ward River Press, 1982.

Fortini, Arnaldo. *Francis of Assisi/Arnaldo Fortini: A Translation of Nova vita di san Francesco by Helen Moak*. New York: Seabury Press, 1981.

Franciscan Christology. Damian McElrath, ed. St. Bonaventure, N.Y.: Franciscan Institute Publications, 1980.

Franciscan Essays II. Manchester: The University Press, 1932.

Francis of Assisi: Early Documents, Volume I: The Saint. Regis J. Armstrong, O.F.M. Cap., J. A. Wayne Hellmann, O.F.M. Conv., William J. Short, O.F.M., eds. New York: New City Press, 1999.

Frances Teresa, O.S.C. *Living the Incarnation: Praying With Francis and Clare of Assisi*. Quincy, Ill.: Franciscan Press, 1996.

____ *This Living Mirror: Reflections on Clare of Assisi*. London: Darton, Longman and Todd Ltd., 1995.

Frugoni, Chiara. *Francis of Assisi*, John Bowden, trans. London: SCM Press LTD, 1988.

Gasnick, Roy M., O.F.M. *The Francis Book*. New York: Macmillan, 1980.

Gaudoin-Parker, Michael L. *A Window on the Mystery of Faith: Mystical Umbria Enlivened by the Eucharist*. New York: Alba House, 1997.

Goudge, Elizabeth. *My God and My All: The Life of Saint Francis of Assisi*. London: Hodder and Stoughton, 1959.

____ *Saint Francis of Assisi*. London: Gerald Duckworth & Co., 1959.

Grant, Zachary, O.F.M. Cap. *Paths to Renewal: The Spirituality of Six Religious Founders*. New York: Alba House, 1998.

Grau, Engelbert, O.F.M., and Cajetan Esser, O.F.M. *Love's Reply*. Ignatius Brady, O.F.M., trans. Chicago: Franciscan Herald Press, 1963.

Green, Julien. *God's Fool*, Peter Heinegg, trans. San Francisco: Harper Publishers, 1985.

Green, Thomas, S.J. *When the Well Runs Dry*. Notre Dame, Ind.: Ave Maria Press, 1979.

Hauser, Walter, with Leonard von Matt, photographer. *St. Francis of Assisi*. Chicago: Henry Regnery Co., 1956.

Hegener, Mark, O.F.M. *The Poverello: St. Francis of Assisi*. Chicago: Franciscan Herald Press, 1956.

Heschel, Abraham, Rabbi. *The Wisdom of Heschel*, Ruth Marcus Goodhill, ed. New York: Farrar, Straus, and Giroux, 1986.

The History of Franciscan Theology, Kenan Osborne, ed. St. Bonaventure, N.Y.: Franciscan Institute, 1994.

Holl, Adolf. *The Last Christian*. Garden City, N.Y.: Doubleday, 1980.

Hugo, William R., O.F.M. Cap. *Studying the Life of Francis of Assisi*. Quincy, Ill.: Franciscan Press, 1996.

Huizinga, Johan. *The Waning of the Middle Ages*. New York: Doubleday Anchor Books, 1954.

Iriarte, Lazaro, O.F.M., *Franciscan History: The Three Orders of St. Francis of Assisi*, Patricia Ross, trans. Chicago: Franciscan Herald Press, 1982.

Jager, Willigis. *Search for the Meaning of Life*. Liguori, Mo.: Triumph Books, 1995.

James, Father. *The Franciscans*. London: Sheed & Ward, 1930.

James, Henry. *Italian Hours*, John Auchard, ed. University Park, Penn.: Pennsylvania State University, 1992.

Jessey, Cornelia. *The Prayer of Cosa: Praying in the Way of Francis of Assisi*. Minneapolis: Winston Press, 1985.

Jobe, Sara Lee. *Footsteps in Assisi*. Mahwah, N.J.: Paulist Press, 1996.

John Climacus, Saint. *The Ladder of Divine Ascent*, Archimandrite Lazarus Moore, trans. London: Faber and Faber, 1959.

John of the Cross. *Ascent of Mount Carmel*, in *Collected Works*, Kieran Kavanaugh, O.C.D., trans. Washington, D.C.: ICS Publications, 1973.

Jörgensen, Johannes. *Saint Francis of Assisi: A Biography*, T. O'Conor Sloane, trans. London: Longmans, 1926.

Kazantzakis, Nikos. *Saint Francis*. New York: Simon & Schuster, Inc., 1962.

Keating, Thomas. *The Heart of the World*. New York: Crossroad Publishing Co., 1999.

_____ *Invitation to Love*. Rockport, Mass.: Element Books, 1992.

_____ *Open Mind, Open Heart*. Amity, N.Y.: Amity House, 1986.

LaCugna, Catherine Mowry. *God for Us*. San Francisco: Harper, 1993.

The Lady Poverty: A XIII Century Allegory, Montgomery Carmichael, trans. and ed. London: John Murray, 1901.

Lafrance, Jean. *Pray to Your Father in Secret*. Sherbrooke, Quebec: Editions Paulines, 1987.

Lambert, M. D. *Franciscan Poverty: The Doctrine of the Absolute Poverty of Christ and the Apostles in the Franciscan Order 1210-1323*. St. Bonaventure, N.Y.: The Franciscan Institute, 1998.

Larrañaga, Ignacio, O.F.M. Cap. *Brother Francis of Assisi*. Jennie M. Ibarra, trans. Sherbrooke, Quebec: Mediaspaul, 1994.

_____ *Sensing Your Hidden Presence: Toward Intimacy with God*. New York: Doubleday Image, 1987.

Lawrence, D. H. "We Need One Another," in *Phoenix: The Posthumous Papers of D. H. Lawrence*, Edward D. McDonald, ed. New York: The Viking Press, 1936.

Leclerc, Eloi, O.F.M. *The Canticle of the Creatures: Symbols of Union*. Matthew J. O'Connell, trans. Chicago: Franciscan Herald Press, 1977.

_____ *Exile and Tenderness*. Abbe Germain Marc'hadour, trans. Chicago: Franciscan Herald Press, 1965.

_____ *Francis of Assisi: Return to the Gospel*. Chicago: Franciscan Herald Press, 1983.

_____ *The Wisdom of the Poor One of Assisi*. Pasadena, Calif.: Hope Publishing House, 1992.

Lekeux, Martial, O.F.M. *Short Cut to Divine Love*. Chicago: Franciscan Herald Press, 1962.

le Monnier, Leon, Abbé. *History of St. Francis of Assisi*. London: Kegan Paul, Trench, Trubner & Co., 1894.

Levoy, Gregg. *Callings: Finding and Following an Authentic Life*. New York: Harmony Books, 1997.

Little, W. J. Knox. *St. Francis of Assisi*. London: Isbister and Company, 1897.

The Little Flowers of St. Francis. Raphael Brown, trans. New York: Image Books, 1971.

The Liturgy of the Hours According to the Roman Rite. Compilation copyright 1974, the hierarchies of Australia, England and Wales, Ireland. London, Sydney, Dublin: Wm Collins Sons & Co. Ltd., E. J. Dwyer Pty., The Talbot Press Ltd., 1974.

Luce, Clare Boothe. *Saints for Now*. San Francisco: Ignatius Press, 1993.

Mackay, H.F.B. *The Message of Francis of Assisi*. London: Society of Ss. Peter and Paul, 1924.

Magro, Pasqual, O.F.M. Conv. *Assisi: History, Art, Spirituality*. Assisi: Casa Editrice Francescana.

Maloney, George A., S.J. *The Breath of the Mystic*. Denville, N.J.: Dimension Books, 1974.

The Marrow of the Gospel: A Study of the Rule of Saint Francis of Assisi by the Franciscans of Germany, Ignatius Brady, O.F.M., trans. and ed. Chicago: Franciscan Herald Press, 1958.

Martin, Eugene. *The Catholicism of St. Francis*, in *Etudes Franciscaines*, 49, Frederick E. Conron, trans., 1937.

Mary Francis, P.C.C. *Spaces for Silence*. Chicago: Franciscan Herald Press, 1964.

____ *Strange Gods Before Me*. Chicago: Franciscan Herald Press, 1976.

Mary Seraphim, P.C.P.A. *Clare: Her Light and Her Song*. Chicago: Franciscan Herald Press, 1984.

Masseron, Alexandre. *The Franciscans*. Warre B. Wells, trans. London: Burns, Oates & Washbourne Ltd., 1931.

____ *Memorable Words of Saint Francis*, Margaret Sullivan, trans. Chicago: Franciscan Herald Press, 1963.

Matura, Thaddee, O.F.M. *Francis of Assisi: The Message of His Writings*. St. Bonaventure, N.Y.: Franciscan Institute Publications, 1997.

Maynard, Theodore. *Richest of the Poor: The Life of Saint Francis of Assisi*. Garden City, N.Y.: Doubleday, 1948.

McElrath, Damian, and Eric Doyle, O.F.M., "St. Francis of Assisi and the Christocentric Character of Franciscan Life and Doctrine," in *Franciscan Christology*. Damian McElrath, ed. St. Bonaventure, N.Y.: Franciscan Institute Publications, 1980.

McMichaels, Susan W. *Journey Out of the Garden*. Mahwah, N.J.: Paulist Press, 1997.

McNamara, William. *Earthy Mysticism: Contemplation and the Life of Passionate Presence*. New York: Crossroad Publishing, 1983.

Medieval Woman's Visionary Literature, Alvilda Petroff, ed. New York: Oxford University Press, 1986.

Melnick, Robert, O.F.M. Conv., and Joseph Wood, O.F.M. Conv. *Franciscans: Conventual Friars of the Community*. Padua: Edizioni Messaggero Padova, 1996.

Merton, Thomas. *The Asian Journal*. New York: New Directions, 1973.

_____ *Bread in the Wilderness*. New York: New Directions, 1997.

_____ *Contemplation in a World of Action*. Notre Dame, Ind.: University of Notre Dame Press, 1968.

_____ *Mystics and Zen Masters*. New York: Dell Publishing Co., Inc., 1961.

_____ *New Seeds of Contemplation*. New York: New Directions, 1962.

_____ *No Man Is an Island*. New York: Harcourt Brace Jovanonich, Publishers, 1955.

_____ *Seasons of Celebration*. New York: Farrar, Straus and Giroux, 1965.

_____ *Seeds of Contemplation*. New York: New Directions, 1949.

_____ *The Sign of Jonas*. New York: Harcourt, Brace and Company, 1953.

_____ *The Silent Life*. New York: Farrar, Straus and Cuhady, 1957.

_____ "Solitude," *Spiritual Life*, 14, Fall 1968.

_____ *Thoughts in Solitude*. New York: Farrar, Straus and Giroux, 1985.

——— *What Are These Wounds?* Milwaukee: The Bruce Publishing Co., 1950.

Metz, Johannes. *Poverty of Spirit*. Mahwah, N.J.: Paulist Press, 1998.

Mockler, Anthony. *Francis of Assisi: The Wandering Years*. Oxford/ New York: Phaidon/ E. P. Dutton, 1976.

Moorman, John. *A History of the Franciscan Order From Its Origins to the Year 1517*. Oxford: Clarendon Press, 1968.

Navone, John J., S.J. *Personal Witness: A Biblical Spirituality*. London: Sheed & Ward, 1967.

Nicholson, D.H.S. *The Mysticism of St. Francis of Assisi*. Boston: Small, Maynard & Company, 1923.

Nouwen, Henri J. M. *The Genesee Diary: Report from a Trappist Monastery*. New York: Image Books, 1981.

—— *Reaching Out*. New York: Doubleday, 1986.

O'Brien, Isidore, O.F.M. *Francis of Assisi: Mirror of Christ*. Chicago: Franciscan Herald Press, 1978.

Omnibus of the Sources for the Life of St. Francis, Marion A. Habig, ed. Chicago: Franciscan Herald Press, 1972.

Paz, Octavio. *Conjunctions and Disjunctions*, Helen Lane, trans. New York: Little, Brown and Company, 1990.

Peck, George T., *The Fool of God*. Birmingham, Ala.: University of Alabama Press, 1980.

Peterson, Ingrid J., O.S.F. *Clare of Assisi*. Quincy, Ill.: Franciscan Press, 1993.

—— and Ramona Miller. *Praying With Clare of Assisi*. Winona, Minn.: St. Mary's Press, 1994.

Petry, Ray C. *Francis of Assisi, Apostle of Poverty*. New York: Duke University Press, 1941.

Picard, Marc. *The Icon of the Christ of San Damiano*. Assisi: Casa Editrice Francescana, 1989.

Polidoro, GianMaria, O.F.M. *Francis of Assisi: Innovator for a New Society*. Firenze, Italy: Vallecchi, 1981.

Rahner, Karl, S.J. *Liturgy of the World*. Collegeville, Minn.: The Liturgical Press, 1991.

—— *The Shape of the Church to Come*. London: SPCK, 1974.

Raymond, Ernest. *In the Steps of St. Francis*. Chicago: Franciscan Herald Press, 1975.

Sabatier, Paul. *Life of St. Francis of Assisi*, Louise Seymour Houghton, trans. New York: Charles Scribner's Sons, 1906.

St. Francis of Assisi: His Life and Writings as Recorded by His Companions, Leo Sherley-Price, trans. New York: Harper & Brothers, 1959.

Saint Sing, Susan. *St. Francis, Poet of Creation: The Story of the Canticle of Brother Sun*. Chicago: Franciscan Herald Press, 1985.

Salvatorelli, Luigi. *The Life of St. Francis of Assisi*, Eric Sutton, trans. New York: A.A. Knopf, 1928.

Schmemann, Alexander. *Lent: A Journey to Pascha*. Crestwood, N.Y.: St. Vladimir's Seminary Press, 1969.

Schneider, Reinhold. *The Hour of St. Francis of Assisi*, James Meyer, O.F.M., trans. Chicago: Franciscan Herald Press, 1953.

Scudder, Vida Dutton. *The Franciscan Adventure: A Study of the First Hundred Years of the Order of St. Francis of Assisi*. London: J. M. Dent and Sons, Ltd., 1931.

Spirit and Life. St. Bonaventure, N.Y.: The Franciscan Institute Press, 1991.

"Starting Points: Images of Women in the Letters of Clare of Assisi to Agnes of Prague," *Spirit and Life*, Vol. 1. St. Bonaventure, N.Y.: The Franciscan Institute Press, 1991.

Steindl-Rast, David. *A Listening Heart*. New York: Crossroad Publishing Co., 1983.

—— with Sharon Lebell, *Music of Silence*. Berkeley, Calif.: Seastone, 1998.

Sticco, Maria. *The Peace of Saint Francis*. New York: Hawthorne Books, Inc., 1962.

Straub, Gerard Thomas. *The Canvas of the Soul*. Unpublished.

—— *Dear Kate*. Buffalo, N.Y.: Prometheus Books, 1992.

—— *Salvation for Sale*. Buffalo, N.Y.: Prometheus Books, 1988.

Stubblebine, James H. *Assisi and the Rise of Vernacular Art*. New York: Harper & Row, 1985.

Sulmasy, Daniel P., O.F.M. "Celebrating the Death of St. Francis," *The Cord*, October 1993.

Talbot, John Michael and Steve Rabey. *The Lessons of St. Francis*. New York: E.P. Dutton, 1997.

Teresa of Avila. *The Interior Castle*, Classics of Western Spirituality, Kieran Kavanaugh, O.C.D., and Otilio Rodriquez, O.C.D., trans. Mahwah, N.J.: Paulist Press, 1979.

Thomas à Kempis. *The Imitation of Christ*. New York: Dorset Press, 1986.

Thomas of Celano. *First Life*, Placid Hermann, O.F.M., trans., in *Omnibus of the Sources for the Life of St. Francis*, Marion A. Habig, ed. Chicago: Franciscan Herald Press, 1972.

—— *Second Life*, in *Omnibus of the Sources for the Life of St. Francis*.

Tolstoy, Leo. *A Calendar of Wisdom*, Peter Sekirin, trans. New York: Scribner, 1997.

Underhill, Evelyn. *The Essentials of Mysticism*. New York: E.P. Dutton Co., Inc., 1960.

—— *The Golden Sequence: A Fourfold Study of the Spiritual Life*. New York: E.P. Dutton, 1933.

—— *Jacopone da Todi, Poet and Mystic*. Freeport, N.Y.: Books for Libraries Press, 1972.

—— *The Spiritual Life*. Wilton, Conn.: Morehouse Barlow, 1955.

—— *The Ways of the Spirit*. New York: Crossroad Publishing, 1990.

van Breeman, Peter G., S.J. *Let All God's Glory Through*. Mahwah, N.J.: Paulist Press, 1995.

van Corstanje, Auspicius, O.F.M. *Francis: Bible of the Poor*. Chicago: Franciscan Herald Press, 1977.

Vanier, Jean. *Community and Growth*, Ann Shearer, trans. London: Darton, Longman and Todd, 1979.

—— *Tears of Silence*. Denville, N.J.: Dimension Books, 1970.

Vatican Council II: The Conciliar and Post Conciliar Documents, Austin Flannery, O.P., general ed. Northport, N.Y.: Costello Publishing Co., 1988.

von Balthasar, Hans Urs, S.J. *The Last Grain of Wheat*, Erasmo Leiva-Merikakis, trans. San Francisco: Ignatius Press, 1995.

von Galli, Mario, S.J. *Living Our Future: Francis of Assisi and the Church of Tomorrow*. Chicago: Franciscan Herald Press, 1972.

von Matt, Leonard, and Walter Hauser. *St. Francis of Assisi*. Chicago: Henry Regnery Company, 1956.

Vorreaux, Damien, O.F.M. *First Encounter With Francis of Assisi*. Chicago: Franciscan Herald Press, 1979.

Walker, Alice. *The Color Purple*. New York: Harcourt, Brace & Company, 1992.

The Way of the Pilgrim and *The Pilgrim Continues His Way*, R. M. French, trans. New York: Seabury Press, 1965.

Weil, Simone. *Waiting for God*, Emma Craufurd, trans. New York: G.P. Putnam's Sons, 1951.

Wilde, Oscar. *De Profundis*. New York: Dover Publications, 1997.

Wood, Joseph, O.F.M. Conv., and Robert Melnick, O.F.M. Conv. *Franciscans: Conventual Friars of the Community*. Padua: Edizioni Messaggero Padova, 1996.

Zehringer, Dr. William C. "This Dark Mystery: The Franciscan Vocation of Saint Clare of Assisi," *The Cord*, October, 1993.

Acknowledgments

Grateful acknowledgment is made to the following for permission to reprint previously published material:

Abbeville Press for excerpts from *Giotto* by Francesca Flores D'Arcais, copyright ©1995 Federico Motta Editore, SpA, Milan, Italy, copyright ©1995 English translation, Abbeville Press; A. P. Watt Ltd., on behalf of The Hierarchies of England & Wales, Ireland and Australia, compilation copyright ©1974, the hierarchies of Australia, England and Wales, Ireland; Ave Maria Press, Inc., for text from *Merton's Palace of Nowhere: A Search for God Through Awareness of the True Self* by James Finley, copyright ©1978 by Ave Maria Press, P.O. Box 428, Notre Dame, IN 46556; Regis J. Armstrong, O.F.M. Cap., for *Clare of Assisi: Early Documents*, edited by Regis J. Armstrong, O.F.M. Cap., copyright ©1988; Burns & Oates Ltd. for excerpts from *The Franciscans* by Alexandre Masseron, copyright ©1931; Casa Editrice Francescana for excerpts from *St. Francis of Assisi* by Bernardino Farnetani, O.F.M. Conv., copyright ©1984; Continuum Publishing Group for excerpts from *Francis of Assisi's Canticle of the Creatures* by Paul M. Allen and Joan deRis Allen, copyright ©1996; The Crossroad Publishing Co. for excerpts from *Hildegard, Prophet of the Cosmic Christ* by Renata Craine, copyright ©1977, *The Ways of the Spirit* by Evelyn Underhill, copyright ©1990, and the Seabury Press books, *The Way of the Pilgrim* and *The Pilgrim Continues His Way*, R.M. French, translator, copyright ©1965; Doubleday Publishing Group, a division of Random House, Inc., for excerpts from *The Little Flowers of St. Francis*, translated by Raphael Brown, copyright ©1958 by Beverly Brown, by Murray Bodo, O.F.M.: *Tales of St. Francis*, copyright ©1988, and *Through the Year With Francis of Assisi*, copyright ©1987, Adolf Holl's *The Last Christian: A Biography of Francis of Assisi*, translated by Peter Heinegg, copyright ©1979 by Deutshe Verlags-Anstalt, Stuttgart, translation copyright ©1980 by Doubleday, and Theodore Maynard's *Richest of the Poor*, copyright ©1948 by Theodore Maynard; Dover Publications for an excerpt from Oscar Wilde's *De Profundis*, copyright ©1997; E.P. Dutton for excerpts from *The Lessons of St. Francis* by John Michael Talbot and Steve Rabey, copyright ©1997, and *Francis of Assisi: The Wandering Years* by Anthony Mockler, copyright ©1976; Farrar, Straus & Giroux Inc. for excerpts from Thomas Merton's *Seasons of Celebration*, copyright ©1965, The Trustees of the Merton Legacy Trust, *The Silent Life*, copyright ©1957, The Trustees of the Merton Legacy Trust, and *Mystics and Zen Masters*, copyright ©1967, The Trustees of the Merton Legacy Trust; Franciscan Institute Press for excerpts from *I Know Christ* by Gratien de Paris, O.F.M. Cap., copyright ©1957, *Song of Brotherhood* by Eric Doyle, O.F.M., copyright ©1997, and *Franciscan Christology*, copyright ©1980; Franciscan Press for excerpts from *Clare of Assisi* by Ingrid J. Peterson, O.S.F., copyright ©1993, Pierre Brunette's *Francis of Assisi and His Conversions*, translated by Paul Lachance, O.F.M., and Kathryn Krug, copyright ©1997, *This Living Mirror* by Sister Frances Teresa, O.S.C., copyright ©1996, and the following published by Franciscan Herald Press: *Omnibus of the Sources for the Life of St. Francis*, edited by Marion A. Habig, copyright ©1972, *The Canticle of the Creatures, Francis of Assisi*, copyright ©1977, and *Exile and Tenderness*, copyright ©1965, by Eloi Leclerc, O.F.M., *Clare: Her Light and Her Song* by Sister Mary Seraphim, P.C.P.A., copyright ©1984, *First Encounter With Francis of Assisi* by Damien Vorreaux, O.F.M., copyright ©1979, *The Hours of St. Francis of Assisi* by Reinhold Schneider, copyright ©1953, Alexandre Masseron's *Memorable Words of Saint Francis*, translated by Margaret Sullivan, copyright ©1963, *The Marrow of the Gospel*, translated and edited by Ignatius Brady, O.F.M., copyright ©1958, *Saint Francis, Poet of Creation* by Susan Saint Sing, copyright ©1985, *St. Francis of Assisi, His Holy Life and Love of Poverty* by Nesta de Robeck, copyright ©1964, and *True Joy From Assisi* by Raphael Brown, copyright ©1978; George Braziller Inc. for excerpts from Bruce Cole's *Giotto*, copyright ©1993; GIA Publications, Inc., for excerpts from *The Psalms* from the Grail translation from the Hebrew, copyright ©1986; HarperCollins Publishers for excerpts from *God's Fool* by Julien Green, copyright ©1985, *Enduring Grace* by Carol Lee Flinders, copyright ©1993, *Francis of Assisi* by Lawrence S. Cunningham, copyright ©1981, and The Grail translation of the Psalms, copyright ©1963, published by Collins in Fontana Books, London; Hawthorne Books for excerpts from Maria Sticco's *The Peace of Saint Francis*, copyright ©1962; Hodder & Stoughton for excerpts from Elizabeth Goudge's *My God and My All*, copyright ©1959; The Merton Legacy Trust for the following whose copyrights are

Other FRANCISCAN RESOURCES *From*
ST. ANTHONY MESSENGER PRESS

Books

The Almond Tree Speaks: New and Selected Writings, 1974-1994 by
Murray Bodo, O.F.M.

*The Autumn of St. Francis of Assisi: Companions of St. Francis of Assisi
Series*, by Roderic Petrie, O.F.M.

Brother Leo Remembers Francis: Companions of St. Francis of Assisi Series,
by Roderic Petrie, O.F.M.

Canticle of Brother Sun, by Rev. Edd Anthony, O.F.M.

Clare, A Light in the Garden, by Murray Bodo, O.F.M.

Day by Day With Followers of Francis and Clare, by Pat McCloskey,
O.F.M.

Following Francis of Assisi: A Spirituality for Daily Living, by Patti
Normile

Francis: The Journey and the Dream, by Murray Bodo, O.F.M.

Francis of Assisi: The Song Goes On, by Hugh Noonan, O.F.M., and Roy
Gasnick, O.F.M.

Francisco: El Viaje y el Sueño, by Murray Bodo, O.F.M., translated by
Alicia Sarre, R.S.C.J.

Lights: Revelations of God's Goodness, by Jack Wintz, O.F.M.

A Retreat With Anthony of Padua: Finding Our Way, by Carol Ann
Morrow

A Retreat With Francis and Clare of Assisi: Following Our Pilgrim Hearts,
by Murray Bodo, O.F.M., and Susan Saint Sing

Ritual of the Secular Franciscan Order, edited by Benet A. Fonck, O.F.M.

St. Anthony of Padua: The Story of His Life and Popular Devotions

Swimming in the Sun: Discovering the Lord's Prayer With Francis of Assisi and Thomas Merton, by Albert Haase, O.F.M.

Tales of St. Francis: Ancient Stories for Contemporary Living, by Murray Bodo, O.F.M.

Through the Year With Francis of Assisi: Daily Meditations From His Words and Life, selected and translated by Murray Bodo, O.F.M.

To Live as Francis Lived: A Guide for Secular Franciscans, by Leonard Foley, O.F.M., Jovian Weigel, O.F.M., and Patti Normile, S.F.O.

The Way of St. Francis: The Challenge of Franciscan Spirituality for Everyone, by Murray Bodo, O.F.M.

Videos

Francis and Clare of Assisi, Oriente Occidente Productions

Franciscan Holy Ground: Where Francis and Clare Found God

Poor Clares: A Hidden Presence, Oriente Occidente Productions

St. Clare of Assisi, Oriente Occidente Productions

St. Francis of Assisi, Oriente Occidente Productions

Audios

Francis and Clare of Assisi: Models of Gospel Living, by Louis Vitale, O.F.M.

Solanus Casey: One Man's Journey Toward Sanctity, by Michael Crosby, O.F.M.Cap.

To order, call our toll-free number, **1-800-488-0488**,
or see our products catalog on our Web site at
http://**www.AmericanCatholic.org**